Special Edition

Using

HTML and XHTML

Molly E. Holzschlag

201 W. 103rd Street
Indianapolis, Indiana 46290

SPECIAL EDITION USING HTML AND XHTML

Copyright © 2002 by Que

International Standard Book Number: 0-7897-2731-5

Library of Congress Catalog Card Number: 2001099408

Printed in the United States of America

First Printing: May 2002

05   04   03   02   4   3   2   1

Trademarks

Warning and Disclaimer

Publisher
David Culverwell

Executive Editor
Jeff Schultz

Development Editor
Laura Norman

Managing Editor
Thomas F. Hayes

Senior Editor
Susan Ross Moore

Project Editor
Tricia Liebig

Copy Editors
Michael Deitsch
Kitty Jarrett

Indexer
Chris Barrick

Proofreader
Kay Hoskin

Technical Editor
Steve Champeon

Team Coordinator
Sharry Lee Gregory

Interior Designer
Ruth Harvey

Cover Designers
Dan Armstrong
Ruth Harvey

Page Layout
Stacey Richwine-DeRome
Mark Walchle

Contents at a Glance

Introduction   1

I   Web Markup for Professionals
1   Working with Specifications   7
2   Writing Conforming Documents   31
3   Dealing with Data Types   61
4   Choosing the Right DTD   81

II   Structuring and Formatting Documents
5   Global Structure and Syntax of Documents   95
6   Managing Text and Lists   111
7   Adding Hypertext and Independent Links   155
8   Working with Tables   177
9   Creating Framesets and Frame Documents   219
10   Building Forms   247

III   Images, Multimedia, and Embedded Objects
11   Adding Images   275
12   Working with Multimedia   301
13   Embedding Objects   325

IV   Style and Scripting
14   Using CSS with HTML and XHTML   345
15   CSS in Depth: Applying Style and Positioning   369
16   Adding Scripting to HTML and XHTML Documents   401

V   Accessibility and Internationalization
17   Creating Accessible Sites   419
18   Designing International Documents   435

VI   Advanced Concepts
19   XHTML Modularization   451
20   Customizing DTDs   467
21   Transforming Documents with XSLT   485
22   Moving Toward XML   511

VII   Appendixes
A   Site Publishing, Maintenance, and Marketing Guide   541
B   Annotated Resources for Web Developers   563
C   XHTML Reference   569
D   CSS2 Reference   631
Index   663

TABLE OF CONTENTS

Introduction 1

I Web Markup for Professionals

1 Working with Specifications 7

A Markup Roadmap for Professionals **8**
SGML and HTML **9**
Enter XML **21**
Redefining HTML as an XML
Application **22**

The W3C **24**

HTML and XHTML: Common Ideologies **25**
HTML 4.0 and 4.01: Concepts **26**
XHTML 1.0 and 1.1: Ideologies and New
Directions **27**

Case by Case: Web Standards Project **28**

2 Writing Conforming Documents 31

Document Conformance **32**
Conformance Definitions in HTML and
XHTML **32**

Conformance Requirements and
Recommendations in HTML 4.01, XHTML
1.0, and XHTML 1.1 **35**
HTML 4.01 **36**
XHTML 1.0 **37**
XHTML 1.1 **43**

Special Characters **45**
Encoding Documents **46**
Clearly Labeling Encoded Documents **48**
Labeling Alternate Character Sets **51**

Validation **54**
What Validation Does **54**
Validating a Document **56**

Case by Case: Working with Templates **58**

3 Dealing with Data Types 61

Dealing with Data Types **62**

About URIs **62**

Representing Colors in HTML and
XHTML **63**

Length Values **65**

MIME Types **66**

Managing Language Codes **66**

Character Encodings **68**

Media Descriptors **78**

Script and Style Data **78**

Target Names **79**

Case by Case: Working with Character
Entities **79**

4 Choosing the Right DTD 81

DTDs: An Overview **82**

Which Is the Right DTD to Use? **82**
Dealing with Client Concerns **83**
Adding New Documents to Older
Web Sites **84**
Determining DTDs During Site
Redesigns **85**
Working with Visual Editors and
CMS **85**

DOCTYPE Declarations and DTDs **86**
New Developments **87**
DOCTYPE Switching in Detail **88**
Differences in Rendering Modes **89**

Case by Case: Transitional Design for
the New York Public Library **90**

II Structuring and Formatting Documents

5 Global Structure and Syntax of Documents 95

About Document Structure 96

Declarations and Document Types 96

The html Element 98

The head Element 98

The body Element 100

Syntax of Documents 101
  Elements 101
  Attributes 103
  Values 104

Case Sensitivity 105
  In HTML 106
  In XML 106
  In XHTML 107

Attribute Quoting 107
  In HTML 107
  In XML and XHTML 108

Case by Case: Troubleshooting Errors with Structure and Syntax 108

6 Managing Text and Lists 111

Working with Text 112

Structuring Text 112
  Phrase Elements 112
  Quotation Elements 113
  Subscripts and Superscripts 114

Adding Paragraphs and Breaks 115

Working with Headers 119

Working with Preformatted Text 121

Using Text Styles 123

Aligning Text 125

Using Lists Effectively 126
  Bulleted (Unordered) Lists 126
  Numbered (Ordered) Lists 130
  Definition Lists 131

Dealing Effectively with Lists 134
  Working with List Attributes 140

Adding Color, Size, and Typefaces to Text 141
  Managing Color for Backgrounds, Text, and Links 142
  Working with the font Element 143

Adding Horizontal Rules 152

Case by Case: Dealing with Text 153

7 Adding Hypertext and Independent Links 155

The Web's Very Essence: Linking 156

The Anchor Element 156
  Absolute Linking 158
  Relative Linking 158
  Linking Images 164
  Intrapage Linking 165
  Mail Links 169

Link Relationships with the link Element 171
  Linking to a Style Sheet 172
  Using the link Element for Navigation 173
  Using link to Point to an Alternate Document 174

Case by Case: Aiding and Abetting Search Engines 175

8 Working with Tables 177

The Importance of Tables **178**

Table Elements **178**
   The Basic Table **179**
   Captions and Table Headers **182**
   Column Grouping **184**
   Table Head, Table Foot, and Table Body **186**

Table Attributes **187**
   Borders **188**
   Table Width **188**
   Creating a Fixed-Width Table **190**
   Padding **192**
   Column Span **195**
   Row Span **198**

Table and Table Cell Alignment **202**
   Horizontal Alignment **202**
   Vertical Alignment **203**

Using Fixed and Dynamic Design **206**
   Applying a Fixed Table Design **206**
   Working with Dynamic Table Design **210**
   Combination Fixed and Dynamic Table Design **211**

Nesting and Stacking Tables **213**

Case by Case: Design First, Then Plan the Table **216**

9 Creating Framesets and Frame Documents 219

To Frame or Not to Frame **220**

Understanding Frame Structure **222**

The Frameset Document **223**

Building a Framed Page **224**

Setting frameset and frame Attributes **226**

Exploring a Frame with Margin, Resize, and Scroll Controls **227**

Targeting Windows **228**
   Creating a Frame Using target and name Attributes **229**
   Magic Target Names **230**

Working with Borderless Frames **233**

Advanced Frame Concepts **236**
   Appropriate Use of Frames **236**
   Fixed and Dynamic Frame Design **238**
   Combining Rows and Columns **240**

Working with Inline Frames (I-Frames) **241**

The noframes Element and Accessibility **242**
   Building Accessible Framed Pages **243**

Case by Case: Special Issues with Frames **244**

10 Building Forms 247

About Forms **248**

Using Proper Form Syntax **248**
   Form Elements and Attributes **249**
   Controls **250**
   Other Elements Used with Forms **251**

Building a Form **253**
   Adding a Text Field **254**
   Making a Checkbox **256**
   Adding a Radio Button **258**
   Making a Menu List **260**
   Creating a Text Area **264**
   Providing Reset and Submit Buttons **267**

Case by Case: Method, Action, and Hidden Fields **270**

III Images, Multimedia, and Embedded Objects

11 Adding Images 275

Working with Web Graphics 276
Graphics Interchange Format (GIF) 276
Joint Photographic Experts Group (JPEG) 278
Portable Network Graphics (PNG) 279

Graphic Optimization 280

Adding Images to Web Pages 282
The img Element 282
Image Attributes 284

Presentational Attributes in Transitional HTML and XHTML 285
width and height 285
Image Borders 286
Alignment 286
The alt Attribute 288
Horizontal and Vertical Space 290

Floating Images 292

Aligning Multiple Images 295

Linking Images 299

Case by Case: Exhibiting Your Work 299

12 Working with Multimedia 301

Action and Interaction 302

Audio and Video on the Web 303

Creating Audio and Video Files 303
Audio Files 303
Video Files 305

Downloadable Audio and Video File Formats 306
Audio Formats 306
Video Formats 308

Adding Audio and Video to a Web Page 308

Audio and Video Plug-Ins 309

Streaming Media Concepts 311
Streaming Audio 312
Streaming Video 312

Producing Streaming Media 313
Creating a Streaming Audio File 313
Working with Streaming Video 315

Incorporating Streaming Media into Your Page 315
Adding Streaming Media Using RealServer G2 316
Adding Streaming Media to a Page with HTTP 316

Multimedia Software: Macromedia Director, Shockwave, and Flash 319

Exploring Flash in Detail 320

Case by Case: Exploring Streaming Media Options 322

13 Embedding Objects 325

About Embedded Objects 326

The object Element in Detail 328
Using object to Add an Image 329
Using object to Add an Applet to Your Page 330

Working with the applet Element 331
Adding a Java Applet Using the applet Element 332
Workarounds for Cross-Browser Support 335

Imagemaps 336

Case by Case: Ensuring Accessibility for Embedded Objects 341

IV Style and Scripting

14 Using CSS with HTML and XHTML 345

Style Sheets and Web Markup 346

Style Sheet Fundamentals 346
  Separation of Presentation from
  Structure 347
  Cascade and Inheritance 347

Style Sheet Methods 350
  Inline Style 351
  Embedded Style 353
  Linked Style Sheets 355

Style Sheet Syntax 358
  Selectors in Detail 359

Exploring Class and Grouping 360
  Working with Class 361
  Using Grouping 364

Case by Case: Anatomy of Style 368

15 CSS in Depth: Applying Style and Positioning 369

Applying Style to Text 370
  Style Sheet Font Families 371
  Type Properties and Values 373

Using CSS for Layout 386
  Creating a Three-Column Layout 387
  Exploring a Two-Column Layout
  Using float 392

Gracefully Degrading CSS Layouts 394

Case by Case: css/edge: Visual and
Dynamic Effects with CSS 396

16 Adding Scripting to HTML and XHTML Documents 401

Scripting and Markup 402
  Adding Scripts to a Page Using the
  script Element 403
  Intrinsic Events 407

JavaScript Overview 408

Using JavaScript 409
  Drop-Down Menu Navigation 410
  Pop-Up Window 411

Case by Case: Merging Scripting, Style,
and Intrinsic Events 413

V Accessibility and Internationalization

17 Creating Accessible Sites 419

Rules and Laws Governing
Accessibility 420
  Historical Policies Leading to
  Accessibility Initiatives 420
  Section 508 421
  Foreign Rules and Laws on
  Accessibility 421

Web Accessibility Initiative 422

Techniques for Working with HTML 4.0
Accessibility 424
  Making Links Understandable with
  the title Attribute 424
  Adding Tab Order to Links 426
  Making Tables Accessible Using a
  Summary 428
  Clarifying Abbreviations with the
  acronym Element and title
  Attribute 430

Case by Case: Testing for
Accessibility 432

18 Designing International Documents 435

Globalization, Internationalization, and
Localization 436

Character Encoding 438

Expressing Encoding via MIME 439

Identifying Language **441**

Dealing with Text Presentation **444**
Setting Direction **444**
Joining Control **446**

Case by Case: Fonts and Font
Utilities **447**

VI Advanced Concepts

19 XHTML Modularization 451

The Need for Modularization **452**
Devices Affected by XHTML
Modularization **452**
Modularization: A Closer Look **453**

What Is Modularization? **454**

The Modules **455**
Abstract Modules **455**
XHTML DTD Modules **458**

Extending XHTML **458**

XHTML Basic **459**
Features in Use Across
Appliances **460**
What's Supported and Why **460**
What's Not Supported and Why **461**
Specific Modules Included in XHTML
Basic **462**

XHTML Basic Document Structure **463**

Case by Case: Creating and Deploying
an XHTML Basic Document **464**

20 Customizing DTDs 467

Understanding DTDs **468**
What Is a DTD? **468**
The DOCTYPE Declaration **468**
DTD Syntax **470**

Reading the XHTML DTDs **476**
Downloading the XHTML DTDs **477**
Structure of the Transitional XHTML
DTD **477**
Structure Versus Semantics **479**

Case by Case: Defining Your Own
DTD **479**
Extending an XHTML DTD **480**
Defining the <embed> tag **480**
Using Your New DTD **483**

21 Transforming Documents with XSLT 485

Understanding XSL **486**
Formatting Objects **486**
Transformations **488**
XSLT Parsers **489**

Creating XSL Style Sheets **491**
Exploring XSLT Syntax **491**
Structure of an XSL Document **491**
Understanding XPath References **497**

Transforming XHTML with XSLT **498**
Using CSS and XSLT with XHTML **498**
Creating Alternate Content Views **505**

Case by Case: Adapting Web Pages for
Specific Audiences **509**

22 Moving Toward XML 511

Making All Things Possible with XML **512**

Understanding the Relationship Between
SGML, XML, and XHTML **513**
SGML **514**
XHTML **515**

XML in Theory and Practice **515**

Practical Examples of XML **515**

Understanding XML Structure **518**

Describing New Vocabularies with
XML **518**
  Understanding Document Type
  Definition Advantages **519**
  Coping with Document Type Definition
  Disadvantages **520**

Is XML Just HTML All Over Again? **521**
  HTML and XML **521**
  Element Name Guidelines **522**

Defining the XML Document **522**
  Document Production **523**
  Understanding Well-Formedness
  Constraints **525**

The Prolog: The XML Declaration **526**

Constructing the XML Document Prolog:
The Document Type Declaration **527**

Constructing the Document Body **528**
  Character Data **529**
  Markup **529**

Understanding How XML Forms Logical
Structures **529**
  How XML Forms Physical Structures **530**
  Normalization **531**
  Element Types **532**
  Attribute Lists and Types **534**
  Unparsed Entities **535**

Case by Case: Real-World Applications of
XML **536**

VII Appendixes

**A Site Publishing, Maintenance, and
   Marketing Guide 541**

You've Built Your Web Site,
What Now? **542**

Transferring Files Using FTP **542**
  FTP Software **543**
  Macintosh and UNIX FTP Software **543**
  Visual Applications **543**

Testing Files Live **544**

Managing Links **545**
  Manual Management **546**
  Link Management Programs **546**

Copyright Guidelines **547**

The Web As a Commercial Venue **548**

Search Engines and Directories As
Marketing Tools **549**
  How to Get Listed **550**
  Preparing Your Site for Submission **551**
  Submission Follow-Up **553**

Banner Advertising **553**
  Pricing Structures for Banner
  Advertising **554**
  Common Design Guidelines **555**
  Banner Placement **556**
  Does Banner Advertising Really
  Work? **556**

Other Online Marketing Techniques **557**
  E-mail Marketing **557**
  Newsgroups **558**
  Links **558**
  Awards **559**

Web Rings **559**

Offline Marketing Strategies **559**

Case by Case: Legal Issues on
the Net **561**

**B Annotated Resources for Web
   Developers 563**

Web Sites of Interest **564**

Mailing Lists **565**

Organizations **566**

Education and Conferences **567**

C XHTML Reference 569

Data Types: XHTML 1.0 Versions and Specifications **570**

Alphabetical XHTML 1.0 Element Listing **570**

    `<!--… -->` Comments **570**

    `<!DOCTYPE…>` **571**

    `<a>…</a>` **571**

    `<abbr>…</abbr>` **573**

    `<acronym>…</acronym>` **574**

    `<address>…</address>` **574**

    `<applet>…</applet>` **574**

    `<area />` **576**

    `<b>…</b>` **577**

    `<base />` **577**

    `<basefont />` **578**

    `<bdo>…</bdo>` **578**

    `<big>…</big>` **579**

    `<blockquote>…</blockquote>` **579**

    `<body>…</body>` **580**

    `<br />` **581**

    `<button>…</button>` **581**

    `<caption>…</caption>` **582**

    `<center>…</center>` **583**

    `<cite>…</cite>` **584**

    `<code>…</code>` **584**

    `<col>` **584**

    `<colgroup>…</colgroup>` **585**

    `<dd>…</dd>` **586**

    `<del>…</del>` **587**

    `<dfn>…</dfn>` **587**

    `<dir>…</dir>` **588**

    `<div>…</div>` **588**

    `<dl>…</dl>` **589**

    `<dt>…</dt>` **589**

    `<em>…</em>` **590**

    `<fieldset>…</fieldset>` **590**

    `<font>…</font>` **591**

    `<form>…</form>` **591**

    `<frame />` **593**

    `<frameset>…</frameset>` **593**

    `<h1>…</h1>` Through `<h6>…</h6>` **594**

    `<head>…</head>` **594**

    `<hr />` **595**

    `<html>…</html>` **595**

    `<i>…</i>` **596**

    `<iframe>…</iframe>` **596**

    `<img />` **597**

    `<input />` **598**

    `<ins>…</ins>` **600**

    `<isindex />` **600**

    `<kbd>…</kbd>` **601**

    `<label>…</label>` **601**

    `<legend>…</legend>` **602**

    `<li>…</li>` **602**

    `<link />` **603**

    `<map>…</map>` **604**

    `<menu>…</menu>` **604**

    `<meta />` **605**

    `<noframes>…</noframes>` **605**

    `<noscript>…</noscript>` **606**

    `<object>…</object>` **607**

    `<ol>…</ol>` **608**

    `<optgroup>…</optgroup>` **609**

    `<option>…</option>` **609**

    `<p>…</p>` **610**

    `<param />` **610**

    `<pre>…</pre>` **611**

    `<q>…</q>` **611**

    `<s>…</s>` **612**

    `<samp>…</samp>` **612**

    `<script>…</script>` **613**

    `<select>…</select>` **613**

    `<small>…</small>` **614**

    `<span>…</span>` **615**

    `<strike>…</strike>` **615**

    `<strong>…</strong>` **615**

    `<style>…</style>` **616**

    `<sub>…</sub>` **616**

    `<sup>…</sup>` **617**

    `<table>…</table>` **617**

    `<tbody>…</tbody>` **618**

    `<td>…</td>` **619**

    `<textarea>…</textarea>` **621**

    `<tfoot>…</tfoot>` **621**

    `<th>…</th>` **622**

    `<thead>…</thead>` **624**

    `<title>…</title>` **624**

    `<tr>…</tr>` **625**

<tt>…</tt> **625**

<u>…</u> **626**

<ul>…</ul> **626**

<var>…</var> **627**

Common Attributes **627**

Intrinsic Events **627**

Data Types **628**

D CSS2 Reference 631

Style Sheet Properties **632**
Selectors **632**
Pseudo Classes **633**
Rules **633**
Properties **634**
Text **634**
Colors and Backgrounds **636**
Fonts **638**
Box Model **640**
Visual Formatting and Positioning **645**
Generated Content and Lists **650**
Tables **653**
Paged Media **655**
Aural Style Sheets **656**

Index 663

ABOUT THE AUTHOR

A writer, instructor, and designer, **Molly E. Holzschlag** brings attitude and enthusiasm to books, magazines, classrooms, and Web sites. Honored by Webgrrls as one of the Top 25 Most Influential Women on the Web, Molly has spent over a decade working in the online world. She has written 20 books on HTML and Web design and development topics, including the best-selling *Special Edition Using HTML 4.0* and the internationally acclaimed *Web by Design*.

Molly's popular column of 2 $\frac{1}{2}$ years, "Integrated Design," appeared monthly in the internationally popular *WebTechniques Magazine*, until the magazine's closing in early 2002. Molly served for a year as the executive editor of *Web Review*, and has contributed features and columns to *Adobe Studios, Adobe.com, Builder.Com, Digital Chicago, Digital New York, IBM developerWorks, MacWorld, MSDN, PC Magazine,* and other developer publications.

When offline, Molly plays guitar and sings in the original acoustic duo Courage Sisters. For books, giveaways, training, speaking events, and other items of fun and interest, drop by her Web site at (where else?) `http://www.molly.com`.

Dedication

For Michael.

ACKNOWLEDGMENTS

Despite the seeming isolation that computer book authors work in, the reality is that writing a computer book is a collaborative event. In fact, there are many people—from the publisher to the day-to-day managers of the book.

From Que Publishing, I would like to thank Executive Editor Jeff Schultz, Development Editor Laura Norman, and the production and copy editors who helped see the book through to fruition.

From Waterside Productions, I thank my literary agent, David Fugate, who is a great friend indeed. Maureen Maloney keeps my authoring logistics in order, and for her attentiveness and expedience I am very thankful.

I am especially grateful that Steven Champeon agreed to tech edit this book. Steve's breadth and depth of knowledge are astonishing and have helped me become so much better at what I do and how I do it. If there is excellence in this book, it is largely due to Steve's influence.

I couldn't have accomplished putting together a book on such a transitional topic without the guidance and contributions of many people in the industry. Their names certainly extend beyond those acknowledged here, but the following individuals helped me in profound ways directly related to the process of creating this book, and for their perspectives I thank them very much: Kynn Bartlett, Cassandra Greer, Christian Jarolim, Jennifer Kettell, Alan K'necht, Anitra Pavka, Lee Anne Phillips, Sebastian Schnitzenbaumer, Simon St. Laurent, Derrick Story, and Randal S. Schwartz.

To my family and friends, I want to say thank you for your blessings of love and kindness.

And last, but most certainly not least, thanks to all the readers of my books. I thank you for your letters, gifts, and ongoing encouragement and support. You make any of the harder days worthwhile.

TELL US WHAT YOU THINK!

As the reader of this book, *you* are our most important critic and commentator. We value your opinion and want to know what we're doing right, what we could do better, what areas you'd like to see us publish in, and any other words of wisdom you're willing to pass our way.

As a Publisher for Que, I welcome your comments. You can fax, e-mail, or write me directly to let me know what you did or didn't like about this book—as well as what we can do to make our books stronger.

Please note that I cannot help you with technical problems related to the topic of this book, and that due to the high volume of mail I receive, I might not be able to reply to every message.

When you write, please be sure to include this book's title and author as well as your name and phone or fax number. I will carefully review your comments and share them with the author and editors who worked on the book.

Fax: 317-581-4666

E-mail: feedback@quepublishing.com

Mail: David Culverwell
          Publisher
          Que
          201 West 103rd Street
          Indianapolis, IN 46290 USA

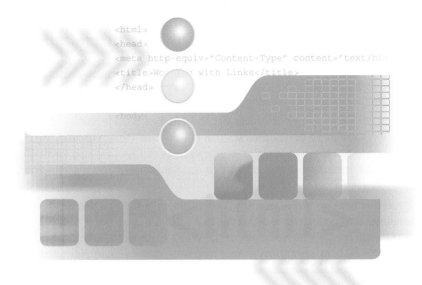

INTRODUCTION

The Web's cool factor is subsiding and now comes the time for the career-level work to begin. This is not to say that innovation is over. If anything, the ideas and methods coming to the forefront of today's Web design and development milieu are paving the way for a new level of innovation and creation.

But the reasons the Web has so rapidly advanced are also reasons that bear examination. We are in a time of great change—and not just in technology. The world, as we all know through the events and circumstances of our recent history, is becoming ever more global and ever more immediate. And I daresay there isn't a soul among us who will disagree that the Internet is as necessary today as it has ever been, and even more so in the changing industrial, technological, multinational, and ideological environments in which we live.

With changes to the world come changes to the way people live and work. Broadband is available and affordable to many more people than ever before. Wireless technologies are becoming more and more a part of our everyday lives. Web sites have grown up in profound and detailed ways. These changes affect not only the way we as individuals use technology but the way we as technologists must accommodate change.

In order to raise the bar from the days of the hobbyist and fledgling design professional to the sophistication of the contemporary designer or developer, information must be collated in such a way that individuals have a multitude of choices at hand. What's more, and perhaps more important, is that our knowledge must continue to deepen as well as broaden—and this is no easy task in our busy lives.

What we clearly need is to go back and spackle the nicks our View Source, read-it-on-Webmonkey, bought-the-book-of-the-month means of education has caused. We are darned good at what we do, and we have so very, very much of which to be proud. But we also have an obligation to the growing professionalism of our industry to make a commitment to solid background. This, in turn, will give us our forward vision.

This means examining Hypertext Markup Language (HTML) very carefully, and gaining an understanding of the ideologies and methodologies inherent to HTML that have often been overlooked. And, while HTML still remains the mainstay of the Web's underbelly, Extensible Hypertext Markup Language (XHTML) offers a great deal of help to shift the limited and often cumbersome HTML methods to a potentially limitless and ideally more logical approach. XHTML is in a sense a bridge, rooted on one side in the territory of existing Web sites, and on the other side in a future of extended and even unknown lands.

XHTML will especially serve to help transition documents to be prepared for new types of delivery that exist today, as well as those to come. Learning XHTML along with those missing principles of HTML will help position you as a Web author to be able to embrace other Web applications and technologies with ease, giving you much more power and flexibility than you've ever had before.

WHO SHOULD READ THIS BOOK

While anyone with an interested in Web site authoring will be able to use this book to learn to create well-authored Web sites, the book is most appropriate for the professional who is interested in strengthening his or her skills in HTML, understanding the rationale and role of XHTML 1.0, and gaining greater insight into the reasons XHTML Modularization decomposes HTML and XHTML, in turn making our daily work both more abstract and more powerful.

The perfect reader of this book is someone who has been writing HTML for at least a little while, is interested in the future of the Web and related technologies, and wants to learn how to improve his or her markup skills.

HOW THIS BOOK IS ORGANIZED

Each chapter in this book is written to stand alone but work in tandem with other chapters in the book. The best way to read the book will be determined by you!

You can start at the beginning and work your way through; this is an especially good technique for intermediate readers to build and refine skills. If you want to know about a specific topic, you can jump right to that topic by using the table of contents as your guide or checking the index for topic references. Within all chapters in this book, I've included cross-references that guide you toward related materials, so you can follow your needs and preferences to the next topic of interest.

Special Edition Using HTML and XHTML has a total of 22 chapters, separated into 6 parts. The goal of the book is to help readers improve their markup knowledge and practice in a sophisticated, learned way. The book uses a combination of W3C guidelines and insights drawn from hands-on experience.

Part I, "Web Markup for Professionals," covers specifications, ideologies, conformance, data types, and document type definitions (DTDs) in detail. This offers people who have been working with HTML or other markup languages a leg up on the technical details of the language.

Part II, "Structuring and Formatting Documents," describes the proper structure and formatting of documents. Although much of this will be familiar at first glance to many readers, you now have professional needs that demand intense detail and accuracy. In Part II, people who have been using HTML workarounds and proprietary markup will learn stricter habits to achieve a greater range of options and skills.

Whether you're adding images, audio, video, Java applets, or Flash to pages, understanding the elements and attributes associated with images, multimedia, and embedded objects is a critical part of creating contemporary Web pages with markup. Part III, "Images, Multimedia, and Embedded Objects," describes these topics.

The goal of Part IV, "Style and Scripting," is to show you how to apply style, scripts, and objects by using markup. You'll gain a more structured view of cascading style sheets (CSS) and how it is inseparable a technology from markup. This is particularly true for XHTML 1.1, which demands that you must use CSS if you want to use the public DTDs and have any options for presentation. Although you won't learn how to write JavaScript or create applets here, you will learn how to address special concerns while adding those technologies to HTML or XHTML documents.

In Part V, "Accessibility and Internationalization," you'll learn about the laws, policies, and technology solutions that affect accessibility concerns worldwide. Internationalization and localization study the various methods user agents use to display other languages and how authors can learn to deal with special fonts, character sets, and display issues for sites around the globe.

In Part VI, "Advanced Concepts," you'll learn that XHTML Modularization is the decomposition of HTML and XHTML 1.0 as we know them. Instead of having a singular set of DTDs, XHTML has discrete modules for text, tables, forms, and so on. It's up to you to put it all together with a custom DTD or tap into one of the few public DTDs based on modules such as XHTML Basic. In Part VI you'll learn about advanced document management processing using Transformations. This exciting technology is empowering authors to take information stored in an XML document and transform it into a number of formats, including HTML and XHTML.

The book also has four appendixes:

* Appendix A, "Site Publishing, Maintenance, and Marketing Guide," is a helpful overview of non-markup-specific techniques to help professionals manage sites.

* Appendix B, "Annotated Resources for Web Developers," is a hand-picked reference list of sites, books, and events that can empower the professional who is interested in advancing his or her skills.

* Appendix C, "XHTML Reference," is a helpful lookup of elements and attributes in HTML and XHTML.

* Appendix D, "CSS2 Reference," will assist you in working effectively with Cascading Style Sheets.

CONVENTIONS USED IN THIS BOOK

Special conventions are used to help you get the most from this book and from Web markup.

Text Conventions

Various typefaces in this book identify terms and other special objects. These special type-faces include the following:

Typeface	Meaning
Italic	Italic is used for new terms or phrases when they are initially defined.
Monospace	This is used for information that you type (such as HTML and XHTML), Web addresses, folder names and filenames, and onscreen messages.
Red monospace	The markup to be added during an exercise, or any markup that is being high-lighted for purposes of discussion, is in red monospaced text.

Case by Case

At the end of each chapter you'll find insights, projects, and case studies that help enhance your skills by providing professional applications, examples, tips, and wisdom.

Special Elements

Throughout this book, you'll find notes, cautions, side-bars, and cross-references. These elements provide a variety of information, ranging from warnings you shouldn't miss to ancillary information that will enrich your learning experience:

Cross-references are designed to point you to other locations in this book that will provide supplemental or supporting information. Cross-references look like this:

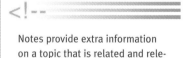 *To learn more about placing images on a page,* **see** *"Adding Images," p. 275.*

`<!--Caution`
Watch your step! Avoid pitfalls by keeping an eye on the cautions available in many of this book's chapters. `-->`

`<!--`
Notes provide extra information on a topic that is related and relevant to the topic but not specific to the given task at hand. `-->`

Sidebars for More Information

Sidebars are designed to provide information that is ancillary to the topic being discussed. Read these if you want to learn more about an application or task.

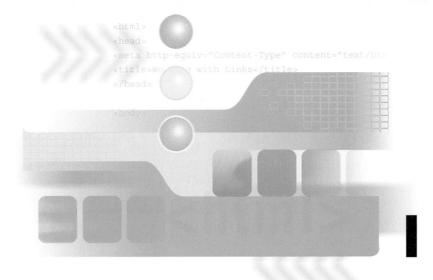

WEB MARKUP FOR PROFESSIONALS

IN THIS PART

1   Working with Specifications   7

2   Writing Conforming Documents   31

3   Dealing with Data Types   61

4   Choosing the Right DTD   81

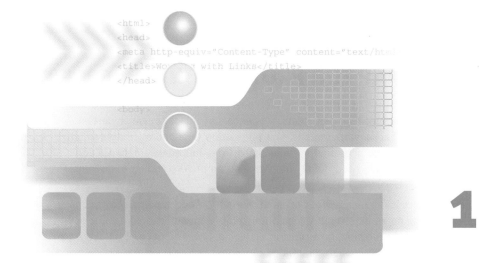

```
<html>
<head>
<meta http-equiv="Content-Type" content="text/html
<title>Wo    g with Links</title>
</head>

<body>
```

1

WORKING WITH
SPECIFICATIONS

IN THIS CHAPTER

A Markup Roadmap for Professionals   8

The W3C   24

HTML and XHTML: Common Ideologies   25

Case by Case: Web Standards Project   28

A MARKUP ROADMAP FOR PROFESSIONALS

It's becoming clear that what we as professional Web designers and developers need today is knowledge—deep as well as broad. In past years, it was commonplace to use Hypertext Markup Language (HTML) hacks, workarounds, and proprietary tags and attributes to build sites. But in a world of disparate operating systems, hardware, and browsers, hacks and workarounds just don't cut it. We need detail, and we need an understanding of how markup really works.

The interesting truth is that the majority of people authoring Web documents professionally come to HTML authoring as an extension of jobs unrelated to communications technology. Rather, most authors are in education, government, medicine, law, and general industry, performing Web authoring as a part of their job-related tasks, but not as their primary chores. Of course, there are many full-time Web builders, too, but the climate and needs of the authoring professional have definitely undergone tremendous changes in recent years.

Whether you're a full-time Web builder or not, it's highly likely that you learned to author Web pages by the bootstrap method—using View Source, books, online resources, and help from friends and colleagues. The bootstrap method worked extremely well in getting people authoring pages. Although early practices were certainly innovative, without a framework of literacy in authoring, it's becoming obvious that we cannot achieve interoperability, nor can we achieve technological advancement.

It's certain that you realize many serious concerns that Web developers face. First, there's the browser dilemma. To ensure that sites are as cross-platform, cross-browser compliant as possible, you have to work extra hard. Imagine if browser developers adhered more rigorously to recommended practices? Our lives would be made much simpler. But browser developers have had their own agendas, and that has done very little to help us. As a result, Web designers in contemporary times typically have to:

- Test work on numerous platforms.

- Test work in numerous browser types.

- Use legacy as well as current browsers in testing.

- Rely on authoritative charts and materials to compare what works and what doesn't work in a given platform/browser environment.

- Learn stress management techniques to cope with the extra-long hours spent trying to make a great site interoperable.

Another profound misfortune is the failure of major Web development software manufacturers to create products that conform to some semblance of recommendations. This is especially disconcerting in today's Web production environment, where many Web authors are being asked to use specific applications that include visual editing tools such as Adobe GoLive, Macromedia Dreamweaver, Microsoft FrontPage and content management systems such as

Vignette to do a job. Given the wealth of collaborative tools and production environments that exist in visual editors, it makes sense in many cases to test work with legacy browsers, rely on authoritative charts, and learn stress-management techniques!

As a result of all these changes, not only do today's Web professionals have to learn markup, but they must understand the limitations of the software products they are using. The good news is that by formally studying markup—and the myriad choices it gives you—you can totally empower yourself. You can become an ace troubleshooter, refine your process, reduce markup overhead as much as possible, and bring documents up to professional level.

A final concern is taking responsibility for our own practices. This is no easy task because the rapid pace of change can be downright maddening! On the other hand, there are more and more authoritative resources available. We must find those resources and turn to them to gain the knowledge we need. Despite our busy lives, if we really want to progress as Web authors, we must read the books, visit Web sites, and practice methodologies that help us become more skilled.

> `<!--`
>
> Although it is common in casual conversation to refer to HTML as *code*, this is inaccurate. HTML and Extensible Hypertext Markup Language (XHTML) are markup languages, not programming languages. Some features distinguish markup languages from programming languages. Typically, markup is human-readable and is interpreted by some agent, such as a Web browser. Programming languages tend to use more abstract syntax than markup, and in most cases they must be compiled and executed in order to run. Because of this difference, I refer to working with HTML as *authoring* and to the text in the languages as *markup*.
>
> `-->`

Learning proper authoring practices brings context to what we do and how we do it. This, in turn, creates an opportunity for a set of best practices to emerge that will ultimately make our work easier and our opportunities more innovative and extensible as a result.

SGML and HTML

In 1995, when the frenzy to build the Web big and strong had just begun, a working Web author needed just a few items: a dog-eared copy of Laura Lemay's HTML book, a text editor, a graphics editor, Web space, and an File Transfer Protocol (FTP) client. Sure, there were learning curves, but those curves are not remotely comparable to the demanding shape of today's sophisticated and complicated technology.

In order to provide the context necessary to move from a casual approach to markup to a professional one, it's my firm belief that digging a bit into the historical foundations can reveal explanations for many of the things you know from experience but never put into words.

HTML's history is very interesting. It began as an application of Standard Generalized Markup Language (SGML) and went through a period of pure application and then a period of total chaos; it is now back to a time in which pure application ideologies are being promoted.

The original goal of HTML was to provide streamlined document markup suitable for exchanging files on the Web. At heart, HTML is simply a document language that works with Internet protocols.

About SGML

SGML is what is sometimes referred to as a metalanguage: Its purpose is to create other document markup methods such as HTML. SGML is complicated and syntactically strict but incredibly powerful—its applications address industry, government, military, and business needs. Some of SGML's features include concern with a document's structure rather than its appearance, the portability of documents, and the ability to port documents to a variety of media, including print and screen.

To learn more about SGML, you can visit `http://www.w3.org/MarkUp/SGML`.

Enter the visual browser, which changed the Web environment from one constructed of hyper-linked text documents to one that promised growing opportunities for visual design. HTML—and Web browsers themselves—were stretched out of proportion in order to accommodate the rapid-fire pace of the Web's visual and interactive growth. Designers, especially, were naturally concerned with creating designs that were visually rich and aesthetically pleasing rather than concerning themselves with the underlying technology.

HTML focuses on the structure of a document. Originally designed for text, it was *never* meant to be a language of design. HTML originally included very few facilities for a document's visual design. In fact, in its original text-based environment, HTML couldn't even display images; you had to download them and view them in a separate application. Over time, a variety of elements were added to make documents more suitable to a visual environment. But the increasing popularity of the Web meant that designers had to do more: Everyone wanted sites that were attractive and interactive.

As a result, HTML was dramatically altered from its original structure with the introduction of browser-centric, proprietary elements and attributes. This resulted in complex markup that was difficult to maintain. Despite the introduction of Cascading Style Sheets (CSS), which are intended to aid in the separation of document structure from presentation, browser support has historically been problematic, forcing Web developers to rely on HTML (with both nonproprietary and proprietary elements and attributes), or a combination of HTML and CSS for presentation. This has also resulted in bloated Web browsers containing plenty of forgiveness checking of poorly written markup.

Because SGML is such a highly structured methodology, when HTML was in its first incarnation, it had clear and straightforward rules. Documents were structured in a simplistic way, using headers, paragraphs, and some limited text formatting. There wasn't a lot to HTML that diverted from the structural concerns of SGML, except that HTML was a whole lot less complex. Some of the early features of the first version of HTML included basic document structure, such as `head`, `title`, and `body`; a variety of document formatting needs, such as `h1-h6`, `p`, and `br`; and the anchor `a` element and related attributes.

<!--
For a look at early HTML, including the original HTML document type definition (DTD), see
`http://www.w3.org/History/19921103-hypertext/hypertext/WWW/MarkUp/MarkUp.html`.
-->

Very few Web designers have a thorough understanding of HTML's rules or principles because many of us missed out on that information in the early rush to build the Web. Time has also proven a critical factor: When you have to get a site to a client quickly, worrying about writing clean markup *seems* less important than simply making the site work. In my experience, and in the experience of many working professionals, good markup is a timesaver because it reduces troubleshooting problems significantly. The fact is, a fair amount of the HTML created today does not conform to any set of rules—it's really not HTML at all in a certain sense, but a conglomerate of nonproprietary and proprietary markup. This is not necessarily a problem for today's browsers, which have been specifically designed to forgive.

However, nonconformance with good authoring practices certainly creates problems. The following are some of the problems that have come about because of what has historically happened with HTML:

- **Style inconsistency between documents**—If more than one person is responsible for updating documents, the variation in authoring style because of haphazard practices can make documents very difficult to maintain.

- **Problems with error correction**—Debugging documents that are full of syntactical and style-oriented errors can be extremely problematic and time-consuming.

- **Interoperability issues**—Despite the myriad hacks and workarounds such as the use of graphic shims and JavaScript for routing browsers, interoperability issues related to documents on the Web remain a major source of trouble to the Web author.

The problem has grown with the introduction of new user agents such as personal data assistants (PDAs) and cell phones. The presentation for these devices is dramatically different from the presentation possible within the context of a Web browser. So, from the perspective of the Web author, without an understanding of the principles of the language, severe limitations on technologic advancement can ensue.

To accommodate the sudden demand to make what was once a simple, text-based markup language flex to a graphic environment, an entire generation of imaginative tags and attributes was born.

Design Woes in HTML

As any designer will tell you, the quality of HTML-based presentation is woefully lacking.

Trying to manipulate HTML to get it to do what you want is pretty frustrating, right? No consistent layout support. No consistent way to control whitespace. No stable way to manage type. This designer's nightmare is a result of the fact that the Web was never intended to be a visual environment. But it became one, and how to manage that reality has been a challenge ever since.

Admittedly, to most designers, presentation always seemed to take a backseat with the committees that work on markup languages. But the committees are not thinking as much about design because presentational issues have historically occurred via methods other than markup. Fortunately, the W3C has made tremendous progress with style languages, specifically CSS, which brings a lot more control to those interested in creating rich visual sites.

Three widely seen examples illustrate how the blurring between structure and presentation occurred in HTML:

- **The center element**—Netscape created the center element (see Listing 1.1), which is used to center text and images on a page (see Figure 1.1). Note that the center element doesn't follow any particular rule structure. It's an arbitrarily named tag, and although it worked, it also signified a break from any formal tradition. HTML, which was originally used for structuring documents, was becoming a de facto language of design.

- **Tables**—Not long after the appearance of center, tables emerged to provide a neater alternative to creating tabular data without having to resort to the difficult pre (preformatted text) element (see Listing 1.2). Preformatted text ensures that anything within it, including spaces and tabs, is kept intact and displayed as is (see Figure 1.2). Although the practice can be justifiable and can be done in accordance with W3C recommendations, it is the truest example of how HTML elements and attributes that were created to solve a practical structural problem turned into a presentation methodology that has found widespread use.

- **The font element**—The font element is one of the most frustrating elements to deal with because of the sheer amount of markup it generates. Tables compound the problem because authors find themselves having to open and close their font tags within each cell of a table to achieve consistent visual results across browsers. This introduces a great potential for error, and it bloats markup unnecessarily.

Listing 1.1   An Early Example of HTML That Uses the *<center>* Tag

```
<html>
<head>
<title>My Page</title>
</head>
<body>
<h1>Welcome To My Web Page</h1>
<p>This Web page contains a bit about me, my family,
and favorite World Wide Web links</p>
<center><a href="more.html">Click Here for More</a></center>
<p>Thanks for visiting, and be sure to send an email!</p>
</body>
</html>
```

Listing 1.2   Using the *<pre>* Tag to Format Tabular Data

```
<html>
<head>
<title>Fruits & Veggies</title>
</head>
<body>
<pre>
```

Listing 1.2   Continued

```
Fruits          Veggies
Avocado         Asparagus
Coconut         Carrot
Strawberry      String Beans
<pre>
</body>
</html>
```

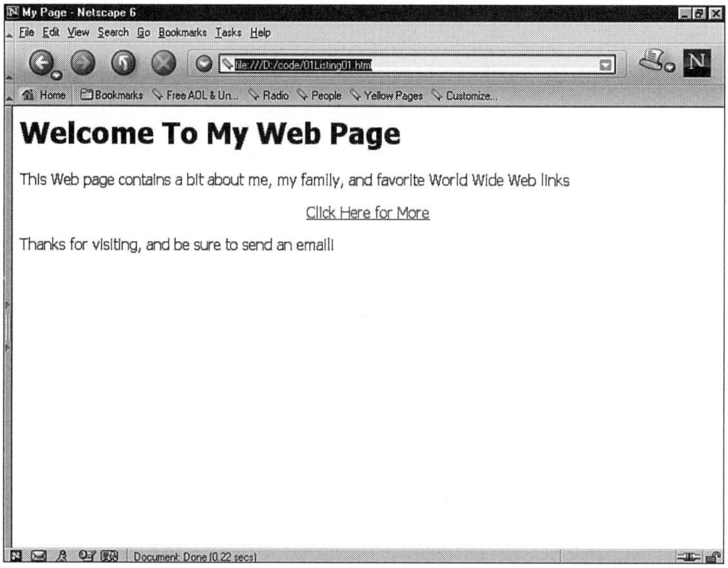

Figure 1.1
Once a solution, now the `<center>` tag is deprecated for not conforming to syntactical integrity.

Figure 1.2
Originally, the preformatted text, `pre`, element was used to create tabular data.

Preformatted text also forces a monospaced font as its default. This is great for showing programming code and markup snippets, perhaps. But tables provide much more precise control
over data (see Listing 1.3), enabling you to position each bit of table content within an individual cell and row (see Figure 1.3).

Listing 1.3   Using Tables for Their Intended Purpose

```
<html>
<head>
<title>Fruits & Veggies</title>
</head>
<body>
<table border="1">
<tr>
<th>Fruits</th>
<th>Veggies</th>
</tr>
<tr>
<td>Avocado</td>
<td>Asparagus</td>
</tr>
<tr>
<td>Coconut</td>
<td>Carrot</td>
</tr>
<tr>
<td>Strawberry</td>
<td>String Beans</td>
</tr>
</td>
</table>
</body>
</html>
```

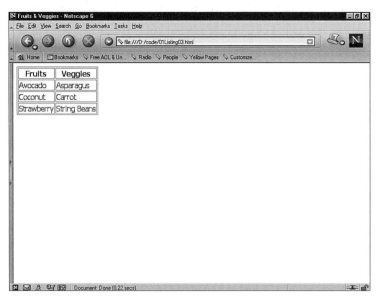

Figure 1.3
A table solution to the same tabular data shown in Figure 1.2. See also Listing 1.4.

Listing 1.4   A Table-Based Layout

```
<!DOCTYPE HTML PUBLIC "-//W3C//DTD HTML 4.0 Transitional//EN"
"http://www.w3.org/TR/REC-html40/loose.dtd">

<html>
<head>
<meta http-equiv="Content-Type" content="text/html; charset=ISO-8859-1">

<meta name="description" content="DynamicTraders.com showcases Robert
Miner's Dynamic Trader Software and DT Reports and provides current
trade recommendations for the futures, stock and mutual fund markets.">

<meta name="keywords" content="Dynamic Trading,Dynamic Traders,Robert Miner,
stocks,bonds,mutual funds,Dynamic Trading Software &amp; Trading Course,trading
course,futures">

<title>Dynamic Traders - Welcome</title>

<link href="css/site.css" rel="stylesheet" type="text/css">

<script src="js/date.js" type="text/javascript">
</script>

</head>

<body>
```

Listing 1.4 Continued

```
<table width="679" cellpadding="0" cellspacing="0" align="center"
border="0">

<tr>

<td width="679" colspan="4" align="center" valign="top">

<img src="images/main_header.gif" width="679" height="87"
alt="DynamicTraders.com: Dramatically Improve Your Trading Results"
border="0"></td>

</tr>
</table>

<table width="679" cellpadding="0" cellspacing="0" align="center"
border="0">
<tr>

<td width="15" align="left" valign="top"><img src="images/date_left.gif"
width="15" height="18" alt="" border="0"></td><td width="215"
bgcolor="#6699FF" align="center" valign="top"><span class="whiteSans">

<script language="JavaScript1.2" type="text/javascript">Greetings();
</script></span></td><td width="44" align="left" valign="top"><img
src="images/date_right.gif" width="16" height="18" alt="" border="0"></td>

<td width="405" align="right" valign="top"><a href="default.htm"><img
src="images/tab_home_blue.gif" width="81" height="18" alt="Home" border="0">
</a><a href="futures.htm"><img src="images/tab_futures.gif" width="80"
height="18" alt="Futures" border="0"></a><a href="stocks.htm"><img
src="images/tab_stocks.gif" width="80" height="18" alt="Stocks" border="0">
</a><a href="funds.htm"><img src="images/tab_funds.gif" width="80"
height="18" alt="Funds" border="0"></a><a href="freestuff.htm"><img
src="images/tab_freestuff.gif" width="80" height="18" alt="Free Stuff"
border="0"></a></td>

</tr>
</table>
<br>

<table width="679" cellpadding="0" cellspacing="0" align="center"
border="0">
<tr>
<td width="135" valign="top">

<table cellpadding="0" cellspacing="0" width="135" border="0">
<tr>
```

Listing 1.4   Continued

```
<td width="135"><img src="images/left_header.gif" width="135" height="19"
alt="" border="0"></td>
</tr>

<tr>
<td bgcolor="#3366CC" width="135">

<div align="left">

<font face="Verdana,Arial,Helvetica,sans-serif" size="1" color="#FFFFFF">
<a href="dtbk.htm" class="whiteSans">  <b>Dynamic Trading<br>
  Book</b></a>
<br><br>
<a href="dt3.htm" class="whiteSans">  <b>DT Software<br>
  &amp; Trading Course</b></a>
<br><br>
<a href="https://www.DynamicTraders.com/PDFStore/main.asp"
class="whiteSans">  DT Reports Online</a>
<br><br>
<a href="DTSubscribers/" class="whiteSans">  
<b>Subscribers </b></a>
<br><br>
<a href="DTOwners/" class="whiteSans">  <b>DT Owners</b></a>
<br><br>
<a href="aboutbob.htm" class="whiteSans">  <b>Robert Miner</b></a>
<br><br>
<a href="whatot.htm" class="whiteSans">  <b>Client Comments</b>
</a>
<br><br>
<a href="https://www.DynamicTraders.com/Secure/dtorder.asp"
class="whiteSans">  Order</a>
<br><br>
<a href="contact.htm" class="whiteSans">  <b>Contact Us</b>
</a>
<br><br>
</font>
</div>
</td>
</tr>
</table>
</td>

<td width="9"><img src="images/spacer.gif" width="9" alt="" border="0"></td>

<td width="350" align="left" valign="top">
<div class="blackSans">
```

Listing 1.4   Continued

```
<p><b>Current Trade Recommendation - The High-Probability Trade of the Week
</b><br>

Updated each Monday evening with the commentary, charts and trade
recommendation of one market from the Dynamic Trader Futures Report.<br>

<a href="curtrec.asp">Go to this week's trade recommendation</a></p>

<p><b>DT Reports Online - New Report Every Saturday</b><br>
The DT Futures and Mutual Funds Report is now available to non-subscribers
from our DT Reports Online Store<br>
<a href="https://www.DynamicTraders.com/pdfstore/main.asp">Go to the DT
Reports Online Store</a></p>

<p><b>Dynamic Trader Futures Report</b><br>
<strong>Comprehensive analysis, trade recommendations and traders education
for the major financial and commodity markets.</strong><br>
The new Dynamic Trader Futures Report is now delivered four days per week.
Daily delivery means expanded coverage, trading recommendations and trading
education. Best of all, there is five times the coverage but no price
increase.<br>
<a href="futures.htm">Complete information on the new Dynamic Trader
Futures Report</a></p>

<p><b>Dynamic Trader Mutual Funds Report</b><br>
<strong>Comprehensive analysis, and switching strategies for bull and bear
index and sector funds.</strong><br>
<a href="funds.htm">Complete information on the new Dynamic Trader Mutual
Funds Report</a></p>

<p><b>Traders Education Tutorial - Updated Every Saturday</b><br>
<strong>Practical technical analysis and trade strategies
education</strong><br>
DynamicTraders.com offers far more comprehensive FREE trading education than
any web site. Each week we provide a Traders Education Tutorial of practical
trading strategies. We archive the past tutorials so you may download them
for a complete trading education.<br>
Go to this week's
<a href="dttraded.asp">Traders Education </a>and the Traders Education
<a href="arc_te.asp">Archives</a></p>

</div>
</td>
<td width="4"><img src="images/spacer.gif" width="4" alt="" border="0"></td>
<td width="181" align="center" valign="top">
```

Listing 1.4   Continued

```
<table width="181" cellpadding="0" cellspacing="0" border="0">
<tr>

<td colspan="3" width="181" align="center" valign="top"><img
src="images/right_header_news.gif" width="181" height="38" alt="News"
border="0"></td>

</tr>

<tr>

<td width="6" bgcolor="#FFFFEC"><img src="images/spacer.gif" width="6"
height="1" alt="" border="0"></td>

<td width="171" valign="top" bgcolor="#FFFFEC">
<div class="smallBlackSans" align="left">
<p><strong>FREE - $300 Subscription with the Purchase of
Dynamic Trader Software and Trading Course </strong>  <br><br>
<span class="redSans"><strong>* Offer Good Through November 19th *</strong>
</span><br><br>
For a limited time, we are offering an additional three-month subscription
to the Dynamic Trader Futures Report with the purchase of the Dynamic Trader
Software & Trading Course. Take advantage of this incredible package of
technical analysis software and trading course now!<br><br>
<a href="dt3.htm">More information on DT Software and Trading Course </a>
</p>
</div>

<br><br>
</td>

<td width="4" bgcolor="#FFFFEC"><img src="images/spacer.gif" width="4"
height="1" alt="" border="0"></td>

</tr>
</table>

</td>

</tr>
</table>

<br>
```

Listing 1.4 Continued

```
<div align="center" class="smallBlackSans">&copy; 2001 Dynamic Traders Group
ALL RIGHTS RESERVED
</div>

</body>

</html>
```

See Figure 1.4 for a complex table layout.

Figure 1.4
This page uses a complex table layout to achieve its design. Note also the use of font tags, which are actually used in tandem with style.

Quicker than you can say "browser wars," new elements and attributes began to appear, along with entirely new technologies such as JavaScript, CSS, and dynamic HTML (DHTML). The way in which these technologies were supported had everything to do with the way the browser manufacturers did or did not incorporate them into a given browser.

HTML was soon in a state of chaos. The World Wide Web Consortium (W3C); for more details, see the section "The W3C," later in this chapter)—a committee of individuals, research organizations, and companies such as Microsoft and Netscape—worked to find some solution to the refinement of HTML. What emerged from the W3C were formal specifications about HTML authoring practices.

Of course, what was agreed upon at the table and what has since appeared in browsers has been inconsistent. It's confounding when you think that vendors never fully implement the details they themselves assist in creating; they continue to support their own proprietary extensions. We have specifications, but working authors in the real world find themselves having to balance the needs of clients with the ideologies inherent to the maturing languages.

Despite that little problem, the W3C has managed to corral many of the renegade aspects of HTML into some refined sense of syntactical integrity. By the time the HTML 4.0 recommendation appeared, formal and intelligent structure was being reexamined as being a main priority within the language.

Enter XML

eXtensible Markup Language (XML) came about as a response to the need to streamline SGML for a networked environment—specifically, the Internet. The focus of XML is always on the data. XML has a very clear separation between structural markup for the data and the presentation of that data.

Like SGML, the common parent it shares with HTML, XML is a metalanguage. It is a specification of rules that enable authors to create applications and subsets that are unique to their needs. For example, if I am interested in writing a memo in XML, I can describe the information as I see fit, as illustrated in Listing 1.5. However, it's up to me to author the presentational components of the document, which I can do by using style methods such as Extensible Style Language Transformations (XSLT) and CSS.

Listing 1.5   An Example of an XML Document That Is Free of Presentational Markup

```
<?xml version="1.0" standalone="yes"?>
<memo>
<recipient>Steve C.</recipient>
<message>We aim to please, how are we doing?</message>
</memo>
```

XML is difficult for some Web designers to learn because of its abstract and seemingly arbitrary methods. However, XML is really a very logical and organized technology. It draws from its parent SGML a syntactic quality referred to as *rigor*. *Rigor*, in very simple terms, means following the rules. Although following rules might not be something Web developers have done much of in the past, the benefits are great. Some of XML's features and subsequent influences on markup languages for the Web include the following:

- **Flexibility**—XML can manage data that is unique to banking and medicine. No matter the data type, XML likely offers a method by which to accommodate that data. The two exceptions to this are binary data and embedded scripting.

- **Customization**—XML's flexibility is directly related to the fact that tags can be customized.

- **Conformity**—XML retains the syntactical integrity and strict structure that its SGML parent defines.

Looking at XML's features, it becomes immediately evident that XML can conceivably replace HTML as a means of marking up Web sites. This is in fact why XML was, when it first hit the press, referred to as the "HTML killer."

*For detailed information on XML, **see** Chapter 22, "Moving Toward XML," p. 511.*

Browsers are beginning to incorporate more and more of XML's intelligence, which is very good news. XML will indeed be able to give Web developers on the client side a lot of power. But even given an environment where browsers completely support XML, there are a couple problems with XML as a client-side language. First, the learning curve with XML is steeper for some people than it is with HTML. Second, there are few tools to generate XML, so its widespread use among more visually oriented authors makes its accessibility and subsequent popularity on the client side limited.

➪ *To learn about XSLT, **see** Chapter 21, "Transforming Documents with XSLT," p. 485.*

<!--
For a comprehensive text on XML, see *Special Edition Using XML* by Lee Anne Phillips (Que Publishing).
-->

<!--
Both Microsoft Internet Explorer 5.0+ and Netscape Navigator 6.0+ contain some support for XML. This support is expected to expand considerably in subsequent browser versions.
-->

Redefining HTML as an XML Application

HTML and XML do different things, and they do things with a certain amount of respectability and historical intelligence. As we look to the future needs and necessities in the way that markup works and accommodates all the interesting technologies coming down the pike, it's easy to see that some combined force is necessary.

To deal with the existence of HTML and XML, a working group connected with the W3C began to discuss ways to give XML structure and extensibility but still honor HTML as a real-world and legacy methodology. What resulted, as you've by now guessed, is XHTML. Essentially, XHTML means that HTML has been redefined as an application of XML. No longer a sibling, HTML is now in essence a child of XML, and it must conform to XML's parental rules (see Figure 1.5).

<!--
XML has related technologies such as Extensible Style Language (XSL) and XSLT that allow options for XML presentation. XSL and XSLT emerged from an earlier technology known as *Document Style Semantics and Specifications Language (DSSSL)*. CSS can also be used with XML.
-->

Figure 1.5
The original and current relationship of SGML, HTML, and XHTML.

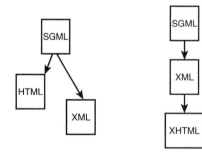

Currently, there is growing interest in the refinement of what is presented within a Web browser as well as in alternative devices. The ideologies born in HTML 4.0 and carried over into XHTML 1.0 and beyond very clearly embrace the concept of multiple-device development.

Table 1.1 shows a time line of markup languages that are significant to Web authors.

Table 1.1   Markup Languages of Current Significance to Web Authors

Language	Year Introduced	Description
SGML	1986	International Organization for Standardization (ISO) standard for specifying a document markup language.
HTML	1992	An early recommendation for marking up documents.
HTML+	1993	An interesting proposed superset of HTML in which anything that determined appearance was left out. HTML+ was specifically concerned with device independence—which has since re-emerged with XHTML.
HTML 2.0	1995	An HTML version created by the Internet Engineering Task Force (IETF).
HTML 3.2	1996	W3C formal recommendation for HTML. A 3.0 version had been under discussion but was never adopted.
XML	1998	Universal format for structured documents and data on the Web.
XHTML	2000	Document markup language for Web and alternative devices.
Module-based XHTML	2001	Means of subsetting and extending XHTML for emerging platforms.
XHTML Basic	2000	Modular subset of XHTML created specifically for alternative user agents that don't support full features of XHTML, such as frames.

XHTML 1.0 revisits the concept of strong markup for documents. Using XHTML helps you strengthen the structure and syntax of your markup. Why is this even important? If you consider the direction that technology is going, it makes a lot of sense. The information designer of the future will have to include numerous user agents in his or her plan. The browser-based Web with which we are so familiar is no longer the only consideration. Documents will need to be aesthetically pleasing on the Web while being pleasing and logical in numerous other environments as well (for example, pagers, PDAs, cell phones).

XHTML enables any creator of documents, whether designer or developer, to stabilize documents, which makes them more interoperable. XHTML can be used with CSS to achieve presentation goals. XHTML also allows you to use XSL with Transformations. By using this XML-based style technology, you can actually transform a document from one type to another (for example, from an HTML document to a PDF document).

Furthermore, learning to author XHTML documents helps designers who are unfamiliar with programming or more abstract markup make the transition into the extensible world. Using XHTML means using vocabulary you're familiar with—the HTML elements and attributes you work with every day. But you do it in the context of XML, and that means that when you move to pick up other XML technologies, it's easier. For many, learning XHTML means that learning such other technologies as the Synchronized Markup Integration Language (SMIL) and Scalable Vector Graphics (SVG) will be much easier.

It's clear that although SGML was the metalanguage on which HTML was based, XML has had profound impact on the growth and changes seen in markup today.

THE W3C

No doubt you've heard the word *standards* bandied about. But just what are standards and how do they apply to the Web author? Enter the W3C.

The W3C (see Figure 1.6) was formalized in October, 1994. It's an independent, international organization made up of people from across the Internet and Web development community from individuals to representatives from major corporations such as Microsoft, IBM, Sun Microsystems, and Netscape.

Figure 1.6
The W3C Web site provides detailed information on current HTML and related technology standards.

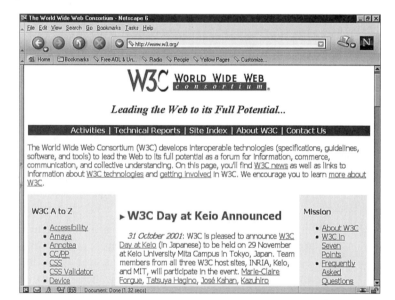

The job of the W3C is to oversee the formal organization of HTML, as well as the various protocols and languages related to the Web, including XML, XHTML, CSS, SMIL, and SVG. The W3C's individual working groups focus on issues within a given technology and make recommendations about the formal practices that they believe should be put into use. A recommendation is a specification that W3C members vote on to demonstrate that they are in agreement about the appropriate and best use of the recommendation's details.

It's important to realize that the processes of the W3C—although based on those of the ISO—do not in fact result in true standards. Web markup languages are not ISO standardized, but are often referred to as standards, despite the fact that they are actually *specifications*.

```
<!--
Access the W3C by pointing your
browser to http://www.w3.org.
                              -->
```

The W3C is not the boss of me or of you. The W3C's role is to study technologies and reach consensus on best practices. How you ultimately apply W3C ideologies is your choice. Following a recommendation is not going to automatically make your Web site development woes go away. In fact, some of the processes might just make your workaday world a little more detailed.

<!--
The ISO (http://www.iso.org) provides detailed information on the concepts and practices for creating formal standards.
-->

⇨ *For more information about developer representation outside the W3C,* **see** *"Case by Case: Web Standards Project," p. 28.*

Whether to follow W3C recommendations is a major concern to the working Web author. I see the concern of following W3C recommendations as being akin to the philosophy "with freedom comes responsibility." Having an understanding of the rules gives you more freedom to innovate, break the rules, or follow the rules in an effort to see how adherence can serve to empower. At the very least, you know why you're doing what you're doing, rather than blindly hoping against hope that your practices will make perfect.

For practical purposes, I like to think of the W3C as a critical resource for three groups:

- **Web developers**—Anyone working on Web sites is affected by the work of the W3C. Keeping up with W3C activities can keep Web developers working cleanly, well, and at the cutting edge.

- **Browser and user-agent manufacturers**—The W3C's recommendations extend to any group building Web browsers and user agents that access Web-based or related documents.

- **Visual software developers**—Companies that are interested in providing Web development software can (and should) use W3C recommendations to oversee the way markup is generated in a given application.

The W3C Web site is frequently updated to keep people posted on what is new in the world of specifications and recommendations. Anyone interested in the history, evolution, use, and future of markup and related technologies should visit the W3C site at regular intervals.

HTML AND XHTML: COMMON IDEOLOGIES

With an understanding of how HTML has grown and changed and how the W3C makes formal recommendations regarding Web markup languages, you can think about how to raise the bar from the more loose practices of the past to the implementation of a professional, learned approach to the job at hand.

As of this writing, HTML and XHTML are both being used to create Web sites. But there are multiple versions of each, with specific changes and ideologies attached. Table 1.2 shows the current W3C HTML and XHTML recommendations of note.

Table 1.2   HTML and XHTML Versions

Version	Introduced	Changes from Prior Versions
HTML 4.0	1997	Deprecation of presentational elements in favor of style sheets, awareness of accessibility and needs of alternative devices, concern with improved rendering of Web documents, introduction of three unique DTDs.
HTML 4.01	1999	A revision of HTML 4.0 to fix minor errors. HTML 4.01 is canonically important because it forms the basis for XHTML 1.0.
XHTML 1.0	2000	An application of XML for solving problems from earlier markup versions, requiring its authors to write stricter documents.
XHTML 1.1	2001	Introduction of modularization and the Ruby Annotation.

⇨ *For further information about document type definitions, **see** "Choosing the Right DTD," p. 81.*

HTML 4.0 and 4.01: Concepts

Within HTML 4.0 are specific ideologies that you need to study in order to have a full understanding of the versions and languages that have followed. Specifically, HTML 4.0 addresses the following critical concepts:

* **Deprecation of presentational elements in favor of style sheets**—You can consider this the heart and soul of contemporary Web design. HTML 4.0 clearly states that the separation of structure and presentation are an imperative goal in order for Web authoring to progress. CSS is the suggested alternative, which upon HTML 4.0's emergence in 1997 was more problematic (due to browser support) than it is today.

> `<!--` XHTML 1.0 Second Edition, in draft form at this writing, is an update of HTML 4.01 with editorial corrections. `-->`

* **Awareness of accessibility and internationalization**—HTML 4.0 is very concerned with ensuring that pages are available to individuals who use alternative user agents. Internationalization concerns are brought forth in HTML 4.0, and discussions about how to internationalize and globalize HTML and XHTML are ongoing.

* **Improved rendering of Web documents**—HTML 4.0 added several elements, specifically in terms of tables, that aid in accelerated interpretation and rendering of markup.

> `<!--` The W3C uses common terminology to describe the status of a component from version to version. *Deprecated* means that the component in question may be used in certain circumstances but that other technologies are available and preferred. *Obsolete* means the component is no longer to be used, and *forbidden* is just that—the component must never be used in that version. `-->`

* **Introduction of three unique DTDs**—HTML 4.0 involves the concept of three unique public DTDs: Strict, Transitional, and Frameset. The Strict DTD is HTML 4.0 at its most ideal, with the presentation of a document relying on CSS almost entirely. The Transitional DTD allows for the use of deprecated

elements, and it also understands the transitional need for authors to use presentational markup in HTML. The Frameset DTD formalizes the use of frames in HTML 4.0 and provides a specific set of rules for their implementation.

For detailed information on changes made between HTML 4.0 and 4.01, see `http://www.w3.org/TR/html4/ appendix/changes.html`.

⇨ *For more details about CSS,* **see** *Chapter 14, "Using CSS with HTML and XHTML,"* **p. 345**.

⇨ *For information on accessibility,* **see** *Chapter 17, "Creating Accessible Sites,"* **p. 419**.

⇨ *For information on internationalization,* **see** *Chapter 18, "Designing International Documents,"* **p. 435**.

HTML 4.0 really upped the ante in terms of offering real options and alternatives to Web developers who are interested in writing documents that conform to W3C ideologies. However, many authors have missed learning these important concepts, which create the foundation for XHTML ideologies.

HTML 4.01 introduced a few errors and editorial changes. These changes are minor in terms of general concept, but they are important because XHTML 1.0 is based on the updated HTML 4.01 DTDs rather than HTML 4.0 DTDs.

XHTML 1.0 and 1.1: Ideologies and New Directions

XHTML 1.0 is the reformulation of HTML as an XML application. This means that documents as well as syntax must strictly conform to the ideologies and DTDs of the language version. The ideologies from HTML 4.0, especially the separation of document structure from presentation and issues concerning accessibility and internationalization, are intact in XHTML 1.0. What's more, the three DTD offerings (Strict, Transitional, and Frameset), which are originally from HTML 4.0 and were later refined by HTML 4.01, are essentially the same DTDs found in XHTML 1.0.

XHTML 1.0 is best seen as a transitional language that helps put professional Web authors in the position of writing specification-oriented markup. It puts browser manufacturers on the hot seat and tells them "get your acts together!" It also moves us toward the extensible intelligence of XML and away from the limitations of HTML.

But transition also means that readying yourself for XML is very important. Fortunately, XHTML can both help strengthen your HTML skills *and* to make those of you unfamiliar with XML more comfortable with its applications. Several of the primary XML ideologies introduced in XHTML 1.0 are as follows:

- **Reintroducing structure to the language**—Picking up on the SGML and XML idea that documents should be written in conformance with the rules set out within the languages, XHTML insists on a variety of syntactic and semantic rules that must be adhered to. One such rule is the idea of *well-formed* documents, which is described in Chapter 2, "Writing Conforming Documents."

- **Providing authors with incentives to validate documents**—The validation of documents is somewhat controversial for a number of reasons. Certain people believe that validation is an unnecessary part of the process if documents are well formed. However, I feel that validation is a powerful learning tool that helps us find mistakes, fix them, and in the process understand the way a specific DTD works. Validation, therefore, is demonstrated and encouraged throughout this book.

- **Accommodating new devices**—Part of the drive to accommodate XML in the Web development environment has to do with an intriguing phenomenon. If the 1990s were the years of information explosion and the movement of the PC from the workplace to the home, this decade will be known for the movement away from the desktop.

Use of Alternative Devices

Instead of PCs, the Web will be increasingly accessed by alternative devices. These include everything from small computers to wireless devices such as PDAs and related devices, cell phones, and pagers. Cell phones and PDAs are often used more frequently overseas than they are in the United States. Many industry pundits have noted that by 2002, the Internet appliance market will begin to saturate the United States.

Of course, a lot of how this will all play out is theoretical. I won't tell you that we have the answers and solutions ready to go today. But I will say that new device applications are up and coming, and when the languages and protocols learn how to play nicely with each other, it's going to be a very different World Wide Web. For that we must all be prepared, and this is a primary reason that XHTML exists. It is also why you, as a developer with concerns about the future, need to know and understand how to put it to work today.

With XHTML 1.1, the concept of separation of structure and presentation is complete. XHTML 1.1 has only one public DTD, based on the Strict DTD found in XHTML 1.0. Web authors have the option to work with modularization. *Modularization* breaks HTML down into discrete modules such as text, images, tables, frames, and forms. The author can choose which modules he or she wants to use—perhaps based on the level of support for those features in the target browser—and then write a DTD that combines those modules into a unique application. This is the first time we really see the extensibility introduced by XML at work, because instead of having only the public DTDs to choose from, authors can now create their own.

➪ *For more details about modularization, **see** Chapter 19, "XHTML Modularization," **p. 451**.*

CASE BY CASE: WEB STANDARDS PROJECT

Although Web authors have to strive to understand and incorporate the important contributions of the W3C, in reality the W3C has no official enforcement status. It exists only as an advisory and consultative organization. It can recommend the adoption of formalized recommendations to facilitate efficient and effective transfer of information.

However, the W3C, while providing a rich array of activities, documentation, and some tutorials, is not an educational or political organization. It is essentially a think-tank. It is also fraught with its own internal issues, and as mentioned earlier, its actions are not always in the best interest of the professional Web author.

Therefore, we Web authors are entrusted with the task of making implementation decisions within the framework and structure of a given site's individual markup needs. It is our responsibility to adopt and administer the recommendation to the best of our abilities and circumstances. Knowing the past, present, and future of Web markup is an undeniable empowerment.

In an effort to encourage fellow authors, browser manufacturers, and software developers to work closely with W3C recommendations, a grass-roots, all-volunteer group of Web designers and developers created an organization known as the Web Standards Project (see Figure 1.7). The WaSP, as it's called, has been aggressive and successful in raising the awareness of all parties involved in the advancement of Web technologies. Further, while encouraging others to follow the W3C, WaSP has also been critical of certain W3C policies that it believes to be counterproductive to progress. As a result, the organization serves as an independent and important public voice.

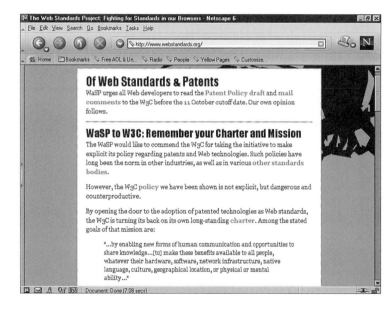

Figure 1.7
The WaSP keeps members and interested parties informed of policy activities regarding markup languages and Web technologies.

```
<!--

For more information on the activities of WaSP, visit
http://www.webstandards.org.
-->
```

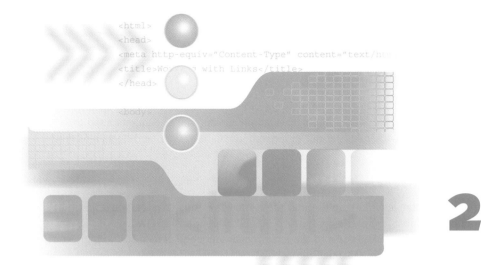

WRITING CONFORMING DOCUMENTS

IN THIS CHAPTER

Document Conformance 32

Conformance Requirements and Recommendations in HTML 4.01, XHTML 1.0, and XHTML 1.1 35

Special Characters 45

Validation 54

Case by Case: Working with Templates 58

DOCUMENT CONFORMANCE

In order to bring HTML and XHTML documents to a professional level, you must understand the concept of *conformance*. For Web authors, this simply means that documents need to follow—that is, conform to—the rules set out in a given language version and document type definition (DTD).

To learn the definition of DTD, **see** "Conformance Definitions in HTML and XHTML," **p. 32.**

When you study the examples and step through the exercises in this chapter, you'll find that the progress of conformance requirements from HTML 4.01 through to XHTML 1.1 has been, for the most part, built on the ideologies of the most recent language versions. The biggest departure you'll find is that from XHTML 1.0 to XHTML 1.1.

Conformance Definitions in HTML and XHTML

To understand conformance requirements, and to follow the sometimes difficult-to-understand language of World Wide Web Consortium (W3C) specifications, it helps to know the terminology used to describe documents and their components.

The following is a list of some of the important terms related to HTML and XHTML:

- **Attribute**—*Attributes* modify elements with a range of types and values. An attribute is made up of two parts, an attribute name and an attribute value. For example, in `div align="center"`, `align` is the attribute name and `center` is the attribute value. Attributes that are in conformance with a given specification are declared in the DTD for that specification (see Figure 2.1).

Figure 2.1
Here, you can see the way an HTML element with related attributes is diagrammed.

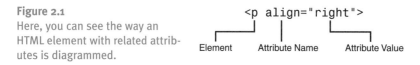

- **Author**—The *author* is the individual who writes the document.

- **Deprecated**—A *deprecated* element or attribute is one where a newer, more suitable method for achieving the goals of that element or attribute has come about. Deprecated elements and attributes can be used with HTML and XHTML Transitional DTDs, and there is a deprecated module in XHTML 1.1 that allows authors to reintroduce a deprecated element or attribute.

- **Document**—In HTML, the document is considered an SGML document that meets the constraints of the HTML specification at hand. In XHTML, the document is considered an XML document.

<!--
The content of this section focuses specifically on HTML 4.01 and XHTML 1.0. Conformance varies with specifications, so if you're using a specification other than HTML 4.01 and XHTML 1.0, check with the specs published on the W3C (http://www.w3c.org) if you have any concerns.
-->

- **Document Type Definition**—This is a master document that identifies and defines the elements, attributes, and other features in a given specification. HTML 4.0, 4.01, and XHTML 1.0 each have three DTDs from which to choose. XHTML 1.1 is based on one of the XHTML 1.0 DTDs and also allows you to create your own DTD.

⇨ *To learn more about DTDs, **see** "Choosing the Right DTD," **p. 81**.*

- **Element**—The mainstay of document structure, an *element* is comprised of a tag or set of tags and any related content, such as paragraph tags surrounding a paragraph of text. As with attributes, elements that are in conformance to a specification are declared in the DTD for that specification (refer to Figure 2.1).

- **Obsolete**—An *obsolete* element is one that has been removed from the specification.

- **User**—The *user* is the individual accessing the document via a Web browser or another user agent.

- **User agent**—A *user agent* is a device that is capable of interpreting (for the purposes of this book) HTML or XHTML markup. It might be a visual Web browser such as Netscape Navigator or Internet Explorer, a text-based browser (remember Lynx?), a browser in a PDA or cell phone, or any other device used by the user to access a document.

These important terms require your specific attention when you're authoring XHTML:

- **Validation**—This is the process in which a document that you write is tested against the DTD that you've declared for that document. It is important in HTML 4.0 and 4.01, but validation is specifically required in XHTML.

- **Well formed**—A *well-formed* document is one in which all elements are properly nested, their attribute values are properly quoted, and the other syntactical constraints are followed. Well-formedness is a critical issue in XHTML.

Listing 2.1 shows poorly formed markup. Look specifically at the welcome sentence, where there both bold and italics are used to format the text. If you drew an arc from the opening bold tag to its closing companion tag, and did the same with the italics tags, you would find that the arcs would intersect (see Figure 2.2). This is because the tags are improperly nested.

Listing 2.1   Improper Nesting of Elements in Poorly Formed Markup

```
<html>

<head>
<title>Poorly Formed Markup</title>
</head>

<body>
```

Listing 2.1 Continued

```
<p><b><i>Welcome to My Web Page</b></i></p>

<p>This Web page contains a bit about me, my family, and favorite
World Wide Web links</p>

<p><a href="more.html">Click Here for More</a></p>

<p>Thanks for visiting, and be sure to send an email!</p>

</body>
</html>
```

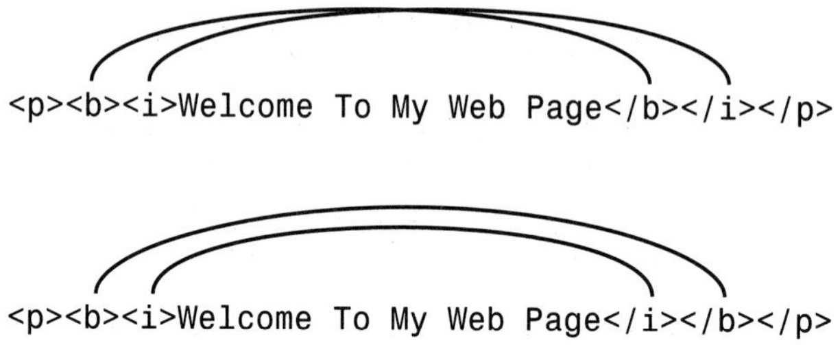

Figure 2.2
The arcs show improper and proper nesting techniques.

```
<p><b><i>Welcome To My Web Page</b></i></p>
```

```
<p><b><i>Welcome To My Web Page</i></b></p>
```

Listing 2.2 shows correct, well-formed markup. In this case, if you drew arcs from the opening and closing tags in question, you would find no intersection, for the tags are properly nested (refer to Figure 2.2).

Listing 2.2 The Proper Nesting of Elements in Well-Formed Markup

```
<html>

<head>
<title>Poorly Formed Markup</title>
</head>

<body>

<p><b><i>Welcome to My Web Page</i></b></p>

<p>This Web page contains a bit about me, my family, and favorite
World Wide Web links</p>

<p><a href="more.html">Click Here for More</a></p>

<p>Thanks for visiting, and be sure to send an email!</p>

</body>
</html>
```

Of course, you could take either one of these examples and load it into the browser of your choice, and it would likely render the page—even the poorly formed one— exactly as you intended (see Figure 2.3). This is due, as expressed in Chapter 1, "Working with Specifications," to the amount of error forgiveness that most browsers have. It's a great example of how bootstrap habits introduced and perpetuated errors into the way HTML should be written instead of the way so many of us have been writing it.

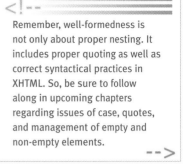

Remember, well-formedness is not only about proper nesting. It includes proper quoting as well as correct syntactical practices in XHTML. So, be sure to follow along in upcoming chapters regarding issues of case, quotes, and management of empty and non-empty elements.

Although the HTML is improperly nested, the browser displays the markup properly.

Figure 2.3
Even poorly formed HTML is for-given by most browsers.

CONFORMANCE REQUIREMENTS AND RECOMMENDATIONS IN HTML 4.01, XHTML 1.0, AND XHTML 1.1

The W3C provides information about what is required for a document to conform and what is recommended for ideal conformance. Requirements must be adhered to, whereas conformance recommendations can be set aside should you find a rationale to do so.

HTML 4.01

In HTML 4.01, three components are necessary to make a document conform:

- **The Document Type Declaration (DOCTYPE) must be in place**—In order for an HTML 4.01 document to conform, it must contain a declaration that states which version of HTML is in use. The Document Type Declaration (DOCTYPE) describes the Document Type Definition (DTD) the document is using.

- **A declarative header section**—This section is delimited by the head element and must contain the title element as well.

- **Document contents**—In a regular document, this is contained within the body element. For frame documents, the frameset element is the delimiter.

As mentioned in Chapter 1, there are three DTDs available in HTML 4.01. The HTML 4.01 specification recommends (but does not require) that the Strict DTD be used. This holds the Web author to a high ideal of writing markup that clearly separates structure from presentation. However, the use of the Transitional DTD is acceptable, and of course the Frameset DTD is necessary when creating HTML 4.01 frame documents that conform to the specification. The Frameset DTD is simply the Transitional DTD plus information on how to properly write framesets.

⇨ For detailed information on using DTDs, **see** Chapter 4, "Choosing the Right DTD," **p. 81.**

Listing 2.3 shows a document that conforms to the requirements and recommendations of the HTML 4.01 specification.

Listing 2.3   Following the HTML 4.01 Conformance Requirements and Recommendations

```
<!DOCTYPE HTML PUBLIC "-//W3C//DTD HTML 4.01//EN"
        "http://www.w3.org/TR/html4/strict.dtd">
<html>

<head>

<title>HTML 4.01 Conformance</title>

</head>

<body>

<p>This document conforms to HTML 4.01 in that:</p>

<ul>

<li>It begins with the DOCTYPE declaration
<li>It has a declarative header section
<li>It contains a body element for content
```

Listing 2.3 Continued

```
<li>It adheres to the recommendation (but not the requirement) that the HTML
4.01 Strict interpretation be used over the transitional one

</ul>

</body>
</html>
```

Figure 2.4 shows the validation results for the page in Listing 2.3, which is in conformance with HTML 4.01.

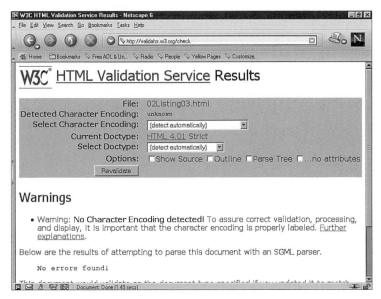

Figure 2.4
Running this page through the W3C validator confirms that the document is a conforming one.

XHTML 1.0

As you are by now aware, the concerns of HTML and the intelligence of XML resulted in XHTML, a more strict version of markup. The document conformance requirements and recommendations for XHTML authoring practices are a bit more detailed than those for HTML.

Necessary practices to create a strictly conforming document in XHTML 1.0 include the following:

- **Validation**—Documents in XHTML 1.0 must be valid, in accordance with one of three DTDs: Strict, Transitional, or Frameset.

- **Root element**—The familiar html element is clearly defined as the root element of an XHTML 1.0 document.

<!--Caution

Despite the fact that the document in Listing 2.3 is valid, the validator is issuing a warning. Warnings are often generated when you could be writing something more efficiently or in accordance with current practices. In this case, I have not denoted a character set, which is ideally done on the server-side. See the section "Special Characters," later in this chapter for more detail regarding how to avoid warnings of this nature.

-->

- **Namespace**—Using the xmlns attribute name, you set the value to the location of the XHTML namespace.

- **DOCTYPE declaration**—As with HTML 4.01, the inclusion of the proper DOCTYPE declaration is imperative. You can choose from the three DTDs in XHTML 1.0: Strict, Transitional, and Frameset.

<!--
In XML, a *namespace* is a collection of element types and attribute names identified by the specific DTD of which they are a part.
-->

Using Alternate Namespaces

The XHTML namespace can be used with other XML namespaces. The resulting documents are not strictly conforming XHTML 1.0 documents, as defined in this section.

The W3C provides an interesting example of the way XHTML 1.0 could be used in conjunction with another XML application, the MathML Recommendation:

```
<!DOCTYPE html
    PUBLIC "-//W3C//DTD XHTML 1.0 Transitional//EN"
    "DTD/xhtml1-transitional.dtd">

<html xmlns="http://www.w3.org/1999/xhtml" xml:lang="en" lang="en">

<head>
<title>A Math Example</title>
</head>

<body>
<p>The following is MathML markup:</p>

<math xmlns="http://www.w3.org/1998/Math/MathML">

<apply> <log/>
<logbase>
<cn> 3 </cn>
</logbase>
<ci> x </ci>
</apply>

</math>

</body>
</html>
```

The highlighted lines show the root and the namespace for XHTML 1.0, which is the namespace in use for the document itself. However, a few lines down into the body, the example shows a new namespace, this time for MathML. For that portion of markup, element types and attributes in the MathML namespace are available to be used between the opening $tag and its companion closing tag,$.

Recommended, Not Required: The XML Declaration

Along with conformance requirements, there is an important recommendation in XHTML 1.0 that you need to examine. In XML, documents can be declared with an XML declaration (also referred to as a *prolog*). At minimum, an XML prolog includes the language and version number, as in the following example:

```
<?xml version="1.0" ?>
```

The prolog might also contain information about character encoding:

```
<?xml version="1.0" encoding="ISO-8859-1" ?>
```

The prolog might also contain the `standalone` attribute. There are two values for this attribute. The value `"yes"` states that there are no external references. The value `"no"` means that the document references an external data type specification. Here we see a standalone example:

```
<?xml version="1.0" encoding="ISO-8859-1" standalone="yes" ?>
```

The XML declaration, as noted previously, describes the XML version and the character encoding (see the section "Special Characters," later this chapter) for the document. Because XHTML is an application of XML, you can use the declaration in accordance with your needs.

However, using the XML declaration causes certain browsers to render the page as text (see Figure 2.5). Table 2.1 shows a detailed breakdown of different browsers, showing where the problems have been found or reported. As a result of these problems, the XML declaration is *recommended but not required* to use.

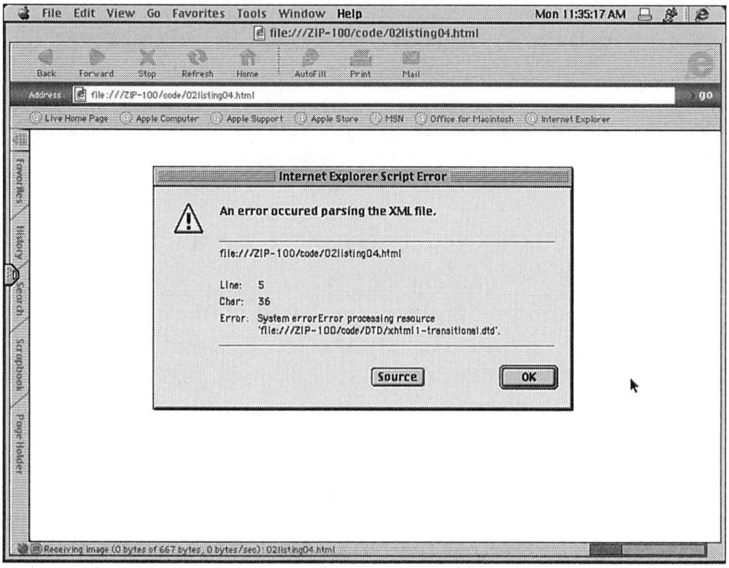

```
<!--
```
To read more about XML namespaces, see "Namespaces in XML," at www.w3.org/TR/1999/REC-xml-names-19990114.
```
-->
```

Figure 2.5
Certain browsers do not render a document as text if the XML declaration is in place.

Table 2.1   Rendering Problems with the XML Declaration*

Browser	Problems with XML Declaration
Amaya 3.1	No
Lynx 2.8.1ver1.1	No
Internet Explorer 3.0, Windows	No
Internet Explorer 3.0, Macintosh	Yes
Internet Explorer 4.0, Windows	No
Internet Explorer 4.0, Macintosh	Yes
Internet Explorer 4.5, Macintosh	Yes
Internet Explorer 5.0x	No
Internet Explorer 6.0	See the sidebar "Compliance Mode in Internet Explorer 6.0"
Mosaic 3.0	No
Netscape 1.0	Yes
Netscape 2.02	Yes
Netscape 3.04	Yes
Netscape 4.0	Yes
Netscape 4.01	Yes
Netscape 4.02+	No
Netscape 6.0+	No
Opera 3.21	No
Opera 3.51	No
Opera 3.60+	Some problems reported
Mozilla	Reported problems with certain builds

*The information in this table was compiled from testing performed by members of the XHTML-L discussion list.

As you can see from Table 2.1, the majority of problems with browser rendering and the XML declaration are found in most 4.0 versions of Netscape (for Windows and Macintosh) and Internet Explorer 4.0 Macintosh versions.

Compliance Mode in Internet Explorer 6.0

Internet Explorer 6.0 has a feature known as *compliance mode,* which switches on or off, depending on the existence and type of a DOCTYPE declaration in a document to be interpreted. This mode provides enhanced support for Cascading Style Sheets (CSS). If the XML declaration is in place, it prevents recognition of the DOCTYPE declaration, causing potential compatibility problems.

For more information on compliance mode in Internet Explorer 6.0, see msdn.microsoft.com/ library/default.asp?url=/library/en-us/dnie60/html/cssenhancements.asp.

To get a good feel for the required and recommended features of an XHTML 1.0 document, step through the following exercise:

1. Open the text or HTML editor of your choice, and create a new document.

2. Add the XML prolog (remember that you can leave this off if you desire):

   ```
   <?xml version="1.0" encoding="UTF-8" ?>
   ```

3. Add the appropriate DOCTYPE definition. In this case, use XHTML 1.0 Transitional:

   ```
   <!DOCTYPE html
        PUBLIC "-//W3C//DTD XHTML 1.0
   Transitional//EN"
        "DTD/xhtml1-transitional.dtd">
   ```

4. Enter the html root element and xmlns attribute name and value:

   ```
   <html xmlns="http://www.w3.org/1999/xhtml">

   </html>
   ```

5. Add the head and title elements (both of which are necessary, just as they are in HTML 4.01):

   ```
   <head>

   <title>XHTML 1.0 Conformance</title>

   </head>
   ```

6. Create the body and content, as follows:

   ```
   <body>

   <p>This document conforms to XHTML 1.0 in that:</p>

   <ul>

   <li>It includes the DOCTYPE declaration</li>
   <li>The root element is &gt;html&lt;<li>
   <li>The namespace is declared using the xmlns attribute</li>
   <li>It validates as an XHTML 1.0 document</li>

   </ul>
   ```

<!--
To avoid rendering problems associated with the XML declaration, you can leave the XML declaration off your documents and, because it's a recommended rather than required declaration, your documents will still be valid. You have to use a workaround (either in the Hypertext Transfer Protocol [HTTP] header or a meta tag) if you want to use character encoding other than U.S. ASCII characters.
-->

```
<p>Note that the XML declaration, which is recommended but not required,
is used in this document.</p>

</body>
```

Listing 2.4 shows the complete document.

Listing 2.4   A Conforming XHTML 1.0 Transitional Document, with the XML Declaration in Place

```
<?xml version="1.0" encoding="UTF-8" ?>

<!DOCTYPE html
     PUBLIC "-//W3C//DTD XHTML 1.0 Transitional//EN"
     "DTD/xhtml1-transitional.dtd">

<html xmlns="http://www.w3.org/1999/xhtml">

<head>

<title>XHTML 1.0 Conformance</title>

</head>

<body>

<p>This document conforms to XHTML 1.0 in that:</p>

<ul>

<li>It includes the DOCTYPE declaration</li>
<li>The root element is &lt;html&gt;</li>
<li>The namespace is declared using the xmlns attribute</li>
<li>It validates as an XHTML 1.0 document</li>

</ul>

<p>Note that the XML declaration, which is recommended but not required,
is used in this document.</p>

</body>
</html>
```

Figure 2.6 shows the document from Listing 2.4 displayed in Netscape Navigator 6.2, which has no difficulty rendering the page even with the XML declaration in place.

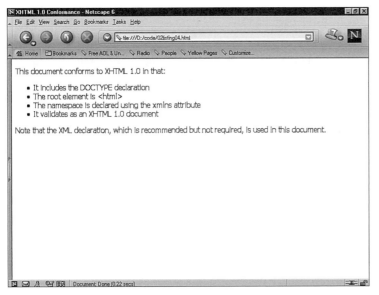

Figure 2.6
The conforming XHTML 1.0 document properly renders in Netscape Navigator 6.2.

As mentioned previously, developers of user agents are also encouraged (and sensible) to develop their agents to the recommendations of the W3C.

Along with the recommendations and requirements that the W3C offers to authors, it also sets out a series of conformance concerns for the manufacturers of user agents, at www.w3.org/TR/xhtml1/#uaconf.

XHTML 1.1

XML's influence is profoundly felt in XHTML 1.1. The introduction of XHTML Modularization offers true extensibility to document authors. The important thing to remember is that although XHTML 1.1 represents a significant departure from the familiar, it offers the potential for enormous power and freedom in the creation of documents.

Documents conforming to XHTML 1.1 must do the following:

- **Restrict elements and attributes to the XHTML namespace**—A strictly conforming XHTML 1.1 document is restricted to the elements and attributes from the XHTML namespace. Using a namespace makes the document more in accordance with XML than anything possible in HTML authoring.

- **Recognize the ideologies of modularization**—Modularization is the decomposition of HTML and XHTML 1.0 into discrete modules. This is a significant influence of better programming practices on markup.

<!--
Examine Listing 2.4 closely, and you'll notice the closing `</li>` list item tags. These are necessary in XHTML 1.0 syntax. You must adhere to numerous syntax rules to for an XHTML 1.0 document to be valid. These syntax issues are addressed in more detail in Chapter 4, "Choosing the Right DTD."
-->

- **Have a root element that is designated as html**—As with XHTML 1.0, the root element is html.

- **Designate a namespace**—The root element designates the namespace as the XHTML namespace by using the xmlns attribute.

- **Have a DOCTYPE definition in place**—With XHTML 1.1, there is only one public DTD, not three as in XHTML 1.0 (or, prior to that, HTML 4.01). That DTD is primarily based on the XHTML 1.0 Strict DTD. With XHTML 1.1, you can also create your own DTD, based on modules, and use a system identifier for that DTD.

Listing 2.5 shows an XHTML 1.1 document that conforms to the public DTD.

Listing 2.5   An XHTML 1.1 Document That Conforms to the Public DTD

```
<?xml version="1.0" encoding="utf-8" ?>

<!DOCTYPE html PUBLIC "-//W3C//DTD XHTML 1.1//EN"
    "http://www.w3.org/TR/xhtml11/DTD/xhtml11.dtd">

<html xmlns="http://www.w3.org/1999/xhtml" xml:lang="en">

<head>

<title>XHTML 1.1: Conforming Document</title>

</head>

<body>

<p>This is a conforming XHTML 1.1 document.</p>

</body>
</html>
```

Should you decide to write your own DTD for XHTML 1.1, remember the rules for conformance to XHTML Modularization.

⇨ *For more about modularization, **see** Chapter 19, "XHTML Modularization," p. 451.*

Table 2.2 summarizes the main conformance concerns for HTML 4.01, XHTML 1.0, and XHTML 1.1.

Table 2.2   HTML and XHTML Conformance Comparison

Conformance Property	HTML 4.01	XHTML 1.0	XHTML 1.1
XML prolog	No	Recommended	Recommended
DOCTYPE declaration	Required	Required	Required
head and title	Required	Required	Required
html	Recommended	Required	Required
Namespace	No	Required	Required
body (or frameset for frame documents)	Required	Required	Required with public DTD

SPECIAL CHARACTERS

An often overlooked but increasingly important area of markup is gaining an understanding of how special characters are dealt with in HTML and XHTML. You'll be reading a great deal more about this in the context of internationalization later in the book. This section gives preliminary information regarding special characters.

➪ *To learn more about internationalization in markup, **see** Chapter 18, "Designing International Documents," **p. 435**.*

Where Character Sets Come From

A number of 8-bit International Organization for Standardization (ISO) character sets are in use for ASCII. Because these characters are 8-bit sets, a limited number of combinations of character entities are possible; ASCII provides a total of 256 characters. Therefore, 8-bit sets are limited in terms of widespread globalization use.

Unicode is a standardized character set, overseen by an organization similar in role to the W3C. Unicode matches binary code for text and script characters. Because it uses 16 bits per character, it is provides a total of more than 65,000 characters. This means Unicode is capable of encoding all the languages of the world—or close to it. Currently, there are more than 34,000 unique characters in Unicode, drawing from 24 languages. Unicode also contains the ASCII character set, most commonly used by Web professionals today to mark up documents in English.

Web professionals use encoding every time they use a character entity (for example, , which is a nonbreaking space). In conforming browsers, the character entity (an entity in this case is a string of characters that together define a symbol to be displayed) displays the space or symbol referred to by the entity. Character entities are taken from several standard encoding methods, including ISO and Unicode standards.

```
<!--
```
For detailed information on the Unicode standard, visit www. unicode.org.

You can find a very helpful article on Unicode, by Mark Davis, at www-106.ibm.com/ developerworks/library/ utfencodingforms.
```
-->
```

Especially important in the internationalization and localization of documents, encoding is a growing area of concern.

Encoding Documents

In order to create characters, including letters, glyphs, symbols, and foreign characters, several encoding methods have been used to provide the many options needed to display text and symbols from any language. Several sets of character entity references are available for use:

The semicolon terminator is not required when writing entities, although it's strongly recommended and to avoid problems, I suggest always using it.

* **ISO 8859-1 (Latin-1) characters**—Numerous entities have been taken from this ISO standard encoding, such as   and © (see Table 2.3 and Figure 2.7).

Table 2.3   Examples of Entities from the ISO 8859-1 Character Set

Entity	Alphabetic	Numeric
Nonbreaking space		
Inverted exclamation point	&iexcl;	&#161;
Cent sign	&cent;	&#162;
Pound sign	&pound;	&#163;
Currency sign	&curren;	&#164;
Yen sign	&yen;	&#165;

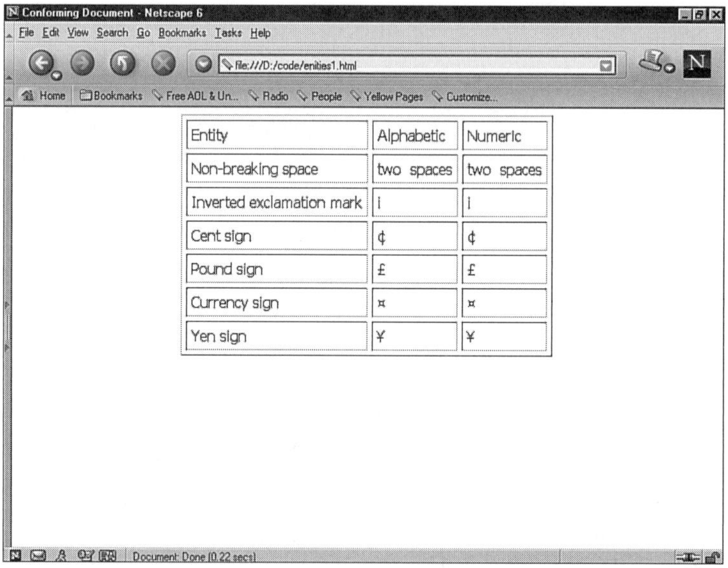

Figure 2.7
Here you see a range of entities from the ISO 8859-1 character set.

- **Symbols, math symbols, and Greek characters**—Using the Adobe Symbol font, these characters can be represented in HTML. Table 2.4 shows the entities taken from the special characters set. Figure 2.8 shows the way these entities are displayed. In Table 2.5, the card-suit glyphs are generated by an individual entity corresponding to each glyph. Figure 2.9 demonstrates symbol entities at work.

Table 2.4   Examples of Special Characters Entities

Entity	Alphabetic	Numeric
En space		
Em space		
En dash	&ndash;	&#8211;
Em dash	&mdash;	&#8212;

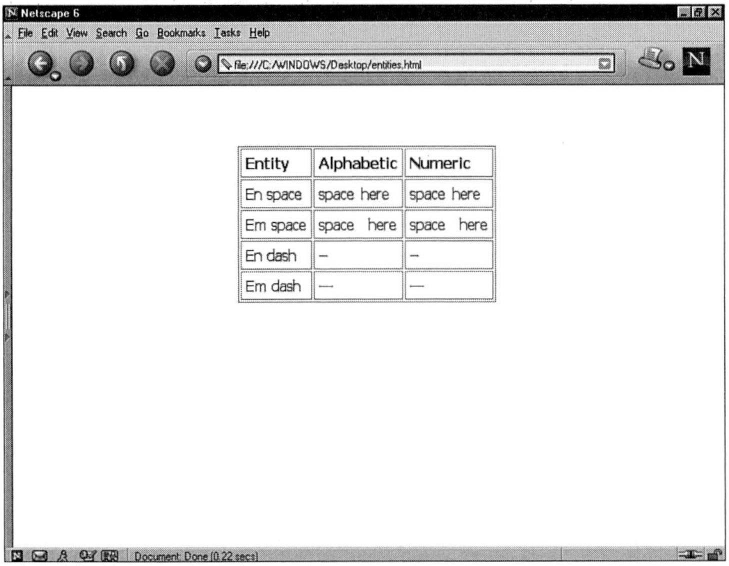

Figure 2.8
A display of special character entities.

Table 2.5   Examples of Symbol Entities

Entity	Alphabetic	Numeric
Spades	&spades;	&#9824;
Clubs	&clubs;	&#9827;
Hearts	&hearts;	&#9829;
Diamonds	&diams;	&#9830;

Figure 2.9
Symbol entities create glyphs.

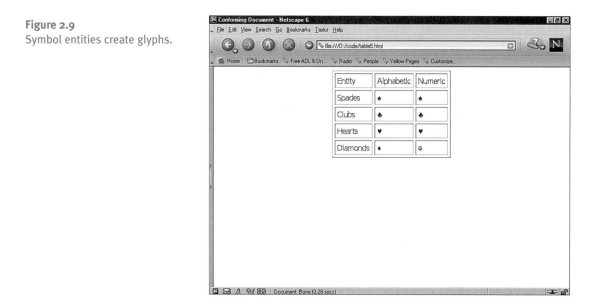

- **Markup-significant and internationalization characters**—These characters are for internationalization, bidirectional text and other special applications.

HTML 4.01 and XHTML have the same entity sets, with minor modifications. You need to be sure to choose from the entity sets that are supported by HTML 4.01 and XHTML and validate your documents (see the section "Validation," later in this chapter).

Another problem with some encoding is browser support. Compare Figure 2.8 from Netscape 6.2 to Figure 2.10 from Internet Explorer 6.0. Netscape supports all the entities shown, but Internet Explorer, has problems properly interpreting the spaces.

Clearly Labeling Encoded Documents

The W3C states emphatically that it is very important for the character encoding of a document to be clearly labeled. Depending on the encoding that you're using, the existence of these labels may or may not have any influence on the way a given browser displays a document.

If, however, you leave encoding out of documents, you might generate warnings when you attempt to validate documents, if the server hasn't provided the character set in the HTTP headers. A warning won't prevent your document from validating (so long as there are no other errors), but it speaks to the concern of proper labeling and the importance that this will have on developments in internationalization practices. And, even more

```
<!--
If you want to demonstrate
markup within a page, such as:
<tag>
you'll need to escape those char-
acters as entities in order for
them to be avoided as being inter-
preted as markup by the browser:
&lt;tag&gt;
-->
```

importantly, using the incorrect character set will cause a jumbled mess for users, especially if their browser has a different default character set (such as those found in international browsers).

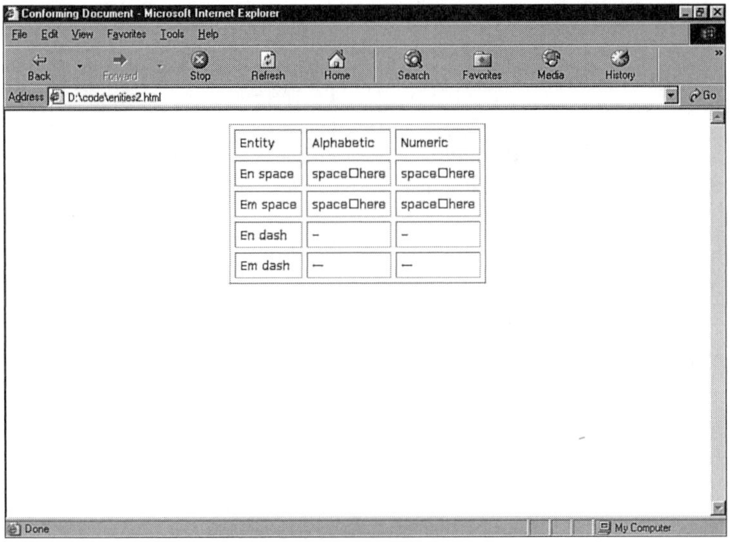

Figure 2.10
Browser support for encoding can be problematic. Here, IE 6.0 in compliance mode, cannot properly render the compliant em and en space entities in either their alphabetic or numeric forms.

Clearly labeling your encoding can be done in any combination of of three ways:

- In the HTTP header. This is appropriate for either HTML or XHTML, as in the following example:

```
Content-Type: text/html; charset=utf-8
```

- In the XML declaration, should you be using one. This is appropriate in XHTML, as in the following example:

```
<?xml version="1.0" encoding="utf-8" ?>
```

- In a meta tag where the encoding is described. This is appropriate in HTML, as in the following example:

```
<meta http-equiv="Content-Type" content="text/html; charset=utf-8">
```

and it is appropriate for XHTML, as in the following example:

```
<meta http-equiv="Content-Type" content="text/html; charset=utf-8" />
```

If you leave character encoding information out of a document and attempt to validate it, you get a warning. The document might still validate, provided that everything else is in order.

```
<!--
```
UTF-8 is Unicode, and therefore it has global properties. You can use UTF-8 as a default for a variety of means of encoding. You can find more information in Chapter 18.
```
-->
```

Common Encoding Practices in Web Markup

Generally, Web document authors who are creating documents in English and are not concerned with localization issues can use the default character set that is valid for the markup version and type in use.

Listing 2.6 shows an HTML 4.01 transitional document with the character set called for in a meta tag. This is recommended by the HTML 4.01 specification.

<!--
The HTML 4.01 specification recommends that the meta information go as high up in the head section of the document as possible. This minimizes any flashing caused by browsers that re-render a page when encountering a new character set.
-->

Listing 2.6   An HTML 4.01 Transitional Document with the Character Set Defined

```
<!DOCTYPE HTML PUBLIC "-//W3C//DTD HTML 4.0 Transitional//EN"
        "http://www.w3.org/TR/REC-html40/loose.dtd">

<html>

<head>

<meta http-equiv="Content-Type" content="text/html; charset=ISO-8859-1">
<title>Defining a Character Set in HTML 4.01</title>
</head>

<body>

<p>This document conforms to HTML 4.01. </p>

</body>
</html>
```

Listing 2.7 demonstrates an XHTML 1.1 document with the character set called for in the XML declaration.

Listing 2.7   An XHTML 1.1 Document with the Character Set Defined

```
<?xml version="1.0" encoding="UTF-8" ?>

<!DOCTYPE  html PUBLIC "-//W3C//DTD XHTML 1.1//EN"
      "http://www.w3.org/TR/xhtml11/DTD/xhtml11.dtd">

<html xmlns="http://www.w3.org/1999/xhtml">

<head>
```

Listing 2.7   Continued

```
<title>Defining a Character Set in the XML Prolog</title>
</head>

<body>

<p>This document is a conforming, valid XHTML 1.1 document with the
Character Set described in the XML declaration.</p>

</body>
</html>
```

Another way to define character sets is by using the `charset` parameter in the `Content-Type` portion of the HTTP header. Because this is a server-related method, it's considered the most efficient means of ensuring that a character set is properly handled.

Labeling Alternate Character Sets

You can use alternate character sets for global or other purposes, by specifying the ISO series or Unicode character set that is appropriate for your needs.

Follow these steps to create an HTML 4.01 document set up to be read in Japanese:

1. Add the DOCTYPE declaration for HTML 4.01 Transitional:

```
<!DOCTYPE HTML PUBLIC "-//W3C//DTD HTML 4.01 Transitional//EN"
          "http://www.w3.org/TR/html4/loose.dtd">
```

2. Enter the root:

```
<html>
```

3. Enter the `head` and `title` elements:

```
<head>

<title>Properly Labeling a Character Set in
HTML 4.01</title>
</head>
```

> <!--
> Consult with your server adminis-
> trator regarding the implementa-
> tion of character sets in the HTTP
> header.
> -->

4. Enter the `meta` tag, with encoding instructions for Japanese:

```
<head>

<meta http-equiv="Content-Type"
content="text/html;
charset=ISO-2022-JP">

<title>Defining ASCII Character Set in HTML
4.01</title>

</head>
```

> <!--
> In XHTML it is perfectly acceptable
> to place the character encoding in
> both the XML declaration and the
> `meta` tag. However, without the
> XML declaration, the `meta` tag
> might not be enough to ensure
> that pages are rendered properly
> in all user agents. In this case,
> you'll want to also be sure the
> character set is included in the
> HTTP header on the server.
> -->

5. Enter the body element and any content:

```
<body>

<p>Content goes here.</p>

</body>
```

6. Close the document by using the `</html>` closing tag:

```
</html>
```

Compare your work to Listing 2.8, which shows the complete markup in context. Figure 2.11 shows the results.

Listing 2.8 An HTML 4.01 Document for Japanese, with the Character Set in Use Labeled Correctly via the meta Tag

```
<!DOCTYPE HTML PUBLIC "-//W3C//DTD HTML 4.01 Transitional//EN"
        "http://www.w3.org/TR/html4/loose.dtd">

<html>

<head>

<meta http-equiv="Content-Type" content="text/html;
charset=ISO-2022-JP">

<title>Properly Labeling a Character Set in HTML 4.01</title>

</head>

<body>

<p><font size="7">&#12398;&#35388;&#21048;&#21462;&#24341;&#12289;&#35519;
&#26619;&#12289;&#12493;</font></p>

</body>
</html>
```

Follow these steps to create an XHTML 1.0 page that is set up for Korean (iso-2022-kr):

1. Open your editor and add the XML prolog, using the encoding for Korean:

```
<?xml version="1.0" encoding="iso-2022-kr" ?>
```

2. Add the DOCTYPE declaration for XHTML 1.0 Transitional:

```
<!DOCTYPE html
      PUBLIC "-//W3C//DTD XHTML 1.0 Transitional//EN"
      "DTD/xhtml1-transitional.dtd">
```

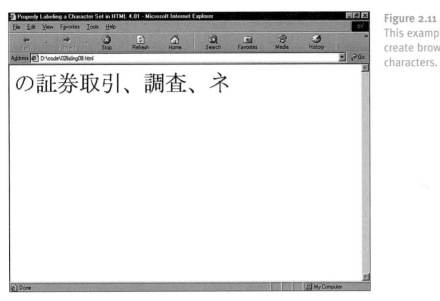

Figure 2.11
This example uses encoding to create browser-based Japanese characters.

3. Add the root and namespace:

```
<html xmlns="http://www.w3.org/1999/xhtml">
```

4. Enter the head and title elements:

```
<head>

<title>Properly Labeling a Character Set in XHTML 1.0</title>

</head>
```

5. Enter the body element and any content:

```
<body>

<p>Content goes here.</p>

</body>
```

6. Close the document by using the </html> closing tag:

```
</html>
```

Compare your work with Listing 2.9, which shows the final document.

Listing 2.9 An XHTML 1.0 Document for Korean, with the Character Set in Use Labeled Correctly via the XML Prolog

```
<?xml version="1.0" encoding="iso-2022-kr" ?>

<!DOCTYPE html
     PUBLIC "-//W3C//DTD XHTML 1.0 Transitional//EN"
     "DTD/xhtml1-transitional.dtd">

<html xmlns="http://www.w3.org/1999/xhtml">

<head>

<title>Properly Labeling a Character Set in XHTML 1.0</title>

</head>

<body>

<p>Content goes here.</p>

</body>
</html>
```

For more information on creating international documents, **see** Chapter 18, "Designing International Documents," **p. 435**.

VALIDATION

Although it is an important idea in HTML, validation is required in XHTML. The goal of XHTML is to encourage Web authors to write conforming, valid documents. This is thought to be important as we move ahead to greater extensibility in XHTML Modularization.

Many validation tools are available online and many are built in to popular editors. It's been my experience that the validation tool at the W3C (validator.w3.org) is by far the most precise.

What Validation Does

The primary role of validation is to compare a document to the DTD the document designates. The validation process does the following:

```
<!--
You can validate documents at
validator.w3.org. Another
good resource is RealValidator, at
http://www.htmlhelp.com/
tools/validator/. For an inter-
esting discussion between syntax
checkers and validators, which
will help explain why validation
should use real validation tools
instead of syntax tools in editors,
see http://www.htmlhelp.
com/tools/validator/
differences.html.
-->
```

- **Returns errors**—The validator reports on any markup errors that are in direct conflict with the DTD reported in the document. An example of this would be the use of an element or attribute that is not found in that DTD or that is found in a part of the document where the DTD does not allow it.

- **Returns warnings**—The validator reports a warning for certain recommended but not required issues. Warnings are often related to accessibility and internationalization concerns. A document can return a warning but still be valid.

- **Returns confirmation of conformance**—If a document has no errors, you receive confirmation that the document is valid markup specific to the DTD identified.

A document can be error free with warnings, it can have errors and no warnings, it can have errors and warnings, and it can have no errors and no warnings.

Pros and Cons of Validation

There are different schools of thought regarding the necessity of validation. Some strong proponents of XML and XHTML follow the W3C conformance ideologies, which infer that if a document is not valid, it is not a conforming document and is therefore not really a document in that language. Although that's technically accurate, you can imagine that in HTML and XHTML it's problematic to suddenly tell people to stop using a proprietary attribute and find a workaround.

Concerned with the limitations that validation itself can impose on people who are transitioning to XHTML and XML-related technologies, some people have vocalized antivalidation sentiments. Simon St. Laurent, a well-known author and speaker on XML topics, has said on the XHTML-L list, "I'm concerned that the emphasis on validation is leaving developers and designers in a straitjacket with very little current benefit." Many of St. Laurent's concerns are based on the fact that there are few browser vendors building software that cares whether a document is valid. It's frustrating indeed.

My own thoughts are that validation is an excellent learning tool for authors who don't have a full and formal understanding of the conformance requirements and recommendations and syntax rules of a given language and version. By validating a document and subsequently fixing the illegal markup, an author can gain a greater understanding of how to create documents.

Whether you choose to validate documents is a personal choice. Without validation, you will have no idea whether your documents are conforming. Even if you're sure of your authoring conformance, mistakes happen. Validation can help ensure that your documents are mistake free. Validation can also give you ammunition while debugging, as it can help you rule out a variety of problems that are caused by invalid document structure before you start really digging into the problem you're trying to solve. Often, fixing the errors found during validation can even resolve problems with a document that isn't behaving the way you want it to.

Validating a Document

Validation can be an easy process. If your documents are filled with errors, however, validation can become very difficult as you sit there and try to debug your markup.

Listing 2.10 is a purposely invalid HTML 4.01 Strict document for testing validation.

> `<!--`
>
> When attempting to debug a lot of errors reported by a validator, you should start by fixing the first error and any other obvious errors. Revalidate, and then try again. In many instances, one error generates other errors. By correcting the obvious error(s) first, the report will likely be reduced significantly, and the time spent debugging will also be reduced.
>
> `-->`

Listing 2.10   An Invalid Document

```
<!DOCTYPE HTML PUBLIC "-//W3C//DTD HTML 4.01//EN"
        "http://www.w3.org/TR/html4/strict.dtd">

<html>
<head>

</head>

<body topmargin="0">

<font size="4">

<p>Welcome to my site</p>

</font>

</body>
</html>
```

Follow these steps to run the invalid markup in Listing 2.10 and make corrections according to the validator's response:

1. Access Listing 2.10 for Chapter 2 from this book's Web site. Copy the markup from the listing and paste it into your editor.

2. Save the file to a local directory.

3. Go to `validator.w3.org/file-upload.html`.

4. Select Browse.

5. Find the file on your local drive, select it, and click Validate. You should receive the following errors:

    Line 7, column 6:

    ```
    </head>
    ```

    Error: missing a required subelement of "HEAD".

Line 9, column 16:

```
<body topmargin="0">
```

Error: there is no attribute "TOPMARGIN" for this element (in this HTML version).

Line 11, column 11:

```
<font size="4">
```

Error: there is no attribute "SIZE" for this element (in this HTML version).

Line 11, column 14:

```
<font size="4">
```

Error: element "FONT" not defined in this HTML version.

Line 17, column 6:

```
</body>
```

Error: missing a required subelement of "BODY".

6. Correct the document according to the errors generated. Table 2.6 shows the errors and warnings, describes the problems, and describes the fixes.

> <!--
> You'll also notice that a "No character encoding detected" warning appears if your server is improperly configured.
> -->

Table 2.6   Debugging Your Markup

Error	Problem	Solution
Line 7	The `title` element is missing.	Add the missing element.
Line 9	`topmargin` is proprietary.	Remove the proprietary attribute.
Line 11	The `font` and `size` are not allowed.	Remove the `font` tag completely.
Line 17	An error is generated from the error in line 7.	Fix line 7.
Warning	Problem with labeling of character set.	Have your server administrator set the HTTP headers to a default character set, or add the `meta` tag and make sure the character set is defined.

Listing 2.11 shows the corrected, valid version of the document.

Listing 2.11   A Valid, Warning-Free Document

```
<!DOCTYPE HTML PUBLIC "-//W3C//DTD HTML 4.01//EN"
        "http://www.w3.org/TR/html4/strict.dtd">

<html>
<head>
```

Listing 2.11   Continued

```
<meta http-equiv="Content-Type" content="text/html; charset=UTF-8">

<title>Validation Test</title>
</head>

<body>

<p>Welcome to my site</p>

</body>
</html>
```

Case Concerns in Validation

Case is an issue with DTDs in HTML and XHTML.

First, the DOCTYPE must *always* be in uppercase. It is a declaration, not an element, and therefore it needs to conform to the rules of case in XHTML.

Interestingly, you'll notice that in HTML DOCTYPE declarations, the HTML is in uppercase:

```
<!DOCTYPE HTML PUBLIC "-//W3C//DTD HTML 4.01//EN"
        "http://www.w3.org/TR/html4/strict.dtd">
```

But, in the XHTML declarations, the HTML is in lowercase:

```
<!DOCTYPE html
     PUBLIC "-//W3C//DTD XHTML 1.0 Strict//EN"
  s
```

Similarly, the word PUBLIC must be uppercase, and the Formal Public Identifier (FPI) is case-sensitive as well. If you fail to use the correct case, your documents will not validate.

For more information about choosing DTDs, *see* Chapter 4, "Choosing the Right DTD," *p. 81*.

CASE BY CASE: WORKING WITH TEMPLATES

Whether you work on your own or in a team, coming up with templates that contain the conforming markup for a document's basic structure can save time and effort. You can then save templates in a specific file on a local network or as a template document in any number of programs. I use Homesite, where saving documents as templates is a very easy process (see Figure 2.12).

```
<!--
```

An alternative approach to rewriting the document would be to change the DTD from a Strict to a Transitional one. This would allow for the use of nonproprietary presentational elements and attributes. The `topmargin` attribute is proprietary, so it would not be available for use in a valid HTML 4.0 or XHTML 1.0 document.

```
-->
```

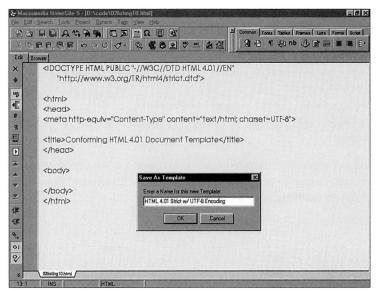

Figure 2.12
Saving documents in Homesite 5.

The focus of this chapter is on ensuring that document structures are correct. The following are the issues of main concern:

- Inclusion of a `meta` encoding statement in HTML (or in XHTML)

- Inclusion of an XML declaration with encoding information in XHTML documents

- Specification of the correct DTD via the DOCTYPE declaration in HTML and XHTML

- Inclusion of the root element and namespace in XHTML

To make life easier, I've created several template resource files as well as a list of useful DOCTYPEs in the Chapter 2 section on the book's Web site, as described in Table 2.7.

Table 2.7   Useful Files for Creating Templates

File	Description
`xml_declaration.txt`	Include this in any XHTML document where you'd like to declare proper encoding. Remember that the XML prolog can be problematic in rendering, so use this as a recommended but not required conformance guideline.
`doctypes.txt`	This file offers all DOCTYPE declarations for authors. It is a great cut-and-paste utility.
`html4.01s.html`	This is a conforming HTML 4.01 template (Strict).
`html4.01t.html`	Use this document when authoring a conforming HTML 4.01 template (Transitional).
`html4.01f.html`	This is a conforming HTML 4.01 template (Frameset).

Table 2.7 Continued

File	Description
XHTML1.0s.html	This file is a conforming XHTML 1.0 template (Strict).
XHTML1.0t.html	Use this file when you want to write a conforming XHTML 1.0 template (Transitional).
XHTML1.0f.html	Here's a conforming XHTML 1.0 template (Frameset).
XHTML1.1.html	If you want to author XHTML 1.1 documents, use this conforming XHTML 1.1 template.

You can download these files and work with them in your environment. For Homesite users, the XML and DOCTYPE declarations can be saved as code snippets and inserted where needed in order to create a custom template.

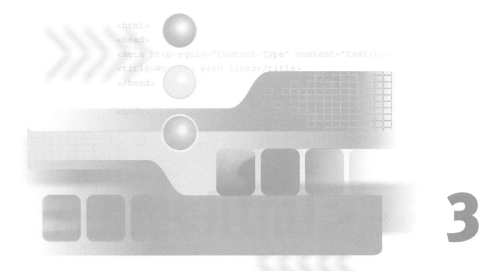

```
<html>
<head>
<meta http-equiv="Content-Type" content="text/ht
<title>Wo    g with Links</title>
</head>

<body>
```

3

DEALING WITH DATA TYPES

IN THIS CHAPTER

Dealing with Data Types   **62**

About URIs   **62**

Representing Colors in HTML and XHTML   **63**

Length Values   **65**

MIME Types   **66**

Managing Language Codes   **66**

Character Encodings   **68**

Media Descriptors   **78**

Script and Style Data   **78**

Target Names   **79**

Case by Case: Working with Character Entities   **79**

DEALING WITH DATA TYPES

This chapter focuses on dealing with various types of information that can be presented within a document. To develop your ability to write conforming, sophisticated documents, it's important to examine the types of key data and how that data is used in HTML and XHTML syntax. Uniform Resource Identifiers (URIs), colors, lengths, language codes, link types, and so forth are governed by a variety of rules and methodologies set forth in the given language and language version specification.

<!--

The W3C provides data management information in its specifications so that browser developers and software manufacturers can produce software that conforms to the specification and so that you, the Web author, can understand how data is typed and processed. As you are by now aware, this information has often been overlooked or mismanaged by browser and software manufacturers as well as Web authors.

-->

ABOUT URIs

There are a lot of resources on the Internet: text, images, animations, video clips, audio files, and executable programs.

A URI, or *uniform resource identifier*, is a string of characters that identifies such a resource. Examples of a URI would include identifiers of FTP, gopher, Web, e-mail, news, and telnet services. URIs consist of the following elements:

- **The means in which the information is accessed—** This is typically some kind of Internet protocol, such as FTP or HTTP.

- **The network location where the information resides—**Specifically, the hostname of the resource host.

- **The path and name of the file in question—** Sometimes this won't appear in the URI as a specific document because a default document or script, such as index.html, is assumed.

<!--

The familiar term URL, or *uniform resource locator*, defines a subset of URI that points to a specific location. Another subset of URI is the *URN* (*uniform resource name*). When describing a Web address, people will use the term URI and URL interchangeably.

-->

Table 3.1 provides a look at an identifier for a variety of resource types.

Table 3.1   URI Schemes

Protocol	URI Example
FTP	`ftp://ftp.aol.com/aim/win95/aim95.exe`
Gopher	`gopher://infoserv.utdallas.edu/11/subject`
HTTP	`http://www.molly.com/`
Mail	`mailto:molly@molly.com`
News	`news:comp.infosystems.www.servers.unix`
Telnet	`telnet://database.carl.org/`

As you can see in the listings, each identifier begins with the protocol, and is followed by the location of the resource.

Managing URIs in your Web documents is a fairly easy process. The main thing to keep in mind is that on certain systems, path names and filenames may be case sensitive. So, `http://www.molly.com/books/index.html` might not necessarily be the same resource as `http://www.molly.com/BOOKS/index.html`. It largely depends on how the specific server is being managed. To properly author URIs, you'll need to be sure of the URI's case.

> `<!--Caution`
>
> Because XHTML is case-specific and asks that element and attribute names are all lowercase, many people become confused and think that attribute values must also be in lowercase. However, attribute values in XHTML are *not* case-sensitive and can therefore accommodate mixed-case URIs.
>
> `-->`

REPRESENTING COLORS IN HTML AND XHTML

Whenever you define colors in HTML and XHTML documents, you must represent those colors according to the allowed data types.

The color representations discussed in this section are based on the use of presentational syntax. Because most presentational elements and attributes are deprecated in HTML 4.0 and 4.01, and XHTML, if you use them at all it will be in transitional documents. In strict document authoring, colors are defined in style sheets. The means for representing color via style include both methods described here as well as a third method, the use of actual RGB values.

To learn more about style sheets, please **see** "Using CSS with HTML and XHTML," **p. 345**, Chapter 14.

There are two means of representing color directly in HTML and XHTML:

* A hexadecimal number
* A color name as defined in the language's specification

Hexadecimal, also referred to as "hex," is a base-16 alphanumeric representation of numbers. It is used in HTML and XHTML to represent the RGB (red, green, blue) color space. This color space is based on *additive synthesis*, which refers to the method used by computer hardware and software to project color onto the screen.

Numbers in hexadecimal as used by HTML and XHTML contain three or six digits and may be made up of any combination of the letters A–F and the numbers 1–9. When writing hex colors as attribute values, you'll precede the number with a hash (#) mark:

`text="#FFFFFF"`

Each consecutive pair of digits in a hex number represents the value of red, green, and blue respectively. In the case of FFFFFF, which represents white, the first FF corresponds to the red value of 255, the second one does also for green, as does the third pair for blue. Using decimal values, this might be written 255, 255, 255. You might also see the color represented using a shorter, three-character version, such as FFF. This has a value equivalent to that represented by FFFFFF.

There are also 16 color names defined for use within HTML and XHTML. If you are using a color name as a value, you simply write the color name:

`text="white"`

Each of the 16 color names in HTML and XHTML has a corresponding hexadecimal representation. Table 3.2 defines the available color names as well as their hexadecimal counterparts.

Although you are limited to the use of one of the available 16 color names, you can use any hexadecimal value you like, including those shown here. However, there are some concerns regarding the use of color and color names, which are addressed in the sidebar, "Web-Safe Color and Browser-Defined Color Names."

There are two other issues of which to be aware when authoring colors in HTML and XHTML:

- **Color combinations**—Background, text, and link colors should be combined in such a way as to ensure readability. This means ensuring that contrast between the colors is high. Another concern with color combining is for the color-blind, where you can use certain color combinations in order to ensure color-blind readers will be able to distinguish the colors appropriately.

- **Setting all properties**—If you use a background color (or a background graphic) be sure to define all the related properties (`text`, `link`, `alink`, `vlink`) as well. If you use a background graphic, I recommend using a similar background color as well as it will load first and subtly prepare the audience for the color scheme. This is simply a choice based on aesthetics, there is no technical rule that says this must be done.

Table 3.2	Color Names in HTML and XHTML
Color Name	Hexadecimal Representation
Black	000000
Silver	C0C0C0
Gray	808080
White	FFFFFF
Maroon	800000
Red	FF0000
Purple	800080
Fuchsia	FF00FF
Green	008000
Lime	00FF00
Olive	808000
Yellow	FFFF00
Navy	000080
Blue	0000FF
Teal	008080
Aqua	00FFFF

*Read more about contrast and the use of color in cases of color-blindness in "Creating Accessible Sites," **p. 419**, Chapter 17.*

LENGTH VALUES

When describing length and width values in HTML and XHTML, values follow three conventions:

- Pixels

- Percentages

- Relative sizing

Pixel values are written numerically. So, if you want to have a table be 500 pixels across, you'd simply write:

```
<table width="500">
```

Percentage values are written numerically with a percent sign following. If you want your table to take up only half of the available screen space, you could write:

```
<table width="50%">
```

Relative sizing in the context of length values is a means of sizing something by having any leftover length be distributed appropriately. A good example of this is with frames, where you can use the "*" symbol to indicate that any remaining available space will be allotted accordingly.

Because length values are written numerically, they are considered to be case-neutral.

<!--
As with colors, length values are presentational and are used in transitional documents. Style sheets are the current recommended method.
-->

MIME TYPES

Also referred to as "content types," this is data type information that describes certain media. The acronym "MIME" stands for *Multipurpose Internet Mail Extensions,* which are used to properly identify the media type of an e-mail attachment.

Sometimes you'll insert type information into syntax, such as when linking to a style sheet, as in this case:

```
<link rel="stylesheet" type="text/css" href="site.css" />
```

Types are classified by the primary type, and the subtype. A primary type refers to the kind of file in question, such as text, multipart, message, application, image, audio, video, and model. Subtypes define the specific file format. In the markup sample above, text is the primary type, and css is the subtype.

Table 3.3 shows samples of content types that can be used in HTML and XHTML.

Table 3.3 Examples of MIME Types in HTML and XHTML

Primary Type	Subtype
text	css
text	html
application	pdf
image	jpeg
image	gif
audio	mpeg
video	mpeg
video	quicktime
model	vrml

MANAGING LANGUAGE CODES

Language codes are the two-letter codes used to define a document's language. They are specifically useful when internationalizing documents. Language codes are standardized by the International Standards Organization (ISO) and are case-insensitive.

Table 3.4 defines the standardized language codes available for use in HTML and XHTML.

```
<!--
For a complete list of registered
media types, see http://www.
isi.edu/in-notes/iana/
assignments/media-types/
media-types.
-->
```

Table 3.4 ISO 639 Two-Character Language Codes

Language	Code	Language	Code
Abkhazian	AB	Lithuanian	LT
Afan (Oromo)	OM	Macedonian	MK
Afar	AA	Malagasy	MG
Afrikaans	AF	Malay	MS
Albanian	SQ	Malayalam	ML
Amharic	AM	Maltese	MT
Arabic	AR	Maori	MI
Armenian	HY	Marathi	MR

Table 3.4   Continued

Language	Code	Language	Code
Assamese	AS	Moldavian	MO
Aymara	AY	Mongolian	MN
Azerbaijani	AZ	Nauru	NA
Bashkir	BA	Nepali	NE
Basque	EU	Norwegian	NO
Bengali; Bangla	BN	Occitan	OC
Bhutani	DZ	Oriya	OR
Bihari	BH	Pashto; Pushto	PS
Bislama	BI	Persian (Farsi)	FA
Breton	BR	Polish	PL
Bulgarian	BG	Portuguese	PT
Burmese	MY	Punjabi	PA
Byelorussian	BE	Quechua	QU
Cambodian	KM	Rhaeto-Romance	RM
Catalan	CA	Romanian	RO
Chinese	ZH	Russian	RU
Corsican	CO	Samoan	SM
Croatian	HR	Sangho	SG
Czech	CS	Sanskrit	SA
Danish	DA	Scots Gaelic	GD
Dutch	NL	Serbian	SR
English	EN	Serbo-Croatian	SH
Esperanto	EO	Sesotho	ST
Estonian	ET	Setswana	TN
Faroese	FO	Shona	SN
Fiji	FJ	Sindhi	SD
Finnish	FI	Singhalese	SI
French	FR	Siswati	SS
Frisian	FY	Slovak	SK
Galician	GL	Slovenian	SL
Georgian	KA	Somali	SO
German	DE	Spanish	ES
Greek	EL	Sudanese	SU
Greenlandic	KL	Swahili	SW
Guarani	GN	Swedish	SV

Table 3.4 Continued

Language	Code	Language	Code
Gujarati	GU	Tagalog	TL
Hausa	HA	Tajik	TG
Hebrew	HE	Tamil	TA
Hindi	HI	Tatar	TT
Hungarian	HU	Telugu	TE
Icelandic	IS	Thai	TH
Indonesian	ID	Tibetan	BO
Interlingua	IA	Tigrinya	TI
Interlingue	IE	Tonga	TO
Inuktitut	IU	Tsonga	TS
Inupiak	IK	Turkish	TR
Irish	GA	Turkmen	TK
Italian	IT	Twi	TW
Japanese	JA	Uigur	UG
Javanese	JV	Ukrainian	UK
Kannada	KN	Urdu	UR
Kashmiri	KS	Uzbek	UZ
Kazakh	KK	Vietnamese	VI
Kinyarwanda	RW	Volapuk	VO
Kirghiz	KY	Welsh	CY
Kurundi	RN	Wolof	WO
Korean	KO	Xhosa	XH
Kurdish	KU	Yiddish	YI
Laothian	LO	Yoruba	YO
Latin	LA	Zhuang	ZA
Latvian; Lettish	LV	Zulu	ZU
Lingala	LN		

CHARACTER ENCODINGS

Character sets are sets of characters which allow a document to be interpreted in a specific way. By using entities from a character set, an author can include letters, glyphs, symbols, and foreign characters in their documents.

Table 3.5 describes a number of popular character sets commonly used to represent characters found in specific languages.

```
<!--
Source: http://www.oasis-open.
org/cover/iso639a.html.
```

For more information on ISO 639 language codes, please see the International Standards Organization Web site, http://www.iso.org.
```
                                    -->
```

Table 3.5   Character Sets by Language (Partial List, Source: W3C Internationalization Documents)

Language	Character Set	Language	Character Set
Afrikaans	iso-8859-1	Inuit	iso-8859-10*
Albanian	iso-8859-1	Irish	iso-8859-1
Arabic	iso-8859-6	Italian	iso-8859-1
Basque	iso-8859-1	Japanese	iso-2022-jp, euc-jp
Bulgarian	iso-8859-5	Lapp	iso-8859-10*
Byelorussian	iso-8859-5	Latvian	iso-8859-13
Catalan	iso-8859-1	Lithuanian	iso-8859-13
Croatian	iso-8859-2	Macedonian	iso-8859-5
Czech	iso-8859-2	Maltese	iso-8859-3*
Danish	iso-8859-1	Norwegian	iso-8859-1
Dutch	iso-8859-1	Polish	iso-8859-2
English	iso-8859-1	Portuguese	iso-8859-1
Esperanto	iso-8859-3*	Romanian	iso-8859-2
Estonian	iso-8859-15	Russian	koi8-r, iso-8859-5
Faroese	iso-8859-1	Scottish	iso-8859-1
Finnish	iso-8859-1	Serbian	iso-8859-5
French	iso-8859-1	Slovak	iso-8859-2
Galician	iso-8859-1	Slovenian	iso-8859-2
German	iso-8859-1	Spanish	iso-8859-1
Greek	iso-8859-7	Swedish	iso-8859-1
Hebrew	iso-8859-8	Turkish	iso-8859-9
Hungarian	iso-8859-2	Ukrainian	iso-8859-5
Icelandic	iso-8859-1		

You'll notice that many languages refer to the same character set, such as English, French, German, and Italian. The reason for this is because the character set in question contains the majority of characters required to represent that language. Character sets with an asterisk (*) beside them are those with known browser-support problems.

Single characters can be embedded into documents using character entity references. These references have a numeric value as well as a named value. You can use either one just so long as it is allowed within the DTD in question.

```
<!--
```

UTF-8 is a universal character set. Support for it is inconsistent, but growing. If you're authoring documents with specific character set requirements, you might still prefer to use the exact character set in question.

```
-->
```

Using character entities is particularly helpful when the encoding set doesn't express all the characters that you might want to use in the document. For example, if I were authoring a document in English and wanted to use an inverted exclamation mark for a Spanish quotation, I'd use an entity to create that character. Other character entity references help control space, symbols, and so on. (See Table 3.6.)

For a complete list of character sets available, see the following registry: http://www.iana.org/assignments/character-sets.

There are three types of character entities available in HTML and XHTML.

- **ISO 8859-1 characters**—This set includes the Latin set of character entities.

- **Symbols, mathematical characters, and Greek letters**—This set includes entities for various symbols (such as copyright symbols and so on), math characters, and Greek letters.

- **Markup-significant characters**—This set includes internationalization characters such as those required for bi-directional text.

➪ *Learn more about internationalization in "Designing International Documents," **p. 435**, Chapter 18.*

Table 3.6   Named Entities

Named Entity	Numeric	Entity Description
nbsp		non-breaking space
iexcl	&#161;	inverted exclamation mark
cent	&#162;	cent sign
pound	&#163;	pound sign
curren	&#164;	currency sign
yen	&#165;	yen sign
brvbar	&#166;	broken vertical bar
sect	&#167;	section sign
uml	&#168;	diaeresis
copy	&#169;	copyright sign
ordf	&#170;	feminine ordinal indicator
laquo	&#171;	left-pointing double angle quotation mark
not	&#172;	not sign
shy	&#173;	soft hyphen
reg	&#174;	registered sign
macr	&#175;	macron
deg	&#176;	degree sign
plusmn	&#177;	plus-minus sign
sup2	&#178;	superscript two

Table 3.6 Continued

Named Entity	Numeric	Entity Description
sup3	&#179;	superscript three
acute	&#180;	acute accent
micro	&#181;	micro signB5
para	&#182;	pilcrow sign
middot	&#183;	middle dot
cedil	&#184;	cedilla
sup1	&#185;	superscript one
ordm	&#186;	masculine ordinal indicator
raquo	&#187;	right-pointing double angle quotation mark
frac14	&#188;	vulgar fraction one-quarter
frac12	&#189;	vulgar fraction one-half
frac34	&#190;	vulgar fraction three-quarters
iquest	&#191;	inverted question mark
Agrave	&#192;	Latin capital letter A with grave
Aacute	&#193;	Latin capital letter A with acute
Acirc	&#194;	Latin capital letter A with circumflex
Atilde	&#195;	Latin capital letter A with tilde
Auml	&#196;	Latin capital letter A with diaeresis
Aring	&#197;	Latin capital letter A with ring above
AElig	&#198;	Latin capital letter AE
Ccedil	&#199;	Latin capital letter C with cedilla
Egrave	&#200;	Latin capital letter E with grave
Eacute	&#201;	Latin capital letter E with acute
Ecirc	&#202;	Latin capital letter E with circumflex
Euml	&#203;	Latin capital letter E with diaeresis
Igrave	&#204;	Latin capital letter I with grave
Iacute	&#205;	Latin capital letter I with acute
Icirc	&#206;	Latin capital letter I with circumflex
Iuml	&#207;	Latin capital letter I with diaeresis
eth	&#208;	Latin capital letter eth
Ntilde	&#209;	Latin capital letter N with tilde
Ograve	&#210;	Latin capital letter O with grave
Oacute	&#211;	Latin capital letter O with acute
Ocirc	&#212;	Latin capital letter O with circumflex
Otilde	&#213;	Latin capital letter O with tilde

Table 3.6 Continued

Named Entity	Numeric	Entity Description
Ouml	&#214;	Latin capital letter O with diaeresis
times	&#215;	multiplication sign
Oslash	&#216;	Latin capital letter O with stroke
Ugrave	&#217;	Latin capital letter U with grave
Uacute	&#218;	Latin capital letter U with acute
Ucirc	&#219;	Latin capital letter U with circumflex
Uuml	&#220;	Latin capital letter U with diaeresis
Yacute	&#221;	Latin capital letter Y with acute
thorn	&#222;	Latin capital letter thorn
szlig	&#223;	Latin small letter sharp
agrave	&#224;	Latin small letter a with grave
aacute	&#225;	Latin small letter a with acute
acirc	&#226;	Latin small letter a with circumflex
atilde	&#227;	Latin small letter a with tilde
auml	&#228;	Latin small letter a with diaeresis
aring	&#229;	Latin small letter a with ring above
aelig	&#230;	Latin small letter ae
ccedil	&#231;	Latin small letter c with cedilla
egrave	&#232;	Latin small letter e with grave
eacute	&#233;	Latin small letter e with acute
ecirc	&#234;	Latin small letter e with circumflex
euml	&#235;	Latin small letter e with diaeresis
igrave	&#236;	Latin small letter i with grave
iacute	&#237;	Latin small letter i with acute
icirc	&#238;	Latin small letter i with circumflex
iuml	&#239;	Latin small letter i with diaeresis
eth	&#240;	Latin small letter eth
ntilde	&#241;	Latin small letter n with tilde
ograve	&#242;	Latin small letter o with grave
oacute	&#243;	Latin small letter o with acute
ocirc	&#244;	Latin small letter o with circumflex
otilde	&#245;	Latin small letter o with tilde
ouml	&#246;	Latin small letter o with diaeresis
divide	&#247;	division sign
oslash	&#248;	Latin small letter o with stroke

Table 3.6 Continued

Named Entity	Numeric	Entity Description
ugrave	&#249;	Latin small letter u with grave
uacute	&#250;	Latin small letter u with acute
ucirc	&#251;	Latin small letter u with circumflex
uuml	&#252;	Latin small letter u with diaeresis
yacute	&#253;	Latin small letter y with acute
thorn	&#254;	Latin small letter thorn
yuml	&#255;	Latin small letter y with diaeresis

Table 3.7 describes general symbols, Greek, and mathematical symbols available.

Table 3.7 Symbols, Greek Symbols, and Math Symbol Entities

Named Entity	Numeric	Entity Description
fnof	&#402;	Latin small f with hook
Alpha	&#913;	Greek capital letter alpha
Beta	&#914;	Greek capital letter beta
Gamma	&#915;	Greek capital letter gamma
Delta	&#916;	Greek capital letter delta
Epsilon	&#917;	Greek capital letter epsilon
Zeta	&#918;	Greek capital letter zeta
Eta	&#919;	Greek capital letter eta
Theta	&#920;	Greek capital letter theta
Iota	&#921;	Greek capital letter iota
Kappa	&#922;	Greek capital letter kappa
Lambda	&#923;	Greek capital letter lambda
Mu	&#924;	Greek capital letter mu
Nu	&#925;	Greek capital letter nu
Xi	&#926;	Greek capital letter xi
Omicron	&#927;	Greek capital letter omicron
Pi	&#928;	Greek capital letter pi
Rho	&#929;	Greek capital letter rho
Sigma	&#931;	Greek capital letter sigma
Tau	&#932;	Greek capital letter tau
Upsilon	&#933;	Greek capital letter upsilon
Phi	&#934;	Greek capital letter phi
Chi	&#935;	Greek capital letter chi
Psi	&#936;	Greek capital letter psi

Table 3.7 Continued

Named Entity	Numeric	Entity Description
Omega	&#937;	Greek capital letter omega
alpha	&#945;	Greek small letter alpha
beta	&#946;	Greek small letter beta
gamma	&#947;	Greek small letter gamma
delta	&#948;	Greek small letter delta
epsilon	&#949;	Greek small letter epsilon
zeta	&#950;	Greek small letter zeta
eta	&#951;	Greek small letter eta
theta	&#952;	Greek small letter theta
iota	&#953;	Greek small letter iota
kappa	&#954;	Greek small letter kappa
lambda	&#955;	Greek small letter lambda
mu	&#956;	Greek small letter mu
nu	&#957;	Greek small letter nu
xi	&#958;	Greek small letter xi
omicron	&#959;	Greek small letter omicron
pi	&#960;	Greek small letter pi
rho	&#961;	Greek small letter rho
sigmaf	&#962;	Greek small letter final sigma
sigma	&#963;	Greek small letter sigma
tau	&#964;	Greek small letter tau
upsilon	&#965;	Greek small letter upsilon
phi	&#966;	Greek small letter phi
chi	&#967;	Greek small letter chi
psi	&#968;	Greek small letter psi
omega	&#969;	Greek small letter omega
thetasym	&#977;	Greek small letter theta symbol
upsih	&#978;	Greek upsilon with hook symbol
piv	&#982;	pi symbol
bull	&#8226;	bullet
hellip	&#8230;	horizontal ellipsis
prime	&#8242;	prime
Prime	&#8243;	double prime
oline	&#8254;	overline
frasl	&#8260;	fraction slash
weierp	&#8472;	script capital

Table 3.7 Continued

Named Entity	Numeric	Entity Description
image	&#8465;	blackletter capital I
real	&#8476;	blackletter capital R
trade	&#8482;	trade mark sign
alefsym	&#8501;	alef symbol
larr	&#8592;	leftward arrow
uarr	&#8593;	upward arrow
rarr	&#8594;	rightward arrow
darr	&#8595;	downward arrow
harr	&#8596;	left right arrow
crarr	&#8629;	downward arrow with corner leftward
lArr	&#8656;	leftward double arrow
uArr	&#8657;	upward double arrow
rArr	&#8658;	rightward double arrow
dArr	&#8659;	downward double arrow
hArr	&#8660;	left-right double arrow
forall	&#8704;	for all
part	&#8706;	partial differential
exist	&#8707;	there exists
empty	&#8709;	empty set
nabla	&#8711;	nabla
isin	&#8712;	element of
notin	&#8713;	not an element of
ni	&#8715;	contains as member
prod	&#8719;	n-ary product
sum	&#8721;	n-ary summation
minus	&#8722;	minus sign
lowast	&#8727;	asterisk operator
radic	&#8730;	square root
prop	&#8733;	proportional to
infin	&#8734;	infinity
ang	&#8736;	angle
and	&#8743;	logical and
or	&#8744;	logical or
cap	&#8745;	intersection
cup	&#8746;	union
int	&#8747;	integral

Table 3.7 Continued

Named Entity	Numeric	Entity Description
there4	&#8756;	therefore
sim	&#8764;	tilde operator
cong	&#8773;	approximately equal to
asymp	&#8776;	almost equal to
ne	&#8800;	not equal to
equiv	&#8801;	identical to
le	&#8804;	less-than or equal to
ge	&#8805;	greater-than or equal to
sub	&#8834;	subset of
sup	&#8835;	superset of
nsub	&#8836;	not a subset of
sube	&#8838;	subset of or equal to
supe	&#8839;	superset of or equal to
oplus	&#8853;	circled plus
otimes	&#8855;	circled times
perp	&#8869;	up tack
sdot	&#8901;	dot operator
lceil	&#8968;	left ceiling
rceil	&#8969;	right ceiling
lfloor	&#8970;	left floor
rfloor	&#8971;	right floor
lang	&#9001;	left-pointing angle bracket
rang	&#9002;	right-pointing angle bracket
loz	&#9674;	lozenge
spades	&#9824;	black (solid) spade suit
clubs	&#9827;	black (solid) club suit
hearts	&#9829;	black (solid) heart suit
diams	&#9830;	black (solid) diamond suit

Table 3.8 shows markup significant characters. It's important to note that some of these characters are considered new and may not be supported by some browsers and language version types.

<!--

If you've noticed a few seemingly missing numeric representations for characters, such as ΢ it's because they've not been defined in this character set.

-->

Table 3.8 Markup Significant Characters

Named Entity	Numeric	Entity Description
quot	&#34;	quotation mark
amp	&#38;	ampersand
lt	&#60;	less-than sign
gt	&#62;	greater-than sign
OElig	&#338;	Latin capital ligature OE
oelig	&#339;	Latin small ligature oe
Scaron	&#352;	Latin capital letter S with caron
scaron	&#353;	Latin small letter s with caron
Yuml	&#376;	Latin capital letter Y with diaeresis
circ	&#710;	modifier letter circumflex accent
tilde	&#732;	small tilde
ensp		en space
emsp		em space
thinsp		thin space
zwnj	&#8204;	zero width non-joiner
zwj	&#8205;	zero width joiner
lrm	&#8206;	left-to-right mark
rlm	&#8207;	right-to-left mark
ndash	&#8211;	en dash
mdash	&#8212;	em dash
lsquo	&#8216;	left single quotation mark
rsquo	&#8217;	right single quotation mark
sbquo	&#8218;	single low-9 quotation mark
ldquo	&#8220;	left double quotation mark
rdquo	&#8221;	right double quotation mark
bdquo	&#8222;	double low-9 quotation mark
dagger	&#8224;	dagger
Dagger	&#8225;	double dagger
permil	&#8240;	per mille sign
lsaquo	&#8249;	single left-pointing angle quotation
rsaquo	&#8250;	single right-pointing angle quotation
euro	&#8364;	euro sign

MEDIA DESCRIPTORS

Media descriptors are used to define the media for which a given document is prepared. The following media descriptors are available in HTML and XHTML (see Table 3.9).

Table 3.9 Media Descriptors

Descriptor	Media
screen	Computer screen
tty	Teletype terminals
tv	Television devices
projection	Projectors
handheld	Small devices with limited screen space
print	Intended for the printed page
braille	Braille (tactile) devices
aural	Speech synthesizers
all	All devices

SCRIPT AND STYLE DATA

When working with scripts, certain concerns arise as to how those scripts are managed. Several important points of which to be aware include

* Script data must not be interpreted as HTML or XHTML. Rather, it is passed on as data to a script engine. For the developer, this means authoring scripts in documents must conform to the specification in order to avoid problems. For the browser manufacturer, this means that they must be written so script data is appropriately passed to the available engine.

* Case sensitivity with scripts is dependent upon the language. In HTML, you can have mixed case scripts. However, this becomes an issue in XHTML. Because XHTML is case-specific, you'll have to modify case concerns when authoring XHTML, so getElementByID will have to be written getelementbyid.

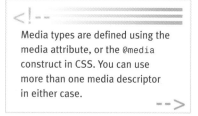

Media types are defined using the media attribute, or the @media construct in CSS. You can use more than one media descriptor in either case.

* Script data that relates to an element may not contain character entities. Script data corresponding to an attribute may do so.

Read about working with scripts in "Adding Scripting to HTML and XHTML Documents," *p. 401*, Chapter 16.

In most instances, style data is dealt with just as script data is. In an HTML or XHTML document, style is defined in the head via the style element, or inline, within the document via the style attribute. User agents should never try to interpret style data as HTML.

As with script data, style data case concerns depend on the style sheet language, and the author's conventions. And, as with script data, element-related style may not contain character entities, whereas attribute-related style may do so.

For more information about style, please *see* "Using CSS with HTML and XHTML," *p. 345*, Chapter 14.

TARGET NAMES

There are four target names (sometimes referred to as "magic target names") that are reserved in HTML and XHTML, and have specific actions related to them (see Table 3.10).

Table 3.10 Reserved Target Names

Target Name	Action
_blank	The document is loaded into a new window.
_self	The document is loaded into the same window as the referring document.
_parent	In frames, the document is loaded into the frameset parent of the current frame. If the frame has no parent, the document is loaded into the referring document.
_top	The document is loaded into the full, original window. In frames, this cancels all other frames in use.

➪ *Learn about frames in "Creating Framesets and Frame Documents," **p. 219**, Chapter 9.*

CASE BY CASE: WORKING WITH CHARACTER ENTITIES

In order to assist you in demonstrating how character entities work, I took several screen shots from each character entity set (see Figures 3.1, 3.2, and 3.3). Your mission is to re-create the appearance of the shot using the appropriate entities.

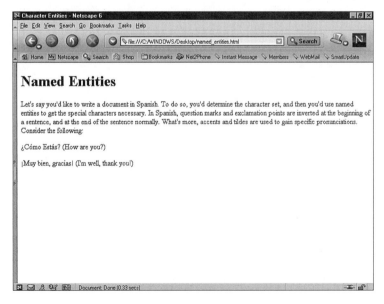

Figure 3.1
Choose from the primary entity set to re-create this image.

Figure 3.2
Using the symbol, Greek, and mathematical entity set, re-create this image.

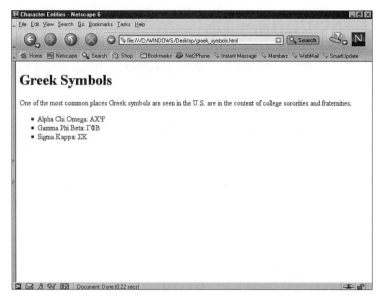

Figure 3.3
Using markup-significant characters, reproduce this image.

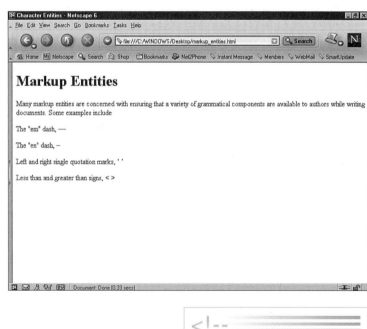

<!-- The em dash character is not supported in IE5 and below, but it is supported in IE 6, as well as Netscape 6. Be sure to test your work with one of those browsers to see the results. -->

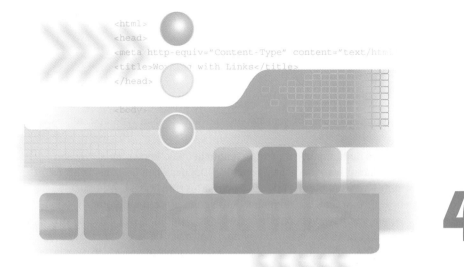

CHOOSING THE RIGHT DTD

IN THIS CHAPTER

DTDs: An Overview   **82**

Which Is the Right DTD to Use?   **82**

DOCTYPE Declarations and DTDs   **86**

Case by Case: Transitional Design for the
New York Public Library   **90**

DTDS: AN OVERVIEW

In this chapter, you'll gain a better understanding of what a Document Type Definition (DTD) is, how to choose the most appropriate one for your needs, and how to deal with special issues regarding DTDs and Web browsers.

Technically speaking, a DTD is a definition for a markup language (also known as a "vocabulary" or "tag set"). If a single markup language has several DTDs, each can be considered its own markup language variant—for example, HTML can be strict or transitional. Additionally, there might be different versions of a markup language, corresponding to the different versions of the DTD (as in HTML, where you have versions 1, 3.2, 4.01, and so on). SGML (Standard Generalized Markup Language) defines the rules and syntax that must be used when creating DTDs. Because HTML has an SGML DTD, it is known as an SGML application, which simply means that someone applied the rules defined by SGML to specify the document type HTML. In simpler terms, I like to think of a DTD as a long laundry list of elements, attributes, and other syntax and structure rules inherent to the particular markup language that the DTD helps to describe.

General features of a DTD include the following:

- A DTD is machine-readable for parsing.

- A DTD is human-readable and understandable.

- A DTD is an ASCII document.

- A DTD expresses syntax and structure.

DTDs are critically important because they are the most precise representation of what is allowed to be used when following a given language version.

➪ *To effectively structure a document with the DOCTYPE declaration included, **see** "Global Structure and Syntax of Documents," **p. 95**, Chapter 5.*

➪ *To learn more detail about the structure and syntax of actual DTDs, **see** "Customizing DTDs," **p. 467**, Chapter 20.*

WHICH IS THE RIGHT DTD TO USE?

With XHTML 1.1 being the most recent version of recommended Web markup, a difficult question for Web authors enters the issue: Which DTD is most appropriate for the job? The answer to this question can seem extremely difficult for several reasons:

- Client expectations sometimes conflict with best markup practices.

- Upon adding new documents to an older Web site, there are often concerns about how to accommodate newer versions of HTML or XHTML without jeopardizing the design of the existing site.

- When redesigning a site, questions about how the site design will be executed come into play.

- If you are in the position of having to rely on certain Web development tools such as visual editors or content management systems (CMSes), you risk having to work to ensure your documents not only define the DTD via the DOCTYPE, but also conform to the rules of that DTD.

Although these difficulties might at first seem insurmountable, they can be addressed with relative ease.

One of the most important things to remember is that even though XHTML 1.1 is the current recommended Web markup language, you do *not* have to use XHTML 1.1 to create Web documents. You can select from any DTD available to address the needs of a project in question. So, if you need to use tables for layout, add presentational elements to the markup, and so on, recognize that you can do so by using Transitional DTDs over Strict ones. Although perhaps this isn't the ideal, it certainly is a better choice than relying on nonconforming documents or proprietary tags and attributes.

Dealing with Client Concerns

Although there is no doubt that clients are becoming more aware of the complexity of the creation, implementation, and deployment of Web sites, there is little question that clients by and large do not understand (nor do many care) how markup influences design and cross-browser compatibility concerns.

The main problem at this time is that relying primarily on CSS for layouts means that the visual design of a site might not look great on all browsers, particularly legacy browsers with no or partial CSS support, especially Netscape 4.x which is still in significant use. Another issue is that in many instances, a Web author will create templates for a client, who then will be making updates to the site. If the client's team doesn't understand markup, or uses a visual editor, the creation of well-formed compliant documents goes right out the window.

You can address these concerns in the following ways:

- **Evaluate the client's audience exhaustively**. If the demographics show that there are backward-compatibility issues, consider using Transitional HTML or XHTML in order to address cross-browser concerns.

- **Educate the client**. Depending on the client, you might want to spend a little time discussing current trends in regards to cleanly structured documents and the move toward CSS for presentational issues. Discuss also issues of accessibility and, where appropriate, internationalization. The more information you can provide your client with, the better you can in turn address the client's concerns.

- **If the client will be making updates to the site, it is especially important to consider an educational or training approach**. This becomes even more true should the client's team be using tools to do the updating. Make recommendations based on the tool in question (see the "Working with Visual Editors and CMS" section later in this chapter).

Client relations can be complicated. Only you will know exactly the right approach to take with your client, but with persistence, you can create conforming documents for the client and still address the client's design needs.

⇨ For more information on accessibility, *see* "Creating Accessible Sites," **p. 419**, Chapter 17.

⇨ To learn about Internationalization, *see* "Designing International Documents," **p. 435**, Chapter 18.

<!--
For a humorous look at clients (and some tips on how to deal with them), enjoy my article *Clients from Hell: Learn to Deal with Devilish Personalities*, http://builder.cnet.com/ webbuilding/pages/Business/ Clients/.
-->

Adding New Documents to Older Web Sites

Many Web authors are finding themselves in the position of having to add new documents to existing Web sites. In most cases, these sites have been designed using a bootstrap methodology: non-conforming markup, proprietary tags and attributes, and a variety of other hacks.

Transitioning an older site to better practices is no easy task, because it's highly likely that the site's owners are going to want to keep the look and feel of that site intact. The heavy use of tables for layout, little or no CSS, and an overabundance of presentational attributes in the markup make your job much more difficult.

Some ways in which to deal with figuring out which DTD to use include the following:

- **Determine whether there is a current DTD in use**. If so, you might wish to stick to the same DTD for consistency's sake.

- **Determine which proprietary elements/attributes are in use**. If there are many, are there appropriate CSS workarounds available? If you determine that you can use solid CSS workarounds to achieve the same, or very similar, results to match the old site's design, consider using a Transitional HTML or XHTML DTD along with a new style sheet that addresses those workarounds.

- **Determine whether there are any CSS style sheets in use**. If so, how can the CSS be expanded on or improved? You can refine the style sheet in order to address certain presentational issues or inconsistencies.

Ideally, the transition to a Strict DTD with CSS for presentation is the goal. However, this can be very difficult to achieve in a situation like this. The good news is that most of these transitional problems can be solved with Transitional DTDs and some CSS.

⇨ For more information on how to work effectively with CSS, *see* "Using CSS with HTML and XHTML," **p. 345**, Chapter 14.

⇨ If you'd like more detail on using CSS for presentation, *see* "CSS in Depth: Applying Style and Positioning," **p. 369**, Chapter 15.

<!--
If resources are limited, you might want to avoid attempting to update archival material. Instead, focus on the ways in which you can best achieve improvement in current and future document production.
-->

Determining DTDs During Site Redesigns

In the past several years, the general consensus is that site redesigns have moved to the forefront of the kind of work most Web authors are doing. Clients, companies, and organizations are looking to get a fresh look or perspective with their sites. This provides the perfect opportunity to upgrade the site to current trends, ideologies, and best practices.

In the case of redesigns, you will greatly benefit from the exploration of these issues:

- **Who is your audience?** Of course, this is a cardinal rule in the creation of any media. The audience will determine your approach. If you're working in an intranet where everyone uses Netscape 4.x browsers, you must address some significant limitations regarding presentation and will likely have to rely on Transitional DTDs. However, if your audience is more sophisticated, you might just be able to create an XHTML 1.1 document and rely completely on CSS for presentation.

- **Think about design from the perspective of CSS**. This is a shift for many Web authors who have traditionally created a design in Photoshop and then used tables to determine layout. But if you have the luxury of relying on CSS for layout, learning and exploring CSS layout methodologies is going to help you create a look and feel for the design in question without relying on old conventions.

- **Create templates!** Once you've decided on the DTD you can employ during the redesign, creating templates will empower you to more quickly take the content from the old site and pour it into the new. The use of templates will also assist in keeping the DOCTYPE and structural information consistent throughout the new site.

Ideally with a redesign, you'll be able to at the very least implement XHTML 1.0 Transitional as the DTD of choice.

Working with Visual Editors and CMS

Visual editors and content management systems (CMS) are currently one of the worst obstacles for the intermediate to advanced Web author to overcome.

Some of the reasons for these obstacles include the following:

- Visual editors by and large do not conform to W3C specifications in the way they generate markup. This is changing to some degree over time, but the reality is that most popular WYSIWYG editing software is still more than inadequate in this regard.

- Some visual editors do not have "round-trip" editing features. This means that even if you are working in the editor window rather than the visual workspace, the software might rewrite your markup to its own particular methodology.

- CMS technology pays precious little attention to specifications, and in most cases, management systems have ignored them out and out. This is extremely problematic, because many such systems do not allow for customization of features, which in turn might enable you as the concerned Web author to effectively author documents. The sad truth is that most of these systems are extremely expensive—from thousands to millions of dollars—and once a company has made an investment in such a system, the Web author has little recourse in promoting better practices.

So how can you as a Web author try to address these concerns? It's not always going to be easy, and in some cases, it's going to be downright impossible.

The following ideas might help:

* **Review the visual editor with which you are working**. Popular software programs such as Dreamweaver, Adobe GoLive, and Microsoft FrontPage have, at least in more recent versions, certain preferences that can be set to enable you to create more compliant documents. For example, you can set up Microsoft FrontPage 2000 to enable you to edit your markup without the program rewriting your work. This way, you can work in the editing window to add DOCTYPE information and make modifications wherever noncompliant markup is generated.

* **Check the version of your visual editor**. If you are using older versions, you might not have the flexibility I've described in my previous point. If the organization or client in question is not amenable to allowing Web authors to produce their own markup via a simple editor, there may be leeway to suggest an upgrade of the software in use, giving you more flexibility.

* **Validate, validate, validate**. No matter which visual editor you are using to create your documents, validate your documents to see whether you've managed to author ones that are conforming.

* **Study the way the CMS works**. In the case of content management systems, you might, as I've mentioned, have little recourse to change anything. However, do see if there's any way you can make modifications to its templates that will result in conforming documents. If your organization is interested in a CMS but has yet to purchase one, speak up about specifications and try to encourage the organization to purchase or build a CMS that has enough flexibility to create compliant pages.

If it seems as though the onus is on you, the Web author, to ensure document compliance, you're right. So many people are unfortunately uninformed about these concerns that you might very well find yourself having to be extremely proactive in ensuring that your clients, organizations, and tools are constructive toward your goals rather than destructive. But, the more you are able to express the importance and rationale of compliance to your colleagues and clients, the more people will become educated, ideally resulting in better document creation and management.

DOCTYPE DECLARATIONS AND DTDS

As you by now understand, you declare the document type using the DOCTYPE declaration. In the past, this declaration was ignored by Web browsers, and became useful only when attempting to validate a document.

New Developments

As if choosing a DTD weren't difficult enough, a new wrench has been thrown into the situation. Referred to as "Quirks Mode" in the industry, many newer browsers implement both a rendering engine that complies with standards, and one that manages nonstandard markup. When a document is received that lacks a DOCTYPE declaration or has a DOCTYPE that is of a certain form, the browser displays the page using the older rendering engine, rather than the newer, more standards-savvy engine.

Because choosing your DTD and declaring it with the DOCTYPE will influence the way your documents are interpreted, I felt it important to include how DOCTYPE declarations work with this mode.

<!--
Much of the information in this section was contributed by Eric A. Meyer via his book, *Eric Meyer on CSS* from New Riders (ISBN: 0-7357-1245-x) and has been used and modified with permission. I highly recommend Meyer's book as an extraordinarily useful companion as you deepen your skills in HTML and XHTML, as it will provide you with practical, creative ideas for CSS presentation and layout.
-->

It was the release of IE 5 for Macintosh that first pointed to a way out of the chaos the Browser Wars had created. The lead programmer of IE5 for the Macintosh, Tantek Çelik, recognized that no browser could afford to break old pages. But, in order to permit a move to standards-based markup, the very behaviors on which those old pages were based would have to be broken.

The solution was to implement both a standards-compliant rendering engine and the old, "bugwards-compatible" behaviors, and then provide a mechanism which would let the author of a document actually choose which rendering mode the browser should use in displaying the document.

The most practical way to achieve this resulted in using the DOCTYPE as a means of deciding between engines.

As you are well aware, every HTML and XHTML document should declare its document type using a directive at the very top of the document:

```
<!DOCTYPE HTML PUBLIC "-//W3C//DTD HTML 4.0//EN"
"http://www.w3.org/TR/REC-html40/strict.dtd">
```

In this case, the document has been marked as using strict HTML 4.0. There are a variety of DOCTYPE values with which you are already familiar. In order to put the concept of how newer browsers are switching modes into context, consider Table 4.1, which provides a sampling of DOCTYPES for your reference.

Table 4.1 A Sampling of DOCTYPE Values

Document Type	DOCTYPE
HTML 3.2	`<!DOCTYPE HTML PUBLIC "-//W3C//DTD HTML 3.2 Final//EN">`
HTML 4.0 Transitional	`<!DOCTYPE HTML PUBLIC "-//W3C//DTD HTML 4.0 Transitional//EN">`
HTML 4.0 Frameset	`<!DOCTYPE HTML PUBLIC "-//W3C//DTD HTML 4.0 Frameset//EN"`
	`"http://www.w3.org/TR/REC-html40/frameset.dtd">`

Table 4.1 Continued

Document Type	DOCTYPE
HTML 4.0 Strict	`<!DOCTYPE HTML PUBLIC "-//W3C//DTD HTML 4.0//EN"` `"http://www.w3.org/TR/REC-html40/strict.dtd">`
HTML 4.01 Transitional	`<!DOCTYPE HTML PUBLIC "-//W3C//DTD HTML 4.01 Transitional//EN">`
HTML 4.01 Strict	`<!DOCTYPE HTML PUBLIC "-//W3C//DTD HTML 4.01//EN"` `"http://www.w3.org/TR/REC-html40/strict.dtd">`
XHTML 1.0 Strict	`<!DOCTYPE html PUBLIC "-//W3C//DTD XHTML 1.0 Strict//EN"` `"http://www.w3.org/TR/xhtml1/xhtml1-strict.dtd">`

As you can see in this table, some of the DOCTYPEs have URIs and some do not. This is not a hard rule because any DOCTYPE can have a URI or leave it off. Thus, they were included at random in the examples shown in the table. As you'll soon see, the presence or absence of a DOCTYPE URI can affect which rendering mode gets picked.

The mechanism of *DOCTYPE switching* is, at its core, fairly sensible and straightforward:

- Documents with older or Transitional DOCTYPEs, or no DOCTYPE at all, are displayed using the quirks mode. This mode, also called "loose mode" and "bugwards compatibility," emulates legacy bugs and behaviors of version 4 browsers.

- Documents with Strict or XHTML DOCTYPEs are displayed using the strict rendering mode. This mode follows W3C specifications for HTML, CSS, and other layout languages as closely as possible.

While incredibly useful for authors, DOCTYPE switching might have remained no more than a curiosity had it only been implemented in IE5 for the Macintosh. Happily, it has since been adopted by Netscape 6 and Internet Explorer 6 for Windows.

`<!--`

Netscape Navigator 4.x came long before DOCTYPE switching was even conceived, so it should be assumed to always be in quirks mode (and a buggy form of it at that). Opera 6 and earlier versions do not bother with DOCTYPE switching, and should be assumed to be in strict mode. Note that it may still have bugs, but its behavior is very close to the strict modes of other browsers.

`-->`

DOCTYPE **Switching in Detail**

Table 4.2 provides a sampling of DOCTYPEs and the effect they'll have in the various Web browsers that recognize DOCTYPE switching at all.

Table 4.2 DOCTYPE Switching in Various Browsers

DOCTYPE	IE6/Win	IE5/Mac	NS6.0	NS6.1	NS6.2
No DOCTYPE provided	Q	Q	Q	Q	Q
Unknown DOCTYPE	S	S	Q	Q	Q
HTML 2.0	Q	Q	Q	Q	Q
HTML 3.2	Q	Q	Q	Q	Q

Table 4.2   Continued

DOCTYPE	IE6/Win	IE5/Mac	NS6.0	NS6.1	NS6.2
HTML 4.0 Frameset	Q	Q	Q	Q	Q
HTML 4.0 Frameset + URI	S	S	Q	Q	Q
HTML 4.0 Transitional	Q	Q	Q	Q	Q
HTML 4.0 Transitional + URI	S	S	Q	Q	Q
HTML 4.0 Strict	S	Q	S	S	S
HTML 4.0 Strict + URI	S	S	S	S	S
HTML 4.01 Frameset	Q	Q	Q	Q	Q
HTML 4.01 Frameset + URI	S	S	S	S	S
HTML 4.01 Transitional	Q	Q	Q	Q	Q
HTML 4.01 Transitional + URI	S	S	S	S	S
HTML 4.01 Strict	S	Q	S	S	S
HTML 4.01 Strict + URI	S	S	S	S	S
Any known XHTML	S	S	S	S	S
Any known XHTML + URI	S	S	S	S	S

S = Strict mode   Q = Quirks mode

Differences in Rendering Modes

If you plan to upgrade your old pages to a new DTD, it will help to know what changes you're likely to encounter. There are profound changes, like an altered meaning for the properties width and height, and subtle changes, like inheritance into tables, that can cause trouble with legacy designs. There might even be differences in the way the CSS can be written, depending on the browser.

The following information, while not a comprehensive list of differences between quirks and strict modes in various browsers, touches on the areas most likely to cause an author trouble:

- **Inheritance and tables**—The biggest area of potential trouble relates to tables and their inheritance (or lack thereof) of styles. In older browsers such as Navigator 4.x and Internet Explorer 5.x (and earlier), styles such as fonts and font sizes were not inherited into tables. In quirks mode, this lack of inheritance is preserved. In strict mode, all styles are inherited by text within tables.

- **Case-sensitivity**—In the HTML 4.01 specification, class and id values are defined to be case-sensitive. Browsers from the version 4 era treated class and id values as being case-insensitive. Because there is no penalty to making sure all of your CSS rules and HTML-based values for class and id have the same case, you should always make sure the case matches between the two.

- **CSS value problems**—This issue belongs entirely to Internet Explorer. IE4.x and IE 5.x for Windows allowed an author to write fairly sloppy values in CSS and would forgive those values. For example, you could leave out hash marks, use too many spaces in your values, or leave out measurement units, and the document would still render more or less in the way you intended. Internet Explorer 6 in strict mode will now interpret any of those sloppy CSS mistakes and render your documents accordingly. If you've not been paying attention to proper CSS authoring techniques, now's the time to start doing so!

- **Changing width and height**—This issue is by far the biggest surprise to authors making the switch from legacy to standards-compliant layout, especially those authors who did any CSS positioning, or attempted pixel-precise layout of elements in Explorer 5.x. If you used the Internet Explorer box model instead of the correct CSS model, you will find significant, perhaps even radical alterations to a page's layout between strict and quirks mode when it comes to width and height values.

About the Box Model

The box model is the model used to describe the way visual formatting is achieved in CSS. Each box has a content area made up of text, or an image, or what have you. Then, there are optional surrounding padding, margins, and border areas.

The W3C box model is different from the IE box model, and this causes some concerns in the proper rendering of box properties in IE.

For more information about visual formatting in CSS, please see http://www.w3.org/TR/REC-CSS2/visuren.html.

Of course, if you are authoring documents according to the specifications and properly declaring your DTD, you won't have to worry about a browser switching to quirks mode.

CASE BY CASE: TRANSITIONAL DESIGN FOR THE NEW YORK PUBLIC LIBRARY

Well-known Web designer Jeffrey Zeldman recently worked on a project with the New York Public Library. The goal was to create a site that was standards-compliant and addressed the needs of the client. Figure 4.1 shows the results.

Working alongside Carrie Bickner, a librarian trained in SGML, the two determined that the site would require a transitional approach to its design.

Zeldman describes his rationale as to how the transitional methodology emerged.

"All who publish Web sites should be concerned about the long-term viability of what they publish. Librarians are particularly concerned with issues of durability. For instance when deciding which published version of a book to stock, a librarian would want to know about the

<!--
Visit the NYPL at http://www.nypl.org/.
-->

quality of the paper and the binding, etc. Librarianship is not disposable; it's about preserving our intellectual heritage."

"A purist might have said, 'we must use XML.' Or, 'we must use XHTML 1.1 Strict, and confine all document stylization to the CSS.'"

Bickner describes why strict XHTML wasn't the best route for the New York Public Library:

"The New York Public Library still has so many N[etscape] 4.7 browsers in our system. We are upgrading to IE 5.0, but in an institution of this size, that process is very slow. I needed to make sure that the N 4.7 user experience was not damaged by our adoption of Web standards. The XHTML 1.0 transitional DTD helps us keep a good balance between keeping N 4 users happy, and having well-formed documents."

And Zeldman summarizes the process by adding:

"So XHTML 1.0 Transitional was chosen as the appropriate markup language, tables were used for page layout (but written to comply with WAI accessibility standards), and two levels of CSS were served so that the pages would look reasonable in old browsers and great in newer, more compliant ones.

"The chosen standards will continue to be supported in browsers, so the strategy makes short-term and long-term sense."

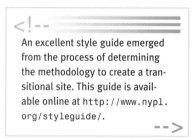

An excellent style guide emerged from the process of determining the methodology to create a transitional site. This guide is available online at http://www.nypl.org/styleguide/.

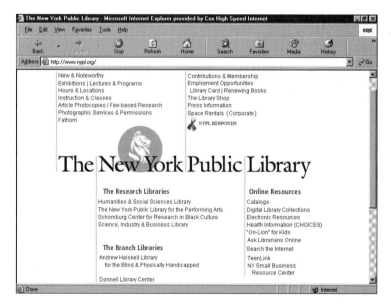

Figure 4.1
Transitional design seen at the New York Public Library online.

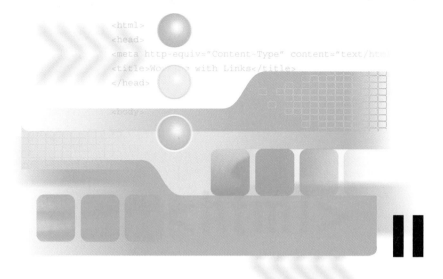

STRUCTURING AND FORMATTING DOCUMENTS

5   Global Structure and Syntax of Documents   **95**

6   Managing Text and Lists   **111**

7   Adding Hypertext and Independent Links   **155**

8   Working with Tables   **177**

9   Creating Framesets and Frame Documents   **219**

10 Building Forms   **247**

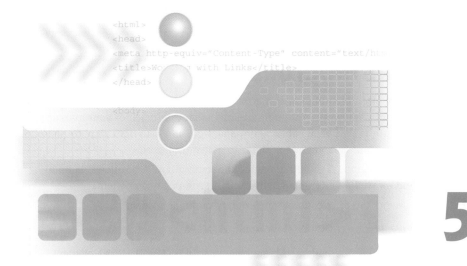

GLOBAL STRUCTURE AND SYNTAX OF DOCUMENTS

IN THIS CHAPTER

About Document Structure   96

Declarations and Document Types   96

The html Element   98

The head Element   98

The body Element   100

Syntax of Documents   101

Case Sensitivity   105

Attribute Quoting   107

Case by Case: Troubleshooting Errors with Structure and Syntax   108

ABOUT DOCUMENT STRUCTURE

Just as a building requires a strong foundation and structural integrity, so Web documents demand strong and consistent framework. Although it might seem that much of your markup works independently, the truth is that each component on a page, and also from page to page, works interdependently with other components in order to deliver the goods.

To ensure that this process is sound, Web authors must understand how a document is built, and learn the independent as well as interdependent roles of each page component.

HTML and XHTML documents typically contain four primary parts, as follows:

- The document type declaration (DOCTYPE) including HTML version information.

- The `html` element, containing the `head` and `body` elements. In HTML, the `html` element may include attributes providing information about language and text direction. In XHTML, the `html` element may include this information as well, but must also include the proper namespace.

- A header section defined by the `head` element and containing the page title and various metadata, scripting, and style data.

- A body section, which is defined by the `body` element, or in the case of framesets, the `frameset` element.

Figure 5.1 shows a diagram of a typical page's structure.

Figure 5.1
The primary structural parts of a conforming Web document.

DECLARATIONS AND DOCUMENT TYPES

You've read detailed information about the DOCTYPE declaration in Chapter 4, "Choosing the Right DTD." This declaration is essential, although most people authoring Web documents leave it out, usually due to lack of awareness, and because it really didn't matter until very recently.

<!--
In XHTML, an additional part, the XML declaration, is a recommended but not required portion of the document appearing above the DOCTYPE declaration. You can see examples of this in Chapter 2, "Writing Conforming Documents."
-->

The failure to include the DOCTYPE declaration also manifests because of a related failure on the part of Web development software manufacturers to adequately include DOCTYPE information in software. The good news is that more and more software manufacturers are becoming aware of the issue, and making DOCTYPES available for Web authors. Macromedia's popular Homesite editor, as of version 5.0, offers XHTML as well as HTML options (see Figure 5.2).

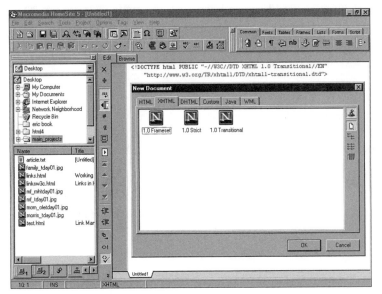

Figure 5.2
Macromedia's popular Homesite editor offers HTML and XHTML DOCTYPES in version 5.0.

So what purpose does the DOCTYPE serve? Well, by declaring the HTML or XHTML version in use, you as an author can validate the document against the DTD. What's more, you can include information about entity sets that are needed in the definition, such as those for Latin, symbolic, or special entities.

An oft-asked question is whether the DOCTYPE has the browser actually download the DTD from the URL located in the definition. Most browsers do not do this, and in fact the DOCTYPE is a fairly passive component in most instances, until a document is passed through a validator.

Figure 5.3 shows a DOCTYPE declaration with its various parts explained.

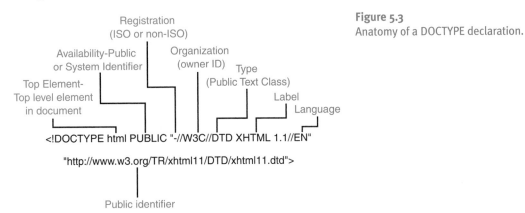

Figure 5.3
Anatomy of a DOCTYPE declaration.

THE HTML ELEMENT

In HTML, this element is optional, believe it or not! But, good form suggests that you should use it. In XHTML, the html element is decidedly not optional. You must include it as it provides information regarding the namespace in use.

There are several attributes that can be used along with the html element in HTML and XHTML:

- **lang**—The language attribute provides information regarding the language in use. The value is a language code. An example of using such a code to denote a document in Azerbaijani, for instance, would be as follows:

```
<html lang="az">
```

- **dir**—This attribute is the *text direction* attribute, which defines the direction of text and tables. Values for this attribute include ltr (left-to-right) and rtl (right-to-left). So, if I were marking up a document in Hebrew, which unlike English is written right-to-left, I would write this:

```
<html lang="he" dir="rtl">
```

Both the lang and dir attributes can be used with other elements, such as paragraphs and divisions.

For a complete listing of language codes, please **see** "Dealing with Data Types," **p. 61**, Chapter 3.

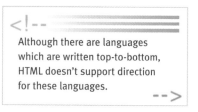

Although there are languages which are written top-to-bottom, HTML doesn't support direction for these languages.

Within the html element the head and body elements are included respectively.

THE HEAD ELEMENT

Most readers are familiar with the head element and its purpose: to provide information about the document. Information contained within the head element is not rendered by the browser as content. However, it may affect the rendering of the content itself, such as with the use of the meta tag to specify a content type or character set, or with the use of style or link to specify styles.

The only required element within the head of a document is the title element. Using this element, you will title your document in a way that accurately describes the content of that document. There are several reasons this is important. First, it helps orient users as to where they are in a given site. Of equal or perhaps greater importance is that titling your page assists with accessibility.

To learn more about accessibility concerns, **see** "Creating Accessible Sites," **p. 419**, Chapter 17.

Typically, you will include the name of the site and then specific details about the particular document:

```
<title>All About Cats: Bringing Your Kitten Home</title>
```

It is very important to remember that you *must* include the title element in any HTML and XHTML document that you write.

Another common and important issue in the head portion of a document is the provision of metadata. Using the meta element and a variety of attributes, you can describe a range of details about the document, including author, http response header name, keywords, and other information.

<!--**Caution**
Although you may use character entities within a title, you cannot use any other markup.
-->

The meta element is a non-empty element. In HTML, it is written as a single tag. In XHTML, the tag terminates with a trailing slash according to XML rules:

HTML: <meta>

XHTML: <meta />

The following attributes set up the structure for meta information:

- name—This attribute identifies the meta information property name. Let's say I want to identify the author of the document. I'd begin with:

  ```
  <meta name="author" />
  ```

- content—Content is used to describe the meta information's property value. So, if I wanted to define myself as the author of the document, I'd add:

  ```
  <meta name="author" content="Molly E. Holzschlag" />
  ```

- http-equiv—Used in place of name, this attribute is used by HTTP servers to grab information for HTTP response message headers. Let's say a document resides in cache, but you'd like to ensure that it expires on a given date, in this case, December 26, 2001. On that date, you want to have the browser deliver a fresh copy of the document. To do this, you'd write:

  ```
  <meta http-equiv="Expires" content="Wed, 26 Dec 2001 01:25:27 GMT" />
  ```

Depending on your needs, a range of additional information can be included within the head element, including:

- **Scripting**—JavaScript and other scripts are often placed in the head of the document, within the script element.

- **Style**—To link a document to a style sheet, you'll use the link element. To embed style information into a document, you'll use the style element and include the style syntax within the element.

- **Document Character Encoding**—As you learned in Chapter 2, "Writing Conforming Documents," some authors will want to include the type of document encoding used for the document within a meta element.

- **Alternate content**—Using the link element, authors can describe alternate content and even create navigational options.

<!--
The meta and link elements, which are empty elements, terminate with a trailing slash according to XML rules. In HTML, these elements take no closing tag and do not require a trailing slash.
-->

⇨ *For detailed information on scripting,* **see** *"Adding Scripting to HTML and XHTML Documents,"* **p. 401,** *Chapter 16.*

⇨ *To learn more about style sheets,* **see** *"Using CSS with HTML and XHTML,"* **p. 345,** *Chapter 14.*

⇨ *Find out how to provide alternate content,* **see** *"Adding Hypertext and Independent Links,"* **p. 155,** *Chapter 7.*

⇨ *Learn how to use metadata to prepare your site for search engines,* **see** *"Site Publishing and Maintenance Guide,"* **p. 541,** *Appendix A.*

THE BODY ELEMENT

The body element's primary goal is to provide user agents with the document content to be displayed. Attributes within the body have typically been used to describe presentational issues. Although you may use such presentational attributes in HTML 4.01 and XHTML 1.0 Transitional documents and have conforming documents, strict documents for both demand that you move these attributes into a style sheet in order to conform to their respective DTDs.

Presentational attributes for transitional documents to be displayed in visual browsers include the following:

- **background**—This attribute defines a background graphic. The attribute value is the URI indicating where the graphic in question resides:

  ```
  <body background="graphics/molly-background.gif">
  ```

- **bgcolor**—To add a background color to a document's entire body content, you can use bgcolor along with a permissible color value:

  ```
  <body bgcolor="white">
  ```

- **text**—This attribute defines the default color of the content's text. However, the use of font tags along with the color attribute, or the use of style sheets applied to text will override this value.

  ```
  <body bgcolor="white" text="black">
  ```

- **link**—To define the color of a link, add a color value:

  ```
  <body bgcolor="white" text="black" link="blue">
  ```

- **alink**—This is *active link* and is the color of the link as the link is activated:

  ```
  <body bgcolor="white" text="black" link="blue" alink="red">
  ```

- **vlink**—The color of a *visited link* can be defined by this attribute:

  ```
  <body bgcolor="white" text="black" link="blue" alink="red" vlink="purple">
  ```

Numerous other attributes can be used in the body tag including id, class, lang, dir, style, and intrinsic events such as onload, onclick, and so on. Please refer to the cross references in the previous section for details as to where you can find more information regarding these attributes.

SYNTAX OF DOCUMENTS

Writing Web markup is hardly different than writing a simple sentence. The central pillar of Web markup is the *element*. Elements are made up of a tag or tag combination. A tag is the identity of markup, which means it acts as a container for content or other elements. Tags become powerful with modification, and that modification begins with an *attribute*.

Attributes define an element's properties. With them, a tag can come to life and not only do something, but do it in a certain way.

Attribute names are modified by attribute *values*. A value defines the way an attribute will be interpreted.

Elements

There are specific as well as general rules and conventions regarding elements. The first is that all standard element identifiers are contained within a less-than and greater-than symbol, as follows:

```
<link>
```

Note that there are no spaces between the symbols and the tag, and no spaces between the letters that denote the tag.

Elements that appear in the body of a document are defined by the concept of *block* or *inline*.

Block-level elements refer to structural elements. Block-level elements can contain other block-level elements (as in a division containing paragraphs) and inline elements. Usually, block level elements are rendered by browsers as beginning on a new line.

Inline elements, also referred to as *text-level* elements, are those elements that contain content. They may also contain other inline elements, but they should not contain a block-level element. Inline elements typically work within the content of a document without causing any line breaks.

In transitional HTML and XHTML, inline elements may appear alone. However, in strict HTML and XHTML, all inline elements must be contained within a reasonable block-level element. So, let's say you are using the img element and you do not place it within a division, paragraph, or other block-level element. In a transitional document, this will cause no problems with validation. However, in strict documents, you will get an error while attempting to validate the document because the inline element must be properly contained by a block-level element.

Other rules and conventions involve non-empty and empty elements.

Non-Empty Elements

A non-empty element is an element that acts as a container, containing its content within an opening and closing tag. A good example of this is the <html> element, which contains the entire document structure information within its opening and closing counterparts, <html> and </html> respectively.

Another non-empty element to study is the paragraph element (<p>). Although in HTML, <p> does not require a closing tag, XHTML requires a tag set of <p> and </p> surrounding the element's contained data. In this case, that data is text, as in the following markup:

```
<p>The text in this paragraph makes up the data that is contained by the
paragraph element.</p>
```

In HTML, it is perfectly legal to use an opening <p> only, despite the fact that there is data contained within the element:

```
<p>The text in this paragraph makes up the data that is contained by the
paragraph element.
```

However, in XHTML, you *must* close any non-empty element. Those of you who are already quite familiar with HTML will know that there are other instances where HTML allowed for non-empty elements to have no terminating tag, such as the list item, or li element. In XHTML, elements that are not empty *must* terminate.

So, although the following markup is valid in HTML:

```
<ul>
<li>One tag
<li>Two tags
<li>Three tags
<li>Four
</ul>
```

It is *not* valid in XHTML. Instead, you must close the non-empty element, as follows:

```
<ul>
<li>One tag</li>
<li>Two tags</li>
<li>Three tags</li>
<li>Four</li>
</ul>
```

A little more to write, but the results are valid, consistent, and well-formed XHTML.

For more information DOCTYPEs and how browsers behave with them, **see** "Choosing the Right DTD," **p. 81,** Chapter 4.

<!--

Some people have asked me whether using an end tag with paragraphs or list items changes the rendering of the content. Sometimes, it does. It depends upon the browser, and the DOCTYPE you're using (see the next cross reference). However, these changes are pretty consistent and easy to get accustomed to. You still will want to test your pages with a variety of browsers and platforms to get the best results.

-->

Empty Elements

An empty element is an element that is sufficient unto itself and needs no additional markup to convey its meaning. For example, the img tag displays an image, but has no closing tag and contains no data outside of the tag and its related attributes and values. The same is true of break tags, horizontal rules, meta tags, the link tag, and so forth.

In HTML, empty elements are simply written as single tags, along with any attributes:

```
<hr>
<br clear="all">
<img>
```

In XML, all empty elements require termination. This is due to the fact that if the author doesn't alert the user agent's parser to stop looking for the close tag, it will keep searching for it, and treat every subsequent element as an error. As a result, XHTML demands this termination. XHTML borrows a markup convention from XML to solve this concern, which was never addressed in HTML. The termination of an empty element is a space and a forward slash after the element and before the greater-than symbol:

```
<element />
```

This means that any empty element will now contain this termination. Here's an example using the img element:

```
<img src="images/molly_logo.gif" width="50" height="50" border="0"

alt="molly.com logo" />
```

Attributes

Many elements can act perfectly fine alone, but there is a variety of tags that *must* have attributes in order to function properly.

An attribute actually consists of two properties, the attribute *name*, and the attribute value.

Many attributes in HTML have historically had to do with modifying the way something on a page looks. In the strict DTDs of HTML 4.0, 4.01 and XHTML 1.0, and the XHTML 1.1 DTD, any attribute that defines a style is not allowed; instead, you are to use style sheets. However, you can use these attributes and their companion values in transitional HTML 4.01 and XHTML 1.0.

Other attributes are fundamental to the proper interpretation of an element and have nothing to do with presentation at all. Examples would be src, alt, href, and so on.

Attribute names can be whole words, partial words or abbreviations, or even acronyms. Some whole word attributes include align, color, link, and face. Partial word examples include src for "source," and vlink for "visited link."

<!--Caution
Attributes *only exist in the start tag*. For example, <body bgcolor="#ffffff"> is correct syntax, and will be closed simply with </body>. I've seen many new Web authors try to close a tag with the attribute, writing the close tag as </body bgcolor="#ffffff">. Seasoned authors will know this is incorrect, but new Web authors should be very cautious as to avoid this common mistake.
-->

Attributes follow the tag and are separated by at least one space:

```
<body bgcolor…
```

and are then set by the attribute value before the tag is closed.

A tag can have more than one attribute, and, in fact, some tags take on many attributes at the same time. In this case, the syntax follows the same concept: first the tag, then a space, and then an attribute. The attribute will receive a value, and then a space is once again introduced *before* the next attribute:

```
<body bgcolor="#ffffff" text="#000000">
```

and so forth, until all the attributes and their values are included.

Values

Values, like attributes, can be made up of a whole word. If I'm using the div, or division, element, and I want to align all the information in that division in a transitional HTML or XHTML document, I can select from several values that will modify the align attribute. Such values include left, right, center, and justify.

A resulting statement would be:

```
<div align="right">
</div>
```

Some attribute values are numeric, referring to pixels or percentages, browser-defined sizes, or hexadecimal numbers to define color. A pixel value example is well described by the width attribute:

```
<table width="768">
```

Similarly, I can use a percentage value in the same instance. The markup would then be:

```
<table width="100%">
```

and in this case, the table would flex to 100% of the available space.

➪ For more information on the table element, including its attributes and values, **see** "Working with Tables," **p. 177**, Chapter 8.

Browser-defined sizes are those sizes that the browser selects. In other words, you cannot predetermine the exact size, such as with pixels, but you can approximate the size. The best example of this is with the deprecated font tag attribute size. The size attribute can opt to take a value ranging from 1 to 7, with 1 being the smallest, and 7 the largest:

```
<font size="5">
```

<!--**Caution**═══

Because different browsers and platforms interpret and display browser-defined sizes differently, you will have to test your pages by using as many browsers as possible to ensure that you are getting results that are satisfactory.

-->

Any text between this and the closing /font tag takes on the browser's interpretation of a size 5. An example of a numeric type of value would be hexadecimal color codes:

```
<body bgcolor="#FFFFFF">
```

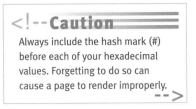

<!--**Caution**

Always include the hash mark (#) before each of your hexadecimal values. Forgetting to do so can cause a page to render improperly. -->

There are other kinds of values of which to be aware. One such value is a relative or absolute link to another document, meaning that a directory, series of directories, and specific filename, can be included in certain attributes to fulfill a value:

```
<a href="http://www.molly.com/">Go to My Home Page</a>
```

This markup will create a link that, when activated, goes to my home page. The a, or anchor element, creates a link; the attribute is href, or hypertext reference; and the value is the URL, http://www.molly.com/.

Similarly, I can point to a directory and an image:

```
<img src="images/molly.gif" />
```

In this case, the tag is img, or image (which, again, is an empty element and must be terminated in XHTML), the attribute is src ("source"), and the value is a combination of the path to the images directory and the specific file, molly.gif.

Another interesting example is the alt attribute. This attribute appears in image or object tags and offers a description of the image or object for those individuals who cannot or do not want to see the image or object:

```
<img src="molly.gif" alt="picture of Molly" />
```

In this situation, you see that the value assigned to the alt attribute is actually a series of words used to describe the picture. You can also see in this example how a tag can have multiple attributes with corresponding values.

➡ *To locate information on the anchor tag and its attributes,* **see** *"Adding Hypertext and Independent Links," **p. 155**, Chapter 7.*

➡ *If you want to examine image syntax in detail,* **see** *"Adding Images," **p. 275**, Chapter 11.*

By now you probably have noticed that all values are preceded by an = symbol (the equal sign), and the value is within quotation marks.

CASE SENSITIVITY

How case is managed in authoring also becomes part of the way documents are properly validated and read. XHTML examined the methods used in HTML and XML, and came up with a happy medium to create its own method.

In HTML

Tags and attributes can be in upper- or lowercase, depending on personal tastes and needs. HTML itself is *not case-sensitive*. As a result you can do any or all of the following in HTML:

- Use all uppercase in tags and attributes

- Use all lowercase in tags and attributes

- Mix upper- and lowercase in tags and attributes

View the source on any arbitrary page out on the Web, and you'll see HTML tags and attributes in uppercase, lowercase, and mixed case. Listing 5.1 shows an HTML 4.01 document using all three combinations.

Listing 5.1   Mixed Case in HTML 4.01

```
<!DOCTYPE HTML PUBLIC "-//W3C//DTD HTML 4.0 Transitional//EN"
"http://www.w3.org/TR/REC-html40/loose.dtd">
<HTML>
<HEAD>
<TITLE>HTML Example of Case</TITLE>
</HEAD>
<BODY>
<P ALIGN="LEFT">These tags and attributes are all uppercase</P>
<p align="right">These tags and attributes are all lowercase</p>
<P align="center">These tags and attributes are all mixed case</P>
</BODY>
</HTML>
```

you can even mix case within a given element and attribute:

```
<P AliGn="LefT"> . . . </p>
```

And this markup will be valid, although it's ugly!

In XML

XML, unlike HTML *is case-sensitive*. This means that case is a critical component within your syntax. So, an XML element that looks like this:

```
<desktop>

</desktop>
```

will be different from:

```
<DESKTOP>

</DESKTOP>
```

<!--
I recommend writing all HTML elements and attributes in lowercase, even though you don't technically have to do so. Your documents will be neater and therefore easier to debug. What's more, if you choose to convert those documents to XHTML later on, the task will be much less difficult.
-->

This element can be added to the mix, too:

```
<DeskTop>

</DeskTop>
```

And all of these elements are *individual, independent, and unique*, because XML is case-sensitive. Simply said, `desktop` is not `DESKTOP` and is not `DeskTop`.

In XHTML

XHTML is *case-sensitive*. You simply cannot use anything but lowercase markup in XHTML elements and attribute names, and that is that. No mixed case, no uppercase. Only lowercase. Anything else departs from conforming XHTML markup.

Attribute values in XHTML may be written in uppercase, lowercase, or mixed case. Take for example a URI that points to:

```
http://www.w3.org/TR/html4/types.html
```

is not the same as:

```
http://www.w3.org/tr/html4/types.html
```

It is my recommendation to use lowercase values everywhere even when it is not necessary to do so, in order to keep your documents clean and consistent.

<!-- ====
You'll probably notice that DOCTYPE in the DOCTYPE declaration is , even though everything in an XHTML document is supposed to be lowercase. The reason? DOCTYPE is not considered to be part of the XHTML markup. Rather, it is a separate entity responsible for declaring the document itself.
-->

ATTRIBUTE QUOTING

As with case, there are significant differences between the way that quotation marks are used in XHTML and HTML. Simply said, HTML is rather loose, whereas in XHTML, rigorous use of quotes is the name of the day.

In HTML

The use of quotations in HTML is relatively unrestricted. For example, you can write:

```
<div align="left">
```

or:

```
<div align=left>
```

and either one is considered acceptable.

Although I can confidently leave the quotations out from around a `width="x"` or `align="center"` attribute value, making the `width=x` and `align=center`, there are many cases in which removing the quotations means trouble. Sometimes, an attribute value will require a quote for a certain browser to understand it, or it won't render properly.

One such instance is around hexadecimal values. In a body tag, for example, I can potentially render my HTML markup unreadable by missing a quotation around those values. The same is true of any time I use a URL or directory/filename value for an anchor or image tag.

I've also seen this happen on occasion when browsers attempt to interpret magic target names:

```
<a href="nextpage.html" target=_blank>
```

Another very common authoring problem is failure to fully quote an attribute value. Certainly, this occurs in XHTML too, accidents, after all, do happen. However, when you aren't required to quote all attribute values, it has been my experience that the problem occurs more frequently:

```
<p align="right">
```

Because there is *never* an instance in HTML where it's improper to quote attribute values, I recommend anyone authoring HTML documents quote all attribute values.

In XML and XHTML

In XML, all attribute values must be quoted. Period. The same is true with XHTML, because XHTML *is* XML. No matter your habits prior to writing XHTML, the bottom line is that if you're using XHTML, you now *must quote all attribute values*.

CASE BY CASE: TROUBLESHOOTING ERRORS WITH STRUCTURE AND SYNTAX

Most common authoring errors in HTML and XHTML occur at the structural or syntactical level. Whether it's the omission of a required structural component such as the DOCTYPE declaration or a `title` element, or a syntax error such as the omission of a quote or improper use of block and inline elements, the reality is these mistakes can cause us a lot of hair-pulling and frustration.

Even more problematic is that many software products do not properly manage structure and syntax. So, you might be introducing errors into a document completely unbeknownst to you because you're placing faith in the software. This is troublesome because even the best software available has flaws in terms of generating markup that is structured properly and is syntactically correct.

To highlight this point, I opened Dreamweaver, my favorite visual editor, and without changing or modifying any settings, I simply typed in a sentence and saved the file. The results are pretty clean and simple, as shown in Listing 5.2. But, when examined for structural integrity, you'll quickly see that the document is missing one important component and has a syntax concern.

Listing 5.2   Examining a Document for Structural Integrity

```
<html>
<head>
<title>Untitled Document</title>
<meta http-equiv="Content-Type" content="text/html; charset=iso-8859-1">
</head>

<body bgcolor="#FFFFFF" text="#000000">
Context is everything, and content is king.
</body>
</html>
```

The structural error in this case is that there's no DOCTYPE declaration. As I mentioned, this is a fundamental issue when it comes to writing conforming documents for the Web, as without the DOCTYPE declaration the document can't be properly validated. And, while all other structural components are in place—html, head, and body elements—unless I know how to format my text, the program won't do it for me, so I have text floating in the body that is completely unstructured. Overall, not too shabby, but if I were to get more detailed with my content, more errors would begin to appear, especially in terms of delineating block-level and inline elements. In other programs, such as Microsoft FrontPage and Adobe GoLive, the structural and syntactical problems are even more complex.

In order to gain better perspective into dealing with structural and syntactical concerns, I'd like you to first grab a document you've written or generated with a software program and examine that document in light of the structure and syntax in light of what we've discussed here. How does the document measure up? Make a list of any structural or syntactical components you think are missing or incorrect. Then, run the document through a validator (I recommend using the online validation service at the W3C) and see what errors are generated.

The W3C online validation service can be found at http://validator. w3.org/.

If you're writing your markup by hand, you'll find that this exercise will help you be more aware of document structure and syntax. If you rely on a commercial software product to generate your markup, this exercise will help you become more intimately familiar with the quirks of the program you're using. As a result, you can research the product more in-depth to see if there are ways to ensure that all components of the document are included, and that syntax is written accurately.

If there are no tools within the program to ensure better structuring and syntax of your document, and you must continue to use that program because of work circumstances or personal preference, you will at least have a greater awareness as to what concerns you'll have to address by hand in order to have well-structured, syntactically accurate documents.

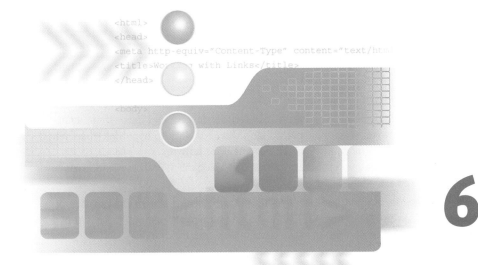

MANAGING TEXT AND LISTS

6

IN THIS CHAPTER

Working with Text   **112**

Structuring Text   **112**

Adding Paragraphs and Breaks   **115**

Working with Headers   **119**

Working with Preformatted Text   **121**

Using Text Styles   **123**

Aligning Text   **125**

Using Lists Effectively   **126**

Dealing Effectively with Lists   **134**

Adding Color, Size, and Typefaces to Text   **141**

Adding Horizontal Rules   **152**

Case by Case: Dealing with Text   **153**

WORKING WITH TEXT

Text formatting is where HTML and XHTML can be the most simple—and the most powerful. After all, Web markup was developed to format text-based documents and make them available on the Internet, with the major enhancement being the capability to hyperlink documents. As you work your way through this chapter, you'll get a feel for how markup was originally intended to work with text and how surprisingly simple, yet elegant, HTML is when it comes to dealing with text.

From the way whitespace is handled, to effectively formatting paragraphs, to the creation of lists, how to deal with text in HTML and XHTML is a skill you need to use daily. Knowing how to do so properly can be an enormous asset, saving time and frustration.

STRUCTURING TEXT

In HTML and XHTML, *structured text* refers to the simple markup of text such as adding headers, paragraphs, and lists. It does not refer to deeply presentational issues such as adding alignment or fonts.

There are three categories of structured text:

- **Phrase elements**—These are elements that add structure to text.
- **Quotation elements**—This category contains elements that manage long and short quotations.
- **Subscripts and superscripts**—These are specialty elements for text management.

Phrase Elements

A number of elements indicate the way text is structured. How browsers render the text when the element is in place might vary somewhat, but generally, browsers are consistent in the way structured text is interpreted, as follows:

- **em**—This element is for emphasis. Most browsers render text that is marked up with em tags in italics.
- **strong**—For emphasis, strong is usually rendered in bold.
- **cite**—This element is used for citations of source. Browsers usually render it in italics.
- **dfn**—This element is a definition of a term, rendered in italics by most browsers.
- **code**—This element is used to show programming code samples. Text structured with this element renders in a browser's default monospace font.
- **samp**—This element is for sample output from programs and scripts. It renders in monospace.
- **kbd**—This element indicates text to be entered by the site visitor. Most browsers render text structured with kbd in monospace.

- **var**—This element is a variable or program argument, and it renders in italics.

- **abbr**—This element is abbreviated text. In most browsers it renders in the default font or any font style that the author calls for.

- **acronym**—This element is used to indicate an acronym, and it causes text to display normally.

<!--Caution

If you're using a strict DTD or writing XHTML 1.1, you need to be sure that any time you use a structure-related element, you contain the element within a block-level element for the document to validate.

-->

All these elements are allowed in HTML 4.0, 4.01, XHTML 1.0 and XHTML 1.1, and all DTDs.

⇨ *To learn more about block and inline elements, **see** Chapter 5, "Global Structure and Syntax of Documents," p. 110.*

Figure 6.1 shows the rendering of structured text in the Netscape browser.

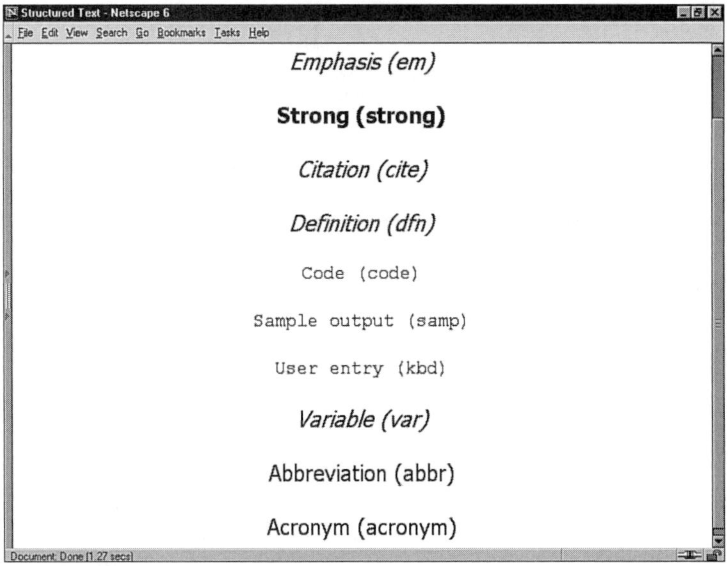

Emphasis (em)

Strong (strong)

Citation (cite)

Definition (dfn)

Code (code)

Sample output (samp)

User entry (kbd)

Variable (var)

Abbreviation (abbr)

Acronym (acronym)

Figure 6.1
Viewing structured text as rendered by Netscape.

Quotation Elements

There are two quotation elements in structured text:

- **blockquote**—This element is meant to structure block-level text quotations. Block-quoted sections of text are generally rendered as an indented block of text.

- **q**—This element is meant for use inline for short quotations. It is rendered with quotations, so you need not add quotation marks when using the q element.

Despite the fact that the q element is alive in all flavors of HTML and XHTML, it's very rarely used. Also, a common design hack is to use `blockquote` to create indented visual components on a page. You can do this and still have a valid document, but the practice is frowned upon.

The point of having structured markup is so that the element name gives meaning to the structure of the element's content. Using the wrong element just to gain a particular visual effect is considered a problematic hack and should be avoided.

In Figure 6.2, you can see how Opera renders quotation elements.

<!--
You should use `blockquote` for bona fide block-level quoting and style sheets to create indentation for visual elements.
-->

Figure 6.2
The quotation marks in the second paragraph are rendered by the browser upon interpreting the q element.

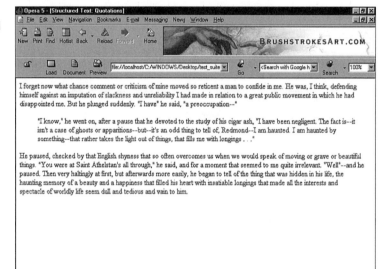

Subscripts and Superscripts

The final category for structured text deals with creating subscripts and superscripts. A subscript is a character that appears immediately below, or below and to the left or right of, the primary character. A superscript is the opposite; the character appears immediately above and to the right of the primary character. Many languages, including English, use subscripts and superscripts.

The elements for structuring subscripts and superscripts are as follows:

* **sub**—Using this element renders the character to which it's applied as a subscript.

* **sup**—Using sup causes the character to which it's applied to render as a superscript in supporting browsers.

<!--Caution
Not all browsers support the q element. In fact, Opera 5 and Netscape 6.0+ render quotes created by the q element perfectly well, but Internet Explorer 6.0 does not.
-->

To use sub or sup, simply place the opening and closing tags around the character that will achieve the special scripting, as in the following example:

```
<p>Molly's 39<sup>th</sup> birthday is coming up!</p>
```

The *th* now renders smaller and to the upper right, just as in standard text formatting (that is, 39th).

ADDING PARAGRAPHS AND BREAKS

By using paragraph element options, you can separate paragraphs into discrete, visible and logical blocks. The paragraph tag formats blocks by making the separation where you determine the beginning and end of a paragraph to be.

Similarly, you can use a break to break a line. However, a break is not rendered with additional whitespace as a paragraph is. Rather, it's simply equivalent to one line break.

As you'll recall from the discussion in Chapter 5, "Global Structure and Syntax of Documents," there are two kinds of elements: *non-empty* and *empty*. A non-empty element is an element that is composed of two tags (opening and closing) and content. An empty element is a tag with no associated content.

The paragraph tag is a non-empty element. However, because in HTML the closing tag is considered optional, there are two ways of marking up paragraphs in HTML. The first way is to simply use the <p> tag before the natural beginning of a paragraph, as shown in Listing 6.1.

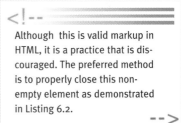

Although this is valid markup in HTML, it is a practice that is discouraged. The preferred method is to properly close this non-empty element as demonstrated in Listing 6.2.

Listing 6.1   Using a Single <p> Tag Before a Paragraph in HTML

```
<!DOCTYPE HTML PUBLIC "-//W3C//DTD HTML 4.01 Transitional//EN"
        "http://www.w3.org/TR/html4/loose.dtd">

<html>
<head>

<meta http-equiv="Content-Type" content="text/html; charset=ISO-8859-1">
<title>Benefits of Exercise</title>

</head>

<body>

<p>Exercise is an excellent way of improving your health. Medical
studies demonstrate that exercise can strengthen your heart and
lungs, lower your blood pressure, and help you maintain a healthy
weight.
```

Listing 6.1   Continued

```
<p>Exercise can also assist with improving your mood. In fact, people who
exercise have demonstrated better self-esteem, stronger decision
making, and a generally more positive outlook on life.

</body>
</html>
```

The second way you could author the HTML document with the open and closing tags, as shown in Listing 6.2.

Listing 6.2   Ideally, Authors Will Close Their Paragraph Tags

```
<!DOCTYPE HTML PUBLIC "-//W3C//DTD HTML 4.01 Transitional//EN"
        "http://www.w3.org/TR/html4/loose.dtd">

<html>
<head>

<meta http-equiv="Content-Type" content="text/html; charset=ISO-8859-1">
<title>Benefits of Exercise</title>

</head>

<body>

<p>Exercise is an excellent way of improving your health. Medical
studies demonstrate that exercise can strengthen your heart and
lungs, lower your blood pressure, and help you maintain a healthy
weight.</p>

<p>Exercise can also assist with improving your mood. In fact, people who
exercise have demonstrated better self-esteem, stronger decision
making, and a generally more positive outlook on life.</p>

</body>
</html>
```

As you've already guessed, because p is a non-empty element, it must be closed in XHTML, so not using a closing tag is *not* allowed when writing to any XHTML specification.

Listing 6.3 shows the same example as in Listing 6.2, this time using the open/close paragraph style in the context of XHTML 1.1.

Listing 6.3   Paragraphs in XHTML

```
<?xml version="1.0" encoding="ISO-8859-1"?>

<!DOCTYPE  html PUBLIC "-//W3C//DTD XHTML 1.1//EN"
```

Listing 6.3 Continued

```
      "http://www.w3.org/TR/xhtml11/DTD/xhtml11.dtd">

<html xmlns="http://www.w3.org/1999/xhtml">

<head>

<title>Health Benefits of Exercise</title>

</head>

<body>

<p>Exercise is an excellent way of improving your health. Medical studies
demonstrate that exercise can strengthen your heart and lungs, lower
your blood pressure, and help you maintain a healthy weight.</p>

<p>Exercise can also assist with improving your mood. In fact, people who
exercise have demonstrated better self-esteem, stronger decision making,
and a generally more positive outlook on life.</p>

</body>
</html>
```

Paragraph rendering relies on the browser or user agent in question. There are inconsistencies between browsers and approaches. For example, if you are writing HTML and not using a closing paragraph tag, you might encounter differences in the way browsers render your paragraphs than if you had used a closing tag. Ideally, you should rely on the power of style sheets to gain more control over the way paragraphs render.

⇨ *To learn how to work with style sheets,* **see** *Chapter 14, "Using CSS with HTML and XHTML," **p. 345**.*

When you want to force a line break, you can use the break element (br). Breaks, unlike paragraphs, are empty elements. Therefore, in XHTML, a break must be terminated with the trailing slash (/>).

Listing 6.4 shows how an address is the perfect place to use the break element in HTML 4.01. Listing 6.5 shows the same markup in XHTML 1.1.

Listing 6.4 Using the Break Tag in HTML

```
<!DOCTYPE HTML PUBLIC "-//W3C//DTD HTML 4.01 Transitional//EN"
      "http://www.w3.org/TR/html4/loose.dtd">

<html>

<head>
<meta http-equiv="Content-Type" content="text/html; charset=ISO-8859-1">
```

Listing 6.4 Continued

```
<title>Getting in Touch</title>

</head>

<body>

Natural Health Products<br>
1 Happy Trails Way<br>
Anytown, USA, 000000<br>

</body>
</html>
```

Listing 6.5 The Break Tag in XHTML

```
<?xml version="1.0" encoding="ISO-8859-1"?>

<!DOCTYPE  html PUBLIC "-//W3C//DTD XHTML 1.1//EN"
    "http://www.w3.org/TR/xhtml11/DTD/xhtml11.dtd">

<html xmlns="http://www.w3.org/1999/xhtml">

<head>

<title>Getting in Touch</title>

</head>

<body>

<p>Natural Health Products<br />
1 Happy Trails Way<br />
Anytown, USA, 000000</p>

</body>
</html>
```

The Break tag in Listings 6.4 and 6.5 forces the line to break and resume at the next available line, with no extra lines in between (see Figure 6.3).

Figure 6.3
Using the Break tag gives you added control over text placement and spacing on a Web page.

Nonbreaking Spaces

There are instances in which you'll want to ensure that a line does *not* break at a certain point. To do this, you can use a nonbreaking space entity: (also,   and) between the words you do not want broken.

Nonbreaking spaces can also be used to create visual space. So, if you want to indent a paragraph by five spaces, you can place five nonbreaking spaces in front of the starting character. Of course, using Cascading Style Sheets for indentation or other presentation is the preferred method.

WORKING WITH HEADERS

A *header* denotes a specific area of a document by titling that individual area. A header element is an alphanumeric combination of an *h* plus a numeric value ranging from 1 to 6 (where 1 is the largest and 6 is the smallest): h1, h2, h3, h4, h5, and h6.

As many seasoned authors know, you can use headers to represent distinct layers of information within the natural progression of text. A document's title, for example, would be a large header, the first subsection could be titled by using a header size one size smaller than the chapter head, and so forth. It's important to note that headers are the same in HTML as in XHTML.

`<!--Caution`

Many people use breaks to create whitespace between elements, and even between images or objects. Although this is not wrong per se, in Strict documents, the preference is to use style sheets. In Transitional documents, you can use table layouts. You can also consider using the pre (that is, preformatted text) element or the vspace attribute when working with images in Transitional documents.

`-->`

Headers work simply, by surrounding the text you want to use as a head with the appropriately sized tag set (Figure 6.4), as in this example:

`<h1>Health Benefits of Exercise</h1>`

<!--**Caution**

Header tags seemingly work backward, with the lowest value, 1, creating the largest visual header. This is a convention born of document structure rules, where a larger header denotes the dominant level of concept. Thus, h1 will constitute a headline, with h2 being a subhead of h1 and so on.
-->

Figure 6.4
Headers of size 1 are used most commonly to format the primary heading of a page.

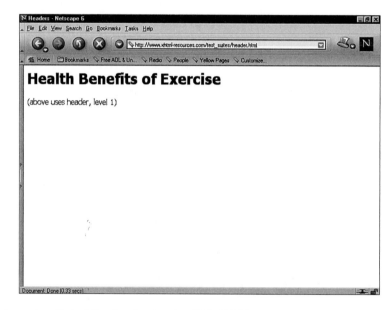

You simply change the numeric value of the header tag to get a different size:

`<h5>Other Benefits of Exercise</h5>`

Figure 6.5 shows a comparison of h1 and h5 headers.

Headers are automatically left-aligned on a page, so if you want to center them or align them to the right, you can apply a style or use an alignment attribute and value in transitional documents.

<!--

Headers maintain relative consistency in default size and appearance across browsers and platforms. However, when a header is viewed at different resolutions, the size naturally changes.
-->

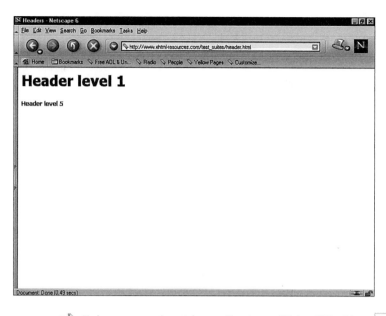

Figure 6.5
The size 5 header will appear smaller on all browsers than the size 1 header.

⇨ *To learn more using style, **see** Chapter 14, "Using CSS with HTML and XHTML," p. 345.*

WORKING WITH PREFORMATTED TEXT

<!--
Use headers sparingly and where absolutely necessary. Keeping to header sizes 1 through 3 is safest, because the smaller-sized headers can be hard to read.
-->

The preformatted text element, pre, was originally developed to create columnar data in an HTML page. This was done before the advent of tables, and it was not an effective way of controlling data.

The way the tag works in both HTML and XHTML is by including all the formatting you place within the tags—including carriage returns, spaces, and text—but *without* the use of any other tags. In other words, you don't need a <p> tag to get a paragraph break; all you need to do is manually enter breaks, as shown in Listing 6.6.

Listing 6.6   Using the pre Element

```
<!DOCTYPE HTML PUBLIC "-//W3C//DTD HTML 4.01 Transitional//EN"
        "http://www.w3.org/TR/html4/loose.dtd">

<html>

<head>
<meta http-equiv="Content-Type" content="text/html; charset=ISO-8859-1">
<title>Preformatted Text</title>
```

Listing 6.6   Continued

```
</head>

<body>

<pre>
This sentence is broken
not by a break tag, but
by the preformatted carriage
returns I've placed within
this section of markup.
</pre>

</body>

</html>
```

Figure 6.6 shows how the markup in Listing 6.6 is rendered, complete with breaks.

Figure 6.6
When you use the pre element, any text formatting options, such as the line breaks shown here, that are used when you type the text, remain part of the text, and no other tags are necessary to invoke the formatting.

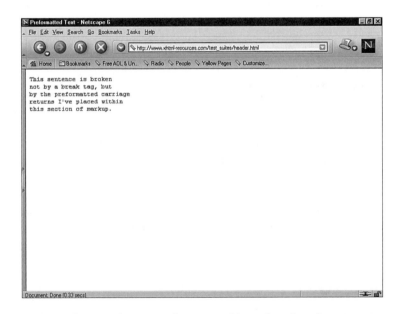

You've probably noticed that the preformatted text tag does something other than format text: It forces a fixed-width, or monospaced, font. This monospaced font is different from the default font, and a page can be unattractive when the two fonts are combined without forethought.

Tables have solved the irregularity problems caused when trying to arrange columnar material with the pre tag. Font tags and style sheets allow you to have infinitely more control over fonts. The pre tag is still used from time to time to add space, however, and you can choose this option over or in addition to paragraphs and breaks when you want more space between elements on a page.

To learn more about creating columnar data with tables, **see** Chapter 8, "Working with Tables," **p. 177**.

Another use for `pre` is to use it to format examples of source code, because of the monospaced font that using it will produce. Another method to do this is to use the `code` element, but it doesn't respect whitespace, which is important in source examples.

The preformatted text tag is still supported by all contemporary browsers, and you can confidently use it for any of its legal applications. However, choosing tables or sticking with paragraph and break tags is usually a more reliable choice than using the preformatted text tag.

USING TEXT STYLES

Writers and designers often want to draw attention to specific information within a text document. There are also conventional methods of formatting text information, such as creating bibliographic references.

Three main text styles—bold, italic, and underline—can be used in HTML and XHTML to accommodate these text formatting concerns. These styles are represented by the following elements:

<!--Caution
You should use text styles sparingly. The point is to emphasize a few words or ideas on a page. If you overuse text styles, you lose the impact that emphasis intends, so tread lightly. Furthermore, you should not use italics, bold, or underline for long sections of body text. For most people, styled text is more difficult to read than standard text.
-->

- **b.** Browsers render the b element as bold.

- **i.** Browsers render the i element in italics.

- **u.** Underlining can be achieved with the u element.

The structural `strong` and `em` tags can be used for emphasis; many authors prefer using these tags in XHTML especially, because they are structural by nature instead of presentational.

Listing 6.7 shows bold, italics, and underline at work.

Listing 6.7   Styling Text with Bold, Italic, and Underline

```
<!DOCTYPE HTML PUBLIC "-//W3C//DTD HTML 4.01 Transitional//EN"
      "http://www.w3.org/TR/html4/loose.dtd">

<html>

<head>

<meta http-equiv="Content-Type" content="text/html; charset=UTF-8">

<title>Styling Text</title>

</head>

<body>
```

Listing 6.7 Continued

```
<p>Sally Forth sallies forth to <b>boldly</b> go where no one has gone before.</p>

<p>Janet did a <i>terrific</i> job organizing this year's conference.</p>

<p>The novel I'm currently reading, <u>Fugitive Pieces</u>, is a poetic look at
the life of a Holocaust survivor.</p>

</body>
</html>
```

Stylized text, because it is in fact presentational, is not available in all language versions. Table 6.1 shows the language and version support for text styles.

Table 6.1 Language and Version Support for Text Styles

Element	HTML 4.0/1 Strict	HTML 4.0/1 Transitional	Version XHTML 1.0 Strict	XHTML 1.0 Transitional	XHTML 1.1
b	Yes	Yes	Yes	Yes	Yes
i	Yes	Yes	Yes	Yes	Yes
u	No	Yes	No	Yes	No

Figure 6.7 shows Listing 6.7 in a Web browser.

Figure 6.7
Bold, italic, and underlined text formatting options should be used for emphasis and only where appropriate.

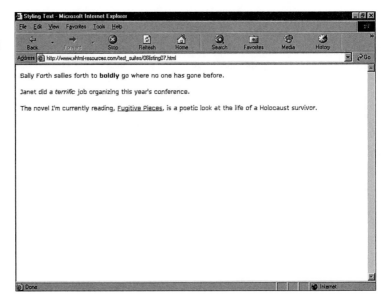

Other text styles, including the following, are worthy of note:

- **tt**—This element (which stands for teletype) usually causes text to be rendered as monospaced text.

- **big**—Browsers render anything marked with the big element in a larger font than the default.

- **small**—Text marked with small is rendered smaller than default.

- **strike**, **s**—These are strikethrough text markup elements. Note that like u, strike and s are deprecated, and if you use them, they must be in Transitional documents.

These text styles are not commonly used, and as you know by now, all presentation should be done by using style sheets.

ALIGNING TEXT

In HTML, you can use the align attribute to align text elements such as paragraphs and headers. Because alignment is presentational, you should use style sheets to align elements on a page. However, if you are using transitional HTML or XHTML, you can use the align attribute for presentation and still be in accordance with the specification.

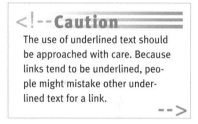

<!--
Even though u is still supported, it has been officially deprecated since HTML 4.0.
-->

<!--Caution
It's very important to maintain well-formed documents in XHTML (and HTML, too). Nesting mistakes are frequently made when an author is using text styles—especially when more than one style is being applied to a portion of text. So be careful to open and close your tags in the appropriate order.
-->

<!--Caution
The use of underlined text should be approached with care. Because links tend to be underlined, people might mistake other underlined text for a link.
-->

To align content, you add the align attribute name to an element that allows for the attribute—such as tables, images, objects, paragraphs, headers, and rules. This is acceptable in Transitional documents, but not strict ones.

When you use the align attribute, you include a value. There are numerous values available, depending on the element in question. For text, there are four values of note:

- **left**—This value causes all lines to be flush left. In desktop publishing, this is sometimes referred to as "rag right" or "ragged right." This is the default rendering for elements.

- **right**—This value causes all lines to be flush right. This causes a ragged left edge and should be used only for short sections of text.

- **center**—This value centers each line. Be wary of centering; the interesting whitespace that results is very attractive to newcomers, but overcentering of text can be very problematic because it is both distracting and difficult to read.

- **justify**—This value justifies text; that is, it spaces characters and/or words within a line to create smooth right and left margins.

To align a paragraph to the center, you would use the following markup:

```
<p align="center"> . . . </p>
```

You change the alignment attribute value as necessary to achieve your needs, bearing in mind that using style sheets for alignment is, again, the preferred contemporary method of aligning elements.

USING LISTS EFFECTIVELY

You can use lists to separate information into a logical series of items. Built on text formatting styles, lists in HTML and XHTML tend to be stable because browsers have supported them from the early days.

This section explains why lists are so valuable, shows how to use them, and explores some of the special concerns to be aware of when using them.

There are several important reasons that lists are valuable, and as you work with HTML and XHTML both semantically and in the context of Web design, you'll see that, time and again, lists play an important role in the way a document appears and the way it functions.

This book often discusses the importance of being clear and concise when presenting information onscreen. Lists help you do just that; when you clarify which items are important, people are drawn directly to the information they need to see, rather than having to wade through a lot of heavy text to find it. Lists not only help to clarify, but they logically order information, allowing you to guide readers from one precise item to the next at a predetermined pace. This allows you to prepare document content in such a way as to get people to the main ideas within that content quickly and in the exact order you specify.

Another powerful aspect of lists is that because they indent information, they create whitespace, and this guides the eye toward important information but also allows for a subtle but important design element to emerge: the flow, rather than the constraint, of space. Visual real estate on a computer screen is so precious that too much constrained information is detrimental to keeping people involved with the material.

Lists, then, strengthen a document logically, organizationally, and visually. This powerful combination can help Web authors create pages with maximum impact.

Bulleted (Unordered) Lists

The bulleted list is probably the list that is most commonly used to achieve logical organization within the text of an XHTML document. A bulleted list places a symbol rather than a numeric value next to each list item. The default symbol of a standard, nonnested bulleted list is a solid disk.

To create a bulleted list, you need two elements:

- **ul**—This is the element that creates the unordered list.

- **li**—This element, the list item element, allows you to create numerous list items. It displays a bullet next to the content of each item.

As with p, li is a non-empty element that has an optional closing tag in HTML. It is acceptable to leave the closing tag off in HTML, but in XHTML the closing tag is required.

Listing 6.8 shows a strict HTML 4.01 document with an unordered list and no closing list item tags. This is a valid HTML 4.01 method of creating a bulleted list. You can also close the list item tag, but again, it's not required in HTML. What's more, in some older browsers, closing the list item might cause the list to be rendered differently (such as the addition of a line break) in newer browsers.

Listing 6.8   A Bulleted List in HTML 4.01

```
<!DOCTYPE HTML PUBLIC "-//W3C//DTD HTML 4.01//EN"
        "http://www.w3.org/TR/html4/strict.dtd">

<html>

<head>

<meta http-equiv="Content-Type" content="text/html; charset=ISO-8859-1">

<title>Bulleted List in HTML 4.01</title>

</head>

<body>

<p>Things on my desk:</p>

<ul>

<li>A pen
<li>A cup of Earl Grey tea
<li>A small, yellow pad

</ul>

</body>
</html>
```

The information in Listing 6.8 appears as single-line items preceded by round bullets, as shown in Figure 6.8.

As mentioned previously, the closing link item tag, </li>, is rarely used in HTML. But because of XHTML's rigorous syntax, the tag must now be closed in order for its document to be a conforming XHTML document. Listing 6.9 shows the correct method to use in XHTML.

Figure 6.8
Creating an unordered list in HTML 4.01.

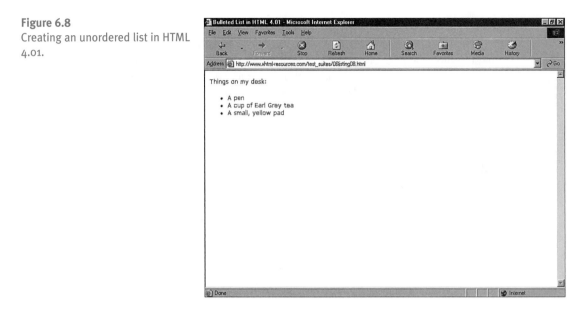

Listing 6.9 An Unordered List in XHTML

```
<!DOCTYPE  html PUBLIC "-//W3C//DTD XHTML 1.1//EN"
     "http://www.w3.org/TR/xhtml11/DTD/xhtml11.dtd">

<html xmlns="http://www.w3.org/1999/xhtml">
<head>

<meta http-equiv="Content-Type" content="text/html; charset=UTF-8" />

<title>Unordered Lists in XHTML</title>

</head>

<body>

<p>Things on my desk:</p>

<ul>

<li>A pen</li>
<li>A cup of Earl Grey tea</li>
<li>A small, yellow pad</li>

</ul>

</body>
</html>
```

If you want more space between individual list items, a workaround is to add a break tag or two, as shown in Listing 6.10. This practice is common, but using style sheets is the preferred method of adding space in most instances.

Listing 6.10   Adding Extra Space Between List Items

```
<!DOCTYPE  html PUBLIC "-//W3C//DTD XHTML 1.1//EN"
    "http://www.w3.org/TR/xhtml11/DTD/xhtml11.dtd">

<html xmlns="http://www.w3.org/1999/xhtml">
<head>

<meta http-equiv="Content-Type" content="text/html; charset=UTF-8" />

<title>Unordered Lists in XHTML</title>

</head>

<body>

<p>Things on my desk:</p>

<ul>

<li>A pen<br /><br /></li>
<li>A cup of Earl Grey tea<br /><br /></li>
<li>A small, yellow pad<br /><br /></li>

</ul>

</body>
    </html>
```

Figure 6.9 shows the extra space added in Listing 6.10.

Some authors use an indentation style to help them navigate markup. Lists are one place where this can be done, as in the following:

```
<ul>

    <li>A pen</li>
    <li>A glass of water</li>
    <li>A small, yellow pad</li>

</ul>
```

> **<!--Caution**
> Different browsers interpret the amount of space between each line item differently. Therefore, if you choose to add a paragraph tag or use another method of adding space, you need to check your work in a variety of environments.
> **-->**

Whether to use indentation is a personal call, or one that will be determined by a company style guide. If indentation will help you with speed and accuracy in your work, then go ahead and use it. However, it is a good idea to be consistent in the style that you choose.

Figure 6.9
Additional space between line items can increase the readability of a list by providing additional whitespace.

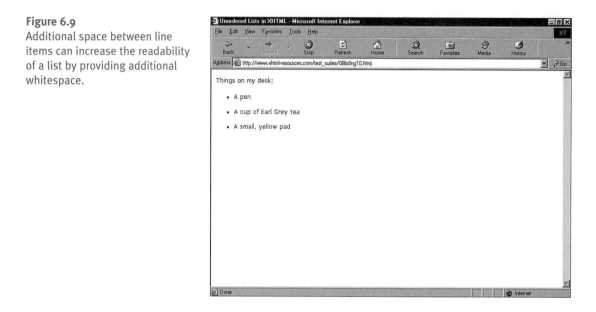

Numbered (Ordered) Lists

Ordered lists work exactly like bulleted lists, with the exception that instead of a round bullet being displayed by the line item tag, sequential numeric values are shown.

The elements used in ordered lists are ol, which behaves as the ul element does, and the now-familiar list item, li. You treat ordered list items in HTML and XHTML the same way you would treat unordered list items. You should use ordered lists wherever numeric ordering makes more sense than using simple bullet points, as in Listing 6.11.

Listing 6.11 Using Ordered Lists

```
<!DOCTYPE  html PUBLIC "-//W3C//DTD XHTML 1.1//EN"
    "http://www.w3.org/TR/xhtml11/DTD/xhtml11.dtd">

<html xmlns="http://www.w3.org/1999/xhtml">
<head>

<meta http-equiv="Content-Type" content="text/html; charset=UTF-8" />

<title>Ordered Lists in XHTML</title>

</head>

<body>

<p>To get to Maple Drive follow these directions:</p>
```

Listing 6.11   Continued

```
<ol>

<li>Go to the first light on Main and take a left.</li>
<li>Drive 3 miles and turn right on High Street.</li>
<li>Follow High Street until you pass the Maple Elementary on your right.
Maple Drive is the first right after the school.</li>

</ol>


</body>
</html>
```

The numeric results of Listing 6.11 are shown in Figure 6.10. Note that standard numerals are displayed.

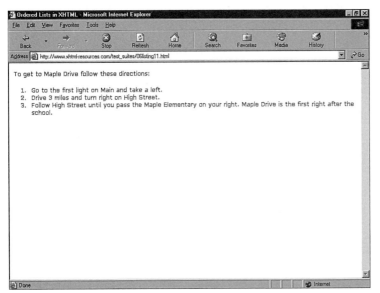

Figure 6.10
An ordered list presents information in a sequential manner.

As with bulleted lists, in numbered lists you can add extra space between each line item by using paragraph or break tags. However, the same caution to testing applies to numbered lists as to bulleted lists.

Definition Lists

Definition lists comein handy when you want to offset information in dictionary-like style. These lists were created to manage information such as glossaries. The

<!--
You can list as many items as you want to on a page, but you cannot stop a list and start another one and have it pick up at the numeric value where you left off. To set values on lists, you can use the value attribute, discussed in the "List Attributes" section, later in this chapter.
-->

syntax for definition lists is a bit odd compared to the straightforward nature of the syntax of ordered and unordered lists.

Definition lists are made up of the following elements:

- **dl (definition list element)**—As with ol and ul, this element sets up the list.
- **dt (definition term)**—This element marks the term to be defined.
- **dd (definition description)**—This element is used to mark the description.

Despite the fact that dd and dt are non-empty elements, in HTML they are like p and li in that the closing tag is optional. Many authors got used to not closing tags in definition lists; for all flavors of HTML, this isfine (see Listing 6.12).

Listing 6.12   A Definition List in HTML

```
<!DOCTYPE HTML PUBLIC "-//W3C//DTD HTML 4.01//EN"
        "http://www.w3.org/TR/html4/strict.dtd">

<html>

<head>

<meta http-equiv="Content-Type" content="text/html; charset=ISO-8859-1">

<title>Bulleted List in HTML 4.01</title>

</head>

<body>

<dl>

<dt>Dreamweaver
<dd>Dreamweaver is a visual Web editor from Macromedia.


</dl>

<dl>

<dt>FrontPage
<dd>FrontPage is a visual Web editor from Microsoft.

</dl>

<dl>
```

Listing 6.12   Continued

```
<dt>GoLive
<dd>GoLive  is a visual Web editor from Adobe.

</dl>

</body>
</html>
```

In XHTML 1.0 and above, since non-empty elements must be properly terminated, both dd and dt must be closed in order for the document to be valid. Listing 6.13 demonstrates this for XHTML.

Listing 6.13   A Definition List in XHTML

```
<!DOCTYPE  html PUBLIC "-//W3C//DTD XHTML 1.1//EN"
    "http://www.w3.org/TR/xhtml11/DTD/xhtml11.dtd">

<html xmlns="http://www.w3.org/1999/xhtml">

<head>

<meta http-equiv="Content-Type" content="text/html; charset=ISO-8859-1" />

<title>Bulleted List in HTML 4.01</title>

</head>

<body>

<dl>

<dt>Dreamweaver</dt>
<dd>
Dreamweaver is a visual Web editor from Macromedia.
</dd>

</dl>

<dl>

<dt>FrontPage</dt>
<dd>
FrontPage is a visual Web editor from Microsoft.
</dd>

</dl>
```

Listing 6.13   Continued

```
<dl>

<dt>GoLive</dt>
<dd>
GoLive  is a visual Web editor from Adobe.
</dd>

</dl>
</body>
</html>
```

Figure 6.11 shows how definition lists are rendered.

Figure 6.11
Examining a rendered definition
list.

DEALING EFFECTIVELY WITH LISTS

Several complications and additional issues must be addressed when working with lists, including nesting lists, using lists for purposes other than their original intent, and working with list attributes.

Nesting Lists

Nesting is the act of putting one set of elements within another. Do you remember those magical Chinese boxes from childhood, where you would open one only to find another, identical but smaller, one inside the first? This concept is akin to nesting.

Lists can be nested, creating an outline style of information. To build an unordered list with one level of nesting, follow these steps:

1. Open a transitional HTML template in your favorite editor:

```
<!DOCTYPE HTML PUBLIC "-//W3C//DTD HTML 4.0 Transitional//EN"
        "http://www.w3.org/TR/REC-html40/loose.dtd">

<html>

<head>
<title>Nested Lists</title>

</head>
<body>



</body>
</html>
```

2. Add the unordered list tags:

```
<!DOCTYPE HTML PUBLIC "-//W3C//DTD HTML 4.0 Transitional//EN"
        "http://www.w3.org/TR/REC-html40/loose.dtd">

<html>

<head>
<title>Nested Lists</title>

</head>
<body>

<ul>

</ul>

</body>
</html>
```

3. Add several list items:

```
<!DOCTYPE HTML PUBLIC "-//W3C//DTD HTML 4.0 Transitional//EN"
        "http://www.w3.org/TR/REC-html40/loose.dtd">

<html>
<head>
<title>Nested Lists</title>

</head>
<body>

<ul>
```

```
<li>Chocolate
<li>Coffee
<li>Sugar

</ul>

</body>
</html>
```

4. Add another unordered list container beneath a list item (I've indented this one for the sake of clarity):

```
<!DOCTYPE HTML PUBLIC "-//W3C//DTD HTML 4.0 Transitional//EN"
        "http://www.w3.org/TR/REC-html40/loose.dtd">

<html>
<head>
<title>Nested Lists</title>

</head>
<body>

<ul>

<li>Chocolate

    <ul>

    </ul>

<li>Coffee
<li>Sugar

</ul>

</body>
</html>
```

5. Place several list items within that element:

```
<!DOCTYPE HTML PUBLIC "-//W3C//DTD HTML 4.0 Transitional//EN"
        "http://www.w3.org/TR/REC-html40/loose.dtd">
<html>
<head>
<title>Nested Lists</title>

</head>
<body>

<ul>
```

```
    <li>Chocolate

        <ul>
        <li>unsweetened
            <li>semi-sweet
            <li>dark

        </ul>

    <li>Coffee<
    <li>Sugar

    </ul>

    </body>
    </html>
```

Listing 6.14 shows the complete markup.

Listing 6.14   Creating a Nested List in HTML

```
<!DOCTYPE HTML PUBLIC "-//W3C//DTD HTML 4.0 Transitional//EN"
        "http://www.w3.org/TR/REC-html40/loose.dtd">

<html>

<head>

<title>Nested Lists</title>

</head>
<body>

<ul>

<li>Chocolate

    <ul>
    <li>unsweetened
        <li>semi-sweet
        <li>dark

    </ul>

</li>

<li>Coffee
<li>Sugar
```

Listing 6.14 Continued

```
</ul>

</body>
</html>
```

Notice in Figure 6.12 that the nested list has a different kind of bullet than the primary-level list. This is the browser's way of helping you and your page visitors distinguish between lists and sublists.

Figure 6.12
Authoring nested lists in HTML.

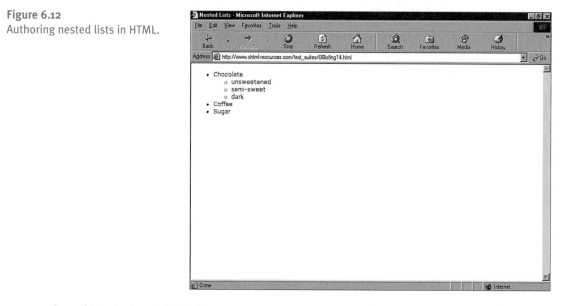

Something that's a little confusing for authors is properly nesting lists when a list item uses the closing li tag. A nested list appears *within* the list item, not in between two list items. So, if you are writing HTML and using the closing li tag, or if you are writing XHTML, a nested list should look like the one shown in Listing 6.15.

Listing 6.15 Properly Nesting Lists

```
<!DOCTYPE  html PUBLIC "-//W3C//DTD XHTML 1.1//EN"
    "http://www.w3.org/TR/xhtml11/DTD/xhtml11.dtd">

<html xmlns="http://www.w3.org/1999/xhtml">

<head>
<meta http-equiv="Content-Type" content="text/html; charset=ISO-8859-1" />
<title>Nested Lists</title>

</head>
<body>
```

Listing 6.15   Continued

```
<ul>

<li>Chocolate

    <ul>
    <li>unsweetened</li>
        <li>semi-sweet</li>
        <li>dark</li>

    </ul>
</li>

<li>Coffee</li>
<li>Sugar</li>

</ul>

</body>
</html>
```

<!--
If you want to nest an ordered list,
simply change the unordered tags
to ordered tags.
-->

You can combine list types when you nest lists. Listing 6.16 shows the same list as in Listing 6.15, but with the primary level an unordered list and the secondary level an ordered list.

Listing 6.16   Mixing Types of Nested Lists

```
<!DOCTYPE HTML PUBLIC "-//W3C//DTD HTML 4.01 Transitional//EN"
        "http://www.w3.org/TR/html4/loose.dtd">

<html>

<head>
<meta http-equiv="Content-Type" content="text/html; charset=ISO-8859-1">
<title>Nested Lists: Mixed Lists</title>
</head>

<body>

<ul>

<li>Chocolate
    <ol>
        <li>Buy the chocolate.</li>
        <li>Unwrap it quickly.</li>
        <li>Eat it immediately!</li>
    </ol>

</li>
```

Listing 6.16   Continued

```
<li>Coffee</li>
<li>Sugar</li>

</ul>

</body>
</html>
```

In this case, the bullets appear in the primary list and the numerals in the secondary list, as shown in Figure 6.13.

Figure 6.13
Combining ordered and unordered nested lists in an HTML document.

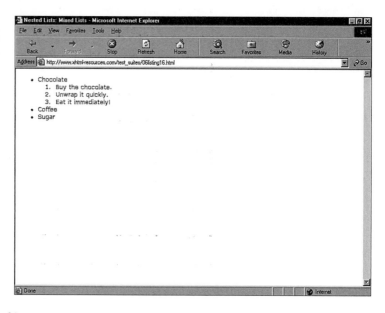

Working with List Attributes

Some people want to be able to control the order or visual appearance of list elements. You can do this by using several list attributes, including value and type.

To pick up where we left off with ordered lists, you can add a numeric value to the list item:

```
<ol>

<li value="30">This is item 30</li>
<li>this is 31</li>
<li>and so forth</li>

</ol>
```

You can change the visual appearance of the bullets by using the type attribute in the list item, as follows:

```
<ul>

<li type="disc">This bullet appears as a disc</li>
<li type="circle">This appears as a circle</li>
<li type="square">and this bullet appears as a square</li>

</ul>
```

Figure 6.14 shows these attributes at work.

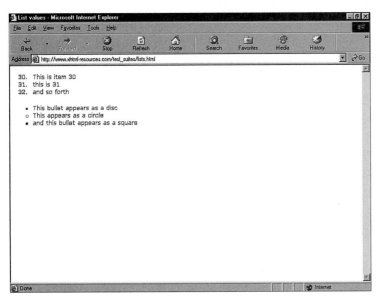

Figure 6.14
Adding value and type to lists can help to differentiate list items, especially when you're nesting one or more lists.

Some people use the type attribute with list items, and it is supported by contemporary browsers. However, instead of using the type attribute, you can use style sheets, which in Strict XHTML 1.0 is the way to go.

ADDING COLOR, SIZE, AND TYPEFACES TO TEXT

This section moves away from the structural issues concerning text and on to the means that HTML and XHTML offer for presenting text with markup elements and not style. As you are by now well aware, it is important to separate presentation from the document structure.

<!--
You can use the type attribute within an ordered list element to specify alphabetical order or even Roman numeration, but this is a deprecated attribute in Strict DTDs. The best method is to use style sheets to define classes for lists. These classes can specify alphabetical or Roman numerical order, as well as other formatting information.
-->

The elements and attributes in this section are, for the most part, presentational in nature but still perfectly acceptable to use in certain versions and flavors of HTML and XHTML.

Managing Color for Backgrounds, Text, and Links

A number of specific attributes can be added to the body element to assist browsers in managing backgrounds, text, and link colors. Values for these attributes are either color names or hexadecimal codes, as described later in this section:

- `text="x"`—This attribute tells the browser what color the default body text is.

- `link="x"`—Without this attribute, browsers usually use blue as a default link color, unless the user has marked or styled another default link color.

- `vlink="x"`—This attribute specifies the visited link. As with the `link` attribute, if you don't set this with a value or style, the browser looks for a default (usually purple), or a user-defined setting.

- `alink="x"`—This attribute specifies the active link. This is a color that appears when the link is made active—when a user clicks the link.

- `bgcolor="x"`—This attribute sets the color that fills the background. Browsers used to default to a basic gray, but now they usually default to white. Users can set this, too, so you should always define it, even if you choose to use a background graphic.

- `background="url"`—You use this attribute when you want to include a background graphic on a page by using markup rather than style sheets.

To add color to an XHTML Transitional document by using the body tag and the attributes listed here, you use an acceptable color name or hexadecimal value with each of the desired attributes for that language or version, as in the following example:

```
<body bgcolor="white" text="black" link="cyan" vlink="dark cyan"
alink="dark goldenrod">
```

For another color scheme in hexadecimal, you could use this markup:

```
<body bgcolor="#999999" text="#FFFFFF" link="#660000" vlink="993300"
alink="#CCCC99">
```

You can also add a background graphic, as in this example:

```
<body bgcolor="#FFFFFF" text="#000000" link="#999999"
vlink="#999999"
alink="#FFFFFF" background="images/gray_paper.gif">
```

⮕ To learn more about allowed colors in HTML and XHTML, **see** Chapter 3, "Dealing with Data Types," **p. 61.**

<!--
Body element attributes, including background graphics, are very popular in HTML. However, in Strict HTML and in XHTML, style sheets are the preferred method for achieving anything that has to do with presentation of material.
-->

Working with the font Element

One of the most problematic elements in HTML is the font element. These are two of the most compelling reasons this is the case:

- For a specific font to display on a user's browser, that font must exist on the user's machine. This can severely limit your choices for fonts, and it also complicates HTML documents, which must contain long strings of alternate font names.

- With every change in color, size, or font, the font element must be opened and closed. This occurs within paragraphs and table cells, and it causes an incredible amount of clutter within a document.

Despite all its ugliness, the font element works. And even though it's deprecated in HTML 4.0, it is perfectly acceptable for use with HTML 4.0+ and XHTML 1.0 Transitional DTDs. So although I strongly encourage you to look at Cascading Style Sheets (CSS) as a viable, necessary alternative means of adding style to text, this section helps you work effectively with the font element.

About basefont

Deprecated along with the font element, basefont is a means of providing a document wide default for font size, color, and face, as in the following example:

```
<basefont face="Arial" size="3" color="#000000">
```

If you use basefont, any relative sizing (see the section "The size Attribute," later in this chapter) is based on the number assigned to the base font.

You can use basefont in Transitional documents, but current practices advise against doing so and prefer using CSS instead.

The font element gives you the only control available when you're relying on markup without style sheets to apply typography to a page. As mentioned previously, this is an area of great instability. With the font element, you can write markup to work with browsers that do not favor HTML 4.0 standards. You can also use style sheets to control typographic design. If you use both style and markup-based presentation, CSS browsers read and apply the styles they interpret first.

➡ *For more information on how to control type by using CSS,* ***see*** *"Designing International Documents," p. 435.*

The font element uses the opening <font> and closing </font> tags, as shown in Listing 6.17.

Listing 6.17   Using the `font` Element

```
<!DOCTYPE HTML PUBLIC "-//W3C//DTD HTML 4.01 Transitional//EN"
        "http://www.w3.org/TR/html4/loose.dtd">

<html>

<head>

<meta http-equiv="Content-Type" content="text/html;
charset=ISO-8859-1">

<title>Working with Fonts: size</title>

</head>

<body>

<p><font>One confidential evening, not three months ago, Lionel Wallace
told me this story of the Door in the Wall.  And at the time I thought
that so far as he was concerned it was a true story.</font></p>

</body>
</html>
```

If you were to load this into a browser, nothing would happen. You need to use attributes to add the color, size, and typeface. The following are the available attributes for the `font` element:

- **`size`**—This attribute helps determine the font's size.

- **`color`**—Using this attribute and a color adds that color to the selection of text.

- **`face`**—This attribute allows you to specify the name of the type you want.

The `size` Attribute

Font sizing is fairly arbitrary; whole-number values from 1–7 determine the size of the font. The default standard size is 3. Obviously, anything higher is bigger and anything lower is smaller, but the rendering varies onscreen from computer to computer because of the differences in computer hardware.

Listing 6.18 is an example of a paragraph that uses different font sizes, and Figure 6.15 shows the different sizes.

Listing 6.18   Exploring Font Sizing in HTML

```html
<!DOCTYPE HTML PUBLIC "-//W3C//DTD HTML 4.01 Transitional//EN"
        "http://www.w3.org/TR/html4/loose.dtd">

<html>

<head>

<meta http-equiv="Content-Type" content="text/html; charset=ISO-8859-1">

<title>Working with Fonts: size</title>

</head>

<body>

<p><font size="5">Working with Font Sizing </font></p>

<p><font size="3">He told it me with such a direct simplicity of
conviction that I could not do otherwise than believe in him.  But in
the morning, in my own flat, I woke to a different atmosphere, and as
I lay in bed and recalled the things he had told me, stripped of the
glamour of his earnest slow voice, denuded of the focussed shaded table
light, the shadowy atmosphere that wrapped about him and the pleasant
bright things, the dessert and glasses and napery of the dinner we had
shared, making them for the time a bright little world quite cut off
from every-day realities, I saw it all as frankly incredible.  "He was
mystifying!" I said, and then: "How well he did it!. . . . .  It isn't
quite the thing I should have expected him, of all people, to do well."
</font></p>

<p><font size="2">Afterwards, as I sat up in bed and sipped my morning tea, I
found myself trying to account for the flavour of reality that
perplexed me in his impossible reminiscences, by supposing they did
in some way suggest, present, convey--I hardly know which word to
use--experiences it was otherwise impossible to tell.</font></p>

<p><font size="1">Well, I don't resort to that explanation now.  I have got over
my intervening doubts.  I believe now, as I believed at the moment
of telling, that Wallace did to the very best of his ability strip
the truth of his secret for me. But whether he himself saw, or only
thought he saw, whether he himself was the possessor of an
inestimable privilege, or the victim of a fantastic dream, I cannot
pretend to guess.  Even the facts of his death, which ended my
doubts forever, throw no light on that.  That much the reader must
judge for himself.</font></p>
</body>
</html>
```

Figure 6.15
The title is set to size 5, the subsequent paragraph to 3, the next to 2, and the bottom to 1.

Anything much bigger than size 5 is ungainly. Smaller sizes, such as 2, allow you to put more body text on a page, but you run the risk of making it difficult for people to read.

You can also size text by using the relative numbering method. To do this, you use a minus or plus sign to adjust the default size down or up, according to the value you use, as in Listing 6.19.

Listing 6.19   Using Relative Sizing for Fonts

```
<!DOCTYPE HTML PUBLIC "-//W3C//DTD HTML 4.01 Transitional//EN"
        "http://www.w3.org/TR/html4/loose.dtd">

<html>

<head>

<meta http-equiv="Content-Type" content="text/html; charset=ISO-8859-1">

<title>Working with Fonts: size</title>

</head>

<body>

<p><font size="-1">I forget now what chance comment or criticism of mine moved so
reticent a man to confide in me.  He was, I think, defending
himself against an imputation of slackness and unreliability I had
made in relation to a great public movement in which he had
```

Listing 6.19   Continued

```
disappointed me.  But he plunged suddenly.  "I have" he said, "a
preoccupation--"</font></p>

</body>
</html>
```

The color **Attribute**

Understanding color theory and how color works on a computer screen and within a browser are very significant when it comes to selecting text and link colors. The reason is two-fold:

- **Aesthetic**—The quality of a page's design is increased when you use color in a sophisticated fashion. It is important to learn how to make an individual palette that unifies your theme and sends a specific, visual message with each page you create.

- **Functional**—If you use colors that don't have enough contrast, site visitors will have trouble reading your pages. You must choose colors that make visual as well as artistic sense.

There are 16 predefined browser color names. By selecting from these colors, you can color text, links, and backgrounds.

The 16 predefined color names aren't enough for most developers, so professionals tend to work from the 216-color Web-safe palette or from any RGB color, using its corresponding hexadecimal code, to achieve visual flavor when adding colors to links.

An example of the font element with the color attribute added is shown in Listing 6.20.

Listing 6.20   Adding Color to Text with the font Element

```
<!DOCTYPE HTML PUBLIC "-//W3C//DTD HTML 4.01 Transitional//EN"
        "http://www.w3.org/TR/html4/loose.dtd">

<html>

<head>

<meta http-equiv="Content-Type" content="text/html; charset=ISO-8859-1">

<title>Working with Fonts: Color</title>

</head>

<body>

<p><font size="2" color="#99999"> "I know," he went on, after a pause
that he devoted to the study of his cigar ash, "I have been negligent.
The fact is it isn't a case of ghosts or apparitions--but--it's an odd
```

```
thing to tell of, Redmond--I am haunted. I am haunted by something--
that rather takes the light out of things, that fills me with longings
. . ."</font></p>

</body>
</html>
```

By using a string containing a hexadecimal (base 16) equivalent of the decimal RGB (red, green, blue) values, Listing 6.20 selects a gray color for text.

⇨ *For more information on hexadecimal codes,* **see** *Chapter 3, "Dealing with Data Type," p. 61.*

<!--
For a good hexadecimal color chart, visit sdc.htrigg.smu.edu/HTMLPages/RGBchart.html or download the nhue.gif file from www.lynda.com/files. These charts put color selection and hexadecimal values right at your fingertips.
-->

The `face` Attribute

If you want to add a typeface to a selection of text, you can do so by using the `face` attribute and then declaring a typeface name.

Listing 6.21 is an example of markup that includes the `face` attribute.

Listing 6.21   Using the `face` Attribute with the `font` Element in HTML

```
<!DOCTYPE HTML PUBLIC "-//W3C//DTD HTML 4.01 Transitional//EN"
        "http://www.w3.org/TR/html4/loose.dtd">

<html>

<head>

<meta http-equiv="Content-Type" content="text/html; charset=ISO-8859-1">

<title>Working with Fonts: Face</title>

</head>

<body>

<p><font face="Arial">He paused, checked by that English shyness that so often
overcomes us when we would speak of moving or grave or beautiful
things.  "You were at Saint Athelstan's all through," he said, and
for a moment that seemed to me quite irrelevant.  "Well"--and he
paused.  Then very haltingly at first, but afterwards more easily,
he began to tell of the thing that was hidden in his life, the
haunting memory of a beauty and a happiness that filled his heart
with insatiable longings that made all the interests and spectacle
of worldly life seem dull and tedious and vain to him.</font>
```

```
</p>


</body>
</html>
```

Figure 6.16 shows the selection and the typeface, which is Arial regular.

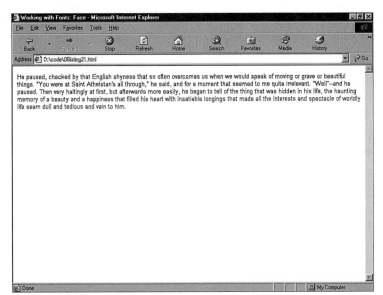

Figure 6.16
The typeface in this paragraph renders in Arial, which is resident on my machine.

Declaring a typeface sounds easy enough—and it is. The caveat, as mentioned earlier, is that if the font isn't resident on a visitor's machine, he or she isn't going to see the typeface that you're using unless you provide more than one font option.

Arial is a font that is native to Windows machines, and it is also found on many Macs. If a computer doesn't have Arial installed, the browser may display a default font, which is normally set to Times. Or, the browser may select a font at random.

The `face` attribute allows you to stack (name several) fonts as the attribute value, delimited by a comma. The browser looks for the first font, and, if it doesn't find that font, moves on to the next named font, and so on.

This stacking method gives you better control than just letting the browser do the thinking for you. You can put as many font names as appropriate and reasonable into the stack. This way, the browser will look for your preferred font and then for a similar font. Helvetica is a sans-serif font that is similar to Arial, so you might want to make it your second choice:

```
<font face="Arial, Helvetica">
```

With this in the string, the browser looks for Helvetica if it cannot find Arial.

You can add another option to the string as well. It's supported only by later Web browser versions, such as most browsers of a 4.0 version and later. This allows you to put the generic family name into the string, as follows:

```
<font face="Arial, Helvetica, sans-serif">
```

If the browser cannot find Arial or Helvetica, it will seek out the first sans-serif font that it can find on the resident machine and use that.

Another important consideration is to make sure you have a good understanding of what fonts are generally resident on standard machines. Below are the standard fonts that are loaded on Macintosh and Windows machines.

Windows	Macintosh
Arial	Chicago
Arial Black	Courier
Arial Narrow	Geneva
Arial Rounded MT Bold	Helvetica
Book Antiqua	Monaco
Bookman Old Style	New York
Century Gothic	Palatino
Century Schoolbook	Times
Courier	
Courier New	
Garamond	
Times New Roman	
Verdana	

If IE is present on a computer (especially Macintosh), the following fonts will be available, if they are not already:

Arial	Georgia	Trebuchet MS
Arial Black	Impact	Verdana
Comic Sans MS	Times New Roman	Webdings
Courier New		

It's a little daunting to think that the *only two fonts* that are cross-platform compatible are Times and Courier. And this is only a PC/Mac comparison! Unix systems are also limited in their crossover font capacity.

Even when you're using style sheets, you need to be aware of these issues when you choose typefaces and stack font names. As mentioned earlier, the Arial font is a particularly good example to work with, because Arial is resident and very readable on Windows. Macintosh computers often have Arial resident, too, especially if any Microsoft products (for example, Office, Internet Explorer) have been installed. But Arial on the Mac is not nearly as readable as Arial on Windows, nor is it as readable as other, similar, Macintosh fonts. For the Mac, Helvetica is a close match to Arial, but Geneva is a more attractive and readable font. Unix machines don't usually have Arial, or Geneva for that matter. So what do you do?

The best solution is to balance order with availability. Because it is very unlikely that Windows or Unix will have Geneva installed, you can put Geneva first in the stack. Macintosh browsers will interpret that, but Windows and Unix will ignore it. Because Windows has Arial, but Unix does not, Arial should come second. Finally, Helvetica is perfectly suitable for Unix, so you can place that at the end of the stack. Here's how you'd do this:

```
<font face="Geneva,Arial,Helvetica">
```

Frustrating? Indeed! But if you combine typographic knowledge with an understanding of the cross-platform limitations of fonts, you can maintain control over the look of your documents.

Listing 6.22 puts together the font element's face, color, and size attributes, to come up with a unique style2.

<!--Caution

You *must* remember that if a typeface isn't available on a given machine, the default typeface appears. The default, at least in the past, has almost always been a serif font such as Times, unless the user has selected another font for his or her default. However, many newer browsers are using sans-serif fonts for the default because they are anecdotally thought to be more readable onscreen.

-->

Listing 6.22   In This Listing, You Can See How Using the font Element with Its Attributes Works

```
<!DOCTYPE HTML PUBLIC "-//W3C//DTD HTML 4.01 Transitional//EN"
        "http://www.w3.org/TR/html4/loose.dtd">

<html>

<head>

<meta http-equiv="Content-Type" content="text/html; charset=ISO-8859-1">

<title>Working with Fonts:  Face</title>

</head>

<body>


<p><font size="4" color="#666666" face="century schoolbook,
times, serif">Now that I have the clue to it, the thing seems written
visibly in his face.  I have a photograph in which that look of
detachment has been caught and intensified.  It reminds me of what
a woman once said of him--a woman who had loved him greatly.
"Suddenly," she said, "the interest goes out of him.
He forgets you.  He doesn't care a rap for you
--under his very nose . . ."</font></p>

</body>
</html>
```

Figure 6.17 shows the results of Listing 6.22: a size 4, dark gray type in the Century Schoolbook typeface.

Figure 6.17
Using font attributes to gain a size 4, dark gray type and the Century Schoolbook typeface.

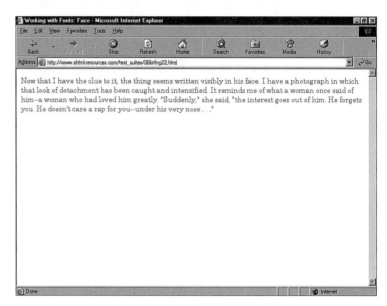

ADDING HORIZONTAL RULES

Rules can be very useful for creating visual breaks between paragraphs. Rules are widely acceptable for use in HTML and XHTML DTDs. However, the attributes used to modify horizontal rules are largely deprecated and can be used only in Transitional documents.

To create a horizontal rule, you need only place the <hr> tag where you want the rule to be. The hr element is an empty element, and therefore in XHTML, it is written with the necessary trailing slash, <hr />.The following attributes (all deprecated in favor of style sheets) are available for rules in transitional documents:

If Web typography interests you, here are some resources to find more information:

DesktopPublishing.Com (www.desktoppublishing.com) is a truly amazing place that contains thousands of resources.

Microsoft's Typography on the Web (www.microsoft.com/typography/web/default.asp) is a good resource for Web typography.

- **align**—You can use the values left, center, and right to align the rule to your taste.

- **noshade**—Most browsers render a standard rule with two colors. If the noshade attribute is in use, only one color renders in supporting browsers. Please note that because this attribute name takes no value in HTML, you have to modify it for use in XHTML 1.0 Transitional files.

  In HTML, you'd use this:

  ```
  <hr noshade>
  ```

In XHTML, you'd use this:

```
<hr noshade="noshade" />
```

- **size**—The size attribute, whose value is specified in pixels, controls the height of the rule.

- **width**—The width attribute, whose value is specified in pixels or as a percentage, modifies the length of the rule. The default value is 100%.

Figure 6.18 shows a variety of attributes applied to rules.

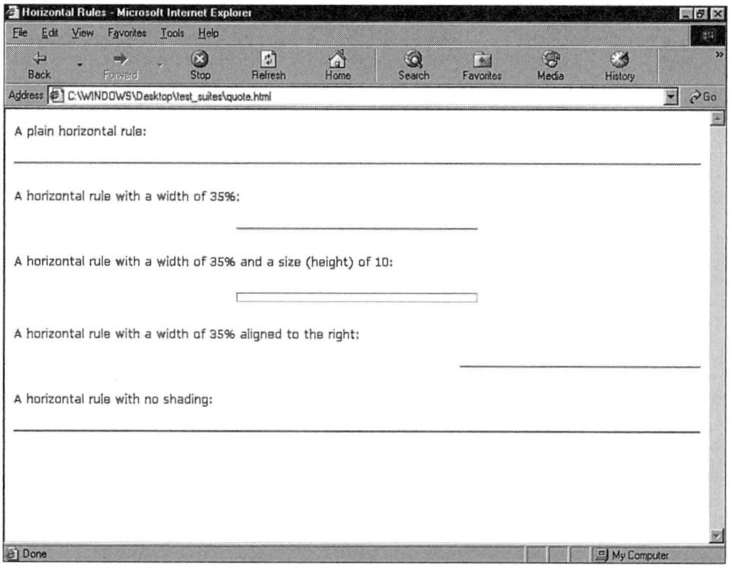

Figure 6.18
Here, the browser displays the results of attributes with rules in Transitional documents.

CASE BY CASE: DEALING WITH TEXT

When approaching text content for a Web page, you should follow a number of helpful guidelines.

Just as you would prepare any professional text document, all Web-based text should be free of grammatical and spelling errors, appropriately written with the audience in mind, and follow a clear, concise pattern of development. A good structure to follow is to begin with an introduction, include several paragraphs that detail the content, and follow this with a conclusion that restates the intent of the communication.

The Web has certain visual constraints. It's important to keep in mind that extremely long pages of text are tiring on the eyes. Furthermore, keeping paragraphs short can be helpful in getting information across to page visitors, who tend not to stay on individual Web pages for very long periods of time.

Following a logical arrangement of text is wise. For example, if you structure text well, you can use headers or text emphasis to bring a site visitor's attention to certain areas. There is a logical order for headers, beginning with the largest size and moving into smaller sizes where necessary. When emphasizing text with bold, italic, or underlined styles, you need to remember that a light touch is wise. Be consistent and logical, and never deviate from the clean and precise output that is so necessary for effective Web communication.

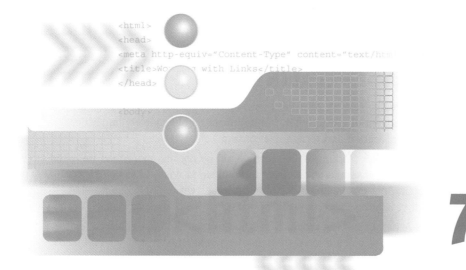

ADDING HYPERTEXT AND INDEPENDENT LINKS

IN THIS CHAPTER

The Web's Very Essence: Linking   156

The Anchor Element   156

Link Relationships with the `link` Element   171

Case by Case: Aiding and Abetting Search Engines   175

THE WEB'S VERY ESSENCE: LINKING

I have a friend, Joe, who lives in Tucson, Arizona. I have another friend, Jo, who lives in southeast Asia. Before the advent of the Internet, the two would probably have had little opportunity to meet—to *link* together and form a relationship.

Linking is the essence of the Web. Without it, the Web would be nothing more than the publication of straightforward text documents on the Internet. Linking is what takes you beyond the framework of connecting not only a single document to other, related, documents—but into the human potential of relating ideas as well as people.

Originally referred to as *hyperlinking,* the technical method to offer linking opportunities to documents has also expanded to include more than just text links. In fact, today's Web uses a variety of media and objects that are active links. The term *hypermedia* encompasses this aspect.

If you attempt to picture this vast network of linked information—from text documents, to entertainment Web sites, to personal home pages to people—you can begin to see what a complex Web is woven by this seemingly simple act of linking.

And, although the syntax for linking is fairly straightforward, there are some details you must become familiar with to harness the Web's potential and facilitate the opportunities that linking enables. Such issues include working with the Anchor element, a, using relative and absolute links, managing specialty links, and working with link relationships via the `link` element.

THE ANCHOR ELEMENT

If the essence of the Web can be defined as linking, the essence of linking can most certainly be exemplified by the element at its core—the anchor element.

It is no accident that the word *anchor* defines this element. The concept is that a link is a relationship between two anchored points—the *source* and *destination*. The source is the originating location, and the destination is the resulting location, which can be a variety of things, such as an HTML or XHTML document, an image, or an application.

Simply put, the a element allows one document to attach, or anchor itself, to another resource. That other resource can be on a local server, or it can be far away, across the world, much like my friends Joe and Jo. If Joe and Jo both had Web sites located in their native areas, components of those sites could be attached, or anchored, to each other by using the anchor element.

Numerous attributes and values are associated with the anchor element. Those of specific note to this chapter include the following:

- **href**—This is the hypertext reference. The value of the reference is the location of the link destination.

- **name**—The name attribute allows you to create a literal name for the anchor. This is used in intrapage links (discussed later this chapter) and for scripting.

- **target**—The target attribute enables you to point the link to another location, such as another instance of the Web browser.

The most necessary attribute in an Anchor is href. This is followed by a value consisting of a *uniform resource indicator (URI)* as shown in Listing 7.1.

Listing 7.1 shows an XHTML 1.0 document with a standard link.

Listing 7.1   Using a Standard Link

```
<!DOCTYPE html PUBLIC "-//W3C//DTD XHTML 1.0 Transitional//EN"
    "http://www.w3.org/TR/xhtml1/DTD/xhtml1-transitional.dtd">

<html>
<head>
<meta http-equiv="Content-Type" content="text/html; charset=utf-8" />
<title>Working with Links</title>
</head>

<body>

<p><a href="http://www.xhtml-resources.com/">Go to XHTML-Resources</a></p>

</body>
</html>
```

Any text or object that is placed between the open tag and the closing tag is considered "hot." This means it is a clickable link that takes you from the page you're on to the page to which the anchor refers. For example, the link in Figure 7.1 takes you to the XHTML-Resources home page.

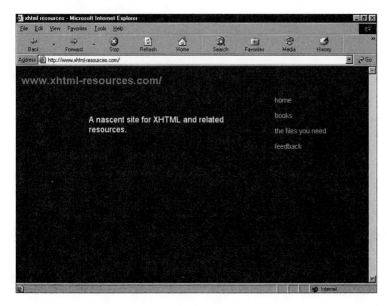

Figure 7.1
When a user users the link source, he or she ends up at the defined destination, in this case www.xhtml-resources.com.

There are two primary linking methods, with which you might already be familiar: *absolute* and *relative*. The following sections describe these linking methods.

Absolute Linking

The example shown in Figure 7.1, which uses a complete URL as its value, is referred to as an *absolute* link. This means that you use *absolutely the entire* destination—not just a part of it. You must include the beginning http: (or ftp: or gopher:, or any acceptable URI), as well as the specific location. This URI takes you to that Web site's default home page.

➡️ *For more information about URLs and URIs,* **see** *Chapter 3, "Dealing with Data Types," p. 61.*

Absolute linking is important when addressing anchors to destinations other than your own. The use of an absolute address allows your browser to query the correct server and actually go to a specific file on that server if you author your anchor to do so. Joe, with his Web page sitting on a server in Arizona, requires an absolute link to Jo's site on a server in southeast Asia.

If you want a link to refer to a particular section within a Web site, you have to include relevant path information. To link to the book area of the XHTML-Resources site, you use the following URL as the value:

```
<a href="http://www.xhtml-resources.com/books/">XHTML
Books</a>
```

This link takes you to the default page set up for the XHTML-resources Books page. To link to a specific page in an area on a Web site, you can define the reference with a specific page's filename, like so:

```
<a href="http://www.xhtml-resources.com/books/authors.html">
Meet XHTML Book Authors</a>
```

This link takes you directly to the author's page within the Books section of the site.

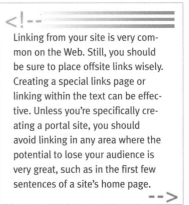

Linking from your site is very common on the Web. Still, you should be sure to place offsite links wisely. Creating a special links page or linking within the text can be effective. Unless you're specifically creating a portal site, you should avoid linking in any area where the potential to lose your audience is very great, such as in the first few sentences of a site's home page.

Relative Linking

Let's say that Joe and Jo are going to set up housekeeping in the same house. However, Joe is in the study, and Jo is in the living room. To link them up, do we need to specify a direct address—an absolute link—as we did when they were half a world away from one another? No! After all, they're already at the same address.

Relative linking allows you to link to files that reside at the same address, on the same server. The files can be in the same directory as one another, or they might be in another directory. In either case, there are methods of linking to these files *relatively* (that is, in relation to on another) rather than absolutely.

Linking to Other File Types

If you want to directly link to an image, sound, or other non-HTML file, you can do so simply by pointing the location anchor directly to the file. If the browser supports the file type, the file then displays in the browser. If the browser does not support the file type, either a configured helper application (such as an MP3 player) spawns, or the user is prompted to download and save the file for use on his or her own.

To link to an image, you use the following:

```
<a href="http://www.molly.com/molly.jpg">Picture of Molly</a>
```

To link to a sound file, you use the following:

```
<a href="happy_days.mp3">Play the Song!</a>
```

To link to a Word document, you use the following:

```
<a href="manual.doc">Download the Manual</a>
```

To link to a PDF document, you use the following:

```
<a href="manual.pdf">Download the manual in PDF format</a>
```

One important issue to be aware of is that a server must have the correct MIME type registered for the file extension in question in order for the browser to recognize the file. In the case of most common files for Web and related resources, this is usually not a problem. However, you should check with your service provider or system administrator if you encounter any problems.

If you are linking from one page to another page within a site, and both files reside in the same directory, you simply use the filename as the hypertext reference value, as in the following example:

```
<a href="jo.html">Jo's Home Page</a>
```

Things get a bit more complex when you want to link to a document in another directory on that server. Let's say I'm authoring a document, and have that document in my main folder, but I had a subfolder called jo where I've placed the file jo.html. I then have to place the path to that file into the hypertext reference, as follows:

```
<a href="jo/jo.html">Jo's Home Page</a>
```

Now the browser knows to look under the jo directory rather than in the same directory as the original document.

You always have to refer to the exact path to the file from your initial page. If I had a subfolder in the jo directory called stories and I wanted to link from the first document in the main folder, I would have to include the entire path to the file I want to have the browser load. In this instance, I want to load the file travels1.html. The markup would look like this:

```
<a href="jo/stories/travels1.html">Read About Jo's Adventures in
Southeast Asia</a>
```

What happens if you are on Jo's home page (jo.html), but you want to link back up to the main page? In relative linking, you can use ../ to go to the folder above the subfolder. So to get from jo.html to index.html in the main folder, you use the following:

```
<a href="../index.html">Go Back Home</a>
```

This takes you to the top directory, where the index.html file exists.

Follow these steps to create a relative link:

1. On your computer, create a folder and name it top.

2. Open root and create a subfolder named articles.

3. Create an XHTML page, as follows:

```
<!DOCTYPE html PUBLIC "-//W3C//DTD XHTML 1.0 Transitional//EN"
"http://www.w3.org/TR/xhtml1/DTD/xhtml1-transitional.dtd">
<html xmlns="http://www.w3.org/1999/xhtml">

<head>

<meta http-equiv="Content-Type" content="text/html; charset=utf-8" />
<title>Relative Link Example</title>

</head>

<body>

<p>This page will appear in the root directory. If I want to link it to
an article in the "articles" directory, I would use relative linking.</p>

</body>
</html>
```

4. Save this file in the top folder as index.html. Now you have an index page within the top directory. You have to have something to link to for relative linking to work.

Now you have an index page within the top directory. You have to have something to link to for relative linking to work.

1. Open your editor and mark up the following page:

```
<!DOCTYPE html PUBLIC "-//W3C//DTD XHTML 1.0 Transitional//EN"
"http://www.w3.org/TR/xhtml1/DTD/xhtml1-transitional.dtd">
<html xmlns="http://www.w3.org/1999/xhtml">

<head>

<meta http-equiv="Content-Type" content="text/html; charset=utf-8" />
<title>Sample Article I</title>
```

```
</head>

<body>

<p>This page will appear in the article directory.</p>

</body>
</html>
```

2. Save this page as `article.html` in the `article` directory (see Figure 7.2).

Figure 7.2
`article.html` is saved to the `article` directory and is ready to be used on your site via a relative link.

Follow these steps to add the link to the original document:

1. Open `index.html` in your editor and add the following highlighted syntax:

```
<!DOCTYPE html PUBLIC "-//W3C//DTD XHTML 1.0 Transitional//EN"
"http://www.w3.org/TR/xhtml1/DTD/xhtml1-transitional.dtd">
<html xmlns="http://www.w3.org/1999/xhtml">

<head>

<meta http-equiv="Content-Type" content="text/html; charset=utf-8" />
<title>Relative Link Example</title>

</head>

<body>

<p>This page will appear in the root directory. If I want to link it to
an article in the "articles" directory, I would use relative linking.</p>

<p>If you <a href="articles/article.html">Click This Link</a>
the articles1.html
page will load. This is a relative link example!</p>

</body>
</html>
```

2. Save the file.

3. Check your link. It should load `articles.html`, as shown in Figure 7.3.

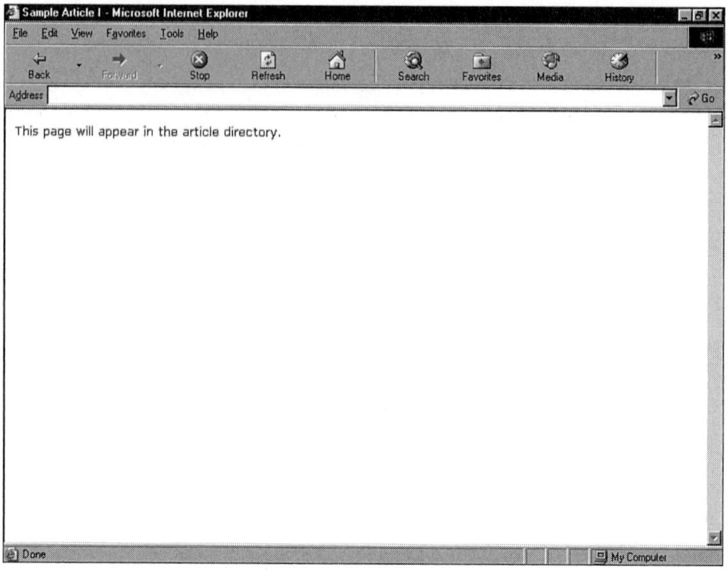

Figure 7.3
Clicking the first relative link loads
the sample article page.

If you want to link back to the index, follow these steps:

1. Open the `articles.html` file in your editor and add the following highlighted relative link:

```
<!DOCTYPE html PUBLIC "-//W3C//DTD XHTML 1.0 Transitional//EN"
"http://www.w3.org/TR/xhtml1/DTD/xhtml1-transitional.dtd">
<html xmlns="http://www.w3.org/1999/xhtml">

<head>

<meta http-equiv="Content-Type" content="text/html; charset=utf-8" />
<title>Sample Article I</title>

</head>

<body>

<p>This page will appear in the article directory.</p>

<p>If you <a href="../index.html">Click Right Here</a>
you'll return to the index
page. This link is also a relative link!</p>

</body>
</html>
```

2. Save the file and test the link. I just did, and the `index.html` file loaded into my browser (see Figure 7.4).

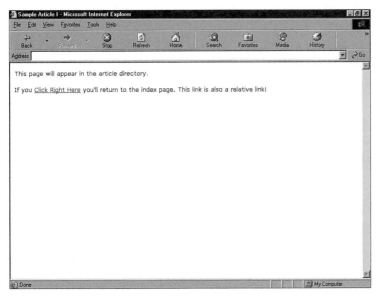

Figure 7.4
Clicking the link causes the referring file to load and returns the user to the home page, which is located in the root directory.

Relative linking is simple and powerful. You use this form of linking every time you are working locally or on the same server, unless you choose to link to the Internet at large.

Listing 7.2 shows the completed sample article page with an external, absolute link added.

Listing 7.2   Demonstrating the Use of Relative and Absolute Links

```
<!DOCTYPE html PUBLIC "-//W3C//DTD XHTML 1.0 Transitional//EN"
"http://www.w3.org/TR/xhtml1/DTD/xhtml1-transitional.dtd">
<html xmlns="http://www.w3.org/1999/xhtml">

<head>
<meta http-equiv="Content-Type" content="text/html; charset=utf-8" />
<title>Sample Article I</title>
</head>

<body>

<p>This page will appear in the article directory.</p>

<p>If you <a href="../index.html">Click Right Here</a> you'll return to the index
page. This link is also a relative link!</p>

<p>If you decide to visit the XHTML-Resources Web site, you can do so by
<a href="http://www.xhtml-resources.com/">following this link</a>.</p>

</body>
</html>
```

When two sites each contain a link to the other, the term used to define this is *reciprocal linking*. The concept of *reciprocity* is an important one because it can promote the flow of traffic between Web sites, which is a helpful aspect in marketing sites.

Linking Images

So far, the examples in this chapter show hypertext links. In other words, text is active. However, as mentioned earlier, a variety of media—particularly images—can be made "hyper" (that is, linkable).

Using images as links is easy to do. You simply need to place the image within the context of the anchor tag, and that image becomes hyper—anchored to the relative or absolute link that you've designated. In this case, I have my computer image linked to a document:

```
<a href="computers.html"><img src="computer_image.gif"></a>
```

Figure 7.5 shows the link image you can click to go to the `computers.html` page.

Figure 7.5
A linked image automatically appears with a border around it, to indicate that the image is acting as a link.

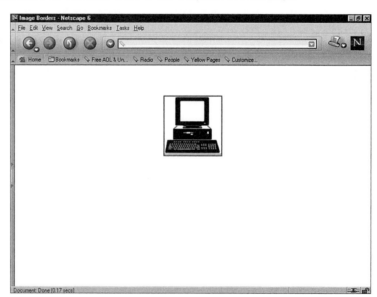

A border surrounding an image is not always aesthetically pleasing. To remove the border, you can add the `border="0"` attribute and value to the `img` attribute in transitional documents. Better still, you can use a style sheet.

▷ *To learn more about style sheets,* **see** *Chapter 14, "Using CSS with HTML and XHTML,"* **p. 345.**

Here's the modified markup, with the border in place:

```
<a href="computers.html"><img src="computer_image.gif" border="0"></a>
```

The link now has no border, as shown in Figure 7.6.

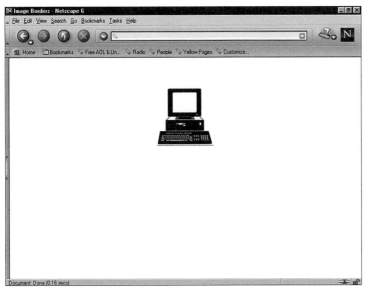

Figure 7.6
A linked image without a border is much more appealing to the eye and won't disturb the visual quality of the overall design of the page the way links with borders tend to do.

Intrapage Linking

A helpful method of navigating within a page is to use a process called *intrapage linking*, in which the destination of the link is within the same document as the originating anchor.

Intrapage linking is convenient for site visitors, and it helps authors organize pages in a succinct, sensible fashion. Here's a look at the link that takes you from the top of a page to the directions:

<!--Caution
Remember that the border attribute can be used in Transitional documents only. You should use style sheets wherever possible instead.
-->

```
<p><a href="#direct">directions</a></p>
```

As you can see, this looks like a regular, relative link. The only difference is that instead of a filename, there's a hash sign followed by a single word (#direct).

Because there is no file to link to, you have to create a place for the link to be anchored to. This is called a *named target*, and it looks like this:

```
<p><a name="direct"><img src="direct.gif" alt="amenities" width="200"
height="42" border="0"></a></p>
```

In this case, the anchor tag names a point on the page for the initial link to the named target. The anchor can be text or, as shown in this example, a graphic. When you click the initial link, directions, you are taken to the target anchor.

To help you understand this method, here is an exercise that illustrates intrapage linking:

1. In your editor, begin with the following:

```
<!DOCTYPE html PUBLIC "-//W3C//DTD XHTML 1.0 Transitional//EN"
"http://www.w3.org/TR/xhtml1/DTD/xhtml1-transitional.dtd">
<html xmlns="http://www.w3.org/1999/xhtml">

<head>

<meta http-equiv="Content-Type" content="text/html; charset=utf-8" />
<title>Intra-Page Link Example</title>

</head>

<body>

</body>
</html>
```

2. Add several link items to the template:

```
<!DOCTYPE html PUBLIC "-//W3C//DTD XHTML 1.0 Transitional//EN"
"http://www.w3.org/TR/xhtml1/DTD/xhtml1-transitional.dtd">
<html xmlns="http://www.w3.org/1999/xhtml">

<head>

<meta http-equiv="Content-Type" content="text/html; charset=utf-8" />
<title>Intra-Page Link Example</title>

</head>

<body>

<p>Gentle Ben's Gem Shop Offers Amethyst, Aquamarine, and Rose Quartz.</p>

</body>
</html>
```

3. Add text that will make a natural target for those items:

```
<!DOCTYPE html PUBLIC "-//W3C//DTD XHTML 1.0 Transitional//EN"
"http://www.w3.org/TR/xhtml1/DTD/xhtml1-transitional.dtd">
<html xmlns="http://www.w3.org/1999/xhtml">

<head>
```

```
<meta http-equiv="Content-Type" content="text/html; charset=utf-8" />
<title>Intra-Page Link Example</title>

</head>

<body>

<p>Gentle Ben's Gem Shop Offers Amethyst, Aquamarine, and
Rose Quartz.</p>

<h1>Amethyst</h1>
<p>Amethyst is a beautiful gem, with clear as well as purple
coloration that ranges in depth and intensity. The depth of the purple
color relates to the age of the gem. The older the gem, the deeper the
color can get.</p>

<h1>Aquamarine</h1>
<p>It's almost as if the depths of the ocean are reflected in this
gem. From clear crystal to the purest aqua, this is a breathtaking
gemstone.</p>

<h1>Rose Quartz</h1>
<p>Rosy pink and smooth, Rose quartz is favored by many gem collectors
for use in making jewelry as well as figurines. It is thought to have
powerful healing properties where the heart is concerned. Some say that
keeping a piece of Rose Quartz near you will help bring a perfect love
into your life.</p>

</body>
</html>
```

4. Name the first target Amethyst:

    ```
    <h1><a name="amethyst">Amethyst</a></h1>
    ```

5. When you're finished, move back up to the top list and link the word *amethyst* to the target you just created:

    ```
    Gentle Ben's Gem Shop Offers <a href="#amethyst">Amethyst</a>,
    Aquamarine, and Rose Quartz.
    ```

6. Save the file and check the link in your browser.

Now that you've stepped through this intrapage link example, you can finish the page. Listing 7.3 shows the final document.

Listing 7.3   Intrapage Linking

```
<!DOCTYPE html PUBLIC "-//W3C//DTD XHTML 1.0 Transitional//EN"
"http://www.w3.org/TR/xhtml1/DTD/xhtml1-transitional.dtd">
<html xmlns="http://www.w3.org/1999/xhtml">

<head>

<meta http-equiv="Content-Type" content="text/html; charset=utf-8" />
<title>Intra-Page Link Example</title>

</head>

<body>

<p>Gentle Ben's Gem Shop Offers <a href="#amethyst">Amethyst</a>,
<a href="#Aquamarine">Aquamarine</a>, and
<a href="#rose">Rose Quartz</a>.</p>

<h1><a name="Amethyst">Amethyst</a></h1>
<p>Amethyst is a beautiful gem, with clear as well as purple
coloration that ranges in depth and intensity. The depth of the purple
color relates to the age of the gem. The older the gem, the deeper the
color can get.</p>

<h1><a name="Aquamarine">Aquamarine</a></h1>
<p>It's almost as if the depths of the ocean are reflected in this
gem. From clear crystal to the purest aqua, this is a breathtaking
gemstone.</p>

<h1><a name="rose">Rose Quartz</a></h1>
<p>Rosy pink and smooth, Rose quartz is favored by many gem collectors
for use in making jewelry as well as figurines. It is thought to have
powerful healing properties where the heart is concerned. Some say that
keeping a piece of Rose Quartz near you will help bring a perfect love
into your life.</p>

</body>
</html>
```

You can compare your page to mine, which is shown in Figure 7.7.

> **<!--Caution**
>
> Although intrapage linking can be a Web author's best helper in organizing material within a page, it's important to keep the length of pages reasonable. Some pages on the Internet that scroll for many screens—and even with intrapage linking, this is not an ideal situation. You should stick to no more than five or six total screens per page, with three screens being best. This way, your users don't have to scroll forever to find information.
>
> -->

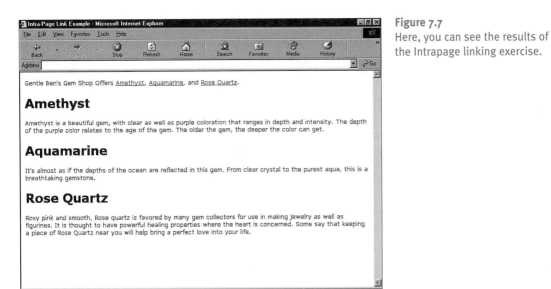

Mail Links

A convenient way of enabling Web site visitors to reach you via your Web page is to provide a link to your mail address. You can do this by using the anchor tag and a reference known as `mailto`. Here is an example:

```
<a href="mailto:molly@molly.com">Send an e-mail to
Molly</a>
```

When you click the link, the browser calls up a mail program that automatically lets you type an e-mail message to the designated account.

Figure 7.8 shows that when I click this link in Netscape 6.2, my e-mail client comes up, with the address portion filled in.

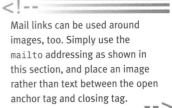 *For more information about creating and managing forms, see Chapter 10, "Building Forms," **p. 247**.*

<!-- ====================================== -->

Mail links can be used around images, too. Simply use the `mailto` addressing as shown in this section, and place an image rather than text between the open anchor tag and closing tag.
-->

<!-- ====================================== -->

Using forms is another popular way to offer mail links to site visitors, and there are other methods to choose from as well.
-->

<!-- ====================================== -->

When using `mailto`, do alert your user that the link is a `mailto:` link by using descriptive text or an icon of some kind. This way, the user is aware that clicking the link or linked image will trigger the browser to attempt to run an external e-mail application.
-->

Figure 7.8
With `mailto`, the browser launches a default mail reader.

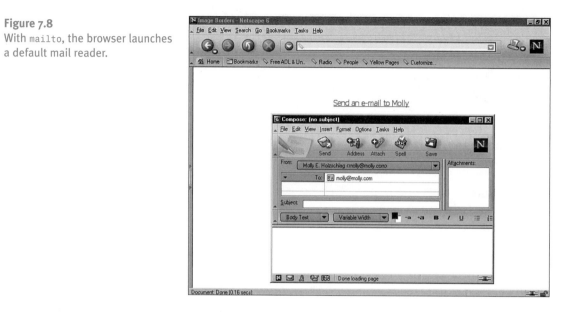

Because mail links are an effective method of getting people to contact you, you might want to put a `mailto` link on every page of your site. You can do this discreetly in the footer information, as shown in Figure 7.9.

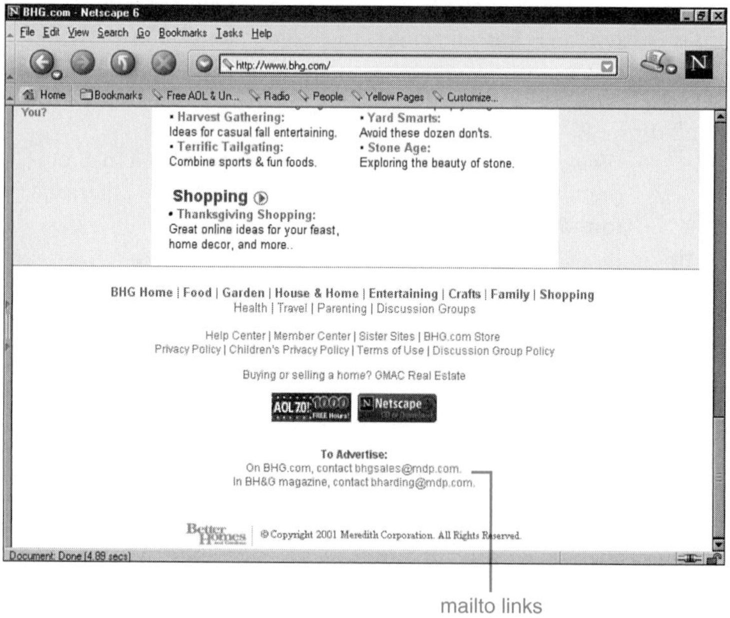

Figure 7.9
`mailto` is often used on every page to make it more convenient for site visitor to contact the site owner.

mailto links

LINK RELATIONSHIPS WITH THE LINK ELEMENT

The link element is used for certain kinds of linking, but it is used quite differently from the anchor element. First, the link element can only appear in the head portion of a document. In this sense, it is meta-information: It is used to dictate certain behaviors that do not appear in the rendered area of a page.

<!--
Pages can have multiple link styles. There's no limitation to how many links or the type of links you can have on a single page. However, it is wise to balance your links throughout a page so that they make sense.
-->

The link element can be used to associate one document with another, such as a document and a style sheet or multiple style sheets. The link element can also be used for forward and reverse navigation, to refer to an alternative document, and to provide information to search engines.

The link element takes numerous attributes. Of importance to this discussion are the following:

- **rel**—This attribute helps describe the type of relationship between the current document and the anchor to which it is relating.

- **rev**—This is a reverse link.

- **type**—The type attribute allows you to designate the content (MIME) type.

- **media**—You can use this attribute to describe the purpose of the link (for example, an alternative document that is especially formatted for either the screen or print.

The link element is an empty element. Therefore, it must be properly terminated with a trailing slash in XHTML.

The title Attribute

You are probably familiar with the alt attribute, which is used with an image to provide an image description. With links (using both a and link elements), there is a similar descriptive attribute, known as title. This is an extremely powerful attribute, but many people are not aware of it.

You can use title to describe a standard link, as follows:

```
<a href="molly.html" title="Link to Molly's web page">Molly's Page</a>
```

You can also use it to describe a link relationship, as in this example:

```
<link rel="Next" href="training.html" title="training your puppy" />
```

Not only does the title attribute add useful information for general purposes, but it is very helpful for individuals who are accessing the Web via screen readers, Braille printers, or alternative devices.

Linking to a Style Sheet

A very common example of link relationships with the link element is linking to a style sheet. To link to a style sheet, you use the link element. Listing 7.4 shows an HTML 4.01 document that uses the link element to link to an external style sheet.

Listing 7.4   Using the link Element in HTML 4.01

```
<!DOCTYPE HTML PUBLIC "-//W3C//DTD HTML 4.01 Transitional//EN"
       "http://www.w3.org/TR/html4/loose.dtd">
<html>

<head>
<meta http-equiv="Content-Type" content="text/html; charset=ISO-8859-1">
<title>Working with the link Element</title>

<link rel="stylesheet" type="text/css" href="site.css">

</head>

<body>

<p> . . . </p>

</body>
</html>
```

In Listing 7.4, notice how the rel attribute is defined with the value stylesheet. This indicates that the kind of document to which the originating document is linked is in fact a style sheet. The type attribute defines the content type as being text-based CSS. The href attribute works with link exactly as it does with a: The value points to the URI (relative or absolute) where the related document is located.

Listing 7.5 shows how the document from Listing 7.4 would be authored in XHTML 1.1.

Listing 7.5   Using the link Element in XHTML

```
<!DOCTYPE  html PUBLIC "-//W3C//DTD XHTML 1.1//EN"
     "http://www.w3.org/TR/xhtml11/DTD/xhtml11.dtd">
<html xmlns="http://www.w3.org/1999/xhtml">

<head>
<meta http-equiv="Content-Type" content="text/html; charset=ISO-8859-1" />
<title>Working with the link Element</title>

<link rel="stylesheet" type="text/css" href="site.css" />

</head>
```

Listing 7.5 Continued

```
<body>

<p> . . . </p>

</body>
</html>
```

Note the proper termination of the empty link element (the meta element is also empty and therefore it is terminated as well).

Using the link Element for Navigation

You can also use the link element for navigation. Using link to describe the relationship of a page to other pages on a site can enable a variety of browsers to interpret both forward and reverse links. This is especially helpful when you're creating documents that will be accessible to those using screen readers, Braille printers, or alternative devices.

To learn more about accessibility, **see** "Creating Accessible Sites," **p. 419**.

To set up navigation using link, you use the rel attribute to describe the relationship of each link and href to point to the associated document (see Listing 7.6).

Listing 7.6 Using link for Navigation

```
<!DOCTYPE  html PUBLIC "-//W3C//DTD XHTML 1.1//EN"
     "http://www.w3.org/TR/xhtml11/DTD/xhtml11.dtd">
<html xmlns="http://www.w3.org/1999/xhtml">

<head>

<meta http-equiv="Content-Type" content="text/html; charset=ISO-8859-1" />
<title>Training Your New Puppy</title>

<link rel="Next" href="training.html" />
<link rel="Previous" href="feeding.html" />
<link rel="Home" href="choosing.html" />
<link rel="Glossary" href="glossary.html" />

</head>

<body>

<p> . . . </p>

</body>
</html>
```

To create forward and reverse links, you add the correct attribute in the link element. Let's say Document A is your starting point, and you want to link it to Document B. To do so, you include the rel attribute as shown in Listing 7.6. To have Document B link back to Document A, you include a link element that uses the rev attribute with an href value of the location of Document A, as shown in Listing 7.7.

Listing 7.7   Using the rev Attribute for Reverse Navigation

```
<!DOCTYPE  html PUBLIC "-//W3C//DTD XHTML 1.1//EN"
      "http://www.w3.org/TR/xhtml11/DTD/xhtml11.dtd">
<html xmlns="http://www.w3.org/1999/xhtml">

<head>

<meta http-equiv="Content-Type" content="text/html; charset=ISO-8859-1" />
<title>Training Your New Puppy</title>

<link rev="Previous" href="feeding.html" />

</head>

<body>

<p> . . . </p>

</body>
</html>
```

You can use as many forward and back links as you like; there is no limit to the number of link elements in a document.

Using link to Point to an Alternate Document

To reference an alternate document such as a text-only, translation, accessible, or printable version of a page, you can do so by using link.

To use link to refer to alternative pages, you first create an alternate version of the page. Then you add the link element to the originating page to redirect capable browsers to the alternate page.

To create a link to an alternate document, follow these steps:

1. Open a completed file in your editor and save the file with a new filename.

2. Edit the file to create a text-only version of the page by eliminating extraneous graphics. Ensure that the links are contextual and identifiable as links, and that the content is laid out in an easy-to-follow format.

3. Save this text-only version of the page.

4. Open the original document.

5. In the original document, add a `link` element that references the text-only page and the media type for which it is intended (see Listing 7.8).

Listing 7.8   Linking to an Alternate Document

```
<!DOCTYPE HTML PUBLIC "-//W3C//DTD HTML 4.01//EN"
        "http://www.w3.org/TR/html4/strict.dtd">
<html>

<head>

<meta http-equiv="Content-Type" content="text/html; charset=UTF-8">
<title>Example of Alternate Page Loading</title>

<link title="Text-only version" rel="accessible" href="text_page.html"
media="aural, Braille, tty">

</head>

<body>

<p>  . . . </p>

</body>
</html>
```

The `media` type attribute values describe what kind of accessibility tools users can use to access the page, as follows:

- **aural**—This refers to speech synthesizers and screen reader software.

- **braille**—This specifies that the document can easily be printed to a Braille printer.

- **tty**—This indicates that the document can be displayed by a teletype terminal.

Browsers that support the alternative media specified by the `link` element automatically load the alternative page referenced by the tag.

CASE BY CASE: AIDING AND ABETTING SEARCH ENGINES

In the constant struggle to ensure good and accurate positioning on search engines, you can look to the `link` element as a means of providing information about pages. This is especially helpful in the following instances:

- If the document in question has been translated into other languages and you'd like to provide links to the translations.

- If alternate media versions are being made available.

- If there is a fully related group of documents in a collection and you'd like to have them noted as being a collection.

To define this information for search engines, you can use the following attributes:

- `hreflang`—This attribute defines the language of the related document.

- `charset`—You're already familiar with character sets from Chapter 2, "Writing Conforming Documents." In this case, you can define the character encoding of the related document.

- `title`—The `title` attribute allows you to describe the purpose of the link.

Listing 7.9 shows an HTML document that has a translation and alternate media and that's part of a collection.

Listing 7.9 Using `link` and Related Attributes to Assist Search Engines

```
<!DOCTYPE HTML PUBLIC "-//W3C//DTD HTML 4.01 Transitional//EN"
        "http://www.w3.org/TR/html4/loose.dtd">
<html>

<head>

<meta http-equiv="Content-Type" content="text/html; charset=ISO-8859-1">
<title>Using the Link Element</title>

<link title="Arabic Version" type="text/html" rel="translation"
hreflang="ar" charset="ISO-8859-6" href="arabic.html">

<link media="print" title="print version" type="application/pdf"
rel="print"  href="arabic.pdf">

<link rel="begin" title="table of contents" type="text/html"
href="index.html">

</head>

<body>

<p> . . . </p>

</body>
</html>
```

By defining any or all related documents via these attributes in the `link` element, search engines are enabled to more explicitly catalog your information. Ideally, not only will the engine catalog the main document, but any related documents as well, making it easier for users to find the best available document for their needs.

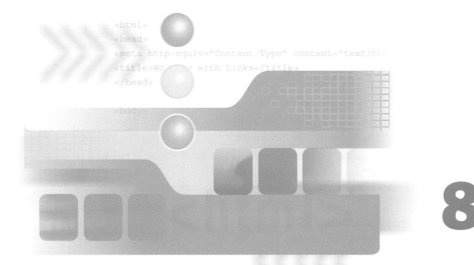

WORKING WITH TABLES

IN THIS CHAPTER

The Importance of Tables   178

Table Elements   178

Table Attributes   187

Table and Table Cell Alignment   202

Using Fixed and Dynamic Design   206

Nesting and Stacking Tables   213

Case by Case: Design First, Then Plan the Table   216

THE IMPORTANCE OF TABLES

Tables were originally introduced to provide a way to table data. As simple as that might seem, it only took a few weeks for savvy authors to realize that the grid system created by tables could be used as a means of controlling the entire layout of pages.

This realization grew beyond a means and into a convention—soon, the vast majority of sites on the Web came to embrace tables as their underlying structure. To this day, the entire infrastructure of most sites uses tables for graphic placement, color arrangement, and text layout control.

But contemporary authoring practices are changing. The use of tables for structural layout of sites, while still dominant, is becoming less of a recommended practice in favor of style sheet layout. As browsers become more sophisticated, it becomes easier to imagine a time where the power of style can replace the limitations of tables as a layout tool.

While I encourage you to learn style for layout, the information in this chapter will provide you with details about tables for both table data and layout so you ultimately will have the option to determine which approach is best for your audience and circumstances.

> *For information on CSS layout, **see** "CSS in Depth: Applying Style and Positioning," **p. 369**, Chapter 15.*

<!--Caution

An important concern for table-based designs involves ensuring that users who are accessing the information with alternative devices can properly display the information. For text-only browsers and screen readers used by many visually disabled, as well as those individuals accessing via PDAs and cell phones, you may have to streamline tables considerably, using fewer graphics and more consideration as to structure. -->

TABLE ELEMENTS

The first step in becoming aware of how best to use tables as a fundamental tool in Web design is to understand the elements used to create them.

- **table**—The main table tag, denoting the beginning and subsequent end of a table.

- **tr**—The table row tag, and its companion closing tag.

- **td**—The table data, or table cell. This tag is used to define individual table cells.

- **th**—Defines a cell with header information. Typically, this will render in bold.

- **caption**—A caption describes the nature of a table. You are only allowed one caption per table. Captions are especially helpful for accessibility and are rarely used in table layout, but rather reserved for table data.

- **thead**—Table head, used for table header information.

- **tfoot**—Table foot, used for footer information.

- **tbody**—Table body, defines the table body.

- **colgroup**—Defines a group of columns. There are two ways to specify the group. One is to use the span attribute to specify the number of columns to be grouped. The other way is to use the `col` element.

- **col**—Used to define columns within a group.

> `<!--Caution`
>
> Many people get confused between the role of table rows and cells. I encourage authors to think of table rows as the horizontal axis, and the top table cells as the vertical, columnar information. Every time you create a row, you're creating a horizontal control. Each new row creates a new horizontal section. Similarly, each time you add a table cell in the top row, you're adding a vertical column to the table. `-->`

The Basic Table

Before you begin, set up a workshop folder on your computer—you will use this to save files that you make for future use. Again, I encourage experienced authors to walk through these steps to learn a highly methodical, clean approach to creating great table layouts.

1. In your favorite editor, set up a transitional XHTML template, with the `html`, `head`, `title`, and `body` tags in place:

```
<!DOCTYPE html PUBLIC "-//W3C//DTD XHTML 1.0 Transitional//EN"
"http://www.w3.org/TR/xhtml1/DTD/xhtml1-transitional.dtd">
<html xmlns="http://www.w3.org/1999/xhtml">
<head>
<title>     </title>
</head>
<body>


</body>
</html>
```

2. In between the `title` tags, type the page's title, `Table Exercise I`:

```
<!DOCTYPE html PUBLIC "-//W3C//DTD XHTML 1.0 Transitional//EN"
"http://www.w3.org/TR/xhtml1/DTD/xhtml1-transitional.dtd">
<html xmlns="http://www.w3.org/1999/xhtml">
<head>
<title> Table Exercise I</title>
</head>
<body>


</body>
</html>
```

3. Now, add the `table` tag below the body tag. This alerts the browser interpreting your markup that a table is beginning. Using the container method, place the closing `table` tag above the body tag:

```
<!DOCTYPE html PUBLIC "-//W3C//DTD XHTML 1.0 Transitional//EN"
"http://www.w3.org/TR/xhtml1/DTD/xhtml1-transitional.dtd">
```

```
<html xmlns="http://www.w3.org/1999/xhtml">
<head>
<title> Table Exercise I</title>
</head>
<body>

<table>


</table>

</body>
</html>
```

4. Directly underneath the table tag, place the tr tag. This defines the beginning of your first table row. Directly above the body tag, place the closing tr tag:

```
<!DOCTYPE html PUBLIC "-//W3C//DTD XHTML 1.0 Transitional//EN"
"http://www.w3.org/TR/xhtml1/DTD/xhtml1-transitional.dtd">
<html xmlns="http://www.w3.org/1999/xhtml">
<head>
<title> Table Exercise I</title>
</head>
<body>

<table>
<tr>


</tr>
</table>

</body>
</html>
```

5. Move down to the line below the opening tr, and type in the tag to determine the starting point of your first table cell, td. Below this, add a line of text, and then close the cell with the td closing tag:

```
<!DOCTYPE html PUBLIC "-//W3C//DTD XHTML 1.0 Transitional//EN"
"http://www.w3.org/TR/xhtml1/DTD/xhtml1-transitional.dtd">
<html xmlns="http://www.w3.org/1999/xhtml">
<head>
<title> Table Exercise I</title>
</head>
<body>

<table>
<tr>
```

```
<td>This is my first table cell.</td>

</tr>
</table>

</body>
</html>
```

6. Repeat step 5, adding a second table cell (remember, cells determine columns):

```
<!DOCTYPE html PUBLIC "-//W3C//DTD XHTML 1.0 Transitional//EN"
"http://www.w3.org/TR/xhtml1/DTD/xhtml1-transitional.dtd">
<html xmlns="http://www.w3.org/1999/xhtml">
<head>
<title> Table Exercise I</title>
</head>
<body>

<table>
<tr>

<td>This is my first table cell.</td>

<td>This is my second table cell.</td>

</tr>
</table>

</body>
</html>
```

7. Save your file as 01listing01.html.

Listing 8.1 shows the markup for a basic table.

Listing 8.1   A Basic Table

```
<!DOCTYPE html PUBLIC "-//W3C//DTD XHTML 1.0 Transitional//EN"
"http://www.w3.org/TR/xhtml1/DTD/xhtml1-transitional.dtd">
<html xmlns="http://www.w3.org/1999/xhtml">
<head>
<title> Table Exercise I</title>
</head>
<body>

<table>
<tr>

<td>This is my first table cell.</td>
```

Listing 8.1 Continued

```
<td>This is my second table cell.</td>

</tr>
</table>

</body>
</html>
```

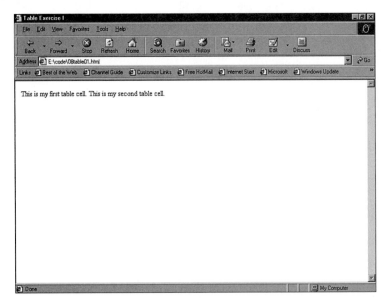

<!--
You'll notice I've kept the closing
/td tag on the same line as the
opening tag and the data. This is
a good practice, because it will
keep your cells tight and help you
avoid gaps in fixed-table designs.
-->

Figure 8.1 shows the results.

Figure 8.1
The final product is a table with
two cells.

As every document has a foundational template, so does
a table layout. This basic exercise can be seen as a simple table grid template.

Captions and Table Headers

As mentioned, a caption enables accessibility and context
by providing a description of the table. Although it's
rarely used in table layouts, it can be helpful when creating tables of data.

Listing 8.2 shows a table with a caption added.

<!--
It's important to remember that
while I'm focusing on how tables
are used for grid layouts, tables
can, and do, serve their original
function: the tabling of data. You
can use the same techniques covered in this chapter to assemble
spreadsheet style information as
well as understand the grid concepts offered.
-->

Listing 8.2   Using the `caption` Element in a Table

```
<!DOCTYPE html PUBLIC "-//W3C//DTD XHTML 1.0 Transitional//EN"
"http://www.w3.org/TR/xhtml1/DTD/xhtml1-transitional.dtd">
<html xmlns="http://www.w3.org/1999/xhtml">
<head>
<title> Table Exercise I</title>
</head>
<body>

<table>
<caption>Adding a Table Caption</caption>
<tr>

<td>This is my first table cell.</td>

<td>This is my second table cell.</td>

</tr>
</table>

</body>
</html>
```

Adding a table header also aids and abets with the provision of descriptions, but in this case, for individual columns within the table (see Listing 8.3).

Listing 8.3   Using Table Headers

```
<!DOCTYPE html PUBLIC "-//W3C//DTD XHTML 1.0 Transitional//EN"
"http://www.w3.org/TR/xhtml1/DTD/xhtml1-transitional.dtd">
<html xmlns="http://www.w3.org/1999/xhtml">
<head>
<title> Table Exercise</title>
</head>
<body>
<caption>Adding a Table Caption</caption>
<table>

<tr>
<th>Table Header I</th>
<th>Table Header II</th>
<th>Table Header III</th>
</tr>
<tr>
<td>table cell I</td>
```

Listing 8.3   Continued

```
<td>table cell II</td>
<td>table cell III</td>
</tr>
</table>

</body>
</html>
```

Column Grouping

Another accessibility feature, column grouping, is useful for streamlining your markup by applying structure- or content-related information to grouped columns within your tables.

As mentioned, you can use the span attribute to define your groups. You may also use the col element. In the case of the span attribute, the number of columns to be grouped is determined by the numeric value of span. So, if I write:

```
<colgroup span="5">
</colgroup>
```

Then the number of columns to be spanned is five.

In Listing 8.4, I've created a table with three rows of four cells each. I've grouped the columns together with the colgroup element, and then applied an alignment to each group using the align attribute in the colgroup tag.

Listing 8.4   Column Grouping

```
<!DOCTYPE HTML PUBLIC "-//W3C//DTD HTML 4.01 Transitional//EN"
        "http://www.w3.org/TR/html4/loose.dtd">

<html>
<head>
<title>Column Grouping</title>
</head>

<body>

<table border="2" width="100%">

    <caption>Column Grouping</caption>

    <colgroup align="right">
    <colgroup align="left">
```

Listing 8.4   Continued

```
<colgroup align="center">
<colgroup align="right">
<tr>
<td>content</td>
<td>content</td>
<td>content</td>
<td>content</td>

</tr>

<tr>
<td>content</td>
<td>content</td>
<td>content</td>
<td>content</td>

</tr>

<tr>
<td>content</td>
<td>content</td>
<td>content</td>
<td>content</td>

</tr>

</table>


</body>
</html>
```

So instead of having to put my alignment in each of the individual table cell tags, I simply applied it using column grouping, and it subsequently applies to all of the grouped columns.

Figure 8.2 shows how the grouping controls look when applied to a table.

<!--
In HTML 4.0 and 4.01, colgroup has an optional closing tag, and col is considered an empty element (closing tag forbidden). So, if you're writing XHTML documents, you'll need to accommodate this by always closing your colgroup element, and terminating the col element:

```
<col width="100%" />
```
-->

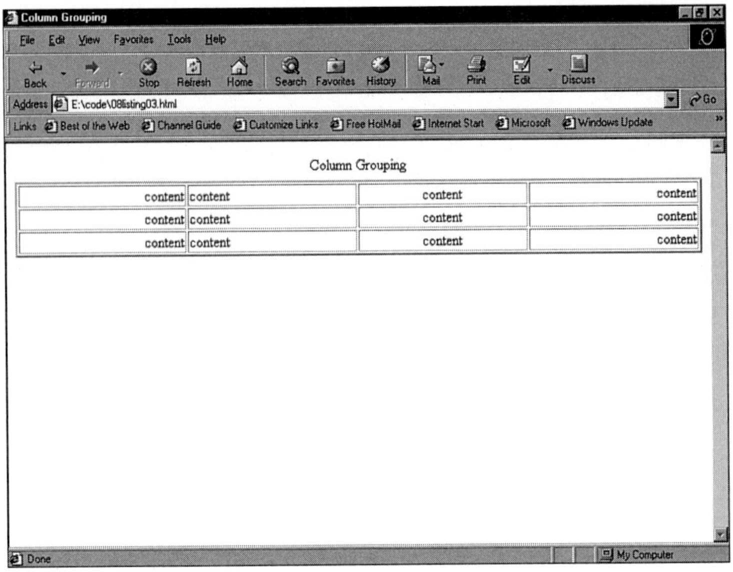

Figure 8.2
Here is an example of a table that uses the colgroup element. Load the markup into your browser to see the actual colors.

Table Head, Table Foot, and Table Body

While colgroup and col work to group columns, these elements within HTML and XHTML can be seen as working to combine rows. Using these elements, rows can be grouped according to their function. There are a few idiosyncrasies when working with these, as follows:

- Each of the thead, tfoot, and tbody elements must contain a row group of at least one row. The tbody element can be left out in HTML for backward compatibility with older table models (see Listing 8.5).

- Interestingly, the tfoot appears *above* the tbody.

- In HTML, tbody end tags may be omitted. In XHTML, you must use the end tag.

- In HTML, when both the thead and tfoot elements are in place, you may use a start tag only. However, in XHTML, you must use both start and end tags.

Listing 8.5 Using thead, tfoot, and tbody

```
<!DOCTYPE HTML PUBLIC "-//W3C//DTD HTML 4.01 Transitional//EN"
        "http://www.w3.org/TR/html4/loose.dtd">
<html>
<head>
<title>Working with Tables</title>
</head>

<body>
```

Listing 8.5   Continued

```
<table>
<thead>
    <tr><td>This is the table head</td></tr>
</thead>
<tfoot>
    <tr><td>This is the table foot</td></tr>
</tfoot>
<tbody>
    <tr><td>This is the table body</td></tr>
</tbody>
</table>

</body>
</html>
```

Figure 8.3 shows the results.

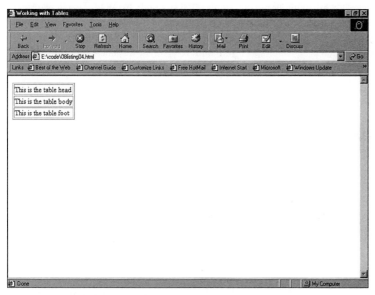

Figure 8.3
Despite the fact that the foot appears in the markup before the head, it visually renders in its appropriate position. Note that I've set the table's borders to "1" to see the structure of the table.

TABLE ATTRIBUTES

The table element has a variety of related attributes and values that turn it from a simple tag into the control tower of table layouts. Because many of these attributes are style related, using them is most appropriate when authoring documents as transitional rather than strict, and of course the preferred layout method for contemporary markup is the style sheet, not attributes such as these.

Table 8.1 shows some of the more common attributes for the table tag.

Table 8.1 Common Table Attributes

Attribute and Value	Results
align="x"	To align entire tables on a page, as opposed to their contents, you can use this attribute. Options allow "x" to equal left, center, or right. Because the default alignment in browsers is to the left, it's commonplace to center tables by using other tags such as the div tag. The only really effective use of this attribute is when you specifically want an entire table placed to the center or far right of the page.
border="x"	The "x" is replaced with a value from 0 on up. This value defines the width of the visual border around the table (see the tip directly after this list to show how to turn borders into a handy design tool).
cellspacing="x"	Cellspacing defines the amount of space between each individual table cell (in other words, between visual columns and rows). The "x" requires a value from 0 on up.
cellpadding="x"	This attribute calls for the space around the edges of each cell within the table—its literal "padding."
summary="x"	The summary attribute allows you to describe the table in detail. This is especially helpful for accessibility concerns.
width="x%" or width="x"	To define the width of a table, you can choose to use a number that relates to the percentage of browser space you want to span, or a specific numeral that will be translated into pixel widths.

Borders

Borders and width are primary control attributes and values for a table. Borders are most powerful for grid design when turned completely off, because this is what gives us the invisible control for our layout. However, there are instances in which you might like to have a table border, such as when you are laying out information in a spreadsheet-style fashion.

Table Width

There are three methods by which to add width to a table using the width attribute:

- **Fixed**—The value is given in pixels, as in width="768". The table will be rendered to the pixel value supplied.

- **Percentage**—Also referred to as *dynamic*, the author determines the percentage of horizontal screen space a given table should take up. So, if you wanted to author a table that took up three-fourths of the available screen space, you'd write width="75%".

<!--Caution

When used as design elements, borders around tables cause a site to appear visually constrained, creating a sense of claustrophobia for site visitors. Although the instinct to place a border around a table is probably born from a desire to keep things neat and orderly, the results are usually problematic. My recommendation is to only use table borders as a power tool while building the site. Later you'll want to set them to a value of "0". The exception to this is when you're creating data that is meant to be tabled and requires the borders to make sense, or has a subtle border appropriate for your overall design.

-->

- **Proportional**—If the author wants the user agent to render equal amounts of screen space to the given columns within the markup, he or she can use a proportional value: width="3*". This method is rarely used in conventional authoring.

Table width is an important issue—one that bears close examination. The reason is because the width of tables will determine how a table interacts with a browser and the resolution settings of your computer screen.

When authoring widths by pixel (referred to as *fixed design* or *fixed-width design)*, this means that anything larger than the page visitor's screen resolution will force a horizontal scrollbar to appear. The lowest standard screen resolution for desktop computers is 640×480, and for a long time, Web authors would fix their table layouts to that width. Over the years, developers began to argue that 800×600 resolution was becoming more common. Currently, it is felt that 800×600 is the most common screen resolution, although some say that 1,024×768 is more common. As a result, should an author desire to write a table layout for general audiences, choosing to accommodate 800×600 is the current convention.

There are some issues when authoring fixed table layouts at 800×600 or lower resolution:

- If you design tables with fixed design for lower screen resolution and the majority of individuals visiting are at higher resolutions, you can still make the site attractive using design-savvy techniques such as centering the table so that it's not flush left and the white space available flows evenly around the layout.

- Often, people using lower resolutions have vision problems. Low resolution means objects appear larger on the page. If your audience has many site visitors that have poor vision (a site for senior citizens would be a good example) you might consider keeping your table layouts to a lower resolution.

- Tables using percentages rather than pixels (referred to as *dynamic table designs)* can be employed where and when appropriate to avoid problems that fixed layouts can cause.

<!--
While working with tables for page layout, you'll find it extremely helpful to turn on borders by adding a value of "1" to the border attribute to see the grid you are creating. Then turn them off to see the results without the borders.
-->

<!--
Wondering why I've used a value of "768" for 800×600 resolution? The answer is simple. Operating system and browser software eats into the total available screen space. To avoid horizontal scrollbars, fixed tables should be less than the total available horizontal width. Always test your work in a range of browsers and OSes in order to get the results you want.
-->

<!--
If you're designing for small-screen access such as PDAs and cell phones, the concerns regarding fixed table widths are especially important because of the very low resolution of these devices. The resolution of such devices varies greatly, check with the device manufacturers for specific resolution information and adjust your table widths accordingly.
-->

Creating a Fixed-Width Table

When do you choose to use pixels, and when are percentages a better choice? Pixels give you more control over your page, but you have to be careful and watch your math. This means that every width within a table must add up precisely. You'll see how this realistically unfolds as you work through the stepped exercises in this chapter.

Percentages are powerful when you want to create a dynamic table—a table that opens up to the entirety of the available screen space. This sounds like a better option, but because you do lose control and design integrity, the technique should only be used in specific instances. We'll now get a feel for adding the primary attributes of border and width to the table tag.

1. Begin by opening the file 08listing01.html in your HTML editor. Change the title to Table Exercise II. You should see the following:

```
<!DOCTYPE html PUBLIC "-//W3C//DTD XHTML 1.0 Transitional//EN"
"http://www.w3.org/TR/xhtml1/DTD/xhtml1-transitional.dtd">
<html xmlns="http://www.w3.org/1999/xhtml">
<head>
<title>Table Exercise II</title>
</head>
<body>

<table>
<tr>

<td>This is my first table cell.</td>

<td>This is my second table cell.</td>

</tr>
</table>

</body>
</html>
```

2. The first attribute you're going to add is the border, which you need to set to a numeric value of "1":

```
<!DOCTYPE html PUBLIC "-//W3C//DTD XHTML 1.0 Transitional//EN"
"http://www.w3.org/TR/xhtml1/DTD/xhtml1-transitional.dtd">
<html xmlns="http://www.w3.org/1999/xhtml">
<head>
<title> Table Exercise II</title>
```

```
</head>
<body>

<table border="1">
<tr>

<td>This is my first table cell.</td>

<td>This is my second table cell.</td>

</tr>
</table>

</body>
</html>
```

3. Now add the width in pixels:

```
<!DOCTYPE html PUBLIC "-//W3C//DTD XHTML 1.0 Transitional//EN"
"http://www.w3.org/TR/xhtml1/DTD/xhtml1-transitional.dtd">
<html xmlns="http://www.w3.org/1999/xhtml">
<head>
<title> Table Exercise II</title>
</head>
<body>

<table border="1" width="765">
<tr>

<td>This is my first table cell.</td>

<td>This is my second table cell.</td>

</tr>
</table>

</body>
</html>
```

4. Save your file as `08table02.html` and view it using your browser. It should match Figure 8.4.

Note that in this instance the border is visible, showing you the grid that you've created.

Figure 8.4
The result of this exercise is a table with two visible cells spanning 768 pixels.

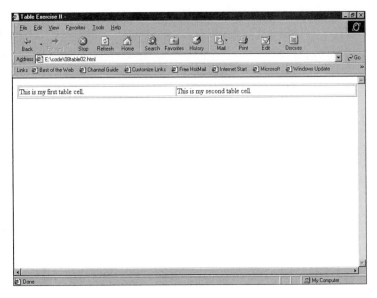

Padding

Cellpadding and spacing are sometimes helpful because they can aid in the addition of white-space when authoring tables without borders. In a desire to gain and maintain control of your layouts, however, cellpadding and spacing become problematic.

The following examples show markup using these techniques so that you can visualize how they work. Let's begin with cellpadding, demonstrated in Listing 8.6.

Listing 8.6   Adding Cellpadding

```
<!DOCTYPE html PUBLIC "-//W3C//DTD XHTML 1.0 Transitional//EN"
"http://www.w3.org/TR/xhtml1/DTD/xhtml1-transitional.dtd">
<html xmlns="http://www.w3.org/1999/xhtml">
<head>
<title>Cellpadding</title>
</head>
<body>

<table border="1" cellpadding="20">
<tr>

<td>This is my first table cell.</td>

<td>This is my second table cell.</td>

</tr>
</table>

</body>
</html>
```

Figure 8.5 shows the results of this table. Note how far apart the border is from the text. This is the result of the padding.

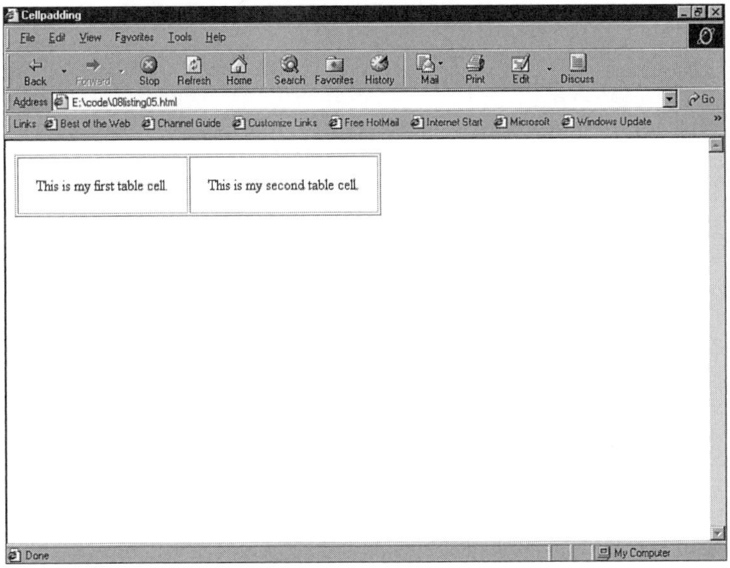

Figure 8.5
Cellpadding within a table adds whitespace between the cell border and its contents so that even when borders are not used, the information on your page won't appear too close to each other, avoiding a cramped feeling on the page.

Listing 8.7 shows you cellspacing only.

Listing 8.7   Using Cellspacing

```
<!DOCTYPE html PUBLIC "-//W3C//DTD XHTML 1.0 Transitional//EN"
"http://www.w3.org/TR/xhtml1/DTD/xhtml1-transitional.dtd">
<html xmlns="http://www.w3.org/1999/xhtml">
<head>
<title>Cellspacing</title>
</head>
<body>

<table border="1" cellspacing="20">
<tr>

<td>This is my first table cell.</td>

<td>This is my second table cell.</td>

</tr>
</table>

</body>
</html>
```

In Figure 8.6, you'll notice that the text is now encased in the cell's border, but there's plenty of space between the cell itself and the edge of the table.

Figure 8.6
In contrast to cellpadding, cellspacing within a table adds space between the cell border and the table border.

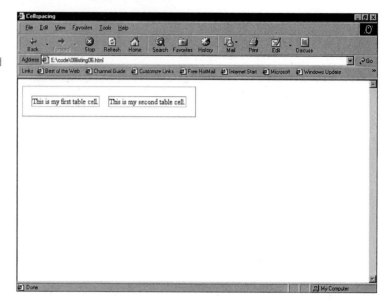

Listing 8.8 shows an example with both cellpadding and cellspacing in action at the same time.

Listing 8.8   Cellpadding and Spacing Together

```
<!DOCTYPE html PUBLIC "-//W3C//DTD XHTML 1.0 Transitional//EN"
"http://www.w3.org/TR/xhtml1/DTD/xhtml1-transitional.dtd">
<html xmlns="http://www.w3.org/1999/xhtml">
<head>
<title>Cellpadding</title>
</head>
<body>

<table border="1" cellpadding="20" cellspacing="20" width="768">
<tr>

<td>This is my first table cell.</td>

<td>This is my second table cell.</td>

</tr>
</table>

</body>
</html>
```

Now there is padding and spacing, giving the text some breathing room within the cell, and some space between the cell's border and the remainder of the table (see Figure 8.7).

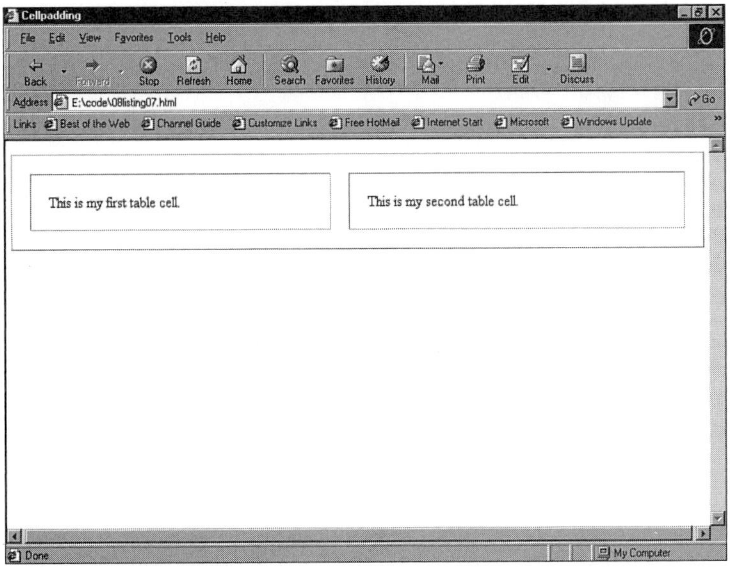

Figure 8.7
Cellpadding and cellspacing work together to help give your page a nice, organized look with plenty of whitespace to aid with readability.

Column Span

Spanning columns enables you to create interesting grids and to manage areas of space within a table more completely. The attribute is as follows: colspan="x", where colspan refers to the number of columns the cell you are working with will span.

Column span works by allowing the table to span a set amount of columns (remember, columns are created with cells). If you don't use the colspan attribute, the table will try to compensate for any undesignated space.

Consider Listing 8.9, which you'll recognize as a standard table sample with two rows. The top row contains four cells set to a width of 100 pixels each, and the bottom row has two—one with a value of 100 pixels, another with a width of 300 pixels.

Listing 8.9   Standard Table with Rows and Columns

```
<!DOCTYPE html PUBLIC "-//W3C//DTD XHTML 1.0 Transitional//EN"
"http://www.w3.org/TR/xhtml1/DTD/xhtml1-transitional.dtd">
<html xmlns="http://www.w3.org/1999/xhtml">
<head>
<title>Column Span</title>
</head>
<body>
```

Listing 8.9 Continued

```
<table border="1" cellspacing="0" cellpadding="0" width="400">
<tr>

<td width="100" valign="top" align="left">
This is my first table cell in the top row.</td>

<td width="100" valign="top" align="left">
This is my second table cell in the top row.</td>

<td width="100" valign="top" align="left">
This is my third table cell in the top row.</td>

<td width="100" valign="top" align="left">
This is my fourth table cell in the top row.</td>

</tr>

<tr>

<td width="100" valign="top" align="left">
This is my first table cell in the bottom row.</td>

<td width="300" valign="top" align="left">
This is my second table cell in the bottom row.</td>

</tr>

</table>
</body>
</html>
```

Logically speaking, the browser should know to set the first table cell in the bottom row to 100 pixels and then stretch, or *span*, the remaining cell to reach across the full 300 pixels available. But this doesn't happen. Instead, the browser applies a blank space (see Figure 8.8) to a section of that row.

The colspan attribute allows you to tell the browser how to manage that space and avoid this problem.

To do this, you have to subtract the number of available cells from the *total sum* of possible columns. Because you have a total of four cells, or columns, in the top row, you have to use that as the amount from which to subtract. You have one cell in the bottom row already, so the second cell, which will span the remainder of the row, must take a colspan of "3". Subtract the first cell from the total available columns to get this value (see Listing 8.10).

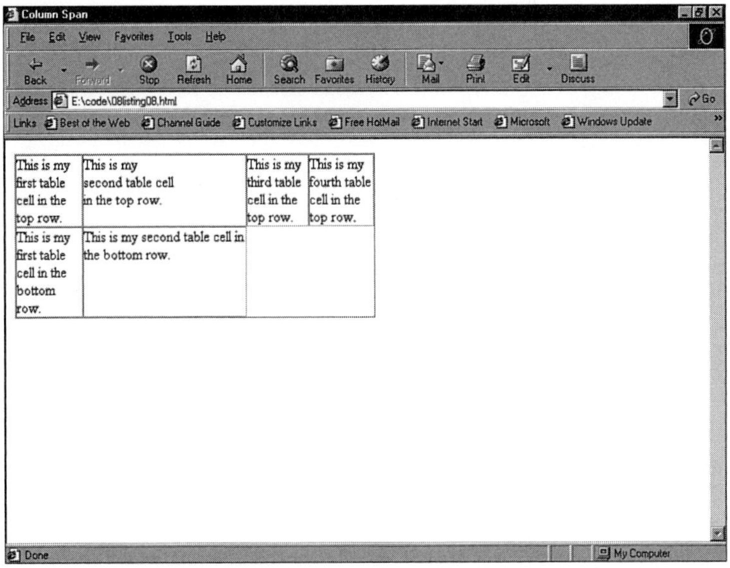

Figure 8.8
Without `colspan`, the browser gets confused!

Listing 8.10   Spanning Columns

```
<!DOCTYPE html PUBLIC "-//W3C//DTD XHTML 1.0 Transitional//EN"
"http://www.w3.org/TR/xhtml1/DTD/xhtml1-transitional.dtd">
<html xmlns="http://www.w3.org/1999/xhtml">
<head>
<title>Column Span</title>
</head>
<body>

<table border="1" cellspacing="0" cellpadding="0" width="400">
<tr>

<td width="100" valign="top" align="left">
This is my first table cell in the top row.</td>

<td width="100" valign="top" align="left">
This is my second table cell in the top row.</td>

<td width="100" valign="top" align="left">
This is my third table cell in the top row.</td>

<td width="100" valign="top" align="left">
This is my fourth table cell in the top row.</td>

</tr>
```

Listing 8.10   Continued

```
<tr>

<td width="100" valign="top" align="left">
This is my first table cell in the bottom row.</td>

<td width="300" colspan="3" valign="top" align="left">
This is my second table cell in the bottom row.</td>

</tr>

</table>
</body>
</html>
```

When I add the colspan attribute and value to the second cell, the browser will now render the table accordingly (see Figure 8.9).

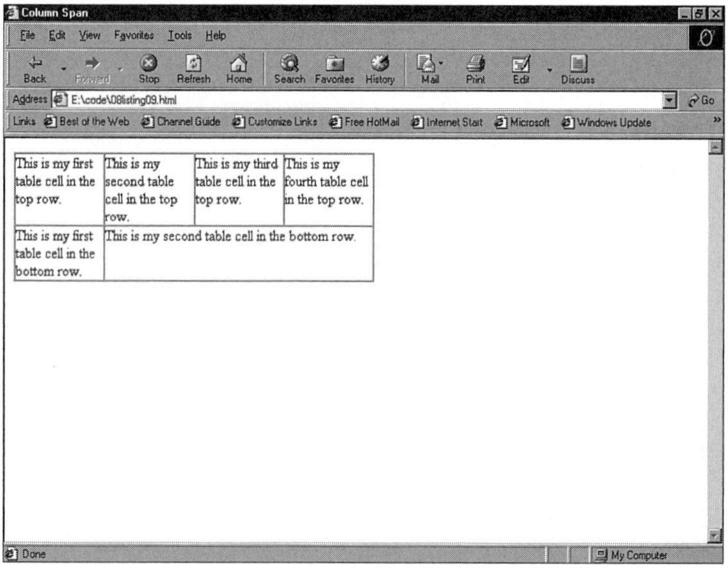

Figure 8.9
The colspan attribute solves the problem.

Row Span

Rowspan works in exactly the same way as colspan, but is applied to the rows. As with colspan, rowspan="x" refers to the span of the cell, in this case how many rows the cell stretches.

The markup in Listing 8.11 shows two rows, each with three cells.

Listing 8.11   A Table with Rows and Cells

```
<!DOCTYPE html PUBLIC "-//W3C//DTD XHTML 1.0 Transitional//EN"
"http://www.w3.org/TR/xhtml1/DTD/xhtml1-transitional.dtd">
<html xmlns="http://www.w3.org/1999/xhtml">
<head>
<title>Row Span</title>
</head>
<body>

<table border="1" cellspacing="0" cellpadding="0" width="300">
<tr>

<td width="100" valign="top" align="left">
This is my first table cell in the top row.</td>

<td width="100" valign="top" align="left">
This is my second table cell in the top row.</td>

<td width="100" valign="top" align="left">
This is my third table cell in the top row.</td>

</tr>

<tr>

<td width="100" valign="top" align="left">
This is my first table cell in the bottom row.</td>

<td width="100" valign="top" align="left">
This is my second table cell in the bottom row.</td>

<td width="100" valign="top" align="left">
This is my third table cell in the bottom row.</td>

</tr>

</table>
</body>
</html>
```

Figure 8.10 shows the simple table that this markup creates.

Now, let's say you want to have the first cell in the top row, width of 100 pixels, span both rows, creating a vertical column. To do this, you have to first remove a column from the bottom row, because you're going to essentially stretch the first cell across that space. Then, you need to add the rowspan attribute and value to the first cell in the top row.

The way you get rowspan value is by simply counting the number of rows you want to span—in this case, "2".

Listing 8.12 is resulting markup.

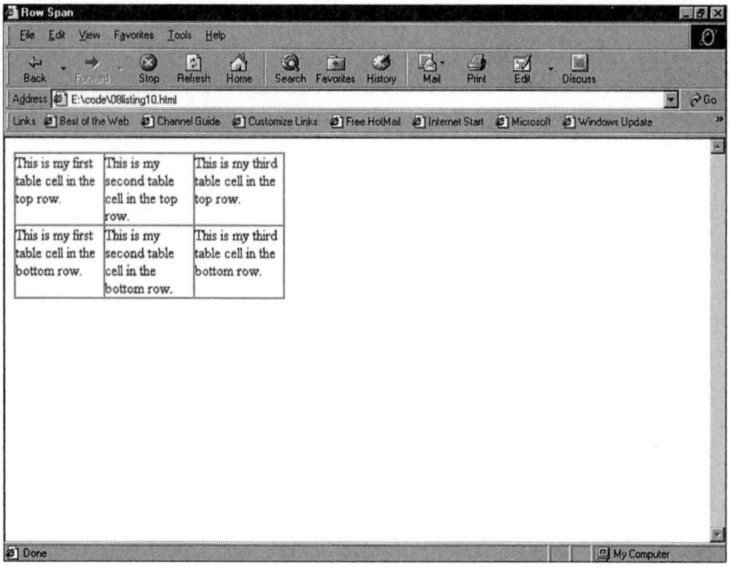

Figure 8.10
The result of Listing 8.10 is a table with two rows and three cells in each row.

Listing 8.12   Spanning Rows

```
<!DOCTYPE html PUBLIC "-//W3C//DTD XHTML 1.0 Transitional//EN"
"http://www.w3.org/TR/xhtml1/DTD/xhtml1-transitional.dtd">
<html xmlns="http://www.w3.org/1999/xhtml">
<head>
<title>Row Span</title>
</head>
<body>

<table border="1" cellspacing="0" cellpadding="0" width="300">
<tr>

<td width="100" rowspan="2" valign="top" align="left">
This is my first table cell, and it spans two rows.
</td>

<td width="100" valign="top" align="left">
This is my second table cell in the top row.
</td>

<td width="100" valign="top" align="left">
This is my third table cell in the top row.
</td>

</tr>
```

Listing 8.12 Continued

```
<tr>

<td width="100" valign="top" align="left">
This is my second table cell in the bottom row.
</td>

<td width="100" valign="top" align="left">
This is my third table cell in the bottom row.
</td>

</tr>

</table>
</body>
</html>
```

Figure 8.11 shows the table with the first cell now spanning two rows.

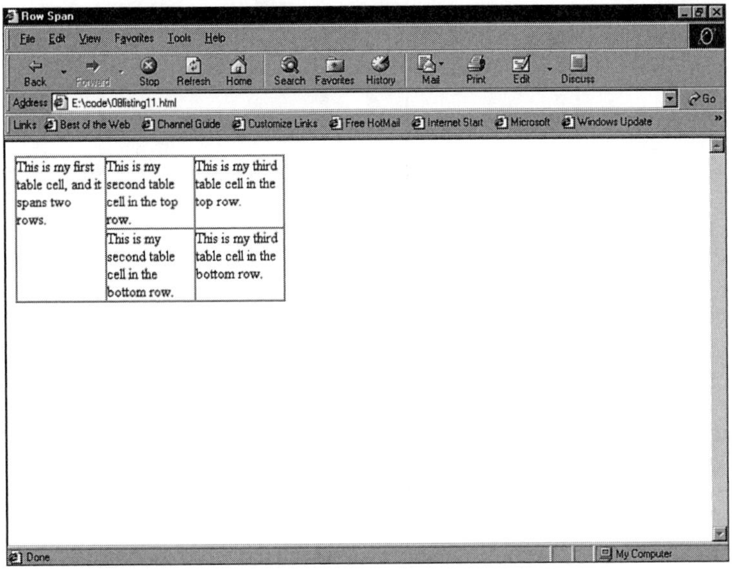

Figure 8.11
Similar to how the colspan attribute enables you to span columns within the table, the rowspan attribute allows you to span rows.

Using these attributes can get fairly complex, particularly when you have a table with many rows, and many cells within those rows. The rule of thumb when working with these attributes is to rely on the mathematical formulas described in this chapter.

Fix your table width, make sure that your table cells total the appropriate width, and when using colspan and rowspan attributes, measure how many cells or rows need to be spanned appropriately.

TABLE AND TABLE CELL ALIGNMENT

As I mentioned, rows make up a table's horizontal axis, and cells its vertical axis. There are ways to control alignment in both. The following section will describe how. As you are well aware, the information in this section is decidedly presentational. While you can't use these attributes in strict HTML or XHTML documents, you can use these techniques in transitional documents. Either way, contemporary markup practices dictate that you still use style sheets.

Horizontal Alignment

The only two attributes ever used within rows are align, which controls the row's spatial alignment, and valign, which determines the vertical placement of all the data within a row. While these attributes are considered legal, they don't offer the kind of control available in attributes related to the table and td elements, so they are rarely used.

<!-- ===
To understand table rows best, think of them as the horizontal structure of the grid, whereas table cells will be the columnar, or vertical, structure of that grid.
--> -->

To show you some of the control issues related to row attributes, take a look at Listing 8.13. The border value is set to "1" and cellpadding and cellspacing are added, so you can see the rows clearly.

Listing 8.13   Row Attributes Are Often Inconsistent

```
<!DOCTYPE html PUBLIC "-//W3C//DTD XHTML 1.0 Transitional//EN"
"http://www.w3.org/TR/xhtml1/DTD/xhtml1-transitional.dtd">
<html xmlns="http://www.w3.org/1999/xhtml">
<head>
<title>Table Row Attributes and Values</title>
</head>
<body>

<table border="1" cellspacing="10" cellpadding="10" width="100%">
<tr valign="top">

<td>This is my first table row.</td>

</tr>

<tr valign="bottom">
<td>This is my second table row.</td>

</tr>

<tr align="center">
<td>This is my third table row, middle alignment.</td>
</tr>
```

Listing 8.13   Continued

```
<tr align="center">
<td align="right">This is my fourth table row.</td>

</tr>
</table>
</body>
</html>
```

When viewed in my browser (see Figure 8.12), you'll notice how the valign attribute used in the first two rows doesn't even apply. Furthermore, although the align attribute in the third row does in fact center the text within that row, the fourths row's table cell alignment value *overrides* that specified by the row.

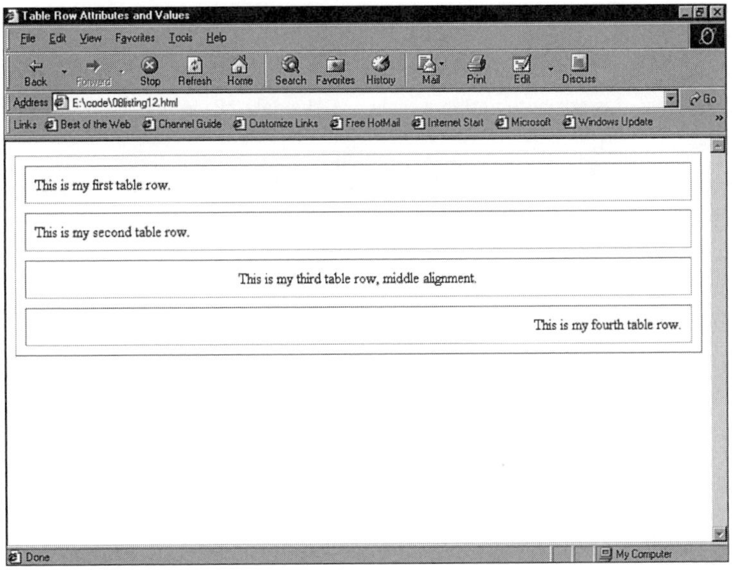

Figure 8.12
Row attributes are inconsistent and do not offer adequate control over the alignment of cells.

Listing 8.3 demonstrated an instance where practical wisdom can override the standard to become a convention. It's important to know that you can use attributes within rows, and many authors do. It's perfectly acceptable in transitional documents, but not always the easiest way to accomplish your table goals.

<!--
Row attributes do not necessarily lend themselves to strong control over tables. The greatest control comes from the relationship between table tags and attributes and table cell tags.
-->

Vertical Alignment

The essence of table design really relies on the table cell, or td element. This element has a variety of important attributes that can be applied for maximum table control. The attributes and values are added to specific sections, depending on what type of control they offer.

Primary attributes and values should generally be placed in all table cells. Column and row spanning attributes and values are more useful in specific grid designs, and specialty attributes such as `height`, and `bgcolor`, are generally used in more advanced or specialized table design.

Primary Attributes

Table 8.2 shows the primary attributes for the table cell tag.

Table 8.2 Table Cell Attributes

Attribute and Value	Results
`width="x%"` or `width="x"`	Setting a percentage width with x% will make the cell dynamic within the context of the table. Fixing the cell width to a pixel value fixes that cell within the table. For example, you can have dynamic cells in a fixed design and vice versa.
`align="x"`	When you use this attribute within a table cell, the data inside the cell will align with the literal value you assign to the attribute. In other words, a `<left>` value will left-justify the text or graphic you place within the cell, the `<center>` value will center the information, and a value of `<right>` will justify the information to the right of the cell.
`valign="x"`	The vertical alignment of a table cell will place the information therein to the top, middle, or bottom of the cell.

Listing 8.14 shows a table with three cells, each cell being completely defined with primary attributes.

Listing 8.14 Defining the Attributes in Every Cell

```
<!DOCTYPE html PUBLIC "-//W3C//DTD XHTML 1.0 Transitional//EN"
"http://www.w3.org/TR/xhtml1/DTD/xhtml1-transitional.dtd">
<html xmlns="http://www.w3.org/1999/xhtml">
<head>
<title>Table Cell Attributes and Values</title>
</head>
<body>

<table border="1" cellspacing="0" cellpadding="0" width="585">
<tr>

<td width="250" valign="top" align="left">
This is my first table cell. Its width is 250 pixels, the information within it
is vertically aligned to the top of the cell, and is justified to the left of
the cell.</td>
```

Listing 8.14 Continued

```
<td width="250" valign="middle" align="right">
This is my second table cell. It, too, has a width of 250 pixels. The
information within this cell is aligned to the middle of the cell, and is
justified to the right.</td>

<td width="90" valign="bottom" align="center">
This is my third table cell. Its values are completely different than the prior
cells.</td>

</tr>
</table>
</body>
</html>
```

Figure 8.13 shows how the table cell attributes are much more consistent.

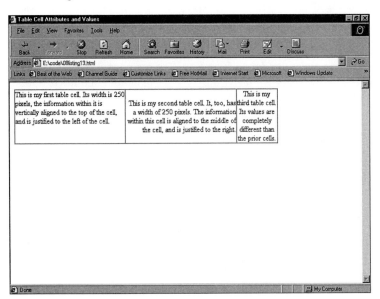

Figure 8.13
These table cells help to clarify just how cells are a critical component of object placement.

In the first cell, the information is vertically aligned to the top of the cell, and justified to the left. The second cell's data is vertically aligned to the middle of the cell and justifies right. Finally, the third cell's content, which is vertically aligned to the bottom of the cell, also is centered. Each cell is fixed to the width called for within the cell and within the table tag itself.

This control relationship between the table cell and the table tag is the most powerful aspect of table authoring. Carefully working with this relationship is certain to help you create stable, compatible tables that allow you to firmly secure your data and design.

```
<!--
When you don't add attributes to a
tag, browsers will seek the de-
fault. Table borders default to 0,
cell padding and cell spacing to 1.
Alignment defaults to the left, and
width becomes dynamic, meaning
that the width of a table and the
cells within adapt to the combina-
tion of browser space and the data
you've placed within the cells.
-->
```

USING FIXED AND DYNAMIC DESIGN

Fixed designs are created for a specific resolution. *Fixed-width* layouts require very accurate measurement on the designer's part. You must work within the parameters of the resolution.

Dynamic layouts, however, stretch to meet the resolution of the screen. These layouts rely on percentages or wild-cards, essentially saying "put this information here, but this information can take up whatever screen space is available."

<!--
In transitional HTML 4.0, 4.01, and XHTML 1.0, background color can be added to individual table cells using the bgcolor="x" (where "x" is a named or hexadecimal color) attribute. Color also can be achieved using style sheets, which of course is the preferred method when dealing with XHTML 1.0 in its strictest sense.
-->

Applying a Fixed Table Design

To fix a page to a 640×480 resolution (with a 585×295 per screen recommendation), follow these steps:

1. Determine how much space is necessary for each section. (For my page, I want 125 pixels for my navigational margin, 10 pixels of whitespace between the margin and my text, and a right margin of 45.)

2. Add up these sections. (In my example, I get a total of 180 pixels. Subtract that number from 585. I end up with 405 pixels available for my body area.)

3. Fix this information into the table. To do so, create a table with the fixed width of 585 pixels. Then create four cells, each with the appropriate number of fixed pixels for each cell.

Listing 8.15 shows the markup necessary to create the grid.

Listing 8.15   HTML Markup for a Fixed, Left-Margin Table

```
<!DOCTYPE html PUBLIC "-//W3C//DTD XHTML 1.0 Transitional//EN"
"http://www.w3.org/TR/xhtml1/DTD/xhtml1-transitional.dtd">
<html xmlns="http://www.w3.org/1999/xhtml">
<head>
<title>Fixed, left-Margin Table</title>
</head>

<body>
<table border="0" width="585" cellpadding="0" cellspacing="0">
<tr>
<td width="125" align="left" valign="top"></td>

<td width="10" align="left" valign="top"></td>
```

Listing 8.15 Continued

```
<td width="405" align="left" valign="top"></td>

<td width="45" align="left" valign="top"></td>

</tr>
</table>
</body>
</html>
```

In authoring the opening `table` tag, note that I included the `border`, `cellpadding`, and `cellspacing` attributes along with the `width`. This approach goes back to the "don't let the browser do the thinking for you" concept.

Along the same lines, every table cell includes the correct width but also the default "left" alignment and top alignment. (You can set these attributes as you ultimately need them to be set; they are the conventions I typically begin with.)

The example in Listing 8.15 isn't the entire picture. Although later generation (4.0 and above) browsers in both the IE and Netscape varieties tend to respect cell widths, you *always* run the risk of a collapsing or drifting table cell unless you fix that cell. One way to do so is to incorporate a graphic into the cell design. My navigation buttons, for example, are all 125 pixels wide, so the cell to the left is going to be sturdy. What about my other cells, however? I either have to do the same thing with a specific graphic, or include a single pixel, transparent GIF (known as a spacer GIF) stretched to the width of the table to ensure that it really *is* fixed.

This technique has long been a controversial one, and it's becoming even more controversial to do this now that style sheets are so much better supported by contemporary browsers. But, because the practice is a convention, I'm including this method here with the oft-expressed caution to consider CSS as the preferred methodology in all cases of presentation.

How to Make a Spacer GIF

In Photoshop or your favorite imaging program, create an image that is 1×1 pixel. Fill the image with a color (I use white). Now, index the color and reduce the bits to the lowest number your imaging program allows. Export the file as a GIF, but before saving, remove all the color and be sure that the image is not interlaced. Save this file as `spacer.gif` and place it in your images directory. You can now call on it at any time.

Listing 8.16 shows the markup with the navigation buttons and spacer graphics in place.

Listing 8.16 Fixed, Left-Margin Design with Spacer Graphics Included

```
<!DOCTYPE html PUBLIC "-//W3C//DTD XHTML 1.0 Transitional//EN"
"http://www.w3.org/TR/xhtml1/DTD/xhtml1-transitional.dtd">
<html xmlns="http://www.w3.org/1999/xhtml">
<head>
```

Listing 8.16 Continued

```
<title>Fixed, left-Margin Table</title>
</head>
<body background="images/bluebak.gif">
<table border="0" width="585" cellpadding="0" cellspacing="0">
<tr>
<td width="125" align="left" valign="top">

<p><a href="new.html"><img src="images/new.gif" border="0" width="125"
height="30" alt="what's new" /></a></p>

<p><a href="about.html"><img src="images/about_us.gif" border="0" width="125"
height="30" alt="About Us" /></a></p>

<p><a href="products.html"><img src="images/products.gif" border="0" width="125"
height="30" alt="products" /></a></p>

<a href="contact.html"><img src="images/contact.gif" border="0" width="125"
height="30" alt="contact" /></a>
</td>

<td width="10" align="left" valign="top">
<img src="images/spacer.gif" border="0" width="10" height="1" alt="" /></td>

<td width="405" align="left" valign="top"><img src="images/company_header.gif"
border="0" width="405" height="50" alt="welcome to the company" />
</td>

<td width="45" align="left" valign="top">
<img src="images/spacer.gif" border="0" width="45" height="1" alt="" />
</td>
</tr>
</table>
</body>
</html>
```

In Figure 8.14, you can see the results. This table will not collapse, because every cell is mathematically accounted for. In Figure 8.15, the table's border is set to 1 so that you can see the grid.

<!--
When using spacer images in a table, be sure to include an alt attribute in the image, and leave the attribute value undeclared. The reason you should do this is so that screen readers for the visually disabled will ignore the spacer image. If you don't do this, the word "image" will be repeated to the user over and over.
-->

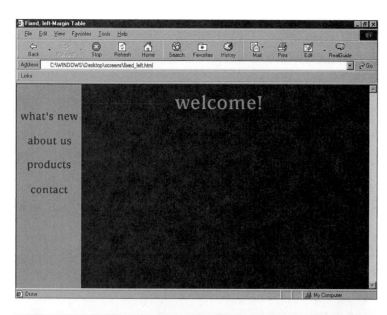

Figure 8.14
Fixed, left-margin table design. This popular design method is used throughout the Web as a method of keeping navigation and content in specific, familiar locations.

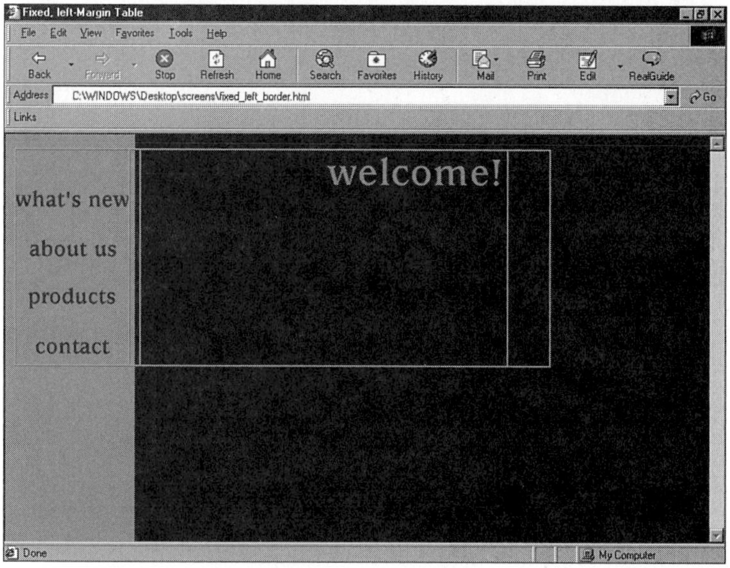

Figure 8.15
This table has a border attribute set to 1 so that you can see the grid—note the cells where the spacer GIFs fill in.

If you want to reverse the process—say you want to fix a table with a right margin—you prepare it exactly the same way. Mark off the exact widths of each section—whether it is whitespace, a navigation area, or a body text area—and do the math.

Of course, one of the problems with designing to the lowest common resolution occurs when someone comes along viewing the page at a higher resolution. In the case

`<!--Caution`

In fixed design you must never exceed a cell's parameters. In other words, if you have a cell that is 125 pixels wide, but you put a 200-pixel–wide graphic in it, you will cause the table to render improperly.

`-->`

of fixed tables, more whitespace is visible at the right and bottom of the page. The design will be set into the left x- and y-axes snugly. Because this design is so prevalent on the Web, most individuals are not distracted by it.

Working with Dynamic Table Design

To create tables that stretch to accommodate any space, you can make them dynamic by using a percentage for widths instead of a fixed layout. Dynamic tables come in handy when designing tables that contain some graphical information, but are more fluidly designed without relying on fixed-pixel positioning.

<!--
If you want to balance whitespace around fixed table designs in transitional documents, center the table inside a div element. It won't be noticeable at low resolution, but at higher resolutions you'll end up with the empty space flowing around the fixed table instead of weighing heavily on one side of the page.
-->

Listing 8.17 shows a dynamic table. I've made the entire table dynamic—placing a 100% value in the `table` tag itself and creating four dynamic columns of 25% each. What's powerful about this table is that it will adjust to the width of the available space, no matter what.

Listing 8.17   A Dynamic Table

```
<!DOCTYPE html PUBLIC "-//W3C//DTD XHTML 1.0 Transitional//EN"
"http://www.w3.org/TR/xhtml1/DTD/xhtml1-transitional.dtd">
<html xmlns="http://www.w3.org/1999/xhtml">
<head>
<title>Dynamic Table</title>
</head>
<body>
<table border="1" width="100%" cellpadding="1" cellspacing="1">
<tr>
<td width="25%" align="left" valign="top">text</td>

<td width="25%" align="left" valign="top">text</td>

<td width="25%" align="left" valign="top">text</td>

<td width="25%" align="left" valign="top">text</td>
</tr>
</table>
</body>
</html>
```

In Figure 8.16, you can see the table at full resolution. If I make the browser window smaller (see Figure 8.17), the table automatically adjusts. If I did this with a fixed table, however, I would obscure all the information that fell outside the exact pixel range of my browser window size.

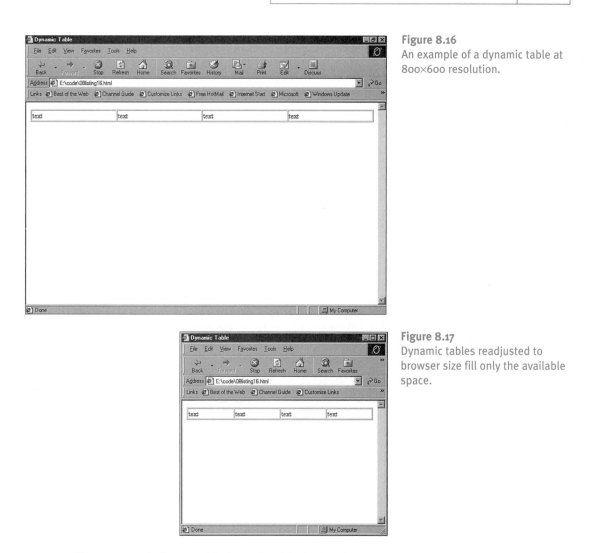

Figure 8.16
An example of a dynamic table at 800×600 resolution.

Figure 8.17
Dynamic tables readjusted to browser size fill only the available space.

The greatest challenge with dynamic table design, however, is that you lose the integrity of the fixed grid that allows you to stabilize a precision design within it.

Combination Fixed and Dynamic Table Design

One way to greatest reach for the best of both worlds is to combine fixed and dynamic approaches. The wisdom here, however, is to ensure that only one cell is fixed to a percentage width, and that width should be 100%. This approach helps you maintain the shape of the layout but allows for dynamic positioning of text.

This approach works well, for example, if I have a left and right margin I want to remain fixed and still have the center, body area dynamic. I could achieve this effect by fixing the cells to the left and right using both a fixed width cell and spacer GIF set to the dimensions of the cell, but leaving the center cell dynamic. Listing 8.18 shows an example of this effect.

Listing 8.18 Fixed and Dynamic Cells

```
<!DOCTYPE html PUBLIC "-//W3C//DTD XHTML 1.0 Transitional//EN"
"http://www.w3.org/TR/xhtml1/DTD/xhtml1-transitional.dtd">
<html xmlns="http://www.w3.org/1999/xhtml">
<head>
<title>Fixed and Dynamic Table</title>
</head>
<body background="images/decorative.gif" text="#FFFFFF">
<table border="0" width="100%" cellpadding="0" cellspacing="0">
<tr>

<td width="75" align="left" valign="top"> <img src="images/spacer.gif" border="0"
width="75" height="1" alt="" /></td>

<td width="100%" align="left" valign="top">
<p>A maid servant then brought them water in a beautiful golden ewer and poured
it into a silver basin for them to wash their hands, and she drew a clean table
beside them. An upper servant brought them bread, and offered them many good
things of what there was in the house, the carver fetched them plates of all
manner of meats and set cups of gold by their side, and a man-servant brought
them wine and poured it out for them.</p>

<p>Then the suitors came in and took their places on the benches and seats.
Forthwith men servants poured water over their hands, maids went round with the
bread-baskets, pages filled the mixing-bowls with wine and water, and they laid
their hands upon the good things that were before them.</p>

<p>As soon as they had had enough to eat and drink they wanted music and
dancing, which are the crowning embellishments of a banquet, so a servant
brought a lyre to Phemius, whom they compelled perforce to sing to them. As
soon as he touched his lyre and began to sing Telemachus spoke low to Minerva,
with his head close to hers that no man might hear.</p></td>

<td width="50" align="left" valign="top"><img src="images/spacer.gif" border="0"
width="50" height="1" alt="" />
</td>
</tr>
</table>
</body>
</html>
```

In this case, you have the advantage of being able to fix margins. Here, you can accommodate a left, decorative background and whitespace to the right (see Figure 8.18). You also can allow for the dynamic wrapping of text (see Figure 8.19).

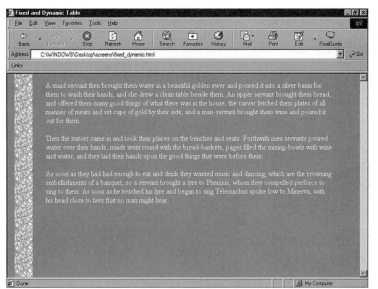

Figure 8.18
Fixed margins over a decorative background allow for better positioning of the text so it does not run into the decorative margin design.

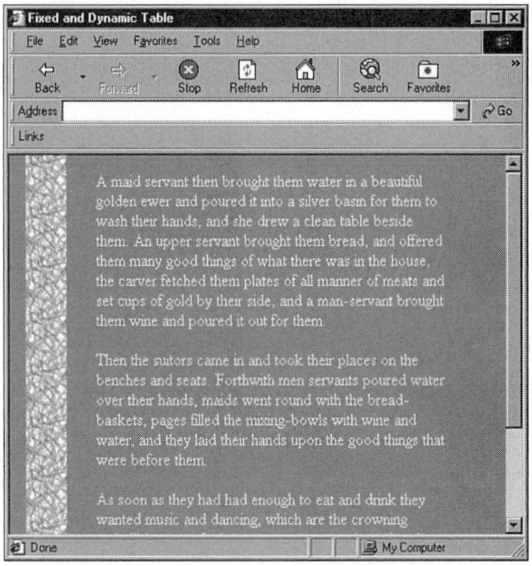

Figure 8.19
The fixed and dynamic combination readjusted. Note how the design adjusts to the screen space, without the appearance of a horizontal scrollbar.

NESTING AND STACKING TABLES

To create complex layouts using tables, you can often employ column and row spanning. Spanning provides options that help designers break from strict column and row design and add some visual diversity.

However, sometimes this technique is limited or cannot provide you with the control you're after. Say you want to create a layout that manages a background margin tile, yet you want to have central sections broken up. And, within those sections, you want to add swatches of background design or color.

One method of enabling complex table design is to nest tables. In this process, you put a table within a table to achieve the layout you require.

Here's the method: Any table cell within a table can accept a complete, new table. Doing so creates a nest:

```
<td>
<table>
<tr>

<td>    </td>
</tr>
</table>
</td>
```

You can take the nest even further:

```
<td>
<table>
<tr>

<td>
    <table>       <tr>

 <td>    </td>
 </tr>
 </table>

</td>
</tr>
</table>
</td>
```

Nesting tables is one of the keys to complex table design. After you've learned the basics, nesting can help you get control over space within space.

You also can stack tables. In this process, you take more than one table and place it above another. The advantage of stacking is that you can separate particular sections of a page, revert to non-table markup in between, return to a table, or combine any variety of options to create varied design.

Listing 8.19 demonstrates a set of stacked tables with a numbered list between the two tables.

<!--Caution

Use nesting creatively, but use it wisely. Nesting anything beyond three levels is a good indicator that you need to go back and examine your grid, looking for a simpler approach to the layout. What's more, deep nests can cause browsers to fail, especially Netscape 4.x browsers.

-->

Listing 8.19   Stacked Tables

```
<!DOCTYPE html PUBLIC "-//W3C//DTD XHTML 1.0 Transitional//EN"
"http://www.w3.org/TR/xhtml1/DTD/xhtml1-transitional.dtd">
<html xmlns="http://www.w3.org/1999/xhtml">
<head>
```

Listing 8.19   Continued

```
<title>Stacked Table Example</title>
</head>

<body background="images/flocked.gif" text="#FFFFCC">

<table border="0" width="595" cellpadding="0" cellspacing="0">
<tr>
<td width="100" align="left" valign="top">

<h3>An Excerpt from Homer's Odyssey</h3></td>

<td width="495" align="left" valign="middle">

<p>A maid servant then brought them water in a beautiful golden ewer and poured
it into a silver basin for them to wash their hands, and she drew a clean table
beside them.</p></td>

</tr>
</table>

<p>Then the suitors came in and took their places on the benches and seats:</p>

<ul>
<li>Men servants poured water over their hands</li>
<li>maids went round with the bread-baskets</li>
<li>pages filled the mixing-bowls with wine and water</li>
</ul>

<p>and they laid their hands upon the good things that were before them.</p>

<table border="0" width="595" cellpadding="0" cellspacing="0">
<tr>
<td width="595" align="left" valign="top">
<img src="images/lyre.gif" width="100" height="69" border="0" alt="lyre image"
align="left" hspace="10" vspace="10" />

<p>As soon as they had had enough to eat and drink they wanted music and
dancing, which are the crowning embellishments of a banquet, so a servant
brought a lyre to Phemius, whom they compelled perforce to sing to them.  As
soon as he touched his lyre and began to sing Telemachus spoke low to Minerva,
with his head close to hers that no man might hear.</p></td>

</tr>
</table>
</body>
</html>
```

Figure 8.20 shows the results.

Figure 8.20
Stacked tables offer even more design flexibility.

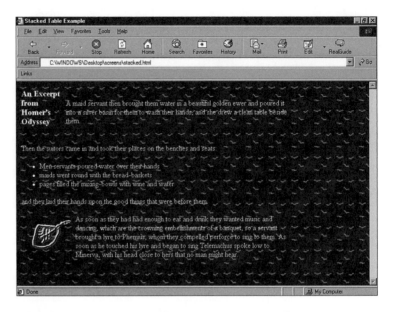

CASE BY CASE: DESIGN FIRST, THEN PLAN THE TABLE

One of the problems many Web developers face is how to create innovative designs within the constraints of table grids. This is one of the reasons that style sheet positioning is so ideal and appealing.

When working to create great designs, do the design work first, and then and only then begin to solve the table necessary to lay out the design.

One way to do this is to first sketch your design ideas out on paper. After you have a sketch, you can move to Photoshop to lay out the design. After you're satisfied with the layout, you can then begin to solve the table problem.

Start out by creating a design—first by sketching it, then by laying it out in Photoshop (or the imaging software you typically use for graphic layout). I want you to think outside the box—literally! Don't try to force the design into the context of tables. Just let the design flow naturally from you.

No matter your level of experience, this is a great exercise to help you come up with innovative designs. In fact, I'm going to do the exercise with you. Here's what I did:

1. I first took out my sketch pad, and I made several sketches. I chose the one with which I was most satisfied.

2. Using the sketch as a guide, I opened up my favorite imaging program, Photoshop. You can use whatever imaging program you are most comfortable with.

3. One by one, I laid out the elements of the design carefully, placing the header, background, and navigation on separate layers so I could make adjustments to them at a later time.

4. I saved my file with the layers intact using Photoshop's native format, PSD.

After you have your design mocked up, follow these steps:

1. Print out the mockup. This gives you an opportunity to move away from the screen and think creatively.

2. Draw a table grid directly over your design. Do this several times, trying out different approaches and ideally minimizing the table's complexity.

3. Move back to your imaging program and set up guides, measuring each table element carefully.

Now you can generate the graphics and markup the table. Ideally, you've worked this process through rigorously enough so that your table is streamlined—achieving what it needs without being too complicated and weighty.

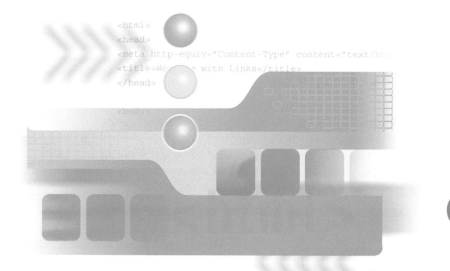

9

CREATING FRAMESETS AND FRAME DOCUMENTS

IN THIS CHAPTER

To Frame or Not to Frame	220
Understanding Frame Structure	222
The Frameset Document	223
Building a Framed Page	224
Setting `frameset` and `frame` Attributes	226
Exploring a Frame with Margin, Resize, and Scroll Controls	227
Targeting Windows	228
Working with Borderless Frames	233
Advanced Frame Concepts	236
Working with Inline Frames (I-Frames)	241
The `noframes` Element and Accessibility	242
Case by Case: Special Issues with Frames	244

TO FRAME OR NOT TO FRAME

Frames have been a source of both frustration and empowerment for Web site designers and visitors alike. The frustration comes from a number of concerns. First, frames divide the available browser space, which is preciously restricted to begin with. Frames, particularly in their bordered manifestation, literally take what is a small, contained space and break up that space into smaller, even more contained spaces (see Figure 9.1). This makes frames an unfortunate choice for certain audiences unless the author knows what he or she is doing.

Figure 9.1
Bordered frames break up the screen's visible space.

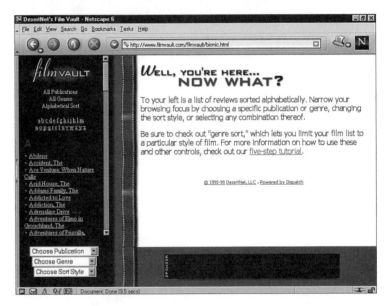

Using frames requires an understanding of accessibility options for the site to be made useful to blind and disabled site visitors. Frames also make it more difficult to bookmark pages within a site in older browsers, or to refer to specific pages within a framed structure via a URL. What's more, frames consume a lot more bandwidth. Finally, frames force the designer to write more markup, because they require more actual pages of markup per visible page.

Because of these difficulties, only the most technologically adept, design-literate of Web authors can use frames as part of a design well, and even then at the risk of upsetting visitors to the pages they built.

Despite all the potential problems, frames can be very empowering from a design perspective. One aspect of this empowerment is that designers can keep sections of a page static whereas other parts of the page can be used to display other pages. Particularly handy for Fixed

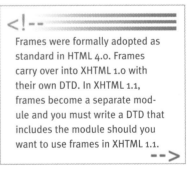

Frames were formally adopted as standard in HTML 4.0. Frames carry over into XHTML 1.0 with their own DTD. In XHTML 1.1, frames become a separate module and you must write a DTD that includes the module should you want to use frames in XHTML 1.1.

navigation, this is a common approach to the development of menu bars and other specialty areas that are to remain in place.

Frames, particularly of the border*less* variety, also give designers another method to create a grid system upon which to base their design (see Figure 9.2).

Figure 9.2
Borderless frames create a design system similar to what is available when using tables, however with other capabilities such as keeping sections of the design static.

⇨ *To see whether tables are a better option for your particular design needs, **see** "Working with Tables,"*
p. 177.

This system expands frames from their original role as an organizational tool to include page format and design control. With borderless frames, as with borderless tables, individual sections of a page can be defined and controlled.

But where tables can only be used on a page-by-page basis, frame technology introduces the static concept, discussed previously, and the aspect of *targets* which offer a variety of powerful controls.

Webmasters and site designers can now make better choices about how to employ frames. Whether the choice is to use borders for an interface or to create pages with frames as the silent and strong foundation beneath a complex and multifaceted design, the Web designer is ultimately empowered by having these choices.

No matter how you feel about frames, it's a good idea to know the ropes in terms of authoring them. This way, you always have the option to use them if you like or to set them aside if you feel using them is problematic for your audience.

UNDERSTANDING FRAME STRUCTURE

Before I introduce the practical aspects of how to design a framed page, I want to demonstrate a fundamental aspect of frame design. Much like tables, frames are built by thinking in columns and rows. Tables, as described in Chapter 8, get a bit complex with the ways columns and rows are spanned, creating a technological blur between horizontal and vertical reference points. Frames approach the issue in a much clearer way. A column is always a vertical control, a row is a horizontal control.

Moreover, the syntax is clear. Rows are created using the rows attribute, columns use the cols attribute. Both columns and rows can be set to a value by using pixels *or* percentages. For example, cols="240, *" calls for a left column with a *width* of 240 pixels, and the right column, denoted by the asterisk, will be the *dynamic remainder* of the available viewing space.

To add more columns, simply define each one in turn. For example, if I wanted to create four columns of equal percent, the syntax would read cols="25%,25%,25%,25%". The results of this sequence are shown in Figure 9.3.

Figure 9.3
Here the frame columns have been designed in equal sizes using percentages, and the borders are turned on.

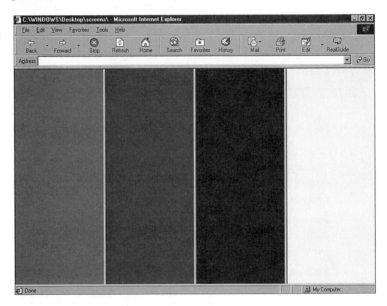

Similarly, if I wanted to create rows rather than columns, I would simply change the syntax to rows="240, *", and the results would be a top row with a *height* of 240 pixels. To create four individual rows of equal percent, I would call for rows="25%,25%,25%,25%", as demonstrated in Figure 9.4.

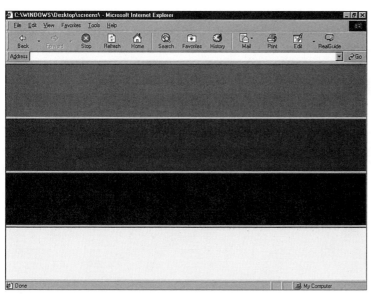

Figure 9.4
Four individual rows of 25% each.

THE FRAMESET DOCUMENT

There are only three components absolutely necessary to build a framed page. Yes, frames can get a bit complicated, depending on the ways you want to employ them, but at the most basic level, all framed sites begin with the factors introduced here.

Any framed page requires a controlling document that gives the instructions on how the framed page is to be set up. This control document is called the *frameset*. Then, a document is required for each individual frame.

The frameset page is the control page of your framed site. In it, you'll define the rows or columns you want to create and the documents that will fill those rows or columns. This is done using two major elements:

- **frameset**—This element defines the frame, and its attributes define rows and columns. The frameset element is non-empty.

- **frame**—The frame element arranges individual frames within the frameset. This includes the location of the document required to fill the frame, using the src="x" (where x assigns the relative or absolute URL to the location of the page). A variety of other frame attributes will be covered later in the chapter. Because frame is an empty element, in XHTML it must be terminated: <frame />.

<!--
Remember your sums! A framed page requires one page per each individually defined area *plus* one page for the control, or frameset, page.
-->

<!--
XHTML 1.0 requires you to identify the frameset document by including the version information. This means you'll need to insert

<!DOCTYPE html PUBLIC
"-//W3C//DTD XHTML 1.0
Frameset//EN"

"http://www.w3.org/TR/xhtml1/
DTD/xhtml1-frameset.dtd">

into an XHTML 1.0 frameset.

Individual pages within the framed site can use either strict or transitional XHTML 1.0, depending on your needs. Be sure to refer to the appropriate DTD accordingly. Note that if you use any frames-related markup in a document, you can no longer use the strict DTD.
-->

It's important to remember that the `frameset` element is a conceptual replacement for the body element in the frameset HTML page. Therefore, in a simple frameset (as in one without `noframes` in place), *no* body *tags* should appear.

BUILDING A FRAMED PAGE

In this case, you're going to build a two-column page, with the left column serving as a simple menu that could eventually be used to guide a visitor through the site.

First, you'll create the page for the left, or menu, column:

1. In your editor, type the following:

```
<!DOCTYPE html PUBLIC "-//W3C//DTD XHTML 1.0 Strict//EN"
    "http://www.w3.org/TR/xhtml1/DTD/strict.dtd">
<html xmlns="http://www.w3.org/1999/xhtml">
<head>
<title>Menu</title>
</head>
<body>

<p><a href="about.html">About the Company</a></p>

<p><a href="clients.html">Company Clients</a></p>

<p><a href="contact.html">Contact Company</a></p>

</body>
</html>
```

2. Save the file as `menu.html`.

3. View the file in your browser to see how it looks before you apply the frameset to it.

4. Now create the main document:

```
<!DOCTYPE html PUBLIC "-//W3C//DTD XHTML 1.0 Strict//EN"
    "http://www.w3.org/TR/xhtml1/DTD/strict.dtd">
<html xmlns="http://www.w3.org/1999/xhtml">
<head>
<title>Main Page</title>
</head>
<body>
<p>Welcome to The Company! We specialize in a variety of high
quality services. Our clients encompass just about everyone who
is anyone.</p>
</body>
</html>
```

5. Save the file as `main.html`.

6. View the file in your Web browser to see what it looks like before adding the frameset command file.

Now you'll create the frameset.

1. Open your editor and begin a new page. Type the following:

```
<!DOCTYPE html PUBLIC "-//W3C//DTD XHTML 1.0 Frameset//EN"
"http://www.w3.org/TR/xhtml1/DTD/xhtml1-frameset.dtd">
<html xmlns="http://www.w3.org/1999/xhtml">
<head>
<title>Frame Control</title>
</head>
<frameset>
</frameset>
</html>
```

2. Now you'll want to add the columns or rows. In this instance, I'm using columns:

```
<!DOCTYPE html PUBLIC "-//W3C//DTD XHTML 1.0 Frameset//EN"
"http://www.w3.org/TR/xhtml1/DTD/xhtml1-frameset.dtd">
<html xmlns="http://www.w3.org/1999/xhtml">
<html xmlns="http://www.w3.org/1999/xhtml">
<head>
<title>Frame Control</title>
</head>
<frameset cols="240, *">
</frameset>
</html>
```

3. The individual frames with their corresponding XHTML pages are added by using the frame tag:

```
<!DOCTYPE html PUBLIC "-//W3C//DTD XHTML 1.0 Frameset//EN"
    "http://www.w3.org/TR/xhtml1/DTD/xhtml1-frameset.dtd">
<html xmlns="http://www.w3.org/1999/xhtml">
<head>
<title>Frame Control</title>
</head>
<frameset cols="240, *">
<frame src="menu.html" />
<frame src="main.html" />
</frameset>
</html>
```

4. Save the document as index.html.

5. Load the frameset page into your browser and view the results. Does it match Figure 9.5? If it does, congratulations!

Pages not matching the examples? Look over your syntax carefully. It's amazing how tiny mistakes can create total havoc.

Figure 9.5
This figure displays a simple, framed page.

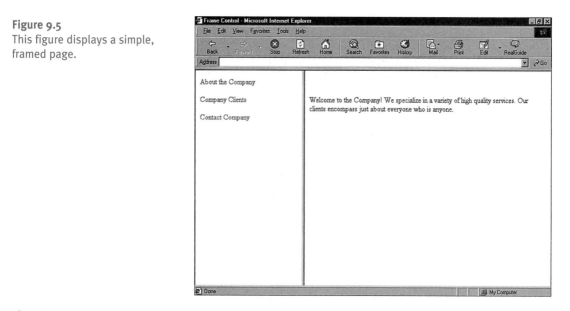

SETTING FRAMESET AND FRAME ATTRIBUTES

There are several powerful attributes available for the frameset and frame elements. The following list covers those used for the frameset.

- **cols="x"**—As covered earlier, this attribute creates columns. An "x" value is given for each column in the framed page and will be either a pixel value, a percentage value, or a combination of one of those plus the "*", which creates a *dynamic* or *relative size* frame, the remainder of the framed space.

- **rows="x"**—This attribute is used to create rows in the same fashion that the column attribute is used.

- **border="x"**—The border attribute is used by Netscape Navigator 3.0, 4.0, and later to control border width. Value is set in pixel width.

- **frameborder="x"**—frameborder is used by the Internet Explorer browser to control border width in pixels. Netscape Navigator 3.0, 4.0, and later uses the attribute with a yes or no value.

- **framespacing="x"**—Used originally by Internet Explorer, this attribute controls border width.

Use the following tag attributes with the <frame> tag:

- **frameborder="x"**—Use this attribute to control frameborders around individual frames. Netscape Navigator requires a yes or no value, whereas Internet Explorer will look for a numeric pixel width value.

- **marginheight="x"**—Argue a value in pixels to control the height of the frame's margin.

- `marginwidth="x"`—This attribute sets a frame's margin width in pixels.

- `name="x"`—This critical attribute enables the designer to name an individual frame. Naming frames permits *targeting* by links within other XHTML pages. Names must begin with an alphanumeric character.

- `noresize`—Simply place this attribute in your string if you don't want to allow resizing of a frame by the user. This fixes the frame into the position and disallows a visitor to alter the size of a frame. You'll note that this is attribute minimization, and in XHTML it must take its own name as a value: `noresize="noresize"`.

- `scrolling="x"`—By using the settings `"yes"`, `"no"`, or `"auto"`, you can control the appearance of a scrollbar. A `"yes"` value automatically places a scrollbar in the frame, a `"no"` value ensures that no scrollbar ever appears. The `"auto"` argument turns the power over to the browser, which will automatically place a scrollbar in a frame should it be required.

- `src="x"`—The `"x"` value is replaced with the relative or absolute URL of the XHTML page you want to place within the frame at hand.

- `title="x"`—To add a human-readable description of the frame's function, use the `title` attribute with a descriptive value, such as `title="navigation frame"`. This is a particularly useful means of ensuring accessibility for those with disabilities.

These choices ultimately lead to a lot of control with frame-based design.

EXPLORING A FRAME WITH MARGIN, RESIZE, AND SCROLL CONTROLS

Listing 9.1 shows the markup for a framed page with `marginheight`, `marginwidth`, `noresize`, and `scrolling` attributes.

Listing 9.1   Frameset with `marginheight`, `width`, `resize`, and `scrolling` Attributes

```
<!DOCTYPE html PUBLIC "-//W3C//DTD XHTML 1.0 Frameset//EN"
"http://www.w3.org/TR/xhtml1/DTD/xhtml1-frameset.dtd">
<html xmlns="http://www.w3.org/1999/xhtml">
<head>
<title>Frame With Numerous Controls</title>
</head>
<frameset cols="240, *">
<frame src="menu.html" marginheight="5" marginwidth="5" noresize=
"noresize" scrolling="auto" />
<frame src="main.html" marginheight="9" marginwidth="9"
noresize="noresize" scrolling="auto" />
</frameset>
</html>
```

The first issue to be aware of is that this is a frameset, therefore no body tag is used. Instead, the `frameset` tag and its companion closing tag are placed around the internal information.

Within the `frameset` tag, I've called for a left margin of 240 pixels, and I've used the * value to allow for the right frame to be dynamic.

Following this information are the two lines of syntax for each of the corresponding frames. The left frame information is placed first, and then the right frame information is written underneath.

In the first frame instance, I've named the source, and I've added margin information of height and width at 5 pixels each. This gives me a bit of whitespace around any of the information appearing within that frame. I've chosen the `noresize` option and set `scrolling` to `auto` so that at lower resolutions individuals will see a scrollbar should it become necessary.

I'm of the opinion that a `"yes"` value for scrolling rarely looks good but is extremely useful when the frame in question contains a long document. A `"no"` value is most valuable for Fixed-column frames used for menus.

If you do your math and are absolutely certain that you have allowed for enough viewing area to contain the information, use the `"no"` value. Setting scrolling on `"auto"` is usually the favorable choice, because it allows the browser to make the decision. An `"auto"` value is especially favorable wherever you've argued for *dynamic* or *relative size* (a `"*"` value) rows and columns.

Resizing is similar in concept. Although offering it can foul up your attractive, well thought out framed pages, resizing can be valuable when you want to give your visitor ultimate control. In this case, I've decided to not allow my visitor that control.

The second frame is authored exactly the same way, with the one distinction of more white-space allotted to the area via the margin controls.

TARGETING WINDOWS

To effectively use frames, a Web author must decide where linked pages will load. For example, in the frame page you've developed so far in this chapter, I've guided you to create a menu on the left, and a larger frame field on the right. This is a natural start for effective design using frames.

There are two basic ways to link, or *target*, HTML pages to specific windows:

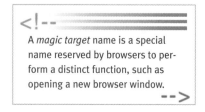

A *magic target* name is a special name reserved by browsers to perform a distinct function, such as opening a new browser window.

- Combine `target` and `name` attributes to specifically target windows.

- Use a magic target name.

`target` and `name` attributes allow you to add more pages to your framed site and to target a specific window by naming that window and targeting the link.

Creating a Frame Using `target` and `name` Attributes

Naming the target is the best place to start. Using the same frameset markup in Listing 9.1 shown previously, I've added a name to the right, or "main," frame:

```
<!DOCTYPE html PUBLIC "-//W3C//DTD XHTML 1.0 Frameset//EN"
"http://www.w3.org/TR/xhtml1/DTD/xhtml1-frameset.dtd">
<html xmlns="http://www.w3.org/1999/xhtml">
<head>
<title>Frames with Targets and Names</title>
</head>
<frameset cols="240, *">
<frame src="menu.html" marginheight="5" marginwidth="5" noresize=
"noresize" scrolling="auto" />
<frame src="main.html" name="right" marginheight="9"
marginwidth="9" noresize="noresize" scrolling="auto" />
</frameset>
</html>
```

After the target window has a name, the target must be added to the link. In the menu file, I'm going to specify the target, as follows:

```
<!DOCTYPE html PUBLIC "-//W3C//DTD XHTML 1.0 Strict//EN"
    "http://www.w3.org/TR/xhtml1/DTD/strict.dtd">
<html xmlns="http://www.w3.org/1999/xhtml">
<head>
<title>Menu</title>
</head>
<body>
<a href="about.html" target="right">About the Company</a>

<p> <a href="clients.html" target="right">Company Clients</a></p>

<p> <a href="contact.html" target="right">Contact Company</a></p>

</body>
</html>
```

As long as I've created each of the pages referred to in the links, each click of the link on this menu will load the appropriate page into the right frame (see Figure 9.6).

> `<!--`
>
> Want all of a site's pages to load into the same window? Follow the name and `target` convention. Within each document you want to load into that window, use the `<base>` tag. To load all pages within the framed site you are building would be to place this syntax within the `<head>` of *every* page to be loaded in that window: `<base target="right">`.
>
> `-->`

Figure 9.6
Targeting the right frame causes the pages referred to in the links to appear in that frame.

[Browser window screenshot: "Frames with Targets and Names - Microsoft Internet Explorer". Left frame contains: About the Company / Company Clients / Contact Company. Right frame contains: "Welcome to the Company! We specialize in a variety of high quality services. Our clients encompass just about everyone who is anyone."]

Magic Target Names

There are several predefined target names that will cause certain actions to occur when a link is clicked.

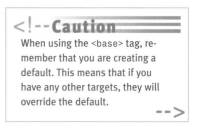

<!--Caution
When using the <base> tag, remember that you are creating a default. This means that if you have any other targets, they will override the default.
-->

- **target="_blank"**—The "_blank" target name causes the targeted document to open in a completely new browser window.

- **target="_self"**—The targeted document will load in the same window where the originating link exists.

- **target="_parent"**—This will load the targeted document into the link's parent frameset.

- **target="_top"**—Use this attribute to load the link into the full window, overriding any existing frames.

You'll notice that magic target names always begin with an underscore to avoid being confused with other target names.

The following are issues to bear in mind when using magic target names:

- You should avoid naming standard targets with anything other than an accepted alphanumeric character. An underscore, or any other symbol, will be ignored.

- The magic target name "_blank" always forces a new browser window to open. Be careful to use this only when a new window is absolutely necessary, otherwise you run the risk of angering Web site visitors, who, depending upon their settings, might end up with numerous, resource-draining browser windows on the desktop. The practice also introduces problems for users with disabilities. It's a good rule of thumb to specifically let the user know that the link destination will open in a new window.

- The `target="_top"` attribute and value is usually the right choice when a link takes the visitor out of your framed site into a new site. Some authors like the idea of keeping external sites inside their own site by targeting the remote site into a local frame, allowing the native site's menu or advertisement to remain live while surfing elsewhere. This is not only considered an annoyance, but might get you into legal trouble. Avoid this at all costs unless you have express permission from the site you are incorporating within your own.

You can now put your magic to use and try out a magic target name exercise:

1. Begin by opening your editor. You'll need to create two more pages to target. Type in the following:

```
<!DOCTYPE html PUBLIC "-//W3C//DTD XHTML 1.0 Strict//EN"
    "http://www.w3.org/TR/xhtml1/DTD/strict.dtd">
<html xmlns="http://www.w3.org/1999/xhtml">
<head>
<title>Magic Targets: About</title>
</head>
<body>
<h2>About the Company</h2>

<p>This page has information about the company.</p>
</body>
</html>
```

2. Save the file as `about.html`.

3. Open another blank editing page and enter the following:

```
<!DOCTYPE html PUBLIC "-//W3C//DTD XHTML 1.0 Strict//EN"
    "http://www.w3.org/TR/xhtml1/DTD/strict.dtd">
<html xmlns="http://www.w3.org/1999/xhtml">
<head>
<title>Magic Targets: Clients</title>
</head>
<body>
<h2>Clients</h2>

<p>This page has information about the clients.</p>
</body>
</html>
```

4. Save this file as `clients.html`.

5. Now create another:

```
<!DOCTYPE html PUBLIC "-//W3C//DTD XHTML 1.0 Transitional//EN"
    "http://www.w3.org/TR/xhtml1/DTD/loose.dtd">
<html xmlns="http://www.w3.org/1999/xhtml">
<head>
<title>Magic Targets: Contact</title>
```

```
</head>
<body>
<h2>Contact</h2>

<p>This page will be set up with a contact form.</p>
</body>
</html>
```

6. Save this page as `contact.html`.

7. Open the `menu.html` file you made earlier. This is the file where the *links* to the pages that will be targeted appear. You should see the following:

```
<!DOCTYPE html PUBLIC "-//W3C//DTD XHTML 1.0 Transitional//EN"
    "http://www.w3.org/TR/xhtml1/DTD/loose.dtd">
<html xmlns="http://www.w3.org/1999/xhtml">
<head>
<title>Menu</title>
</head>
<body>
<p><a href="about.html">About the Company</a></p>

<p><a href="clients.html">Company Clients</a></p>

<p><a href="contact.html">Contact Company</a></p>
</body>
</html>
```

8. You're going to add the syntax first for the "about" page, which you'll make target over the menu frame. The syntax is as follows:

```
<a href="about.html" target="_self">About the Company</a>
```

   Save the file, open the frameset page, and in the menu frame you will notice that About is now hot. Click that link and watch how `about.html` loads into the menu frame.

9. Return to your HTML editor and add the following syntax to the clients reference:

```
<a href="clients.html" target="_blank">Company Clients</a>
```

10. Save the file, and open the frameset page in your browser. `Clients` is now hot. When you click this choice, you'll note how `clients.html` is loaded into an entirely *new* browser window (see Figure 9.7).

11. Finally, add a link to the contact page itself:

```
<!DOCTYPE html PUBLIC "-//W3C//DTD XHTML 1.0 Transitional//EN"
    "http://www.w3.org/TR/xhtml1/DTD/loose.dtd">
<html xmlns="http://www.w3.org/1999/xhtml">
<head>
<title>Magic Targets: Contact</title>
```

```
</head>
<body>
<h2>Contact</h2>

<p>This page will be set up with a contact form.</p>

<p><a href="menu.html" target="_top">Reload the Menu Only</a></p>
</body>
</html>
```

12. Click the link, which loads the menu page over the contact form.

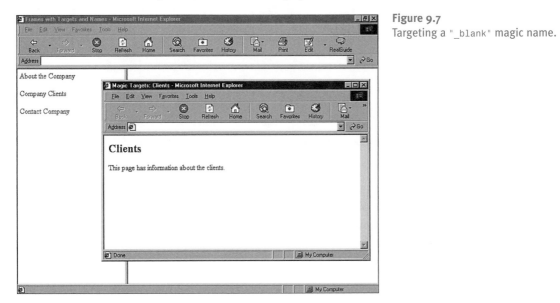

Figure 9.7
Targeting a "_blank" magic name.

You've now tackled some of the most difficult aspects of markup for frames. I encourage you to try a few variations using targets and attributes of your own selection. You'll learn a lot from experimentation, and have fun in the process.

WORKING WITH BORDERLESS FRAMES

Choosing to use borderless frames is a critical issue because using or not using borders is the point where the designer makes decisions about how to use frame technology as a layout method. Removing borders makes laying out a frame appear as a seamless, single unit, and this is a powerful and popular method of designing pages.

The first rule in cross-browser design is to know which browsers you are attempting to reach. With borderless frames, that rule is clarified by the fact that only certain browsers, and certain browser versions, interpret borderless frames in the correct manner.

The first thing to remember is that borderless frames are not supported in the Netscape and Microsoft browsers earlier than the 3.0 version.

The challenge of borderless frames doesn't lie in the markup per se, but in the differences in the way popular browsers interpret the markup, or require the markup to read.

Fortunately, there's a workaround: You can stack attributes within tags, and if a browser doesn't support that attribute or its value, it will ignore it and move on to the attribute and related value that it does interpret.

In HTML 4.0 and XHTML 1.0, authoring borderless frames is easy. You simply add the attribute and value `frameborder="0"` within the `<frame>` tag.

However, browsers without strict HTML 4.0 support, which includes most popular browsers before 4.0 and later versions, require a little jostling to get the borderless effect.

The Netscape browser (3.0+) allows for borderless frames when

- The `border` attribute is set, in pixels, to a numeric value of `"0"`.

- The `framespacing` attribute is assigned a `"no"` value.

Microsoft's Internet Explorer, browser version 3.0, produces borderless frames if

- The `frameborder` attribute is set, in pixels, to a numeric value of `"0"`.

- The `framespacing` attribute is assigned a width, in pixels, to a numeric value of `"0"`.

If it seems like there's a conflict, well, there really isn't, because each browser requires either a different attribute to control width or a different value to control spacing. It looks confusing, but if you stack attributes, you can easily create borderless frames that will be read by both browsers without difficulty.

This technique results in two syntax options:

```
<frameset frameborder="0" framespacing="0" border="0">
```

or

```
<frameset frameborder="no" framespacing="0" border="0">
```

The problem with this markup, however, is that it will not validate. Therefore, if you want to create a borderless frame in a valid Frameset document for HTML or XHTML, you'll have to leave certain attributes out, as they are not part of the DTD.

Here's the method described above to achieve a borderless effect (see Listing 9.2).

Listing 9.2   Authoring Borderless Frames—This Is Invalid XHTML

```
<!DOCTYPE html PUBLIC "-//W3C//DTD XHTML 1.0 Frameset//EN"
"http://www.w3.org/TR/xhtml1/DTD/xhtml1-frameset.dtd">
<html xmlns="http://www.w3.org/1999/xhtml">
<head>
<title>Borderless Frames</title>
</head>
<frameset frameborder="0" framespacing="0" border="0" cols="240,
```

Listing 9.2 Continued

```
*">
<frame src="menu.html" marginheight="5" marginwidth="5" noresize=
"noresize" scrolling="auto" />
<frame src="main.html" marginheight="9" marginwidth="9"
noresize="noresize" scrolling="auto" />
</frameset>
</html>
```

For contemporary browsers, this isn't a problem. All that's required is the `frameborder="0"` attribute in each frame element. Listing 9.3 shows the correct results for a contemporary frameset with borders turned off.

Listing 9.3 Authoring Borderless Frames—This Is Valid HTML

```
<!DOCTYPE HTML PUBLIC "-//W3C//DTD HTML 4.01 Frameset//EN"
        "http://www.w3.org/TR/html4/frameset.dtd">
<html>
<head>
<title>Borderless Frames</title>
</head>
<frameset cols="240,*">
<frame frameborder="0" src="menu.html" marginheight="5" marginwidth="5" noresize
scrolling="auto">
<frame frameborder="0" src="main.html" marginheight="9" marginwidth="9" noresize
scrolling="auto">
</frameset>
</html>
```

Your results should match Figure 9.8.

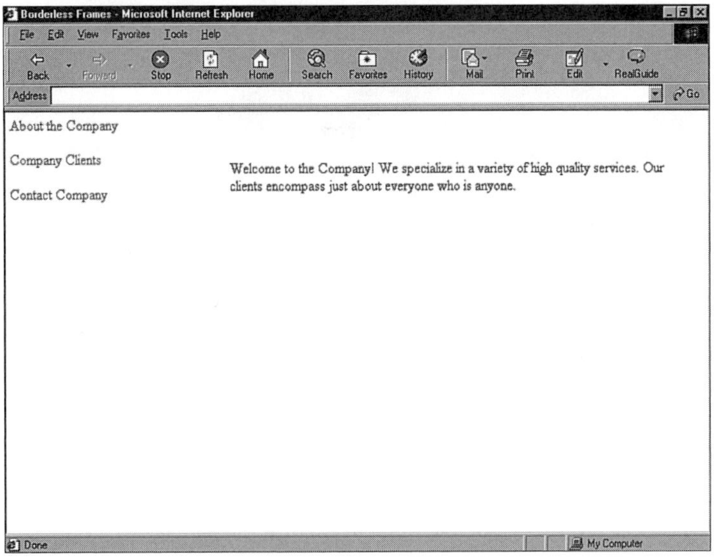

Figure 9.8
A borderless frame gives a cleaner and more professional look to your pages.

ADVANCED FRAME CONCEPTS

Frames are problematic; there's no denying that. For one thing, they require extra work from you, the author. For each framed page, you have to markup, design, and manage more than one page.

Next, frames upset site visitors. As discussed earlier in the chapter, part of the reason is that frames break up space. So, unless you're using borderless frames, the visual clutter they add to a page is detrimental.

Another headache is that they are more difficult to navigate, search for, and print.

So how do you design a sophisticated, advanced frame-based page? The absolutely, positively, most imperative place to begin is to determine whether your site really needs frames at all. If you can create the same layout with basic HTML or XHTML, with tables, or with CSS, then do it one of those ways.

Appropriate Use of Frames

There's only one really, really good reason to use frames in a page's design, and that is to create an interface that has both static and active parts (see Figure 9.9). In other words, say you want your company logo to dominate the user experience, and you have a standard navigation bar that you always want to be present. Put them in frames. This approach makes sense because the user's experience becomes enhanced rather than problematic.

Figure 9.9
This is an example of an elegant site that uses frames with static navigation (top) and active parts (center).

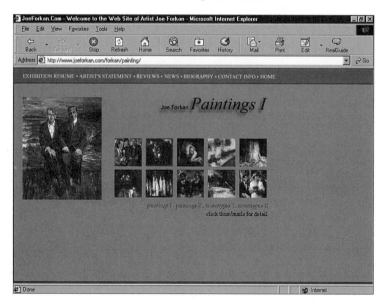

If you are going to choose to work with frames instead of CSS, I would also recommend that you use borderless frames. They reinforce the fact that you're using the frames not to constrain design, but to create perpetual information.

You also can use frames for design, such as when creating bleeding or blurred edges. These techniques can't be achieved without frames unless you use background graphics, which limit your options. However, you should never use more frames than are absolutely necessary to achieve your goal—especially in the primary body section of your layout. Can you create a page with seven columns and five rows? Absolutely! Unless you can tell me why that's important other than as an exercise to understand how to create such a page, I don't think you should do it.

Finally, the use of tables or CSS layout within the framed pages—especially the content pages—can give you maximum design power when you're laying out complex sites.

Listing 9.4 shows the frameset for the frame design in Figure 9.9. The top frame handles the navigation, and the central frame handles content. A bottom frame handles a bleed along the bottom. Note that the <noframes> tag is also employed.

Listing 9.4   Sophisticated Frameset Design

```
<!DOCTYPE html PUBLIC "-//W3C//DTD XHTML 1.0 Frameset//EN"
"http://www.w3.org/TR/xhtml1/DTD/xhtml1-frameset.dtd">
<html xmlns="http://www.w3.org/1999/xhtml">
<!-- frames -->
<head>
<title>Frameset Design</title>
</head>
<frameset rows="30,3,*,5">
<frame name="topnav" src="top_nav.html" marginwidth="0"
marginheight="0" scrolling="no" frameborder="0" noresize=
"noresize" />
<frame name="topline" src="topline.html" marginwidth="0"
marginheight="0" scrolling="no" frameborder="0" noresize=
"noresize" />
<frame name="main" src="main.html" marginwidth="0" marginheight=
"0" scrolling="auto" frameborder="0" noresize="noresize" />
<frame name="bottom" src="bottom.html" marginwidth="0"
marginheight="0" scrolling="no" frameborder="0" noresize=
"noresize" />
<noframes>
<body>
<p>Welcome to the online portfolio of the illustration,
cartooning, and painting of Joe Forkan. This site is
predominantly visual and requires frames.</p>

<p>Visitors without graphic or frames support can email Joe
Forkan for more information at <a href=
"mailto:joe@joeforkan.com">joe@joeforkan.com</a></p>

<p>Thank you for visiting!</p>
</body>
</noframes>
</frameset>
</html>
```

Fixed and Dynamic Frame Design

Frames, as with tables, can be Fixed (see Figure 9.10), or allowed to stretch dynamically to fit a specific resolution or screen size. Similarly, you can combine the techniques to achieve a combination of Fixed and dynamic frame design.

Figure 9.10
Remember that fixing frame widths becomes more important as you add more than two frame columns or rows. Fixing the frames helps secure each frame in place.

To make frames dynamic, use percentages rather than numeric values when you're creating your rows or columns:

```
<frameset rows="50%,25%,25%">
<frame src="red.html" noresize="noresize" scrolling="no" />
<frame src="black.html" noresize="noresize" scrolling="no" />
<frame src="yellow.html" noresize="noresize" scrolling="no" />
</frameset>
```

Note that I've split the browser area into three sections (see Figure 9.11). You can split the area into as many sections as you like, actually; however, the concern is to always add up to 100%. This way, when you resize the browser (see Figure 9.12), the frames will dynamically adjust.

To make a portion of a frame Fixed and another dynamic, you use the * (asterisk symbol) in place of a numeric value or percentage. This symbol simply means that the browser should evaluate what space is available and flex to accommodate that space:

```
<frameset rows="*,90, 90">
<frame src="red.html" noresize="noresize" scrolling="no" />
<frame src="black.html" noresize="noresize" scrolling="no" />
<frame src="yellow.html" noresize="noresize" scrolling="no" />

</frameset>
```

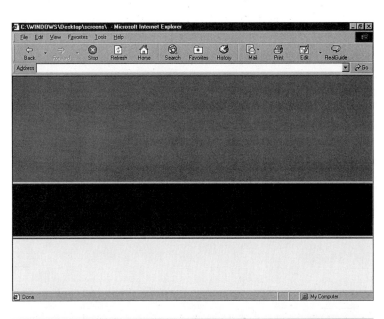

Figure 9.11
Dynamic frames adjust to the available screen space of the browser, making the design more compatible across a variety of environments.

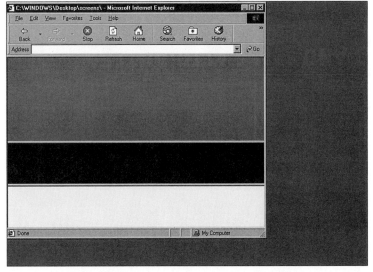

Figure 9.12
Dynamic frames adjust to the browser or resolution size.

Figure 9.13 shows the results full-frame. In Figure 9.14, I've once again collapsed the browser. Note that the top row stays Fixed at 250 pixels, but the bottom row is dynamic.

Figure 9.13
Combination of Fixed and dynamic frames. The top row is Fixed at 90 pixels; the bottom is dynamic.

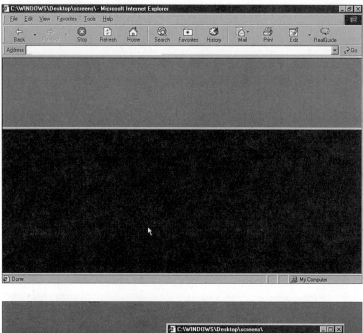

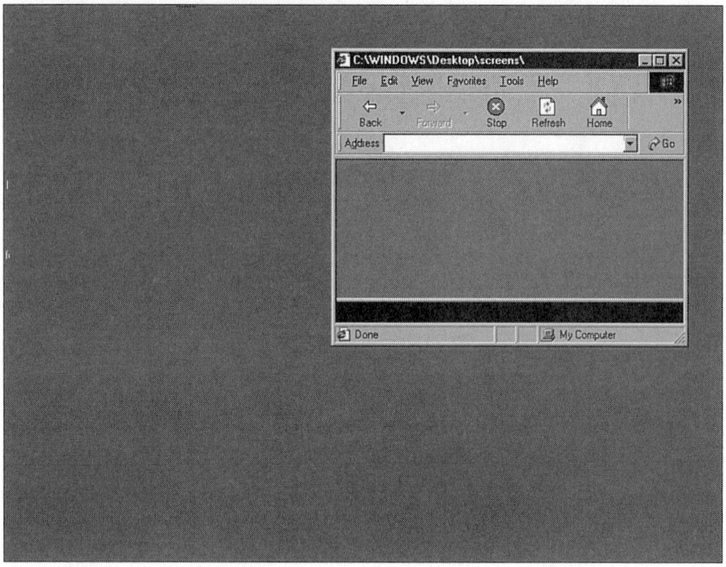

Figure 9.14
After I resized the browser, the dynamic portion collapsed but the top, Fixed row, remained intact.

Combining Rows and Columns

There are instances in frame-based layouts where you'll want to reserve two or more static sections with some in rows and some in columns. A good example of this is when you'd like your navigation to appear in one static portion of the page, and headers, footers, or ads in another static portion. Perhaps your navigation runs along the left, and your ad runs along the top, with your content in the right bottom section.

To accomplish this, a combination of rows and columns is used in a frameset nest (see Listing 9.5).

Listing 9.5 Combining Rows and Columns

```
<!DOCTYPE html PUBLIC "-//W3C//DTD XHTML 1.0
Frameset//EN"
"http://www.w3.org/TR/xhtml1/DTD/xhtml1-frameset.dtd">
<html xmlns="http://www.w3.org/1999/xhtml">
<frameset rows="100, *">
<frame src="top.html" />
    <frameset cols="200, *">
    <frame src="nav.html" />
    <frame src="main.html" />
    </frameset>
</frameset>
</html>
```

<!--
Frame design is most elegant when borders are turned off and the use of graphics and layout within the framed pages is maximized. More important, however, frame design should never be frivolous. You should always use frames for a good reason, such as when you want static navigation, banner, or branding areas, or you are using borderless frames for Fixed layout.
-->

<!--Caution
Be absolutely sure you close each nest with the closing </frameset> element or your browser may not render the nested frames properly.
-->

WORKING WITH INLINE FRAMES (I-FRAMES)

Originally introduced by Internet Explorer 3.0, I-Frames—*inline,* or *floating* frames—were officially adopted in HTML 4.0. This is good news because they're very effective when put to appropriate use. The bad news, however, is that they aren't supported by Netscape 4.61 and many other browsers. Netscape 6.0+ does have inline frame support.

I-Frames work a bit differently from standard frames. First, you don't create a separate frameset for the frame. You place the I-Frame information directly inline in any HTML or XHTML page.

Here's a snippet of I-Frame syntax:

```
<iframe width="350" height="200" src="text.html">

</iframe>
```

This syntax looks a bit like an image or `object` tag in action, and in fact, it works in a similar way, too, with the width and height defined in the tags. As with standard frames, you can add scrolling and border attributes:

```
<iframe width="350" height="200" src="text.html" scrolling="no"
frameborder="0">

</iframe>
```

You can align and space inline frames just as you would an image:

```
<iframe width="350" height="200" src="text.html" scrolling="no"
frameborder="0" align="right" hspace="10" vspace="10">

</iframe>
```

Figure 9.15 shows a page using an I-Frame.

<!--
Inline frames support the name attribute, as well as magic target names.
-->

Figure 9.15
Inline frames can be placed any-where on a page. Unlike stan-dard frames, they do not require a frameset, but as with standard frames, I-Frames do require an additional resource such as an HTML or XHTML page to work.

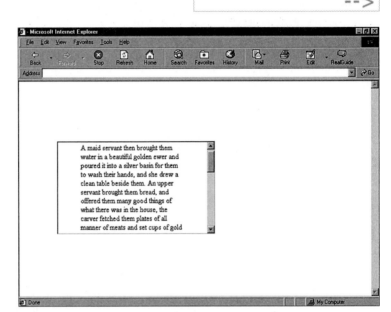

THE NOFRAMES ELEMENT AND ACCESSIBILITY

One of the most important considerations when designing with frames is, as mentioned earlier, ensuring that individuals who cannot use frames, such as the blind or mobility impaired (who, if using mouth sticks or pointers, have additional woes trying to navigate framed pages), can still have access to important information on a Web site.

The Internet, with its vast wealth of information and communications opportunities, has been empowering for a wide variety of individuals with different needs and circumstances world-over.

Sadly, the graphically rich environment of the Web is at best cumbersome and at worst inaccessible to people who use screen readers, special access tools, or who are accessing sites at slower speeds than those to which we are accustomed.

<!--
It's important to point out that tables also are problematic in terms of accessibility, but slightly less so. Line-based browsers can read tables fairly well, assuming they are authored properly. Graphical browsers used with screen readers often do not perceive table columns as separate entities and therefore will read right across columns. However, frames, without the noframes element in use, are inaccessible in either case.
-->

Keeping to the current trends *and* incorporating no-frame and text access addresses cross-browser issues by enabling not only those who *require* text access, but those who prefer it as well.

One of the ways to achieve this in a framed site is by employing the noframes element. This is placed in the *frameset*. Critical information can then be provided at the same URL as the frameset page, and an entirely accessible site can be formed by using the same pages as the framed site. See Listing 9.4 for a sample of frame markup that includes full use of the noframes tag, and follow the steps in the section below to create accessible frames.

Building Accessible Framed Pages

Using the noframes element, as described earlier in the chapter, the following steps show you how to build accessible framed pages:

1. Create a frameset in your editor:

```
<!DOCTYPE html PUBLIC "-//W3C//DTD XHTML 1.0 Frameset//EN"
"http://www.w3.org/TR/xhtml1/DTD/xhtml1-frameset.dtd">
<html xmlns="http://www.w3.org/1999/xhtml">
<head>
<title>Frame with noframes Element</title>
</head>
<frameset cols="240,* ">
<frame src="menu.html" marginheight="5" marginwidth="5" noresize="noresize"
scrolling="auto" />
<frame src="main.html" name="right" marginheight="9" marginwidth="9"
noresize="noresize" scrolling="auto" />
</frameset>
</html>
```

2. Add the <noframes> tag and its companion </noframes> in the following fashion:

```
<!DOCTYPE html PUBLIC "-//W3C//DTD XHTML 1.0 Frameset//EN"
"http://www.w3.org/TR/xhtml1/DTD/xhtml1-frameset.dtd">
<html xmlns="http://www.w3.org/1999/xhtml">
<head>
<title>Frames with NOFRAMES Element</title>
</head>
<frameset cols="240,*">
<frame src="menu.html" marginheight="5" marginwidth="5" noresize="noresize"
scrolling="auto" />
<frame src="main.html" name="right" marginheight="9" marginwidth="9"
noresize="noresize" scrolling="auto" />
<noframes>
</noframes>
</frameset>
</html>
```

3. Now add all the HTML syntax necessary to create a fully functional page within the
   `<noframes>` tag:

```
<!DOCTYPE html PUBLIC "-//W3C//DTD XHTML 1.0 Frameset//EN"
"http://www.w3.org/TR/xhtml1/DTD/xhtml1-frameset.dtd">
<html xmlns="http://www.w3.org/1999/xhtml">
<head>
<title>Frames with NOFRAMES Element</title>
</head>
<frameset cols="240,*">
<frame src="menu.html" marginheight="5" marginwidth="5" noresize="noresize"
scrolling="auto" />
<frame src="main.html" name="right" marginheight="9" marginwidth="9"
noresize="noresize" scrolling="auto" />
<noframes>
<body>
<p>Welcome. We're happy to provide this non-frames access to our
Web site. If you prefer to view our site using frames, please
upgrade your browser to a recent one that fully supports frames.
Otherwise, please visit our <a href="index_noframes.html">
non-framed</a> version of this site.</p>
</body>
</noframes>

</frameset>
</html>
```

4. Save the page. You've now made the page completely
   accessible to non-frame browsers.

The results of this exercise will be a framed site accessible to text-based line browsers such as Lynx, or voice
browsing software used by people with visual impairments.

<!--
Because you can format an entire
document within the noframes
element, consider using the index
page as the Welcome page to
your site. From there, link to internal pages that are external to the
frame design.
-->

CASE BY CASE: SPECIAL ISSUES WITH FRAMES

Many people like to link to sites and load the external site into their framed site. Can you do
this? Technically speaking, yes. Legally speaking? Questionable. People have argued over this
and in general agree that it's a bad practice.

What's more, it doesn't make experienced Web visitors very happy—when I get to a site I
want to experience *that* site, not a hybrid. Newcomers to the Web might be completely confused by this action as well.

When this confusion occurs, it raises several legal issues, including:

* Copyright infringement

* Passing off

- Defamation

- Trademark infringement

The controversy came to the forefront of the media when a company known as Totalnews appeared on the Web scene in 1996. Their site developers used frame technology, where one frame displayed icons of other, well-known news sources such as CNN, MSNBC, and so forth.

When a user selected the link to CNN, the content was then loaded into one of Totalnews' frames. This practice resulted in a complaint in federal court, describing that the practice allegedly violated various state and federal laws with the U.S.

A lawsuit filed in February of 1997 consisted of five counts as follows:

- Misappropriation

- Unfair competition

- Federal trademark dilution

- Trademark infringement

- Copyright infringement

The lawsuit was settled when Totalnews agreed to cease the practice of using frames in this way.

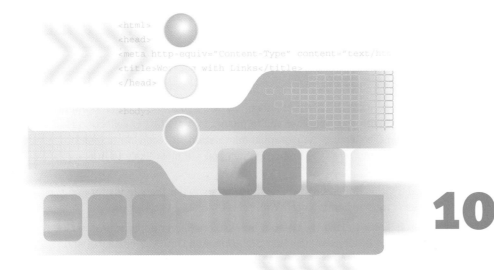

10

BUILDING FORMS

IN THIS CHAPTER

About Forms   248

Using Proper Form Syntax   248

Building a Form   253

Case by Case: Method, Action, and Hidden Fields   270

ABOUT FORMS

Forms are one of the oldest and most flexible methods of allowing your site visitors to interact with your site, and ultimately, with you. Whether you're providing a method of collecting feedback for the site's improvement, collecting demographic information, or receiving orders for products on your site, forms are the interface through which you are most likely to interact with your audience.

Unlike more static methods, forms depend upon a relationship between the site visitor and the page you create *as well as* scripts residing on the Web server.

Typically, this relationship is helped along by a server application. Server applications can be any number of technologies and interfaces, including CGI (Common Gateway Interface) and Perl scripts, Microsoft technologies such as ASP or ASP.NET, Java Server Pages (JSP), PHP, or Macromedia ColdFusion. These applications act as the conduit through which the information passes, and hands off the information server-side for processing.

Forms can encompass a wide range of functions, including the simple gathering of a user's name, address, and contact information which is then sent to an e-mail address, to the creation of games based on user input.

In this chapter, I'm going to focus specifically on how to create a standard form interface—how to prepare it for processing, create input fields, and control the behavior of various form elements.

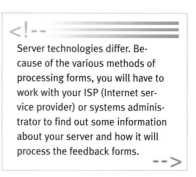

Server technologies differ. Because of the various methods of processing forms, you will have to work with your ISP (Internet service provider) or systems administrator to find out some information about your server and how it will process the feedback forms.

USING PROPER FORM SYNTAX

Forms employ some unique elements and attributes to enable diverse input options to be displayed and made functional by the form. These elements are interpreted and displayed as *controls* and I'll be showing you how to make the most out of setting up and using your form controls.

An important thing to remember is that there are several syntactical differences in the way HTML and XHTML forms are written. Specifically, in HTML there is a method referred to as *attribute minimization* in which you can write certain attributes using the attribute's name only. Form syntax provides two clear examples of this in the `checked` and `selected` attributes, which take no value in HTML:

```
<input type="checkbox" checked>
```

However, attribute minimization is not allowed in XML, and therefore it's not allowed in XHTML either. In XHTML, an attribute must take a value, so you'll use the attribute name as the attribute value:

```
<input type="checkbox" checked="checked" />
```

Attribute minimization is a fairly uncommon occurrence in HTML, you've rarely if ever used it. But, it's critical to remember that XHTML demands well-formed markup and as such, you must accommodate these concerns when writing XHTML rather than HTML documents.

Form Elements and Attributes

There are numerous key form elements and associated attributes that you'll need to know to create forms:

- **form**—The foundational element of all forms, `form` is a container element. The element accepts a variety of attributes. The two most critical are `action`, which combines with a URL to the form processor, and `method`, which takes the value of `get` or `post` depending upon the way the form technology is set up.

- **input**—The input element is responsible for managing the input attributes that will be added to the element. These attributes dictate the type of form control to be displayed. Note that `input` is an empty element, and therefore must terminate in XHTML as `<input />`. Commonly used attributes for the `input` element are as follows:

  type—This specifies the type of control being called upon. See the "Controls" section for details.

  name—The `name` attribute names the control.

  value—Value describes the input control, determining the value for input, labels for buttons, and the value to be sent back in the event that a checkbox or radio button is checked The use of `value` is optional with all controls except for `radio` or `checkbox`.

  size—The width of the input control in pixels. Sometimes the number of characters determines the size of the control, as is the case with the `text` and `password` controls. Size is considered a presentational attribute, so in strict HTML and XHTML documents, you'll want to use style sheets instead of the `size` attribute.

  maxlength—The maximum numbers of input characters allowed in an input control.

  checked—This option pre-selects a given radio button or checkbox within a form. Note that the attribute name is minimized (stands alone) in HTML, but must be written as an attribute name *and* value in order to conform to the rules of XHTML.

  src—Allows you to determine the location of an image to be used for graphical button elements within the form.

  alt—Specifies alternative text for graphical buttons.

- **textarea**—This element creates a text input area. The attributes it accepts are `name` (see above), `rows="x"` where *x* defines the numbers of lines in the box, and `cols="x"`, where *x* specifies the width of the box.

- **select**—The `select` element creates a menu. You can add the `multiple` attribute if you'd like to have a site visitor be able to choose more than one option in the list menu.

<!--
Rows and columns in a text area do not constrain the amount of data allowed. For example, if I have a text area that is 40 columns wide and 20 rows high, I can type into that box continuously. Scrollbars will become available to help me work within the box most effectively. In fact, there's no way to limit the maximum character length in a text area except using JavaScript, which is unreliable.
-->

- **option**—This element defines each individual list item within a menu. Both the opening and closing tags are required. Note that the end tag in HTML 4.0 was *optional* with the option element, but is necessary in XHTML because the element is a non-empty element. It contains the text to display in each list item and the value to be submitted if the item is selected.

Controls

Controls define the kind of input option that will appear onscreen. Controls are produced in HTML and XHTML syntactically an attribute *value* and are placed along with the name attribute within an input element string. This in turn alerts the browser to display the desired control.

The controls available include

- **text**—Creates an input text box that consists of a single line. Width of the box is controlled by the size attribute.

- **password**—Exactly like text, except the characters input by the site visitor will reflect back as asterisks. No additional security is added by using this option, it's merely a display feature.

- **checkbox**—Creates a box that can be checked. You can have multiple checkboxes in a selection, and all of them may be checked if applicable.

- **radio**—This creates a radio button. You can have as many radio buttons as you want in a given subject area, but only one may be selected.

- **submit**—This control creates the familiar "Submit" button, which appears as a raised button with a push-button look in visual browsers. The label on the control can be customized using the value attribute.

- **reset**—The same in appearance and customization features as submit, this control will return the form to the original values it had when loaded. This could be a completely clear form, or if the form was prepopulated with information, using reset will return the form to those values.

- **file**—This creates a file selection control. The site visitor can then upload a file from the local hard drive to the server.

- **hidden**—Hidden controls are those that don't render in the browser. They are used to insert information for the recipient of the form data (see "Case by Case" later in this chapter). For example, this can be used to send additional information to a form processing script, such as script version information, saving information from a prior form, and so on. However, "hidden" in this context only means that the information is not rendered. It is still viewable in the source.

- **image**—Allows for the insertion of a custom image. This gives the designer the ability to use a graphic for submit and reset instead of the default option.

- **button**—Creates a push button. These must be associated with a script in order to work, because there is no built-in action for them.

> `<!--`
> There is also a button element, which can be used to create graphical options for Submit with a slightly different interpretation. It creates a visible button and allows for the insertion of an image and descriptive content. This approach is used less than the standard input plus the button value for the type attribute.
> `-->`

Other Elements Used with Forms

There are several other elements that have been used or can be used when building forms:

- **label**—The label element is used to provide hooks for information to be attached to a given control. Using the for attribute, you can then associate the label attribute with the form control being defined. The for control is associated with the control in question using the id attribute and the name provided for the for attribute (see Listing 10.1).

- **isindex**—Used for creating single-line text input control, this element has been deprecated in favor of using the input element to create text controls.

- **fieldset**—This element allows you to group related controls and labels. This adds context to like sections of information, as well as providing tabbing navigation via the tabindex attribute for a variety of user agents, helping to facilitate forms accessibility (see Listing 10.2).

- **legend**—Using legend, you can give your fieldset a caption. This again is used to enhance accessibility.

Listing 10.1   Using the Label Attribute

```
<form action="..." method="post">
<label for="name">Name:</label>
<input type="text" name="customer_name" id="customer">
<label for="dob">Date of Birth</label>
<input type="text" name="date_of_birth" id="dob">
</form>
```

Listing 10.2   Using fieldset and legend

```
<!DOCTYPE html PUBLIC "-//W3C//DTD XHTML 1.0 Strict//EN"
    "http://www.w3.org/TR/xhtml1/DTD/xhtml1-strict.dtd">

<html xmlns="http://www.w3.org/1999/xhtml">
<head>
```

Listing 10.2   Continued

```
     <title>Using Fieldset and Legend</title>
</head>

<body>

<form method="post" action="http:::://www.myserver.com/apps/cgi-bin/mailscript">
 <fieldset>
 <legend>Contact Information</legend>
<p>Please provide your contact information:</p>
<p> Last Name: <input name="last_name" type="text" tabindex="1" /></p>
<p>First Name: <input name="first_name" type="text" tabindex="2" /></p>
<p>Address: <input name="address" type="text" tabindex="3" /></p>
 </fieldset>

<fieldset>
<legend>Favorite Newspapers</legend>
<p><input name="new_york_times" type="checkbox" value="NYT" tabindex="4" /> New York
Times</p>
<p><input name="new_Orleans_picayune" type="checkbox" value="NOP" tabindex="5" /> New
Orleans Picayune </p>
<p><input name="usa_today" type="checkbox" value="USA" tabindex="6" /> USA Today</p>
 </fieldset>
</form>
</body>
</html>
```

Figure 10.1 shows the results. Please note how the browser renders a distinguishing line around each fieldset.

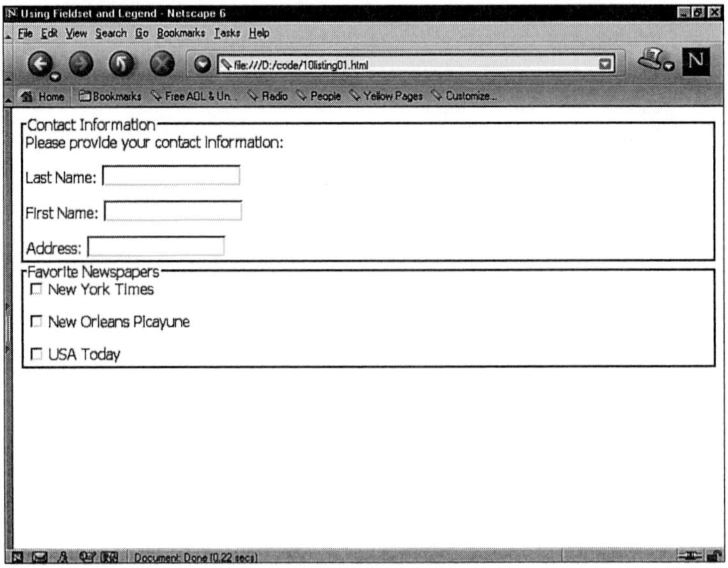

Figure 10.1
Notice the use of `tabindex` to identify the numeric order in which tabbed navigation should occur.

BUILDING A FORM

The exercises in the following sections will each focus on the design of a form. I'll first review the foundational elements of the form. Each subsequent section will then examine how a specific control can be used to enhance or customize the form to your design needs. In these examples, I'm using XHTML 1.0 Transitional to show you how form syntax is presented in XHTML.

A form can begin anywhere within the body of your document. You'll use the `<form>` tag and its companion closing tag `</form>` to indicate the beginning and end of the document.

<!--
Tab order is dictated by the value of the `tabindex` attribute. In Listing 10.1, the tab order is sequential from input to input. However, you can change tab order to any pattern you require simply by changing the value. So if I want a person using tabbed navigation to fill in the first input on the page third, I'd simply make the first input's `tabindex` value "3".
-->

1. Open a template that you've created, or an existing page where you'd like to introduce a form.

```
<!DOCTYPE html PUBLIC "-//W3C//DTD XHTML 1.0 Transitional//EN"
    "http://www.w3.org/TR/xhtml1/DTD/xhtml1-transitional.dtd">

<html>
<head>
<title>Building Forms</title>
</head>

<body>



</body>
</html>
```

2. Add the `form` tag and its companion closing tag. Make sure to leave several spaces in between so you can effectively add form elements to come.

```
<!DOCTYPE html PUBLIC "-//W3C//DTD XHTML 1.0 Transitional//EN"
    "http://www.w3.org/TR/xhtml1/DTD/xhtml1-transitional.dtd">

<html>
<head>
<title>Building Forms</title>
</head>

<body>

<form>

</form>

</body>
</html>
```

3. To set up the way in which your form sends information to the server, you'll need to add the `method` attribute and an appropriate value. Values are `get` and `post`.

```
<!DOCTYPE html PUBLIC "-//W3C//DTD XHTML 1.0 Transitional//EN"
    "http://www.w3.org/TR/xhtml1/DTD/xhtml1-transitional.dtd">

<html>
<head>
<title>Building Forms</title>
</head>

<body>

<form method="post">

</form>

</body>
</html>
```

4. Naturally, you'll want to ensure that the data you send goes to the correct place for processing. To do this, you'll use the `action` attribute, combined with the path to the script on the server that will help perform the action.

```
<!DOCTYPE html PUBLIC "-//W3C//DTD XHTML 1.0 Transitional//EN"
    "http://www.w3.org/TR/xhtml1/DTD/xhtml1-transitional.dtd">

<html>
<head>
<title>Building Forms</title>
</head>

<body>

<form method="post" action="http:://www.myserver.com/apps/cgi-bin/mailscript">

</form>

</body>
</html>
```

Adding a Text Field

At this point, you'll want to begin adding areas where people can input data in to the form. One of the most common input areas is known as a *text field* (also referred to as a *text box*). You will use text fields for information that is entered on a single line, such as a name, address, phone number, and e-mail address.

<!--
Check with your ISP for both the method of preference (get or post) and the location and name of the script available. This will help you properly fill out your method and action attributes. There are numerous reasons why you will use GET versus POST, including security and limitations on how the transfer of data is handled.
-->

You'll set up the text field by using the input element and the type attribute. Fields are defined by the type attribute's value. There are also a number of additional attributes and values you'll want to add to your text field, including name, size, and the maximum amount of characters the box will allow.

1. Within the form, add the input tag, type attribute, and text value.

```
<form method="post" action="/cgi-bin/mailscript">

<input type="text" />

</form>
```

2. Add the descriptive text that will appear on the page, and give the field a name.

```
<form method="post" action="/cgi-bin/mailscript">

First Name: <input type="text" name="firstname" />

</form>
```

3. You can set the size (width) of the text field by using the size attribute and a numeric value.

```
<form method="post" action="/cgi-bin/mailscript">

First Name: <input type="text" name="firstname" size="25" />

</form>
```

4. Text fields can receive more or fewer characters than their visual size. For example, if I set the size of the field to be 25, I can still allow the page visitor to input 0 or 250 characters if I so choose.

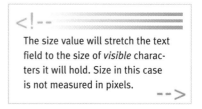

The size value will stretch the text field to the size of *visible* characters it will hold. Size in this case is not measured in pixels.

```
<form method="post" action="/cgi-bin/
mailscript">

First Name: <input type="text" name="firstname" size="25" maxlength="0" />

</form>
```

5. Continue adding as many text fields as your form requires, modifying the attributes to your needs and tastes.

```
<form method="post" action="/cgi-bin/mailscript">

First Name: <input type="text" name="firstname" size="25" maxlength="0" />
<br />
```

```
Last Name: <input type="text" name="lastname" size="25" maxlength="0" />
<br />

Email: <input type="text" name="email" size="25" maxlength="0" />

</form>
```

In this case, I've added line breaks between the lines, formatting the form's input areas using breaks as I go.

Check your work against Figure 10.2, which displays the information you've added to the form so far.

<!--
If you'd like to use the text fields for passwords and have the "*" character echoed rather than the actual characters, use "password" in place of "text" for the type attribute.
-->

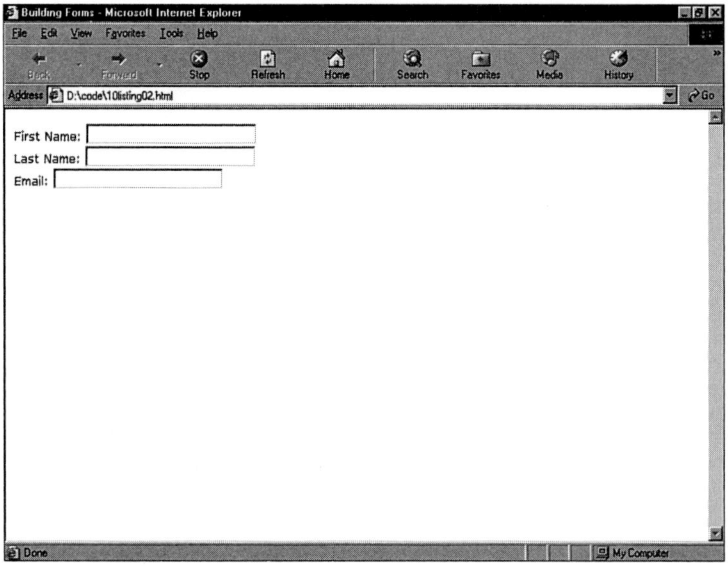

Figure 10.2
This unfinished form contains three text fields, complete with name and maxlength attributes.

Making a Checkbox

Text fields are powerful, but sometimes you'll want to offer a group of choices for your site visitor to make. Checkboxes will help you set up these choices and then take the user's selection to the server for processing. You'll use the `<input />` tag as before, but this time your `type` value will be `checkbox`.

1. Add the first choice, which in this case is a favorite activity.

```
<form method="post" action="/cgi-bin/mailscript">

First Name: <input type="text" name="firstname" size="25" maxlength="0" />
<br />
```

```
Last Name: <input type="text" name="lastname" size="25" maxlength="0" />
<br />

Email: <input type="text" name="email" size="25" maxlength="0" />

<p>Favorite Activity:</p>

<p>Reading</p>

</form>
```

2. Type in the input tag and the proper attributes.

```
<form method="post" action="/cgi-bin/mailscript">

First Name: <input type="text" name="firstname" size="25" maxlength="0" />
<br />

Last Name: <input type="text" name="lastname" size="25" maxlength="0" />
<br />

Email: <input type="text" name="email" size="25" maxlength="0" />

<p>Favorite Activity:</p>

<p>Reading <input type="checkbox" name="reading" /></p>

</form>
```

3. Continue to add checkboxes as necessary. You can even preselect a checkbox for your site visitor by using the `checked` attribute.

```
<form method="post" action="/cgi-bin/mailscript">

First Name: <input type="text" name="firstname" size="25" maxlength="0" />
<br />

Last Name: <input type="text" name="lastname" size="25" maxlength="0" />
<br />

Email: <input type="text" name="email" size="25" maxlength="0" />

<p>Favorite Activity:</p>

<p>Reading <input type="checkbox" name="reading" /></p>


<p>Listening to music <input type="checkbox" name="music" checked="checked" /></p>

</form>
```

In Figure 10.3, I've taken a screen shot of the form as it is so far, with text boxes and check-boxes.

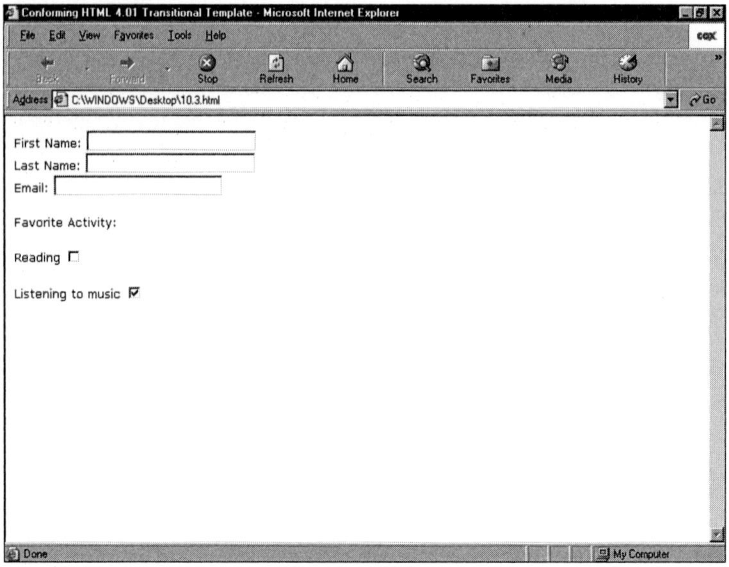

Figure 10.3
The form now contains check-boxes. When the form is com-pleted and activated, site visitors will be able to click the checkbox most appropriate to them.

Adding a Radio Button

As with checkboxes, radio buttons allow you to make a selection. However, radio buttons will not allow more than one choice if they have the same name.

1. Add the selection options required in your form. I'm using gender in my example.

```
<form method="post" action="/
cgi-bin/mailscript">

First Name: <input type="text" name="firstname"
size="25" maxlength="0" />
<br />

Last Name: <input type="text" name="lastname" size="25" maxlength="0" />
<br />

Email: <input type="text" name="email" size="25" maxlength="0" />

<p>Favorite Activity:</p>
```

<!--
Checkboxes also allow you to set up choices where an individual can check more than one box. For example, if you were setting up a selection of choices of films seen in the past six months, you'd want your site visitors to check as many as apply to them.
-->

```
<p>Reading <input type="checkbox" name="reading" /></p>


<p>Listening to music <input type="checkbox" name="music" checked="checked"
/></p>

<p>Gender:</p>

<p>Male</p>

<p>Female</p>

<p>Prefer not to say</p>

</form>
```

2. Using the `input` tag, add the type attribute, radio value, and attributes of your choice.

```
<form method="post" action="/cgi-bin/mailscript">

First Name: <input type="text" name="firstname" size="25" maxlength="0" />
<br />

Last Name: <input type="text" name="lastname" size="25" maxlength="0" />
<br />

Email: <input type="text" name="email" size="25" maxlength="0" />

<p>Favorite Activity:</p>

<p>Reading <input type="checkbox" name="reading" /></p>


<p>Listening to music <input type="checkbox" name="music" checked="checked"
/></p>


<p>Gender:</p>

<p><input type="radio" name="gender" value="male" /> Male<br />
<input type="radio" name="gender" value="female" checked="checked"  />Female<br
/>
<input type="radio" name="gender " value="undisclosed" />Prefer not to say</p>

</form>
```

The form now contains both radio and checkbox options (see Figure 10.4).

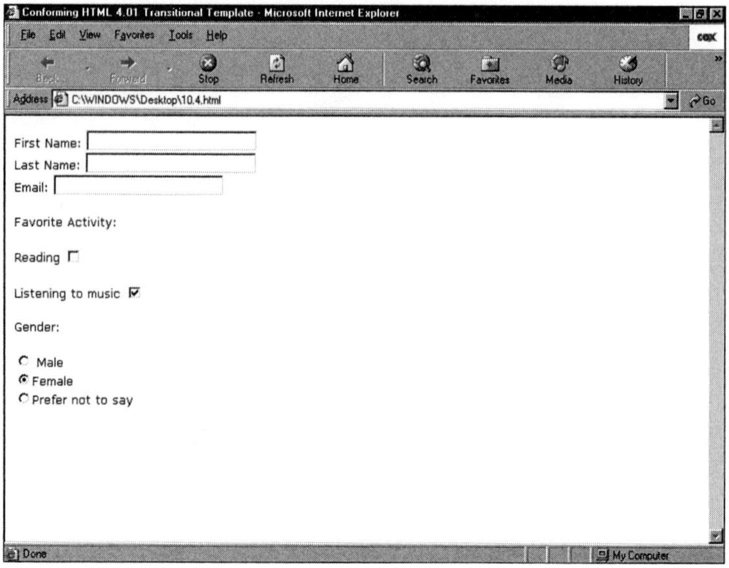

Figure 10.4
With both checkboxes and radio buttons, the form is beginning to become both more technically and visually complex.

Making a Menu List

Another powerful method of offering form selections for your visitors is a menu with options. These are especially helpful when you have numerous items in a list, such as a list of states or countries.

Drop-down lists are created by using the `select` element and individual `option` tags. There are several attributes that can modify both, which will be explained as we step through the process.

1. In the area where you'd like to place your drop-down list, input your display text, and the opening and closing `select` tags.

```
<form method="post" action="/cgi-
bin/mailscript">

State:
<select>

</select>

</form>
```

<!--
Radio buttons can also contain the "checked" attribute. After the user clicks another radio button, the previous button will clear and the user's choice will be selected instead. Note also that `checked` is a minimized attribute in HTML but because XHTML does not allow for attribute minimization, the attribute name and value must be described, `checked="checked"`.
-->

2. If you'd like to set the amount of rows to be visible in the menu, you can do so by using the `size` attribute. If you give the numeric value of "4," four items will be shown in the resulting a list box.

```
<form method="post" action="/cgi-bin/mailscript">

State:
<select size="4">


</select>

</form>
```

If you have four items and specify a size of four, the menu will be rendered in most Web browsers as a list box, with all options fully visible on screen.

3. You can also allow for multiple items to be selected. To do this, add the `multiple` attribute. Note that `multiple` is a minimized attribute in HTML, but in XHTML must be treated just as the `checked` attribute is.

```
<form method="post" action="/cgi-bin/mailscript">

State:
<select multiple="multiple">


</select>

</form>
```

4. Now, add the `option` tag and the first option. Here I've added the `value` attribute to the option tag. This sets up the form so the results will display the selected option.

```
<form method="post" action="/cgi-bin/mailscript">

State:
<select size="4" multiple="multiple">
<option value="arizona">Arizona</option>

</select>

</form>
```

5. Continue adding options as necessary. You can use the `selected` attribute for the option that you'd like to have set as the default menu selection. The `selected` attribute is a minimized attribute in HTML, but in XHTML must be written out as below:

```
<form method="post" action="/cgi-bin/mailscript">

State:
```

```
<select>
<option value="arizona">Arizona</option>
<option value="california">California</option>
<option value="nevada" selected="selected">Nevada</option>
</select>

</form>
```

Figure 10.5 shows two menu variations. The first is the drop-down menu (you'd need to click on the arrow to see the other options), the second is a list menu (all of the options are visible). The list variation was created by ensuring that the number of list items and the size of the menu are equal.

Figure 10.5

Two variations on a menu theme: The left menu is a drop-down menu, and the right menu is a list menu. The markup difference is in the attributes used to describe the select and option elements.

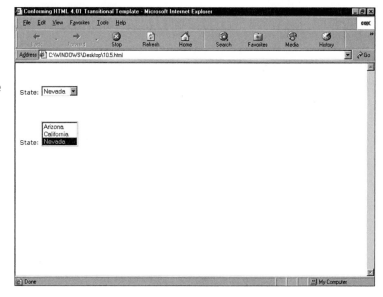

Using optgroup **with Menu Selections**

The optgroup element allows authors to organize their menu items. This is helpful in several situations:

- When the menu list is especially long, optgroup can help by reducing the length of the list.

- Ensures ease of use for those individuals with disabilities as it provides additional context for any related information, making the form easier to understand

To use optgroup, you begin with the select element, and then subcategorize where necessary, as shown in Listing 10.3.

> `<!--`
> As with the checked and multiple attributes, selected was minimized in HTML. In XHTML, you must write out the full attribute value pair, selected="selected" or your document will not be well-formed.
> `-->`

Listing 10.3   Using optgroup for Logical Option Grouping

```
<select name="dailymenu">
    <option selected label="menu" value="menu">none</option>
    <optgroup label="breakfast">
      <option label="omelet" value="omelet">Cheese Omelet</option>
      <option label="bacon" value="bacon">Side of Bacon</option>
      <option label="coffee" value="coffee">Pot of Coffee</option>
    </optgroup>
    <optgroup label="lunch">
      <option label="salad" value="salad">Chef Salad</option>
      <option label="soup" value="soup">Soup of the Day</option>
    </optgroup>
    <optgroup label="dinner">
      <option label="fish" value="fish">Fresh Salmon</option>
      <option label="chicken" value="chicken">Stuffed
      Chicken Breast</option>
      <option label="steak" value="steak">Filet Mignon
      </option>
    </optgroup>
</select>
```

Figure 10.6 shows how the optgroup element breaks down menu selections.

<!--
It's important to point out that optgroup is new as of HTML 4.0, and therefore won't be supported by older browsers. What's more, the display shown in Figure 10.6 is only one way a browser might display this markup. Test it out in a number of browsers to see the results.
-->

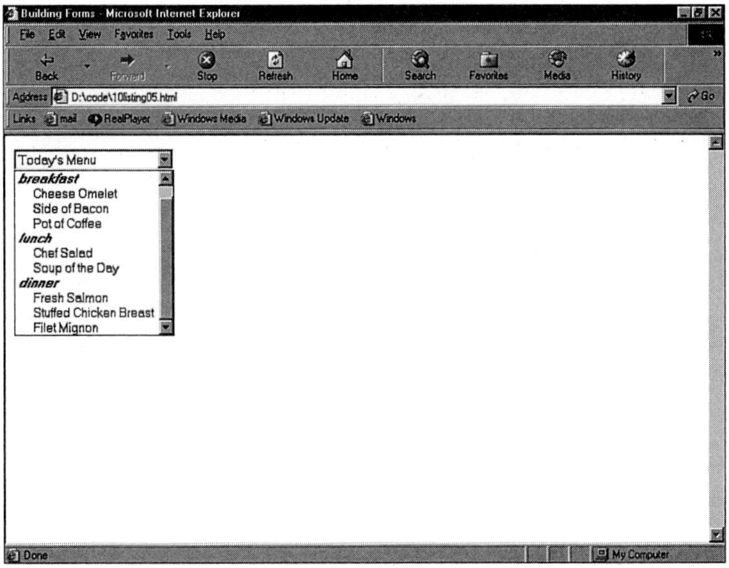

Figure 10.6
The sub-categories in this menu were created using the optgroup element.

Creating a Text Area

Text fields are handy for one-line sections of input. However, if you want to give your visitors more room to add their own feedback and thoughts, you can accommodate them by providing them with a text area.

Text areas are created using the `<textarea>` tag, and its companion closing `</textarea>` tag. You'll also add attributes including `rows` and `cols` to create one visible cell. The rows will determine how many rows of characters the text area can manage, and the cols will determine how wide the resulting box will be.

1. In the portion of the form where you'd like to add the text area, type in the display text and opening and closing `textarea` element tags.

```
<form method="post" action="/cgi-bin/mailscript">

First Name: <input type="text" name="firstname" size="25" maxlength="0" />
<br />

Last Name: <input type="text" name="lastname" size="25" maxlength="0" />
<br />

Email: <input type="text" name="email" size="25" maxlength="0" />


<p>Favorite Activity:</p>

<p>Reading <input type="checkbox" name="reading" /></p>


<p>Listening to music <input type="checkbox" name="music" checked="checked"
/></p>


<p>Gender:</p>

<p><input type="radio" name="gender" value="male" /> Male<br />
<input type="radio" name="gender" value="female" checked="checked"  />Female<br
/>
<input type="radio" name="gender " value="undisclosed" />Prefer not to say</p>

<p>State:</p>
<select>
<option value="arizona">Arizona</option>
<option value="california">California</option>
<option value="nevada" selected="selected">Nevada</option>
</select>

<p>Do you have additional concerns?</p>
```

```
<textarea>

</textarea>

</form>
```

2. To set the rows (how high the text area will be), add the row with a numeric value.

```
<form method="post" action="/cgi-bin/mailscript">

First Name: <input type="text" name="firstname" size="25" maxlength="0" />
<br />

Last Name: <input type="text" name="lastname" size="25" maxlength="0" />
<br />

Email: <input type="text" name="email" size="25" maxlength="0" />


<p>Favorite Activity:</p>

<p>Reading <input type="checkbox" name="reading" /></p>


<p>Listening to music <input type="checkbox" name="music" checked="checked"
/></p>


<p>Gender:</p>

<p><input type="radio" name="gender" value="male" /> Male<br />
<input type="radio" name="gender" value="female" checked="checked" />Female<br
/>
<input type="radio" name="gender " value="undisclosed" />Prefer not to say</p>

<p>State:</p>
<select>
<option value="arizona">Arizona</option>
<option value="california">California</option>
<option value="nevada" selected="selected">Nevada</option>
</select>

<p>Do you have additional concerns?</p>

<textarea rows="5">

</textarea>

</form>
```

3. To set the width in characters, use the cols attribute with a numeric value.

```
<form method="post" action="/cgi-bin/mailscript">

First Name: <input type="text" name="firstname" size="25" maxlength="0" />
<br />

Last Name: <input type="text" name="lastname" size="25" maxlength="0" />
<br />

Email: <input type="text" name="email" size="25" maxlength="0" />


<p>Favorite Activity:</p>

<p>Reading <input type="checkbox" name="reading" /></p>


<p>Listening to music <input type="checkbox" name="music" checked="checked"
/></p>


<p>Gender:</p>

<p><input type="radio" name="gender" value="male" /> Male<br />
<input type="radio" name="gender" value="female" checked="checked"  />Female<br
/>
<input type="radio" name="gender " value="undisclosed" />Prefer not to say</p>
<p>State:</p>
<select>
<option value="arizona">Arizona</option>
<option value="california">California</option>
<option value="nevada" selected="selected">Nevada</option>
</select>

<p>Do you have additional concerns?</p>

<textarea rows="5" cols="25">

</textarea>

</form>
```

Figure 10.7 shows the form.

More About Text Areas

Setting the name attribute to the text-area element will help ensure that the form submission works as expected. So, you can add the name attribute using a descriptive value as follows:

```
<textarea rows="5" cols="25" name="feedback">

</textarea>
```

Note also that if you place content within the text area, that content will display in the text area. Some Web authors use this method as a means to cue the site visitor to type something into the area, such as:

```
<textarea rows="5" cols="25" name="feedback">

Type Comments Here!

</textarea>
```

Providing Reset and Submit Buttons

With the bulk of your form designed, it's time to offer the ability of the page visitor to submit the form, or reset the form data and start over.

1. To add a submit button, use the input tag with the type attribute. The value "submit" will create the button.

```
<form method="post" action="/cgi-bin/mailscript">

<input type="submit" />

</form>
```

2. You can customize what the submit button says by adding a value.

```
<form method="post" action="/cgi-bin/mailscript">

<input type="submit" value="send it!" />

</form>
```

3. The reset button works using the same logic. Simply use the `reset` value in the `type` attribute to create a reset button. If you'd like to customize how the button is labeled, use the `value` attribute.

```
<form method="post" action="/cgi-bin/mailscript">

<input type="submit" value="send it!" />

<input type="reset" value="do it over" />

</form>
```

Figure 10.8 shows the results of our completed form, which is fully designed but will not function until properly connected with the server-side script.

Submit: Mac Versus Windows

On the Macintosh platform, the Submit button is usually (but not always) found on the right, near the bottom of any system dialog box, so Mac users have different expectations than do Windows or Unix users with regard to what each button does.

There's much controversy regarding which to use and where, and it always divides along Mac versus Win lines; Windows users want it on the left or earlier in the tab order, whereas Mac users will try to click the rightmost/bottommost button to submit, regardless of whether it's actually the submit button.

This can cause huge problems if you change the labels and then make the reset button rightmost/bottommost; especially in long forms, where users will lose everything they've typed.

If you'd like to use an image to customize your Submit and Reset buttons, you can do so by first creating the image, and then following one of two options.

The first option is to insert the image directly into the Submit or Reset control, as follows:

```
<input type="image" src="images/go.gif" width="50"
height="25" alt="go"
value="submit" />
```

<!--
If you want your forms to be very neat and organized, use style sheets to lay out the form's input controls. Many authors use tables for forms layout, which is allowed but not encouraged in contemporary authoring practices.
-->

This will result in a seamless look, with the button fitting into the design of the page.

The second option is to use the `button` element, which is a non-empty element, containing some text description. This sets the image *into* the submit button:

```
<button name="submit" value="submit" type="submit">
Send <img src="images/go.gif" width="50" height="25"  alt="go"></button>
```

As mentioned in the note early on in this chapter, the second option is rarely used. Figure 10.9 shows an example of both styles.

⇨ *For more information on working with images, **see** "Adding Images," **p. 275**, Chapter 11.*

<!--**Caution**

Although you can use an image for `submit`, this technique will unfortunately not work for `reset` unless you add JavaScript to make it do so.

-->

<!--**Caution**

You cannot use an image map with the button element. The image must be static.

-->

Figure 10.9
Customized Submit buttons. The
top example uses an image for a
seamless look, whereas the bottom uses the button element to
insert the image into the standard
form interface submit button.

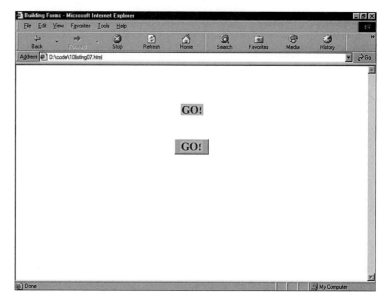

CASE BY CASE: METHOD, ACTION, AND HIDDEN FIELDS

A lot of confusion comes about for certain authors who are trying to create forms. Largely, this confusion is due to the fact that while you'll be authoring your forms using HTML or XHTML, the processing of those forms depends on server-side scripts, whose methods might vary greatly.

In this section, I'd like to look more closely at method, action, and hidden fields so you can gain a little more insight into how these things work, at least from a meta-perspective. Having this insight can empower you to speak with your ISP about your specific needs.

The following syntax is taken from the contact form on one of my Web sites. I want to have you look closely at two issues. First, let's examine the form's method and action attributes.

```
<form method="post" action="http://opus1.com/htbin/mailto">
```

As you can see, "post" is the recommended method for my ISP's mailto script. Also, the action points to a specific script on the server. The first part of the URL is the ISP's address (opus1.com), the directory htbin is the location of the script, and mailto is the name of the script. This simple syntax is what connects my form to the server's script so any information entered into the form can be processed and sent to me via e-mail.

The second issue is the use of *hidden fields*. These are input entries that use the type="hidden" attribute and value to invisibly include them within the form. The first entry in my form is as follows:

```
<input name="from" type="hidden" value="site visitor" />
```

This information will insert the words "site visitor" into the from line of any e-mail processed by the form. This next example is similar:

```
<input name="subject" type="hidden" value="Feedback:
Molly's Web Site" />
```

In this case, the subject line of the e-mail from this form will clearly note that it is in regards to Feedback: Molly's Web Site.

<!--Caution

Remember, this information is based on the way that my ISP's email script works, not necessarily the way your ISP's scripts will work.

-->

Hidden fields are very powerful. In this example, I can use this information to create filters within my e-mail program so all incoming mail from this form goes directly to a specific box. This helps me stay organized and discriminate between information coming from my personal site versus any other Web sites I have.

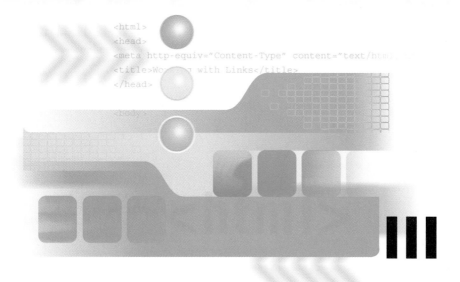

IMAGES, MULTIMEDIA, AND EMBEDDED OBJECTS

11 Adding Images   **275**

12 Working with Multimedia   **301**

13 Embedding Objects   **325**

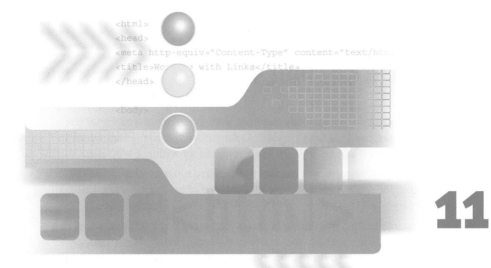

```
<html>
<head>
<meta http-equiv="Content-Type" content="text/htm
<title>Wo      g with Links</title>
</head>

<body>
```

11

ADDING IMAGES

IN THIS CHAPTER

Working with Web Graphics   276

Graphic Optimization   280

Adding Images to Web Pages   282

Presentational Attributes in Transitional HTML and XHTML   285

Floating Images   292

Aligning Multiple Images   295

Linking Images   299

Case by Case: Exhibiting Your Work   299

WORKING WITH WEB GRAPHICS

Whereas most of this book is dedicated to assisting professional Web designers and developers achieve sophisticated markup skills, occasionally the lines between markup and visual concerns intersect. In this chapter, the goal is to provide all readers with a basis from which to create great Web graphics as well as implement them appropriately within a Web page.

To that end, the first part of this chapter will discuss the primary types of Web graphics, and the second part of the chapter will dig more deeply into the use of markup to place and manage Web graphics on a page.

The main goal when it comes to Web graphics is to keep your sizes small without sacrificing quality. Regardless of the media with which you're working—audio, video, animations, or graphics—ensuring that your files are light and your design still bright is a sure way to successful site design.

Understanding the available file formats used in Web graphic design is essential. Whereas many readers of this book will already know the information in this section, there are other readers who will require the review. After all, one of the most daunting aspects of constructing a Web site is the need for high-quality, well-designed graphics. The designer's responsibility isn't just limited to creating visual appeal: This is the Web, not clay or canvas, and working in a digital medium brings with it uniquely digital responsibilities.

Web graphic design is rife with myths about what Web graphics are and how they are created. On one hand, the core ideas are incredibly simple; on the other hand, many try working with graphics and just can't seem to get the process right.

Whether you're a well-studied, professional designer or are just learning how to create Web graphics, there is no reason your Web site should be any less visually strong and technically well-optimized than any other professional site.

File optimization—the act of working with files to achieve both quality appearance and acceptable download times—begins with an understanding of the file formats that are available. I'll begin by describing file formats available on the Web, and which options are available to you within those formats. I'll also recommend a range of tools that might be suitable for your Web graphic design needs.

Graphics Interchange Format (GIF)

GIF is a file format that uses a type of compression known as *lossless*. Compression is based on complicated, mathematical algorithms that work, in a nutshell, by figuring out how much of the image uses the same color information. At that point, the compression algorithm saves those sections by using a numeric pattern.

GIFs are limited to a total of 256 colors so that the resulting numeric pattern is very specific. So, if you have 15 shades of blue within your graphic saved in GIF format, that translates to 15 individual patterns. If there are more than 256 patterns, the compression algorithm has to decide what to leave out. It does this by limiting those blues to just a few or even just one total blue color.

Because of this process, your neon blue might end up being interpreted when saved to GIF format as a sky blue, and so forth. This is where experience and a skilled hand comes into play—knowing when and how to deal with color and file types will enable you to gain control over colors within your graphics.

GIFs are one of the longest supported graphic file types on the Web, and they are extremely useful for a number of graphic file applications.

There are several important guidelines to determine if you should choose the GIF compression method for a specific graphic:

- **Line-drawn images**—Any graphic that uses few lines, especially horizontal lines, is a good choice for GIF compression.

- **Images with few, flat colors**—With only a few colors and no light sources or gradations in that color, there's not going to be a lot of competition for those 256 colors in the compression method.

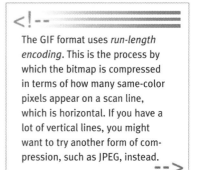

The GIF format uses *run-length encoding*. This is the process by which the bitmap is compressed in terms of how many same-color pixels appear on a scan line, which is horizontal. If you have a lot of vertical lines, you might want to try another form of compression, such as JPEG, instead.

The image in Figure 11.1 shows a line-drawn cartoon. This image is an excellent choice for GIF compression. Figure 11.2 uses black, white, and two shades of gray—and all the colors are flat, with no light sources or gradations. This makes the Any image perfect for GIF compression.

Figure 11.1
A line-drawn cartoon image by cartoonist Joseph Forkan is a perfect choice for GIF format.

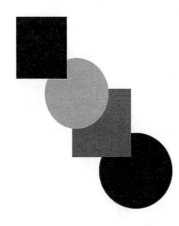

Figure 11.2
This image, using only black, white, and two shades of flat gray, is also a good choice for the GIF format.

Joint Photographic Experts Group (JPEG)

A group of photographic experts went to work on compression methods that would allow high quality compression while retaining millions of colors. The results are what we know today as *Joint Photographic Experts Group* (JPEG, also written JPG).

JPEG defines a *lossy* compression method. The algorithm focuses on removing data that is felt to be unimportant, instead of first mapping out areas of information that should be saved.

```
<!--
```
The appropriate file extension, or suffix, for JPEG files is .jpg. There's a lot of confusion around this issue, because of the JPEG name. Always follow standard file-naming conventions and use the .jpg suffix for all JPEG images.
```
-->
```

The JPEG method does this by dividing the image data into rectangular sections before applying the algorithm. On the one hand, this method gives you a lot of control in terms of how much information you're going to toss away; but, at high compression ratios, you can end up with a blocky, blotchy, blurry result.

These blocky sections are known as *artifacts*. Artifacts occur when you've over-compressed an image. Working with JPEGs, just as with GIFs, requires a bit of skill and a fine hand to achieve the best results.

Because the JPEG format was specifically designed to manage files with a lot of color, there are certain types of images that best lend themselves to JPEG compression. The following list is a helpful guide to use when determining if JPEG is the best format for your image:

- Images with a lot of colors, such as with color photographs

- Graphics using gradient fills (see Figure 11.3)

- Graphics using light sources

- Grayscale images that have subtle gradations

- Photographs with much gradation, such as skies, sunsets, and oceans (see Figure 11.4)

Figure 11.3
Gradient fills are appropriate for JPEG format. The reason has to do with JPEGs ability to compress files without reducing the number of colors. If you tried this with a GIF, you'd lose the smooth transitions from one hue to the next.

Figure 11.4
Sunset pictures, particularly when in full color, contain a lot of gradation and will normally be processed by using JPEG format.

Portable Network Graphics (PNG)

The PNG graphics format was defined during 1995–1996 to overcome copyright issues surrounding the GIF format at the time. Like GIF, PNG is a lossless format. However, aside from the goal of creating a public domain image format, the developers also attempted to improve on the standard set by GIF. This has resulted in a number of enhanced features:

- Indexed color, grayscale and true-color image support

- From 1 to 16 bit depth per pixel

- True color via 8–16 bits per sample, allowing for 24–48 bits per pixel

- Alpha channel for transparency

- Better interlacing, resulting in faster display of a usable image

One of the big features in which PNG outperforms GIF is the ability to store images that include an alpha-channel. This enables proper antialiasing; eliminates the jagged edges around fonts and images, and allows for the creation of transparent images.

Although the current versions of the major Web browsers and some of the graphic image packages have added support for this new format, GIF and JPEG are still far more common.

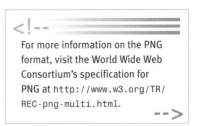

For more information on the PNG format, visit the World Wide Web Consortium's specification for PNG at http://www.w3.org/TR/REC-png-multi.html.

GRAPHIC OPTIMIZATION

Optimizing graphics is the technique by which a Web graphic designer reduces the file size of a graphic for acceptable download times, while maintaining the highest quality image he or she can produce.

The first step in optimization is to determine which file format is appropriate for the file. Using the general guidelines given earlier for GIF and JPEG formats will help you to achieve that crucial first step.

Interestingly, the guidelines discussed within this chapter for GIFs and JPEGs are not always accurate. Take for example a black-and-white photograph, or even a color photograph, with very little color information, light source, and gradients. With this example, it's going to take a little experimentation to determine which file type will help you achieve the smallest file size while retaining the most important information.

There's no cut-and-dry answer to this except through trial-and-error or by using one of the many graphic optimization tools available. Many tools, such as the Save for Web feature in Adobe Photoshop (Figure 11.5) version 5.5 and higher, have preview windows in which you can determine numerous combinations of an image's features to see which combination will result in the highest quality and lowest weight possible.

Figure 11.5
Working with the Save for Web interface in Adobe Photoshop helps you achieve well-optimized Web graphics.

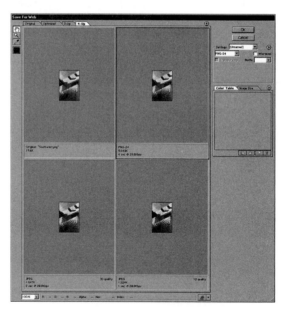

Popular Tools for Graphic Optimization

You can optimize graphics with a wide range of tools from shareware to expensive. For more information about Web graphic design collections, visit the following popular vendors:

Adobe Systems makes high-end graphic design products for the professional; see http://www.adobe.com/.

Macromedia has powerful Web production software; http://www.macromedia.com/.

Corel products, such as CorelDraw and PhotoPaint, have a range of tools geared toward the Web graphic designer; http://www.corel.com/.

Jasc makes a very popular program, Paint Shop Pro, that appeals to folks looking for a low-cost but still powerful imaging option; http://www.jasc.com/.

Ulead offers a number of compression and design products for Windows users; http://www.ulead.com/.

The GNU Image Manipulation Program (GIMP) is a popular open source graphic design and image manipulation program; http://www.gimp.org.

Here's a list of helpful terms (see Table 11.1) that you'll find in use in many popular graphic optimization programs.

Table 11.1   Terms and Definitions for Web Graphic Optimization

Term	Definition
Color palette	A color palette is a table of specified colors. There are several types of color palettes. These are numerically determined sets of colors within the graphic program that enable the designer to make specific choices regarding how an image is processed. Examples include RGB (red, green, blue: used in screen color) and CMYK (cyan, magenta, yellow, black) used for print.
Adaptive palette	This palette allows you to make adaptations to a given image, including controlling color, depth, and dithering.
Indexed color	A software program such as Photoshop will take an image file and count its colors. If there are more than 256 colors in an image, indexing will reduce the image's palette to 256 colors—making it ready for GIF production. At that point, you can use the adaptive palette to further control aspects of the palette.
Exact palette	You'll see this appear when an image already has fewer than 256 colors—because the colors fit within the indexing limits, the specific number of colors used will appear. You can then determine whether to keep this number, or reduce it further with the adaptive palette.
Bit depth	Also known as *color depth*, this is the amount of total bit data that will be saved with your image. The optimization of images into the GIF format depends on your ability to control bit depth.
Number of colors	In GIF optimization, there can be as few as 2 colors or as many as 256 colors. Limiting the number of colors is how you reduce the size of a GIF file during the optimization process.

Table 11.1 Continued

Term	Definition
Dithering	The process of interspersing pixels of a given color with pixels of another color in an attempt to trick the eye into seeing a third color.
Maximum, High, Medium, Low	These settings are specific to JPEG optimization and refer to how much information is removed during the lossy compression process. Depending on your platform and graphic applications program, you might see percentage sliders that quantify the JPEGs quality.

ADDING IMAGES TO WEB PAGES

Adding images to a Web page is the first step in moving away from simple document formatting and into the world of design. Images add identity, color, shape, and presence. The proper use of images is a powerful and important aspect of the Web, yet one that eludes many Webmasters.

There are several ways to position an image on a page. You can use transitional tags and attribute combinations that are in widespread conventional use; you can use tables; and you can choose to use CSS style sheet positioning which of course is the encouraged practice in contemporary markup.

For a discussion on how to accomplish similar results with style sheets, **see** "CSS in Depth: Applying Style and Positioning," **p. 369,** Chapter 15.

The img Element

You'll begin by using the img element to place images on a page. The img element is an empty element. In HTML, you will write it as follows:

```
<img>
```

In XHTML, you'll adhere to the practice of terminating the element, as follows:

```
<img />
```

So to display an image, the img requires a source that is called with the src attribute. The source directs the HTML to get the image in question:

```
<img src="guitar.gif" />
```

This markup alone is sufficient to add an image to your page, provided the image resides in the same location as the referring document. However, you should add the alt attribute for accessibility purposes:

```
<img src="guitar.gif" alt="molly's guitar" />
```

We'll discuss more about the alt attribute and additional img attributes throughout the chapter.

Typically, developers place images in a specific directory below the bottom directory. This directory is aptly named *images* or *graphics*, depending on your preference. If your image resides in such a subdirectory and your document is in the root directory, you'll need to address the source appropriately, by using relative linking:

```
<img src="images/guitar.gif alt="molly's guitar" />
```

➪ *To gain insight into how to manage relative links,* **see** *"Adding Hypertext and Independent Links,"* **p. 155,** *Chapter 7.*

Images always go within the body section of a document. Listing 11.1 shows a transitional XHTML document with a graphic.

Listing 11.1   Adding an Image to an HTML Page

```
<!DOCTYPE html PUBLIC "-//W3C//DTD XHTML 1.0 Transitional
//EN"
"http://www.w3.org/TR/xhtml1/DTD/xhtml1-transitional.dtd">
<html xmlns="http://www.w3.org/1999/xhtml">
<head>
<title>Adding an Image to an XHTML Page</title>
</head>
<body>
<img src="guitar.gif" alt="molly's guitar" />
</body>
</html>
```

Figure 11.6 shows the results. You'll notice that the image appears on the left of the page. It has no special position, other than that determined according to the browser's default settings.

<!--**Caution**
Many server administrators recommend against the use of relative links. Depending on the configuration of the server on which your site resides, there may be other options for structuring your directories.
-->

<!--**Caution**
Some people will link to an image that resides off their site by using an absolute URL to reach the location of an image. This is not a recommended practice for several reasons. One consideration is that you risk a bad connection and the image might never load any time you go off your own server. Another concern is ownership: If that graphic element isn't yours and you link to it without the owner's express permission, you could be in violation of copyright. The third consideration is that bandwidth costs money, and by using an image on someone else's site, you're essentially stealing from them. Unsuspecting image thieves have often found previously innocuous images replaced by their owners with pornography, annoying animations, and even messages announcing the theft to all of their site's visitors. If you're going to use an image you found somewhere else, make your own local copy.
-->

Figure 11.6
Using the `img` with no presentational attributes. As a result, the
guitar is positioned on the page
to the default left position within
the browser.

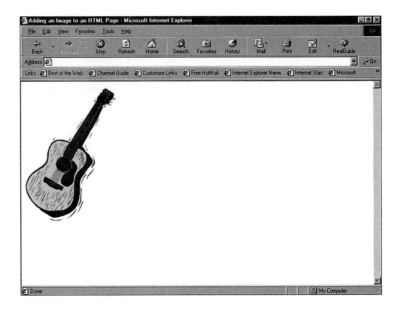

Figure 11.6
Using the `img` with no presentational attributes. As a result, the
guitar is positioned on the page
to the default left position within
the browser.

Image Attributes

A variety of attributes can be added to an `img` tag to control the way a browser manages the
image. These attributes include the following:

- **src="x"**—As mentioned, this is the source attribute, and is used with either an absolute
  or relative URL that points to the location of the image.

- **width="x"**—This allows a browser to predetermine the width, in pixels, that your image
  requires.

- **height="x"**—Along with the `width` attribute, the browser can prepare the necessary
  space for your image in advance. This controls the way your images are loaded on a page.

- **border="x"**—To add or remove a border, use this attribute, where `"x"` is a numeric value.
  Again, although this is useful in transitional documents, the ideals of CSS ask that you
  use a style sheet if you want to modify this attribute.

- **align="x"**—You can align an image horizontally and vertically on a page by using this
  attribute. Alignment is presentational and in strict situations must be relegated to style
  sheets.

- **alt="*description of image*"**—The powerful `alt` attribute allows you to describe the
  image to text-only browsers, tagging the image before it loads onto a page, and allows a
  ToolTip to appear with the description as a mouse passes over the image. You should
  always include the `alt` attribute and a logical value no matter which DTD is being used
  for your document.

- **hspace="x"**—*Horizontal space* is used to add space, with a numeric value, around the
  horizontal axis of the image.

- **vspace="x"**—*Vertical space* controls the spacing of the image along the vertical axis. Both `hspace` and `vspace` are considered presentational and should be controlled with style sheets in strict documents.

PRESENTATIONAL ATTRIBUTES IN TRANSITIONAL HTML AND XHTML

Although in the contemporary practice of authoring strict HTML 4.0+, XHTML 1.0, and XHTML 1.1 documents the separation of presentation and document formatting is required, in transitional HTML and XHTML documents there are a variety of attributes which are acceptable to use.

The sections to follow take a more in-depth look at these attributes and how they work.

> What if your image can't be described by a short alt description? Rather than add an excessively long alt attribute, use the `longdesc` attribute instead. A value for `longdesc` is not a text description at all but rather a URL that points to a Web page where the image is described in further detail. Here's an example:
>
> ```
> <img src="guitar.
> gif longdesc="image1_
> description.html" />
> ```

width **and** height

Including `width` and `height` in your img tag in a transitional XHTML document is a common practice. Many feel this information assists certain browsers manage the image data throughout the page, with the end result in the page being rendered more promptly.

A main concern is using inaccurate `width` and `height` values for any image except for single pixel GIFs. Standard image values must *always* be exact, or you'll cause your browser to abnormally stretch or minimize an image.

You might be thinking: "But Molly, I've seen people create thumbnails of large images by making the `width` and `height` values smaller. I thought that was a clever idea!" It's clever, and it's very problematic.

This is because your large image *still* has to download to the browser. Let's say you have 5 images of 50KB each, and you resize them on your page by using the `width` and `height` attributes. You haven't resized the image by doing this—only the *appearance* of the image. Your browser must retrieve all 200KB of those images even though it will display them as being smaller than their actual dimension. The weight remains the same—and your site visitors might not remain on your site waiting for the downloads.

Following the rules, this markup shows my guitar image with the proper width and height:

```
<img src="images/guitar.gif" alt="molly's guitar"
width="200" height="284" />
```

To find the exact `width` and `height` of your image, look at it in your imaging program. The image size is available there (see Figure 11.7).

> Another way to determine the `width` and `height` of your image is to open the graphic in Netscape Navigator or IE 5.x on the Mac. The image's dimensions will be noted along the top bar of the interface.

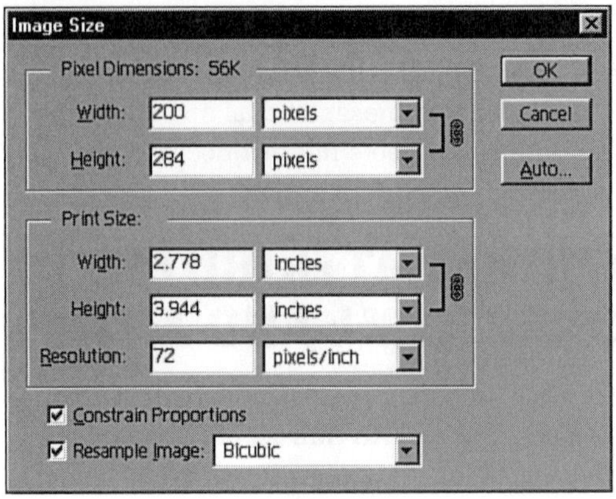

Figure 11.7
Image `width` and `height` information can be found by checking the image in a graphics software program, such as what is seen here in Adobe Photoshop.

Image Borders

Borders around images were once the default of most Web browsers, particularly if the image was linked. The default now is to have no border.

If you prefer that your graphics always appear without borders, it's wise to include a value of `"0"` with the `border` attribute in transitional documents:

```
<img src="images/guitar.gif" width="200" height="284" border="0" alt="molly's guitar" />
```

This syntax protects your image from appearing with borders in older browsers or browsers that still use a border as its default if no border information is included in the img string.

If you really want a border around an image, you can set it by setting a numeric value in the `border` attribute:

```
<img src="images/guitar.gif" width="200" height="284" border="4" alt="molly's guitar" />
```

Figure 11.8 shows the image with the border.

Borders pick up the color of your text if they are not linked. If they are linked, borders appear in the browser defaults of blue for an unvisited link and purple for a visited link; the user's custom colors; or the `link`, `alink`, and `vlink` colors that you personally specify within the body tag or style sheet.

> `<!--`
> When writing strict documents, you'll want to be sure to turn off borders using style.
> `-->`

Alignment

There are a number of ways to align your image. On the horizon line, the default is left for a solitary object. You also can set the alignment to a value of `left` (this is important when wrapping text, discussed in the "Floating Images" section later in this chapter) or a value of `right`.

```
<img src="images/guitar.gif" alt="molly's Guitar" width="200"

height="284" border="0" align="right" />
```

In Figure 11.9, you can see that this alignment value has caused the image to appear along the right of the browser.

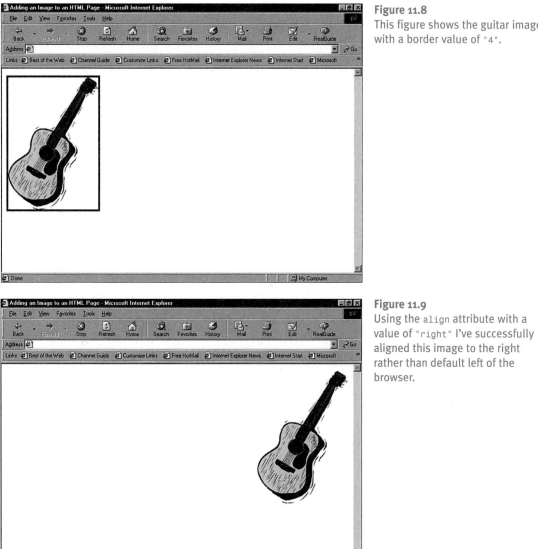

Although the horizontal alignment values of left and right are likely to be used most frequently, you also can use the align attribute to align an image vertically:

```
<img src="little_guitar.gif" alt="little guitar" align="top" />
```

A range of conventional values for this include the following:

- **top**—This puts the image along the topmost part of the horizon line.

- **middle**—The image is aligned with the middle or baseline of the horizon.

- **bottom**—With this value, the image is aligned with the bottom of the horizon line.

I've set up an example of each of these, which you can see in Figure 11.10.

Figure 11.10
Vertical alignment of an image. Note the way the image relates to the text. In this case, I've added a border so you can see the alignment clearly.

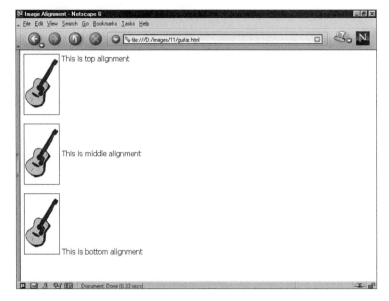

There are several other browser-specific, conventional alignment values, rather than standard methods. I've included the following here for your information:

- **texttop**—Aligns with the top of highest text or image on that line.

- **absmiddle**—Aligns with the *absolute* middle of the highest surrounding text or image.

- **baseline**—Aligns to the bottom.

- **absbottom**—Aligns the bottom of the image with the lowest image or text along the line.

These are sometimes helpful, but because they are browser-specific, they are not necessarily going to be in compliance with a given W3C-recommended practice. In fact, vertical alignment of images by using the align attribute is reserved for instances when the need for precise alignment is desired. In XHTML 1.0, such alignment is handled with tables in transitional documents and style sheets in transitional and strict documents.

<!--Caution
The align attribute was deprecated in HTML 4.0. It can be used in transitional, but not strict documents.
-->

The alt **Attribute**

This extremely important attribute allows you to write out a description of the image. For example, because my guitar image is actually a drawing rather than a photo, I could describe the image as a "drawing of a guitar" as follows:

```
<img src="images/guitar.gif" width="200" height="284" border="0"
alt="drawing of a guitar" />
```

For those individuals without graphics—whether using text browsers due to blindness, limited Internet resources, or for those individuals who surf the Web with graphics turned off—the alt attribute provides a great way to describe the visual nature of what's going on (see Figure 11.11). You're required to use the alt attribute in all HTML 4.x and XHTML 1.x documents in order to be compliant.

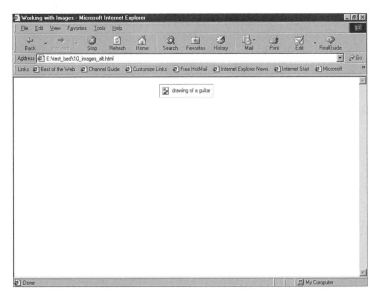

Figure 11.11
The alt description appears when image loading is turned off.

The alt description appears in two other instances. One is as a page is loading graphics. The description shows up before the associated graphic is loaded. This is a helpful way of keeping visitors interested in what's coming. Descriptions defined with this attribute also appear when a mouse passes over a given image (see Figure 11.12).

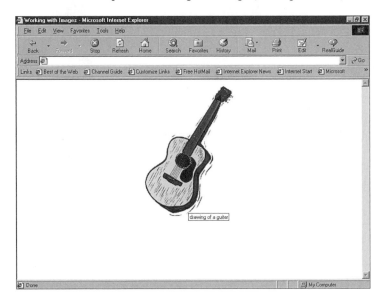

Figure 11.12
The alt description also appears when a mouse passes over the image.

You should use this attribute with an appropriate text value, with one exception: when an image is a single-pixel graphic used for fixing graphic placement. In this case, the alt attribute should be left blank by leaving the attribute in, but placing no value within the quotes:

```
<img src="images/spacer.gif" width="20" height="1"
border="0 alt="" />
```

<!--
Why add an alt attribute with quotes and no value? Well, when you do this, there will be *no demarcation* of the image in a text-based environment. If you don't use this clever technique, [inline] appears where the graphic should be.
-->

Horizontal and Vertical Space

Values for hspace and vspace are numeric. For demonstration purposes, I'm going to use values that are a bit exaggerated for these attributes:

```
<img src="images/guitar.gif" width="200" height="284" border="1" align="right"
alt="drawing of a guitar" hspace="100" />
```

Compare Figure 11.13 and Figure 11.14. In Figure 11.13, I use no horizontal spacing; but in Figure 11.14, I use the horizontal spacing value of "100". I've added a border of "1" to the image so that you can easily see how this puts space between the text and the image.

Figure 11.13
Normal spacing between text and image.

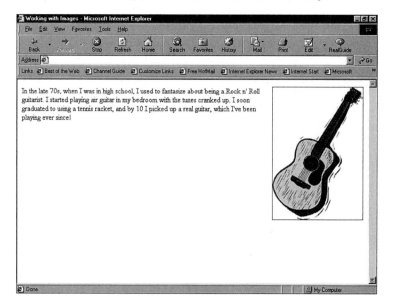

Now compare Figure 11.13 and Figure 11.15, where I've used a vertical spacing of "40". Here's the markup:

```
<img src="images/guitar.gif" width="200" height="284" border="0" align="right"
alt="drawing of a guitar" vspace="40" />
```

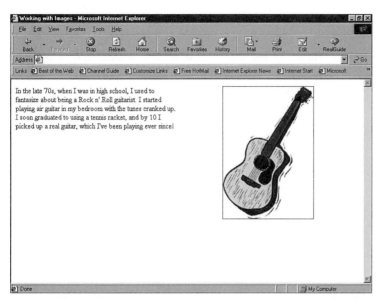

Figure 11.14
Horizontal space added between text and image.

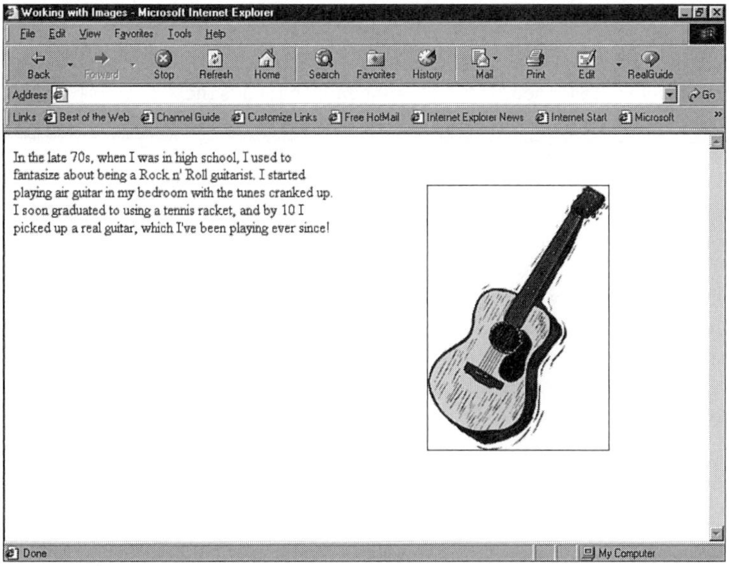

Figure 11.15
In this case, vertical space appears between text and image, providing necessary white space in between. Without that space, the text and image would be too close together, making the text difficult to read and diminishing the unique importance of the image.

Using the hspace and vspace attributes is particularly helpful when wrapping text around images. This is called *dynamic* text wrapping, or *floating* images. You'll learn more about this technique in the next section.

FLOATING IMAGES

Using a combination of attributes within the img tag, you can achieve attractive, dynamic layout of graphics and text. Although tables and style sheets are more sophisticated ways of addressing this matter, it's good to understand the technique.

To float images, you first must align the image. Even if you want to place your image to the left, which is typically the default position, you must use the align attribute to achieve this technique.

Listing 11.2 shows an XHTML page with text and a left-aligned image.

Listing 11.2   Floating Image and Dynamic Text

```
<!DOCTYPE html PUBLIC "-//W3C//DTD XHTML 1.0 Transitional//EN"
"http://www.w3.org/TR/xhtml1/DTD/xhtml1-transitional.dtd">
<html xmlns="http://www.w3.org/1999/xhtml">
<head>
<title>Floating Image and Dynamic Text: Left</title>
</head>
<body>
<img src="images/little_guitar.gif" width="75" height="107" border="0"
align="left" alt="drawing of a guitar" />
In my other life, I'm a guitar player and vocalist. I've been singing since I
was a child, and was formally trained as a vocalist.  spent many years singing
soprano in a variety of school choirs and other music organizations.  My first
instrument was the piano, which I like but never had the discipline to achieve
any level worthy of impressing anyone!  In the late 70s, when I was in high
school, I used to fantasize about being a Rock n' Roll guitarist. I started
playing air guitar in my bedroom with the tunes cranked up.  I soon graduated
to using a tennis racket, and by 10 I picked up a real guitar, which I've been
playing ever since! I've been playing in a duo named  Courage Sisters, with my
music partner, Patti Sundberg, for the last several years. We play a variety of
original, acoustic music typically comprised of two guitars and two voices.
We're especially known for complex harmonies.
</body>
</html>
```

Figure 11.16 shows the left-aligned image and the text that wraps *dynamically* around the graphic.

I also can have my image aligned to the right. Listing 11.3 is the same image and text, but the alignment is now right, with the text wrapping around the image from the left.

<!--
The word *dynamic* is used frequently but often improperly in the Web design field. In the case of text wrapping, dynamic refers to the fact that the text naturally finds its way around the image, taking up whatever available space exists. This is also often referred to as *fluid* or *liquid* design.
-->

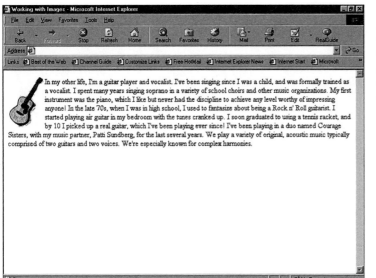

Figure 11.16
A left-aligned image with text wrapping. This dynamic approach to relating text and visual objects creates a natural flow that is both visually appealing and easy on the eyes.

Listing 11.3   Right-Aligned Floating Image and Dynamic Text

```
<!DOCTYPE html PUBLIC "-//W3C//DTD XHTML 1.0 Transitional//EN"
"http://www.w3.org/TR/xhtml1/DTD/xhtml1-transitional.dtd">
<html xmlns="http://www.w3.org/1999/xhtml">
<head>
<title>Floating Image and Dynamic Text: Right</title>
</head>
<body>
<img src="images/little_guitar.gif" width="75" height="107" border="0"
align="right" alt="drawing of a guitar" />
In my other life, I'm a guitar player and vocalist. I've been singing since I
was a child, and was formally trained as a vocalist.  spent many years singing
soprano in a variety of school choirs and other music organizations.  My first
instrument was the piano, which I like but never had the discipline to achieve
any level worthy of impressing anyone!  In the late 70s, when I was in high
school, I used to fantasize about being a Rock n' Roll guitarist. I started
playing air guitar in my bedroom with the tunes cranked up.  I soon graduated
to using a tennis racket, and by 10 I picked up a real guitar, which I've been
playing ever since! I've been playing in a duo named  Courage Sisters, with my
music partner, Patti Sundberg, for the last several years. We play a variety of
original, acoustic music typically comprised of two guitars and two voices.
We're especially known for complex harmonies.
</body>
</html>
```

Figure 11.17 shows the right-aligned image and floating text.

Figure 11.17
Right alignment and text wrap. If you're using a square image with no padding or with a distinct border, be sure to add hspace and vspace.

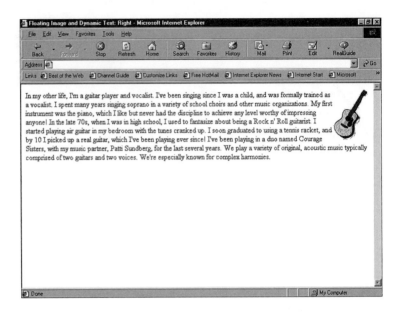

You might notice that the text bumps into the edges of the image a bit. It's slightly less noticeable in this particular instance, because my image is angled and has some whitespace around it. However, if you're using a regular photograph, square image, or image with a border, alignment and text wrapping without the use of hspace and vspace can make a page looked cramped and cluttered (see Figure 11.18).

Figure 11.18
Bordered image and text are too close, cramping the page's style.

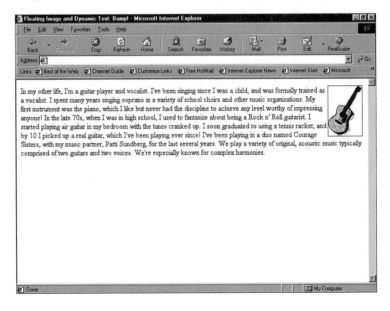

To avoid this problem, add a numeric value of about 5–15 to each of the spacing attributes:

```
<img src="images/little_guitar.gif" width="75"
height="107" border="0"
align="right" alt="drawing of a guitar" hspace="15"
vspace="10" />
```

This adds a nice amount of whitespace (see Figure 11.19), and makes the image and text relationship more harmonious and readable.

⇨ *For more about working with text, **see** "Managing Text and Lists," **p. 111**, Chapter 6.*

<!--
If you're using transitional HTML 4.x or XHTML, and want to put some distance between an aligned graphic and another element, such as another image or text? To break out of the dynamic wrapping, use a br element with the `clear="all"` attribute and value.

```
<img src="guitar.gif" alt=
"molly's guitar" align=
"right">
<br clear="all">
```
-->

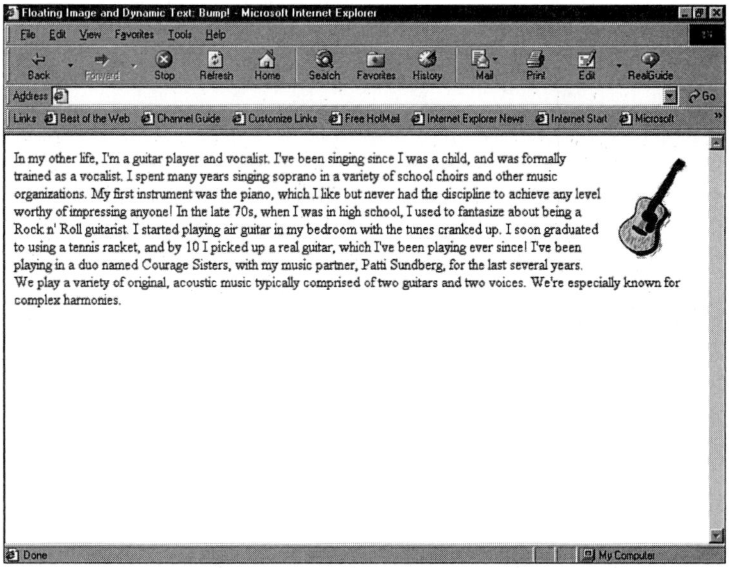

Figure 11.19
More whitespace makes the text readable.

ALIGNING MULTIPLE IMAGES

As Web pages become more complex, you'll want to effectively place images so they look balanced and in proportion to other elements on the page. The example that follows walks you through a page that has a graphic header, an image, and dynamic text:

1. Begin in your editor with a transitional HTML or XHTML template:

```
<!DOCTYPE html PUBLIC "-//W3C//DTD XHTML 1.0 Transitional//EN"
"http://www.w3.org/TR/xhtml1/DTD/xhtml1-transitional.dtd">
<html xmlns="http://www.w3.org/1999/xhtml">
<head>
<title>An Excerpt from Homer's Odyssey</title>
```

```
</head>
<body>

</body>
</html>
```

2. Add the text and page formatting:

```
<!DOCTYPE html PUBLIC "-//W3C//DTD XHTML 1.0 Transitional//EN"
"http://www.w3.org/TR/xhtml1/DTD/xhtml1-transitional.dtd">
<html xmlns="http://www.w3.org/1999/xhtml">
<head>
<title>An Excerpt from Homer's Odyssey</title>
</head>
<body>

<p>A maid servant then brought them water in a beautiful golden ewer and poured it
into a silver basin for them to wash their hands, and she drew a clean table
beside them. An upper servant brought them bread, and offered them many good
things of what there was in the house, the carver fetched them plates of all
manner of meats and set cups of gold by their side, and a man-servant brought
them wine and poured it out for them.</p>

<p>Then the suitors came in and took their places on the benches and seats.
Forthwith men servants poured water over their hands, maids went round with the
bread-baskets, pages filled the mixing-bowls with wine and water, and they laid
their hands upon the good things that were before them.</p>

<p>As soon as they had had enough to eat and drink they wanted music and dancing,
which are the crowning embellishments of a banquet, so a servant brought a lyre
to Phemius, whom they compelled perforce to sing to them. As soon as he touched
his lyre and began to sing Telemachus spoke low to Minerva, with his head close
to hers that no man might hear.</p>

</body>
</html>
```

3. Add the header image, aligned right, with all the appropriate attributes. I used the `<br clear="all" />` trick to break out of the right alignment:

```
<!DOCTYPE html PUBLIC "-//W3C//DTD XHTML 1.0 Transitional//EN"
"http://www.w3.org/TR/xhtml1/DTD/xhtml1-transitional.dtd">
<html xmlns="http://www.w3.org/1999/xhtml">
<head>
<title>An Excerpt from Homer's Odyssey</title>

</head>
<body>
```

```
<img src="images/odyssey_hed.gif" width="350" height="50" border="0"
align="right" alt="an excerpt from homer's odyssey" />
<br clear="all" />

<p>A maid servant then brought them water in a beautiful golden ewer and poured it
into a silver basin for them to wash their hands, and she drew a clean table
beside them. An upper servant brought them bread, and offered them many good
things of what there was in the house, the carver fetched them plates of all
manner of meats and set cups of gold by their side, and a man-servant brought
them wine and poured it out for them.</p>

<p>Then the suitors came in and took their places on the benches and seats.
Forthwith men servants poured water over their hands, maids went round with the
bread-baskets, pages filled the mixing-bowls with wine and water, and they laid
their hands upon the good things that were before them.</p>

<p>As soon as they had had enough to eat and drink they wanted music and dancing,
which are the crowning embellishments of a banquet, so a servant brought a lyre
to Phemius, whom they compelled perforce to sing to them. As soon as he touched
his lyre and began to sing Telemachus spoke low to Minerva, with his head close
to hers that no man might hear.</p>

</body>
</html>
```

4. Add the image you intend to float with all the necessary attributes, including
`<br clear="all" />`, which forces anything that's to come after the image to the next
available line:

```
<!DOCTYPE html PUBLIC "-//W3C//DTD XHTML 1.0 Transitional//EN"
"http://www.w3.org/TR/xhtml1/DTD/xhtml1-transitional.dtd">
<html xmlns="http://www.w3.org/1999/xhtml">
<head>
<title>An Excerpt from Homer's Odyssey</title>

</head>
<body>

<img src="images/odyssey_hed.gif" width="350" height="50" border="0"
align="right" alt="an excerpt from homer's odyssey" />
<br clear="all" />


<p>A maid servant then brought them water in a beautiful golden ewer and poured it
into a silver basin for them to wash their hands, and she drew a clean table
beside them. An upper servant brought them bread, and offered them many good
things of what there was in the house, the carver fetched them plates of all
manner of meats and set cups of gold by their side, and a man-servant brought
them wine and poured it out for them.</p>
```

```
<p><img src="images/schooner2.jpg" width="270" height="140" border="0"
align="right" hspace="5" vspace="5" alt="image of schooner" /></p>

<p>Then the suitors came in and took their places on the benches and seats.
Forthwith men servants poured water over their hands, maids went round with the
bread-baskets, pages filled the mixing-bowls with wine and water, and they laid
their hands upon the good things that were before them.</p>

<p>As soon as they had had enough to eat and drink they wanted music and dancing,
which are the crowning embellishments of a banquet, so a servant brought a lyre
to Phemius, whom they compelled perforce to sing to them. As soon as he touched
his lyre and began to sing Telemachus spoke low to Minerva, with his head close
to hers that no man might hear.</p>

</body>
</html>
```

Figure 11.20 shows the page. Notice how there's plenty of whitespace and balance between the graphics and the text, and the text and images flow naturally along the page.

Figure 11.20
Images and text define the two most critical elements of visual design.

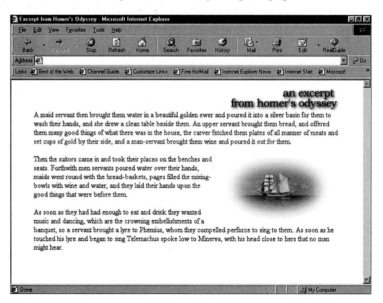

This technique demonstrates not only the appeal images add to a Web page, but the strong relationship that exists between text and images.

LINKING IMAGES

Images, like text, can be linked. Making an image "hot" is a common practice and a foundational part of navigation.

Linking images is easy. All you need to do is surround the image with the standard linking element, the a, or *anchor* element.

⇨ *For more about links,* **see** *"Adding Hypertext and Independent Links," p. 155, Chapter 7.*

The following is a sample linked image:

```
<a href="index.html"><img src="images/home_button.gif"
width="50" height="100"
border="0" alt="follow this link  to go home" /></a>
```

<!--

If you want an image to clearly be noted as a link, you can set the border to a numeric value to show the link border. With the border set to off ("0"), this image will appear seamless with the rest of the page. A smoother, more consistent design is achieved by leaving borders off—my preferred method.

-->

CASE BY CASE: EXHIBITING YOUR WORK

Artistic images on the Web add culture and visual appeal to the slick, information-rich and often commercial focus of today's Web site. Using the Web to display art is a wonderful opportunity to balance the way we use the Web—and to share and promote your artistic works.

In fact, some of the most fascinating visual sites are museums, which have a natural reason to want their Web graphics to be of exceptional quality. Visit the sites recommended below and closely study the use of images. You will also want to view source to see what kind of alignment and other attributes are being used to manipulate the images. Look at any markup problems and make note of both the strengths and weaknesses in the integration of markup with visual design.

The sites to visit are

- Museum of Modern Art, New York, `http://www.moma.org/`. On this site, focus on the excellent quality of the graphic images. Also, the use of thumbnails linking to complete pages with larger images is exceptionally well-handled on this site

- Museum of Modern Art, San Francisco, `http://www.sfmoma.org/`. Like its New York sister, this site offers beautiful visual design. Here, I want you to study the use of vibrant color. Each section of the site uses another color as an area identifier. Note the quality and richness that the site designers have achieved with their graphics no this site

- The Louvre, `http://www.louvre.fr/`. Take a close look at the collections area, where you'll find tables with cell-alignment in use to create balanced visual space between images.

- Guggenheim Museum, `http://www.guggenheim.org/`. The main page of this site is an excellent study in the use of cropping and refined visual effects to achieve a mood.

For more museums, check out the links at the Virtual Library Museums page, `http://vlmp.museouphile.com/`.

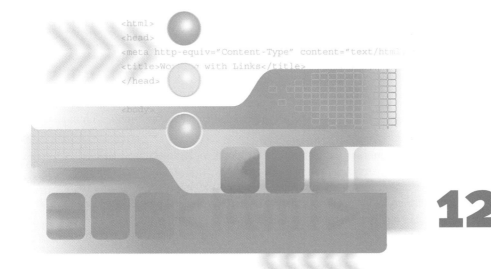

WORKING WITH MULTIMEDIA

IN THIS CHAPTER

Action and Interaction **302**

Audio and Video on the Web **303**

Creating Audio and Video Files **303**

Downloadable Audio and Video File Formats **306**

Adding Audio and Video to a Web Page **308**

Audio and Video Plug-Ins **309**

Streaming Media Concepts **311**

Producing Streaming Media **313**

Incorporating Streaming Media into Your Page **315**

Multimedia Software: Macromedia Director, Shockwave, and Flash **319**

Exploring Flash in Detail **320**

Case by Case: Exploring Streaming Media Options **322**

ACTION AND INTERACTION

Multimedia has been around for a long time and has been used in many circumstances, including corporate and information-based presentations, educational activities, and recreation in the form of video and other games.

It's only natural, then, that businesses, educational institutions, and entertainment-based developers are interested in exploring multimedia options for their Web sites. For this reason, I'm going to spend some time focusing on important tools and techniques that go into the creation and delivery of multimedia via Web documents. In this chapter, I'll provide some markup examples and special concerns, but for those readers interested in getting into serious detail about the markup techniques for embedding objects, applets, and image maps, jump ahead to Chapter 13, "Embedding Objects."

There's a serious caution that must be expressed to Web developers, however, and that is simply the point that multimedia is *not* ideal on most sites. There are certainly many appropriate ways to use multimedia, but using it should be something that is very carefully thought out. Study your audience, know the reason you want to use a given type of media, and think carefully about how to use it in a manner that enhances your user's experience and does not impede it.

As you by now know, a single graphic is best compressed so that it weighs very little to load effectively across browser and platform types, and through a variety of bandwidth situations.

That's just one graphic! Multimedia includes graphics—often many graphics—to create animation and movement, input areas, and responses. And, true to its name, the concept is *multiple*—to have more than one media event occurring in the same environment, meaning the addition of audio and video as well as static graphics and special effects.

How to get all this information compressed and delivered to a Web browser has limited developers to a large degree. Bandwidth is the issue, and although we're certainly seeing more affordable bandwidth options become available in certain parts of the United States, there's an entire world out there with a wide range of special circumstances.

Multimedia specialists such as Macromedia have made some significant advances addressing this concern with their suite of tools; and as the years pass, those tools are more and more closely integrated with one another. That concentration and integration has paid off in the form of some impressive options for multimedia design and delivery over the Web.

Furthermore, changes to hardware and software have been made. The PowerPC and higher-level Macintosh systems have always been graphically oriented, so the addition of multiple media isn't a big step. MMX technology has swept the Windows platform market, with Windows 98, ME, and 2000 offering full support for the technology, which is improving the ease of use of multimedia on the Windows platform.

> `<!--`
>
> MMX (Multimedia Extensions) is a set of 57 new instructions that Intel added to certain processors to speed up and enhance multimedia. This new technology means improved performance for image processing, video, audio, video-conferencing, and similar functions.
>
> `-->`

Improvement in bandwidth and processing power also suggests that multimedia presentations over the Internet, and intranets, may become more effective and ultimately an essential part of the Internet industry as time goes on.

AUDIO AND VIDEO ON THE WEB

Well-managed audio and video can bring your Web pages to life. Poorly managed audio and video can drive your audience away. Who hasn't quickly left a site to escape a droning background sound clip? Who hasn't been excited to see a great video on the Web only to find out that you must commit a good part of an afternoon to downloading it? Audio and video can add a great deal to your site, but it will take some thought and experimentation on your part to make it work for your audience.

If you are interested in venturing into the world of audio and video, there are many factors you must consider. How can you produce high-quality audio and video? How much quality should you sacrifice for efficiency? Should you use downloadable files or streaming technology? Will your audience have the software they need to experience the results of your work? In this section, I'll help you make productive decisions and guide you through methodology that will get you up and running with audio and video. First, we'll look at standard audio and video files, and then we'll look more closely at streaming media.

CREATING AUDIO AND VIDEO FILES

The first step to adding audio and video to your Web site is to create the source files or gather prerecorded source files. It's important to remember that good media content on the Web is the result of good media sampling. If you create a sound clip by taking your tape recorder to a concert and recording your favorite song from the twentieth row, you will have quite a different quality clip than one produced in a studio.

You need a good microphone and good sound editing software if you're recording your own sound sample. For a good video sample, you need a high-quality capture device and encoding software.

Audio Files

Most recording devices create analog recordings. To digitize an analog audio source, the signal must be processed through an analog-to-digital (A/D) converter. Most computers now come equipped with the sound cards that have A/D converters. If your computer has a sound input jack, it already has an A/D converter. If your computer has only a sound output jack or an internal speaker, you probably only have digital-to-analog conversion capabilities. Even if you are recording audio from a digital source, such as a digital audio tape (DAT) or compact disc (CD), some kind of A/D conversion is usually involved, because most computers do not come with digital audio inputs yet.

How Audio Is Digitized

An A/D converter uses a "sample and hold" circuit that records the voltage levels of the input signal at a fixed interval. This interval, or rate, at which the signal is sampled is determined by the A/D converter's "sampling rate." The sampling rate also determines the highest frequency that can be recorded or played back. It is important that the recording be played back at the same sampling rate at which it was recorded. For example, 8KHz is a telephony standard that is emerging as a standard for 8-bit *.au mono files. 44.1KHz is the standard audio CD-ROM sampling rate.

After you create your sound file, you need to edit it with a good sound-editing application. There are many shareware packages that will do the trick for simple projects. It wouldn't hurt to first try some shareware options before deciding to invest in professional software.

The following programs will help get you started with audio editing.

Cool Edit

Cool Edit (by Syntrillium: `http://www.syntrillium.com/`) is a digital sound editor for Windows (see Figure 12.1). With this company you have a variety of software choices from a simple shareware package, Cool Edit 2000, to a more sophisticated tool, Cool Edit Pro.

`<!--`

If you decide you need more serious functionality (and you are willing to pay serious money for it), you will want a professional package like Pro Tools by Digidesign (`http://www.digidesign.com/`). A good in-between application, both in terms of price and features, is SoundEdit 16 by Macromedia (`http://www.macromedia.com/`).

`-->`

Figure 12.1
Cool Edit's Home Page. Begin with a simple shareware package, and if you enjoy using it, upgrade to the more sophisticated Cool Edit Pro.

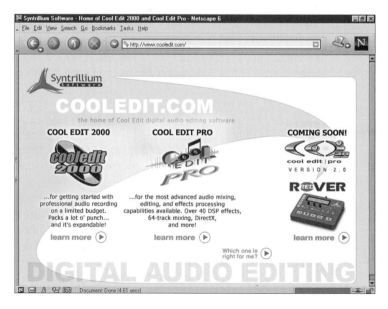

Sound Forge

Sound Forge by Sonic Foundry (http://www.soundforge.com) is professional sound editing software for Windows (see Figure 12.2) that includes an extensive set of audio processes, tools, and effects for manipulating audio. Sound Forge offers full support for the latest streaming technology, including Microsoft Windows NT Server NetShow Services and RealNetworks's RealAudio/RealVideo. Sonic Foundry also has numerous other sound and multimedia editing software to take a look at.

Figure 12.2
Sound Forge has an extensive set of audio editing tools, including MP3 support and streaming audio.

Waves

Waves' AudioTrack is a good audio editor for musicians. It combines audio processors including equalization, compression/expansion, and gating. WaveConvert Pro is a good tool for converting your audio files into another format (http://www.waves.com/).

Other Digital Audio Resources

You can find a great deal of information about digital audio recording online. Macintosh fans will appreciate MacMusic, which covers music, audio, and MIDI for Macintosh platform, http://www.macmusic.org/. Another very explicit resource is Pure Digital Audio, which has articles as well as thousands of links to more information including digital editing software for virtually every platform conceivable, http://www.puredigitalaudio.org/.

Video Files

When considering the possibility of adding video to your Web site, you must look at a hardware investment as well as purchasing software. It was already mentioned that you must begin with a very high-quality audio source file before compressing it and adding it to your

Web page. That point is even more important when it comes to producing video content. There are two steps in the process of creating video when you will sacrifice quality if you do not have good tools.

When you encode video, you capture it to your hard drive. The faster the computer, the faster the video because frames are lost if your computer cannot keep up with the video capture. To produce professional quality video, you need a powerful processor and plenty of RAM. PowerPCs and contemporary Windows machines will fit the bill. You also will require a high-quality video capture card.

<!--
To make video-capturing decisions easier for you, RealNetworks has developed a range of tools that you can use. You can find a list of these tools at http://www. realnetworks.com/resources/.
-->

DOWNLOADABLE AUDIO AND VIDEO FILE FORMATS

There are two methods for delivering audio and video to your audience—downloading and streaming. Downloadable files are ones that are completely loaded on to the user's hard drive before they are played. Streaming files are delivered to the browser in a somewhat steady stream of information. Intermediate formats, such as QuickTime, allow you to create audio and video that can be downloaded or streamed.

With streaming media, the user does not need to wait for the entire file to be received before a player begins to play back the source. Both methods have advantages and disadvantages. This section focuses on downloadable formats, with streaming media discussed later in the chapter.

<!--
Because displaying or playing downloadable media often requires a suitable application, you might consider adding a note to your page about the audio or video file type in use, and a link or selection of links where individuals who do not have suitable players can acquire them.
-->

Audio Formats

All the following formats require a complete download before starting the sound. This can be a great disadvantage if your sound clip is large, because your audience might not be willing to wait for long.

You must always try to make your audio files as small as possible. One important factor that directly impacts file size is quality. The quality of sound clips varies greatly, and different file formats are better suited for different quality clips.

Higher sampling rates and *resolutions* (the number of bits allocated for each "sample") require more storage and throughput. You must decide whether you want to sacrifice disk space and bandwidth for high-quality audio files.

A one-minute clip of an 8-bit mono file sampled at 8KHz is approximately 150KB in size. A 16-bit stereo file sampled at 44.1KHz can take up 10MB. Sometimes a lower quality recording will meet the needs of your site's viewers.

The following is a list of the most used audio file formats followed by each one's commonly used file extensions.

- **AVI *.avi; video/x-msvideo avi**—The Audio/Video Interface is used in Windows operating systems to provide sound and video, with the sound being primary. It may drop frames to keep the sound playing, thereby allowing the format to work on almost any Windows machine, from the least powerful to the most powerful.

- **WAV *.wav; audio/x-wav wav**—A proprietary format sponsored by Microsoft and IBM, it is most commonly used on Windows-based PCs. It is the audio portion of an AVI file.

- **MPEG; *.mp3; audio/x-mpeg mp3**—The International Standard Organization's Moving Picture Expert Group designed this format for both audio and video file compression. The MPEG codecs (compression/decompression methods) have made enormous fans of many Web users. The compression technique yields relatively small files of higher quality than other formats.

- **RMF; *.rmf; audio/x-rmf**—Rich Music Format is a relatively new format that is proprietary to the Beatnik music player. RMF uses JavaScript in order to add the sound file to a page, and its files are extremely small and fast-loading. If an individual does not have the Beatnik player, they simply won't hear the sound (Figure 12.3).

- **MIDI *.mid; audio/x-midi mid midi**—Unlike the other formats discussed here, Musical Instrument Digital Interface (MIDI) is not a specification for sampled digital audio. Rather, it contains a bank of digitized sounds and control information for replaying the file— similar to an electronic synthesizer. MIDI files are much smaller than digitized audio files.

Many people find that they like to provide numerous audio options for download. You can do this, and then provide information about the file, such as size and download times, on the page for the site visitor's convenience.

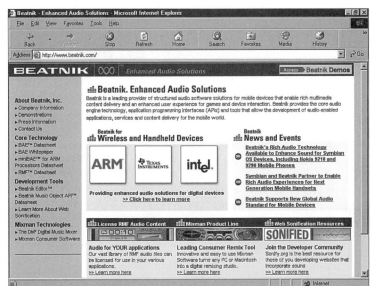

Figure 12.3
The Beatnik home page http://www.beatnik.com/ shows a worthy way of adding sounds to pages without disrupting load times.

Video Formats

Selecting a video format will depend on a variety of factors, including platform availability, which tools you like to use for editing, and personal preference.

The MPEG format is a very commonly used video format on the Web. It is also a highly efficient format because it has an excellent compression technique. Many developers prefer QuickTime files or AVI files because they are usually smaller and don't require as long to download. MPEG and QuickTime tend to be a popular choice over AVIs because MPEG is very widely supported platform-wise, and QuickTime tools and plug-ins are popular. AVI tends to be Microsoft-centric, and although it runs inline in the IE browser, support does vary with other browsers.

If you want to add video to your Web site, you should experiment with these formats to find what works best for you and your audience. You also must consider that not all video-editing tools support all three formats.

ADDING AUDIO AND VIDEO TO A WEB PAGE

There are two ways in which you can place and access most Web-based audio and video that will be read successfully across browsers: by using the anchor tag and the embed element.

⇨ *For detailed coverage of the anchor element,* **see** *"Adding Hypertext and Independent Links,"* **p. 155**, *Chapter 7.*

⇨ *For detailed information about embedding media using* `object`, **see** *"Embedding Objects,"* **p. 325**, *Chapter 13.*

Using the anchor element is the same as placing any link within an document:

```
<a href ="mydogs.mov">see a clip of Bowie and
Kelsey</a>
```

If you use this method, your users will either save the file to their desktops, launch a plug-in application, or load a new browser page, depending on which file type you're linking to, the browser they're using, and how they have set their preferences.

<!--
MPEG 3 files (MP3s) have taken the Web world by storm in the past years. You can find innumerable audio resources that use this format. Since Napster, more people have the resources to play MP3s as well as create them. The format is now supported within the operating systems for both Windows and Macintosh. An update to this compression format is underway, and will be released as MPEG 4 (MP4).
-->

<!--
Beatnik is a proprietary technology that uses HTML and JavaScript to accomplish its audio delivery goals. You can check out the Beatnik Web site, where a range of easy-to-follow tutorials exist, http://www.beatnik.com/.
-->

<!--Caution
The embed element is *not* included in the HTML 4.0 strict DTD and therefore is not available in XHTML 1.0 in deference to the `object` tag. You can choose to use the `object` tag to embed media; however, you won't have the flexibility and interoperability because of cross-browser and platform problems. At this time, it's still recommended that you use `embed` or combine `embed` and `object` when working across platforms and browsers.
-->

If you want the video to appear on the same page as the rest of the content, you must embed the clip in the page by using the embed element. Use of the embed tag is similar to the use of the img tag. However, the embed tag requires users to have the appropriate plug-in installed, or they will not see your work.

The following sample is for a video clip, but the embed tag also works for audio files, as well as for streaming video and audio.

```
<embed src="/home/dogs/rope.mov" height="105" width="100"
controller="false" autoplay=" true" pluginspage="getplug.html"
loop="palindrome" />
```

embed attributes and values are managed as follows:

- **height="*pixel/percent*"**—Unless you need your movie to scale, set this in pixels according to the dimensions of your movie.

- **width="*pixel/percent*"**—Width is best controlled by pixels, but you can use a percentage to describe how much space within the browser frame you want the embedded object to take up.

- **autoplay="true/false"**—Answer with true, and your movie starts when the page is first accessed. Answer with false, and the user must click the play button on the console for the movie to play.

- **controller="true/false"**—This adds user controls to the movie. If you set this for true, you must find out how many pixels your controller needs for the display and then add that amount to the height of your movie. Otherwise, the movie and the controller will be forced into the space required for the movie.

- **loop="true/false/palindrome"**—If you want the movie to play over and over, set this to true. If you want to play it once and stop, set it to false. Palindrome plays from beginning to end and backwards in a continuous loop.

- **pluginspage="gohere.html"**—This takes users who don't have the right to a page that tells them where to get it.

<!--
If you're loading a sound into the background using embed, place the code *at the bottom* of the page, still within the body tag. This allows everything else to load first, with the audio loading last. Your site visitors won't have to stare at a blank page until the audio has loaded.
-->

AUDIO AND VIDEO PLUG-INS

Not too long ago you *had* to download a special program, or "plug-in," to view many audio and video files. Although some file formats still require you to get a special plug-in, many come bundled with operating systems and browsers.

<!--
For a list of audio and video plug-ins supported by Netscape, visit http://www.netscape.com/plugins/audio-video.html.
-->

Some of the primary and important plug-ins you'll want to have include the following:

- **Apple QuickTime, `http://www.apple.com/quicktime/`**—Apple QuickTime plug-in allows your audience to view your QuickTime (.mov) video clips as well as many other audio and video formats (see Figure 12.4). It has come along with browsers since Netscape Navigator 3.0, and works with Navigator 2.0 and as an ActiveX control in Internet Explorer 3.0 and later, so QuickTime's distribution is pretty vast.

- **Microsoft Windows Media Player, `http://www.microsoft.com/windows/windowsmedia/`**—The new and improved Microsoft Windows Media Player is shipped with the later releases of Windows 98 (see Figure 12.5) and above, and is available as a free download for Windows 95 users. This is one-stop shopping for most audio and video formats you will encounter including ASF (a Microsoft format), RealVideo/RealAudio 4.0, MPEG 1, MPEG 2, WAV, AVI, MIDI, MOV, VOD, AU, MP3, and QuickTime files. The Media Player can run as a standalone or can be viewed within Internet Explorer and Netscape. Despite the name, it is also available for Macintosh.

- **Beatnik Player, `http://www.beatnik.com/`**—Beatnik supports Beatnik RMF files. There's also a terrific amount of developer information, tools, and community support.

- **RealPlayer Basic or Plus by RealNetworks, `http://www.real.com/products/player/`**—RealPlayer Basic and Plus support all three Real data types: RealAudio, RealVideo, RealFlash, as well as AVI, WAV, MIDI, MPEG, JPEG, VIVO, VRML, and others. RealNetworks is considered a major leader in delivering audio and video over the Web.

Figure 12.4
Apple's QuickTime Page. QuickTime supports video, audio, and proprietary virtual reality media as well as having many attractive tools and dedicated developer resources.

Figure 12.5
Microsoft Windows Media Player runs as a standalone or inline, and is also available for Macintosh.

When you're deciding on the best format for your audio and video files, you should consider the likelihood that your users will already have the software they need to see your work. Too often, users will not take the time to download a plug-in, so you are better off to provide your files in formats they can already access.

Bandwidth is a significant concern with any media files, due to the size of those files and the limitations of streaming technologies. Another concern is accessibility—if a site visitor can't see or hear, the message you are sending with your video or audio can be lost without due consideration.

Corporate intranets are especially good candidates for using streaming technology because they most often have high-speed connections and standardized software for viewing the material. Intranets provide an opportunity to develop Web sites for a specific audience, though in many large companies you can't even count on a homogeneous platform; the only real benefit is being able to demand that a specific browser be used.

But, if you are preparing audio and video to be streamed on the Internet to a broad audience, you must remember that not all users have the same hardware and software capabilities. Although the average connection speed today is 56Kbps, some users are still accessing your site at slower speeds and, of course, some connections are much faster. You should consider providing your users with options.

If you are streaming a video, consider offering two speeds for viewing the video, for example, 28.8Kbps and 56Kbps. This will help optimize the video for your user. If you are providing media content that the user might not have the necessary plug-in to view, always offer a link to where the software can be downloaded.

STREAMING MEDIA CONCEPTS

An attempt to avoid the eternal bandwidth problem is streaming technology. In 1994, RealAudio introduced a way of delivering Internet audio based on the User Datagram Protocol

(UDP) rather than the usual Transmission Control Protocol (TCP). This technology was later used for transferring video files as well.

UDP technology does not require confirmation of the receipt of all the data; instead, it delivers the packet as quickly as possible. This means that a user can begin playing the audio or video file even before the whole file is received. The user's wait time is cut dramatically. Over time, Real has expanded its line of products and services to include a range of enhanced services to bring streaming media to the Web.

The disadvantage of streaming media is that you lose some control over the quality of your data as it travels over the Internet. The quality of the streaming audio and video depends on the line quality, which varies greatly. However, with the growing proliferation of fast connections such as T1 and ISDN lines, many of these problems are minimized.

Streaming Audio

Adding streaming audio to your Web site is not a decision to be made lightly. You and your client may agree that streaming audio will greatly enhance the site, but you must also weigh the expense in terms of both time *and* money.

The first steps for creating a streaming audio clip are the same as those for creating a downloadable clip. But the next step is to convert the digital recording into the streaming format.

RealNetworks's RealProducer has long been the most popular software for converting files for streaming. The encoding process compresses the files until they are very small. During the compression, some parts of the sound file are left out.

To have the best quality content after compression, you must start with a good source file. If you're creating sound from scratch, you must use professional quality microphones. If you are using content that has already been recorded, you should use CD-ROM or DAT recordings.

<!--
Some excellent hints for creating a good source file can be found at the RealNetworks electronic library at http://www.realnetworks.com/resources/.
-->

Streaming Video

Creating streaming video content is the same process as creating downloadable video content, but you must convert the file to a streaming format. Once again, RealProducer is a popular tool for making videos ready for streaming technology.

Currently RealProducer supports .AVI and .MOV *input* files. If your input files are of any other type, you must find another tool to convert that type to .AVI or .MOV files.

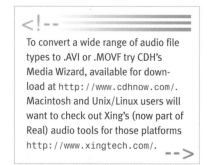

<!--
To convert a wide range of audio file types to .AVI or .MOVF try CDH's Media Wizard, available for download at http://www.cdhnow.com/. Macintosh and Unix/Linux users will want to check out Xing's (now part of Real) audio tools for those platforms http://www.xingtech.com/.
-->

PRODUCING STREAMING MEDIA

In this section, I'll focus on RealNetworks products, because of the availability of free and inexpensive resources for their use. If you are interested in other methods mentioned earlier in this chapter, please visit their Web sites for more information.

Creating a Streaming Audio File

To add a streamed audio clip to your page, you will need some special tools and skills.

For my example, I already have an MP3 file that I want to use, which I prepared from a digital sampling by using the techniques discussed earlier in the chapter.

> `<!--`
> The RealSystem Producer Basic is free for download from `http://www.realnetworks.com/products/producer/basic.html`.
> `-->`

The next step is to convert the MP3 file to a streaming format. To do this, use the RealNetworks product RealSystem Producer Plus. This application allows you to quickly and easily change the MP3 file into the appropriate streaming format.

Follow these steps to convert a MP3 file to RealMedia format (my specific choices are provided as an example):

1. When Producer starts up, it offers a New Session dialog box. In the Input Source section, click the File option button, click Browse, Find and then select the MP3 file you want to encode. The Output section loads the file location and name under RealMedia file (see Figure 12.6).

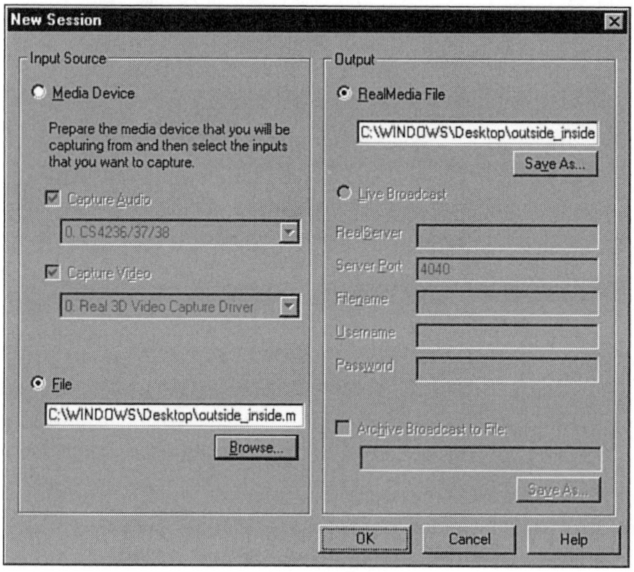

Figure 12.6
Select the input and output files in RealProducer.

2. Click Save As and type the location and name you want to save the encoded file as (in this case my file is named `whale_call_28.rm`, as shown previously in Figure 12.6).

3. Click Save, and then click OK.

4. In the Clip Information area, add the name of the file, your name, the copyright date, a description, and keywords describing the file.

5. In the Target Audience area there are several checkboxes you can use to customize the file to your audience's needs. (I chose the 28K Modem checkbox, see Figure 12.2, because I want to make sure that I can provide 28.8 access—many of the people coming to the Web site I'm creating are on standard modems.)

6. Under Audio Format, choose the type of audio that is most accurate for your music selection from the drop-down menu (I selected Music) as shown in Figure 12.7.

Figure 12.7
Click the appropriate checkboxes to determine audience format.

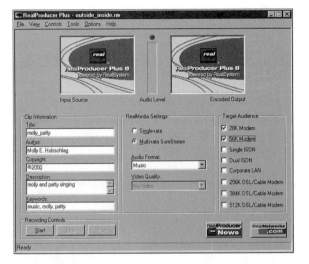

7. In the File Type area, you must choose between Multi-rate and Single-rate. Choose Multi-rate SureStream if you are not using a Web server to deliver your file.

8. Now click Start under Recording Controls.

9. RealProducer encodes the file with an .rm extension, saving it to the location you identified in step 2.

If you want to provide a higher bandwidth access option, follow these steps again, optimizing the file for T1 access, and then save the file under a new name (mine is saved as `molly_patty_t1.rm`).

```
<!--
If you're looking at high-volume
video and audio streaming situations
such as Web broadcasting or intranet
solutions, consider a specialty server
for streaming media. More informa-
tion on servers for Internet and
intranet services can be found at
http://www.realnetworks.com/
solutions/infrastructure/cdn/
index.html.
-->
```

Working with Streaming Video

Streaming video works similarly to streaming audio. In this case, you begin the process with an .AVI file—I am using one that a friend took while feeding fish on the Great Barrier Reef.

I thought this would be a nice addition to a Web page, so I prepared to encode the file by using the RealProducer as I did for streaming audio. Here's the process to follow with my specific choices in parentheses:

```
<!--
```
You can create as many bandwidth options as you want by simply working through this process and letting RealProducer process the files with the specific bandwidth preferences you set.
```
-->
```

1. From RealProducer New Session dialog box, select the .AVI file you want to encode in the Input Source section.

2. Type the name you want to save the encoded file as (in my case, `feeding_fish_28.rm`).

3. Click Save As and then click OK.

4. In the RealProducer main screen, locate the area called Clip Information, and give the title to the video, name the author, and provide a copyright date, description, and keywords.

5. Choose one of the several checkboxes to determine your target audience. (I chose the 28K Modem checkbox because I want to make sure that I can provide 28.8 access—many of the people coming to the Web site I'm creating are on 28.8 modems.)

6. Under Audio Format, you can choose to add audio by selecting the audio most appropriate to your .AVI from the drop-down menu (I chose No Audio). Set Video Quality to Normal Motion Video.

7. In the File Type area, choose either Multi-rate or Single-rate; choose Multi-rate SureStream unless you are preparing the file to be played from a Web server.

8. Under Recording Controls, click Start.

9. RealProducer encodes the file with an .rm extension saves it to the location you identified in step 2.

Now you have a streaming version of the video to place in a Web page.

INCORPORATING STREAMING MEDIA INTO YOUR PAGE

There are two ways to add streaming media to a Web page. The first involves the need to set up or have access to streaming software. The second is setting up the media to stream via HTTP, the Hypertext Transfer Protocol.

Adding Streaming Media Using RealServer G2

If you have access to a RealServer G2, you can stream files using the full gamut of RealServer services. This includes working with the RTSP protocol, which is a special protocol designed for streaming media. It streams data with timelines, adjusting the stream with the idea of allowing it to play as smoothly as possible as it transfers. What's more, there's a feature known as Ramgen, which generates a Ram file—a specialized file that will invoke the RealPlayer.

To have your audio or video run from a RealServer, follow these steps:

1. Place your prepared file on the RealServer.

2. Place a link from the referring page to the file as follows:

   ```
   <a href="http://realserver.yourserver.com:8080/ramgen/molly_patty56.ram">download
   molly's audio clip</a>
   ```

3. Test your file to see if it works properly. The link should automatically invoke the RealPlayer, and the audio or video should begin to stream immediately.

Adding Streaming Media to a Page with HTTP

If you don't have access to a RealServer, you can stream your audio and video directly via HTTP. There are some services, such as live broadcast, that you will not be able to tap into doing it this way, but even so, this method doesn't have the costs associated with RealServer technology.

You will have to contact your ISP to make sure that the MIME types are properly configured on the server. The MIME types you'll want to have to support all Real streaming media, including SMIL, are laid out in Table 12.1.

<!--Caution
The .smi extension is also used by Apple for "Self Mounting Image" files. Depending upon the type of ISP service you're using, the MIME type might be set for Apple's .smi rather than Real's .smi extension. -->

Table 12.1 MIME Types for RealMedia Files

File Type	Extension	MIME Type
Ram	.ram	audio/x-pn-realaudio
Embedded Ram	.rpm	audio/x-pn-realaudio-plugin
SMIL	.smil & .smi	application/smil
RealAudio	.ra	audio/x-pn-realaudio
RealVideo	.rm	application/x-pn-realmedia
RealPix	.rp	image/vnd.rn-realpix
RealText	.rt	text/vnd.rn-realtext

To add streaming media to your page, follow these steps:

1. Prepare your file using RealProducer just as you would for use with RealServer.

2. Create a Ram file. To do this, simply open your editor and type in the URL where your clip resides. Save the file with a .ram extension, such as molly_and_patty.ram.

3. Put the Ram file and the audio or video file into the desired directory on your Web server.

4. Link to the Ram file from your Web page, and voila!

> <!--
>
> RealProducer generates the HTML for you when you click Create Web Page in the Web Publishing section of the application. A wizard is launched that walks you through the process. However, if you want your code to be XHTML compliant, you will need to edit the generated code.
>
> -->

Be sure to test your link. The streaming clip should stream when the link is activated.

In Listing 12.1, I've linked from my page to the files, which reside in a directory on my Web server called "audio." You can run files locally, too.

Listing 12.1   Embedding Streaming Audio

```
<!DOCTYPE html PUBLIC "-//W3C//DTD XHTML 1.0 Transitional//EN"
"http://www.w3.org/TR/xhtml1/DTD/xhtml1-transitional.dtd">
<html xmlns="http://www.w3.org/1999/xhtml">
<head>
<title>Audio Sample</title>
</head>
<body>
<p>My singing partner, Patty Sundberg, and I, are in a duo called Courage Sisters. We
write and perform original acoustic music.</p>
<p>Please enjoy the following RealAudio clip:</p>
<a href="audio/molly_and_patty.ram">Molly and Patty in Concert</a>
</body>
</html>
```

Figure 12.8 shows the RealMedia player with the file playing after the link has been clicked.

Figure 12.8
RealMedia provides a control panel that allows the site visitor to control play of the audio file.

Adding streaming video is essentially the same process. Listing 12.2 is the XHTML code demonstrating how adding a video clip to a Web page was accomplished.

Listing 12.2   Adding Streaming Video

```
<!DOCTYPE html PUBLIC "-//W3C//DTD XHTML 1.0 Transitional//EN"
"http://www.w3.org/TR/xhtml1/DTD/xhtml1-transitional.dtd">
<html xmlns="http://www.w3.org/1999/xhtml">
<head>
<title>Video Sample</title>
</head>
<body>
<p>My friend Kelly, who sadly passed away last year, was a truly inspirational person.
Kelly was a paraplegic. She was paralyzed from the mid-chest area down. But nothing
stopped her from having a very adventurous and active lifestyle. She was a scuba diver,
mountain climber, devoted kayaker, and ski maven, using adaptive equipment to assist her
in achieving her athletic goals.</p>
<p>So if you've been a little concerned about scuba diving, para-sailing--even extreme
sports, Kelly's active life can serve as a great inspiration.</p>
<p>Several years ago, Kelly went scuba diving along the Great Barrier Reef. In this
video, she can be seen feeding beautifully colored fish.  Note: this file is optimized
for 28.8 connections.</p>

<p><a href="video/feeding_fish_28.ram">Kelly Feeding Fish</a></p>

</body>
</html>
```

When a site visitor clicks the link or the Real icon, the RealPlayer will launch. In Figure 12.9, you can see the streaming video in the RealPlayer after the link has been activated.

Figure 12.9
Activating the video in RealPlayer.

MULTIMEDIA SOFTWARE: MACROMEDIA DIRECTOR, SHOCKWAVE, AND FLASH

High interactivity, lower bandwidth. That's what these programs strive for, and in some cases, truly achieve.

Macromedia has excelled in the procurement and development of multimedia tools, including Director, which is considered one of the premier multimedia development packages. With applications that far exceed Web interests, Director can create interactive, multimedia presentations for kiosks, CD-ROM computers, games, and other interactive media.

The Director Studio package includes many useful tools—including the Aftershock utility. Aftershock generates the HTML that can deliver Director and Flash Shockwave movies and Java applets to all platforms and browsers.

Director is a big package and a serious commitment. The learning curve is high, and therefore it is recommended for only the very serious multimedia developer.

Using Director, Shockwave technology works by streaming information to a Web browser via a plug-in.

Shockwave hit the Web scene with a serious splash. However, because browser technology remains fickle when it comes to integrating advanced support for such a complex program with plug-in style delivery, it has only caught on in certain situations.

<!--
For more information on working with Director, check out *Special Edition Using Director 8.5*, from Que.
-->

Shockwave does, however, have many advantages over most Web-based media programs. It supports audio, animation, and advanced interactive events. Web pages with Shockwave are considered to be "shocked," and they are popular among certain Web enthusiasts. Shockwave Flash (see below), due to its lower cost and incredible popularity, has overshadowed Shockwave in recent years.

Figure 12.10 shows the Shockwave site. Stay on the page a few moments, and you can enjoy the action. Figure 12.11 shows a different scene with the very weird but popular Joe Cartoon (http://www.joecartoon.com). Definitely a fun experience, taking the days of static pages to a very different level.

<!--
For a gallery of Director multimedia presentations and Shockwave sites, visit the following:

Director Gallery: http://www.macromedia.com/software/director/gallery/_director/

Shockwave.com: http://www.shockwave.com/
-->

Figure 12.10
The Shockwave site—enjoyable, colorful, and full of promise.

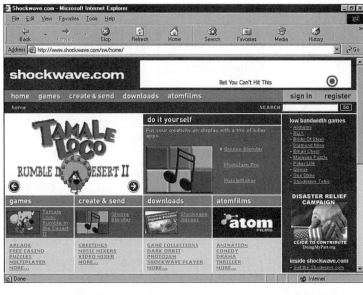

Figure 12.11
Promise fulfilled, especially for Joe Cartoon fans.

EXPLORING FLASH IN DETAIL

Originally a compact animation tool called FutureSplash and later modified to include sound, with intense support from Microsoft, Macromedia Flash was quickly included as a native part of Internet Explorer. At the time of this writing, Flash is in its 5.0 incarnation, with a lot of interface and publishing improvements having been added over its growth cycle.

What's especially interesting about Flash is that it is a vector-based drawing tool, much like Illustrator or Macromedia Freehand, but with the sole purpose of creating Web content.

What this means is that the resulting files are very compact, and can include a wide range of high-quality, low-bandwidth design. Add audio to the mix, and you've got a sophisticated and widely accessible tool.

Adobe has a product it is positioning for competition with Macromedia Flash. LiveMotion 2.0 contains scripting features that move it away from the comparatively limited first version. You can add audio and animation, and it's a vector-based drawing package. It also has the added advantage of a familiar and easy to use interface.

One drawback is that Flash still requires a plug-in, although the plug in does ship with most 4.x and later browsers. However, Flash is wise: It offers output not only to its native vector-based formats, but to animated GIFs, which can be used in place of the vector movies in those circumstances where Flash is not supported. Flash hasn't been on every Web developer's list of sensible Web site choices because of these difficulties. But, it is a powerful option and enthusiastically used by many.

<!--
Macromedia Flash is not the only product that can produce .swf files. CorelDraw 10 has .swf support, and Beatware's e-Picture Pro software (see http://www.beatware.com/) is an excellent tool for animation with full export to .swf.
-->

<!--
Earlier versions of Flash (3.0 and below), despite their lack of these advanced publishing tools, do come with a utility known as Aftershock. This utility is a one-step marvel: It takes what you create in Flash and processes it to work across browsers and across platforms, writing the HTML code, the JavaScript, *and* creating an animated or still GIF for those who can't access the Flash file.
-->

Flash is affordable, and the learning curve not anywhere near as complex as for Director. Although I've always thought the interface (see Figure 12.12) could be a bit more intuitive, Flash still remains an impressive method of creating enhanced visuals.

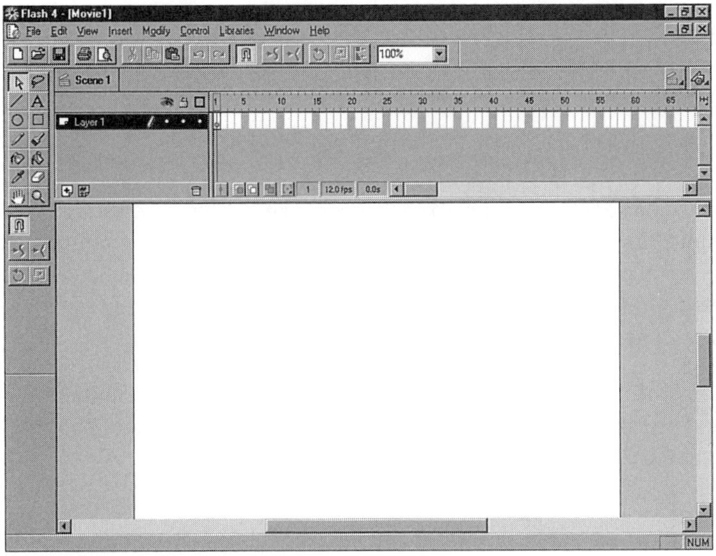

Figure 12.12
The Flash interface complete with menus, timeline, tools, and workspace.

CASE BY CASE: EXPLORING STREAMING MEDIA OPTIONS

After you decide to add audio and video to a site, you will find that there is no shortage of companies that want to try to make your job easier. It can make your head spin when you realize how many companies are vying for a piece of the growing online multimedia market.

The following is a tour of some of the leading companies in the audio/video industry and their products. Visit the sites and download any tools and players. Become familiar with both using and working with audio and video online.

- **Microsoft Advanced Streaming Media Format (ASF),** `http://www.microsoft.com/windows/windowsmedia/`—Using proprietary streaming technology referred to as *advanced streaming media*, Microsoft has developed a suite of streaming media products and applications. FM stereo sound can be streamed over modem connections, and the ASF format is considered to offer better compression than MP3.

- **VivoActive,** `http://www.vivo.com/`—Vivo Software (now part of RealNetworks) is a leader in the streaming media market. VideoNow and VideoProducer are easy-to-use and affordable tools that allow you to make synchronized streaming video and audio Web pages by using AVI or WAV files. This technology is great for the Web because the content can be played back on any platform by using the VivoActive Player. The Player works on 486/66 or higher systems running Windows 3.1 or later and Power Macintosh systems running Mac OS 7.5 or later.

- **Apple QuickTime,** `http://www.apple.com/quicktime/`—Ensures cross-platform and Internet compatibility for your QuickTime files. Prior to QuickTime 3, a tool called the Internet Movie Tool was sometimes used to prepare movies for Web delivery. Apple recommends that you no longer use this tool for movie preparation because QuickTime and MoviePlayer now prepare the movie for the Internet automatically.

- **RealNetworks's RealProducer/Real Publisher,** `http://www.realnetworks.com/resources/`—RealProducer contains all the tools needed to create RealAudio (WAV, AU, MOV, and SND) and RealVideo (AVI and QuickTime format) content, and it's free! RealPublisher is marketed as an upgrade to RealProducer, but auto coding and uploading them to the Web are the only functions exclusive to RealPublisher.

- **Adobe Premiere,** `http://www.adobe.com/prodindex/premiere/`—This is an expensive but powerful tool designed for video professionals. Unlike other tools available to you, this one was not designed specifically for making online video and probably has much more capability than you need. One big benefit of this product is that it can smoothly integrate other Adobe products such as Photoshop and Illustrator.

Adding streaming media is not for every Web designer, nor is it appropriate for every audience. It is important to take a close look at, however, because it is becoming a more popular option as both the streaming technology gets better and connectivity gets faster.

I have rarely used streaming media in standard Web designs. I have had occasion to create streaming media for specific projects, such as an adventure travel site where video and audio of underwater diving or water skiing can really enhance the site visitor's experience. Other instances where streaming media can make a site more powerful include sites for real estate, music, history, art, and education.

In business, streaming media is extremely attractive as a method of communications between distant offices. Of course, the interest in Internet radio and live videocasts has brought a lot of enthusiasm to the medium. Still, as with any media that demands additional software, asks your hardware to work harder, and requires the maximum bandwidth available, careful consideration must be used by the developer before adding it to a given site.

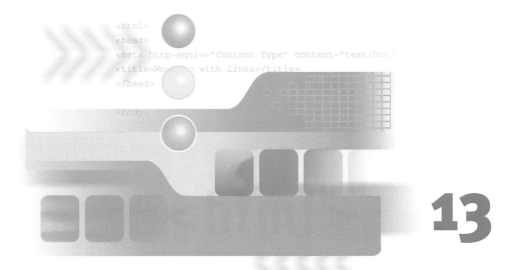

EMBEDDING OBJECTS

IN THIS CHAPTER

About Embedded Objects   326

The `object` Element in Detail   328

Working with the `applet` Element   331

Imagemaps   336

Case by Case: Ensuring Accessibility for Embedded Objects   341

ABOUT EMBEDDED OBJECTS

Any time you add multimedia to an HTML or XHTML document, you are associating an *object* with that document. Objects, in terms of Web authoring, include the following:

- **Images**—This includes standard images such as GIF, JPEG, and PNG images that are embedded into a page.

- **Imagemaps**—An imagemap is a form of object.

- **Applets**—Java applets (small programs written in Java to carry out some interactive task).

- **Multimedia**—Different forms of media, including Macromedia Flash files.

- **ActiveX**—Developed by Microsoft, ActiveX allows developers to create ActiveX components. These are self-sufficient programs that can be run in Web browsers that support ActiveX. ActiveX can be thought of as Microsoft's comparable technology to Java.

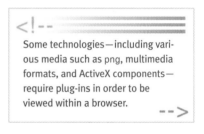

Some technologies—including various media such as png, multimedia formats, and ActiveX components—require plug-ins in order to be viewed within a browser.

For further information on using images in your Web development, **see** "Adding Images," **p. 275**, Chapter 11.

For more information on working with audio, video, and multimedia, **see** "Working with Multimedia," **p. 301**, Chapter 12.

Over the course of HTML's history, different elements and related attributes emerged from the W3C as well as individual browser vendors in an effort to manage the growing variety of media types available via Web pages.

It became apparent that several limitations existed with the way objects were being handled:

- The elements for objects in existence prior to HTML 4 were not flexible enough to allow for new and future media types.

- The applet element could only be used with a Java applet, limiting its availability for use with other objects of a similar nature.

- Objects in general pose accessibility problems, and the elements and attributes used before HTML 4 were less aware of accessibility concerns and therefore are less flexible in addressing this important issue (see "Case by Case" at the end of this chapter).

It was apparent that a unifying element was needed that Web developers would be able to use for almost any kind of media object, including images. As a result, the object element was introduced. This element is much more flexible and addresses a variety of concerns.

Because independent frames (iframes) are added to pages just as any other media, the object element can be used to create them, too.

⇨ *For more about iframes, **see** "Creating Framesets and Frame Documents," **p. 219,** Chapter 9.*

But what's the caveat, you might be thinking? Well, there is a significant one, and that's that browser support for the `object` element has been problematic and buggy, even in relatively recent browsers.

Figure 13.1 shows Netscape 6.2 for Windows rendering a test of the `object` element perfectly. Compare this to Figure 13.2, in which Internet Explorer 6.0 for Windows doesn't render the same results. In Figure 13.3, Netscape 4.76 for Windows completely ignores the results because the `object` element was not available during its development.

Figure 13.1
Netscape 6.2 for Windows renders the object without any problem.

Figure 13.2
Internet Explorer renders the object with problems.

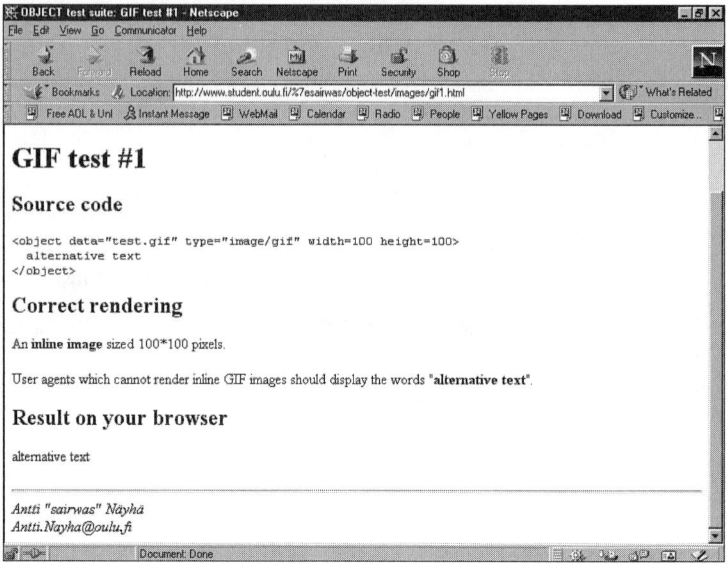

Figure 13.3
Netscape 4.76 doesn't render the object at all.

Figure 13.3
Netscape 4.76 doesn't render the object at all.

For this reason, it makes sense that when working with images, you'll want to use the img element for now, and not the more global object element. However, when it comes to applets and other multimedia objects, the problem becomes significant, because the only real workaround is to employ deprecated or proprietary elements, such as applet or embed.

<!--
A great test suite for object compliance resides at http://www.student.oulu.fi/%7esairwas/object-test/.
-->

THE OBJECT ELEMENT IN DETAIL

Despite compatibility problems, the object element is part of current W3C recommendations for HTML 4 and XHTML. In order to have conforming documents, you will have to use it in some instances. In the instance of images, for example, you may use object instead of img, but you will have to do so with the browser concerns mentioned in mind.

The object element has a number of attributes and other elements associated with it as follows:

- **classid**—Used to point to the location of an object's implementation via a URI. You can use this together with the data attribute, or as an alternative to it, depending on your needs.

- **codebase**—Use this attribute to specify the base path for relative URIs specified by other attributes.

- **codetype**—This attribute is used to describe the content type of the data being downloaded. This requires you to include a MIME type and subtype value.

- **data**—Used to specify the location of the object's data. If a relative URI is used, the location will be interpreted relative by that defined in the codebase attribute.

- **type**—Use this attribute to define the type of data specified in the data attribute. Type also asks that you define the MIME type in use.

- **archive**—This attribute can be used to preload archives related to the object in question.

- **declare**—Using declare makes the current object element a declaration. In order to create a real instance, you'll need another object definition.

- **standby**—Here, you can specify a message for the browser to display while the object is being loaded.

Numerous, more global attributes are associated with object, depending upon the language version. Table 13.1 describes this in greater detail.

Table 13.1 Global Attributes Available in object

Attribute Type	Action
id, class (document identifiers)	Assigns name or class name to an element.
lang, dir (language information and text direction)	Provides information about the language and text direction being defined in a document.
title	Offers additional information about the element in use.
style	Used to provide inline styles.
Intrinsic Events	All legal intrinsic events can be used to attach scripts to an HTML or XHTML document.
tabindex	Provides tabbing information, useful in accessibility.
usemap	Necessary when using object to define client-side imagemaps.
name	Used with forms and scripts. Note that in XHTML you should use id instead.
Presentational Attributes including: width, height, align, border, hspace, vspace	These attributes are used to place and identify the object. They are all deprecated in favor of style sheets in HTML 4 and XHTML Transitional, and cannot be used at all in Strict documents.

As you can see, object is meant to be an extremely utilitarian, backward-compatible, *and* forward-thinking element.

Using object **to Add an Image**

While it is rarely done, it's important to point out that the concept behind object is to provide a more generic element for media. As a result, you can use object to place an image on your page should you so desire.

As discussed in Chapter 11, "Adding Images," you can use the img element to place a variety of graphic file types on your page. There are a variety of presentational attributes such as width and height that can be used to enhance presentation in HTML and XHTML transitional documents. If you were to have an img element used in XHTML, it would appear as:

```
<img src="images/birthday_picture.gif" alt="picture from my birthday" />
```

But, if for some reason you'd like to use `object` as a means of placing an image in a document, you can do so in this fashion:

```
<object data="http://www.molly.com/images/birthday_
picture.gif"
type="image/gif">A picture from my birthday.</object>
```

You can use any number of presentational attributes to manage the placement of the object on the page. Listing 13.1 shows the use of `object` with an image, and several attributes.

<!--
Always include descriptive text content within the `object` element. If the object won't display in a given browser, the text content will, providing some context for users. This is especially important when working to create accessible documents.
-->

Listing 13.1   Using `object` to Place an Image in a Document

```
<!DOCTYPE html PUBLIC "-//W3C//DTD XHTML 1.0 Transitional//EN"
    "http://www.w3.org/TR/xhtml1/DTD/xhtml1-transitional.dtd">

<html xmlns="http://www.w3.org/1999/xhtml">

<head>
<title>Working with Objects</title>
</head>


<body>

<object data="http://www.molly.com/images/birthday_picture.gif"
type="image/gif" border="0" align="right" hspace="10" vspace="10">
A picture from my birthday.</object>

</body>
</html>
```

<!--Caution
Of course, the use of presentational attributes can only be done in Transitional documents. For Strict documents, you'll want to use style sheets for layout.
-->

Using `object` to Add an Applet to Your Page

You can use `object` to add applets or other objects to your pages. In fact, `object` specifically allows you to specify the location of an object, the data to be rendered, and any runtime parameters that the object might call for.

Along with the various attributes available for the `object` element is the `param` element. This element specifies values that the object requires at runtime. Typically, a number of `param` values will exist for a given object. The `param` element is an empty element, so in XHTML, it will require a trailing slash:

```
<param name="bgcolor" value="000000" />
```

Listing 13.2 shows the `object` element pointing to an applet, along with several attributes in use.

Listing 13.2 Using the object Element to Specify a Java Applet

```
<!DOCTYPE html PUBLIC "-//W3C//DTD XHTML 1.0 Transitional//EN"
    "http://www.w3.org/TR/xhtml1/DTD/xhtml1-transitional.dtd">

<html xmlns="http://www.w3.org/1999/xhtml">


<head>
<title>Working with Objects</title>
</head>


<body>

<object codetype="application/java-archive" classid="java:custom.class"
width="200" height="200">If your browser doesn't support the object
element, you will see this text instead.
</object>


</body>
</html>
```

As mentioned, the object element was developed to address limitations with several elements, including the applet element. But, since the object element is not well supported by all browsers, Web authors will likely be using applet to ensure cross-browser compatibility despite the fact that it is deprecated.

WORKING WITH THE APPLET ELEMENT

The applet element, like the object element, has a variety of available attributes, including:

- **codebase**—Use this attribute to denote the location of the applet (by URI).

- **code**—This attribute is used to specify the class file, either by name or by path to the file.

- **name**—Use name to identify the applet as a unique entity within the document.

- **archive**—As with the object element, the archive attribute can be used with applet to provide a list of URIs for archives and other resources to be preloaded, improving the applet's performance.

- **object**—This attribute names a resource, just as code does. One or the other must be present for the applet to work. If both are present, the class names should be the same, or an error will result.

```
<!--
The Java applet used in this sample
was written by Giuseppe Gennaro
and is available at http://
javaboutique.internet.com/
Fade/.
-->
```

The width and height attributes are also available for applet, but again, these can only be used in Transitional authoring. Other attributes available for use with the applet element (depending upon the DTD in use) include id, class, title, style, alt, align, vspace, and hspace.

Adding a Java Applet Using the `applet` Element

In the following exercise, you'll see how the `applet` element can be used in a valid HTML 4.01 Transitional document.

1. With the proper class files available, begin with an XHTML Transitional template:

```
<!DOCTYPE HTML PUBLIC "-//W3C//DTD HTML 4.01 Transitional//EN"
        "http://www.w3.org/TR/html4/loose.dtd">

<html>

<head>
<title>Working with Objects</title>
</head>


<body>

</body>
</html>
```

2. Add the applet element:

```
<!DOCTYPE HTML PUBLIC "-//W3C//DTD HTML 4.01 Transitional//EN"
        "http://www.w3.org/TR/html4/loose.dtd">

<html>

<head>
<title>Working with Objects</title>
</head>


<body>

<applet>

</applet>

</body>
</html>
```

3. Add the code attribute and Java applet name, alternate text description, and any presentational values:

```
<!DOCTYPE HTML PUBLIC "-//W3C//DTD HTML 4.01 Transitional//EN"
        "http://www.w3.org/TR/html4/loose.dtd">

<html>
```

```
<head>
<title>Working with Objects</title>
</head>


<body>

<applet code="Fade.class" alt="Java Applet" width="300" height="50">

</applet>

</body>
</html>
```

4. Add any parameters and related features. For this applet, there's a variety of text, font, and color parameters:

```
<!DOCTYPE HTML PUBLIC "-//W3C//DTD HTML 4.01 Transitional//EN"
        "http://www.w3.org/TR/html4/loose.dtd">


<head>
<title>Working with Objects</title>
</head>


<body>

<applet code="Fade.class" alt="Java Applet" width="300" height="50">
<param name="bgcolor" value="000000" />
<param name="txtcolor" value="ffffff" />
<param name="changefactor" value="5" />
<param name="text1" value="Welcome to Molly.Com." />
<param name="url1" value="http://www.molly.com/" />
<param name="font1" value="Helvetica,Plain,14" />
<param name="text2" value="New Events!" />
<param name="url2" value="http://www.rmolly.com/molly/events.html" />
<param name="font2" value="TimesRoman,italic,18" />
<param name="text3" value="Get in Touch!" />
<param name="url3" value="http://www.molly.com/molly/contact.html" />
<param name="font3" value="Courier,BOLD,18" />
</applet>

</body>
</html>
```

5. Validate and test your work. Figures 13.4 through 13.6 show the applet rendered in a browser.

Figure 13.4
Here's the applet, running inline in IE 6.

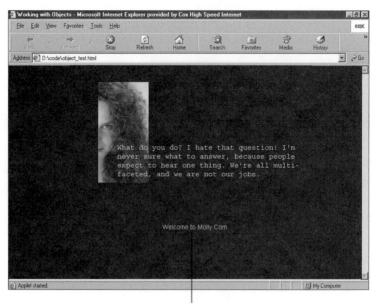

First applet screen

Figure 13.5
The previous image's text fades out, and this new text fades in.

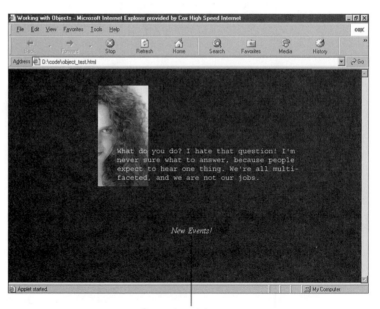

Second applet screen

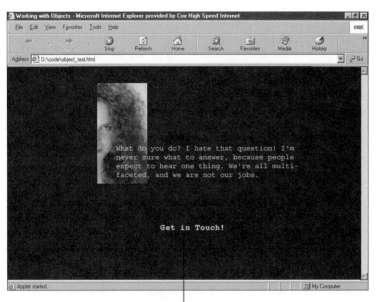

Third applet screen

Workarounds for Cross-Browser Support

Using the applet element ensures that your applet will be available in most Web browsers. Using the object element for this applet would have limited the browser support for it. As a result, the choice to use Transitional documents and the deprecated applet element is one means of ensuring this interoperability and achieving a valid document. Another means is to use both the applet *and* the object elements together, as shown in Listing 13.3.

<!--
Use the alt attribute with applet to enhance accessibility.
-->

Listing 13.3   Combining object and applet for Cross-Browser Compatibility

```
<!DOCTYPE html PUBLIC "-//W3C//DTD XHTML 1.0 Transitional//EN"
    "http://www.w3.org/TR/xhtml1/DTD/xhtml1-transitional.dtd">

<html xmlns="http://www.w3.org/1999/xhtml">

<head>
<title>Working with Objects</title>
</head>

<body>

<object codetype="application/java-archive" classid="java:custom.class"
width="200" height="200">
```

Listing 13.3   Continued

```
<applet code="custom.class" archive="myclasses.jar"
width="200" height="200">
</applet>
</object>

</body>
</html>
```

<!--Caution

If a browser can detect both object and applet, it will probably try to render the object twice if you use this method. If you must use an applet, I recommend sticking to the applet element in a Transitional document for the time being.

-->

IMAGEMAPS

No doubt you are familiar with imagemaps, which are images overlaid with shapes that are defined by coordinates. Each section of the map relates to a different location via URI. Very popular in the early days of the Web, imagemaps have somewhat lost their popularity in favor of more streamlined navigation methods. However, they are still quite useful, and very much a part of W3C specifications.

Originally, imagemapping could only be done with the coordinate information residing on the server. This is referred to as *server-side imagemapping*. Browsers quickly added a means by which to interpret *imagemapping*, and this in turn provided *client-side imagemapping*, the preferred current methodology. The W3C explains the reasoning for this preference as being twofold. First, client-side *imagemaps* can be made accessible to disabled users; and second, there is instantaneous visual response as to whether a given region is active—the mouse pointer changes to indicate an active link.

Client-side *imagemaps* can be created using the img or object elements, along with the map and area elements and a variety of attributes. The map element specifies the map information, the area element helps define the shape, coordinates, and URI, and the img or object element are associated with the map information via the usemap attribute.

Attributes for the map element include

- **name**—This attribute is used to assign a unique identity to the *imagemap*.

- **shape**—To define the shape of a map's region, you can use a value of rect for rectangle, circle for circle, and poly for polygon. There is another value, default, which specifies any region of the map not mapped to another URL.

- **coords**—The coords attribute defines the way the map is positioned on screen. There are a number of value combinations, as follows:

  rect—left-x, top-y, right-x, bottom-y
  circle—center-x, center-y, radius
  Poly—x1, y1, x2, y2, ..., xN, yN

- **nohref**—Use this to define a region with no link.

<!--

Coordinates always begin at the upper-left of the object, and all coordinate values are measured in lengths and separated by commas.

-->

Figure 13.7 shows a Web page with two active *imagemaps*. One is the site navigation (on the left side), and the other is the map of Arizona State Parks. Listing 13.4 shows the markup for the navigation map (corrected from the original and updated to conform with XHTML), using the img, map, and area elements.

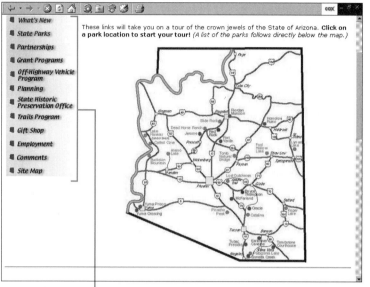

Navigation map

Figure 13.7
This page has two imagemaps. We're going to work with the navigation map on the left.

Listing 13.4 An Imagemap Using the img Element

```
<!DOCTYPE HTML PUBLIC "-//W3C//DTD HTML 4.01 Transitional//EN"
        "http://www.w3.org/TR/html4/loose.dtd">

<html>

<head>
<title>Working with Objects</title>
</head>


<body>

<map name="indexMap3">
<area shape="rect" coords="4,56,124,84"
href="http://www.pr.state.az.us/partnerships/partners.html"
alt="go to partners">
<area shape="rect" coords="5,294,114,321"
```

Listing 13.4 Continued

```
href="mailto:feedback@pr.state.az.us"
alt="send feedback">
<area shape="rect" coords="4,265,127,291"
href="http://www.pr.state.az.us/employment/hrmain.html"
alt="go to main">
<area shape="rect" coords="5,237,111,262"
href="http://www.pr.state.az.us/giftshop.html"
alt="go to giftshop">
<area shape="rect" coords="7,209,129,234"
href="http://www.pr.state.az.us/partnerships/trails/statetrails.html"
alt="go to state trails">
<area shape="rect" coords="6,177,155,207"
href="http://www.pr.state.az.us/partnerships/shpo/shpo.html"
alt="go to state historic preservation office">
<area shape="rect" coords="6,148,115,173"
href="http://www.pr.state.az.us/partnerships/planning/planning.html"
alt="go to planning">
<area shape="rect" coords="6,119,157,146"
 href="http://www.pr.state.az.us/partnerships/ohv/ohv2.html"
alt="go to off-highway vehicle program">
<area shape="rect" coords="6,88,134,114"
href="http://www.pr.state.az.us/partnerships/grants/grants.html"
alt="go to grants">
<area shape="rect" coords="6,31,112,53"
href="http://www.pr.state.az.us/parksites.html"
alt="go to parksites">
<area shape="rect" coords="4,5,112,24"
href="http://www.pr.state.az.us/download.html"
alt="go to what's new">
</map>

<img src="Images/index.gif" width="164" height="354" align="left" border="0"
alt="navigation bar" usemap="#indexMap3">

</body>
</html>
```

Figure 13.8 shows the imagemap results using image.

Figure 13.8
The imagemap results in
Netscape 6.2.

The same thing can be done using the `object` element. Listing 13.5 shows how the markup would look in that case.

Listing 13.5   Using the `object` Element to Create an Imagemap

```
<!DOCTYPE HTML PUBLIC "-//W3C//DTD HTML 4.01 Transitional//EN"
        "http://www.w3.org/TR/html4/loose.dtd">

<html>

<head>
<title>Working with Objects</title>
</head>


<body>

<map name="indexMap3">
<area shape="rect" coords="4,56,124,84"
href="http://www.pr.state.az.us/partnerships/partners.html"
alt="go to partners">
<area shape="rect" coords="5,294,114,321"
href="mailto:feedback@pr.state.az.us"
alt="send feedback">
```

Listing 13.5   Continued

```
<area shape="rect" coords="4,265,127,291"
href="http://www.pr.state.az.us/employment/hrmain.html"
alt="go to main">
<area shape="rect" coords="5,237,111,262"
href="http://www.pr.state.az.us/giftshop.html"
alt="go to giftshop">
<area shape="rect" coords="7,209,129,234"
href="http://www.pr.state.az.us/partnerships/trails/statetrails.html"
alt="go to state trails">
<area shape="rect" coords="6,177,155,207"
href="http://www.pr.state.az.us/partnerships/shpo/shpo.html"
alt="go to state historic preservation office">
<area shape="rect" coords="6,148,115,173"
href="http://www.pr.state.az.us/partnerships/planning/planning.html"
alt="go to planning">
<area shape="rect" coords="6,119,157,146"
href="http://www.pr.state.az.us/partnerships/ohv/ohv2.html"
alt="go to off-highway vehicle program">
<area shape="rect" coords="6,88,134,114"
href="http://www.pr.state.az.us/partnerships/grants/grants.html"
alt="go to grants">
<area shape="rect" coords="6,31,112,53"
href="http://www.pr.state.az.us/parksites.html"
alt="go to parksites">
<area shape="rect" coords="4,5,112,24"
href="http://www.pr.state.az.us/download.html"
alt="go to what's new">
</map>

<object data="images/index.gif" width="164" height="354" align="left"
border="0" type="image/gif" usemap="#indexMap3">
</object>

</body>
</html>
```

Figure 13.9 shows the results in IE 6, which renders the image in as an iframe.

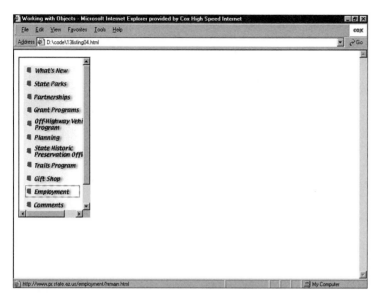

Figure 13.9
Using object for imagemapping can be problematic in certain browsers, in this case, IE 6.

CASE BY CASE: ENSURING ACCESSIBILITY FOR EMBEDDED OBJECTS

There are several ways to ensure that embedded objects are properly dealt with in terms of accessibility.

Here are some things to do to work toward creating an accessible document with embedded objects:

- If you are using the object element to define objects on a page, you can provide text descriptions that will be helpful to everyone, including the disabled, as follows:

```
<object> Text description goes here . . .
</object>
```

- When using the applet element, use the alt attribute to describe the applet's purpose.

- Put descriptive cues within the text so people can understand the relationship between the object and the page in a very clear way. This is especially important if you are using objects for navigation.

- Use the alt attribute and a description to define each link in an imagemap.

For further information about accessibility, **see** "Creating Accessible Sites," **p. 419**, Chapter 17.

<!--

There are many applications that assist with the creation of image-maps. Almost all graphic design software used for Web, such as Photoshop, LiveMotion, Fireworks, Paint Shop Pro, and so on, can produce imagemaps.

Some popular small utilities include

Mapedit is a strong, affordable utility available for Windows, Mac, Unix, and Linux. From Boutell.Com, Inc., at http://www.boutell.com/mapedit/.

CoffeeCup Image Mapper for Windows offers a free version so you can check it out before you buy, at http://www.coffeecup.com/mapper/.

LiveImage is another Windows-platform imagemapping program, considered to be very user friendly— http://www.mediatec.com/.

-->

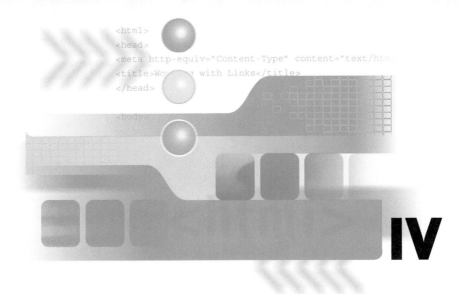

STYLE AND SCRIPTING

14 Using CSS with HTML and XHTML   **345**

15 CSS in Depth: Applying Style and Positioning   **369**

16 Adding Scripting to HTML and XHTML Documents   **401**

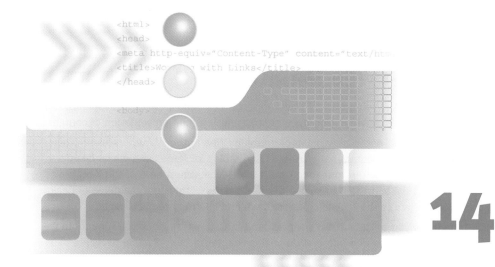

14

USING CSS WITH HTML
AND XHTML

IN THIS CHAPTER

Style Sheets and Web Markup   346

Style Sheet Fundamentals   346

Style Sheet Methods   350

Style Sheet Syntax   358

Exploring Class and Grouping   360

Case by Case: Anatomy of Style   368

STYLE SHEETS AND WEB MARKUP

Web markup is changing. As Web browsers that support styles become more widespread, the easier it is to reach the goals of separating document formatting from presentation of content.

Of course, this introduces an entire new realm of study for Web authors. Authors were previously accustomed to using presentational attributes and tables for layout and visual design, perhaps with a bit of CSS thrown in to manage some style. The atmosphere of the Web now suggests, however, that we learn CSS to such a degree that it becomes our language of design. HTML and XHTML are left as the technologies with which we structure documents.

This chapter introduces you to the main concepts found in CSS and teaches you how to implement them in your pages. All of the information in this chapter is as applicable to HTML as it is to XHTML.

The study of style sheets is complex enough to warrant its own in-depth books and resources. Because style is so critical to working with contemporary Web markup, I will provide you here with the foundational information I believe to be most immediately useful to you as you work on your HTML and XHTML documents. Then, in the next chapter, I'll focus on using CSS for style and positioning.

I do feel compelled to warn you that the information in this chapter (and the following one, too) simply cannot be as detailed as what will be found in those more comprehensive resources dedicated to style. So, as ancillary material to this chapter, I highly recommend you also explore Eric A. Meyer's excellent collection of CSS-related information at http://www.meyerweb.com/eric/css/. I will be making more resource suggestions throughout both this chapter and the following so you can more deeply pursue your study of CSS.

STYLE SHEET FUNDAMENTALS

Cascading Style Sheets (CSS) is the broad term used to refer to the application of presentational properties to documents. In this case, think of a style as any kind of design characteristic: typeface, background, text, link colors, margin controls, and placement of objects on a page.

Why should you use style sheets if markup can do at least some of this work by itself? The developers of HTML originally intended for HTML to be only a markup language, responsible for the basic structure of a page, including body, headers, paragraphs, and a few specific items such as bulleted lists. Web designers and browser developers are the ones who have pushed and pulled at HTML to make it accommodate aspects of presentation, and as a result HTML and XHTML have inherited this legacy.

To gain some separation between HTML's original function as a structural markup tool but still offer a powerful

<!--Caution

Web browsers don't all fully support CSS. Although Internet Explorer introduced CSS in the Windows 3.0 browser version, it had some bugs with the implementation. Netscape, in a rush to meet the competition, built Navigator 4.0 to support CSS. But the compliance is very incomplete at best. Add to this the fact that many Web visitors do not keep up-to-date with the latest and greatest browsers, and the usefulness of completely following the separation of structure and content from presentation should still be carefully considered in many cases.

-->

addition to the designer's toolbox in terms of style, Cascading Style Sheets were developed. In fact, as of the HTML 4.0 recommendation, many of the style-oriented elements (such as <font>) were deprecated (considered undesirable and may not be present in future language versions) in favor of CSS.

Separation of Presentation from Structure

Until Cascading Style Sheets entered the picture, HTML was missing an important component. Although some control of style with headers and font tags is possible, these techniques are limited because of the limitations of HTML. In many ways, style sheets provide a long-awaited solution for many of HTML's restrictions. The results are better font control, color management, margin control, and even the addition of special effects such as text shadowing. Another powerful benefit is the ability to control multiple pages within a site from a single sheet, and use multiple types of style sheets in a sequence for very precise control.

<!--
You can find a significant source for information on style sheets at the World Wide Web Consortium's site at http://www.w3.org/Style/.
-->

The logic and power of style sheets outweigh the current problems with browser support, and for this reason, designers clearly must learn the concepts and techniques and be at the ready to employ them where necessary.

<!--
CSS is now in its second version, CSS2. Work on CSS3 is underway.
-->

Cascade and Inheritance

One of the powers of style sheets is that there is a hierarchy of relationships. *Cascade* in this context refers to the order in which style is applied. Multiple sheets and types of sheets can be used, each one being applied one after another. This creates a hierarchy of application.

For example, you can combine inline, embedded, and linked styles, or any number of individual types of style sheets (see "Style Sheet Methods," later in this chapter), for maximum control. Say you have a large site that you're controlling with a single style sheet. However, you have a page on which you want to alter some of the styles. No problem! You can simply place the modified style as an embedded sheet within the individual page. The browser will first look for the embedded style and apply that information. Whatever isn't covered in the embedded sheet the browser will seek out in the linked sheet.

You also can override both styles by adding an inline style. When all three forms are in place, the style sheet–compliant browser looks for that style first, then the embedded style, and then the linked sheet; it reads the information in that order.

I've created a page with a link, an embedded sheet, and some inline styles, as you can see in Listing 14.1.

Listing 14.1   Linked, Embedded, and Inline Styles Applied to the Same Page

```
<?xml version="1.0"?>
<!DOCTYPE html PUBLIC "-//W3C//DTD XHTML 1.0 Transitional//EN"
"http://www.w3.org/TR/xhtml1/DTD/xhtml1-transitional.dtd">
<html xmlns="http://www.w3.org/1999/xhtml">
<head>
<title>Combination Style Sheet Example</title>

<link rel="stylesheet" href="mystyle_1.css" type="text/css" />

<style type="text/css">

<!--

p {
font: 13pt Verdana;
}

-->

</style>
</head>

<body>

<h1 style="font-family: Garamond; font-size: 22pt;">
A Midsummer Night's Dream</h1>

Act I Scene I<br />

<p>Either to die the death or to abjure <br />
For ever the society of men. <br />
Therefore, fair <a href="hermia.html">Hermia</a>,
question your desires; <br />
Know of your youth, examine well your blood, <br />
Whether, if you yield not to your father's choice, <br />
You can endure the livery of a nun, <br />
For aye to be in shady cloister mew'd, <br />
To live a barren sister all your life, <br />
Chanting faint hymns to the cold fruitless moon. <br />
Thrice-blessed they that master so their blood, <br />
To undergo such maiden <a href="pilgrim.html">pilgrimage</a>; <br />
But earthlier happy is the rose distill'd, <br />
Than that which withering on the virgin thorn <br />
Grows, lives and dies in single blessedness.</p>
</body>
</html>
```

In Figure 14.1, you can see the concept of cascade in action—with the inline style overpowering the embedded style, and so forth. In a sense, the linked sheet becomes the default. If you load the samples from the chapter into your browser, you can replicate the cascade in action yourself.

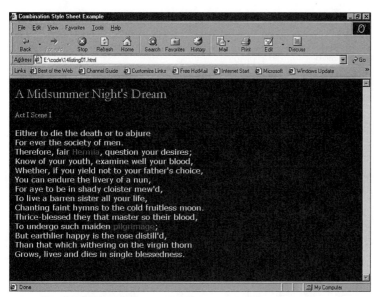

Figure 14.1
In this case, I combined style methods to achieve the page's look and feel.

Another example of a cascade concept within CSS is the use of multiple external sheets in the same document:

```
<head>
<link rel="stylesheet" type="text/css" href="molly1.css" />
<link rel="stylesheet" type="text/css" href="molly2.css" />
<link rel="stylesheet" type="text/css" href="molly3.css" />
</head>
```

The last style sheet in the list will first apply any styles that aren't in the middle one, and the middle one will then apply any styles that aren't in the first one. This is another example of cascade.

Another aspect of CSS is *inheritance*. This concept defines specific elements as being parents, and elements within those elements as children. Take for example the body element. This element contains all other markup that affects the way the content of the page is displayed. Elements within the body are considered *children* of the body element.

This concept continues down the markup hierarchy, referred to as a *tree*. Think of it as a family tree, in fact.

<!--
Whenever possible, streamline the style sheets in a cascade. If you can accomplish the same results using a single linked sheet or an embedded sheet, do so. Use the cascade concept whenever you need to override a linked sheet at specific points in the style relationship, such as linked to embedded to inline, or linked to inline, or embedded to inline and so forth.
-->

So, if you have a paragraph, the elements within that paragraph are the *children* of that parent, and so on. This system is referred to as *containment hierarchy*. Figure 14.2 shows how containment hierarchy works.

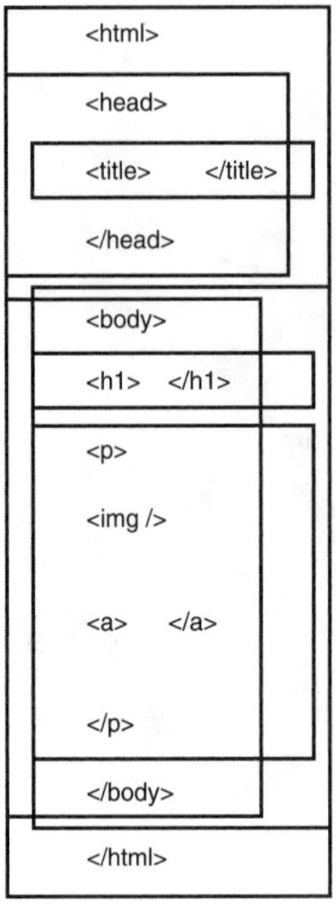

Figure 14.2
Containment hierarchy. Notice how each container is nested in another.

```
<html>
    <head>
        <title>     </title>
    </head>

    <body>
        <h1>   </h1>

        <p>

        <img />

        <a>     </a>

        </p>
    </body>
</html>
```

Inheritance claims that unless you specify differently, style will be inherited by the child of a parent. For example, if you write a style asking that a specific text color be applied to a paragraph, all tags within that paragraph will inherit that color unless you state otherwise.

<!--**Caution**
While browsers are becoming much more mature in their ability to render style, support for inheritance tends to be inconsistent.
-->

STYLE SHEET METHODS

Style can be delivered to a document by a variety of methods including:

- **Inline**—This method allows you to take any tag and add a style to it. Using the inline method gives you maximum control over a precise aspect of a Web document. Say you want to control the look and feel of a specific paragraph. You could simply add a `style="x"` attribute to the paragraph tag, and the browser would display that paragraph using the style values you added to the code.

- **Embedded**—Embedding allows for control of a full document. Using the `style` element, which you place within the `head` section of a document, you can insert detailed style attributes to be applied to the entire page.

- **Linked**—Also referred to as an "external" style sheet, a linked style sheet provides a powerful way for you to create master styles that you can apply to an entire site. You create a main style sheet document using the `.css` extension. This document contains the styles you want a single page or even thousands of pages to adopt. Any page that links to this document takes on the styles called for in that document.

- **Imported**—This method works similarly to linked style except that it uses the `@import` rule. Although I won't discuss imported style in this chapter, I will in Chapter 15, "CSS in Depth: Applying Style and Positioning," when I discuss layout methods.

- **User Defined**—These are style sheets that you can create to override any other style sheets. You can learn more about how to create a user defined style sheet via the external resources I've provided in this chapter.

In the following examples, you'll see a variety of syntax that will look unfamiliar if you are new to style sheets. Bear with me through these examples. You first need to understand the methods used to apply style. Then I'll provide a closer look at style sheet syntax itself.

> `<!--`
> Although you can use any of the style methods in Web documents, it is *highly recommended* that you begin to use linked style sheets with XHTML, avoiding any rendering problems and truly living up to the "separate document structure from presentation" concept inherent to HTML 4.0 and XHTML.
> `-->`

Inline Style

You can add inline style to any element that makes sense. Such elements include paragraphs, headers, horizontal rules, anchors, and table cells. Each is a logical candidate for inline style. Here's a standard paragraph

```
<p>The text in this paragraph will display as text using the
default font.</p>
```

The following example uses the paragraph tag along with the `style` attribute to achieve inline style:

```
<p style="font: 13pt Verdana">The text in this paragraph will display as
13 point text using the
verdana font.</p>
```

Figure 14.3 shows two paragraphs, one with the standard default typeface for a Windows machine (Times) and one with the Verdana typeface applied.

Two elements can help you apply inline style to sections of a page. These elements are particularly useful not only for style sheets, but also later when you combine style sheets with dynamic events through DHTML. They are the division, or `div` element, and the `span` element.

`div` and `span` specify a defined range of text, so everything between them adopts the style you want to use. The primary difference between `div` and `span` is that `div` is a block-level element, meaning it can contain a variety of other elements, including other block-level elements.

However, span can only be used inline and may not contain any block-level elements. For example, you can align a table with div, but you couldn't do the same with span. Another major difference is that div, being a block-level element, creates a line break after the division, whereas span does not. For this reason, span is especially useful within sentences or paragraphs, and div is most appropriate when used to define larger sections of text, including paragraphs, headings, lists, and nested elements.

<!--
Use span to modify the style of any portion of text shorter than a paragraph.
-->

Figure 14.3
Using inline style, I applied the Verdana font to the second paragraph.

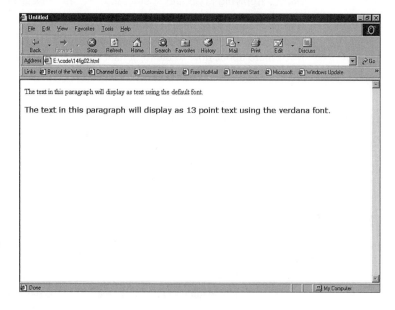

The following is an example of the division element at work:

```
<div style="font-family: Garamond; font-size: 14pt;">

<p>All of the text within this section is 14 point Garamond.</p>
</div>
```

This example shows the <span> tag:

```
<p><span style="color: #999999">This text appears in the color gray, with no
line break after the closing span tag </span> and the rest of the text.</p>
```

Figure 14.4 shows the combined results of the div and span elements with style attributes applied.

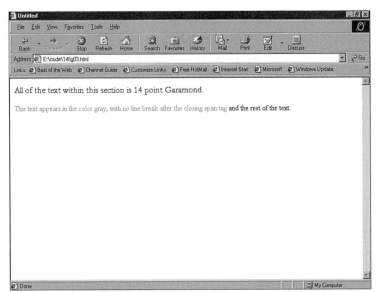

Embedded Style

Embedded styles use the style element, which you place within the head section of an HTML document, as shown in Listing 14.2.

Listing 14.2 Using the style Element

```
<?xml version="1.0"?>
<!DOCTYPE html PUBLIC "-//W3C//DTD XHTML 1.0 Transitional//EN"
"http://www.w3.org/TR/xhtml1/DTD/xhtml1-transitional.dtd">
<html xmlns="http://www.w3.org/1999/xhtml">
<head>
<title>Embedded Style Sheet Example I</title>

<style type="text/css">

<!--

body {
background: #FFFFFF;
color: #000000;
}
h1 {
font: 14pt Verdana; color: #CCCCCC;
}
```

Listing 14.2 Continued

```
p {
font: 13pt Times;
}
a {
color: #FF0000; text-decoration: none;
}

-->

</style>
</head>
<body>

<h1>a Midsummer Night's Dream: Act I Scene I</h1>

Either to die the death or to abjure <br />
For ever the society of men. <br />
Therefore, fair <a href="hermia.html">Hermia</a>, question your desires; <br />
Know of your youth, examine well your blood, <br />
Whether, if you yield not to your father's choice, <br />
You can endure the livery of a nun, <br />
For aye to be in shady cloister mew'd, <br />
To live a barren sister all your life, <br />
Chanting faint hymns to the cold fruitless moon. <br />
Thrice-blessed they that master so their blood, <br />
To undergo such maiden <a href="pilgrim.html">pilgrimage</a>; <br />
But earthlier happy is the rose distill'd, <br />
Than that which withering on the virgin thorn <br />
Grows, lives and dies in single blessedness.

</body>
</html>
```

As you can tell from the preceding example, a document using a style sheet begins to look quite a bit different from older HTML documents, but following the logic is not difficult. In this case, the page's body calls for a background color, a text color, an h1 font style, a paragraph style, and a link style.

Figure 14.5 shows the results of the embedded style sheet in Listing 14.2.

> `<!--`
>
> To ensure that your embedded style sheet is hidden from older browsers, you can place comment tags such as `<!-- style sheet goes here -->` around the sheet. Begin the comment tag underneath the `<style>` tag and end the comment immediately before the `</style>` tag. Note that this technique is only for embedded style sheets, not linked.
>
> `-->`

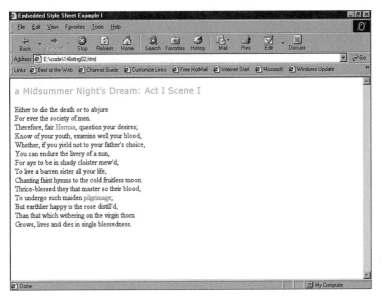

Figure 14.5
In this case, I used embedded style to add color and type styles to the page.

Notice how the level one heading, h1, calls for a font using the font's name as well as a literal point size. This figure is a prime example of one reason why Cascading Style Sheets are so powerful: Not only can you choose to control sizing in points, but you also can use pixels (px), percentages (75%), and other, more effective means of working with sizing.

Another interesting aspect of this style sheet includes the difference in fonts as defined by the header and paragraph style; they're different in color and face. With style sheets, the days of having a document littered with <font> tags are limited. Style is handled in a nice, compact fashion.

The a (anchor) selector in the style sheet shows yet another handy piece of syntax. The text-decoration: none declaration forces underlining to be removed from links, allowing for clean, attractive design results—something that is attractive to designers but somewhat controversial for usability experts, who feel that removing the underlining from links can conceivably confuse site visitors.

Linked Style Sheets

Linked style sheets, also called *external* style sheets, extend the possibilities of embedded style. Using the same code contained within the style element as you saw in the embedded sample, you can place this information in a separate document. You then can save the document with the file extension .css. You should be sure that this document is either in the root directory with the files that you intend to have it affect or that you author the link properly when linking to the sheet.

The power of linked style is that you can link all the pages in a site that you want to be influenced by the style to this single sheet. You can link one page or one thousand pages to a single style sheet.

Listing 14.3 shows the syntax for a linked, or external, style sheet.

Listing 14.3   A Linked Style Sheet

```
body {
background: #000000;
color: #FFFFCC;
}
h1 {
font: 14pt Garamond; color: #CCCCCC;
}
p {
font: 13pt Arial;
}
a {
color: #FF0000; text-decoration: none;
}
```

> `<!--`**Caution**
> Style sheets should not contain any HTML or XHTML tags, simply the selectors, properties, values and comments.
> `-->`

Now, you can take this style sheet and step through the process of making it into an actively linked external sheet:

1. Make sure that you have a template that has been markup up and saved to a directory. Here's my page, saved as `14style01.html`:

```
<?xml version="1.0"?>
<!DOCTYPE html PUBLIC "-//W3C//DTD Xhtml 1.0 Transitional//EN"
"http://www.w3.org/TR/xhtml1/DTD/xhtml1-transitional.dtd">
<html xmlns="http://www.w3.org/1999/xhtml">
<head>
<title>Linked Style Sheet Example</title>

</head>
<body>

<h1>A Midsummer Night's Dream: Act I Scene I</h1>

Either to die the death or to abjure <br />
For ever the society of men. <br />
Therefore, fair <a href="hermia.html">Hermia</a>, question your desires; <br />
Know of your youth, examine well your blood, <br />
Whether, if you yield not to your father's choice, <br />
You can endure the livery of a nun, <br />
For aye to be in shady cloister mew'd, <br />
To live a barren sister all your life, <br />
Chanting faint hymns to the cold fruitless moon. <br />
```

```
Thrice-blessed they that master so their blood, <br />
To undergo such maiden <a href="pilgrim.html">pilgrimage</a>; <br />
But earthlier happy is the rose distill'd, <br />
Than that which withering on the virgin thorn <br />
Grows, lives and dies in single blessedness.

</body>
</html>
```

2. Open your editor and add the markup shown in Listing 14.3.

3. Save the file as `mystyle_1.css`.

4. Place this file in the directory where the `14style01.html` file resides.

5. Reopen `14style01.html`.

6. Add the following link element in the `head` section of the document:

```
<?xml version="1.0"?>
<!DOCTYPE html PUBLIC "-//W3C//DTD Xhtml 1.0 Transitional//EN"
"http://www.w3.org/TR/xhtml1/DTD/xhtml1-transitional.dtd">
<html xmlns="http://www.w3.org/1999/xhtml">
<head>
<title>Linked Style Sheet Example</title>
<link rel="stylesheet" href="mystyle_1.css" type="text/css" />

</head>
<body>

<h1>A Midsummer Night's Dream: Act I Scene I</h1>

Either to die the death or to abjure <br />
For ever the society of men. <br />
Therefore, fair <a href="hermia.html">Hermia</a>, question your desires; <br />
Know of your youth, examine well your blood, <br />
Whether, if you yield not to your father's choice, <br />
You can endure the livery of a nun, <br />
For aye to be in shady cloister mew'd, <br />
To live a barren sister all your life, <br />
Chanting faint hymns to the cold fruitless moon. <br />
Thrice-blessed they that master so their blood, <br />
To undergo such maiden <a href="pilgrim.html">pilgrimage</a>; <br />

But earthlier happy is the rose distill'd, <br />
Than that which withering on the virgin thorn <br />
Grows, lives and dies in single blessedness.

</body>
</html>
```

7. Save the file.

8. View the file in a style sheet–compliant browser. It should match the results shown in Figure 14.6.

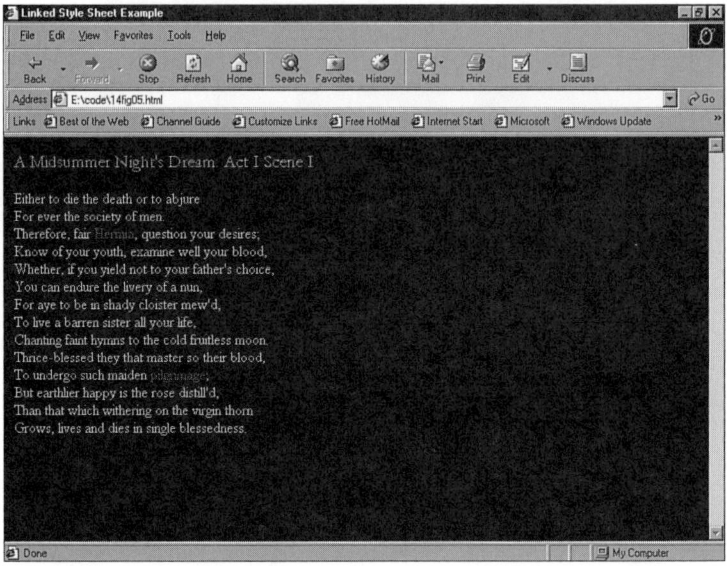

Figure 14.6
Any page containing this link adopts the styles defined in mystyle_1.css.

If you want to have 1,000 documents globally affected by this one style sheet, you can do so by linking them to this page. Then, if you want to make style adjustments to those 1,000 pages, you simply have to change the *one* file—mystyle_1.css.

STYLE SHEET SYNTAX

If you recall the discussion about syntax from earlier in the book, sentences require specific elements, as do mathematical equations. Style sheets are similar to both in that if their syntax does not follow a specified order, they might not function properly.

⇨ *For a refresher on syntax, **see** "Global Structure and Syntax of Documents," **p. 95,** Chapter 5.*

Whatever method you choose to deliver your style to Web documents, the syntax is going to be similar in all cases. Style sheets, like sentences, are made up of very specific parts. These parts include the following:

- **Selectors**—Selectors represent the elements that receive the properties and values you assign. Selectors are usually familiar elements, such as a header, h1, or a paragraph, p. Style sheets allow for a variety of selectors, including class selectors, which are discussed later in the chapter.

- **Properties**—A property describes the appearance of the elements corresponding to a selector. For example, if you have a paragraph, p, as a selector, properties you include will help describe that selector. Margins, fonts, and backgrounds are some property concepts. Style sheets contain many properties, and you can use a variety of properties to define a rule.

- **Values**—Values describe properties. Say you have a level one header, h1, as your selector, and you've included a type family, font-family, as a property. The face that you actually define is the value of that property.

Properties and values combined make up a *declaration*. A selector and a declaration make up a *rule*, as shown here:

```
h1 {
font-family: garamond, times, serif;
}
```

Note that the curly brackets are used to contain the declaration. This syntax is only true for embedded or linked styles. Whenever using inline style, you use quotations to contain your declaration. Selectors aren't defined in this case, as the application of the declaration is inherent to the tag to which the style is being applied:

```
<h1 style="font-family: Garamond, Times, serif;">This text will
be defined by the declaration</h1>
```

Any time you have multiple declarations, you'll end each individual declaration with a semicolon (;). In the case of a single declaration, it's not necessary to use the semicolon, but many practitioners prefer to do so.

> `<!--` Even though a semicolon is unnecessary when ending a single style declaration, many working developers, WYSIWYG programs, and XHTML editors use the semicolon anyway. This can reduce errors down the road. I always use the final semicolon myself when authoring style sheets. `-->`

Selectors in Detail

There are several types of selectors of which to be aware:

- **Element selectors**—These selectors refer directly to an HTML or XHTML element, such as p, h1, a, and so on.

- **Class selectors**—Class selectors can be considered "custom" selectors. They are defined by you, the author, with a name preceded by a period, such as .blue, and an appropriately written rule defining the style. Then, they are applied within the HTML or XHTML document using the class attribute:

  ```
  <p class="bluePara">This paragraph will take on the style you've defined
  for the class selector "bluePara".</p>
  ```

- **ID selectors**—Similar to class selectors, ID selectors have several differences. First, they begin with a hash mark (#) instead of a period. They are called on in the document with the id attribute. IDs also differ from class selectors in that a specific ID is used only once within a document.

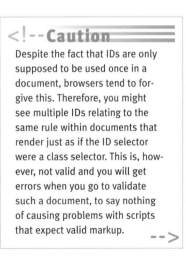

`<!--Caution` Despite the fact that IDs are only supposed to be used once in a document, browsers tend to forgive this. Therefore, you might see multiple IDs relating to the same rule within documents that render just as if the ID selector were a class selector. This is, however, not valid and you will get errors when you go to validate such a document, to say nothing of causing problems with scripts that expect valid markup. `-->`

There are other kinds of selectors, and there are numerous properties and related values. More examples of these will be available in Chapter 15.

EXPLORING CLASS AND GROUPING

Using class selectors is pretty straightforward. Suppose you want two different kinds of h1 headings in your documents. You can create a style class for each one by putting the following text in the style sheet:

```
<style type="text/css">

<!--

.serif {
font: 24pt "Century Schoolbook";
}
.sans {
font: 14pt Arial;
}

-->

</style>
```

You then assign the class serif or sans inline to achieve the results.

Grouping is achieved when style properties and values are condensed, resulting in tighter rules. Consider the following class example:

```
p {
font-family: arial;
font-size: 13pt;
line-height: 14pt;
}
```

In this example, all paragraphs with the class of 1 will show up as a 13-point Arial font with a line height of 14 points. If you apply grouping to this selector, you end up with the following results:

```
p {
font: 13pt/14pt arial;
}
```

The design will be the same, either way. Notice that you place the font size first, the line height after the forward slash, and then the name of the font.

<!--Caution
Grouping requires a specific syntactical order to work properly. With type, the font size comes first, the line height comes second, and then the font name is included. -->

Working with Class

To get the most variation in style, assign classes to individual selectors. You do so very simply by adding a named extension to any selector.

If you have two headers and two paragraph styles that you want to add attributes to, you can name each one and assign styles to the individual paragraphs. You then can call on the name within the specific tag in the body of the document, as shown here:

```
<style type="text/css">

<!--

h1.left {
font: arial 14pt;
color: #FF0033;
text-align: left;
}

H2.right {
font: arial 13pt;
color: #FF6633;
text-align: right;
}

-->

</style>
```

In the HTML or XHTML document, you place the class name:

```
<h1 class="left">This is my Left Heading</h2>
```

All the h1 headers that you name class="left" will have the h1.left class properties. Similarly, the H2 headers with an attribute of class="right" will have the properties defined for that class.

In Listing 14.4, I show an XHTML page with the embedded style sheet and class combination used to achieve the page style.

Listing 14.4   Working with Classes

```
<?xml version="1.0"?>
<!DOCTYPE html PUBLIC "-//W3C//DTD Xhtml 1.0 Transitional//EN"
"http://www.w3.org/TR/xhtml1/DTD/xhtml1-transitional.dtd">
<html xmlns="http://www.w3.org/1999/xhtml">
<head>
```

Listing 14.4   Continued

```
<title>style sheet sample: class</title>
<style type="text/css">

<!--

p.center {
font-family: Garamond, Times, serif;
font-size: 14pt;
text-align: center;
}

p.right {
font-family: Verdana, Helvetica, sans-serif;
font-size: 13pt;
text-align: right;
}

p.name {
font-family: Garamond, Times, serif;
font-size: 10pt;
text-align: center;
text-weight: bold;
text-style: italic;
}

-->

</style>

</head>

<body>

<p class="center">
Brain researchers estimate that your unconscious data base outweighs the
conscious on an order exceeding ten million to one. This data base is the
source of your hidden, natural genius. In other words, a part of you is much
smarter than you are. The wise people regularly consult that smarter part.
</p>

<p class="right">
Crazy people who are productive are geniuses. Crazy people who are rich are
eccentric. Crazy people who are neither productive nor rich are just plain
crazy. Geniuses and crazy people are both out in the middle of a deep ocean;
```

Listing 14.4   Continued

```
geniuses swim, crazy people drown. Most of us are sitting safely on the shore.
Take a chance and get your feet wet.
</p>

<p class="name">
-- Michael J. Gelb
</p>
</body>
</html>
```

Figure 14.7 shows class in action.

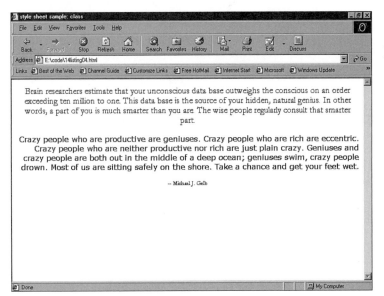

Figure 14.7
Using class, I varied the paragraph alignment and text appearance on this page.

If you'd like to create a custom class, you can do so by simply naming the class—it doesn't have to be attached to a familiar element selector. For example, let's say I'd like to have the style assigned to "right" in the previous example be globally useful to *any* XHTML tag rather than just a paragraph tag. In this case, you'd write the style code as follows:

```
.right {
font-family: Verdana, Helvetica, sans-serif;
font-size: 13pt;
text-align: right;
}
```

Then, you'd add the style to any tag you like using the custom class. The information contained within that tag will pick up the style information described using the `right` custom class.

Using Grouping

To group style sheets, you can do the following:

- Group multiple selectors

- Group properties and values

Say you want to assign the same properties to a number of header styles. One reason you might do so is to force all headers to update to a single style after being linked to the sheet.

Without grouping, the syntax would look like this:

```
<style type="text/css">

<!--

h1 {
font-family: Arial;
font-size 14pt;
color: #000000;
}

h2 {

font-family: Arial;
font-size 14pt;
color: #000000;
}

h3 {

font-family: Arial;
font-size 14pt;
color: #000000;
}

-->

</style>
```

Here's the same example grouped:

```
h1, h2, h3 {

font-family: Arial;
font-size 14pt;
color: #000000;
}
```

The processes of grouping properties and grouping values are similar in concept. Without grouping, an example of properties and values within the body would look like this:

```
body {
font-family: Arial, san-serif;
font-size: 13pt;
line-height: 14pt;
font-weight: bold;
font- style: normal;
}
```

With grouping, you can simply use the font property and then stack the arguments like this:

```
body {
font: bold normal 13pt/14pt Arial, san-serif;
}
```

To exemplify how order in grouping works, you can group margins using the margin property. However, you must follow the property with the top, right, left, and bottom margin values in that order. Be sure to specify all these values when grouping; otherwise, you'll end up with the same value applied to all:

```
body {
margin: .10in .75in .75in .10in;
}
```

Note that no commas appear between the values. However, the declaration can end with a semicolon.

Listing 14.5 describes a style sheet using class and grouping.

Listing 14.5 Class and Grouping

```
<?xml version="1.0"?>
<!DOCTYPE html PUBLIC "-//W3C//DTD XHTML 1.0 Transitional//EN"
"http://www.w3.org/TR/xhtml1/DTD/xhtml1-transitional.dtd">
<html xmlns="http://www.w3.org/1999/xhtml">
<head>
<title>Class and Grouping</title>

<style type="text/css">

<!--

body {
margin: 0.10in 0.50in 0.50in;
}

h1.left {
font: 16pt Helvetica;
```

Listing 14.5 Continued

```
text-align: left;
}

h2.right {

font: 14pt Helvetica;
text-align: right;
color: #FF0033;
}

p.left {
font: 13pt/11pt Garamond;
text-align: left;
}

p.right {
font: 13pt Arial;
text-align: right;
margin: 0in .75in .50in;
}

a {

text-decoration: none;
font-weight: bold;
}

-->
</style>

</head>
<body>

<h1 class="left">A Midsummer Night's Dream</h1>

<p class="left">
Either to die the death or to abjure
For ever the society of men.
</p>

<p class="right">
Therefore, fair <a href="hermia.html">Hermia</a>,
question your desires;
```

Listing 14.5   Continued

```
Know of your youth, examine well your blood,
Whether, if you yield not to your father's choice,
You can endure the livery of a nun,
For aye to be in shady cloister mew'd,
To live a barren sister all your life,
Chanting faint hymns to the cold fruitless moon.
</p>

<p class="left">
Thrice-blessed they that master so their blood,
To undergo such maiden <a href="pilgrim.html">pilgrimage</a>;
But earthlier happy is the rose distill'd,
Than that which withering on the virgin thorn
Grows, lives and dies in single blessedness.
</p>

<p class="right">From Act I, Scene I</p>

</body>
</html>
```

Figure 14.8 shows the combination of class and grouping.

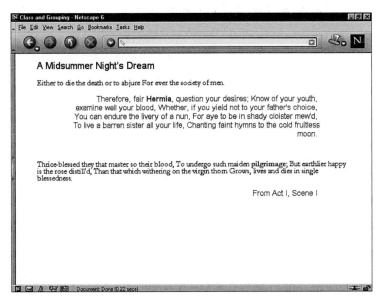

Figure 14.8
By combining class and grouping, you can achieve concise code and varied style.

CASE BY CASE: ANATOMY OF STYLE

You will definitely require more information about style sheets if you find that you are using them regularly in your design work. Up-to-date style sheet resources are available on the Web, and many books address working with styles.

A primary online resource for style sheet information is the World Wide Web Consortium's style sheet section at `http://www.w3c.org/Style/`. In this area, you can find the complete specification and latest information on XHTML style sheets.

Because Microsoft's Internet Explorer pioneered popular browser support of style sheets, Microsoft has accumulated some excellent references on its developer site at `http://msdn.microsoft.com/`.

Another powerful style reference is the Web Review Style Sheets Reference Guide at `http://style.webreview.com/`. This page contains general information, and links to excellent style compatibility browser charts.

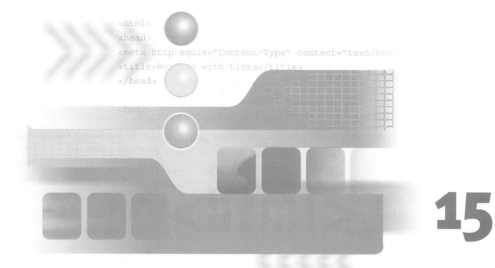

CSS IN DEPTH: APPLYING STYLE AND POSITIONING

IN THIS CHAPTER

Applying Style to Text 370

Using CSS for Layout 386

Gracefully Degrading CSS Layouts 394

Case by Case: css/edge: Visual and Dynamic Effects with CSS 396

APPLYING STYLE TO TEXT

The scope of CSS is becoming broader and more complex than ever before. This is largely because, in many cases, we can now confidently use CSS in our professional applications.

In this chapter, I'm going to provide information and exercises that will help you address two primary and important issues in CSS: how to style text, and how to use CSS to create layouts. This will get you working immediately with sophisticated style, but this chapter can by no means address the level of detail that professional Web authors will require in coming months and years in regards to CSS. To that end, I encourage you to seek out resources that will help you get the depth of information you'll need. I will provide ample Web sites and other recommendations to assist you in this goal.

➪ *For a listing of helpful books and general resources, **see** "Annotated Resources for Web Developers," p. 563, Appendix B.*

Setting type using style sheets is one of the most exciting design aspects that CSS offers. Not only do you have the ability to call for many type styles to appear on a page or a site, but you also have additional control over a variety of typographic conventions otherwise unavailable when using presentational elements and attributes in HTML and XHTML.

➪ *Don' t forget the fundamentals! **See** "Using CSS with HTML and XHTML," p. 345, Chapter 14.*

This control becomes especially important when you're creating large sites. Instead of having to work with multiple, worrisome `font` tags and attributes, with CSS you can create a single style sheet that will define all the styles required for the entire site, including a variety of links types, headers, text, lists, and so on.

Instead of the `font` element, you now can use the style sheet property `font`. You can then add a variety of values along with it, or you can use classes and grouping to fully flex the power of type through the use of style sheets. What's more, you can add a wide variety of typographic conventions to type that extend far above and beyond the `font` element, providing you with extended options and more refined design results.

The Trouble with Fonts

The reality of font support in style sheets is much the same as those issues encountered by the designer when employing the `font` element and its attributes. The specific typeface must be available on the computer viewing your page. And, as with the `font` element, style sheets do allow you to stack any number of typefaces so that you can maximize the chances that your browser will pick up a typeface that you want your audience to see.

If the people viewing your pages don't have Arial, for example, they'll probably have Helvetica, and so forth. Although these typefaces have some minor differences, they are similar enough to be considered workable in the context of style sheet design.

Style Sheet Font Families

Style sheets recognize five font families, attempting to address the major family groups available in typography.

For style sheets, five font categories, or master families, are defined:

- **Serif**—Serif faces are those faces with strokes. These strokes are said to aid in readability; therefore, serif typefaces are often very popular for printed body text. Some examples of serif faces include Times, Garamond, and Century Schoolbook.

<!--
In CSS, font categories, or master families, are simply referred to as *families*. This terminology is one of the confusing differences found between the technology of the Web and the older, venerable typographic naming conventions.
-->

- **Sans Serif**—These typefaces tend to be rounded and have no strokes. Common sans-serif faces include Helvetica, Arial, Avant Garde, and Verdana. The rounded letterforms of many sans-serif faces are thought to be easier to read on screen than serif faces. This issue, however, is still debated by many Web developers and typographers.

- **Script**—A script face is one that looks similar to cursive writing or handwriting. Common script typefaces include Park Avenue and Lucida Handwriting.

- **Monospace**—These faces look like typewriter fonts. They are called monospace fonts because each letter within the face takes up the same width as another. For example, the letter *w*, which is wider in most faces than an *i*, is actually the same width in a monospace font. Courier or Courier New are the common monospace fonts found on both the Windows and Macintosh platforms.

- **Fantasy**—Referred to by most typographers as *decorative,* the fonts available in this category are best used for headers and artistic text rather than body text. Decorative fonts include Whimsy and Party.

To apply a family inline, you follow the stacking convention such as is found with the `font` tag. You do so in all cases of style, whether using the inline, embedded, or linked methods.

<!--
You can also use Wingdings and Webdings, which now come packaged with a variety of software programs, including browsers.
-->

Here's an inline example:

```
<p style="font-family: Arial, Helvetica, sans-serif">
In this selection, the browser will search the user's computer for the Arial
font. If it's found, it will be displayed. If it isn't found, it will look for
Helvetica. If neither is found, the browser will display the first sans-serif
typeface available.</p>
```

In Listing 15.1, I've taken this paragraph and added it to an HTML page with other text that has no style or font information added.

Listing 15.1   Style Applied to a Single Paragraph

```
<!DOCTYPE HTML PUBLIC "-//W3C//DTD HTML 4.01 Transitional//EN"
        "http://www.w3.org/TR/html4/loose.dtd">

<html>

<head>

<title>Style Sheet Sample</title>

</head>

<body>

<p>This paragraph has no style or font information added to it. Therefore, it
relies on the browser's own defaults for a typeface. You'll see this paragraph
appear in Verdana (IE 6.0).</p>

<p style="font-family: Arial, Helvetica, sans-serif">
In this selection, the browser will search the user's computer for the Arial
font. If it's found, it will be displayed. If it isn't found, it will look for
Helvetica. If neither is found, the browser will display the first sans-serif
typeface available. </p>

</body>
</html>
```

Figure 15.1 shows the difference between the first paragraph, with only the browser's defaults to figure out which typeface to include, and the second paragraph, where the typeface is controlled by style.

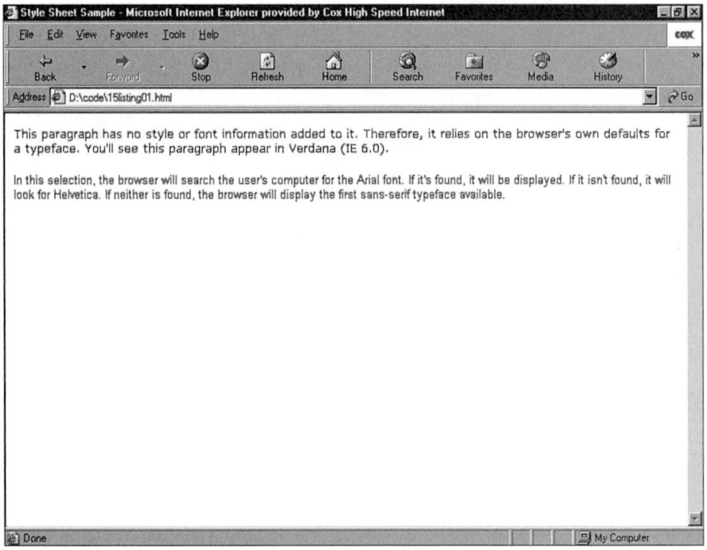

Figure 15.1
The default font compared to the Arial font created with style sheets.

Type Properties and Values

You can modify a range of typeface properties using style sheets, and you can apply an admirable selection of values to those properties. I'll focus on the most immediate and familiar here so that you can get started quickly using them in your designs.

As with the `font` element attributes, properties are available in CSS to control size and color. With style sheets, unlike with presentational HTML or XHTML, you can also control such things as the weight and style of a typeface; line height, also known as *leading*, which is the measurement between individual lines of set type; and numerous other properties to enhance your typographic control.

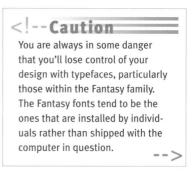

<!--**Caution**
You are always in some danger that you'll lose control of your design with typefaces, particularly those within the Fantasy family. The Fantasy fonts tend to be the ones that are installed by individuals rather than shipped with the computer in question.
-->

Furthermore, the available methods to control font size are very specific, and far exceed anything that presentational elements and attributes in HTML and XHTML have to offer.

Size

You can accomplish sizing by using the `font-size` property or using short-cut properties.

Type size in style sheets can be defined using points, pixels, inches, centimeters, millimeters, and picas. For Web designers, pixels are going to be the most natural choice, although this choice will ultimately depend on your preferences.

The following is an example of inline style setting the size of the typeface in pixels:

```
<p style="font-family: Garamond, Times, serif; font-size: 18px;">
"The most beautiful thing we can experience is the mysterious; It is the source
of all true art and science"
<br />
-- Albert Einstein</p>
```

Figure 15.2 shows how the font face and size are applied to this quote.

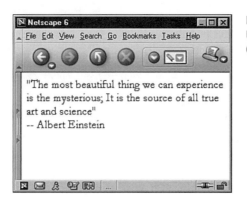

Figure 15.2
Using inline style, I applied the Garamond font at 18 pixels.

In this instance, I've set up a style sheet that can be embedded into a single page or linked to from a page. The style then affects any standard paragraphs on that page:

```
<style>

<!--

p {

font-family: Arial, Helvetica, sans-serif;
font-size: 18px;

}

-->

</style>
```

> <!--**Caution**
> If you create a linked style sheet out of the above markup, be sure to remove the `style` and comment tags, and simply leave the style rules, or the linked sheet won't work. -->

In Figure 15.3, you can see the embedded style sheet in action. The text is now made up of 18-pixel Arial text.

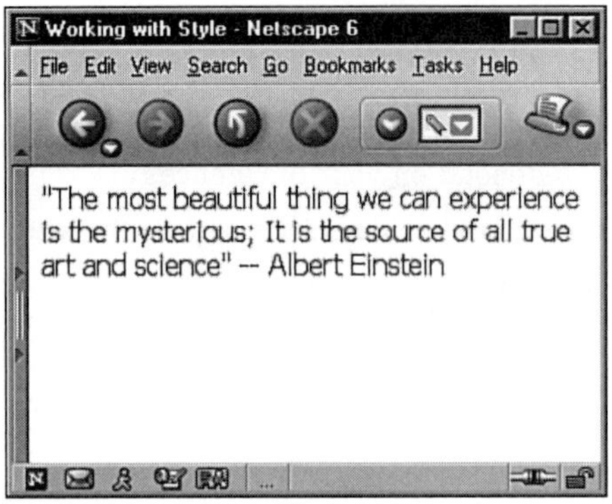

Figure 15.3
In this case, an embedded style sheet set the text to 18-pixel Arial.

Color

Style sheets allow you to choose from the 16 valid color names defined by HTML and XHTML, hexadecimal values, or RGB values.

➡ *To learn about color names, **see** "Dealing with Data Types," p. 61, Chapter 3.*

You can add color, like all style properties, to any reasonable HTML tag using inline, embedded, or linked-sheet methods, with the `color` property.

For this example, I'm going to add a typeface, type size, and color to an XHTML document:

1. Begin with a basic document:

```
<?xml version="1.0" encoding="UTF-8" ?>

<!DOCTYPE html
```

```
        PUBLIC "-//W3C//DTD XHTML 1.0 Transitional//EN"
        " http://www.w3.org/TR/xhtml1/DTD/xhtml1-transitional.dtd ">


<html xmlns="http://www.w3.org/1999/xhtml">

<head>

<title>Working with Style</title>

</head>

<body>

</body>
</html>
```

2. Add text:

```
<?xml version="1.0" encoding="UTF-8" ?>

<!DOCTYPE html
        PUBLIC "-//W3C//DTD XHTML 1.0 Transitional//EN"
        " http://www.w3.org/TR/xhtml1/DTD/xhtml1-transitional.dtd ">


<html xmlns="http://www.w3.org/1999/xhtml">

<head>

<title>Working with Style</title>

</head>

<body>

A human being is a part of the whole called by us universe, a part limited in
time and space. He experiences himself, his thoughts and feeling as something
separated from the rest, a kind of optical delusion of his consciousness. This
delusion is a kind of prison for us, restricting us to our personal desires and
to affection for a few persons nearest to us. Our task must be to free our-
selves
from this prison by widening our circle of compassion to enhance all living
creatures and the whole of nature in its beauty -- Albert Einstein


</body>
</html>
```

3. Add the paragraph tags:

```
<?xml version="1.0" encoding="UTF-8" ?>

<!DOCTYPE html
        PUBLIC "-//W3C//DTD XHTML 1.0 Transitional//EN"
        " http://www.w3.org/TR/xhtml1/DTD/xhtml1-transitional.dtd ">


<html xmlns="http://www.w3.org/1999/xhtml">

<head>

<title>Working with Style</title>

</head>

<body>

<p>A human being is a part of the whole called by us universe, a part limited in
time and space. He experiences himself, his thoughts and feeling as something
separated from the rest, a kind of optical delusion of his consciousness. This
delusion is a kind of prison for us, restricting us to our personal desires and
to affection for a few persons nearest to us. Our task must be to free our-
selves
from this prison by widening our circle of compassion to enhance all living
creatures and the whole of nature in its beauty -- Albert Einstein</p>


</body>
</html>
```

4. To the opening paragraph tag, add a style attribute containing the font-family property and its associated values:

```
<?xml version="1.0" encoding="UTF-8" ?>

<!DOCTYPE html
        PUBLIC "-//W3C//DTD XHTML 1.0 Transitional//EN"
        " http://www.w3.org/TR/xhtml1/DTD/xhtml1-transitional.dtd ">


<html xmlns="http://www.w3.org/1999/xhtml">

<head>

<title>Working with Style</title>
```

```
</head>

<body>

<p style='font-family: "Courier new", Courier, monospace;'>
A human being is a part of the whole called by us universe, a part limited in
time and space. He experiences himself, his thoughts and feeling as something
separated from the rest, a kind of optical delusion of his consciousness. This
delusion is a kind of prison for us, restricting us to our personal desires and
to affection for a few persons nearest to us. Our task must be to free our-
selves
from this prison by widening our circle of compassion to enhance all living
creatures and the whole of nature in its beauty -- Albert Einstein</p>


</body>
</html>
```

5. Add the font's size:

```
<?xml version="1.0" encoding="UTF-8" ?>

<!DOCTYPE html
      PUBLIC "-//W3C//DTD XHTML 1.0 Transitional//EN"
      " http://www.w3.org/TR/xhtml1/DTD/xhtml1-transitional.dtd ">


<html xmlns="http://www.w3.org/1999/xhtml">

<head>

<title>Working with Style</title>

</head>

<body>

<p style='font-family: "Courier new", Courier, monospace; font-size: 18px;'>
A human being is a part of the whole called by us universe, a part limited in
time and space. He experiences himself, his thoughts and feeling as something
separated from the rest, a kind of optical delusion of his consciousness. This
delusion is a kind of prison for us, restricting us to our personal desires and
to affection for a few persons nearest to us. Our task must be to free our-
selves
from this prison by widening our circle of compassion to enhance all living
creatures and the whole of nature in its beauty -- Albert Einstein
</p>

</body>
</html>
```

6. Choose a color and add the color property and value to the string:

```
<?xml version="1.0" encoding="UTF-8" ?>

<!DOCTYPE html
        PUBLIC "-//W3C//DTD XHTML 1.0 Transitional//EN"
        " http://www.w3.org/TR/xhtml1/DTD/xhtml1-transitional.dtd ">


<html xmlns="http://www.w3.org/1999/xhtml">

<head>

<title>Working with Style</title>

</head>

<body>

<p style='font-family: "Courier new", Courier, monospace; font-size: 18px;
color: #999999;'>

A human being is a part of the whole called by us universe, a part limited in
time and space. He experiences himself, his thoughts and feeling as something
separated from the rest, a kind of optical delusion of his consciousness. This
delusion is a kind of prison for us, restricting us to our personal desires and
to affection for a few persons nearest to us. Our task must be to free
ourselves from this prison by widening our circle of compassion to enhance all
living creatures and the whole of nature in its beauty -- Albert Einstein
</p>

</body>
</html>
```

Save and then view the file in your browser. The paragraph should appear in gray. Compare your results with mine, shown in Figure 15.4.

Figure 15.4
Adding gray to a typeface.

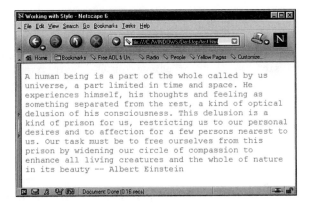

In Listing 15.2, I use another color, type selection, and type size employing the `style` element.

Listing 15.2   Embedded Style with Face, Size, and Color

```
<?xml version="1.0" encoding="UTF-8" ?>

<!DOCTYPE html
    PUBLIC "-//W3C//DTD XHTML 1.0 Transitional//EN"
    "http://www.w3.org/TR/xhtml1/DTD/xhtml1-transitional.dtd">



<html xmlns="http://www.w3.org/1999/xhtml">

<head>

<title>Working with Style</title>

<style type="text/css">

<!--

p {
font-family: Garamond, Times, serif;
font-size: 18px;
color: #CC9966;
}

-->

</style>

</head>

<body>

<p>Brain researchers estimate that your unconscious data base outweighs the
conscious on an order exceeding ten million to one. This data base is the
source of your hidden, natural genius. In other words, a part of you is much
smarter than you are. The wise people regularly consult that smarter part.</p>

<p>Crazy people who are productive are geniuses. Crazy people who are rich are
eccentric. Crazy people who are neither productive nor rich are just plain
crazy. Geniuses and crazy people are both out in the middle of a deep ocean;
geniuses swim, crazy people drown. Most of us are sitting safely on the shore.
Take a chance and get your feet wet.</p>

<p> - Michael J. Gelb</p>

</body>
</html>
```

Figure 15.5 shows the results. The font face is Garamond, the color is sienna (which will show up as gray in the figure but sienna if you test the results in your browser), and a font size of 18 pixels.

Figure 15.5
With an embedded style sheet, I set the font to Garamond, the font color to sienna, and the font size to 18 pixels.

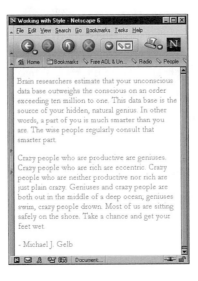

Weight

Weight is how thick or thin a typeface is. The Arial face, for example, has variations in weight including black (a very heavy face), bold, light, and so forth.

Because typefaces have different variants, unless you are absolutely sure that visitors to your site have a specific typeface, you generally should apply a value that is going to be available to all typefaces you are using in a value. The one near-global value for typefaces is bold.

The primary purpose, then, for the `font-weight` property is to make a given typeface bold.

Here's an example of weight applied inline:

```
<p style="font-family: Arial, Helvetica, sans-serif; font-weight: bold;
font-size: 16px; color=#CCCCCC;">
"I studied the lives of great men and famous women, and I found that the men and
women who got to the top were those who did the jobs they had in hand, with
everything they had of energy and enthusiasm." -- Harry S. Truman
 </p>
```

You can also apply weight to an embedded or linked sheet. In Listing 15.3, I've applied the bold to a header size 1 but have left the paragraph at a standard weight.

Listing 15.3   Using the `font-weight` Property in a Header

```
<?xml version="1.0" encoding="UTF-8" ?>

<!DOCTYPE html
     PUBLIC "-//W3C//DTD XHTML 1.0 Transitional//EN"
```

Listing 15.3   Continued

```
    "http://www.w3.org/TR/xhtml1/DTD/xhtml1-transitional.dtd">


<html xmlns="http://www.w3.org/1999/xhtml">

<head>

<title>Working with Style</title>

<style type="text/css">
<!--

h1 {
font-family: Helvetica, Arial, sans-serif;
font-weight: bold;
color: #CC9966;
}
p {
font-family: Garamond, Times, serif;
color: #999999;
}

-->
</style>

</head>

<body>
<h1>Quotations from Michael J. Gelb</h1>
<p>"Brain researchers estimate that your unconscious data base outweighs the
conscious on an order exceeding ten million to one. This data base is the source
of your hidden, natural genius. In other words, a part of you is much smarter
than you are. The wise people regularly consult that smarter part."</p>

<p>"Crazy people who are productive are geniuses. Crazy people who are rich are
eccentric. Crazy people who are neither productive nor rich are just plain
crazy. Geniuses and crazy people are both out in the middle of a deep ocean;
geniuses swim, crazy people drown. Most of us are sitting safely on the shore.
Take a chance and get your feet wet."</p>

</body>
</html>
```

Figure 15.6 shows how the header and paragraph text take on the different styles called for in the embedded style sheet.

Figure 15.6
The header and paragraph in this
example take on different styles
as defined by an embedded sheet.

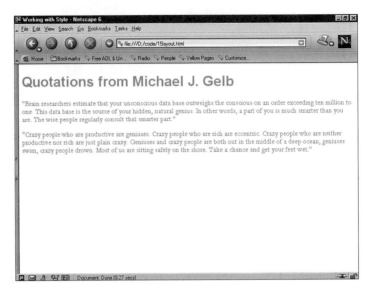

Font Style

In this context, *style* refers to the slant of a given typeface. The three styles are *normal*, *italic*, and *oblique*. As with weight variations, oblique is a rare option and should be used cautiously. However, italic style is available in most typefaces, so you're pretty safe using it wherever you require italics.

The following is an example of inline font style:

```
<p style="font-family: Garamond, Times, serif; font-style: italic;
font-size: 18px; color=#999999;">

"I studied the lives of great men and famous women, and I found that the men and
women who got to the top were those who did the jobs they had in hand, with
everything they had of energy and enthusiasm."  -- Harry S. Truman</p>
```

Figure 15.7 shows this passage in Garamond italics.

Figure 15.7
Applying italics with the
`font-style` property.

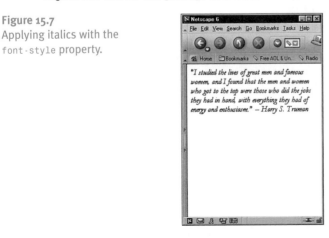

Line Height

Line height is the space between individual lines of text. Normal default leading is usually the same or very near to the point size of the type being used. For example, when you have 16-pixel type, the leading is going to look very natural at 16–18 pixels, too.

To control line height with style sheets, you can use the `line-height` property. Its value is numeric, in whatever measurement you're using. Listing 15.4 shows normal default line height, followed by a larger value, and in the last paragraph, the line height is a smaller value—making the distance between the lines shorter.

> `<!--`**Caution**
>
> Consider using italics and bold sparingly. Their primary function in body type is to emphasize passages of text. Excessive use of bold or italics compromises readability.
> `-->`

Listing 15.4   Adding Line Height

```
<?xml version="1.0" encoding="UTF-8" ?>

<!DOCTYPE html
     PUBLIC "-//W3C//DTD XHTML 1.0 Transitional//EN"
     "http://www.w3.org/TR/xhtml1/DTD/xhtml1-transitional.dtd">


<html xmlns="http://www.w3.org/1999/xhtml">

<head>
<title>Working with CSS</title>

</head>
<body>

<p style="font-family: Arial, Helvetica, sans-serif; font-size: 16px;
color: #000000;">
Call you me fair? that fair again unsay.
Demetrius loves your fair: O happy fair!
Your eyes are lode-stars; and your tongue's sweet air
More tuneable, than lark to shepherd's ear,
When wheat is green, when hawthorn buds appear.</p>

<p style="font-family: Arial, Helvetica, sans-serif; font-size: 16px;
line-height: 22px; color: #000000;">
Sickness is catching: O, were favour so,
Yours would I catch, fair Hermia, ere I go;
My ear should catch your voice, my eye your eye,
My tongue should catch your tongue's sweet melody.</p>

<p style="font-family: Arial, Helvetica, sans-serif; font-size: 16px;
line-height: 9px; color: #000000;">
Were the world mine, Demetrius being bated,
The rest I'd give to be to you translated.
```

Listing 15.4   Continued

```
O, teach me how you look, and with what art
You sway the motion of Demetrius' heart.</p>

</body>
</html>
```

Figure 15.8 shows how leading affects each paragraph. The first is normal, the second is wider leading, and the final example is leading that is a bit too close for comfort!

Figure 15.8
Varying line heights, are applied to this selection of text to adjust the leading.

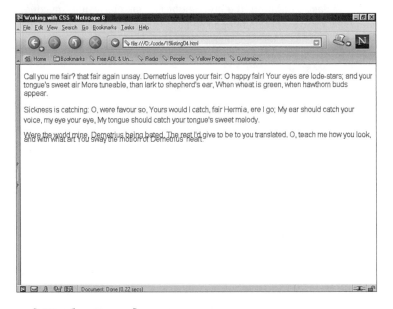

Text Decoration and Background

You also should be aware of several other type options, including the following:

- **text-decoration**—This property is extremely useful for turning off link underlining within an anchor. To do so, set `text-decoration` to a value of `none`. The values of `underline`, `italic`, and `line-through` are also supported.

- **background**—If you want to place a color or image behind text, you can do so by using this property. Either use a hexadecimal color or a URL (address) where that address points to a background image tile. Note that you can assign this option not only to the `<body>` tag, but also to any tag or span of text to "highlight" an area on a page.

Caution

The practice of removing underlines from links is controversial in usability circles. The reason is that many Web site visitors use the underline as a visual cue for a link. If your audience is largely made up of newcomers to the Web, then you may consider not removing link underlines. For broader audiences, it's very common to remove link underlining.

Listing 15.5 demonstrates a page with the use of text decoration and background.

Listing 15.5   Text Decoration and Background Settings

```
<?xml version="1.0" encoding="UTF-8" ?>

<!DOCTYPE html
     PUBLIC "-//W3C//DTD XHTML 1.0 Transitional//EN"
     "http://www.w3.org/TR/xhtml1/DTD/xhtml1-transitional.dtd">


<html xmlns="http://www.w3.org/1999/xhtml">

<head>


<title>Working with Style</title>

</head>

<body>

<p style='font-family: "Courier new", Courier, monospace; font-size: 16px;
color: #000000;'>
Call you me fair? that fair again unsay.
<a href="demetrius.html" style="text-decoration: line-through;">Demetrius</a>
loves your fair: O happy fair!
Your eyes are lode-stars; and your tongue's sweet air
More tuneable, than lark to shepherd's ear,
When wheat is green, when hawthorn buds appear.
Sickness is catching: O, were favour so,
Yours would I catch, fair <a href="hermia.html"
style="text-decoration: none">Hermia</a>, ere I go;
My ear should catch your voice, my eye your eye,
My tongue should catch your tongue's sweet melody.
</p>
<p style='background: #000000; font-family: "Courier
new", Courier, monospace;
font-size: 16px; color: #FFFFFF'>
Were the world mine, Demetrius being bated,
The rest I'd give to be to you translated.
O, teach me how you look, and with what art
You sway the motion of Demetrius' heart.
</p>

</body>
</html>
```

```
<!--
```

There are many other things you can do with style properties to design text on your pages, including such things as hover effects and padding. There are many style sheet resources online, a few sites to help you out include

Guide to Cascading Style Sheets, http://www.htmlhelp.com/reference/css/

Ask Dr. Web about Style Sheets, http://www.zeldman.com/askdrweb/css_index.html

A List Apart's Fear of Style Sheets, http://www.alistapart.com/stories/fear/

```
-->
```

In Figure 15.9, you can see that the first link has been struck through and has the default underline in place. The second link, however, has no underline. Finally, I've used black to set a background against the final paragraph. This trick can be very handy when you're creating sidebars or offsetting text for emphasis.

Figure 15.9
The first link in this case has a strikethrough and no link underline, and the second has no underline.

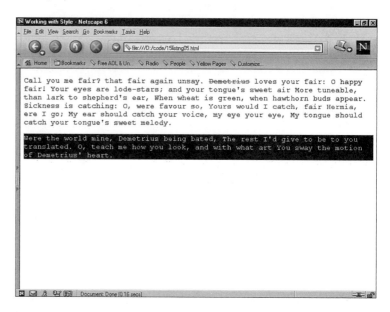

USING CSS FOR LAYOUT

The full promise of style sheets is finally coming to fruition. While Opera and Internet Explorer have each had some support for CSS over the past several years, Netscape was slow to the plate, providing only some CSS support in its version 4.0 browsers. However, all new releases of popular Web browsers have very good style sheet support.

This means that Web authors can turn to style sheets for more than just styling text. We can begin to look at true separation of presentation and document formatting in the context of CSS layout.

While tables remain the de facto methodology by which to create layouts, and probably will do so for some time to come, Web authors would do well to study CSS layout options and begin to employ them wherever possible.

The following examples will help you get started using CSS layouts.

Most of the CSS layout methods described in this chapter are based on the collected works of author and Web developer Eric Costello. Check out his site at http://www.glish.com/. Additional information came from Jeffrey Zeldman and A List Apart, http://www.zeldman.com/ and http://www.alistapart.com/ respectively.

Creating a Three-Column Layout

In this case, you'll create a layout that has three columns, a very popular approach to layout. The left and right columns are going to be positioned absolutely, while the center "content" layout will be fluid.

This example will use an embedded style sheet, but you can also use a linked sheet if you prefer.

1. Begin with a document—in this case I'm using XHTML 1.1:

```
<?xml version="1.0" encoding="UTF-8" ?>


<!DOCTYPE  html PUBLIC "-//W3C//DTD XHTML 1.1//EN"
     "http://www.w3.org/TR/xhtml11/DTD/xhtml11.dtd">


<html xmlns="http://www.w3.org/1999/xhtml">


<head>


<title>CSS Layout Techniques</title>


</head>


<body>



<body>
</html>
```

2. Add the style tags:

```
<?xml version="1.0" encoding="UTF-8" ?>


<!DOCTYPE  html PUBLIC "-//W3C//DTD XHTML 1.1//EN"
     "http://www.w3.org/TR/xhtml11/DTD/xhtml11.dtd">


<html xmlns="http://www.w3.org/1999/xhtml">


<head>


<title>CSS Layout Techniques</title>


<style type="text/css">


</style>
```

```
</head>

<body>


<body>
</html>
```

3. Create an ID selector for the column:

```
<style type="text/css">

#left

</style>
```

4. Create a rule to position the column absolutely, using the `position` property with a value of `absolute`:

```
<style type="text/css">

#left {
    position: absolute;
}

</style>
```

5. Add the positioning information, in pixels:

```
#left {
    position: absolute;
    left:10px;
    top:50px;
    width:200px;
}
```

You've now created a left margin set to a width of 200 pixels that will be positioned in a compliant browser at 50 pixels from the top, and 10 pixels from the left. You can change these values to suit your needs.

Next, you'll create the fluid center. To do so, follow these steps:

1. Create an ID selector for the center column:

```
#center
```

2. Now create a rule for the left-margin value:

```
#center {
    margin-left: 200px;
}
```

3. And a rule for the right-margin value:

```
#center {
    margin-left: 200px;
    margin-right: 200px;
}
```

Save your file before continuing.

You'll now want to create the style rules for the right column.

1. Create an ID selector to denote the right column:

   ```
   #right
   ```

2. Position the column using an absolute value:

   ```
   #right {
       position: absolute;
   }
   ```

3. Add the position values:

   ```
   #right {
       position: absolute;
       right:10px;
       top:50px;
   }
   ```

To implement the layout within your document, you'll employ the `div` tag along with the appropriate ID. Listing 15.6 shows the completed markup and style. I've added some content so you can see the results in Figure 15.10.

Listing 15.6 A Three-Column Layout with a Dynamic Center

```
<?xml version="1.0" encoding="UTF-8" ?>


<!DOCTYPE  html PUBLIC "-//W3C//DTD XHTML 1.1//EN"
    "http://www.w3.org/TR/xhtml11/DTD/xhtml11.dtd">

<html xmlns="http://www.w3.org/1999/xhtml">

<head>

<title>CSS Layout Techniques</title>

<style type="text/css">
```

<!--**Caution**

Internet Explorer 5.x implements the box model improperly. As a result, this design won't be pixel-perfect in IE 5.x.

Some designers recommend a workaround to trick IE 5.x into properly rendering the layout. This workaround is explained in detail at http://www.glish.com/css/hacks.asp. However, other designers consider this improper use of style grammar, and advise against it.

-->

Listing 15.6 Continued

```
#left {
    position: absolute;
    left:10px;
    top:50px;
    width:200px;
}
#center {
    margin-left: 200px;
    margin-right: 200px;
}
#right {
    position: absolute;
    right:10px;
    top:50px;
}

</style>


</head>

<body>

<div id="left">
<p>Navigate:</p>
<p><a href="index.html">Home</a><br />
<a href="news.html">News</a><br />
<a href="about.html">About Us</a><br />
<a href="contact.html">Get in Touch</a></p>
</div>


<div id="center">

<p>Lorem ipsum dolor sit amet, consectetuer adipiscing elit, sed diam nonummy
nibh euismod tincidunt ut laoreet dolore magna aliquam erat volutpat. Ut wisi
enim ad minim veniam, quis nostrud e XErcitation ulliam corper suscipit lobortis
nisl ut aliquip ex ea commodo consequat. Duis autem veleum iriure dolor in
hendrerit in vulputate velit esse molestie consequat, vel willum lunombro dolore
eu feugiat nulla facilisis at vero eros et accumsan et iusto odio dignissim qui
blandit praesent luptatum zzril delenit augue duis dolore te feugait nulla
facilisi.</p>
```

Listing 15.6   Continued

```
<p>Li Europan lingues es membres del sam familie. Lor separat existentie es un
myth. Por scientie, musica, sport etc., li tot Europa usa li sam vocabularium.
Li lingues differe solmen in li grammatica, li pronunciation e li plu commun vocabules.
Omnicos directe al desirabilit‡ de un nov lingua franca: on refusa continuar payar cus-
tosi
traductores. It solmen va esser necessi far uniform grammatica, pronunciation e plu som-
mun
paroles.</p>

</div>

<div id="right">

<p>Of Interest:</p>

<ul>
<li>Headlines</li>
<li>Today's weather</li>
<li>Sports Scores</li>
</ul>

</div>
</body>
</html>
```

<!--
When you work with table layouts, setting the border to a value
of "1" can help you see the layout
as you develop it. With CSS, you
can employ the border property
and set it to a value of 1 pixel in
order to view the layout as you
develop your design.
-->

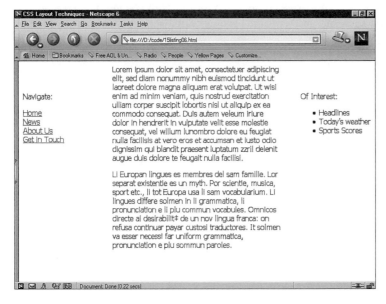

Figure 15.10
The three-column layout as
viewed in Netscape 6.2 for
Windows.

Exploring a Two-Column Layout Using `float`

This technique was documented by Jeffrey Zeldman (see note above for reference) and is now gaining widespread popularity as a simple means to laying out pages using CSS.

You'll define the left and right columns using ID selectors and the `float` property to anchor the design. In this example, you'll create a style sheet that is external so it can be linked or imported. You can, however, embed the style should you so desire.

1. Open a new document to create the external style sheet, and add a class ID for the left portion, which in this case is being used as a content portion, to the document:

   ```
   #content
   ```

2. Create a rule using the float property with a value of left:

   ```
   #content    {
       float:left;
   }
   ```

3. Set the width (in percentages, making it dynamic) of the column, along with a right margin to create a gutter between the content column and the right column:

   ```
   #content {
       float:left;
       width:70%;
       margin-right: 25px;
   }
   ```

4. You can go ahead and create an ID selector and rule for the right column, adding any additional rules as you so desire. In this case, I simply added some padding to the top of the column:

   ```
   #right {
       padding-top: 20px;
   }
   ```

Listing 15.7 shows the complete CSS listing, and Listing 15.8 shows the XHTML document.

Listing 15.7   CSS Syntax for Two-Column Layout

```
#content {
     float:left;
     width:70%;
     margin-right: 25px;
}

#right {
     padding-top: 20px;
}
```

Listing 15.8   XHTML Document Linked to the Layout CSS

```
<!DOCTYPE html
     PUBLIC "-//W3C//DTD XHTML 1.0 Transitional//EN"
     "http://www.w3.org/TR/xhtml1/DTD/xhtml1-transitional.dtd">


<html xmlns="http://www.w3.org/1999/xhtml">

<head>

<title>Working with Style</title>

<link rel="stylesheet" type="text/css" href="layout2.css" />

</head>

<body>

<div id="content">
<h3>Quotations</h3>
<p>"Brain researchers estimate that your unconscious data base outweighs the
conscious on an order exceeding ten million to one. This data base is the source
of your hidden, natural genius. In other words, a part of you is much smarter
than you are. The wise people regularly consult that smarter part."</p>

<p>"Crazy people who are productive are geniuses. Crazy people who are rich are
eccentric. Crazy people who are neither productive nor rich are just plain
crazy. Geniuses and crazy people are both out in the middle of a deep ocean;
geniuses swim, crazy people drown. Most of us are sitting safely on the shore.
Take a chance and get your feet wet."</p>
</div>

<div id="right">
<p>Navigate:</p>
   <p><a href="index.html">Home</a><br />
   <a href="news.html">News</a><br />
   <a href="about.html">About</a><br />
   <a href="contact.html">Get in Touch</a></p>
   </div>
</body>
</html>
```

You now have a two-column, dynamic layout suitable for refining and improving upon.
Figure 15.11 shows the results.

Figure 15.11
This is an example of a two column layout using float.

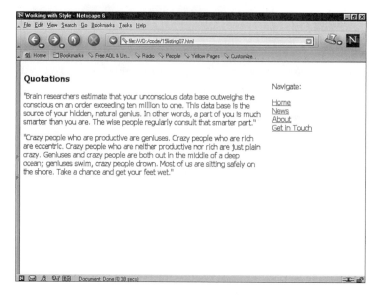

GRACEFULLY DEGRADING CSS LAYOUTS

Because of Netscape 4.x's problematic implementation of style sheets, CSS layouts aren't effective. Because this particular browser is still in fairly widespread use, designers have tapped into both a flaw in the browser and a CSS technique that combined help gracefully degrade the layout so that the page is at least readable.

Figure 15.12 shows a Web page from my site using CSS layout in Netscape 6.2 for Windows. Compare this figure to Figure 15.13, which is a shot of the page as viewed in Netscape 4.76. As you can see, the layout is lost. However, the information is still logically structured, readable, and navigable.

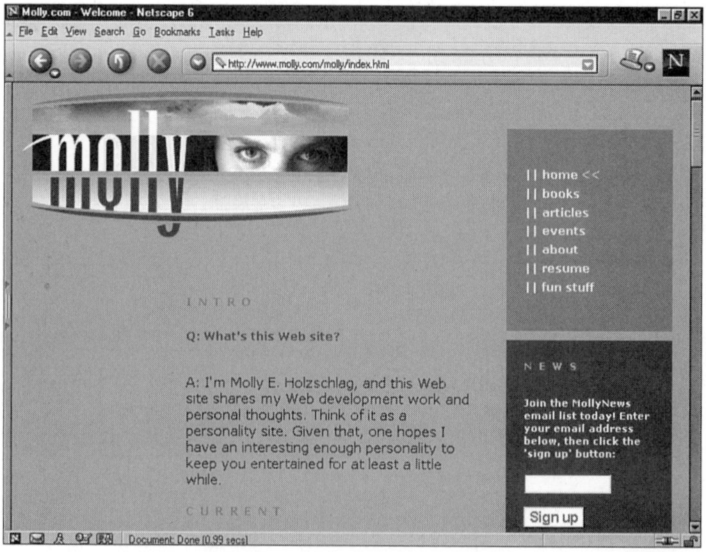

Figure 15.12
CSS was used to create this layout.

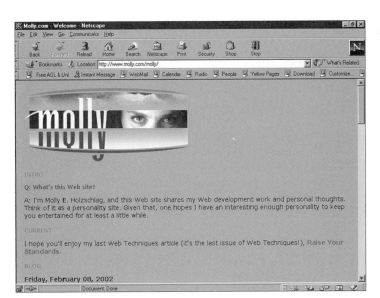

This is done using the `@import` workaround, which exploits the fact that Netscape 4.x doesn't understand it. As a result, you can link to one style sheet with styles that Netscape 4.x *does* understand, and use the `@import` method to bring in another style sheet for the layout. This will create a readable page in Netscape 4.x, and allow browsers that can interpret both the `@import` rule and the layout styles to properly lay out the document. Without this workaround, my page would be unreadable in Netscape 4.x, as shown in Figure 15.14.

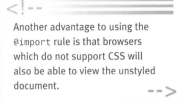

Another advantage to using the `@import` rule is that browsers which do not support CSS will also be able to view the unstyled document.

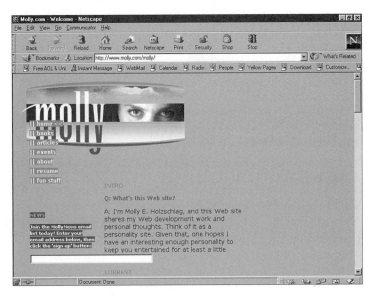

Figure 15.14
Without the import rule in place, Netscape 4.76 completely mangles the layout.

Listing 15.9 shows how the @import rule at work alongside a linked style sheet for styles supported by Netscape 4.x.

Listing 15.9   Using the `@import` Rule for Graceful Degradation of Layouts

```
<head>

<title>Molly.com - Welcome</title>

<!-- begin style sheet for site-wide styles supported by
many browsers -->

<link rel="stylesheet" type="text/css" href="site.css"
/>

<!-- begin style sheet for positioning. it is imported
so Netscape 4.x excludes it
and displays the content in readable format -->

<style type="text/css" media="all"> @import
"position.css";</style>

</head>
```

`<!--` There are current technical and aesthetic debates regarding the use of `@import` to seemingly trick Netscape 4.x browsers into graceful degradation.

Web authors and programmers are discussing whether the method is a hack, a workaround, or a justifiable use of CSS.

Since tables provide more consistent results with layout, many designers argue that this method is not viable for their clients. `-->`

CASE BY CASE: CSS/EDGE: VISUAL AND DYNAMIC EFFECTS WITH CSS

As CSS layouts, visual effects, and dynamic effects come to the forefront of contemporary Web design, several industry leaders are creating great resources for those interested in learning more about how to use CSS to create all kinds of special treatments.

One such site, by Eric A. Meyer, is css/edge. On this site, Meyer demonstrates a variety of effects using *only* well formed markup and CSS—no scripts!

Some of the CSS effects that Meyer is demonstrating, and makes available for your use and inspiration, include:

- **CSS text pop-ups**—In this example, Meyer demonstrates how to create a dynamic text pop-up without using any script whatsoever (see Figure 15.15).

- **CSS pop-ups with images**—Expanding on the text pop-up idea, this example shows pop-ups with images (see Figure 15.16).

- **Visual designs using angles, curves, and embedded bo XEs**—These examples are very compelling because they can inspire the Web author to see just what can be done visually using CSS (see Figures 15.17 through 15.19).

Link   Pop-up

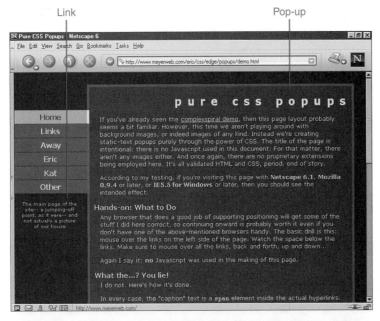

Figure 15.15
CSS text pop-ups can be created
using a variety of display and positioning properties.

Figure 15.16
CSS image pop-ups are created
the same way that text pop-ups
are, but using images.

Figure 15.17
Creating visual angles using CSS adds interest to the page without having to rely on graphics.

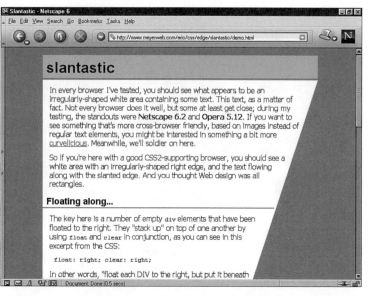

Figure 15.18
In the past, the only way to achieve curves was to use graphics. With CSS, curves can be easily created and quickly rendered.

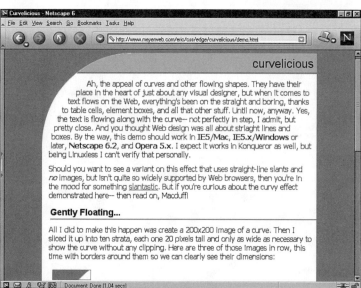

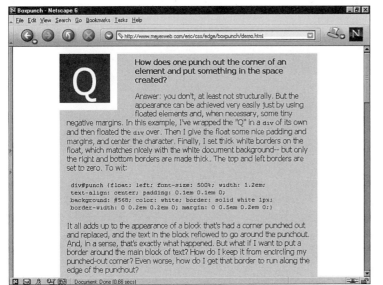

Figure 15.19
Embedding bo XEs using CSS to create a unique look.

There is no denying that CSS layout is the way Web authors will be working with sites in the not-too-distant future, if they aren't already. What excites me most about this shift in approach is that we'll really need to examine how to design for the Web, using Web technologies, instead of the past practice of bending and breaking Web technologies to try and design pages that look more like print or other media. Now the real innovation begins!

<!--
Check out css/edge at http://www.
meyerweb.com/eric/css/edge/.
-->

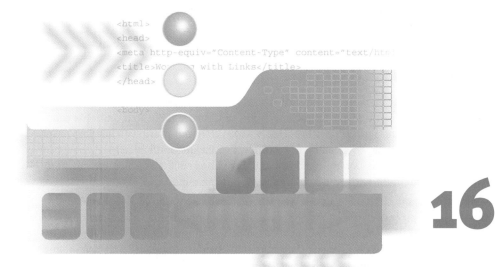

ADDING SCRIPTING TO HTML AND XHTML DOCUMENTS

IN THIS CHAPTER

Scripting and Markup   402

JavaScript Overview   408

Using JavaScript   409

Case by Case: Merging Scripting, Style, and Intrinsic Events   413

SCRIPTING AND MARKUP

This book is primarily about markup, so the goal is to focus less on details about ancillary technologies and more on how a given technology works with markup. To that end, this chapter introduces you to working with scripts in HTML and XHTML and provides some important guidelines you'll want to follow. To sweeten the journey, I've included a few script demos for commonly used features such as pop-up windows and navigation. But, the primary focus here is on the way scripts integrate with your conforming Web documents.

There are some significant differences in the way you'll manage scripting in HTML and XHTML, but the basic process is the same. Scripts used with a document and interpreted by the browser are referred to as *client-side* scripts. These scripts are most often JavaScript, but can be other kinds of scripts, such as Visual Basic Script (VBScript). Scripts can be used inline (embedded scripts) or linked to using the src attribute along with the script element.

It's also important that I mention the Document Object Model (DOM). The DOM is an interface within browsers that allows programs and scripts to dynamically modify various aspects of a document including its structure, its presentation, and its contents.

However, the implementation of the DOM in browsers has varied enormously over the past years. This has led to a lot of confusion about how browsers interpret and deal with scripting. The DOM is especially important in scripting and the creation of dynamic pages in general, and specifically to what has become known as Dynamic HTML (DHTML).

> `<!--`
> For more details about DOM-related activities and resources check out http://www.w3.org/DOM/.
> `-->`

Many readers will be familiar with DHTML, but many others will want to better understand just what DHTML is. The first thing to address is what DHTML is *not*. DHTML is not a language in and of itself. It is instead a combination of technologies, as follows:

- **HTML or XHTML**—An HTML or XHTML document and its elements provides the matrix.

- **DOM**—The interface provided by the DOM is necessary to carry out script-related tasks.

- **CSS**—Using Cascading Style Sheets, numerous presentational effects can be accomplished.

- **Scripting**—Some form of scripting, such as JavaScript, is used to carry out dynamic events.

The major frustration with DHTML has focused on two main concerns. The first is that the implementation of the DOM from one browser type and version to the next has been very different, due to the fact that there was no standardized DOM. The second is that proprietary elements that did not make it into specifications have caused many DHTML authors frustration.

> `<!--`
> The W3C is working toward standardization of the DOM. To learn more about their development work regarding DOM technology, see http://www.w3.org/DOM/.
> `-->`

A powerful case in point for this kind of frustration is how Netscape created the `layer` element, widely used in the first years of DHTML, and then dropped it from its 6.0 version browsers when it was not made part of W3C recommendations.

As a result, pages built to conform to Netscape's perspective on early DHTML using the `layer` element will no longer function in Netscape's own browsers. In some ways, Netscape should be commended for its desire to adhere to W3C recommendations. On the other hand, many sites have been rendered useless, frustrating the individuals who created them.

Because of the many changes in scripting languages, browsers and DOM implementation, and non-standard authoring practices, there's a lot of resulting frustration and inconsistency surrounding scripting. In all cases, testing your pages in a variety of browsers is an imperative, as is validating your documents for conformance.

Adding Scripts to a Page Using the `script` Element

To add a script to a page, you'll use the `script` element, which is placed in the `head` and/or body portion of a document, depending on the requirements of the script. The `script` element is a container element, so be sure to include a closing tag at all times.

Several attributes of importance to the script element are

- **src**—If you'd like to link to an external script, you can use a URI with this attribute.

- **type**—The type attribute defines the content type of the language in question, such as `<script type="text/javascript">` . . . `</script>`. Browsers use this type to decide whether to bother downloading or executing the script, based on whether they support the language specified.

- **language**—This attribute was used in the past to identify the language and version in which the script was written. It was deprecated in HTML 4.0 in favor of the type attribute, which means that while you can use it in transitional HTML 4 documents, it is no longer available in XHTML.

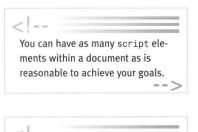

```
<!--
```
You can have as many `script` elements within a document as is reasonable to achieve your goals.
```
-->
```

```
<!--
```
Because the `type` attribute can be used in HTML 4 or in XHTML, avoid using the `language` attribute, but always define the script's content type using the `type` attribute. This way, whether in HTML or XHTML, you'll always be correct.
```
-->
```

To embed a script in your document, follow these steps:

1. Begin with an HTML or XHTML document. I began with an HTML 4.01 Transitional Document:

```
<!DOCTYPE HTML PUBLIC "-//W3C//DTD HTML 4.01 Transitional//EN"
        "http://www.w3.org/TR/html4/loose.dtd">

<html>
```

```
<head>

<title>Working with Scripts</title>

</head>

<body>


</body>
</html>
```

2. Add the `script` element and MIME type to the head portion of the document:

```
<!DOCTYPE HTML PUBLIC "-//W3C//DTD HTML 4.01 Transitional//EN"
        "http://www.w3.org/TR/html4/loose.dtd">

<html>

<head>

<title>Working with Scripts</title>

<script type="text/javascript">


</script>

</head>

<body>


</body>
</html>
```

3. You'll want to place comments around the script. This helps hide the JavaScript from search engines:

```
<!DOCTYPE HTML PUBLIC "-//W3C//DTD HTML 4.01 Transitional//EN"
        "http://www.w3.org/TR/html4/loose.dtd">

<html>

<head>

<title>Working with Scripts</title>
```

```
<script type="text/javascript">

<!--



// -->
</script>

</head>

<body>


</body>
</html>
```

4. Now add the script. In this case, I've used a simple script to display a page-last-updated date for demonstration purposes:

```
<!DOCTYPE HTML PUBLIC "-//W3C//DTD HTML 4.01 Transitional//EN"
        "http://www.w3.org/TR/html4/loose.dtd">

<html>

<head>

<title>Working with Scripts</title>

<script type="text/javascript">

<!--

document.write("This page last updated: " +
document.lastModified + "");

// -->
</script>

</head>

<body>


</body>
</html>
```

5. Save the file and test it in your browser. Figure 16.1 shows my results.

Figure 16.1
Testing an embedded JavaScript.

Similarly, you can link to the script using the `script` element and `src` value. Simply place the script by itself in a file with no markup and save that file using a .js extension. Then, you'll link to the file as shown in Listing 16.1.

Listing 16.1   Linking to an External Script

```
<!DOCTYPE HTML PUBLIC "-//W3C//DTD HTML 4.01 Transitional//EN"
        "http://www.w3.org/TR/html4/loose.dtd">

<html>

<head>

<title>Working with Scripts</title>

<script type="text/javascript" src="update.js">

</script>

</head>

<body>


</body>
</html>
```

Load the document into a JavaScript-compliant browser and test your script. There should be no difference in the way the script works.

Another issue in scripting is the use of the `noscript` element. This element is used in a way similar to the `noframes` element in framesets. The idea is to provide alternatives for browsers that do not support scripting, or for those browsers where users have turned JavaScript off.

> `<!--`**Caution**
>
> When creating external scripts, be sure to use only the script and no markup—such as the `script` element in the external document. As with external style, the only data in the external document should be the script or style data. `-->`

Let's say you want to provide an alternate page for individuals who do not have scripting features in their browsers, or have scripting turned off. To do so, you would use the `noscript` tags, placed in the body of the document, along with the link to the alternate page:

```
<body>
<noscript>
<p><a href="alternate.html">Alternate page for those
without scripting capabilities.</a></p>
</noscript>
</body>
```

You can use `noscript` in any kind of HTML or XHTML document. The placement of `noscript` in the body of the document means that it will be treated as regular markup, and you can put additional markup within it, as shown in the previous snippet.

Intrinsic Events

Intrinsic event attributes are built-in attributes within the specifications that enable you to associate an action to an element where the action is defined by a script. So, if you wanted a specific event to occur when the document is loaded, you'd use an intrinsic event attribute to specify the script to be run when that event is encountered by the browser.

Table 16.1 shows the available intrinsic events in HTML and XHTML with their associated actions.

Table 16.1   Intrinsic Events and Their Associated Actions

Intrinsic Event	Action and Related Elements
onload	This attribute is used with the body or frameset elements, and the related script executes when the browser finishes loading the document or all frames of the frameset.
onunload	Also for use with body and frameset, this action can be associated with scripts that perform some operation upon the removal of the document from the browser.
onclick	Usable with almost every element, when a mouse or another pointing device is clicked over that element, this event will occur.
ondblclick	Same action as onclick, but requiring a double click to be activated.

Table 16.1 Continued

Intrinsic Event	Action and Related Elements
onmousedown	This event will affect almost any element that you'd like to apply as the mouse or pointer is pressed down.
onmouseup	When the pointer or mouse is released, this event can be used to attach an element to a script in order to activate a given action.
onmouseover	The desired action occurs as the mouse or pointing device moves onto an element.
onmousemove	If the pointing device or mouse is moved while over the element, a variety of effects can be achieved by attaching this event to a script.
onmouseout	This occurs when the pointing device or mouse moves away from an element, an effect can occur.
onfocus	This attribute is used to specify a script action to be taken when one of the following elements gets the focus: a, area, label, input, select, textarea, and button.
onblur	When any of the elements listed for onfocus lose focus, a scripting event can occur.
onkeypress	When a key is pressed, an action can be scripted here.
onkeydown	When a key is in the downstate, it can trigger a scripted action.
onkeyup	When the key is released, an action can occur.
onsubmit	This event can only be applied to the submit element in a form. An action can be attached to this event.
onreset	As with onsubmit, an event can only be applied to the submit element within a form.
onselect	An event can take an action when text is selected in a text field via input or textarea in a form.
onchange	When a form control loses focus and its value has been modified while it had focus, an event can occur. Applies only to input, select, and textarea.

The following snippet shows how you can associate scripting with event types by way of an HTML attribute, in this case, the anchor:

```
<a href="new.html" onmouseover="hiLite('b0','images/new_off.gif')"
onmouseout="hiLiteOff('b0','images/new_on.gif')">
```

In this case, the full script is embedded into the head of the document (or it can also be linked), and then within the links, images are toggled as the mouse passes over the anchor, and as the mouse leaves the anchor.

JAVASCRIPT OVERVIEW

The power of JavaScript has become extremely significant to Web developers. Used originally to enhance sites, JavaScript has become a sophisticated method of addressing many previously confounding site development concerns.

JavaScript History and Standardization

JavaScript is a scripting language that was originally Netscape's LiveScript. Sun Microsystems, developer of the Java language, took an interest in this powerful script and, along with Netscape, made some adjustments and reintroduced the script under the new name JavaScript.

Not long thereafter, Microsoft decided to come out with its own implementation of JavaScript, known as JScript. Moves to standardize JavaScript have resulted in ECMAScript.

ECMAScript is a standardized (not merely a recommendation but a true formal standard) Internet scripting language based on JavaScript 1.1. The standard, overseen by the European Computer Manufacturers Association (ECMA) announced the adoption of the standard in June of 1998. Since that time, browser vendors have worked to adopt the standard.

Unlike Java, with which JavaScript is often confused, JavaScript is an interpreted language. Java is a compiled language that can be used to develop entirely standalone applications, including applets. JavaScript works primarily with Web pages. JavaScript, on the other hand, is usually included within the document (or linked to it) and interpreted line-by-line by the browser.

JavaScript is used frequently to

- Add visual functions such as alert boxes and pop-up windows.

- Create animations.

- Detect browser, browser version, and platform.

- Dynamically update documents.

- Validate form data.

Some general JavaScript rules to remember include the following:

- JavaScript is case-sensitive.

- It's possible that even if someone is using a JavaScript-enabled browser, the JavaScript is turned off. So, you need to plan your designs to be nonJavaScript–reliant, too.

- JavaScript code should always be commented out so search engines skip the code while cataloging a site.

<!--
Comment tagging in JavaScript is a bit different than in HTML or XHTML. The opening portion, <!-- is the same as in both, but the closing portion is //-->. The two slashes alert the JavaScript that this is the end of the script syntax.
-->

USING JAVASCRIPT

There are many script repositories on the Web. You can find JavaScripts that do all kinds of things: navigation, time stamping, clocks, calculators, and forms enhancements. In the following section, I'll provide you with a few popular scripting features.

<!--Caution
Be careful about using scripts found in repositories; some have copyrights and other restrictions.
-->

Drop-Down Menu Navigation

Listing 16.2 demonstrates how to create the drop-down menu in XHTML and control its actions with JavaScript. In this example, I'll use the standard select element with option tags holding the names of different Web sites for the menu. The value attributes of the option elements will be the URLs of the Web sites.

For a description of the select and option tags, **see** "Building Forms," **p. 247**, Chapter 10.

Listing 16.2   A Drop-Down Menu

```
<!DOCTYPE html PUBLIC "-//W3C//DTD XHTML 1.0 Transitional//EN"
"http://www.w3.org/TR/xhtml1/DTD/xhtml1-transitional.dtd">
<html xmlns="http://www.w3.org/1999/xhtml">
<head>
<title>JavaScript Drop Down Menu</title>

<script type="text/javascript">
<!--
function goToLink(form)
   {
location.href = form.options[form.selectedIndex].value;
    }
//-->
</script>
</head>

<body>
<br />
<br />
<br />
<br />
<br />

<div align="center">

<form id="URLmenu" action="null">
<select name="choices">
<option value="http://www.molly.com/">Molly.com</option>
<option value="http://www.webstandards.org/">Web Standards Project (WaSP)</option>
<option value="http://www.quepublishing.com">Que Publishing</option>
</select>
<input type="button" value="Go!" onclick="goToLink(this.form.choices)" />
</form>

</div>

</body>
</html>
```

<!--
Note the onclick intrinsic event in this script, found in the input element.
-->

Figure 16.2 shows the drop-down menu. When the user clicks the Go! button, he or she will end up at the selected URL.

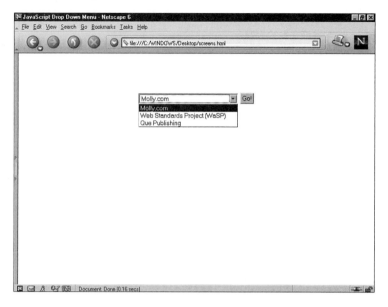

Figure 16.2
Here is an example of a JavaScript drop-down menu navigation. Select your location in the text box and click Go!.

The JavaScript comes in when a user clicks the button. At that point, the goToLink function is called. The value in the parentheses (this.form.choices) uses a JavaScript shortcut for the name of the form object. this refers to the current object. this.form refers to the form of which the object is a part.

The choices part is the name of the select element. When this is passed to the goToLink function, it takes a look to see which of the options in that element have been selected, and then takes the value of that option and makes it the current URL of the Web page.

Pop-Up Window

The pop-up window is one of the mainstays of JavaScript functionality. It can be used any time you want to have a customized page pop-up to display some page component, such as a help menu or code snippet.

You can control a variety of attributes in this script, such as whether or not there is a toolbar or status bar in the window.

To add this script, follow these simple steps:

1. Add this script into the head of an HTML or XHTML document where you'd like to have a pop-up window. I used an XHTML Transitional document:

```
<!DOCTYPE html
     PUBLIC "-//W3C//DTD XHTML 1.0 Transitional//EN"
     "http://www.w3.org/TR/xhtml1/DTD/xhtml1-transitional.dtd">
```

```
<html xmlns="http://www.w3.org/1999/xhtml">

<head>

<title>Working with Scripts</title>

<script type="text/javascript">
<!- -
function openpopup(){
var popurl="code.html"
winpops=window.open(popurl,"","width=400,height=338,resizable,")
}
//-->
</script>


</head>

<body>


</body>
</html>
```

2. Create the XHTML file you'd like to have loaded in the pop-up window. Name and save the file. It should match the filename you have placed in the popurl value.

3. Type this line of JavaScript into the body of your original document:

```
<!DOCTYPE html
      PUBLIC "-//W3C//DTD XHTML 1.0 Transitional//EN"
      " http://www.w3.org/TR/xhtml1/DTD/xhtml1-transitional.dtd">


<html xmlns="http://www.w3.org/1999/xhtml">

<head>

<title>Working with Scripts</title>

<script type="text/javascript">
<!--
function openpopup(){
var popurl="code.html"
winpops=window.open(popurl,"","width=400,height=338,resizable,")
}
//-->
</script>
```

```
</head>

<body>

<p><a href="javascript:openpopup()">check out
the sample code!</a></p>

</body>
</html
```

4. Test your page. It should look similar to mine (in Figure 16.3).

Figure 16.3 shows the pop-up in action.

<!--
As helpful as pop-up windows can be, they also can be overused (especially when made automatic and used for advertising). My advice is to use them where they enhance the site: providing help, additional navigation, and code samples. Try to avoid automating pop-ups on page load, and reserve them for user-initiated tasks such as in the example just provided.
-->

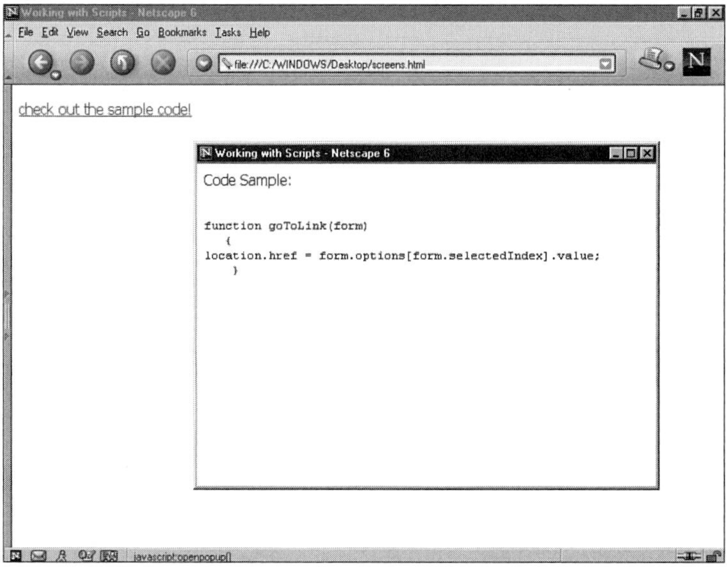

Figure 16.3
This JavaScript pop-up window is handy for adding additional information such as a help page or code sample without having to invoke an entirely new browser window.

CASE BY CASE: MERGING SCRIPTING, STYLE, AND INTRINSIC EVENTS

In this example, you'll see how scripting, style, and intrinsic events work together to create a dynamic behavior.

Let's assume you want to change the font size of a link as a person clicks on that link. To do so, you'd attach style and scripting to the a element via an event handler attribute, in this case, onmouseclick.

To create this action:

1. Begin with an HTML or XHTML document. I chose XHTML 1.0 Transitional:

```
<!DOCTYPE html PUBLIC "-//W3C//DTD XHTML 1.0 Transitional//EN"
"http://www.w3.org/TR/xhtml1/DTD/xhtml1-transitional.dtd">
```

```
<html xmlns="http://www.w3.org/1999/xhtml">
<head>

<title>JavaScript and Style</title>
</head>

<body>

</body>
</html>
```

2. Build an embedded style sheet containing the a selector and add type attributes:

```
<!DOCTYPE html PUBLIC "-//W3C//DTD XHTML 1.0 Transitional//EN"
"http://www.w3.org/TR/xhtml1/DTD/xhtml1-transitional.dtd">
<html xmlns="http://www.w3.org/1999/xhtml">
<head>

<title>JavaScript and Style</title>

<style type="text/css">
<!--
a {
    font: 16px times;
}
-->
</style>

</head>

<body>

</body>
</html>
```

3. Add a link in the body of the document:

```
<!DOCTYPE html PUBLIC "-//W3C//DTD XHTML 1.0 Transitional//EN"
"http://www.w3.org/TR/xhtml1/DTD/xhtml1-transitional.dtd">
<html xmlns="http://www.w3.org/1999/xhtml">
<head>

<title>JavaScript and Style</title>

<style type="text/css">
<!--
a {
```

```
font: 16px times;
}
-->
</style>

</head>

<body>

<p><a href="http://www.molly.com/">Vist Molly's Web page!</a></p>

</body>
</html>
```

4. Add the intrinsic event and script:

```
<!DOCTYPE html PUBLIC "-//W3C//DTD XHTML 1.0 Transitional//EN"
"http://www.w3.org/TR/xhtml1/DTD/xhtml1-transitional.dtd">
<html xmlns="http://www.w3.org/1999/xhtml">
<head>

<title>JavaScript and Style</title>

<style type="text/css">
<!--
a {
font: 16px times;
}
-->
</style>

</head>

<body>

<p><a href="http://www.molly.com/" onclick="this.style.fontSize='24px';">Vist
Molly's Web page!</a></p>

</body>
</html>
```

5. Save and test your file. Compare your results with mine (see Figure 16.4).

You can continue making modifications to this file by adding style, events, and additional links.

Techniques found in this chapter can be very useful in making sites more user-friendly. For example, if I want to provide my site visitors with an option to make the text larger for better reading, I can do so. Other similar techniques can be used to switch font faces, so if a visitor prefers to read sans-serif onscreen, he or she can select that option.

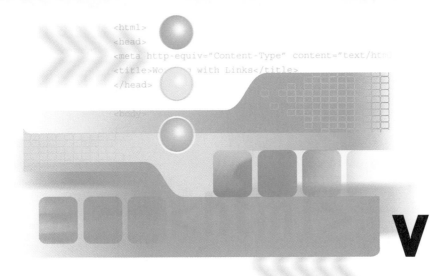

ACCESSIBILITY AND INTERNATIONALIZATION

17 Creating Accessible Sites   **419**

18 Designing International Documents   **435**

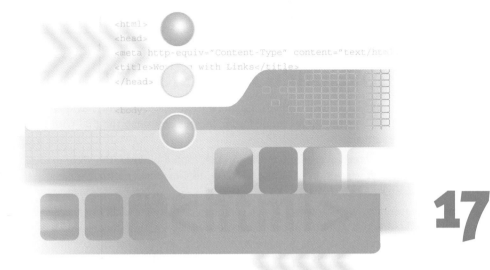

CREATING ACCESSIBLE SITES

IN THIS CHAPTER

Rules and Laws Governing Accessibility 420

Web Accessibility Initiative 422

Techniques for Working with HTML 4.0 Accessibility 424

Case by Case: Testing for Accessibility 432

RULES AND LAWS GOVERNING ACCESSIBILITY

When I first got online using BBSes in the late 1980s, I made a friend named David. David is completely blind, and at the time we met in an online forum, he was accessing the BBS with screen reader hardware and software.

This was just prior to the widespread availability of the Internet (and a bit later, the Web) on the personal desktop. In the first year of the Web's text-based life, David had no trouble navigating, and in fact was delighted by it.

But soon came complex graphical Web browsers which compromised David's ability to access many Web sites. Suddenly, this rich resource of community, knowledge, entertainment, and shopping became difficult to access. I cannot imagine what it must have felt like to have finally achieved access to these resources, only to have it taken away. Accessibility is the initiative that's trying to return the Web to David, and to people like him, by ensuring that its documents are easy to get to.

Accessibility in Web authoring is the process by which Web authors can ensure their documents are created in such a way as to facilitate easy understanding and functionality for the blind, deaf, and physically impaired. While some Web authors have long been sensitive to this issue, many have not been aware of its importance, or just didn't care.

However, legislation in the United States and worldwide has changed all of that. Depending on where you live and what kind of site you're developing, you might not only have to be aware of accessibility guidelines, but conform to them based on public policy.

Historical Policies Leading to Accessibility Initiatives

In the United States in 1973 a bit of legislation was designed to bring provisions for the needs of the disabled community into Federal agencies. Known as *The Rehabilitation Act of 1973*, this legislation insisted that access be provided for the disabled. In this case, access referred to numerous issues: access to buildings, access to work, and so on.

By 1990, increased awareness and attention to the needs of the disabled led to a critical document in U.S. history—*The Americans with Disabilities Act*. This act addressed the access concerns first enunciated in the *Rehabilitation Act*. Now, however, compliance with the act had become law.

Eight years later, another document was designed to update the Rehabilitation Act. Referred to as *The Workforce Investment Act of 1998*, this act specifically calls out accessibility issues in electronic and information technology.

Section 508 of this act is very clear in its directives, demanding that anyone providing electronic information via the Internet who is part of Federal government or any agency that receives Federal monies must adhere to accessibility guidelines. What's more, the act implies that all Web developers will have some responsibility in making their sites accessible.

<!--
For more information on the ADA, see the ADA home page at the U.S. Department of Justice, http://www.usdoj.gov/crt/ada/adahom1.htm.

Information on Section 508 can be found at the U.S. Department of Justice site as well, http://www.usdoj.gov/crt/508/508home.html. A site dedicated to Section 508 specifically is http://www.section508.gov/.
-->

Section 508

In the most clear terms, Section 508 *requires* that U.S. Federal agencies make any electronic and information technology accessible to people with disabilities. This applies to both Federal employees and members of the public.

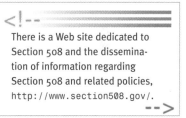

<!--
Interestingly, Section 508 has one exemption. National security systems do not have to be accessible.
-->

Here's the exact language that Section 508 sets forth:

"Section 508 requires that when Federal agencies develop, procure, maintain, or use electronic and information technology, Federal employees with disabilities have access to and use of information and data that is comparable to the access and use by Federal employees who are not individuals with disabilities, unless an undue burden would be imposed on the agency. Section 508 also requires that individuals with disabilities, who are members of the public seeking information or services from a Federal agency, have access to and use of information and data that is comparable to that provided to the public who are not individuals with disabilities, unless an undue burden would be imposed on the agency."

<!--
There is a Web site dedicated to Section 508 and the dissemination of information regarding Section 508 and related policies, http://www.section508.gov/.
-->

Most U.S. agencies are in the process of working to establish and practice compliance with Section 508 and have plans in place to be compliant within the next 24 months.

Foreign Rules and Laws on Accessibility

There are numerous foreign policies in the making across the world to provide the same access that Section 508 is attempting to provide in the U.S.

Table 17.1 provides a look at some of the foreign activity and policy regarding accessibility.

Table 17.1 International Policies Relating to Accessibility

Country	Current Status of Disability Policies, Legislation, or Discussions
Australia	Disability Discrimination Act, 1992 (legislation)
Canada	Canadian Human Rights Act of 1977 (legislation)
Denmark	Action plans and discussions underway, no policy or legislation has yet emerged
European Union	Action plans and discussions are underway with recommendations
France	Action plans and discussions
Ireland	Government guidelines for accessible sites in place with no specific policy or legislation
Italy	Directives and discussion underway
Portugal	Mandatory accessibility
United Kingdom	Disability Discrimination Act of 1995 (legislation)

Interestingly, Portugal was the first European nation to make accessibility mandatory.

WEB ACCESSIBILITY INITIATIVE

The *Web Accessibility Initiative* (*WAI*) is a W3C project dedicated to promoting awareness and accessibility for those with disabilities.

The initiative comprises a variety of important activities, including the preparation of guidelines and checklists for Web authors as well as browser developers and tools manufacturers. Information as to working groups, various events, and helpful resources are each available via the WAI Web site.

In this section, I'll provide an overview of author guidelines as well as checklists to ensure accessibility.

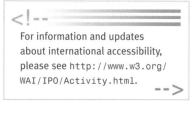

For information and updates about international accessibility, please see http://www.w3.org/WAI/IPO/Activity.html.

Visit the WAI at http://www.w3.org/WAI/.

The Web Accessibility Initiative of the W3C has an official document involving 14 guidelines, which Web developers are encouraged to follow. Here, I'm providing you with the guidelines and an explanation; however, there are checklists and examples that are much more detailed than can be presented here. Please see the note at the end of this section to find more information regarding these guidelines.

1. **Provide equivalent alternatives to auditory and visual content.** If you're using sound or graphics, include text descriptions and employ HTML-based aids, such as the `alt` attribute in images, wherever possible.

2. **Don't rely on color alone.** Since many people cannot see color, have problems with color blindness, or are accessing the Web via non-color devices, relying solely on color to convey information is problematic. To address this guideline, be sure to include explanations wherever color is being used to express important facts, and make sure that foreground and background colors have high enough contrast to be visible.

3. **Use markup and style sheets and do so properly.** This guideline is an important one! It encourages the creation of well-formed documents in accordance with recommendations. What's becoming very evident is that the more separation you can get between presentation and document structure, the more accessible your pages will automatically become.

4. **Clarify natural language usage.** Any foreign pronunciations, acronyms, or abbreviations should be spelled out or accommodated using the `title` attribute in related elements.

5. **Create tables that transform gracefully.** Ideally, you're only using tables now for tabular data. Tables present specific problems, such as screen reader software reading across table cells, which can be very confusing. Some browsers support certain elements and attributes that can be used to make tables more accessible.

➡ *For more information, see "Working with Tables," p. 177, Chapter 8.*

6. **Ensure that pages featuring new technologies transform gracefully.** All pages should be accessible no matter which technologies are being employed.

7. **Ensure user control of time-sensitive content changes.** Many disabilities are affected by things that move and blink. For example, a few members of my family have migraine headaches, and one sure trigger is a fast-moving, blinking object. Moreover, other people have mobility impairments and cannot keep up with any kind of moving object. Others with learning disabilities might become confused. Anything that moves, blinks, or auto-updates should have controls that allow the user to stop, start, and pause the object to make the page more effective and usable.

8. **Ensure direct accessibility of embedded user interfaces.** If you're placing an embedded object within your page, such as an applet or Flash design, be sure that users have access to the interface of that embedded object.

9. **Design for device independence.** Individuals accessing the Web may be doing so using a number of devices, including keyboards, mice, voice commands, a head or mouth stick, and so on. General guidelines to manage this issue include using client-side imagemaps instead of server-side maps, and in forms, provide tab order mechanisms for easier navigation.

10. **Use interim solutions.** Older browsers and assistive devices often do not operate properly, yet many are in abundance in various government organizations, including those that provide services to disabled communities. So, if I wrote a document with a consecutive list of links (very common in navigation schemes) my screen reader might read the link as one uninterrupted link and attempt to resolve it, to no avail. Another problem is the pop-up window, often used in advertising.

11. **Use W3C technologies and guidelines.** The W3C provides recommendations for all browser and tools manufacturers as well as Web authors. When conformance is achieved, accessibility guidelines are that much more readily implemented.

12. **Provide context and orientation information.** The more complex a page or site, the more helpful it is to ensure that visitors know what they are doing at a given location, and why.

13. **Provide clear navigation mechanisms.** Clear and consistent navigation is not only an imperative in accessibility, it's an imperative in user interface design. Links should be clearly identified and organized, and graphical options should have appropriate alternatives available.

14. **Ensure that documents are clear and simple.** The easier your content is to understand, the more you'll get your point across, no matter who the audience is.

<!--
To learn more about checklists and additional guidelines, see http://www.w3.org/TR/WCAG/.

For additional tips on creating an accessible site, see http://www.w3.org/WAI/References/QuickTips/.
-->

TECHNIQUES FOR WORKING WITH HTML 4.0 ACCESSIBILITY

To work toward the ideal of creating accessible documents, I'm going to step through several examples that demonstrate how accessibility techniques can be added to your pages.

There are many accessibility techniques that I've covered in chapters focusing on a given methodology such as tables and forms. Here, I'm including techniques that have not been mentioned previously, or have only been given a passing mention. I'll provide additional cross references so you can move to the chapters containing details on how to approach a given accessibility feature.

Making Links Understandable with the `title` Attribute

I mentioned the `title` attribute briefly in Chapter 7, "Adding Hypertext and Independent Links." It is important for links to be descriptive, but even contextual links can be confusing when taken out of that context. Trying to fashion each link to be descriptive both in and out of context can cause awkward content, however. The `title` attribute allows you to add extra context to your links without detracting from the flow of your content. (See Figure 17.1.)

1. Within the body of your document, type the following paragraph.

```
<!DOCTYPE HTML PUBLIC "-//W3C//DTD HTML 4.01 Transitional//EN"
        "http://www.w3.org/TR/html4/loose.dtd">

<html>

<head>

<title>Accessibility Techniques</title>

</head>

<body>

<p>The new cat owner must be prepared to feed, train, play with,
and give plenty of love to their new pet.</p>

</body>
</html>
```

2. Add links to the words "feed," "train," and "play with" to contextually link those words to other pages in your site.

```
<!DOCTYPE HTML PUBLIC "-//W3C//DTD HTML 4.01 Transitional//EN"
        "http://www.w3.org/TR/html4/loose.dtd">

<html>

<head>
```

```
<title>Accessibility Techniques</title>

</head>

<body>

<p>The new cat owner must be prepared to <a href="feeding.html">feed</a>,
<a href="training.html">train</a>, <a href="playing.html">play with</a>
and give plenty of love to their new pet.</p>

</body>
</html>
```

3. Add the `title` attribute to the link, feeding.html.

```
<!DOCTYPE HTML PUBLIC "-//W3C//DTD HTML 4.01 Transitional//EN"
        "http://www.w3.org/TR/html4/loose.dtd">

<html>

<head>

<title>Accessibility Techniques</title>

</head>

<body>

<p>The new cat owner must be prepared to <a href="feeding.html" title="feeding
your cat">feed</a>,
<a href="training.html">train</a>, <a href="playing.html">play with</a>
and give plenty of love to their new pet.</p>

</body>
</html>
```

4. Repeat and add the `title` attributes to the other links.

```
<!DOCTYPE HTML PUBLIC "-//W3C//DTD HTML 4.01 Transitional//EN"
        "http://www.w3.org/TR/html4/loose.dtd">

<html>

<head>

<title>Accessibility Techniques</title>

</head>

<body>
```

```
<p>The new cat owner must be prepared to <a href="feeding.html" title="feeding
your cat">feed</a>,
<a href="training.html" title="training your cat">train</a>, <a
href="playing.html" title="playing with">play with</a>
and give plenty of love to their new pet.</p>

</body>
</html>
```

Figure 17.1
As the mouse passes over the link, more information is offered about the link in a tool tip.

Adding Tab Order to Links

You can assign an explicit tab order to your links through use of the `tabindex` attribute. This attribute can be used with the `a`, `area`, `button`, `input`, `object`, `select`, and `textarea` elements.

When used on a page, people who are utilizing keyboard navigation will be able to tab first to links with a set tab order. Elements that do not support the `tabindex` attribute are displayed next, in the order in which they appear in your file.

<!--
This technique is not supported in Netscape Navigator 4.x versions. It is fully supported in Netscape 6.0 and IE 4.0 and above.
-->

1. Type a paragraph into the body of your document.

```
<!DOCTYPE HTML PUBLIC "-//W3C//DTD HTML 4.01 Transitional//EN"
        "http://www.w3.org/TR/html4/loose.dtd">

<html>
```

```html
<head>

<title>Accessibility Techniques</title>

</head>

<body>

<p>The new cat owner must be prepared to feed, train, play with,
and give plenty of love to their new pet.</p>

</body>
</html>
```

2. Add links to several words to contextually link those words to other pages in your site. I chose "feed," "train," and "play with."

```html
<!DOCTYPE HTML PUBLIC "-//W3C//DTD HTML 4.01 Transitional//EN"
        "http://www.w3.org/TR/html4/loose.dtd">

<html>

<head>

<title>Accessibility Techniques</title>

</head>

<body>

<p>The new cat owner must be prepared to <a href="feeding.html">feed</a>,
<a href="training.html">train</a>, <a href="playing.html">play with</a>
and give plenty of love to their new pet.</p>

</body>
</html>
```

3. Add the `tabindex` attribute to each of your links:

```html
<!DOCTYPE HTML PUBLIC "-//W3C//DTD HTML 4.01 Transitional//EN"
        "http://www.w3.org/TR/html4/loose.dtd">

<html>

<head>

<title>Accessibility Techniques</title>

</head>
```

```
<body>

<p>The new cat owner must be prepared to <a href="feeding.html"
tabindex="1">feed</a>,
<a href="training.html" tabindex="2">train</a>, <a href="playing.html"
tabindex="3">play with</a>
and give plenty of love to their new pet.</p>

</body>
</html>
```

> The tabindex *attribute can also be used to set the tab order in Forms,* **see** *"Building Forms,"* **p. XXX**, *Chapter 10.*

<!--
The tabindex attribute does not necessarily have to correlate to the order in which the links are presented on the page—put them in the order you like. In the example above, the last link in the paragraph is the first link in the tab order.
-->

Making Tables Accessible Using a Summary

I briefly describe the summary element when discussing tables. The summary element adds a lengthier description of your table. The summary element enables you to explain the information included in your table, thereby making it easier for people to understand it when using accessibility tools. The summary appears as a link to this description within most visual browsers.

1. Add a table to the page within the body of the file:

```
<!DOCTYPE HTML PUBLIC "-//W3C//DTD HTML 4.01 Transitional//EN"
        "http://www.w3.org/TR/html4/loose.dtd">

<html>

<head>

<title>Accessibility Techniques</title>

</head>

<body>

<table>
<tr>
<td>Name</td>
<td>Country</td>
<td>Days</td>
</tr>
<tr>
<td>Jody</td>
<td>Japan</td>
<td>5</td>
</tr>
```

```
<tr>
<td>Molly</td>
<td>Spain</td>
<td>10</td>
</tr>
</table>

</body>
</html>
```

2. Add a summary attribute with a description of the table as the value to the table tag:

```
<!DOCTYPE HTML PUBLIC "-//W3C//DTD HTML 4.01 Transitional//EN"
        "http://www.w3.org/TR/html4/loose.dtd">

<html>

<head>

<title>Accessibility Techniques</title>

</head>

<body>

<table summary="This table shows the name of each traveler, the country he or
she visited, and the duration of their trip.">
<tr>
<td>Name</td>
<td>Country</td>
<td>Days</td>
</tr>
<tr>
<td>Jody</td>
<td>Japan</td>
<td>5</td>
</tr>
<tr>
<td>Molly</td>
<td>Spain</td>
<td>10</td>
</tr>
</table>

</body>
</html>
```

➪ *For additional accessibility techniques for tables, **see**
"Working with Tables," **p. 177** Chapter 8.*

> `<!--`
> Make summaries concise, but
> descriptive. The objective is to
> *summarize*, after all!
> `-->`

Clarifying Abbreviations with the `acronym` Element and `title` Attribute

The acronym element enables you to define the acronyms and abbreviations within your pages without detracting from the content. This ensures that your acronym is clearly defined. Let's say you're writing the abbreviation "ASP." The acronym element allows you to clarify whether you mean "active server pages" or "application service provider." (See Figure 17.2.)

1. Add a sentence with an acronym to the body of the document:

```
<!DOCTYPE HTML PUBLIC "-//W3C//DTD HTML 4.01 Transitional//EN"
        "http://www.w3.org/TR/html4/loose.dtd">

<html>

<head>

<title>Accessibility Techniques</title>

</head>

<body>

<p>Welcome to the ASP newsletter, where this month, you can read all about
ASP.</p>

</body>
</html>
```

2. Add the acronym element to your acronyms:

```
<!DOCTYPE HTML PUBLIC "-//W3C//DTD HTML 4.01 Transitional//EN"
        "http://www.w3.org/TR/html4/loose.dtd">

<html>

<head>

<title>Accessibility Techniques</title>

</head>

<body>

<p>Welcome to the <acronym>ASP</acronym> newsletter, where this month, you can
read all about <acronym>ASP</acronym>.</p>
```

```
</body>
</html>
```

3. Add the title attribute to define "ASP" in each case:

```
<!DOCTYPE HTML PUBLIC "-//W3C//DTD HTML 4.01 Transitional//EN"
        "http://www.w3.org/TR/html4/loose.dtd">

<html>

<head>

<title>Accessibility Techniques</title>

</head>

<body>

<p>Welcome to the <acronym title="Application Service Provider">ASP</acronym>
newsletter, where this month, you can read all about <acronym title="Active
Server Pages">ASP</acronym>.</p>

</body>
</html>
```

Figure 17.2

In compliant browsers, the tool tip shows the acronym spelled out and easy to understand.

CASE BY CASE: TESTING FOR ACCESSIBILITY

There are several ways that agencies working to comply with Section 508 and other accessibility initiatives can ensure that their sites are accessible.

The WAI provides guidelines and resources for testing for accessibility. The first recommended step is to do a preliminary review of the document or documents in question. This review involves the following five steps:

1. Select a sampling of documents from the site you want to review. The WAI asks that you include the home page in this sampling.

2. Using a graphical browser such as Netscape, IE, or Opera, examine the documents following these guidelines:

   - Turn off all images and see if the document is still logical.

   - Turn off any sound to ensure the document is understandable without it.

   - Change the font size, making it larger and then smaller. Your content is ideally still readable.

   - Set the screen resolution to 640×480. If this forces horizontal scrolling, realize that this can cause problems for the mobility impaired.

   - Change your monitor's display to black and white and see if the contrast is high enough to provide good readability.

   - Tab through links and form fields using the keyboard rather than a mouse, making sure you can get to all of the links and fields easily.

3. Test your documents with voice or text browsers. Perform these two checks:

   - Is the information you're hearing or seeing equivalent to what is experienced in a graphic browser?

   - Does the information follow a logical, sequential order?

4. Validate your documents using at least two accessibility validators. See the sidebar at the end of this numbered list for more information on available accessibility validators.

5. Summarize your results, make recommendations as to how any problems can be addressed, and make recommendations as to any follow-up steps to reach full conformance.

Using Validators for Accessibility Checks

Using validators for accessibility checks is an important part of the testing process. It's necessary to realize, however, that there is some controversy as to whether these validators are as intuitive as they need to be. For example, I passed a page through one validator only to be considered invalid because I'd used the words "blue" and "pink" in the document. The validator thought I was using color to convey information, when I was simply talking about colors in the body text.

So, use these validators as you would grammar or spell-checking—as a tool to expand on your existing knowledge.

The WAI recommends the following validators:

WAVE—As of the 2.2 version, tests for Section 508 compliance are included, `http://www.temple.edu/inst_disabilities/piat/wave/`.

Bobby—The most well-known of accessibility validation services with WAI and Section 508 tests, `http://www.cast.org/bobby/`. You can use Bobby to validate one page at a time, and a commercial download of the produce is available that checks entire sites, available for any platform with a Java Virtual Machine installed.

A-Prompt—A downloadable accessibility and usability evaluation program for use on your local computer. Only available for Windows platform currently, `http://aprompt.snow.utoronto.ca/`.

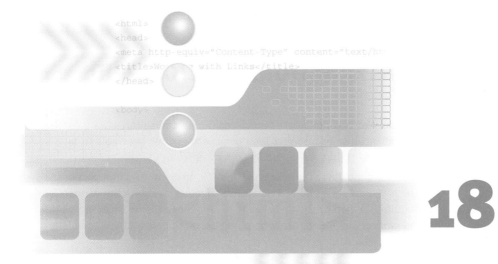

DESIGNING INTERNATIONAL DOCUMENTS

IN THIS CHAPTER

Globalization, Internationalization, and Localization   436

Character Encoding   438

Expressing Encoding via MIME   439

Identifying Language   441

Dealing with Text Presentation   444

Case by Case: Fonts and Font Utilities   447

GLOBALIZATION, INTERNATIONALIZATION, AND LOCALIZATION

There is no question that the Web has proliferated across countries and cultures. As a result, its developers are being challenged to ensure that Web pages are not only viewable in the languages of the areas they support, but are culturally correct as well.

International documents seem difficult for those of us in the U.S. to create. A large part of the reason has to do with the way hardware and software work together to create the various characters and glyphs required to display the wide range of languages that exist in the world. But whether you live and work in the U.S. or elsewhere, the desire to create multilingual sites might still be relevant to your needs.

While reliance on proper character encoding and description of language is a growing markup concern, ultimately, fonts are required to display most foreign characters. These fonts are usually installed via the operating systems found in other languages. For example, an Arabic version of Windows will have Arabic fonts available. When you reach a foreign page with embedded fonts, you'll be able to download that font so you can view the page.

In Figure 18.1, I show a page in Hindi, which uses a Hindi font I downloaded for my browser to properly display the page.

Figure 18.1
This page contains content written in the Hindi language and displayed using a Hindi font.

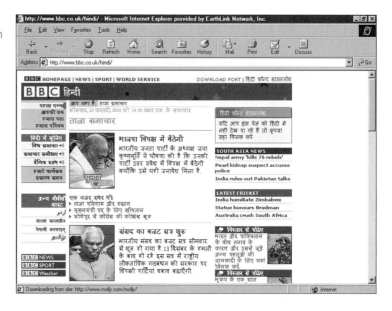

Figure 18.2 shows a page in Chinese, which requires another font altogether.

Figure 18.2
Chinese also requires the presence of special fonts in order to be properly viewed by users who aren't using Chinese operating systems and software.

Before I begin demonstrating how a document becomes internationalized, I want to clarify a bit of terminology for you. You'll read or hear the following words in relation to the internationalization of documents:

- **Globalization**—The concept of globalization in computer languages and software development means to create the end results so they work in multiple locales equally well.

- **Internationalization**—This is the planning and implementation of documents or software so they can be easily ported to any number of locales.

- **Localization**—This is the adaptation of a given global and international product to a specific locale.

- **Multilingual site development**—This is how to create sites from a technical standpoint that appear in multiple languages.

Now let me get this down to real-world sense. Internationalization is specifically the act of making a Web site friendly to visitors from other countries. This can include items such as ensuring you have specific currency declarations (U.S. dollars versus pounds, for example) and being aware of specific limitations about who the site serves. Are you shipping products worldwide, or just in North America? Depending on the scenario needed, specified content can be generated for specific regions.

This content should reflect the cultural expectations of the country. This is localization in action and may include language-specific content. In regard to language, the appropriate version of the language must be used. For example, you don't write English content for the United Kingdom using American English.

A multilingual site offers content in multiple languages. Generally there is virtually no attention to cultural issues, such as which graphic images or colors are acceptable to the French versus the Japanese.

Basically, the site is simply translated but reads left to right rather than right to left. In this example, a U.S.-based site might offer its content in American English and American Spanish (the one used in Puerto Rico; not Florida-Cuban Spanish). No attention is given to trying to communicate or sell products to South America or Spain.

To truly understand these subtleties, let's assume that molly.com wants to start promoting itself to South America. The first thing to do would be to have the site translated into South American Spanish and Brazilian Portuguese. After the content is translated, the choice of graphics, colors, and so on needs to be reviewed so as not to be offensive to that target market and to be appropriate for the general technology used in that region. When completed, molly.com would be marketed to South America. This is what I would call an international site. On the site, you might have icons that say USA, Brazil, and Rest of South America.

In Web development, your audience's needs and the intent of your site will determine the extent of internationalization that is required. If your audience is predominantly English speaking and located in the U.S., the likelihood that you will want to internationalize your documents is low. However, if you are building sites that span the globe, such as eBay or Amazon, the need for internationalization and localization becomes imperative.

CHARACTER ENCODING

Earlier in this book I discussed character encodings and entity sets. In that context, I expressed what they were used for, and why, and in some cases provided examples.

➡ To read more about character encoding, **see** Chapter 3 "Character Encodings," **p. 68**.

Character encodings take many forms. Table 18.1 shows the variety of character encoding types available in HTML and XHTML, and discusses certain features of these encoding types.

Table 18.1   Encoding Standards in HTML and XHTML

Encoding Type	Description	Problems or Features
7-bit ASCII	This encoding, also known as US ASCII, actually uses 8 bits per character, but reserves the first as a 0 value. This results in 128 available characters.	Limited number and type of characters.
8-bit encodings	This encoding uses the full 8 bits, allowing for additional characters.	Multiple versions of 8-bit encodings exist, which the ISO attempted to standardize. ISO 8859-1, the Latin character set, is the result.
16-bit encodings	This encoding uses 16 bits and has been especially useful in creating foreign character sets.	16 bit encoding has been standardized under Unicode.
ISO 10646 / UTF-8	32-bit encoding.	Defines a universal character set.

Using character encoding enables you to serve documents that are encoded specifically for the language character sets you require. This includes all documents, including those being created in the U.S. for U.S. markets.

EXPRESSING ENCODING VIA MIME

Originally developed to extend the capabilities of e-mail, MIME has become standardized for use in numerous contexts, including HTTP and HTML.

By adding header fields that describe the character encoding of a document, and using encoding that is taken from the official registries of data types and MIME-related classifiers, character encoding can be made possible if the responding user agent understands how to interpret those encodings.

In HTML and XHTML, adding information about character encoding is accomplished in a variety of ways:

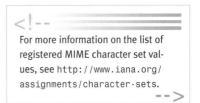

If you'd like to know technical details about character encodings, here are a few resources to help out.

For more information on ASCII, a short description with samples is available at `http://www.webreference.com/js/tips/000205.html`. ASCII is an ANSI standard; you can read more about ANSI at `http://www.ansi.org/`.

For more information on Unicode, try the article at `http://www.webreference.com/js/column25/unicode.html` and `http://www.unicode.org/`.

- The proper character encoding for documents is set by the server administrator on the server.

- Web authors can add the character-encoding information into their documents via the `meta` element.

For more information on the list of registered MIME character set values, see `http://www.iana.org/assignments/character-sets`.

- Web authors can add the character-encoding information into an XHTML document via the XML prolog.

To set the character encoding using the `meta` element, follow these steps:

1. Begin with an HTML or XHTML template. Here, I've used XHTML Strict:

```
<!DOCTYPE  html PUBLIC "-//W3C//DTD XHTML 1.1//EN"
    "http://www.w3.org/TR/xhtml11/DTD/xhtml11.dtd">

<html xmlns="http://www.w3.org/1999/xhtml">

<head>

<title>Internationalization</title>

</head>

<body>

<p>Content here.</p>

</body>
</html>
```

2. Add the `meta` element and http-equiv attribute with a "Content-Type" value:

```
<!DOCTYPE  html PUBLIC "-//W3C//DTD XHTML 1.1//EN"
      "http://www.w3.org/TR/xhtml11/DTD/xhtml11.dtd">

<html xmlns="http://www.w3.org/1999/xhtml">

<head>

<title>Internationalization</title>

<meta http-equiv="Content-Type" />

</head>

<body>

<p>Content here.</p>

</body>
</html>
```

3. Add the content attribute and character encoding required:

```
<!DOCTYPE  html PUBLIC "-//W3C//DTD XHTML 1.1//EN"
      "http://www.w3.org/TR/xhtml11/DTD/xhtml11.dtd">

<html xmlns="http://www.w3.org/1999/xhtml">

<head>

<title>Internationalization</title>

<meta http-equiv="Content-Type" content="text/html; charset=ISO-8859-1" />

</head>

<body>

<p>Content here.</p>

</body>
</html>
```

To set the character encoding using the XML prolog, you'll simply place the character encoding in the encoding attribute of the prolog. Listing 18.1 shows how.

Listing 18.1   Denoting Character Encoding in the XML Prolog

```
<?xml version="1.0" encoding=" ISO-8859-1"?>
<!DOCTYPE  html PUBLIC "-//W3C//DTD XHTML 1.1//EN"
      "http://www.w3.org/TR/xhtml11/DTD/xhtml11.dtd">

<html xmlns="http://www.w3.org/1999/xhtml">

<head>

<title>Internationalization</title>

</head>

<body>

<p>Content here.</p>

</body>
</html>
```

> <!--
> To set the encoding on a server,
> check with your server administra-
> tor. He or she will know how to set
> encoding on the specific type of
> server in use.
> -->

IDENTIFYING LANGUAGE

With HTML 4.0 and the rise in awareness that managing international documents is a major hurdle to overcome, the lang attribute was developed. This attribute can be used with any element, and combined with the correct language code, describes the language in use.

The language can be specified in the html element in HTML 4.0, XHTML 1.0, and XHTML 1.1.

> <!--
> In XHTML 1.1 the lang attribute
> has been removed from the speci-
> fication in favor of the xml:lang
> attribute.
> -->

For a complete list of language codes, **see** "Managing Language Codes," **p. 66**, Chapter 3.

To add a language code to an HTML 4.0 document:

1. Begin with an HTML template. I chose HTML 4.01 Transitional:

```
<!DOCTYPE HTML PUBLIC "-//W3C//DTD HTML 4.01 Transitional//EN"
       "http://www.w3.org/TR/html4/loose.dtd">

<html>

<head>

<title>Internationalization</title>
```

```
</head>

<body>


</body>
</html>
```

2. Add the `lang` attribute and appropriate language code, in this case I used `es` for Spanish:

```
<!DOCTYPE HTML PUBLIC "-//W3C//DTD HTML 4.01 Transitional//EN"
        "http://www.w3.org/TR/html4/loose.dtd">

<html lang="es">

<head>

<title>Internationalization</title>

</head>

<body>


</body>
</html>
```

3. You can also add additional language codes via any element should the language change:

```
<!DOCTYPE HTML PUBLIC "-//W3C//DTD HTML 4.01 Transitional//EN"
        "http://www.w3.org/TR/html4/loose.dtd">

<html lang="es">

<head>

<title>Internationalization</title>

</head>

<body>

<p>Esta frase es escrito en español.</p>

<p lang="en">This sentence is written in English.</p>

</body>
</html>
```

To add a language code in XHTML 1.1, follow these steps:

1. Begin with an XHTML 1.1 document template:

```
<!DOCTYPE  html PUBLIC "-//W3C//DTD XHTML 1.1//EN"
    "http://www.w3.org/TR/xhtml11/DTD/xhtml11.dtd">

<html xmlns="http://www.w3.org/1999/xhtml">

<head>

<title>Internationalization</title>

</head>

<body>

<p>Content here.</p>

</body>
</html>
```

2. Add the xml:lang attribute to the html tag:

```
<!DOCTYPE  html PUBLIC "-//W3C//DTD XHTML 1.1//EN"
    "http://www.w3.org/TR/xhtml11/DTD/xhtml11.dtd">

<html xmlns="http://www.w3.org/1999/xhtml" xml:lang="es">

<head>

<title>Internationalization</title>

</head>

<body>

<p>Content here.</p>

</body>
</html>
```

3. Add your content, save your file, and validate the file to ensure it validates as an XHTML 1.1 document.

In XHTML 1.0 documents, you can use the lang attribute and the xml:lang attributes together as a means to describe the language in use as seen in Listing 18.2.

Listing 18.2   Using the `lang` and `xml:lang` Attributes Together in XHTML 1.0

```
<!DOCTYPE html PUBLIC "-//W3C//DTD XHTML 1.0 Transitional//EN"
        "http://www.w3.org/TR/xhtml1/DTD/xhtml1-transitional.dtd">


<html xmlns="http://www.w3.org/1999/xhtml" lang="es" xml:lang="es">

<head>

<title>Internationalization</title>

</head>

<body>


</body>
</html>
```

DEALING WITH TEXT PRESENTATION

As the challenge to manage international documents increases, methods for handling direction, joining or non-joining of text elements, and the special presentation of characters have emerged.

Line Height in Multilingual Sites

With English, there are no letters that have accents, but in other Latin-based languages such as French, Spanish, Italian, Polish, German, and so on, there are many characters with accents or special marks above and below a letter. Authors may need to create a different style sheet to adjust the distance between lines within a paragraph so that the accent and specialty marks are clearly visible.

Setting Direction

HTML 4.0 attempted to deal with direction issues, and this attempt has continued on into XHTML. While English is written left to right, many languages are not. Hebrew and Arabic are both written right to left, for example. HTML and XHTML enable you to use the `dir` attribute along with two possible values:

- `ltr`—Left-to-right. This value defines the language direction as being read left to right.

- `rtl`—Right-to-left. If the language in question should be read right to left, use this direction value.

Listing 18.3 shows an example of a document that has two different languages and directional values described.

Listing 18.3 Working with Text Direction

```
<!DOCTYPE html PUBLIC "-//W3C//DTD XHTML 1.0 Transitional//EN"
    "http://www.w3.org/TR/xhtml1/DTD/xhtml1-transitional.dtd">


<html xmlns="http://www.w3.org/1999/xhtml">

<head>

<title>Internationalization</title>

</head>

<body>

<p lang="ar" dir="rtl">Arabic characters would be inserted here, and would appear right
to left.</p>

<p lang="en" dir="ltr">English characters, left to right.</p>

</body>
</html>
```

In Figure 18.3 you can see a Hebrew news page in which the dir attribute has been used to set the text direction.

Figure 18.3
Using the dir attribute and the rtl value, the text in this document is positioned right to left.

If you are working in a situation where more than one language is in use in a document, and you want to override the language direction, you can use the bdo (bidirectional override) element:

```
<bdo dir="ltr">This will override any previously
defined text direction.</bdo>
```

For example, in Hebrew, the language is written right to left, but the use of a numeral value such as 200,000 or $30.00 is written left to right in the middle of the paragraph. Using bdo, you can ensure that from the opening tag until the closing tag, the information included will override to the text direction not defined.

<!--Caution

There are inherent conflicts between Unicode, the dir attribute and its values, and the bdo element. You should avoid using Unicode with directional markup. If you are using Unicode, ensure proper nesting of elements and check your documents for conflicts.

-->

Another issue in directionality in the context of internationalization is the inclusion of graphics. Do they align to the left or right of the page? If you're making a document multilingual and are using the English version of the document, there's a head shot of a person on the left of the page looking toward the right side of the page. This will likely have to be flipped so the person is looking from the right side of the page to the left side of the page. If no change is made, the person appears to be looking against the flow, which is confusing. If the image is not flipped but only *moved* to the right side, the individual will be looking off the page.

Joining Control

Another interesting issue in foreign text display is the joining of characters. Typically, when characters are joined or not joined in a given language, the browsers and fonts for that language will usually interpret that joining properly. However, if you want to force two characters to join, or prevent them from joining, you can do so using two special characters available for this purpose. They are

- ‌—This character is the *zero width non joiner*. Use this when you want to prevent characters from joining where they would normally do so.

- ‍—Zero width joiner; use to force characters to join.

Listing 18.4 shows the use of both characters.

Listing 18.4   Forcing and Preventing Character Joining

```
<!DOCTYPE html PUBLIC "-//W3C//DTD XHTML 1.0 Transitional//EN"
     "http://www.w3.org/TR/xhtml1/DTD/xhtml1-transitional.dtd">


<html xmlns="http://www.w3.org/1999/xhtml">

<head>

<title>Internationalization</title>
```

Listing 18.4   Continued

```
</head>

<body>

<p>Characters will be joined: S&zwj;E.</p>
<p>Characters will not be joined: S&zwnj;E.</p>
</body>
</html>
```

Figure 18.4 shows how joining and non-joining work using two Arabic characters. The top and second characters are the individual characters. The third character from the top is the individual character joined with the zero-width joiner, and the bottom character is forced apart with the zero-width non-joiner entity.

```
<!--
```
Joining problems occur mostly in non-Latin character sets, such as Arabic, as shown by Figure 18.4.
```
-->
```

Figure 18.4
Joining and non-joining character entities.

CASE BY CASE: FONTS AND FONT UTILITIES

As you work with international sites, you'll find you require a variety of utilities to assist you in your goals.

To put together a good toolkit for working with international characters, consider the following:

- **Fonts**—You'll want the fonts appropriate for the language you're working with.

- **Keyboard translation**—A keyboard translator is a software program that allows you to emulate a foreign keyboard and thereby generate foreign characters.

- **Font conversion utilities**—Converting fonts from one platform to another is notoriously difficult. A few utilities do exist to help.

You can find a variety of fonts, keyboard emulators, and font utilities online.

For Multilanguage support in Windows, you'll find all the fonts and software you need at `http://www.microsoft.com/typography/multilang/default.htm`.

Macintosh OS 8 and higher have built-in language support. Should you require multilingual support for an older OS version, you can visit Apple's support page and select "multilingual" support from the drop-down menu, `http://www.apple.com/support/`. There are a number of multilingual support pages, by country, which will provide you with the resources you require.

For Unix systems, see the "Unicode fonts and tools for X11" page at `http://www.cl.cam.ac.uk/~mgk25/ucs-fonts.html`.

For keyboard translation, try Keyman for Windows, `http://www.tavultesoft.com/`, or SILkey for Macintosh, `http://www.sil.org/computing/silkey.html`.

Font conversion utilities are, as mentioned, often problematic. Several conversion programs are listed here for you to try out, `http://www.fontsnthings.com/tools/conversion.html`.

Finally, Macromedia's Fontographer is a very powerful font program that allows you to create, convert, and modify fonts, `http://www.macromedia.com/software/fontographer/`.

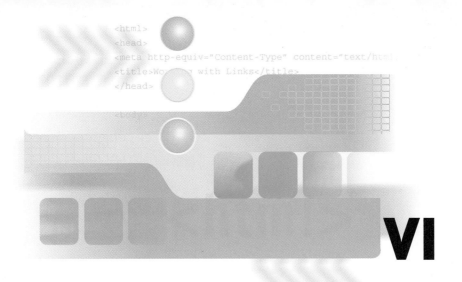

VI

ADVANCED CONCEPTS

19 XHTML Modularization   **451**

20 Customizing DTDs   **467**

21 Transforming Documents with XSLT   **485**

22 Moving Toward XML   **511**

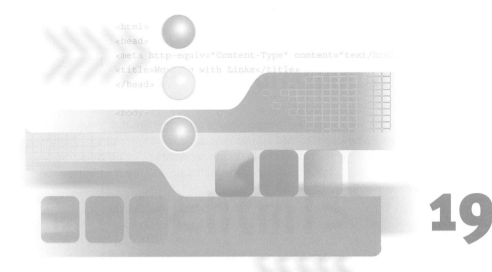

19

XHTML MODULARIZATION

IN THIS CHAPTER

The Need for Modularization 452

What Is Modularization? 454

The Modules 455

Extending HTML 458

XHTML Basic 459

XHTML Basic Document Structure 463

Case by Case: Creating and Deploying an XHTML Basic Document 464

THE NEED FOR MODULARIZATION

While there's no doubt that one of a site designer's or developer's primary goals is to provide positive user experiences on the Web sites they design, there's also no doubt that the wireless age is upon us. Whether you've developed for wireless yet or not, increasingly industry pundits are saying that access to Web content via wireless and alternative devices will be more common than with PCs in a year or two. While this seems to be taking time in the U.S., Europe and Asia are advancing more rapidly in this arena.

XHTML 1.1 incorporates the technology known as *XHTML Modularization*. This is a much more extended version of XHTML that reaches out to accommodate a wide range of needs. So as you grow as an author, developer, or designer, the primary challenge becomes how to write documents that work on a range of devices. Doing that is no simple task. It's hard enough to get our designs working successfully on today's myriad of browsers! XHTML Modularization is the first step toward giving us the flexibility—and extensibility—we need to author documents for devices with different capabilities.

Devices Affected by XHTML Modularization

Here's a short overview of the kinds of alternative devices currently available and how they might be used in the near future:

- **Digital television**—DTV has come to our homes already, in the form of set-top boxes, Web broadcast, and so on. With a set-top box connected to a modem, the TV becomes interactive with the outside world. Tests researching bi-directional communication via the TV set are already being run, but the infrastructure for this has yet to be built.

- **Smart phones**—Modern life requires certain devices for functioning to full capacity. One of these devices is the phone. In the near future, there will be very few people without a cell phone, because most people will want to be available all the time. This idea goes both ways, however. People want to have access to information and services at any time. Cellular phones are getting smaller every month. But the clutter factor is motivating phone manufacturers to prepare for even smarter phones, which incorporate the functions of other handheld devices, integrating many systems into one. Smart phones will need to support the upcoming Web standards. We'll see some cellular displays become smaller and others, larger. But no matter the innovation in terms of phones, the size of the display and the bandwidth will stay far below the standards we're used to on desktop computers.

- **Handheld devices**—I haven't been without a PDA device for several years now. Whether I'm using it for my calendar or phone book, to check e-mail from the airport, or to play games on the plane, my PDA is a device I don't like leaving behind. But, it is doubtful whether a PDA will ever be as popular as a notebook or desktop PC. Part of the reason for this is that cellular phones are becoming more and more "intelligent" and could eventually elbow out handheld devices.

- **Two-way pagers**—Pagers were once only able to receive one-way data, but now they can send and receive e-mail, instant messages, and information from the Web. With notoriously small screens and processing power ensuring that pagers are able to work quickly in part relies on reducing any overhead, including the markup that's used to format the data being exchanged.

- **Desktop browsers**—Familiar Web browsers such as Netscape, Internet Explorer, and Opera will continue to play an important if not major role for authors. As time goes on, the differences between platforms and browsers will likely be significantly reduced or disappear altogether, and we can start to forget about cross-browser authoring. We're already seeing this shift occur, although it seems to be taking some time. But, with the separation of document formatting and presentation, we can begin to concentrate on creating better Web documents that, via conformance, are interpreted equally by browsers.

- **Car navigation systems**—People have always loved their cars, and getting from place to place as quickly, safely and efficiently as possible has always been top priority. In some high-end automobiles, we're beginning to see navigation systems that use satellites and global positioning to aid with travel, traffic management, and the like. What is stopping us from using that same satellite link to browse the Internet for local hotels, restaurants, or entertainment when we are on the road? Eventually, even economy vehicles will be built with some form of navigation system, and markup will be a part of the way that data is exchanged.

- **Printers**—While many people once lauded the Internet Age as also being the paperless age, the opposite is proving true. We are printing now more than ever! While that's not good for ecology, it is often necessary in terms of documenting and distributing important information for education, government, military, and other services. Through modularization it could become a standard to set up your printing device via an XHTML-based driver directly connected to the World Wide Web.

Modularization: A Closer Look

XHTML Modularization is seen as the "decomposition" of HTML as we know it to be. While XHTML is a reformulation of HTML as an XML application, it was the first to move away from the limitations of HTML toward the extensibility offered by XML. But XHTML 1.0 is somewhat limited in that it allows only for the by now familiar three document type definitions (DTDs), each modeled after those found in HTML 4.0: Strict, Transitional, and Frameset.

While XHTML 1.0 is well structured and well formed, many authors are still learning to tap into some of the most powerful aspects of XML and related technologies. You can't write your own DTDs in XHTML 1.0 (although you can extend existing ones). You can't use schemas. You can combine templates with embedded, well-formed but not necessarily valid markup that gets translated into valid HTML or XHTML using a variety of XML tools.

XHTML 1.0 can be viewed as a means of allowing HTML authors—many of whom bootstrapped their way into the field—to painlessly gain entrance to the world of XML. Combining the familiar vocabulary of HTML with the strong syntactical influence of XML, XHTML 1.0 provides authors with a means of working with XML that makes perfect sense. Move to another XML application such as *Synchronized Multimedia Integration Language (SMIL)*, *Scalable Vector Graphics (SVG)*, or *Wireless Markup Language (WML)*, and authoring those applications becomes much less daunting. An author can immediately see how XML, as a metalanguage for creating applications, can influence a wide range of languages. Learn one, and another becomes accessible. This relationship is the most compelling argument that XHTML is not only reasonable but necessary.

WHAT IS MODULARIZATION?

With XHTML 1.0 comes organization. So, why decompose that organization? It seems a bit bizarre at first glance to take Web markup, shore it up, then knock it down. But there's a method to the madness, and anyone interested in developing for multiple devices will come to appreciate this method.

Decomposing XHTML simply means that many familiar parts of XHTML 1.0 (and therefore HTML 4.0) are broken into separate modules. Programmers should be quite comfortable with the modularization concept. When writing Perl, for example, a programmer can use a module as a quick way to add an entire chunk of necessary goods. Instead of lines and lines of code, he or she adds just one line calling the module.

But for the client-side developer, the module concept might be a little harder to grasp. Here's an analogy I've found useful in describing it: To reduce the number of bruises on my body from hauling 15 pounds of computer equipment around on cramped airplanes, I bought a Sony Vaio. The beauty of this computer is that I can have all the extended capabilities of a CD-ROM, DVD, floppy drive—whatever my heart desires—by simply adding that component. But leave them all off, and I've still got a completely functional computer. Begin with a core, add what you need. That's modularization.

XHTML Modularization is basically the same thing. It includes a list of defined modules that express specific aspects of functionality. Then, these modules can be implemented using a DTD, which can, in a sense, be seen as the core. You can combine one, or two, or five, or more. You can even write your own additions, provided that you follow the recommended DTD and driver syntax. XML schemas are also expected to be implemented into this model, which means there's more than one way to approach a given challenge. Hence, if you want to write documents for a PDA, you can choose only those modules that let you do that. Extend that to a Web page, and you may want to add some extra modules to support your needs. In turn, these DTDs create XHTML subsets. Subsets can be shared by many (as is the case with XHTML Basic, which I'll describe later in this chapter), or completely customized for a given application.

If you're following along with this concept, you should begin to see the method to the madness, that herein lies the "X" in XHTML. Finally, extensibility has arrived via the power an author has over DTDs and the potential addition of XML schemas.

THE MODULES

An XHTML module is designed in such a way that it can tell any browser how best to display site content, regardless of what kind of browser it is, and regardless of what kind of hardware requirements happen to limit the content in size and function. To make this easier, XHTML is currently partitioned into two module sections:

- **Abstract modules**—An abstract module defines a type of data that is distinct from others within the document type. One example of an abstract module would be frames, and another would be forms.

- **DTD modules**—A document type definition module details elements, attributes, and content declarations. In XHTML 1.0, there are only three DTDs. But modularization of XHTML enables the development of unique DTDs using a DTD module.

<!--
In addition to these basic modules, there are specific rules, which allow you to create your own XHTML modules and use them in combination with or instead of the already existing XHTML modules. These rules were developed by the W3C HTML Working Group and can be found at http://www.w3.org/TR/ xhtml-building/.
-->

Abstract Modules

XHTML abstract modules define the XHTML elements, their attributes and the rules concerning what kind of data a specific element can contain and how these elements can be nested.

The abstract modules are broken down into basic, presentational, forms, tables, and modules that identify various media types, as described in the following section.

Core Modules

These modules cover the basics of an XHTML document:

- **The Structure Module**—This delivers the structure for the XHTML document and, together with the document type (DOCTYPE) declaration and the XML declaration, builds its framework. The elements included in this module are html, head, title, and body.

- **The Text Module**—This defines the text container elements, their attributes, and content modules such as p h1–h6, and span.

- **The Hypertext Module**—This consists of the a element, which defines hypertext links to other resources.

- **The List Module**—This provides elements for unordered lists, ordered lists and definition lists. The elements are ul, ol, li, dl, dt, and dd.

- **The Applet Module**—This module delivers the applet element if an applet is used.

Text Extension Modules

Presentational modules describe the presentation of text within an XHTML document:

- **The Presentation Module**—This provides elements (b, big, g, hr, i, small, sub, sup, tt), their attributes, and a minimal content model for simple presentation-related markup.

- **The Edit Module**—This module defines elements (del, ins) and attributes for use in editing-related markup.

- **The Bi-Directional Text Module**—This defines an element (bdo) that can be used to declare the bi-directional rules for the element's content.

The Forms Modules

As the name implies, these modules exist to support forms:

- **The Basic Forms Module**—This module defines two content sets: Form with form and Formctrl with input, select, and textarea. The form content set defines the block in which the elements of the Formctrl content set can work as they are supposed to. This module basically represents the forms concept found in HTML 3.2.

- **The Forms Module**—This provides all of the forms features found in HTML 4.0. This module also defines two content sets: The Form content set with form and fieldset and the Formctrl content set with input, select, textarea, label, and button. As you see, this module contains also all the content sets and their elements as seen above in the Basics Forms Module. It is a superset of the Basic Forms Module, and therefore, these modules might not be used together in a single document.

The Tables Modules

Modules in this group are used for creating tables:

- **The Basic Tables Module**—This provides table-related elements (caption, table, td, th, tr), but only in a limited form. Again, this is basically the table model found in and before HTML 3.2.

- **The Tables Module**—This provides all of the table-related elements (caption, table, td, th, tr, col, colgroup, tbody, thead, tfoot). They are accessed easier by non-visual user agents. Like we saw in the Forms Module, this module is a superset of the Basic Tables Module. You cannot use the Basic Tables Module and the Tables Module together.

Additional Modules

A number of additional modules exist to control media and scripting:

- **The Image Module**—This provides basic image embedding, and may be used in some implementations independently of client-side imagemaps.

- **The Client-side Image Map Module**—This provides the elements a&, area, img&, map and object& for client-side imagemaps. It requires that the Image Module (or another module that supports the img element) is included.

- **The Server-side Image Map Module**—This provides support for image-selection and transmission of selection coordinates. It requires that the Image Module (or another module that supports the img element) is included.

- **The Object Module**—This provides the elements object, param for the inclusion of objects of general-purpose.

- **The Frames Module**—This provides the frame-related elements frameset, frame, noframes, a&, area&.

- **The Target Module**—Frames allow authors to determine specific destinations, or *targets* from the frame contents to the destination. This is done using the target element.

- **The Iframe Module**—This defines an element that can be used to define a base URL against which relative URIs in the document will be resolved.

- **The Intrinsic Events Module**—These are the attributes onblur, onfocus, onreset, onsubmit, onload, onunload, onchange, onselect and are used in conjunction with the elements (a&, area&, form&, body&, label&, input&, select&, textarea&, button&) that can have specific actions occur when certain events are performed by the user.

- **The Meta-information Module**—This defines the meta element that describes information within the XHTML documents head element.

- **The Scripting Module**—This defines the elements script and noscript that are used to contain information pertaining to executable scripts or the lack of support for executable scripts.

- **The Stylesheet Module**—This enables the processing of style sheets and is used to define the layout of an XHTML document and the appearance of its elements.

- **Style Attribute Module**—This module defines the style attribute, used in inline style. Note that it's a deprecated module.

- **Ruby Module**—This module was added to XHTML 1.1 in order to accommodate the Ruby annotation, which is a means of annotating Asian text characters.

- **Name Identification Module**—This deprecated module defines the name attribute. The name attribute in XHTML 1.1 has been supplanted with the id attribute.

- **The Link Module**—This defines an element that can be used to define links to external resources. These resources often enhance the user agent's ability to process the associated XHTML document.

- **The Base Module**—This defines an element that can be used to define a base URL against which relative URIs in the document will be resolved.

- **The Legacy Module**—This defines elements and attributes that have been earmarked as deprecated by the W3C in previous versions of HTML and XHTML. While the use of these elements and attributes is no longer encouraged, they facilitate the step from backward compatibility to current standards.

XHTML DTD Modules

But what of character entities and other language methodologies? These concerns are addressed in the XHTML DTD modules, as follows:

- **The XHTML Character Entities Module**—This defines a collection of named character entities made available by the respective XHTML DTD.

- **The XHTML Modular Framework Module**—This consists of a set of support modules, which define tools to simplify the definition of XHTML DTD content models.

- **The XHTML Module Implementations Module**—This contains the formal definition of each of the XHTML Abstract Modules as a DTD module and therefore is a type of "template" describing how to write a Document Type Definition.

- **The XHTML DTD Support Modules**—These are elements of the XHTML DTD that are hidden from regular users but need to be understood when creating other XHTML family members.

Between the Abstract and DTD modules, authors now have a full range of options when seeking to create new applications and subsets on their own.

EXTENDING XHTML

Extending XHTML will be the ultimate challenge for client manufacturers, document authors, and content providers when they realize they need to provide more than just presentational markup in order to reach their goals. Anyone can use the extensible architecture of XHTML to set up document types that meet their needs. Of course, you will have to follow the rules of XHTML Modularization to be integrated within the growing number of XHTML family members.

To become XHTML family members, modules will have to share certain characteristics:

- **Standards**—They must implement methods defined by the W3C.

- **Unique identifiers**—They must use unique identifiers to tell the client agent (for example, a browser) that it should use the exchanged module that is found in a certain DTD instead of the original module.

- **Required modules**—They will need a minimum set of modules: the Basic Structure Module, the Hypertext Module, the Basic Text Module, and the List Module within the respective DTD.

- **Namespaces**—Additional elements and attributes have to be defined in their own unique XML namespaces.

- **Validation**—Documents written with this language must validate against their DTD.

There is little doubt that the best example of XHTML modularization and the extension of XHTML in action is a subset of XHTML known as *XHTML Basic*. This subset is specifically set up for wireless devices, and examining it in detail will give you insight into just how applications and subsets are developed from modular XHTML.

XHTML BASIC

XHTML Basic exists as minimalist method by which to deliver XHTML documents to specialty clients such as those on mobile phones, PDAs, pagers, and set-top boxes.

As many readers are by now aware, HTML, despite its origins, rapidly became an authoring system for Web-based design. This involves powerful computers, plenty of visual space (at least in comparative terms), and complex methods such as the use of frames. But small devices cannot support these issues, and so new methods have to evolve. XHTML Basic is one of those methods.

The goal of XHTML Basic is to use certain parts of HTML within the context of XHTML, including only those parts of HTML that can be sensibly applied to an alternative environment.

As with XHTML Modular in general (see "Devices Affected by XHTML Modularization" earlier this chapter for more detail), the appliances XHTML Basic is geared to accommodate are

- Mobile and "smart" phones

- Television sets

- PDAs such as Palm Pilots

- Computerized vending machines

- Pagers

- Navigation systems in automobiles

- Game machines

- Electronic book devices

- "Smart" watches and similar appliances

XHTML Basic is meant to include only those methods in HTML and XHTML which make *sense* to these kinds of appliances. Given that, many elements and methodologies created for standard Web design are moved out of XHTML Basic so as to simplify the process by which to deliver consistent information to special appliances.

Features in Use Across Appliances

A number of HTML and XHTML features can be used safely across appliances with little risk of causing problems with rendering. These include the use of text and basic text formatting, such as standard headings, paragraphs, and lists.

A critical feature for all hypermedia is, of course, the link. Basic forms are important to manage input, and basic tables—in this case not for design or layout, but for their original intent: the tabular formatting of data. Images can be used in many instances, although they should be kept very small. Meta information can also be included, and is helpful for document identification, character set encoding, and search engine keywords.

XHTML Basic draws from these foundational methods. In some ways, XHTML Basic is much like early HTML—simple, clean, logical.

What's Supported and Why

So if XHTML Basic is a pared-down version of HTML and XHTML, what actually makes it tick? Well, there are many things that *can* be included in XHTML Basic, and some things that cannot. Sometimes, a technology is included, but only in part.

Here's a closer look at what *is* included in XHTML Basic.

> `<!--`
> XHTML Basic inherits the HTML 4.0 and XHTML 1.0 concept of separating presentation from formatting. Presentation of an XHTML Basic document beyond the most simplistic is relegated to a style sheet.
> `-->`

- **Text**—Standard text is in fact supported in XHTML Basic. Formatting including paragraphs, headers, breaks, and lists are also supported. Emphasis is supported, but italics are not.

- **Forms**—Very basic text forms are allowed. Forms must comply with the XHTML 1.1 Basic Forms Module. This module supports form elements common to HTML 3.2: `form`, `input`, `select`, `option`, and `textarea`.

- **Tables**—Tables textfrom the Basic Tables Module in XHTML 1.1 are supported, including the following elements: `caption`, `table`, `td`, `th`, and `tr`.

- **Style sheets**—External text style sheets are supported via the `link` attribute. Elements including `div`, `span`, and `class` are also supported to allow the use of style. It's recommended that developers ensure graceful degradation for those user interfaces that do not support style.

- **Images**—Images are text supported using the `img` element, but it's recommended that images be used very sparingly, and then only when they are extremely small in size.

> `<!--`**Caution**
> Using tables in XHTML Basic in accordance with the XHTML 1.1 Table Module is acceptable, but not necessarily recommended. Tables are difficult for very small devices to display. What's more, no nesting of tables is allowed. Developers are also encouraged to make their tables accessible.
> `-->`

 *To learn more about accessibility, **see** "Creating Accessible Sites," **p. 419,** Chapter 17.*

So, with XHTML Basic, I could have body markup that looks like this:

```
<p>Welcome to Molly's Wireless Web</p>
```

or like this:

```
<h2>Welcome to Molly's Wireless Web</h2>
<p>Here you will find:</p>
<ul>
<li>Book Updates</li>
<li>Speaking Engagements</li>
<li>Contact Information</li>
</ul>
```

or even this:

```
<img src="welcome.gif" /><br /><br />
<p>Select One:</p>
<table border="0" width="100%">
<tr>
<td><a href="updates.html">Book Updates</a></td>
<td><a href="speaking.html">Speaking Engagements</a></td>
<td><a href="contact.html">Contact Information</a></td>
</tr>
</table>
```

For my forms page, I could have a complete (but simple) form, and I could also choose to use an external style sheet to apply style as I saw fit.

> `<!--`
> Most standard attributes for supported elements, such as `border`, `width`, `height`, and so on are allowed in XHTML Basic.
> `-->`

What's Not Supported and Why

So what's been left out of XHTML basic? Lots! The limitations of alternative appliances at this time make it very difficult for many aspects of Web authoring—things with which we've all become intimately familiar—to make sense in restricted environments.

Here's a look at what you *can't* use in XHTML Basic:

- **Scripting**—The `script` and `noscript` elements are not supported. Scripts demand processing power, which many of the smaller, alternative devices simply do not have.

- **Frames**—Frames are based on the interfaces provided by a Web browser. Because the user agents in alternative devices are very limited, and very small, frames don't make sense (some people feel they've never made sense in any context). As such, frames are completely unsupported in XHTML Basic.

- **Imagemaps**—Because mapping requires input from a pointing device, and only a few alternative devices use pointers (for example, PDAs do, but pagers do not), imagemaps have been left out of XHTML Basic.

So, any inline script using the `script` element will not be allowed. Conceivably, I could use [CDATA] or the `link` attribute to link to an external script. However, the use of scripting for alternative devices is very limited if useful at all, at least at this time. You'll never see a frameset in XHTML Basic, because the user agents don't have the power to support them.

The same is true of objects. Imagine trying to deliver a Flash file to a pager? Hardly! And, while small images are supported, the mapping features are not. Consider that original mapping was a server-side process, and later mapping was browser-based. Most user agents for small devices need to be lean and mean, so there simply isn't the support. What's more, the point-and-click options available to us on a computer are not available on most alternative devices.

If all this feels limited, well—it is! But these limitations empower you to deliver content to alternative devices. XHTML Basic doesn't exist for standard browser design. Rather, it is pared down especially because alternative devices are, as a group, limited.

<!--
It's important to point out that the W3C expects that XHTML Basic will be expanded upon. This means that as alternative devices become more supportive of various technologies, elements that are currently not allowed will become allowed, or new elements or methodologies will be introduced. It's critical to remember that XHTML and its related technologies are truly in an evolutionary phase.
-->

Specific Modules Included in XHTML Basic

With an understanding of the fundamental concepts found in XHTML Basic, it becomes very easy to grasp how XHTML Basic uses XHTML 1.1 modules.

The following modules and associated elements are demonstrated in Table 19.1.

Table 19.1   Modules Found in XHTML Basic

Module	Elements Included
Structure Module	`body`, `head`, `html`, `title`
Text Module	`abbr`, `acronym`, `address`, `blockquote`, `br`, `cite`, `code`, `dfn`, `div`, `em`, `h1`, `h2`, `h3`, `h4`, `h5`, `h6`, `kbd`, `p`, `pre`, `q`, `samp`, `span`, `strong`, `var`
Hypertext Module	`a`
List Module	`dl`, `dt`, `dd`, `ol`, `ul`, `li`
Basic Forms Module	`form`, `input`, `label`, `select`, `option`, `textarea`
Basic Tables Module	`caption`, `table`, `td`, `tr`, `th`
Image Module	`img`
Object Module	`object`, `param`
Meta Information Module	`meta`
Link Module	`link`
Base Module	`base`

As you can see, it's modularization that provides the building blocks of any XHTML 1.1 subset. There are other modules available, but only these modules are allowed in XHTML Basic, as it is specifically designed for a precise use.

XHTML BASIC DOCUMENT STRUCTURE

An XHTML Basic document follows what should now be very familiar rules. Documents must conform, must validate, and must contain specific syntax to enable this conformance and validation.

An XHTML Basic document must conform to the following guidelines:

- The document must validate to the XHTML Basic Document Type Definition (DTD).

- The document must contain a DOCTYPE definition denoting the proper DTD.

- The root element of the document (as in XHTML itself) must be `html`.

- The root element must contain the default namespace for XHTML, further defining it as an XHTML-based document.

Conformance is an absolute in XHMTL, and therefore in XHTML Basic. As a result, XHTML Basic documents must validate against the named Basic DTD.

In order to establish the document as an XHTML Basic document, and to allow for validation, the DOCTYPE definition must be included. The root element is `html` because HTML is the vocabulary in use within the context of XHTML Basic markup.

Listing 19.1 Basic shows an XHTML Basic document with all the structure elements in place.

> `<!--` If the rules for XHTML Basic sound to you to be exactly like those found in standard XHMTL 1.0, but with a different DTD, you're correct! XHTML Basic is a perfect example of modularization—a primary concept in XHTML 1.1—at work. `-->`

Listing 19.1   The XHTML Basic Document Template

```
<?xml version="1.0"?>
<!DOCTYPE html PUBLIC "-//W3C//DTD XHTML Basic 1.0//EN"
"xhtml-basic10.dtd" >

<html xmlns="http://www.w3.org/1999/xhtml" xml:lang="en" >
<head>
<title>          </title>
</head>

<body>

<p>example</p>

</body>
</html>
```

> `<!--` As in XHTML 1.0 and 1.1, the XML declaration is suggested, but not required. `-->`

CASE BY CASE: CREATING AND DEPLOYING AN XHTML BASIC DOCUMENT

You can put XHTML Basic to work today. To do so, follow these steps:

1. Create an XHTML Basic Document. Begin with the DOCTYPE declaration:

```
<!DOCTYPE html PUBLIC "-//W3C//DTD XHTML Basic 1.0//EN"
"xhtml-basic10.dtd" >
```

2. Add the html root and namespace element:

```
<!DOCTYPE html PUBLIC "-//W3C//DTD XHTML Basic 1.0//EN"
"xhtml-basic10.dtd" >
<html xmlns="http://www.w3.org/1999/xhtml" xml:lang="en" >
</html>
```

3. Add the head and title element to the document:

```
<!DOCTYPE html PUBLIC "-//W3C//DTD XHTML Basic 1.0//EN"
"xhtml-basic10.dtd" >
<html xmlns="http://www.w3.org/1999/xhtml" xml:lang="en" >
<head>
<title>My First XHTML Basic Page</title>
</head>
</html>
```

4. Add the body element:

```
<!DOCTYPE html PUBLIC "-//W3C//DTD XHTML Basic 1.0//EN"
"xhtml-basic10.dtd" >
<head>
<title>My First XHTML Basic Page</itle>
</head>
<html xmlns="http://www.w3.org/1999/xhtml" xml:lang="en" >
<head>
<title>My First XHTML Basic Page</title>
</head>
<body>


</body>
</html>
```

5. Add content (I've kept mine simple):

```
<!DOCTYPE html PUBLIC "-//W3C//DTD XHTML Basic 1.0//EN"
"xhtml-basic10.dtd" >
<head>
<title>My First XHTML Basic Page</itle>
</head><html xmlns="http://www.w3.org/1999/xhtml" xml:lang="en" >
<head>
```

```
<title>My First XHTML Basic Page</title>
</head>
<body>
<h2>Welcome to Molly's Wireless Web</h2>
<p>Here you will find:</p>
<ul>
<li>Book Updates</li>
<li>Speaking Engagements</li>
<li>Contact Information</li>
</ul>
<p><a href="next.html">Follow this link to continue</a></p>
</body>
</html>
```

6. Save the file as index_basic.html.

7. Upload to your Web server. If you have a PDA or other alternative device, look up the page using that device and test it out.

<!--Caution

You can use the XML declaration in your document if you so desire. However, if certain standard Web browsers come to this page, it may render improperly. Therefore, I've left it off in this example. -->

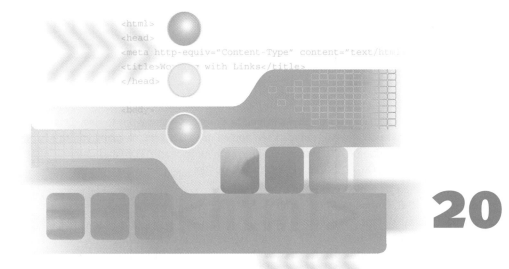

CUSTOMIZING DTDS

IN THIS CHAPTER

Understanding DTDs   **468**

Reading the XHTML DTDs   **476**

Case by Case: Defining Your Own DTD   **479**

UNDERSTANDING DTDS

In previous chapters, you've used the DOCTYPE declaration at the beginning of your Web documents to specify which type of DTD—Strict, Transitional, or Frameset—you want to use. This chapter explains exactly what you've been doing when you've used DOCTYPE, teaches you the basics of *Document Type Definition (DTD)* syntax, shows you how to read DTDs, and demonstrates how you can modify XHTML DTDs to extend the language.

An XML DTD is the method by which you define the syntax and structure of an XML language. You'll recall that XML itself is a meta-language that lets you build markup languages that follow certain rule sets. A DTD adds additional rules that state which elements can be used with others, which attributes are allowed in a tag, and what the default values of an attribute should be.

> `<!--` While you can write your own DTDs to extend XHTML, in the context of XHTML 1.1 they are especially helpful in adding modules. `-->`

What Is a DTD?

A DTD is a formal specification for a language. It's designed to be machine-readable for automatic parsing, but also understandable and capable of being produced by a human with a text editor—as is the case with HTML, XHTML, and XML. DTDs are written in a language that will seem familiar to you, as it includes tags, brackets, and values, although a few differences—such as needing no closing tags or even closing "/" marks—might be a little confusing at first.

The concept of DTDs originated with SGML. Until XHTML 1.0, all HTML DTDs have been written in accordance with the SGML rules for DTDs; now, the simplicity and power of XML has been applied to HTML to produce DTDs available for use in XHTML.

A DTD for a given language defines the structure of that language and the acceptable syntax that's used in that language. For example, the XHTML DTD specifies that <img> tags must have alt attributes, and that <a> tags cannot be nested. DTDs are limited, however, to only expressing syntax and structure. Actual semantics, such as what is meant by an <h1> or how to display a <b> tag, cannot be expressed in DTDs, unless it's done so within comments.

The DOCTYPE Declaration

Whenever you use the DOCTYPE declaration, you are referencing a DTD. Here's the DOCTYPE declaration that refers to the XHTML 1.0 DTD:

```
<!DOCTYPE html PUBLIC "-//W3C//DTD XHTML 1.0 Strict//EN"
"http://www.w3.org/TR/xhtml1/DTD/xhtml1-strict.dtd">
```

Look at each component of the DOCTYPE declaration. First is the word DOCTYPE itself, complete with an exclamation point at the start. This is what's called a declaration, and it's not an XML "element" itself—which means that no closing tag is necessary, not even a slash at the end of the tag. It's also the reason it doesn't conform to case rules in the given language it declares—it should always be uppercase. Declarations *never* having closing tags.

The next item is the word html— note the case, as it's important. This identifies the root element of the document, which is the <html> tag for XHTML. It's important that the html is in lowercase in XHTML, because XML is case-sensitive, and XHTML is properly written with lowercase tags. You'll notice in HTML DTDs, the HTML is often written in uppercase.

The word PUBLIC means that the DTD has a public name, referred to as a *formal public identifier (FPI)*. Contrasted with public identifiers are system identifiers, which are identified by a URL or local file and tell where the DTD can be found. Your XHTML DOCTYPE statement provides both an FPI and a system identifier. The first long quoted string is the public identifier, and the second is the system identifier.

Not all DTDs will have FPIs; usually this is reserved for well-known or famous DTDs. You can think of an FPI as being like a proper name for a famous building, and a system identifier as being like a street address. For example, you might say "The White House" (a public name) or you might say "1600 Pennsylvania Avenue" (a street address) to indicate the residence of the U.S. President. However, if you wanted to speak of a local post office that you go to, saying "the post office" wouldn't be specific to many people, so you would want to include the actual street address.

Here's what the XHTML 1.0 FPI looks like:

```
"-//W3C//DTD XHTML 1.0 Strict//EN"
```

An FPI is composed of four parts, each of which is separated by double slashes. The first part indicates whether the DTD was created by an international standards body, such as the International Standards Organization (ISO); if so, a plus sign is used; if not, then a hyphen is used. The second part names the organization or company that created the standard. The third part is a name or title for the language. The fourth defines the language which was used to document or define the document type—"EN" indicates the English language.

The system identifier is always a URI that identifies a location where the DTD itself can be downloaded. The system identifier is optional for well-known DTDs with FPIs, but it is always prudent to include the system identifier URL anyway, which is why it is included in your DOCTYPE declaration.

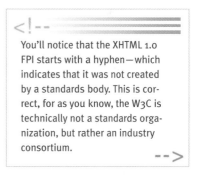

You'll notice that the XHTML 1.0 FPI starts with a hyphen—which indicates that it was not created by a standards body. This is correct, for as you know, the W3C is technically not a standards organization, but rather an industry consortium.

A DOCTYPE declaration without an FPI uses the keyword SYSTEM instead of PUBLIC and skips the FPI entirely, such as this:

```
<!DOCTYPE html SYSTEM
"http://www.w3.org/TR/xhtml1/DTD/xhtml1-strict.dtd">
```

This is a working DOCTYPE for identifying the XHTML 1.0 Strict DTD, just like 1600 Pennsylvania Avenue is a valid address even if we don't mention that it is the White House.

DTD Syntax

So what does a DTD look like? The simplest way to get you familiar with XML DTDs is to show you one, so I've included a rather simple DTD in Listing 20.1. This DTD defines an XML language for describing which cars are in my friend's garage.

Listing 20.1   A Simple DTD for Describing the Cars in a Garage

```
<!--
  cars.dtd
  By Molly E. Holzschlag molly@molly.com

  A simple DTD for describing the cars in a garage.
  SYSTEM "http://molly.com/dtd/garage.dtd"
-->


<!--============= Define some parameter entities ============-->
<!ENTITY % Quality       "(excellent|good|fair|poor|terrible)">
<!ENTITY % Date          "CDATA">  <!-- (DD-)Mon-YYYY -->
<!ENTITY % ModelYear     "CDATA">  <!-- YYYY -->
<!ENTITY % LicPlate      "CDATA">  <!-- 7 letters or digits -->
<!ENTITY % State         "CDATA">  <!-- 2-letter postal code -->

<!ENTITY % CommonAttrs
    "condition      %Quality       #IMPLIED
     modified       %Date          #IMPLIED"
   >


<!ENTITY % AppContent "color|detailing|windows|tires">

<!--============= The root element is "garage" ==============-->
<!ELEMENT garage (car)*>

<!ATTLIST garage
   date            %Date;       #IMPLIED
   >


<!--============= Each car is a separate element ============-->
<!ELEMENT car (license, type, appearance)>

<!ATTLIST car
   %CommonAttrs;
   name            CDATA        #IMPLIED
   >


<!ELEMENT license EMPTY>
```

Listing 20.1   Continued

```
<!ATTLIST license
    state           %State;         #REQUIRED
    expires         %Date;          #IMPLIED
    plate           %LicPlate;      #REQUIRED
    >

<!ELEMENT appearance (%AppContent;)*>

<!ELEMENT color       (#PCDATA)>
<!ELEMENT tires       (#PCDATA)>
<!ELEMENT windows     (#PCDATA)>
<!ELEMENT detailing   (#PCDATA)>

<!ATTLIST color
    %CommonAttrs;
    area            CDATA           "body"
    >

<!ATTLIST tires
    %CommonAttrs;
    brand           CDATA           #IMPLIED
    >

<!ATTLIST windows
    %CommonAttrs;
    >

<!ATTLIST detailing
    %CommonAttrs;
    >

<!ELEMENT type (make, model, style?)>

<!ELEMENT make    (#PCDATA)>
<!ELEMENT model   (#PCDATA)>
<!ELEMENT style   (#PCDATA)>

<!ATTLIST model
    year            %ModelYear;     #REQUIRED
    >
```

Some of this might be obvious and some may be a little harder to understand, so I'll explain each part in order. What does this DTD do? It defines the syntax and the structure of a markup language which can describe the cars in a garage. A sample listing of an XML file written in this language is included as Listing 20.2.

Listing 20.2   An XML File Written According to `garage.dtd`

```
<?xml version="1.0" standalone="no"?>
<!DOCTYPE garage SYSTEM "http://www.molly.com/dtd/garage.dtd">
<garage date="4-Sep-2000">
  <car name="Beverly">
    <license state="CA" expires="Dec-2000" plate="3BVY900" />
    <appearance>
      <color area="upper body">white</color>
      <color area="lower body">orange</color>
      <color area="interior">black</color>
      <windows>tinted</windows>
    </appearance>
    <type>
      <make>Volkswagen</make>
      <model year="1974">bus</model>
    </type>
  </car>
  <car name="Nixby">
    <license state="CA" plate="1NXB337" />
    <appearance>
      <color>metallic green</color>
    </appearance>
    <type>
      <make>Toyota</make>
      <model year="1986">Tercel</model>
      <style>Station Wagon</style>
    </type>
  </car>
</garage>
```

Structure of a DTD

As I mentioned before, DTD syntax is similar to the markup you've been working with before. This is because DTDs are composed of declarations—which begin with <! and end with >—and not elements which have to worry about nesting and closing tags. The comment syntax should be familiar to you; it's the same as in HTML and XHTML, as it is derived from SGML.

The declarations used in this DTD are listed in Table 20.1.

Table 20.1   XML DTD Declarations

XML DTD Syntax	Function
`<!ENTITY>`	Declares an entity—parsed, parameter, or other types
`<!ELEMENT>`	Defines an element in the DTD
`<!ATTLIST>`	Defines attributes for an element
`<!-- Comment -->`	A simple comment

Entities

Entities, in XML DTDs, are a way of defining objects that will be replaced by specific strings or characters wherever they are included in a document. You're actually familiar with a number of entities, even if you're not aware of it. These are a specific type known as character entities. Character entities include <, >, ", Κ, and other such references to characters in XHTML.

➡ *To learn more about character entities,* ***see*** *"Dealing with Data Types," **p. 61**, Chapter 3.*

The syntax for declaring an entity is

```
<!ENTITY name "value">
```

The value of the entity, in the document, is then referenced by using the following in the markup:

```
&name;
```

A parsed entity can be more than just a single character, though; for example, consider the following:

```
<!ENTITY myname "Molly E. Holzschlag">
```

If I write a document in an XML language with the above declaration in the DTD, I can then use the &myname; entity in the document itself, such as

```
<para>The sign on my door reads &myname;.</para>
```

This would expand to

```
<para>The sign on my door reads Molly E. Holzschlag.</para>
```

In the XHTML DTD, entities are most commonly used to define the character entities.

Parameter Entities

Parameter entities are different from parsed entities—while parsed entities are used in the *document*, parameter entities are meant for use in the DTD itself. The value of the parameter entity is substituted into the DTD whenever the entity is used, and this allows for a more modular, organized method of constructing DTDs.

The syntax for a simple parameter entity is similar, but not identical, to parsed entities:

```
<!ENTITY % name "value">
```

Notice the % before the name—that's what indicates that it's a parameter entity. To use the value of a parameter entity, you use a slightly different manner as well:

```
%name;
```

Parameter entities can also be external, which means that the value of the entity is the contents of a file identified by FPI or URL. Declarations of external entities look like one of the following:

```
<!ENTITY % name PUBLIC "FPI" "URI">
<!ENTITY % name SYSTEM "URI">
```

This allows you to include an external file in a DTD declaration; for example, the XHTML 1.0 Transitional DTD contains the following declaration, which says that the xhtml-lat1.ent file should be included:

```
<!ENTITY % HTMLlat1 PUBLIC
    "-//W3C//ENTITIES Latin 1 for XHTML//EN"
    "xhtml-lat1.ent">
%HTMLlat1;
```

Note that simply declaring the entity doesn't actually import the contents of the file—you must then invoke the entity itself, which explains the presence of the %HTMLlat1; above.

Element Declarations

When declaring an element, you declare not only the name, but the content model of the element, using the ELEMENT declaration. The attributes are declared separately using ATTLIST. The syntax for ELEMENT is

```
<!ELEMENT identifier contentmodel>
```

A content model is a description of which types of content—elements and text—can be validly included within the container of the element. Values for the content model are listed in Table 20.2. Parentheses can be used to group elements together, commas to define sequences, and vertical bars to indicate a choice from among several valid options.

Table 20.2   Content Models in XML DTDs

Syntax	Description
ANY	Any text and elements can be contained by the element.
EMPTY	The element is not a container, and must always be empty.
(#PCDATA)*	The element can contain textual data or markup.
(tag1, tag2)	The element can only contain the elements tag1 and tag2, in that order.
(tag1 | tag2)	The element can contain either tag1, or tag2 (but only one of them, and just one such element).
(tag1)*	The element can contain zero or more tag1 elements.
(tag1)+	The element must contain at least one tag1 element, and can contain more than one.
(tag1)?	The element may contain one (and only one) tag1 element, but it's optional.
(#PCDATA|tag1)*	The element can contain either text or markup, or tag1 elements.

Complex sequences can be built using parentheses, vertical bars, commas, and other indicators. To understand these, you'll just need to break them down into simpler groups. For example, consider the following content model:

```
<!ELEMENT aaa (#PCDATA | (bbb, (ccc | ddd))*>
```

This indicates that the <aaa> tag can contain zero or more occurrences of #PCDATA (text or markup, including entities) or <bbb> tags followed by either <ccc> or <ddd> tags.

A simple example from the cars DTD is the root element, <garage>, which can contain zero or more <car> elements:

```
<!ELEMENT garage (car)*>
```

You can use parameter entities in ELEMENT declarations, as in the declaration of the <appearance> tag in the cars DTD:

```
<!ELEMENT appearance (%AppContent;)*>
```

To interpret the possible values for the <appearance> tag, you'll have to look at the definition for the %AppContent; entity:

```
<!ENTITY % AppContent "color | detailing | windows | tires">
```

This tells you that the <appearance> tag consists of zero or more tags from <color>, <detailing>, <windows>, or <tires>.

Attribute List Declarations

You declare the valid attributes for an element by using the ATTLIST declaration. The syntax for ATTLIST is

```
<!ATTLIST element
    attribute    type    default
    attribute    type    default
    >
```

The most common types of attributes you'll encounter are listed in Table 20.3. The type of each attribute determines which kinds of values can legally be assigned to the attribute. The default value indicates whether the attribute has a default value assigned, or if a value is required to be set. The options for the default value are listed in Table 20.4.

Table 20.3 Common Attribute Types Used in XML DTDs

Syntax	Description
(value1 | value2 | ...)	These are literal enumerated values; the attribute can only be one of these values.
CDATA	The attribute must be character data, which means any normal text (although special characters such as < or " must be escaped).
ID	The value of this attribute must be an "id"—XML IDs must be unique with a document, must start with a letter, and can only contain letters, numbers, hyphens, periods, or underscores.
IDREF	The attribute must reference an ID elsewhere in the document.

Table 20.4 Default Values for Attributes in XML DTDs

Syntax	Description
#IMPLIED	There is not a default value for this attribute, and setting a value is not mandatory.
#REQUIRED	A value *must* be set for this attribute, and there is no default value.
"value"	The default value is "value".
#FIXED "value"	The value of this attribute is set to "value", and cannot be changed.

You can mix parameter entities with literal values for the attribute type and default values. For example, here is the ATTLIST declaration for the <license> tag from the sample DTD:

```
<!ATTLIST license
    state         %State;         #REQUIRED
    expires       %Date;          #IMPLIED
    plate         %LicPlate;      #REQUIRED
    >
```

To figure out what values are valid for the state attribute—which is a required attribute for the license tag—you'll need to look up the %State; parameter entry, which reads:

```
<!ENTITY % State     "CDATA">  <!-- 2-letter postal code -->
```

This tells you that values for the state attribute can legally be set to any text value (CDATA) but should only be set to two-letter codes (such as CT or MA) as described by the comment which follows the declaration.

You can even use parameter entities to make whole sets of lists. Here's the declaration for the %CommonAttrs; entity:

```
<!ENTITY % CommonAttrs
    "condition      %Quality       #IMPLIED
     modified       %Date          #IMPLIED"
    >
```

This makes it easy to add a whole set of attributes at once, as in the declaration of the <color> element:

```
<!ATTLIST color
    %CommonAttrs;
    area               CDATA             "body"
    >
```

The <color> tag can take three attributes—condition, modified, and area. Note that if a value is not specified for area, it defaults to "body."

READING THE XHTML DTDS

As a Web author, you'll want to become familiar with the XHTML DTDs and what they contain. While reading XML DTDs can seem intimidating at first, the concepts are actually quite simple and you can learn about the structure of the language by examining the formal syntax definitions. As the authoritative source on XHTML, the XHTML DTDs can help you understand validation errors and, if you want to extend the language by adding (or removing) elements (and modules), you will need to understand how the DTDs are structured.

Downloading the XHTML DTDs

To work with the XHTML DTDs, you'll want to have your own copy of the DTDs. You can read them online, or you can download them to your hard drive. I recommend keeping a local version so that you can read it whenever you like as well as being able to modify it yourself, as you'll do later in this chapter.

There are three distinct DTDs—one each for the Strict, Transitional, and Frameset versions of XHTML 1.0. The XHTML 1.1 DTD is simply the XHTML 1.0 Strict DTD.

In addition, there are three files that contain the parsed entities used in all versions of XHTML. Table 20.5 shows the files you need.

<!--

You can download the files individually, from http://www.w3.org/TR/xhtml1/#dtds, but I recommend that you grab the zip file at http://www.w3.org/TR/xhtml1/xhtml1.zip as it contains the files you need in the DTD subdirectory. The XHTML 1.1 DTD is essentially the same as the XHTML 1.0 DTD, but has additional parameters to deal with modularization.

-->

Table 20.5   XHTML 1.0 DTD Files

Filename	Contents
xhtml1-strict.dtd	DTD for Strict XHTML 1.0
xhtml1-transitional.dtd	DTD for Transitional XHTML 1.0
xhtml1-frameset.dtd	DTD for Frameset XHTML 1.0
xhtml1-lat1.ent	Entity definitions for Latin 1 character set
xhtml1-symbol.ent	Entity definitions for mathematical, Greek, and symbolic characters
xhtml1-special.ent	Entity definitions for "Special" (miscellaneous) characters

As the Transitional DTD tends to be the richest in terms of attributes and elements, as well as the one you are most likely to use in practice, we'll focus on that DTD. The principles you'll learn will enable you to read all three of the XHTML DTDs, however.

Structure of the Transitional XHTML DTD

The Transitional XHTML DTD is arranged in sections, with each section set off by a divider in the form of a long comment. Each section has a specific function and defines different parts of the XHTML specification. These section dividers are listed in Listing 20.3, with the content between them removed so you can more easily see the structure and order of the DTD.

Listing 20.3   Excerpted Section Divider Comments from XHTML 1.0 Transitional DTD

```
<!--========== Character mnemonic entities ==========-->
<!--========== Imported Names ====================-->
<!--============ Generic Attributes ===============-->
```

Listing 20.3 Continued

```
<!--============ Text Elements ====================-->
<!--=========== Block level elements ==============-->
<!--=========== Content models for exclusions =====-->
<!--========= Document Structure ==================-->
<!--========= Document Head ======================-->
<!--================ Frames ======================-->
<!--=========== Document Body ====================-->
<!--=========== Paragraphs =======================-->
<!--=========== Headings =========================-->
<!--=========== Lists ============================-->
<!--=========== Address ==========================-->
<!--=========== Horizontal Rule ==================-->
<!--=========== Preformatted Text ================-->
<!--=========== Block-like Quotes ================-->
<!--=========== Text alignment ===================-->
<!--=========== Inserted/Deleted Text ============-->
<!--=========== The Anchor Element ===============-->
<!--=============== Inline Elements ==============-->
<!--============ Object ==========================-->
<!--=========== Java applet ======================-->
<!--=========== Images ===========================-->
<!--=========== Client-side image maps ===========-->
<!--========= Forms ==============================-->
<!--=============== Tables =======================-->
```

You should skim through the DTD at this time, and look over the structure. One important thing to notice is the way parameter entities are declared in two general locations: at the start of the document (such as in "Generic Attributes") and in some sections just before they are used.

The first section of the DTD loads the parsed entity lists. These are included in the additional files in the DTD directory of the specification. This is where various character entities are defined, such as γ, ♠, · Á, or >.

Within the DTD there some groups of attributes and elements which appear repeatedly, and are represented by parameter entities. These allow for grouping and consolidation of these repeated sections, so that they don't need to be listed each time. A short list of some of the more notable parameter entities is shown in Listing 20.4.

Listing 20.4 Useful Attribute and Element Groups in the XHTML 1.0 Transitional DTD

Parameter Entity	Purpose or Function
%coreattrs;	Attributes found on most elements: id, class, style, and title
%i18n;	Attributes for internationalization: lang, xml:lang, and dir
%events;	Intrinsic events such as onClick and onKeyPress
%focus;	Attributes for elements which can hold "focus": accesskey, tabindex, onfocus, onblur

Listing 20.4 Continued

Parameter Entity	Purpose or Function
%attrs;	All attributes found in %coreattrs;, %i18n;, and %events;
%special;	"Special" inline text elements, such as , <img>, and <object>
%fontstyle;	Elements which affect the presentation of text, such as: <tt>, <big>, <i>, or <font>
%phrase;	Elements which give semantic meaning to a phrase, including: <strong>, <abbr>, and <q>
%inline.forms;	Form elements which should be rendered inline, instead of on separate lines, such as <input> and <select>
%misc;	A catch-all category for elements that can be inline or "block": <ins>, <del>, <script>, and <noscript>
%inline;	Inline tags: the <a> element, and all the elements included in %special;, %fontstyle;, %phrase;, %inline.forms;, and %misc;

As you can see, parameter entities can consist of other parameter entities, and are used throughout the DTD to build up the declarations of the elements and their attributes. You may have to backtrack through several layers of parameter entities to decipher the content models or attributes for a specific element.

Structure Versus Semantics

One thing you'll notice as you read the DTDs is that they do not contain all the information one would need to know in order to write XHTML, or to write a browser to display it. Apart from the comments, nothing describes the *meaning* of the various tags—only the syntax and structure of the markup. For example, the declarations for each of the headers—<h1>, <h2>, to <h6>—are all identical. Data types are assigned to parameter entities, such as %DateTime; or %Number;, but these are all designated as CDATA.

The semantic meaning of each tag is described in the specification, in text that describes the purpose of each tag, the valid values for each attribute, and how a browser should display them. Because XHTML 1.0 is a direct translation of HTML 4.01, you can find you'll the meaning of each tag by looking it up in the HTML 4.01 specification.

CASE BY CASE: DEFINING YOUR OWN DTD

Being able to read the XHTML DTDs is a useful skill; however, you don't want to stop there. The X in XHTML stands for extensibility, and part of the true power of XHTML is the fact that it can be extended as needed.

In XHTML 1.0 and especially 1.1, you can extend the language by editing the DTD. This will give you a new DTD you can use in your DOCTYPE declarations and demonstrate some of the flexibility and adaptability inherent to XHTML.

Extending an XHTML DTD

Apart from the fact that it can be done, why would you *want* to extend the DTD you're using? There are a number of possible reasons, depending on exactly what you're trying to accomplish:

- You may be working on integrating XHTML with another specialized XML-based language.

- Your Web publishing system may require certain tags to be added which are not exposed to the browsers, but are processed on the server side, and you want to use XML tools on those tags.

- Your browser may have additional support for tags which are not defined in the specification, and you want to take advantage of the benefits of writing markup to specification, such as validation.

One tag that is very common is <embed>, which is used to embed multimedia objects in Web pages. Unfortunately, <embed> is not part of the HTML 4 or XHTML 1.0 specifications—instead, the specification promotes the use of the <object> tag, which is really a more elegant and general solution to adding multimedia objects to Web pages.

However, <embed> remains well-supported by the browsers, while there are several serious problems the implementation of <object> in some of the major browsers. This has left Web designers with difficult choices: use <object> and risk browser support problems, or use <embed> and not be able to write to the specification?

For these reasons, <embed> will make a good example of how the XHTML 1.0 specification can be extended.

*For more specific information on how you can use <embed> to add multimedia—including movies and background sounds, **see** "Embedding Objects," **p. 325**, Chapter 13.*

Defining the <embed> tag

The first thing you will need to do when extending XHTML is decide which attributes of the <embed> tag you want to support. Because each browser implements a different set of attributes for <embed>—and because there is no W3C specification which defines it—you'll have to be selective when you put the tag together.

I've summarized the most important—and most supported—attributes in Table 20.6.

Table 20.6   The Attributes of the <embed> Tag

Attribute	Values
src	A URL address
height	Pixels or percentages
width	Pixels or percentages
pluginspage	A URL address

Table 20.6 Continued

Attribute	Values
autoplay	"true" or "false"
controller	"true" or "false"
loop	"true", "false", or "palindrome"

These attributes will give you a good start on defining the <embed> tag. The tag itself will be an EMPTY tag as it has no content. (Actually, this is a matter of debate, as described in the blooberry.com listing for the <noembed> tag, but for this exercise we'll go with the simplest alternative.) Now I'll show you how to modify the DTD and add this element.

1. First, make a copy of the base DTD that you retrieved from http://www.w3.org/TR/xhtml1/xhtml1.zip. You'll want to start with the XHTML 1.0 Transitional DTD, so copy the xhtml1-transitional.dtd file to another name, and edit that file. Call it xhtml1-embed.dtd.

2. Open the new copy in your text editor and go to the very end of the file. We will add our new element there. Add the following at the end of the DTD:

```
<!--===================== Embed =====================-->
<!ELEMENT embed EMPTY>
```

3. This would be a good time to define some parameter entities—both because they might be useful, and also because it will give you practice. On the line below the one where you declared the embed element, add the following lines to define the Boolean and Booloob entities:

```
<!ENTITY % Boolean "(true | false )">
<!ENTITY % Booloob "(true | false | palindrome)">
<!-- Why booloob? It is boolean plus palindrome -->
```

4. Now that you've defined those entities, you can use them and other generic parameter entities from the rest of the XHTML 1.0 DTD to list attributes. First create an attribute list shell for the embed element; leave some spaces between the lines so you can fill them in later. Don't forget the closing angle bracket.

```
<!ATTLIST embed

>
```

5. As you've seen from reading the XHTML specification, many elements use the attrs parameter entity, which includes the core attributes, intrinsic events, and internationalization attributes. These are appropriate for the <embed> tag, so add the attrs entity, as shown here:

```
<!ATTLIST embed
    %attrs;
  >
```

6. Next you need to consider each of the attributes, as listed previously in Table 20.6. The src and pluginspage attributes should be URLs, so use the %URI; entity. The height and width attributes will use the %Length; entity. Add those to the attribute list:

```
<!ATTLIST embed
      %attrs;
      src               %URI;              #REQUIRED
      height            %Length;           #IMPLIED
      width             %Length;           #IMPLIED
      pluginspage       %URI;              #IMPLIED
    >
```

7. Now we will use the parameter entries we defined before, Boolean and Booloob. The autoplay and controller attributes take Boolean values and the default should be "false"; the default for loop is "false" as well, but should use the Booloob entity. Add those attributes and your attribute list is complete:

```
<!ATTLIST embed
      %attrs;
      src               %URI;              #REQUIRED
      height            %Length;           #IMPLIED
      width             %Length;           #IMPLIED
      pluginspage       %URI;              #IMPLIED
      autoplay          %Boolean;          "false"
      controller        %Boolean;          "false"
      loop              %Booloob;          "false"
>
```

8. With the <embed> element and its attributes defined, you are almost done. Locate the part of the DTD marked "Text Elements" and add embed to the "special" entity. Why the special entity? It includes the <object> tag, which is the closest in function and syntax to the <embed> tag, and is a reasonable place to add the tag. If it is not added, then the tag will exist—but there will be no legal place to use it. Here's what your modified %special; declaration should look like:

```
<!--=============== Text Elements ===========================-->
<!ENTITY % special
    "br | span | bdo | object | applet | img | map | iframe | embed">
```

9. Finally, edit the first comment at the beginning of the page to reflect the fact you have changed the DTD. Choose a public identifier and a system identifier URL—here's what I've used:

```
<!--
    Extensible HTML version 1.0 plus Embed DTD
    This is based on the XHTML 1.0 DTD with the addition
    of the embed tag.
    This DTD module is identified by the PUBLIC and SYSTEM identifiers:
    PUBLIC "-//molly.com//XHTML 1.0 plus Embed//EN"
    SYSTEM "http://molly.com/dtd/xhtml1-embed.dtd"
    $Revision: 1.0 $
    $Date: 2002/01/01 23:52:20 $
-->
```

You'll notice that I gave this an FPI—the first part indicates that I am not a standards body; the second identifies me as the author by using my domain name. The third part is the name of the DTD, and the last part identifies this as English. The system identifier is a URL on my Web site where I've placed the new DTD. You can use your own values in your DTD, using this as an example.

Using Your New DTD

Now you'll create a document that actually uses this DTD, and you can validate the page against the DTD. Please fill in your own values where you see mine (this is just a sample), and upload your DTD to the correct path on a server to validate the final results.

1. First, create the framework for the page as you usually would, using the basic template for a strict XHTML 1.0 document:

```
<!DOCTYPE html PUBLIC "-//W3C//DTD XHTML 1.0 Strict//EN"
"http://www.w3.org/TR/xhtml1/DTD/xhtml1-strict.dtd">
<html xmlns="http://www.w3.org/1999/xhtml">
<head>
<title> Document Exercise</title>
</head>
<body>

</body>
</html>
```

2. Change the `<!DOCTYPE>` declaration so that it references your public and system identifiers, instead of the XHTML 1.0 DTD:

```
<!DOCTYPE html PUBLIC "-//molly.com//XHTML 1.0 plus Embed//EN"
"http://molly.com/dtd/xhtml1-embed.dtd">
```

3. Add some content that includes the `<embed>` tag. If you don't have any multimedia handy, that's okay—you're just going to validate this page to see if your DTD works. Use a dummy filename for the `src`, but be sure to include something as it was declared required:

```
<body>
<h1> This is our test </h1>
<embed src="dummy.mov" height="30" width="30" />
</body>
```

4. Save this file, and if you can, upload it to a Web server so that you can test it using the W3C's HTML and XHTML validator at `validator.w3.org/`. Also, make sure that you have saved your new DTD at the location specified by the system identifier, as well as a copy of each of the parsed external entity files included with the XHTML 1.0 DTDs.

5. Validate your file by entering the URL into the W3C's validator. It will validate correctly, even though the <embed> tag isn't normally a valid element for XHTML. You can play with this a little to confirm that it's working—remove the src attribute and check if it truly is required, or add an extra attribute to <embed> (or make it a container). You'll see that the validator now respects your new DTD as strictly as it matches against the XHTML specification.

This example is especially important because it shows, in detail, how extensibility works, and what can happen not just with XHTML 1.0, but how XHTML 1.1 itself works in the sense of modularization.

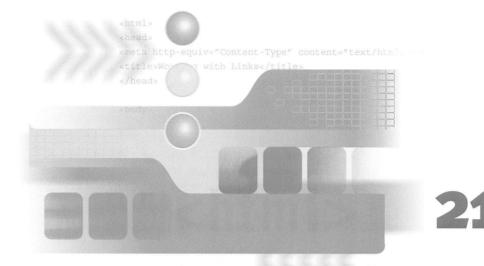

TRANSFORMING DOCUMENTS
WITH XSLT

IN THIS CHAPTER

Understanding XSL   486

Creating XSL Style Sheets   491

Transforming XHTML with XSLT   498

Case by Case: Adapting Web Pages for Specific Audiences   509

UNDERSTANDING XSL

As you by now know, one way to separate presentation from structure is to use Cascading Style Sheets (CSS). This chapter looks at a different way in which structure and presentation can be separated using XSL.

Extensible Stylesheet Language (XSL) was developed by the World Wide Web Consortium to serve two functions—to create an XML-based syntax for expressing style, and to provide a way to transform from one XML language to another. XSL is composed of three related W3C specifications:

- **XSL Formatting Objects (XSL-FO)**—XSL-FO is an XML vocabulary for describing how an XML document should be displayed.

- **XSL Transformations (XSLT)**—XSLT is a template-based language for changing the structure of an XML document or converting it to a different XML-based dialect.

- **XPath**—XPath is a "sub-language" used by XSLT to identify specific parts of an XML document.

Unlike Cascading Style Sheets, an XSL style sheet is not simply a set of presentational styles that are applied to an HTML or XHTML document. Instead, when using XSL you are creating an entirely new document formed by applying the XSLT document to your XML document. This new document can be in any XML-based language, such as XHTML, the Wireless Markup Language (WML), or XSL-FO.

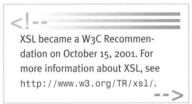

XSL became a W3C Recommendation on October 15, 2001. For more information about XSL, see http://www.w3.org/TR/xsl/.

Because XSL Transformations can be used with any XML-based language, you can use XSL with your XHTML files as easily as you can with any other well-formed XML documents.

Formatting Objects

The XSL Formatting Objects (XSL-FO) language offers an alternative to the use of HTML and CSS as a formatting language, one that is based on XML syntax. As you may have noticed, the syntax for CSS is not very similar to that of XHTML or other XML-based markup languages. Selectors and rules are defined in a very different manner.

To remedy this, the XSL-FO specification was created to allow presentational styles to be defined as XML markup. There are several advantages to this, including better processing by advanced browsers (which only have to speak one type of language instead of two), compatibility with XML-based tools, and ease of transformation to and from XML-based languages.

XSL-FO tags look similar in appearance to XHTML tags, and serve some of the same functions as the presentational markup found in XHTML 1.0 Transitional and earlier versions of HTML. XSL-FO tags are identified by the `fo:` prefix to indicate the XSL-FO namespace, which has the URI `http://www.w3.org/1999/XSL/Format`. In addition to the tags, XSL-FO also defines a number of attributes that affect the styles of those tags. Many of these attributes will be very familiar from CSS, as they serve roughly the same function as CSS rules.

For an explanation about namespaces, please see "Writing Conforming Documents," p. 31.

Short listings of XSL-FO tags and attributes are provided in Tables 21.1 and 21.2. The XSL-FO specification, as noted before, is very long and contains many more tags and elements than these, allowing for a fine degree of control over how your page is displayed.

<!--
XSL also allows for graphics whose data are contained in the document itself, rather than in a separate file. An example of this would be the use of scalable vector graphics (SVG) within an XML or XHTML document. SVG is a language for describing images via XML, rather than using an external file format such as GIF, JPG, PNG, and so on, that dictates the graphic information. For more information on SVG please see `http://www.w3.org/Graphics/SVG/`.
-->

Table 21.1 Common XSL-FO Tags

XSL-FO Tag	Function
fo:block	Define a rectangular block, such as a paragraph or a heading (like <div>)
fo:external-graphic	Include an inline graphic (like <img>)
fo:inline	A inline section of text (like <span> or <b>)
fo:list-block	The container for list items
fo:list-item	A container for each item in a list, that holds the label and body
fo:list-item-body	The content of a list item
fo:list-item-label	The name or number of a list item
fo:simple-link	Identifies something to be used as a hypertext link
fo:title	Give a title to a page

Table 21.2 Common XSL-FO Attributes

XSL-FO Attribute	Function
background-color	Sets a background color
background-image	Sets a background image
border-left-color	Sets the color of the left border
border-bottom-width	Sets the width of the bottom border
font-family	Sets the font
font-weight	Sets the boldness
height	Sets the height
max-height	Defines a maximum height
min-height	Defines a minimum height
text-align	Sets text alignment

In order to use XSL-FO to format your page, you will need to make use of XSL Transformations to change your Web page from an ordinary XHTML (or XML) document into a document written in XSL-FO.

XSL-FO

When would you use XSL-FO? Formatting objects have been designed to allow a large degree of control over the layout, and are meant to be used in situations such as printing a book. Their applicability to Web use is very limited, even discounting the lack of browser support. Håkon W. Lie, the author of the Cascading Style Sheets specification and Chief Technology Officer at Opera Software, went so far as to suggest "Formatting Objects Considered Dangerous" in an April 1999 essay. His argument is that XSL-FO (called XFO in his essay) when used on the Web ignores the semantics of a document in favor of pure presentation, damaging the accessibility and usability of the Web. You can read his essay online at `http://www.operasoftware.com/people/howcome/1999/foch.html`.

Transformations

The XSL Transformations language plays a very important role in the XML family—it serves as a translator, converting between one dialect of XML and another. For this reason, XSLT is crucial to the adoption of XML as a universal data communications language. Applications for XSLT range from business-to-business e-commerce to wireless Web networking.

Because XHTML is defined according to the rules for XML, you can use XSLT with your XHTML files to change them into other XML-based languages. You can also use XSLT to display XML files, using your knowledge of XHTML to good effect by converting the XML into XHTML. Alternate presentations of your page can be created by applying an XSLT style sheet for Wireless Application Protocol (WAP phones) or other specialized Web access devices. You can even extract specific information from your XHTML files and create a completely different view of the same content by applying XSLT and XPath.

XSL Transformations are based on templates. The tags that comprise these templates are a combination of XSLT tags—identified by the XSLT namespace and most often by the `xsl:` prefix—and of the tags belonging to the "target" XML-based language. So if you are converting an XML document to XHTML, your templates will consist of XSLT tags mixed in with XHTML tags.

`<!--`

WAP is a communications protocol and an application environment. It works with wireless networks and wireless devices to facilitate delivery of network information and services to a variety of wireless appliances. For more information about WAP, see `http://www.wapforum.org/`.

`-->`

`<!--`

Because of the way namespaces work in XML, it's not as important that the tags be prefixed by `xsl:`, but they should start with some namespace prefix that references the XSLT namespace, which is identified by `xmlns:xsl= "http://www.w3.org/1999/XSL/Transform`. As long as the namespace identifier is `http://www.w3.org/1999/XSL/Transform`, it doesn't matter what the prefix is—but for most cases, and for the purposes of this chapter, using `xsl:` makes the most sense.

`-->`

Each XSLT template consists of two parts—a pattern to match, and the tags of the template itself. Patterns are defined using the XPath syntax, which includes wildcards such as * as well as functions and expressions for greater flexibility.

A very important concept in XSL is the representation of a document as nodes in a tree. This way of thinking about XML data will be familiar to you if you have a computer science background or if you've worked with the HTML DOM before.

In brief, you can think of a document as a tree-like structure—like a family tree in genealogy. At the top of the tree is the "root node," and each subsequent part of the document is a child node of the root—or a child of a child of the root, or further descendants. For XSLT purposes, nodes are of several important types. Element nodes consist of one element in the document, and its children are the content contained by the tags that comprise the element, plus one node for each attribute. The content in an element node can be other elements or text nodes. Attribute nodes can't have any elements.

When XSL Transformations occur, there are three trees involved, as follows:

- **Source tree**—This is the original file, written in an XML-based language (which might or might not be XHTML).

- **Transformation tree**—This is the XSLT file.

- **Result tree**—This is created by applying the XSLT to the source tree. In order to create the result tree, you will have to build it up from the templates in the transformation tree and decorate it—like a holiday tree—with the content in the source tree.

XSLT Parsers

The actual assembly of the result tree occurs when the source document and the XSLT style sheet are combined by an *XSLT parser*. The XSLT parser reads in the source tree and the transformation tree, and produces a result tree according to the instructions encoded in the XSLT templates.

When using XSLT in a Web environment, there are two places where this parsing can occur—the client side in the user's browser, or the server side.

Client-Side Parsing

For XSLT parsing to happen in the browser, the Web browser must be able to understand both XML and XSLT. Currently, Microsoft's Internet Explorer 5.0 (and higher) has support for XSLT parsing, many Mozilla builds support XSLT to some degree, and Netscape 6.0 and above have some support as well.

<!--
Early versions of Internet Explorer contain a version of Microsoft's XML/XSL parser based on a draft version of the XSL specification, which is not in compliance with the later W3C Recommendation. Newer versions of the MSXML package are available from Microsoft which adhere more closely to the XSL standard; you should download the latest version from http://msdn. microsoft.com/ if you intend to work with client-side XSLT. Further information on using MSXML with XSLT can be found in the unofficial MSXML FAQ, at http://www. netcrucible.com/xslt/ msxml-faq.htm.
-->

Parsing XSLT on the client side is quite similar in procedure to using Cascading Style Sheets. You need to add a tag in the XML (or XHTML) document that tells the browser where to find the XSLT style sheet. To set an XSLT style sheet in Internet Explorer 5, use the following:

```
<?xml-style sheet type="text/xsl" href="transform.xsl" ?>
```

Naturally, you'll want to fill in the name of your style sheet file instead of `transform.xsl`. Note that this tag doesn't follow the normal rules for XML and XHTML tags—it's actually a processing instruction, and those are marked by the <? and ?> at the beginning and end of the tag. There are no closing tags for processing instructions.

Unfortunately, the limited number of browsers supporting XSLT makes it difficult to rely on client-side parsing of XSLT. One solution is to use scripting to detect the browser type and serve up XSLT for client-side parsing only when Internet Explorer 5 and up, Netscape 6 and up, and certain Mozilla builds are recognized. In other cases, an XHTML page would be sent—possibly generated by an XSLT parser on the server.

Server-Side Parsing

When you do server-side processing of XSLT, you are creating the output file on the server and the XSLT style sheet is never actually seen by the Web user—just the end result. This means that the Web browser doesn't have to understand XML and XSLT at all, as long as you send it a result file that is in a language it can understand. For example, you can send XHTML to desktop Web browsers or WML to WAP-enabled phones.

Server-side parsing can occur when you process a request from a Web browser; this is dynamic application of the style sheet. When a request is received from the browser, the Web server selects a style sheet (if there's more than one available) and formats the XML file, sending the result back to the user's browser on-the-fly. This approach is more flexible and allows for greater customizing of the result to fit the user, and is compatible with database-driven Web designs.

You can also apply style sheets on the server in a "batch" mode, or when the content is updated. This enables you to generate static pages based on templates, with the content stored separately in XML files and the pages re-created whenever the content is updated. In effect, you are using a content-management system based on XSLT. The advantage over dynamic application is in speed, but you lose out on some of XSLT's flexibility and power.

This chapter presents source files, XSLT style sheets, and result files for each example. The result files were generated using the second method described above; this way I can display the resulting XHTML. In practice, you will find yourself using client-side parsing, dynamic server-side parsing, and batch server-side processing on different projects as your needs vary.

There are a number of different XSLT parsers available, including offerings from Microsoft, IBM, the Apache Group, and others. I've generated the examples using Saxon, a Java-based XSLT parser engine, available from `http://users.iclway.co.uk/mhkay/saxon/`; because it's written in Java, it runs on a variety of computers including Windows desktop machines. A comprehensive list of XSL-related software, including parsers, is located at `http://www.xmlsoftware.com/xsl/`.

CREATING XSL STYLE SHEETS

To create an XSLT style sheet, you'll need to know several things. First you need to understand the original format of your source document. It has to be compatible with XML, and you'll need to know what it consists of. You can't create an XSLT style sheet without knowing your document's structure. Is it in an XML content description language? In XHTML?

You'll also need to specify what kind of output you're generating. Will it be XHTML for Web browsers, XSL-FO for high-end printing machinery, WML for WAP phones, or another XML-based format for business-to-business data transfer? In this chapter, the examples will concentrate on XHTML.

Exploring XSLT Syntax

As an XML vocabulary, XSLT syntax should be familiar to you. It is composed of well-formed, structured tags, some of which serve as containers for other tags and content, and some of which are empty tags. Attributes set on the tags control their behavior. XSLT tags are identified by the use of `xsl:` before the tag name, to indicate the use of the XSLT namespace.

A short listing of common XSLT elements is shown in Table 21.3. The full specification for XSLT is available online at `http://www.w3.org/TR/xslt/`.

Table 21.3 Common XSLT Elements

Element	Function
`<xsl:style sheet>`	Defines an XSLT style sheet; the wrapper around all XSL content
`<xsl:strip-space>`	Directs the parser to ignore spaces in XML/XHTML documents
`<xsl:output>`	Specifies the format and properties of the result document
`<xsl:template>`	Defines an XSLT template
`<xsl:value-of>`	Inserts the value of a source XML node
`<xsl:for-each>`	Defines a section that is repeated once per matching source node
`<xsl:apply-templates>`	Applies templates to the specified nodes
`<xsl:sort>`	Defines an order by which templates will be applied
`<xsl:comment>`	Creates a comment in the result tree

As you look at the examples later in this chapter, I'll explain the use and syntax of each tag.

Structure of an XSL Document

To examine what an XSLT style sheet looks like, I'll provide a look at a typical application of XSLT—formatting an online book.

In Listing 21.1, you can see a very simple way to describe a chapter of a book in XML. The file consists of a book element which contains a title, an author, and one or more chapters. Each chapter has a chapnum (which shows the chapter number), a title for the chapter, and one or more para tags containing paragraphs of text.

Listing 21.1   A Simple Way to Describe a Book Chapter in XML

```
<book>
 <title>A Tale of Two Cities</title>
 <author>Charles Dickens</author>
 <chapter>
  <chapnum>I</chapnum>
  <title>The Period</title>
  <para>
   It was the best of times, it was the worst of
   times, it was the age of wisdom, it was the age of
   foolishness, it was the epoch of belief, it was the epoch
   of incredulity, it was the season of Light, it was the
   season of Darkness, it was the spring of hope, it was the
   winter of despair, we had everything before us, we had
   nothing before us, we were all going direct to Heaven, we
   were all going direct the other way--in short, the period
   was so far like the present period, that some of its
   noisiest authorities insisted on its being received, for
   good or for evil, in the superlative degree of comparison
   only.
  </para>
  <para>
   There were a king with a large jaw and a queen with
   a plain face, on the throne of England; there were a king
   with a large jaw and a queen with a fair face, on the
   throne of France. In both countries it was clearer than
   crystal to the lords of the State preserves of loaves and
   fishes, that things in general were settled for
   ever.
  </para>
 </chapter>
</book>
```

Since this isn't written in XHTML, it won't be much use in a browser that displays just XHTML. So it will need to be transformed for use in a Web environment. Listing 21.2 shows a style sheet which has been written to change the XML into XHTML. Read over this sample code and notice how the style sheet consists of both `xsl:` tags and familiar XHTML tags.

Listing 21.2   A Sample XSLT Document, for Presenting a Chapter from an Online Book

```
<xsl:stylesheet
 xmlns:xsl="http://www.w3.org/1999/XSL/Transform"
 version="1.0"
 xmlns="http://www.w3.org/1999/xhtml">

 <xsl:strip-space elements="*"/>
 <xsl:output indent="yes"/>
```

Listing 21.2   Continued

```
<xsl:template match="/">
 <html>
  <head>
   <title>
    <xsl:value-of select="book/title" />
   </title>
  </head>
  <body>
   <xsl:apply-templates select="book/*" />
  </body>
 </html>
</xsl:template>

<xsl:template match="title">
 <h1>
  <xsl:apply-templates/>
 </h1>
</xsl:template>

<xsl:template match="chapnum">
 <h1>
  Chapter
  <xsl:apply-templates/>
 </h1>
</xsl:template>

<xsl:template match="author">
 <h2>
  Written By
  <xsl:apply-templates/>
 </h2>
</xsl:template>

<xsl:template match="para">
 <p>
  <xsl:apply-templates/>
 </p>
</xsl:template>

</xsl:stylesheet>
```

You should be able to recognize some patterns in the code sample, such as the use of `<xsl:template>` and `<xsl:apply-templates>`, and the match and select attributes.

xsl:stylesheet

The `<xsl:stylesheet>` is a container that contains the XSLT style sheet. The attributes on `<xsl:stylesheet>` apply to the whole style sheet and define how the rest of the tags should be interpreted. The version attribute specifies that we are writing to the 1.0 specification of XSLT.

The `xmlns:xsl` attribute defines the `xsl:` prefix as referring to tags in the XSLT namespace. The `xmlns` attribute—with no `:xsl` suffix—indicates that the default namespace for non-XSLT tags is XHTML.

If you are writing your own XSL, you will probably not need to change these attributes on the `<xsl:stylesheet>` tag, with the exception of the `xmlns` attribute. If you are writing a style sheet to transform to something besides XHTML, you will change this to the appropriate namespace reference.

An `<xsl:stylesheet>` can contain two types of tags—further instructions about how to apply the transformations, and templates for matching

xsl:strip-space and xsl:output

To indicate that extra whitespace in the source document—such as indentations—should be ignored, use the `<xsl:strip-space>` tag as shown here, with the attribute `elements="*"` to show that this applies to all elements in the source tree. If you don't do this, you may run into problems with *whitespace nodes* which are counted as invisible text elements in your source tree. `<xsl:strip-space>` is always an empty element.

You use the `<xsl:output>` tag to provide details on how the final result tree's output should appear. In this case, I've specified the attribute `indent="yes"`, which will make our result document listings much more readable. Like `<xsl:strip-space>`, `<xsl:output>` is an empty tag.

xsl:template and xsl:apply-templates

An XSLT style sheet is primarily composed of `<xsl:template>` instructions. A template is composed of two things—a pattern that matches what the template is applied to, and the body of the template itself. To tell the XSLT processor to apply templates to portions of the source document, you use the `<xsl:apply-templates>` tag.

When the XSLT processor begins applying the style sheet to the source document, the first thing it looks for is a template that matches the root node. If it doesn't find it, then there's not much to process. The root node is indicated by `match="/"`—the "/" is an XPath expression which means "the root of the source document."

> `<!--`
> XPath is a language that can be used along with XSLT. Its role is to help locate and process items in XML documents. I'll be discussing XPath a bit more in this chapter, and you can read the XPath specification at `http://www.w3.org/TR/xpath`.
> `-->`

Other templates match specific tags in the source tree—for example, the second template in Listing 21.2 will only match `title` tags. Different tags will pass by this template.

The root template is used to start building the result tree. The contents of the root template form the basic structure of the result document, and any XSLT tags in the root template are applied to flesh out that structure and insert content from the source document.

To tell the processor to match against certain tags in the source tree and insert the output into the result tree a given location, the `<xsl:apply-templates>` tag is used. The tag `<xsl:apply-templates select="book/*" />` indicates that matches should be found for specific tags in the source document, and that the results of applying those templates should be placed at the point in the result tree where the `<xsl:apply-templates>` is located.

The expression `select="book/*"` is more XPath—in this case, it means "select all children of the `<book>` element from the source tree, and apply any templates which match." Whenever you apply a new template, the "current location" in the node switches to that location in the source tree, which means that XPath expressions are relative to the new current node.

You can think of each template as one hole in a child's toy, which has holes cut out in the shape of squares, triangles, stars, and circles of various sizes. Some parts of the source tree will match one or more templates, and some will simply not fit in any of the holes.

Default Templates in XSLT

If a selected node of the source tree matches more than one template, the first one matched will be used. If the node matches none of the templates, then the default template will be used. XSLT defines a default template for all nodes which inserts the value of the node—which is the text content, not including any attributes, of the node and all its children nodes—at the appropriate location in the result tree.

In Listing 21.2, we use the default template in this manner to get the text of the `<title>` element. The second template calls `<xsl:apply-templates/>` with no select parameter, which means "match all the children of this node"—but the only child node of `<title>` is the text node consisting of the title text itself. Since the value of a text node is the text, this gives us what we want.

xsl:value-of

Another way to get the value of a node is to use the `<xsl:value-of>` tag. The select attribute is an XPath expression to identify the specific part of the source document whose value you would like to insert.

Applying the Style Sheet

So what does this style sheet do? Take a look at Listing 21.3, which is the result of applying the XSLT style sheet in Listing 21.2 to the source document in Listing 21.1.

Listing 21.3 The XHTML Created by Applying the XHTML Style Sheet to the XML Document

```
<?xml version="1.0" encoding="utf-8" ?>
<!DOCTYPE html PUBLIC "-//W3C//DTD XHTML 1.0 Transitional//EN"
        "http://www.w3.org/TR/xhtml1/DTD/xhtml1-transitional.dtd">

<html xmlns="http://www.w3.org/1999/xhtml">
  <head>
   <title>A Tale of Two Cities</title>
  </head>
  <body>
   <h1>A Tale of Two Cities</h1>
   <h2>
   Written By
   Charles Dickens</h2>
   <h1>
   Chapter
   I</h1>
   <h1>The Period</h1>
   <p>
   It was the best of times, it was the worst of
   times, it was the age of wisdom, it was the age of
   foolishness, it was the epoch of belief, it was the epoch
   of incredulity, it was the season of Light, it was the
   season of Darkness, it was the spring of hope, it was the
   winter of despair, we had everything before us, we had
   nothing before us, we were all going direct to Heaven, we
   were all going direct the other way--in short, the period
   was so far like the present period, that some of its
   noisiest authorities insisted on its being received, for
   good or for evil, in the superlative degree of comparison
   only.
   </p>
   <p>
   There were a king with a large jaw and a queen with
   a plain face, on the throne of England; there were a king
   with a large jaw and a queen with a fair face, on the
   throne of France. In both countries it was clearer than
   crystal to the lords of the State preserves of loaves and
   fishes, that things in general were settled for
   ever.
   </p>
   </body>
</html>
```

As you can see, the result document is XHTML, and consists of the content from the XML document and the structure and tags from the XHTML document. Figure 21.1 shows the results as they appear in a browser.

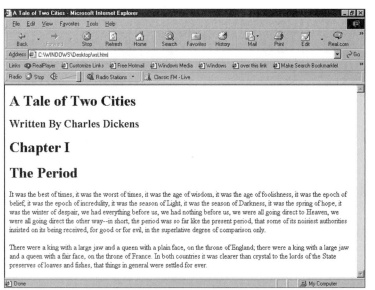

Figure 21.1
The XHTML result document displayed in a Web browser.

Understanding XPath References

XPath is the language used in XSLT select and match attributes (and a few other places) to identify specific parts of the source document. If the source document is thought of as a tree, XPath can be thought of as instructions on how to traverse that tree and reach a specific branch or leaf of the tree.

XPath syntax is similar to that used to describe file systems. The root node is called /, and subnodes are named and separated by slashes. The XPath expression "car/make/year" can be read as "the node named year, which is a subnode of make, which is a subnode of car."

Several simple functions are also built into XPath, such as count(), which calculates how many children there are in a given set of nodes.

A list of XPath syntax and functions is seen in Table 21.4 and will be explained when used in examples in this chapter.

Table 21.4 XPath Syntax and Functions

XPath Expression	Matches
/	Root node
.	Current node
..	Parent node of current node
grape	Subnode "grape"
grape/lime	Subnode "lime" of subnode "grape"
grape/*	All children of subnode "grape"
/grape	Node "grape" that is a direct child of the root node
@tangerine	Attribute "tangerine" of current node

Table 21.4   Continued

XPath Expression	Matches
@*	All attributes of current node
grape@tangerine	Attribute "tangerine" of "grape" subnode
grape/lime@tangerine	Attribute "tangerine" of "lime" subnode of "grape" subnode
..@tangerine	Attribute "tangerine" of parent node
//	Any number of intervening nodes
grape//lime	All nodes "lime" which have "grape" as an ancestor
[]	Introduces a predicate expression
grape[lime]	Node "grape" that has a child "lime"
grape[lime='Key']	Node "grape" that has a child "lime" whose value (text content) is "Key"
grape[@tangerine]	Node "grape" that has an attribute "tangerine"
grape[@tangerine="3"]	Node "grape" that has an attribute "tangerine" whose value is 3
count(grape/*)	The number of children of subnode "grape"

TRANSFORMING XHTML WITH XSLT

As noted before, XSLT can be used with XHTML as easily as it can be used with any other XML-based language. As it's a language to transform documents, XSLT is especially good for producing alternative versions of your pages, as well as inserting presentational markup or CSS to style unformatted XHTML Strict.

Using CSS and XSLT with XHTML

Although they approach style from different perspectives, CSS and XSL are not incompatible at all, and they can be used together to produce sophisticated styling techniques.

When you generate an XHTML document using XSLT, you can create embedded style sheets, reference external CSS documents, or insert CSS into style attributes.

In Listing 21.4, I've created an XHMTL document that consists of just a plain table with some data. This table is a listing of the Tibetan Mastiff dogs owned by the Bartlett family. The name, sex, and age of each dog is included in this data table. (I've used the th element—table header—to identify which line of the table is a header for the rest.)

For more information on tables, *see* "Working with Tables," *p. 177.*

Listing 21.4   An Ordinary XHTML Table

```
<!DOCTYPE html PUBLIC "-//W3C//DTD XHTML 1.0 Transitional//EN"
        "http://www.w3.org/TR/xhtml1/DTD/xhtml1-transitional.dtd">

<html xmlns="http://www.w3.org/1999/xhtml">
```

Listing 21.4 Continued

```
<head>
<title>A Simple Data Table</title>
</head>
<body>
<table>
 <tr>
  <th>Dog Name</th>
  <th>Sex</th>
  <th>Age</th>
 </tr>
 <tr>
  <td>Angie</td>
  <td>female</td>
  <td>10</td>
 </tr>
 <tr>
  <td>Xena</td>
  <td>female</td>
  <td>2</td>
 </tr>
 <tr>
  <td>Sunny</td>
  <td>male</td>
  <td>7</td>
 </tr>
 <tr>
  <td>Kim</td>
  <td>male</td>
  <td>10</td>
 </tr>
 <tr>
  <td>Nying</td>
  <td>female</td>
  <td>10</td>
 </tr>
 <tr>
  <td>Perkyi</td>
  <td>female</td>
  <td>5</td>
 </tr>
</table>
</body>
</html>
```

When you display this in a Web browser, as in Figure 21.2, you can see that all the information is presented—but it's not very exciting. How can this presentation be spiced up using XSLT? With a very simple set of transformations to reformat the page.

Figure 21.2
This very basic XHTML table contains important content but it is quite plain to look at.

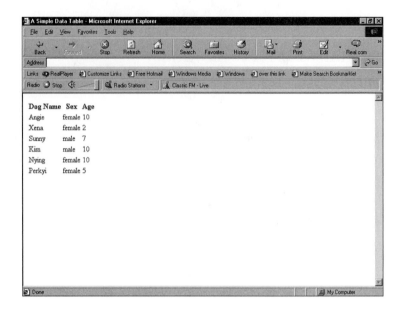

The XSLT style sheet I created for this page will not only reformat the table, it will also reorder the data and insert a header. The style sheet is shown in Listing 21.5.

Listing 21.5   An XSLT Style Sheet

```
<xsl:stylesheet
 xmlns:xsl="http://www.w3.org/1999/XSL/Transform"
 version="1.0"
 xmlns="http://www.w3.org/1999/xhtml">

<xsl:strip-space elements="*"/>
<xsl:output indent="yes"/>

<xsl:template match="/">
 <html>
  <head>
   <title>Bartlett Dogs</title>
  <style type="text/css">
   <xsl:comment>
    <![CDATA[
    p.note { font-family: Arial, sans-serif;
         border: 5px solid blue;
         padding: 3px;
         width: 585px; }
   ]]>
   </xsl:comment>
  </style>
 </head>
```

Listing 21.5 Continued

```
  <body>
   <h1 style="font-family: Arial;">
    Bartlett Family Tibetan Mastiffs
   </h1>
   <p class="note">
    Our dogs are listed in order from oldest to
    youngest.
   </p>
   <xsl:apply-templates select="html/body/*" />
  </body>
 </html>
</xsl:template>

<xsl:template match="table">
 <table border="0" width="585" cellspacing="4"
     style="background-color: green; font-family: Arial;">
  <xsl:apply-templates select="tr[th]" />
  <xsl:apply-templates select="tr~" >
   <xsl:sort select="td[position()=3]"
        data-type="number" order="descending" />
  </xsl:apply-templates>
 </table>
</xsl:template>

<xsl:template match="tr">
 <tr>
  <xsl:apply-templates />
 </tr>
</xsl:template>

<xsl:template match="th">
 <th align="left"
  style="background-color: white; font-weight: bold;">
  <xsl:apply-templates />
 </th>
</xsl:template>

<xsl:template match="td">
 <td align="left" style="background-color: yellow;">
  <xsl:apply-templates />
 </td>
</xsl:template>
</xsl:stylesheet>
```

This style sheet includes a number of XSLT and XPath functions that you haven't seen before, such as CDATA, xsl:comment, predicates in XPath selections, xsl:sort, and the XPath position() function.

`xsl:comment` **and CDATA**

To prevent our CSS from being interpreted as text by older browsers, I need to wrap the embedded style sheet in comments inside the `<style>`...`</style>` tags. To do this, I had to use the `<xsl:comment>` tag—if I just used normal `<!-- comments -->` they would be interpreted as comments in the XSLT document, and not actual markup to be passed along in the result document. If you want a comment to appear in your results, use the `<xsl:comment>` tag as shown here.

I also used the CDATA tag to enclose the text of the style sheet. CDATA is an XML instruction that basically says "pass this along as is—don't bother to check to see if it's markup, well formed, or anything else." Whenever you are using embedded style sheets in your XSLT document, you want to use both `xsl:comment` and CDATA, as shown, so that it appears correctly in your result document. This is also how you want to embed scripts (such as JavaScript) in your XSLT style sheet.

*For more on embedded Cascading Style Sheets, **see** "Using CSS with HTML and XHTML," **p. XXX**, Chapter 14.*

XPath Predicates

In the template that matches `table`, you'll notice that I used two `xsl:apply-templates`—one with `select="tr[th]"` and one with `select="tr~"`. This is an example of XPath predicates at work—a predicate is indicated by square brackets following an XPath expression, and refines the selection.

In the first case, `tr[th]` means "select all tr elements which contain a th element." In the second, `tr~` means "select all tr elements which contain a td element." The effect of this is that the table rows containing a header are included first, and then the table rows containing table data.

`xsl:sort` **and** `position()`

In many cases, `xsl:apply-templates` will be an empty element and you will open and close it at the same time, with `<xsl:apply-templates />`. However, if you want to sort the way in which you apply your templates, you can use `xsl:apply-templates` as a container, one which can only contain the `<xsl:sort>` tag.

The select attribute for `<xsl:sort>` is an XPath expression to identify what you use as your key for sorting. In this example, I've said to use the td attribute—and I added a predicate, `[position()=3]`. That predicate means that the third td child object should be matched, which in this case is the "age" column for our dogs. The XPath `position()` function calculates the position in the list of child nodes. The other attributes of `<xsl:sort>` are data-type, which can be "text" or "number", and order, which takes the values "ascending" or "descending."

So what does all this produce? The resulting XHTML file is shown in Listing 21.6, and Figure 21.3 displays that file in a Web browser. Notice that the dogs are sorted by age.

Listing 21.6   The XHTML File Produced by the Preceding XSLT File

```
<?xml version="1.0" encoding="utf-8" ?>
<!DOCTYPE html PUBLIC "-//W3C//DTD XHTML 1.0 Transitional//EN"
        "http://www.w3.org/TR/xhtml1/DTD/xhtml1-transitional.dtd">

<html xmlns="http://www.w3.org/1999/xhtml">
  <head>
   <title>Bartlett Dogs</title>
   <style type="text/css"><!--

     p.note { font-family: Arial, sans-serif;
         border: 5px solid blue;
         padding: 3px;
         width: 585px; }

   --></style>
  </head>
  <body>
   <h1 style="font-family: Arial;">
    Bartlett Family Tibetan Mastiffs
    </h1>
   <p class="note">
    Our dogs are listed in order from oldest to
    youngest.
    </p>
   <table border="0" width="585" cellspacing="4" style="background-color: green; font-
family: Arial;">
      <tr>
       <th align="left" style="background-color:
        white; font-weight: bold;">Dog Name</th>
       <th align="left" style="background-color:
        white; font-weight: bold;">Sex</th>
       <th align="left" style="background-color:
        white; font-weight: bold;">Age</th>
      </tr>
      <tr>
       <td align="left" style="background-color:
        yellow;">Angie</td>
       <td align="left" style="background-color:
        yellow;">female</td>
       <td align="left" style="background-color:
        yellow;">10</td>
      </tr>
      <tr>
       <td align="left" style="background-color:
        yellow;">Kim</td>
```

Listing 21.6 Continued

```
        <td align="left" style="background-color:
         yellow;">male</td>
        <td align="left" style="background-color:
         yellow;">10</td>
       </tr>
       <tr>
        <td align="left" style="background-color:
         yellow;">Nying</td>
        <td align="left" style="background-color:
         yellow;">female</td>
        <td align="left" style="background-color:
         yellow;">10</td>
       </tr>
       <tr>
        <td align="left" style="background-color:
         yellow;">Sunny</td>
        <td align="left" style="background-color:
         yellow;">male</td>
        <td align="left" style="background-color:
         yellow;">7</td>
       </tr>
       <tr>
        <td align="left" style="background-color:
         yellow;">Perkyi</td>
        <td align="left" style="background-color:
         yellow;">female</td>
        <td align="left" style="background-color:
         yellow;">5</td>
       </tr>
       <tr>
        <td align="left" style="background-color:
         yellow;">Xena</td>
        <td align="left" style="background-color:
         yellow;">female</td>
        <td align="left" style="background-color:
         yellow;">2</td>
       </tr>
     </table>
    </body>
</html>
```

Creating Alternate Content Views

XSL Transformations can accomplish a lot more than simply presenting the existing structure of the page in a new light—the ability to completely transform the source document means that XSLT can be used to create completely different views of the same information. For example, a page with navigation graphics can be reformatted to use text and CSS, a set of layout tables can be converted to frames, markup can be simplified for handheld access devices, or a data table can be summarized in text paragraphs.

I'll take the same data I used before—the table of Tibetan Mastiffs shown in Listing 21.6— and apply a different style sheet that will create a completely different representation of the content.

The new XSLT style sheet is designed to provide a different structure on the same content, and is shown in Listing 21.7.

Listing 21.7   A New XSLT Style Sheet

```
<xsl:stylesheet
 xmlns:xsl="http://www.w3.org/1999/XSL/Transform"
 version="1.0"
 xmlns="http://www.w3.org/1999/xhtml">

 <xsl:strip-space elements="*"/>
 <xsl:output indent="yes"/>
```

Listing 21.7 Continued

```
<xsl:template match="/">
 <html>
  <head>
   <title>Summary Report on Bartlett Dogs</title>
  </head>
  <body>
   <h1>
    Summary of Dogs
   </h1>
   <p>
    The Bartletts have
    <xsl:value-of select="count(html/body/table/tr~)" />
    dogs.
   </p>
   <p>
    They have
    <xsl:value-of
     select="count(html/body/table/tr[td='female'])" />
    female dogs and
    <xsl:value-of
     select="count(html/body/table/tr[td='male'])" />
    male dogs.
   </p>
   <p>
    The male dogs are:
   </p>
   <ul>
    <xsl:for-each select="html/body/table/tr[td='male']">
     <li>
      <xsl:value-of select="td[position()=1]"/>
      --
      <xsl:value-of select="td[position()=3]"/>
      years old
     </li>
    </xsl:for-each>
   </ul>
   <p>
    For more about Tibetan Mastiffs, please see
    <a href="http://www.tibetanmastiffs.com">
     http://www.tibetanmastiffs.com
    </a>
   </p>
  </body>
 </html>
</xsl:template>

</xsl:stylesheet>
```

count() **and More XPath Predicates**

In the first paragraph, I used the XPath count() function. This function takes an XPath expression—html/body/table/tr~— and returns a numeric value which is inserted into the result document by the <xsl:value-of> tag. This XPath expression identifies all table rows that have a td element, and counts them —which tells me how many dogs are in the data table. Later, I use the predicates [td='male'] and [td='female'] to only select dogs of a certain gender.

xsl:for-each

In this example, I used <xsl:for-each> instead of calling <xsl:apply-templates>. The xsl:for-each element defines a section of XSLT that is executed once for each node in the select of the <xsl:for-each> tag, and that block of XSLT is treated as if it were a template itself. You can use <xsl:for-each> for simple loops in this manner.

When the XSLT style sheet is applied, the result is the XHTML document presented in Listing 21.8. Figure 21.4 shows how it looks in a browser. Compare this to the original document—you can see how much the structure has changed and how XSLT has provided a different way of looking at the same content.

Listing 21.8   The Results of Applying the XSLT Style Sheet to Listing 21.6

```
<?xml version="1.0" encoding="utf-8" ?>
<!DOCTYPE html PUBLIC "-//W3C//DTD XHTML 1.0 Transitional//EN"
      "http://www.w3.org/TR/xhtml1/DTD/xhtml1-transitional.dtd">

<html xmlns="http://www.w3.org/1999/xhtml">
  <head>
   <title>Summary Report on Bartlett Dogs</title>
  </head>
  <body>
   <h1>
     Summary of Dogs
    </h1>
   <p>
     The Bartletts have
     6
     dogs.
    </p>
   <p>
     They have
     4
     female dogs and
     2
     male dogs.
    </p>
```

Listing 21.8 Continued

```
<p>
  The male dogs are:
 </p>
<ul>
  <li>Sunny
    --
    7
    years old
  </li>
  <li>Kim
    --
    10
    years old
  </li>
</ul>
<p>
  For more about Tibetan Mastiffs, please see
  <a href="http://www.tibetanmastiffs.com">
   http://www.tibetanmastiffs.com
  </a>
</p>
</body>
</html>
```

Figure 21.4
By using XPath to identify specific content in the XHTML file, we're able to create a new page that summarizes the original page.

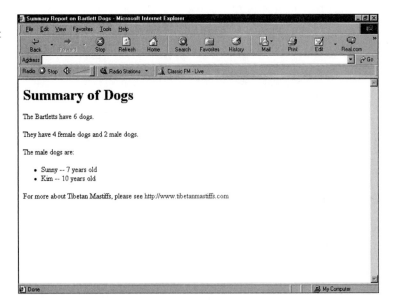

CASE BY CASE: ADAPTING WEB PAGES FOR SPECIFIC AUDIENCES

One of the biggest challenges of Web authoring is making content accessible to everyone, including people with disabilities who use assistive technologies such as screen readers or Braille terminals. One approach is to create pages that degrade gracefully and offer text alternatives to graphic content. This strategy has worked well and made the World Wide Web much more usable by people with special needs.

The advent of XSLT offers the opportunity to use a different approach—the chance to make Web sites that can actually "morph" to meet the specific needs of its users. It's possible to apply XSL technology in order to solve the accessibility problems of the Web.

Starting with a Web site written in XML or XHTML, XSLT can transform the site for each user, presenting a user interface that is optimized for their capabilities and preferences. For example, users of screen readers experience Web pages in a linear fashion. XSLT can be used to create a new interface that puts the main content up front and the navigation at the bottom, along with creating a short index with anchors at the start of the page, optimized for screen reader use.

This same technique can be used to create alternate interfaces for any other access device, from a TV set-top box to a handheld PDA. Through applying XSLT style sheets, access can be guaranteed for a very wide number of Web users.

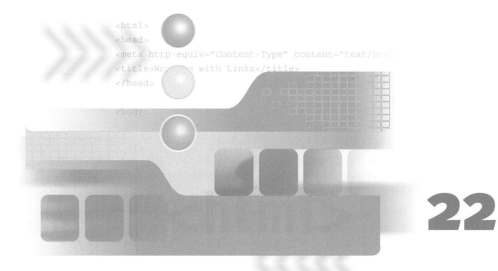

MOVING TOWARD XML

22

IN THIS CHAPTER

Making All Things Possible with XML 512

Understanding the Relationship Between
SGML, XML, and XHTML 513

XML in Theory and Practice 515

Practical Examples of XML 515

Understanding XML Structure 518

Describing New Vocabularies with XML 518

Is XML Just HTML All Over Again? 521

Defining the XML Document 522

The Prolog: The XML Declaration 526

Constructing the XML Document Prolog:
The Document Type Declaration 527

Constructing the Document Body 528

Understanding How XML Forms Logical Structures 529

Case by Case: Real-World Applications of XML 536

MAKING ALL THINGS POSSIBLE WITH XML

What I think all readers will find somewhat humorous is to come to the end of a book on HTML and XHTML, begin reading about XML, and realize that through the process of learning markup *the way it was meant to be learned*, the seemingly abstract nature of XML becomes crystal clear.

As you read through the information in this chapter, little will seem new to you. In part, that's because authoring XHTML is, in fact, authoring XML. So you're familiar with XML because you've been working with it throughout the process of this book.

But XML is, of course, a topic that extends (if you'll pardon the obvious pun) beyond what you've learned here. Although many of the ideas in this chapter will seem familiar, the context is much broader and will help you understand not only where you've been in terms of Web markup, but where the future is likely to go.

The Internet community is pouring an enormous amount of energy, money, and effort into developing an extensive suite of related standards centered around XML, Extensible Markup Language, the new generation of document delivery methods on the Web. In 1999, more standards and drafts, almost all XML-related, had been delivered or proposed than in the history of the World Wide Web Consortium (W3C). In 2000, several dozen more XML-related standards have been delivered, doubling the number of W3C standards and extending the cohesive power of XML into all corners of the World Wide Web. Here, in 2002 and beyond, XML is now shaping almost every technology to come out of the W3C.

XML and its related standards allow you to replace or extend proprietary tagging systems, such as Macromedia's ColdFusion and Microsoft's .NET platform, with platform-independent languages that fit the problem space of your page precisely. Instead of (or in addition to) inserting special tags or comments explaining what a particular field means, the field itself can be made meaningful to both applications and human readers. So an annotated price list in HTML which might look like this:

```
<!--Price list for individual fruits -->
<dl>
  <!-- Fruit -->
  <dt>Apples</dt>
    <!-- Price -->
    <dd>$1</dd>
  <!-- Fruit -->
  <dt>Oranges</dt>
    <!-- Price -->
    <dd>$2</dd>
</dl>
```

can be made to look like this:

```
<FruitPriceList>
  <Fruit>Apples</Fruit>
    <Price>$1</Price>
  <Fruit>Oranges</Fruit>
    <Price>$2</Price>
</FruitPriceList>
```

The above shows a tiny example of what can be accomplished in making data easier to access using XML. Not only is the information less cluttered and more clearly presented, but also the fields are identifiable by a search engine. So, apples to eat can be readily distinguished from the Big Apple (New York City) or the apple of one's eye (a person or thing one is fond of). Whereas we had to fit our HTML data into the Procrustean bed of an HTML definition list to lay out the list in the manner we wanted, in XML we can let the data structure flow from the data itself, and use XML-related standards CSS or XSL to format the page.

Also, the XML version allows us to retain information about the type of data entered in every field. HTML allows us to identify only a half-dozen or so datatypes: abbreviations, acronyms, addresses, block quotes, citations, and variables. And even these are most often (mis)used to effect formatting rather than to identify a logical field.

XML enables you to describe your document exactly in a way that can be "understood" by a machine. Although humans have no trouble looking at a page and deducing what certain layouts mean—an invoice, for example—computers aren't quite that smart. They need help. Descriptive XML tags such as `<seller>` and `<price>` make far more sense to machines than do the anonymous layout tags that HTML currently provides. XML provides a mechanism, the Document Type Definition (DTD), that lets you share knowledge about the structure of your data with anyone you choose.

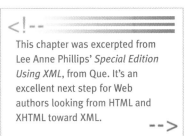

This chapter was excerpted from Lee Anne Phillips' *Special Edition Using XML*, from Que. It's an excellent next step for Web authors looking from HTML and XHTML toward XML.

This chapter introduces you to XML and helps you understand the relationships between HTML, XML, XHTML, and their parent—SGML. It also gets you started with basic principles and syntax for XML.

UNDERSTANDING THE RELATIONSHIP BETWEEN SGML, XML, AND XHTML

XML is a *meta-language*, a special language that allows you to completely describe a class of other languages, which in turn describe documents. It's like an island in the sea of SGML, another and more powerful meta-language. XML is defined as a "proper subset" of SGML, which means no pieces are added to SGML to make XML, but pieces are taken away to make the language easier to parse, understand, and use. XHTML is a production of XML, as HTML is a production of SGML.

Because XML is designed to be extensible, the languages created with XML are *extensible* as well. As in SGML, the language descriptions created by XML are called DTDs, Document Type Definitions.

⇨ Looking for more information on DTDs? **See** Chapter 4, "Choosing the Right DTD," **p. 81.**

SGML

As you read at the very beginning of this book, SGML, the Standard Generalized Markup Language, is a more powerful ancestor of XML and also a meta-language used to describe markup languages. Although it has many useful features, the complexity of the language makes it extremely hard to use and learn. It's also not quite true that nothing was added to SGML to make XML. For example, when multiple ATTLIST declarations defining the same ELEMENT were needed in XML, they were added to SGML and then worked back into XML so that you could still call XML a proper subset.

Although document-description languages such as SGML, Hy-Time, and Text Encoding Initiative (TEI) are used by many major corporations and government organizations, the expense and difficulty of learning and using these languages made it difficult for laypersons and smaller organizations to access the tremendous power of these languages to format structured data. XML is an attempt to make the most of the power of SGML and the rest accessible to non-specialists. Another goal is to make stable implementations of a structured document language easy to create so that the cost of editors, validators, and other tools comes within reach of ordinary people.

IBM, one of the largest publishers in the world, with hundreds of millions of pages of documentation required for its computers and other systems, has used SGML from the earliest days as a data repository and prepress layout engine.

<!--
If your XML project relates to a major industry, asking major firms and associations questions that address the needs of that industry may reveal existing SGML DTDs. If so, you might be able to use these as a basis for XML DTDs and enable your project to address a larger audience than if you just started from scratch. It pays to investigate your target market thoroughly.
-->

The Federal the government uses SGML for procuring parts, producing manuals, automating bids on government contracts, and controlling inventory, as well as for many sophisticated database systems. The armed services, the space program, and the U.S. Government Printing Office all use SGML to ensure interoperability and data accessibility.

Because XML is a subset of SGML, many applications originally coded in SGML are being ported to XML. For the most part, the changes required are more or less mechanical in nature, although some difficulties exist. For technical reasons, many of these problems will be resolved by simplifying the descriptions and making them more exact.

Remember that SGML has been around for a long time, at least in computer lifetimes. Many problems have already been solved and have huge installed user bases. Being able to communicate with these existing systems and users may mean the difference between success and failure for startups looking for a market. Although XML can be used to access SGML databases, it takes some DTD design work.

<!--
If your target market includes government agencies or contractors, there are probably existing SGML DTDs exactly suited to at least part of their problem space. If so, there are probably industry groups already translating those DTDs to XML. So, it pays to do your homework before undertaking XML DTD development. An appropriate DTD might already be available.
-->

Although you don't have to know SGML to learn and use XML, it is fairly common to modify existing or legacy SGML DTDs into XML DTDs in the course of daily life as an XML expert. You will learn enough about this process to be able to do it with some confidence.

XHTML

XHTML redefines HTML as an XML application. This makes it more useful in an XML world. In particular, this means that the XHTML language is extensible, allowing users and groups of users to extend the language in powerful ways. Implications of this extensibility include:

- Simplified document management that encapsulates databases, printed user manuals, and Web display functionalities in one file.

- Tremendous opportunities for extended e-commerce transactions and information exchange automation using standardized XML vocabularies.

- An easy way to reuse or convert many of the millions of HTML Web pages in existence today, retaining compatibility with existing browsers while enabling new features for those using XML-enabled agents.

- Allowing XML Web pages to be automatically validated, completely eliminating many common coding errors while retaining compatibility with legacy browsers.

- Providing simple mechanisms that enable the Web to evolve to meet the needs of the diverse communities it encompasses without requiring proprietary or non-standard additions that make life difficult.

XML IN THEORY AND PRACTICE

XML is so logical you may wonder why it took so long to be described. Part of the answer is that the basic concepts have been around for a long time but were only recently applied to computer data files. A component-based parts list, for example, is a trivial requirement for putting together any complex mechanical device. But the idea of extending this paper tool to the electronic one, and generalizing the concept so it could be used for anything made up of component parts, including non-physical objects, was a flash of insight very typical of human progress over the centuries.

People organize almost everything into hierarchies. It's a very good way to handle truly complex tasks, from buying supplies for the Department of Defense to building space shuttles. Any hierarchical structure can be described with XML, from the parts list that makes up an airliner to the corporate structure of IBM.

PRACTICAL EXAMPLES OF XML

So, applying your existing knowledge of HTML and XHTML is one good way to start learning about XML. It's a language of tags and attributes, just like XHTML, and uses many of the same conventions. In HTML and XHTML, matching pairs of tags surround most content, an opening tag and a closing tag, like this:

HTML and XHTML: `<h1>Headline</h1>`

XML works the same way. XML encourages, but doesn't enforce, slightly more verbosity than HTML does, so the preceding markup in a real XML application might look like this:

XML: `<headline1>Headline</headline1>`

Now might be the time to point out that, unlike HTML, *all* XML languages (including XHTML) are case-sensitive. How the tag is defined, case-wise, is the way you have to use it. So, many XML applications use all lowercase and none can accept different capitalizations of their keywords or attributes.

Attributes, as with XHTML, must be quoted every time. So although you can get away with this in HTML:

`<IMG height=20 width=20 src="myimage.gif">`

in any XML-based language you would use this:

`<image height="20" width="20" source="myimage.gif />`

And of course, you notice the now-familiar slash at the right end of the `<image>` tag, and understand this to be the result of proper element closure in XHTML.

XML isn't as loose about the order of tags either. Tags must be closed in the context in which they were opened. Always. So putting tags in the wrong order, allowed by most HTML browsers in spite of the fact that it's officially disallowed, is forbidden in XML. The first tag opened is always the last one closed:

Wrong: `<i><b>Italics Bold Text</i></b>`

Right: `<i><b>Italics Bold Text</b></i>`

As you well know, proper nesting of elements is a fundamental requirement in XHTML. This is a direct result of XML's rule described here.

It doesn't matter how far away the tags are from each other. The tag context acts like a push-down stack of plates in a serve-yourself restaurant. The tags have to come off the stack in the exact reverse order as when they were pushed down. Alternatively, you can't traverse the document structure tree by swinging from limb to limb like an ape. You have to walk it like an ant.

Speaking of trees, most of the things you use every day have component parts that are more or less invariant and can be organized into a tree-like hierarchy. A bottle of aspirin, for example, has component bits, a body, a lid or top of some sort, one or more labels that describe the contents, and the contents themselves. If you were given the job of assembling aspirin bottles from their components, you would find that there is an order in which you have to do things to avoid spilling the pills. Labels go on first, then tablets, then top. Top, label, tablets won't work

`<!--` First in, last out. This simple rule is easy to follow and, if your source is attractively printed, easy to see. Every nesting level has to close all its tags before exiting. And, all these metaphors are implied by the tree structure of XML documents. `-->`

at all. Tablets, label, top *might* work but you do risk spilling tablets if the bottle goes on its side. So an XML description might go as shown in Listing 22.1.

Listing 22.1   An Aspirin Bottle Broken Down to Components

```
<bottle>
  <top>
    type 3 childsafe
  </top>
  <body>
    <body-type>
      100 count plastic
    </body-type>
    <contents>
      <count>
        100
      </count>
      <content-type>
        aspirin
      </content-type>
    </contents>
  </body>
  <labeling>
    <frontlabel>
      XYZ brand generic
    </frontlabel>
    <rearlabel>
      XYZ directions and warning
    </rearlabel>
  </labeling>
</bottle>
```

Every sub-element is properly nested inside its container element and there is exactly one root element, the bottle. This is most of what's truly necessary for an XML file to be considered well-formed. Of course, there are many ways of describing an aspirin bottle and every description is somewhat arbitrary. A particular bottle might come in a box, for example, and have a printed package insert. Or it might be blister-packed for a different market. Or it might have many different labels for different languages.

The possibilities are as endless as the world of goods and services. However, the bottle as a whole is made up of a container body, the labeling, the top, and the aspirin contained within it. One can easily understand that aspirin tablets are nested within the bottle. It may be slightly less obvious that the bottle itself is made up of parts that are logically nested within the concept of "bottle" used here. But overall, because it's a container, an aspirin bottle is about the most intuitive and accessible example of nesting commonly available.

If aspirin bottles aren't clear, try thinking of any other object or idea with a hierarchy. People do this kind of classification all the time, from the organization chart for your firm (absent dotted lines) to the scientific classifications of plants and animals. Anything with a parts list is a hierarchy. Those little nested Russian Easter dolls are also a good example, or a set of nested mixing bowls.

UNDERSTANDING XML STRUCTURE

XML provides a set of rules for producing well-formed XML documents, and another set of rules for producing an XML DTD which allows the structure of the XML document to be constrained and validated against those constraints. The distinction between these two actions is often blurred, because a complete XML document includes at least the *optional* presence of a DTD, whether it's actually present or not. To complicate things further, the DTD may consist of two parts, an *internal subset* and an *external subset*.

This chapter looks at the XML document without dwelling too much on the DTD, because it's possible to create an XML document without reference to a DTD. For performance reasons, many XML documents will be used without ever validating against the DTD, even if the DTD is available. Over slow connections, reading in a DTD located external to your local machine may be tediously slow, and because DTDs may contain references to other documents, resolving all the external references may take an inordinate amount of time even with a high-speed connection. Users are accustomed to seeing HTML documents load incrementally, so they can be read before the document finishes loading, but validating XML parsers aren't allowed to display the document unless it's valid, so the document won't appear on the user's screen until everything is loaded. This can be disconcerting.

However, every document is created with a DTD in mind, whether the DTD is explicit or not. Even when creating documents without a DTD, a tentative sort of DTD has to be floating around in your mind as you create the document, because a DTD describes a data structure.

⇨ For more information on writing DTDs, **see** Chapter 20, "Customizing DTDs," **p. xxx.**

DESCRIBING NEW VOCABULARIES WITH XML

XML is dual-natured—a meta-language that allows you to describe new document structures and vocabularies as well as the language used to express that structure and vocabulary in a document instance. There is a clear difference between an XML document, which may or may not be associated with a DTD expressed in the XML meta-language, and an XML DTD. They use completely different synta XEs to describe an XML document, the one by example and the other prescriptive.

XML Document Type Definitions (DTDs) describe instances of XML languages, which are sometimes called *XML vocabularies*. XML documents are created using those languages. Unfortunately, that distinction is sometimes lost in casual speech, and particular XML vocabularies and associated DTDs are described loosely as "XML."

Although you need to know both to fully master XML, it's actually not necessary to define a DTD to create and use an XML vocabulary as long as you obey the rules. A user of an XML language or vocabulary may never see nor care about the DTD used to describe her particular application any more than the thousands of individuals working in Web design using HTML may know or care about the W3C HTML 4.0 SGML DTD used to describe HTML. In fact, a DTD might not even exist. It just doesn't matter all that much at the application level. Because you're reading this book, however, it's assumed that you will be called upon to design or work with DTDs in some way, and a truly deep knowledge of XML requires that you understand how and why a DTD is constructed and used.

Understanding Document Type Definition Advantages

Although DTDs are optional because an XML processor can infer a reasonable DTD from an instance of XML, having a DTD available offers many advantages:

- A DTD describes the organization of a document in a way that can be easily shared.

- A DTD allows a designer to create a *robust* transformation between a given type of XML document and another format for display or transfer. Because you know everything possible about documents with a DTD, you'll know how to handle structures that may not exist in a particular sample but are allowed by the document type, even if you've never seen them.

- A DTD allows a *validating* parser to determine whether a particular document is constructed according to the rules set up by the originators of the specification. This is extremely important for EDI and other applications in which documents will be shared and used by other processes.

- Without a DTD, an XML authoring environment cannot give hints about which elements are required or optional at a given point and which attributes the current element can take. Context-sensitive menus or hints are an enormous help in speeding document development and preventing errors.

- Without a DTD, the creator of an authoring manual or style document has no way of knowing how the defined document should be constructed. An authoring manual is an embodiment of the knowledge expressed in a DTD, although not a DTD in itself.

- Specifying the DTD used in a document identifies the revision level of the standard used to create it. When documents evolve in functionality and syntax, this can be an important clue about how to display or transform a document in new situations.

Having a DTD available conveys significant information and benefits, *if* you need those benefits. But like everything else in life, there's a cost involved.

Coping with Document Type Definition Disadvantages

For all their advantages, DTDs are not without problems. They use a different syntax than the rest of XML, so it requires a slightly different skill set to construct one. In addition, like any technical description, getting involved in the DTD design before thinking about the way you want your data structures to look in the document itself can bog you down in detail when you should be looking at the overall structure. Many people design the XML document using the intended XML vocabulary and then use an automatic DTD-extraction tool to generate a DTD from the document itself. After this is done, the DTD can be fine-tuned by adding to or tweaking the source code.

The following disadvantages of DTDs exist as well:

- With a DTD, a validating XML user agent requires at *least* one extra read operation to access the location where the DTD is available. Although caching may lessen the performance hit for some network users, many foreseeable uses of XML documents will preclude the use of cache storage.

- A DTD greatly increases the complexity of the parser required to determine whether a document should be displayed. For some devices, this might not be feasible.

- Some *validating* authoring environments that use a DTD make it difficult to save your workspace at the end of the day or restore it the next day unless the document is in a valid state. This can be annoying if you have a lot of work left to do and need to leave it for a while.

- A DTD is theoretically capable of continuing external reads without limit because a DTD can incorporate other DTDs and entity sets. It's possible that some complex documents might take unacceptable amounts of time before they render on the display device when using a validating parser.

The basic tradeoff in deciding whether to use a DTD is between the free-wheeling ability you're used to with HTML—being able to do pretty much whatever you want and patch things up on-the-fly—and a much more structured environment in which every "i" must be dotted and every "t" crossed. In many situations, such as when you are creating documents meant for general availability and distributed creation, you need that strict enforcement of rules and will want a DTD. In others, such as when you are developing a new XML document type, you won't need or want strict enforcement and can do without a DTD, at least during initial design.

After development has led to a stable product, you'll want to formalize your design so it can be easily distributed. Although you might also want to create a user's manual, a DTD is a simple way of letting users test their document to be sure that they truly follow the guidelines they read in the manual. At that point, you might even regret that DTDs allow so much flexibility. If you intend a field to contain a phone number, defining the field as CDATA leaves a lot to be desired.

In fact, XML Schema allows even stricter rule-making capabilities, which can be useful in situations that demand very strict control over field content.

IS XML JUST HTML ALL OVER AGAIN?

XML is a language of tags and attributes much like HTML, but an HTML mutated almost beyond recognition. XML is HTML on steroids.

XML is far more structured than HTML. Where HTML processors routinely accept wildly inaccurate and malformed code and attempt to make sense of it on the screen, XML is *required* to abort when it encounters a fatal error, which is almost any error at all. This is a throwback to the early days of data processing in some ways, when any error in code was punished with a core dump that you could spend hours deciphering. Expect to spend a bit more time debugging XML than you have previously spent on HTML.

Along with this unforgiving behavior, however, XML is far more powerful. Where HTML contented itself with 77 elements or so, depending on who was counting, XML has a potentially infinite number, structured in almost any way you choose.

HTML and XML

The basics are still the same, however, and your experience with HTML will make it easy to accept the evolutionary step that XML and its associated standards represent. Using XML is not quite as easy as rolling off a log but it's not like climbing Mount Everest either. With a little discipline and knowledge you'll be coding XML before you know it.

In fact, in a way you've been working with XML all along with your previous use of HTML. Not only is well-made HTML awfully close to XHTML—the XML-compliant replacement for HTML—but *clean* HTML 4.0 code is quite readable as XHTML 1.0. Because HTML 4.0 was structured as an SGML application and XML is a subset of SGML, this makes a lot of sense. The minor syntactic differences between XHTML, an XML vocabulary, and HTML, an SGML vocabulary, can be automatically adjusted if desired.

An XML document author is usually issued an authoring or coding manual (or sheet, for small DTDs) describing the elements used in the XML application, their attributes and possible values, and how they nest within each other. Following such a coding manual is no more difficult than remembering that a table row <tr> has to nest inside a table <table> and has, or should have, no meaning outside that context.

For most purposes, this is enough. XML authors are no more likely to be technical gurus who can instantly extrapolate the structure and use of an application from a glance at the DTD than are freeway commuters likely to be expert automobile mechanics. XML is able to give authors quite a bit of help in learning how to use a particular application, because they're encouraged to give tags meaningful names that are easy to remember. The creator of an application *should* provide an authoring manual that explains how to use it in simple terms. The theory is that any future data analyst could look at your XML code and figure out what it is and how it's structured without recourse to the original design documentation (presumably lost in the dust of history) based on structure and element names alone.

<!--
Although any XML processor can tell you whether your code is well-formed and a manual can help you construct a valid document, the DTD enables you to check your work unambiguously. This can be a separate step from the writing process, however, depending on the type of authoring tool used.
-->

Element Name Guidelines

Whether your code fulfills that ideal is largely up to your use of element names within some tiny limits:

- Element names starting with the string xml in any case combination are reserved; that is, you're not permitted to create them no matter what the provocation. Don't invent them on your own. If you feel you *must* have one, submit it to W3C as part of a Member Submission (assuming, of course, that you are a member) and see what happens.

- Element names containing a colon are apt to be interpreted as identifiers with an associated namespace, so using colons in element names is strongly discouraged and may eventually be forbidden. Why take a chance? Avoid them.

- An element name has to start with a "letter," which in this context is any Unicode/ISO/IEC 10646 letter or ideograph, or an underscore (or a colon, which you already know to avoid to prevent confusion with namespaces).

After that, a tag name can include any Unicode/ISO/IEC 10646 "letter," ideograph, or digit, plus the combining characters, extenders, periods, hyphens, spaces, or colons. A few human languages have otherwise legal characters that cannot begin a legal name in that language. These characters are excluded from the list of characters if they're in a position which could be viewed as "first" after a hyphen or other logical word break. But if you know the language, that will be obvious.

The Thai character *mai yamok* (looks like a backward f without a crossbar), for example, looks like a letter but can't be used to begin a word because it signifies repetition of the previous letter.

The combining characters are special characters used to add an accent to another character, many of which normalize to a single accented character. This is a convenience for keyboard entry, because many languages that include accented characters allow you to enter them using special "zero-width" accent characters, which can attach themselves to any other character.

The extenders are various special punctuation marks such as (in European languages) middle dot, triangular colon, and half-triangular colon. The extended characters are similar in other world scripts, not alphabetic exactly, but fitting in there somehow. If you need to use one in a language other than English, you'll probably know what they are so they're easy to find. But if you don't speak or write Arabic, using an Arabic "tatweel" in your element name is probably an affectation, although strictly allowed.

DEFINING THE XML DOCUMENT

An XML document is a collection of entities, which can be either parsed or unparsed. *Unparsed data* is anything that the XML processor can't understand, binary data or data that is only meaningful to other applications. *Parsed data* is anything that XML can understand, either as characters or markup.

An XML document must:

- Taken as a whole, it matches the production labeled *document*.

- It meets all the well-formedness constraints given in this specification (the XML 1.0 Recommendation).

- Each of the parsed entities referenced directly or indirectly within the document is well-formed.

The first constraint says that to be well-formed, an XML document has to obey all the rules that describe a document in the XML 1.0 Recommendation. Those rules essentially say that an XML document has to contain a prolog and a single element that forms the root element of the document together with optional comments and processing instructions.

The rules also say that you can tack on comments and processing instructions to the end of the document but, unfortunately, the XML parser has no way of telling whether these tacked on comments and processing instructions are associated with the document.

Because they can follow the closing tag, an XML parser can't even tell whether all tacked on processing instructions and comments were received. This violates the general rule in XML that the parser must be able to tell whether a document is complete. If you use processing instructions or comments, put them in the prolog where they are far safer and can't get lost.

The second constraint says that the document follows the well-formedness constraints described in the document. What's more, a document cannot refer to itself, even indirectly through an external entity. It can't refer to an external entity unless that too doesn't refer to itself, even indirectly. Non-validating parsers may not catch this error, but it's still an error. Logically, it's apparent that if document A includes document B, defining B as containing A leads to an endless loop. It's the endless loop that's forbidden.

Although being well-formed might be considered enough because a well-formed document has a DTD that describes it, an infinitely large number of DTDs can be constructed that also describe it. So for full validity, an associated DTD is required.

Document Production

Document production is defined in only two statements, again quoting from the XML 1.0 Recommendation:

- It contains one or more elements.

- There is exactly one element, called the *root* or *document element*, no part of which appears in the content of any other element. For all other elements, if the start tag is in the content of another element, the end tag is in the content of the same element. More simply stated, the elements, delimited by start and end tags, nest properly within each other.

The first statement says that there has to be at least one element in a document or, alternatively, that a well-formed document can't be empty.

The second statement says that the document has to be a tree in the narrow sense. It has to be complete so you can tell the difference between a successful download and a partial one.

A partial download is possible in HTML, because HTML doesn't require a closing `</html>` tag, or indeed almost any closing tags. Sometimes the browser can detect the interruption but it's not guaranteed. This means that a partial document can masquerade as complete and the user has no way of knowing unless there's some obvious fault in the text. XML prevents these problems, which might be important if a user later claims that a license agreement, for example, wasn't displayed in total. Insisting on a complete tree, an example of which is shown in Figure 22.1, eliminates these potential problems.

Figure 22.1
This depicts a well-formed tree. You could make an XML document out of the structure represented by this tree.

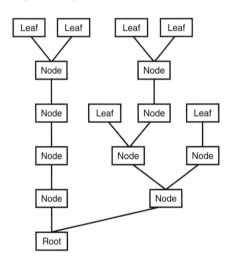

A graph that doesn't form a tree, on the other hand, cannot be made into an XML document unless the graph can be pruned to eliminate any non-tree features. In Figure 22.2, for example, the graph on the left could be pruned by eliminating one path from the topmost leaf to either node. In the same figure, the graph on the upper right would have to have one root eliminated, because an XML document can have only one root.

Figure 22.2
This illustration depicts two graphs that are not trees. They are not capable of being turned into XML documents.

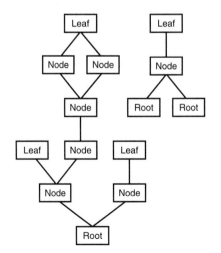

You should also be aware that trees are often depicted growing upside down, with the root at the top and the branches growing downward. This is done to accommodate our habit of reading pages from top to bottom, so the first thing we encounter on this upside-down tree is the root, just as an XML parser would, and scanning down the page brings us deeper into the foliage of the tree.

Understanding Well-Formedness Constraints

Besides the basic properties required in an XML document as listed in the previous "Defining the XML Document" section, an XML document must meet certain extra criteria called constraints.

Here are some constraints that XML requires:

- The name in an element's end tag must match the name in the start tag. This is almost trivial. Few of us would expect to be able to close a `<cite>` tag with a `</citation>` tag.

- An attribute name cannot appear more than once in the same start tag or empty-element tag. Again, this is fairly obvious. What are you supposed to do with a malformed line of code like this?

  ```
  <image src="one.gif" src="two.gif" />
  ```

- Attribute values cannot contain direct or indirect references to external entities. This is more subtle and was done to simplify life for XML processors. In an environment in which arbitrary character encodings are possible in external entities, it would be hard to handle them all correctly in an attribute.

- The replacement text of an entity referred to directly or indirectly in an attribute value (other than `"&lt;"`) must not contain a <. This is for simplicity and error handling. If you allowed an unescaped < inside an attribute, it would be hard to catch a missing final quote mark. Also, because you have to escape < in running text anyway, treating it differently inside an attribute value would be inconsistent.

- Characters referred to using character references must be legal characters. In other words, you can't hide characters that would otherwise be illegal by indirection or by defining them as numeric equivalents. So, for example, `&#x0000;` is not a legal character no matter how you refer to it.

- In a document without a DTD, a document with only an internal DTD subset containing no parameter entity references or a document with a value of `"standalone='yes'"` on the XML declaration, the name given in the entity reference must match that in an entity declaration. One exception is that well-formed documents need not declare any of the following entities: &, <, >, ', or ".

  Basically, the declaration of a parameter entity must precede any reference to it, but there are some situations in which a non-validating XML processor stops processing entity declarations. So if the non-validating processor is confident that all declarations have been read and processed, then it can declare a well-formedness error and abort processing if it finds an undeclared entity. On the other hand, if any of the ways in which the non-validating XML processor stops processing entities have occurred, then it's not an error to encounter an undeclared entity. This is a complicated way of saying that non-validating XML processors may or may not catch undeclared entities, depending on the situation.

- An entity reference must not contain the name of an unparsed entity. In short, you can't plunk binary data into the middle of text without some sort of handling mechanism declared. So, the following code is permitted and the value passed on to the user agent or browser if and only if it represented an external unparsed entity which had already been declared as a notation:

```
<image &myimage; />
```

- A parsed entity must not contain a recursive reference to itself, either directly or indirectly. Although dictionary makers may like to declare that a hat is a chapeau and a chapeau is a hat as if this means something, XML won't let you get away with it.

- Parameter-entity references may only appear in the DTD. In other words, you can't carry processing data into the final document and expect it to mean anything. You might as well expect that you could insert a C statement, say `printf("Hello, world"\n);`, onto your typewritten page and expect it to be replaced with some value and have the carriage returned for you. On the other hand, although it's a logical error if you *expect* it to happen, such text wouldn't actually break anything either, any more than printing the above line of C code in your text generates an error. Because % is only a character and doesn't have to be escaped inside your document, it's hard to see how such an "error" would be found out. Although factually interesting, this is a null statement as far as error processing goes.

THE PROLOG: THE XML DECLARATION

Every XML document should begin with an XML declaration that identifies the file as an XML file and also identifies the version of XML being used in this particular document. The fact that this is not mandatory is due only to the fact that there are many HTML and SGML files lying about on the Web that were perfectly well-formed XML as well. Why break what's already working? The XML declaration is also the place you declare your encoding and whether the document is standalone. The order shown in the following snippet is mandatory, although the encoding and standalone attributes are both optional:

```
<?xml version="1.0" encoding="ISO-8859-1" standalone="yes">
```

The standalone attribute allows you to turn off an external DTD if you want to. It may have other effects as well but it's difficult to say exactly what in a few words. You'll learn more about this attribute in the "Standalone Documents" section later in this chapter.

According to the W3C XML 1.0 Recommendation, "Standalone documents have no external markup declarations which affect XML information passed from the XML processor to an application."

This is a stunningly terse and obscure way of saying that `standalone="yes"` means that

* There are no default attribute values which aren't explicitly declared in the document.

* There are no entities other than &, <, >, ', and " used which have not been declared locally or possibly read in from a file by reference.

* There are no elements with only element content containing whitespace in any form.

* There are no external attributes subject to normalization, which means that the contents of attributes cannot have whitespace in them, or character or entity references.

It *doesn't* mean there is nothing external to the document. There might be. It mainly means that at whatever point the non-validating XML processor stops reading external documents, the processing of *all* declarations stops.

External data which is not markup is not within the scope of this statement. So, you can still have graphics files, included text files, and anything else as long as they aren't markup and as long as you declare them in the internal DTD subset.

After all that, the XML processor isn't required to notify the application as to whether the document is standalone. In fact, the processor isn't required to do much of anything with this information or behave in any particular way when it encounters this information.

Basically, the designer of the DTD has to figure out whether documents authored using that DTD can be standalone and tell people, including authors. Authors who know that the DTD has been designed to be standalone or who have converted a document not designed to be standalone into the alternative format, can insert `standalone="yes"` into their XML declaration as documentation of that fact:

```
<?xml version="1.0" standalone="yes" ?>
```

Documents which are not standalone can be automatically or manually converted.

CONSTRUCTING THE XML DOCUMENT PROLOG: THE DOCUMENT TYPE DECLARATION

The prolog of an XML document contains several statements. The first, the XML declaration, declares that the following document is XML. The second, the Document Type Declaration, is the method you use to identify the Document Type Definition (DTD) used by a particular document. The fact that the abbreviation DTD might apply to the Document Type Declaration is an unfortunate coincidence. DTD refers only to Document Type Definition. There can be only one Document Type Declaration in an XML document, so it's entered on the document instance itself. Because multiple DTDs can be combined to make a single document, this allows control of DTD loading to reside in each individual document.

The Document Type Declaration (DOCTYPE) has two parts, both optional. The first references an external DTD and uses the keywords PUBLIC or SYSTEM to identify a catalog entry or a URI, respectively. If catalogs aren't implemented in your XML processor, you can specify both parts at once without the second keyword:

```
<!DOCTYPE your-doc-name PUBLIC "{catalog }">
<!DOCTYPE your-doc-name PUBLIC "{catalog }" "{uri}">
<!DOCTYPE your-doc-name SYSTEM "{uri}"
```

The second optional part of the DOCTYPE declaration allows you to enter an internal DTD subset directly into your document. The internal DTD subset is surrounded by square brackets like this:

```
<!DOCTYPE your-doc-name [ {internal DTD declarations} ]>
```

You can also combine the two, allowing you to add certain types of declarations and entities almost at will:

```
<!DOCTYPE your-doc-name PUBLIC "{catalog}"

"{uri}" [

{internal DTD declarations}

]>
```

For clarity, the internal subset is usually set off with carriage returns like this:

```
<!DOCTYPE your-doc-name PUBLIC "{catalog}" "{uri}" [
 {internal DTD declarations}
]>
```

The DOCTYPE declaration must use the name of the root ELEMENT of the DTD, whether internal or external, as the field labeled your-doc-name in the previous examples. So, if the name of the root element of your DTD is Dave, your DOCTYPE declaration should start like this:

```
<!DOCTYPE Dave ... >
```

Your manual or sheet tells you what to say on the DOCTYPE if you are an author. If you are a DTD designer, you should supply such a manual or sheet to every author.

When you have a mix of functionality that allows you to create the document structure you need, you can publish the resulting DTD and save the trouble of doing it again and again for each new document.

CONSTRUCTING THE DOCUMENT BODY

An XML document consists of text, which usually consists of mingled markup and character data. The prolog contains markup only, but that isn't the interesting part, because you need data to go with your markup before it's anything other than empty boxes to put things in. The body of your document contains almost everything that counts from an application (and human) perspective, sprinkled liberally within your markup.

Character Data

A DTD can declare many types of data that might be used in your document, but the default datatype is always CDATA, for ordinary character data. The coding sheet or manual tells you what sort of data can be entered into each attribute or element content field.

Assuming that the type is CDATA, you can put just about anything you want into the field as long as it doesn't contain unescaped markup.

It's entirely possible to construct a DTD that contains no text within elements. Instead, one can put the significant data inside attributes associated with each element, which can all be declared as empty or containing element content only.

Markup

Markup consists of the entirety of the non-character data content of an XML file. The various forms that markup can take are shown in Table 22.1.

Table 22.1   XML Markup Syntax

Markup Type	Markup Syntax
start tags	`<elementName attributes] >`
end tags	`</elementName>`
empty-element tags	`<elementName attributes] />`
entity references	`&entityName; or %parameterEntityName;`
character references	`&#decimalNumber; or &#xhexNumber;`
comments	`<!-- comment -->`
CDATA section delimiters	`<![CDATA[ cdata stuff ]]>`
document type declarations	`<!DOCTYPE name externalID? [DTDstuff]>`
processing instructions	`<?processorID data ?>`
XML declaration	`<?xml version encoding standalone ?>`

Everything else is character data.

Markup always starts with either the < character, in which case it always ends with the > character. Entities start with the & character, and always end with the ; character.

UNDERSTANDING HOW XML FORMS LOGICAL STRUCTURES

The nesting of elements is the only mechanism used to indicate logical structure in an XML document. The start and end tags in the text stream tell the XML processor that a node has been encountered.

If the XML processor encounters another start tag before the matching end tag, the processor knows that it's either on a new node in the tree or a leaf. If no new start tag is encountered and the end tag is found, the processor knows that this is a leaf and can proceed iteratively at that level of the tree until another start or end tag is encountered. Processing proceeds stepwise based on this simple rule. If the processor is validating the document, each node can be associated with a rule governing what sorts of content can appear within it. An empty tag is, by definition, a leaf because it can contain no further content.

The rest of the logical structure of the document is defined by the attributes associated with each element. In addition, the logical structure can vary based on the contents of conditional sections contained within the document or its subparts.

> `<!--`
> Most of the data structure contained in an XML document can be accessed sequentially and without building the structure in memory. A start tag starts a node or leaf and the matching end tag ends it. Any tags encountered between a start tag and its matching end tag start a new node or leaf. This principle is the basis of SAX and other event-driven XML processors.
> `-->`

How XML Forms Physical Structures

The nesting of entities is the only mechanism used to indicate physical structure in an XML document. The entity definitions encountered in the text stream tell the XML processor that a separate entity has been encountered.

There are many types of entities, from the tiny entities that form individual characters like this: or &sp; (space), to the external entities that allow you to incorporate portions of other XML documents into your own or include references to unparsed data, such as multimedia files in a document for later rendering by a user agent.

An XML document is a collection of such entities. Each of those subentities must be complete in and of itself. This means that because the structure of the document as a whole must be a simple tree, each subentity must be a single node or must also be a simple tree. You build larger structures by grafting on subentity nodes or trees as portions of your larger tree.

If you look at Figure 22.1, shown previously, you could partition that diagram into sub-trees only as long as you could take a pencil and circle all the elements of your proposed tree and only cross one line, the branch that joins your group of elements to the main tree. If you cross more than one line, you can't form a legal sub-tree. This means that you have to include a single lowest node which will form the root of your new sub-tree.

If your documents contain multiple sub-trees in different files, every sub-tree file must be a complete XML document tree in and of itself.

Look at the two connected graphs shown previously in Figure 22.2. You see that either there are two roots, which you'll remember is forbidden in XML, or a simple circuit (a loop) in the graph, which prevents it from being an XML structure in the first place. There are, in fact, substructures of that tree that seem to be simple trees; however, the one loop is a fatal flaw. As a whole, these structures cannot be made into XML documents. In the first case, by rearranging the structure, you could probably turn it into a simple tree, but one root would become a leaf in the new structure.

In the second case, you could isolate a large portion of the structure as a simple tree and make that part into an XML structure. But you would have to find some other way of representing that part which is not a tree unless you cut one of the circular paths and transform it into a simple tree.

Normalization

Normalization in the context of XML refers to the process of resolving entity references in locations in which such references can occur, and regularizing linefeeds to account for the several different ways of treating them in different operating systems.

It turns out that there are two places where whitespace might be encountered: in character data within the document and in character data argued in element attributes.

In the first case, it's difficult to distinguish significant whitespace within the markup from insignificant whitespace in parsed entities. It seemed best to the designers to pass on all whitespace to the application along with the processor's best guess, based on the DTD, about which data is definitely insignificant and which might or might not be. This passing of the buck makes sense because the application is in the best position to know what to do with extra whitespace.

With end-of-line handling, also a form of whitespace, there's another problem. Newlines are treated differently on different systems. The common alternatives are a line-feed (Unix), a carriage return (Mac OS), and both carriage return and linefeed characters (Microsoft Windows). It's also common for applications to insert anomalous sequences of any of these in any order when they encounter a file from a foreign system. W3C decided they couldn't do everything and chose a set of reasonable rules. If the parser sees either `;#x0D;&#x0A;` (carriage return, linefeed) or `&#x0D;` (carriage return) it replaces it with `&#x0A;` (linefeed), the Unix newline character.

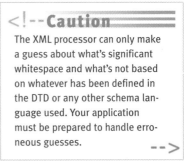

<!--
The designer rarely has to worry about normalization except in a negative way. The XML parser should perform all needed normalizations, so the only thing the document architect need think about is whether normalization will affect his data when making a round trip from un-normalized form to normalized and back again.
-->

<!--Caution
The XML processor can only make a guess about what's significant whitespace and what's not based on whatever has been defined in the DTD or any other schema language used. Your application must be prepared to handle erroneous guesses.
-->

In attributes, there is a standard transformation sequence and then special added processing for everything except CDATA:

- Character references are processed by appending the referenced character to the output attribute value.

- Entity references are processed by recursively processing the replacement text of the entity.

- Whitespace characters—`#x20` (space), `#x0D` (carriage return), `#x0A` (linefeed), `#x09` (horizontal tab)—are processed by appending `#x20` (space) to the normalized output value, except that only a single `#x20` (space) is appended for a `#x0D#x0A` (carriage return, linefeed) sequence that is part of an external parsed entity or the literal entity value of an internal parsed entity.

- Other characters are processed by appending them to the normalized output value.

- Yet another transformation is applied if the attribute datatype is *not* CDATA, the default. Leading and trailing spaces are stripped and multiple spaces are collapsed into one space.

Both types of normalization serve to refine data without modifying element content.

Element Types

Surprisingly, if you're validating, it's not an error to use an element type that hasn't been declared, although the parser may issue a warning. In fact, allowing undeclared element types within other elements, no matter what their content model says, is the basis of being able to supplement a document's DTD with elements from other namespaces. So all you have to do is use the undeclared element in a correct, well-formed manner while possibly identifying the namespace it comes from. Because you've already explored what well-formed means, take a look at the more interesting case, a valid document.

Every element in a valid XML document has been defined in the DTD associated with that document by the DOCTYPE declaration. The DTD declares the following:

- Actual names of the elements

- Rules used to determine which elements can nest within other elements and in what order

- Possible attributes and their default or constant values

- Character values of enumeration types

- Unparsed entities used in the document and how they are referenced by name

- Language encodings used in the document

- Character entities used in the document

- Other information important for the processing and rendering of the document

Following those rules, you're able to create documents according to the template the document designer had in mind when she created the DTD. In a non-validating environment, you can just make up elements and attributes as you go along.

The coding sheet or manual lays all this out in an easy-to-read and understand format, *if* your DTD author has done her job. When authoring an XML document or correcting an error, you might not have the luxury of a full authoring environment. You may be using vi over telnet from a thousand miles away. It's always important to keep the coding documentation handy in case you're called up in the middle of the night and asked if you wouldn't mind fixing your million-dollar database access system, please?

Figure 22.3, later in this chapter, shows a validating authoring environment that can save a lot of time and make life easier for you by automatically encapsulating the DTD information that might otherwise have to be presented in a coding document in programmatic form. However, such tools are neither infallible nor available on every platform. Although they may generate "helpful" error messages when they stop processing your file, the actual message may have little or nothing to do with the error you actually made. You'll have to use your head, not a tool, in many cases.

Entity names must start with a character, which is any character glyph within a given writing system that corresponds to our usual idea of a Latin character plus the ASCII characters underscore and colon. The first character can be followed by characters, digits, and a selection of accents and extenders representing glyph combinations of one sort or another. Processing instructions must not start with the ASCII letters XML, xml, or any mi XEd-case variations of those three characters. It's a very bad idea to use the ASCII colon character except when using namespaces, although it's possible to do so legally, since the presence of a string followed by a colon in a name *looks* like it refers to a namespace even when it doesn't.

The only place that *some* ASCII is mandatory is in a DTD. Literals that name public identifiers—the characters that fill the literal parts of a `<!DOCTYPE PUBLIC "-//public identifier" "uri">` declaration—must be ASCII characters because that's an Internet standard. Numeric character references such as `&#x0D;` must be entered using a very limited ASCII number set. The ISO 639 language codes and the ISO 3166 country codes used in the `XML:lang` and XHTML `lang` attributes must also be in ASCII, again because these are Internet standards. There are a few other places such as quote marks, which must be ASCII quotes, special markup characters like `&gt;`, keywords, like `<!ELEMENT ... >` and IDREF, and so on, where ASCII is required; however, in general you don't have to worry about using equivalent characters from the national language character sets defined in the Unicode/ISO/IEC 10646 standards.

The rest of XML is friendly to speakers of languages other than English.

After years of Eurocentric, even Anglocentric, dependence on ASCII and extended ASCII on the Web, XML has evened the playing field somewhat for all players at the Web level, including the myriad of users who will be able to access information in their native languages and scripts. Having a single standard means of communicating in, say, Chinese, in which there are three main "standards" and a number of variations, is sure to improve the availability of rendering engines as well as reduce their cost.

`<!--`
Surprisingly, many explanations of XML get this part wrong. Although everyone agrees that you can use encodings in content, the fact that this freedom extends to markup as well is harder to grasp. Everyone is so used to the limitations of HTML that it's difficult to remember to embrace this freedom.
`-->`

`<!--Caution`
Although it's great that XML allows Chinese characters in markup and content, that doesn't mean your system actually supports the display and entry of Chinese characters, or any other of the many ideographic, syllabic, and alphabetic writing systems in use around the world. You'll need a character set as well as a keyboard and operating system support for full functionality.
`-->`

Attribute Lists and Types

In your XML coding sheet, you'll find a list of attributes for each element. If you're using a validating editor such as XML Pro 2.0, you'll probably have a menu of available attributes whenever you place the working cursor on an element in the document tree view. There is also a menu of elements that can be inserted at this point in the file.

Such an editor can be a tremendous timesaver because it takes away some of the burden of learning a coding sheet or manual. However, a good coding sheet can give a far more accessible general overview and explain the rationale behind the document structure, something even a validating editor cannot do.

Figure 22.3 shows some of the strengths of this sort of editor. The tree structure of the document is clearly displayed although a large or complex document can quickly overwhelm the limits of readability on a small screen. The highlighted cursor shows where you are in the document at any given time. A list of available attributes for the element you've highlighted is visible on the screen as well. You can scroll down through them and pick the ones you want to employ for this particular element.

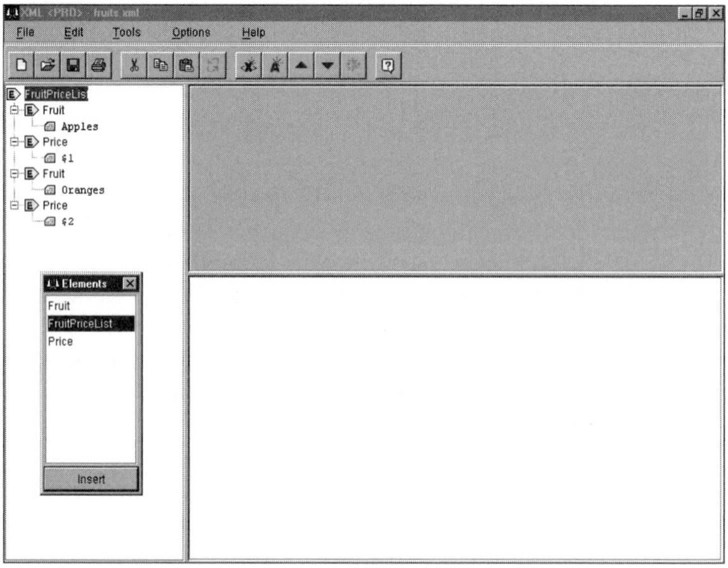

Figure 22.3
XML Pro 2.0 is being used to edit an XHTML file. Note the list of available attributes for an anchor element based on the position of the element cursor.

There is very little checking of your attribute values that can be done at the processor level. XML by itself doesn't offer facilities to validate attributes and element content in detail beyond checking that enumerated choices have been entered correctly, which a validating editor does automatically, and a few other minor details. XML Pro and other authoring environments may offer you a pull-down list of enumerated values so you can't make a mistake, but that's about it. The solution to this dilemma is XML schemas.

Even the little field checking provided may not be reasonable in actual use. If you think telephone numbers have to be numeric, for example, you're flying in the face of various language-dependent conventions which might use periods, hyphens, commas, slashes, parentheses, or even spelled-out words on the telephone keypad to represent numbers. For some purposes, the U.S. military uses a hexadecimal telephone keypad which adds the "digits" A, B, C, and D to the usual 0–9 plus * and #. Telephone TouchTone standards, officially called DTMF (Dual Tone Multi-Frequency) tones, allow for this, so you should too. Postal (ZIP) codes in many countries include letters as well as digits. And large numbers and decimal fractions may have punctuation marks inside them that vary from country to country, often a comma and period respectively but quite often period and comma in an exact reversal of meaning. In general, everything is more complicated than you think, and adding silly restrictions on input is almost guaranteed to cause problems and make you look bad.

Although an XML application may only be enforcing constraints in an underlying database, before finalizing your analysis, consider the fact that the database may be designed in an insular or shortsighted manner that doesn't meet the real demands of a global marketplace. Some data is inherently regional in nature, and a mature individual is cognizant of that fact. Whether one eats with the fork in the right hand or the left is a matter of taste, not error checking. In the case of cosmetic differences, consider normalizing the data before error checking or storage. There's no earthly reason a British user has to guess that we often surround area codes with parentheses in the U.S. and Canada before her input is accepted.

Unparsed Entities

An unparsed entity is anything the XML processor can't recognize, whether it be binary data such as an image or audio file, or text that should be passed to an application without being processed in any way. HTML uses comments to hide such text from the HTML browser, but XML has several mechanisms that work more reliably. In fact, XML is not required to pass comments onto the application at all, so they can't be used as freely as they are in HTML. This was, I think, a bit of pique on the part of some of the designers, who hated the idea of using comments for real data. In HTML, the contents of a `<script>` tag are defined to be PCDATA, which can contain anything at all.

An unparsed entity must first be declared as a NOTATION, a special declaration that names a helper application that knows how to deal with entities of a particular type. You give the notation a name, an optional public identifier, and then the less optional name of the helper application, like one of these options:

> `<!--Caution`
>
> By redefining the way scripts behave in the presence of comments, the designers of XML have introduced an incompatibility problem between XML and HTML. In all likelihood, XML processors will continue to pass on comments to the application because many pages will break without that behavior. Also, the processors are *permitted* to pass on the commented information by the same language by which they're *permitted* not to.
>
> `-->`

```
<!NOTATION mnemonic-name PUBLIC "public-identifier">
<!NOTATION mnemonic-name PUBLIC "public-identifier" "application-name.e XE ">
<!NOTATION mnemonic-name SYSTEM "application-name.e XE ">
```

CASE BY CASE: REAL-WORLD APPLICATIONS OF XML

In this section, I'll provide an overview of some of the many XML DTDs, as follows:

- Health Level-7 (HL7), the Health Informatics Standard was founded in 1987 to develop standards for the electronic interchange of clinical, financial, and administrative information among health care computer systems. The HL7 focus is on using SGML and XML as a transport mechanism between differing health care information systems.

- Real Estate Transaction Standard (RETS) is an XML-based method of exchanging real estate transaction information. A competing standard is Real Estate Markup Language (RELML) which uses XML DTDs to describe residential, commercial, and open land listings for posting on the Web.

- RosettaNet, the Lingua Franca for Business, is an EDI/E-Commerce initiative aimed at procurement for the computer industry.

- MathML and ChemML are two scientific XML standards that allow mathematicians to publish equations and chemists to present chemical formulae.

- SMIL, the Synchronized Multimedia Markup Language, is HyTime for Everyman, a multimedia markup language that lets content providers produce sophisticated visual and audio presentations.

- ICE, Information and Content Exchange, although not strictly an XML application being a transport mechanism, allows the exchange of online assets and personal information over the Web.

- SAE J2008 is an XML-based ordering and inventory system for the automotive industry; MISTI, the Missile Industry Supply-chain Transaction Infrastructures, does the same for the space industry.

- Chinese DTDs provide the specialized structure needed for Chinese language publishing. Similar DTDs exist for Japanese, Korean, Vietnamese, and many other human languages.

- GedML, a genealogy XML standard, encourages the free flow of genealogical data over the Web. Software already exists to convert standard GEnealogical Data COMmunication (GEDCOM) files to GedML.

The list goes on and on. As you can see, the range of applications is immense, touching almost every field of human endeavor. Few businesses can safely ignore XML, although there are so many existing and proposed standards in many fields that there's bound to be some sort of shakeout as major contenders jockey for pole position in a fracas of dueling proposals.

Public Resources for DTDs

With so many proprietary proposals on the table, you might wonder what the differences are between them. For the most part, you'll have to ask potential vendors to disclose their DTD as there are comparatively few DTDs available on the Web. There are two sites that may give you a start. On Microsoft platforms, the BizTalk consortium at `http://www.biztalk.org/` has a searchable list, although it's not easy to use and requires you to guess what the appropriate keywords might be that describe the sort of DTD you're looking for. The Organization for the Advancement of Structured Information Standards (OASIS), at `http://www.oasis-open.org/` plans another but only has the DocBook DTD and a subset of the CALS table model DTD called Exchange Table Model up for public view right now. Many vendors are treating their DTDs as if they were state secrets.

Each browser maker has proposed standards which the others cry are slanted toward themselves. Just as the browser wars led to the development of proprietary "extensions" to HTML, which tended (or tried) to lock out other browsers creating a Babel of incompatible methods that still plague us today, XML is going to be in flux for some time to come.

The basics are already there, however, and a user community increasingly demanding of open standards is driving the various proposals toward convergence. Many of the major successes have been with standards from ISO and ANSII, which sell documentation to support their standards-making efforts but provide neutral ground for all partners. For the price of the documentation, usually a few hundred dollars, anyone can play on the same level ground.

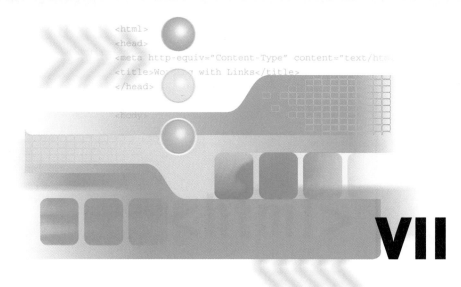

VII

APPENDIXES

A   Site Publishing, Maintenance, and Marketing Guide   **541**

B   Annotated Resources for Web Developers   **563**

C   XHTML Reference   **569**

D   CSS2 Reference   **631**

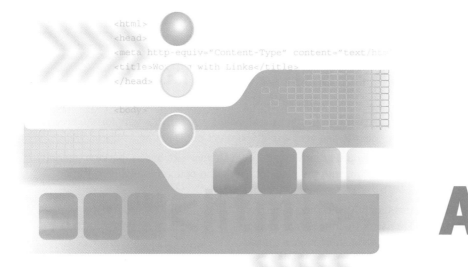

A

SITE PUBLISHING, MAINTENANCE, AND MARKETING GUIDE

IN THIS APPENDIX

You've Built Your Web Site, What Now? 542

Transferring Files Using FTP 542

Testing Files Live 544

Managing Links 545

Copyright Guidelines 547

The Web As a Commercial Venue 548

Search Engines and Directories As Marketing Tools 549

Banner Advertising 553

Other Online Marketing Techniques 557

Web Rings 559

Offline Marketing Strategies 559

Case by Case: Legal Issues on the Net 561

YOU'VE BUILT YOUR WEB SITE, WHAT NOW?

You've developed your Web site. You've come up with a consistent design, spell-checked your content, and tested all your pages for broken links and invalid markup. It's time for the accolades to come. But nobody's going to see your site if you don't publish it somewhere.

This appendix is geared to help you do three things: publish your site online, perform general maintenance tasks, and gain insight into the kinds of marketing options available to you as you take your site to the Web.

Most Internet service providers (ISPs) include some amount of Web space along with their access accounts. This is referred to as *hosting*, and simply means that an ISP provides and maintains the server. *If* you are developing a small home page, this amount of space should be more than adequate. Larger sites, or those with a corporate purpose, will require much more server space and might necessitate the co-location or on-site delivery of services. Co-location is different than hosting in that you build and run the server yourself, but it is housed at the ISP rather than on-site. On-site delivery means that all servers are on the company site and administered by the company rather than a provider.

There are hundreds of Web-hosting services available, and the rates vary greatly. One of the best resources for finding a Web-hosting service is The List, which can be found at http://www.thelist.com/. This site offers information about thousands of ISPs and Web-hosting services.

Keep in mind that you do not necessarily have to choose a local Web-hosting service. Many national ISPs offer commercial Web hosting, with the added benefit of local access numbers all over the country, so you can access the Internet and maintain your Web site even if you're on the road.

Even if you have a local ISP, you may still choose a Web-hosting service that is more distant if it offers competitive rates. You would use the same local ISP to access the Internet, but your Web site would then be hosted elsewhere.

Prices for Web hosting vary widely depending on the type of service and the amount of space you require. You can generally find an adequate amount of space and bandwidth (amount of usage your site is allocated per month before additional charges accrue) for a medium business site for under $75 per month.

Larger sites—and especially those requiring specialty services such as secure transactions—will cost upward of $100 per month for hosting. If you choose to operate your site under a registered domain name, it will cost you on average an additional $70 to register that name, depending upon how you go about doing it. This cost covers the initial registration and the first two years of service. You'll be billed an additional $35 per year after the first two years to maintain your own domain name.

TRANSFERRING FILES USING FTP

Uploading your Web site files requires a communications standard known as File Transfer Protocol (FTP). You use FTP to transfer all the files relating to your Web site, including your document files, image files, and any audio or video files, to the remote Web server.

There are many FTP packages available today, including the following:

- **Dedicated packages**—These are standalone software products that help you manage your FTP needs.

- **Built-ins**—Many Web development software packages have FTP services built right into the application.

Dedicated FTP packages offer capabilities that built-in components do not offer, such as the ability to delete old Web pages and rename files on the server.

FTP Software

The most popular FTP programs are WS_FTP and CuteFTP for the PC, and Fetch for the Macintosh. Each of these programs is available as shareware on the Web. As with all shareware, you are expected to register the software if you use it beyond a reasonable trial period.

The method for transferring your files to a Web server is similar for each of these programs. First, you configure the software to locate the remote server and log in with your user ID and password. You locate the directory to which you're transferring your files and identify the files you want to transfer. Then you let the software do its work.

<!--
Download Fetch from http://
fetchsoftworks.com/.

You can also search for FTP tools
at http://www.shareware.com/,
or from the InformIT download
site, http://www.informit.
com/downloads/.
-->

Macintosh and UNIX FTP Software

Fetch is a Macintosh-based FTP program developed by Dartmouth University and now owned by Fetch Softworks. It's the most convenient and popular of the Macintosh-based FTP programs. Its interface is extremely user friendly, making the FTP process especially simple for those new to the game.

Most UNIX systems come with pre-installed FTP packages. For more options, visit your favorite shareware and software sites for a wide range of choices of FTP applications for all platforms.

Visual Applications

Many popular visual applications such as Microsoft FrontPage, Adobe GoLive, and Macromedia Dreamweaver, have FTP capabilities built right into the software. As with all aspects of these types of editors, the focus is on ease of use.

FrontPage will keep track of which pages have changed on your site. Both FrontPage and Adobe GoLive will upload your pages at the touch of a button after you have configured the software to access your Web server.

<!--
If your site is nested several directories deep on your remote Web server, you'll need to pay close attention to how you configure FrontPage's Web Publishing Wizard.
-->

I recommend you try uploading one sample page to test your configuration before attempting to FTP your entire site. This can save you a lot of time—and embarrassment with your Web-hosting service—in case the wizard needs to be tweaked a bit to find the right directory.

Dreamweaver (see Figure A.1) allows you to keep a connection with your Web server open as you edit your files. This allows you to easily transfer files back and forth between your local computer and the Web server as you work.

Figure A.1
Dreamweaver supports FTP, too.

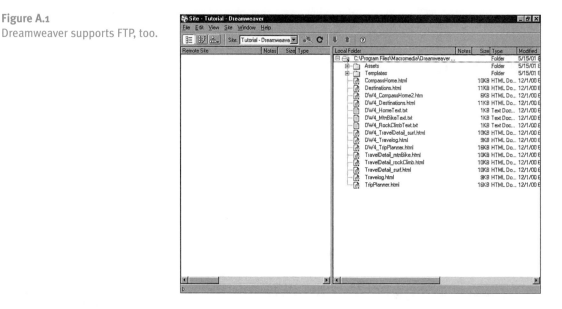

Dreamweaver will automatically re-create on the remote server the same file structure, including subdirectories that you have on your local machine. This will ensure that any relative links you create will remain accurate on the remote server.

TESTING FILES LIVE

After you've uploaded your files to your remote Web server, it's time to begin the testing process all over again. No matter how good everything looked on your local machine, it's a good idea to visit every page again and click every link. Did you forget to upload an image file? Did you create an absolute link where you intended to create a relative link? All these little problems can be easily fixed in this testing phase.

When testing your site, look for the following:

- Does it look good at lower resolutions? Many computers these days can handle 800×600 and above, but there are still people out there viewing your pages at 640×480. Choose your preferred common denominator, but do check out how your pages look at lower resolution even if you're designing for a higher optimal resolution. Or, go the contemporary route and create dynamic (also referred to as *fluid* or *liquid*) sites, where your visual content flows into the available space.

- Can you navigate your site without graphics turned on? Unless you have a specific audience in mind that can definitely handle a graphics-intensive site, you'll want to make sure that any graphic navigation also has a text counterpart.

- How does it look in 256 colors? Again, more and more Web visitors have video cards that can handle higher color modes, but 256-color is still a common issue in certain arenas, especially education. Even if you stuck with the Web-safe color palette, it's a good idea to view all your pages in 256-color to make sure there aren't any horrifying surprises.

- How does it look in different browsers? Internet Explorer and Netscape Navigator can make the same page look very different, particularly if you're using table background colors and other design tricks. It may be impossible to have your pages look exactly the same in each browser, but you want the site to still look good in each.

<!--

Want to make sure your sites are available to a variety of user agents? Disable all scripts, graphics, and media. Test the site using a browser or PDA. Does it make conceptual sense? If not, you may need to look more closely at Web page accessibility methods.

-->

- How long does it take to load? Even if you've kept page weight in mind when you're building your site, you'll still want to download the pages after you've put them on the Web server to see how everything is loading and check the download time.

To learn how to write accessible sites, *see* "Creating Accessible Sites," **p. 419**, Chapter 17.

Follow these guidelines, and you've improved your chances of having a very stable site.

MANAGING LINKS

Every time you add or revise a page on your Web site, you'll want to test your links on the live server. As your site grows, it's very easy to move a page from one directory to another and forget to update the link reference on another page.

If you have links to other sites on your pages, you'll also want to check those links on a regular basis. The Web is a moving target with sites coming and going on a daily basis. You might link to a wonderful related site today only to find that it has moved to another location or disappeared completely by next week.

The topic of a site may change over time, too. Don't let your members be surprised by clicking to an erotic poetry site when they (and you) think they're clicking to a discussion of Shakespeare's sonnets.

Even large, commercial sites can be redesigned in such a way that they're either no longer appropriate for your site or might be a better resource for your viewers if you link to a specific page.

Manual Management

The best and quickest way to manage links on a small site is to maintain a list of all your links. You can do this in a database such as Access. Another, very convenient method is to create a simple HTML file for yourself with hot links to every site and page referenced from your Web site. Perhaps the easiest way to check your links is to bookmark each linked site using your browser. You can then navigate from link to link directly from that list.

Once a week or so, run through your list, calling up each of those sites in your browser. If a site is being redirected, it's best to change your link to the actual URL of the site. Be sure to scan the site briefly to make sure the material hasn't changed to something objectionable to your audience. And, of course, remove any links to sites that have disappeared.

Link Management Programs

As your site grows, manually checking all the links on every page will become cumbersome. That's where a good link management program can come in handy.

A link management program will automatically check every link on a page or site, including both intra-page and inter-site links and will indicate which links are invalid. There are dozens of programs available, ranging from freeware applications that will check a limited number of links to commercial packages that can check hundreds of links at once. Some packages will also generate a site map of your entire Web site. Several packages are mentioned later, under HTML validators.

⇨ For more on intra-page linking, *see* *"Adding Hypertext and Independent Links," p. 155,* Chapter 7.

There are also Web services that will provide link checks on a page. Website Garage will check one page of a site free of charge (see Figure A.2). If you want to check your entire site and do regular link checks, you can pay an annual fee that entitles you to automatic monthly updates with results e-mailed to you.

Figure A.2
The Web Site Garage services page.

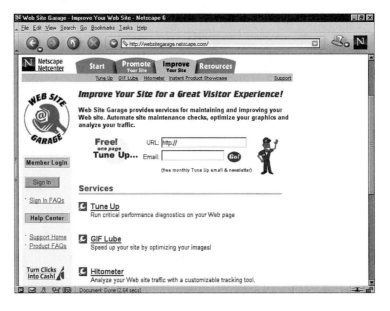

Another favorite is Doctor HTML. The good Doctor will check your links as well as give you feedback on your HTML code.

<!--
Visit Website Garage at http://
www.websitegarage.com/, and
Doctor HTML at http://www.
imagiware.com/RxHTML/.
-->

COPYRIGHT GUIDELINES

Plagiarism may be the sincerest form of flattery, but it is also illegal. Copyright law is just as applicable on the Internet as offline, no matter what you might see on other sites or read about on Usenet. Any work that is published in a book, magazine, newspaper, or even elsewhere on the Internet is most likely copyrighted.

Graphic images, songs, and video clips are also normally copyrighted. Be very careful about "borrowing" copyrighted material for your Web site. Not only do you risk your reputation, but you also risk serious legal repercussions.

This doesn't necessarily mean that you cannot use copyrighted work, however. If you are quoting a few lines from an article, for example, and cite the original copyright of the author and publisher, you are making "fair use" of the material, which is permitted under U.S. law. The trick is in using just enough material to get your point across without repurposing entire passages of the work.

You can also obtain written permission to use excerpts from a copyrighted work. You do this by contacting the author, publisher, agent, or license-holder of the material. If you want to use a passage from a book or newspaper, the best place to start is with the publisher. If you want to use an audio file, you should contact ASCAP (American Society of Composers, Authors, and Publishers), (http://www.ascap.com/) or BMI (http://www.bmi.com). Whether or not you obtain the permission you seek is up to the copyright holder, and they may require a fee before they'll grant permission.

Stock photography and music sites are another source of high-quality, copyrighted material. One such site is Photodisc (http://www.photodisc.com/). Photodisc allows you to browse thousands of stock photos at its site and will let you download test images to use as you're building your site.

If you wish to use the images on a live site, you can purchase a license at a small price. The price per image runs about $20. If you find you are using several images from the same group, you can purchase a license for an entire CD-ROM of images.

Another popular source of stock images is ArtToday (http://www.arttoday.com/). Unlike Photodisc, which charges per image, ArtToday charges an annual fee to access its site. The quality and depth of the images is generally not as high as Photodisc, but it offers fonts, clip art, Web buttons, and icons in addition to stock photography.

If you are developing a personal home page, it is probably not worth paying a steep fee to license background music or pay for stock graphic images. For commercial sites, however, licensed material can improve the image of the site and may be worth the investment.

As you can see, while the technical aspects of turning your Web site live are quite easy, there are many other considerations and resources to be considered first. Choose the level of complexity that is appropriate for your site, your time constraints, and your technical competence, and you'll do fine.

THE WEB AS A COMMERCIAL VENUE

As the Web continues to grow in popularity as a means for commercial ventures, more and more companies are feeling that an online presence is not only necessary to have, but to maintain and grow. Additionally, there are many companies that are emerging solely on the Web, with no offline counterpart.

With so much commercialism on the Web, it didn't take long for the advertising and marketing firms to step into the act—first to use a Web site as an advertising medium, and now recognizing that many Web sites are not simply the means to a product but the product itself.

Whether you intend to use your Web site as an addition to your offline business, to provide products or services, or as a forum for your expression, you have to put some effort into marketing it. With the millions of Web pages available today, your content could be lost and, as fabulous as your site is, it might never get seen.

Every good Web designer knows how important it is to know your target audience. You wouldn't use elegant fonts and understated colors to appeal to the audience of a rock music site, you would use funky fonts and bright vibrant colors.

The same can be said about marketing your site. You wouldn't waste your time marketing your music site to members of a quilting club. Sure, there could be some music fans there, but the probability is slim.

You have to know your audience before you can effectively market to it. You need to know the following information about your target audience:

- Age

- Gender

- Locale

- Language spoken

- Computer platform

- Marital status

- Financial status

You should also include categories that specifically apply to your Web site.

After you have determined your primary audience, you should also consider secondary markets. Although your main target audience for a quilting Web site is affluent women over 45, you should also include young teen girls just learning to quilt.

If you are unfamiliar with demographic research and want to be aggressive in your online marketing techniques, it

```
<!--
```
If you are running your own servers, consider installing one of the many statistic analysis products available for tracking users and user activity. If you are purchasing Web space via an ISP, many offer statistical services as part of their business packages. Viewing statistics on a regular basis can help you make and adjust marketing decisions. Unix administrators recommend Webalizer, and Analog is an extremely popular statistics tool available on most platforms.
```
-->
```

might be a good idea to investigate the type of information you can get from a professional marketing firm or advertising agency. As the composition of the Internet community begins to more closely mirror that of society at large, however, you should also make yourself aware of demographics in general.

After you have a good understanding of your audience, you can then market your site directly to them. You could place ads on the search engines they are most likely to use and on the Web sites they frequent. You can also take your advertising offline and target the magazines and newspapers they read or the radio station they tune to.

> <!--
> If you want to learn more about demographic research, you can visit the American Demographics Web site at http://www.demographics.com. The site offers archives of their magazine from the last several years. Many of these issues include demographic information about Internet usage for various markets.
> -->

Marketing your site blindly, without consideration of your target, is counterproductive. An audience that isn't interested will view your ads, and your target audience may never know your site exists.

SEARCH ENGINES AND DIRECTORIES AS MARKETING TOOLS

Search engines and directories can be powerful online marketing tools, but you must first understand how they work and how to best use them. Search engines "spider" the Web finding Web pages to add to their databases of listings. Directories allow you to submit URLs to categorized listings.

With search engines, users access the database by entering a keyword or phrase that interests them. The search engine then returns a list of Web pages from within its database that matches the query of the user. The results are ranked from most to least relevant, and there are often hundreds of thousands of listings returned with a single query. Directories allow users to submit URLs— usually via a feedback form—and then the information is processed.

There are hundreds of search engines and directories, some appealing to very specific audiences. The most popular search engines appeal to a broad audience and have an easy-to-use interface (see Figure A.3).

> <!--
> Here's a selection of popular search engines and directories:
>
> Yahoo!: http://www.yahoo.com/
>
> AltaVista: http://www.altavista.com/
>
> Excite: http://www.excite.com/
>
> Lycos: http://www.lycos.com/
>
> HotBot: http://www.hotbot.com/
>
> Infoseek: http://www.infoseek.com/
>
> Dogpile: http://www.dogpile.com/
>
> Google: http://www.google.com/
> -->

Figure A.3
Yahoo! has broad appeal and an easy-to-use interface.

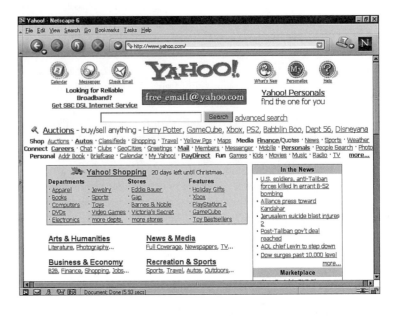

How to Get Listed

There are three ways you can get your site listed with a search engine or directory:

- Wait for search engines to find their way to your site.

- Submit your site to the search engines and directories with which you want to be listed.

- Use a listing service or software, usually for a fee.

Although your first choice is by far the easiest, it is also extremely ineffective. It's like an aspiring actress sitting in a Hollywood restaurant waiting to be discovered. It could happen, but it might take a long, long time, or it might never happen at all.

Submitting your site to be included in a search engine or directory database is remarkably easy. You simply go to the engine you are interested in and look for the "Submit URL" or "Add URL" button or link.

After filling in a few lines of information on a form, your site is submitted, and all that's left to do is wait for your site to appear in the listing.

If you find this process time-consuming, you can subscribe to the services offered at listing services such as Microsoft bCentral, `http://www.bcentral.com/` or `http://www.register-it.com/`, Netscape Netcenter's similar service.

These services submit your site to many search engines and directories, often charging different amounts for the type and/or number or search engines to which they submit your site, or offering free services along with subsidized advertising banners.

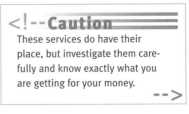

<!--Caution

These services do have their place, but investigate them carefully and know exactly what you are getting for your money.

-->

Preparing Your Site for Submission

Before submitting your site, make sure it is complete. With some engines taking weeks to list sites after submission, it is tempting to submit your site before it is finished. This may work in some cases, but many engines verify that your site is valid on the day of submission, and if they don't find your index or home page, your submission could be deleted.

Most engines only require that you submit your home page, because they will seek out links on that page and go down two or three levels to find other pages to include in their database. It doesn't hurt to submit a few of your most important pages in addition to your home page. It is not advisable to submit every single page within your site, however. Many engines are taking a stand against people they feel are abusing their service. Some monitor the number of pages a person submits and often limit the number of pages you can submit in one day.

Although submitting your site is easy, it is not enough to make search engines an effective marketing tool. Unless your site is returned within the first two or three pages of listings, it may never be seen. The challenge when submitting your site is to improve your ranking.

Using the `meta` Element and Attributes to Improve Your Ranking

Engines use two primary methods to rank Web pages: the text of the page and the information provided via the `meta` element's attribute values.

Investing some time in the use and placement of keywords within the text of your document and in your `meta` elements can improve your chances of a high rank.

For more information about the `meta` element, **see** "Global Structure and Syntax of Documents," **p. 95,** Chapter 5.

Consider your keywords carefully, and try to imagine the experience the user has when trying to find your product or service. For example, a user will undoubtedly come up with thousands of results if he or she enters "restaurants." But if a user was looking for a restaurant in Las Vegas, he or she would instinctively type "Las Vegas restaurants."

As a Las Vegas restaurateur, you would be wise to include "Las Vegas restaurants" in your keywords and leave out the vague "restaurants." It is also wise to include common misspellings in your keywords and international spellings of words like color (colour).

Include keywords within the text of your pages, and be aware of their placement. Prominent keywords are weighted higher than words or phrases that occur near the bottom of the page, and some engines only read the first 200 words of a Web page.

Many search engines take the number of keywords being searched and divide it by the number of words within a document. A short document with frequently repeating phrases or keywords can increase its relevancy and, in turn, its rank. However, what is good for the rank of your page isn't always good for the design and layout of your page.

```
<!--
An excellent site for detailed infor-
mation on how search engines
work, and how you can leverage
your power, try http://www.
searchenginewatch.com/.
-->
```

A common way to circumvent this is to create doorway pages that draw a user into your site through the search engine and then point the user to your home page. If you sold subscriptions to political magazines, you could have doorway pages for each of your magazine titles, and they could have keywords tailored specifically for them.

When users look up "Republicans Unite," they will find your doorway page with a short paragraph and a link saying, "Click Here for more information on Republicans Unite." Because you have only a short paragraph, the keywords and phrases only need to be mentioned a few times to be given more significance.

Because these secondary pages will only be used as an entrance for search engines, there is no need to link to them from your home page, so you won't affect the design of your site and users won't find them accidentally.

Keep keywords in mind when naming your HTML documents and titling your pages. If a user is searching for information on Roses, `http://www.yourpage.com/roses.html` will get a higher rank than `http://www.yourpage.com/redros1.html`. Giving your pages an appropriate title not only makes good design sense, but the title is also used by search engines and can increase the rank of your page if it includes the keywords.

Finding the right combination of keywords is not a science. It is impossible to predict exactly what someone will type into a search engine when looking for information on your product or service. You can do some research into the habits of searches by doing a few simple things. Ask your friends and colleagues what they would type in while searching for your product or service. You could even sit them down at a computer and write down the words and phrases they use when they are actively searching.

Another helpful device is Metaspy. This page (see Figure A.4) shows you exactly what keywords and phrases people are using when using the MetaCrawler search engine. The page automatically refreshes every 15 seconds and gives you a new perspective on how people search.

Figure A.4
Metaspy lets you take a look at how people type in search terms.

Avoiding Keyword Spam

As important as the preceding steps are to achieving a high ranking, there are some equally important things that you shouldn't do when preparing your pages for submission.

Avoid excessive repetition of keywords. Unscrupulous personalities have sometimes intentionally overused keywords to gain the attention of sites. This is a form of abuse and should be avoided at all costs! If you repeat a keyword more than six or seven times, a red flag goes up at many search engines, and your page could be disqualified from the listing. It is also not a good idea to include popular keywords that don't have any relevance to your site.

You should also be wary of using trademarked names in your keywords. *Playboy* successfully sued the owner of an adult entertainment site that used the *Playboy* name in its `meta` tags to attract users to his site. Although the Web has often had an aura of freedom, big business has been known to pay attention and crack down on trademark infringement.

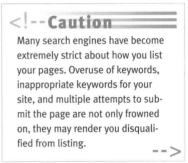

`<!--` Metaspy is located at `http://www.metaspy.com/`. There, you can choose from a general or adult option to see what keywords are being used. `-->`

`<!--Caution` Many search engines have become extremely strict about how you list your pages. Overuse of keywords, inappropriate keywords for your site, and multiple attempts to submit the page are not only frowned on, they may render you disqualified from listing. `-->`

Submission Follow-Up

After you have submitted your pages to the search engines you have selected, you have to plan your follow-up. Each search engine has its own turn-around time. Some take only a few hours to list your page, although others can take up to six weeks. It is important to record these turn-around times and check back to see if your site was accepted and, if so, its ranking. If your site has not been listed, you must resubmit it. Some search engines require that you e-mail any resubmissions; record this next to the turn-around time.

If your site was listed but had a poor ranking, visit some of the sites that made the highest ranking and use your browser to view the HTML markup. Compare their markup to that from your page and try to determine why their page was given a higher rank.

Hundreds, if not thousands, of new pages are submitted to search engines daily. Even if you get a high ranking, you could get moved down in the relevancy by new pages that are submitted. This is why follow-up is so important. You should monitor your rank on a regular basis, evaluating and resubmitting if your rank falls.

BANNER ADVERTISING

Banner ads are the most common form of advertising on the Web to date. It is rare to find a public site that doesn't include some form of banner ad somewhere within its pages. Such ads offer a unique approach to advertising not found in print or offline marketing. How often in offline advertising can the reader be at your store within seconds of viewing the ad? With banner advertising, potential customers are virtually one mouse click from your product.

This type of advertising also offers concrete results that you can analyze to better refine your advertising strategy.

To better understand this popular form of online advertising, it is important to be familiar with some industry buzzwords.

- **Banner ad**—This is a graphical advertisement, usually a GIF image and often animated. Standard industry size is 468×60 pixels, with weight between 5 and 10KB. However, new sizes have been emerging, as have different kinds of banner ads.

- **Click-through**—The number of people who click a banner ad and get to the advertiser's Web site.

- **Page impressions or page views**—These terms refer to the number of visitors who view a page.

- **CPM/Cost–per-Thousand**—When paying for advertising through CPM, you are paying for how many times your ad is displayed each month. This is the most common type of payment structure, and many larger sites require that you purchase a minimum amount of impressions.

- **Flat fee**—This is where a site owner charges you a flat fee per month for advertising on the site. This price structure is rare and is usually found on smaller sites.

Pricing Structures for Banner Advertising

Banner advertising can cost anywhere from thousands of dollars to no cost by using a banner exchange. There are a variety of price structures when dealing with paid advertising. The two most common include:

- **Impressions**—This is how many times the banner ad is actually seen onscreen.

- **Click-through**—When a site visitor clicks on a banner ad to visit the advertised site, this is referred to as *click-through*.

For example, Yahoo!, the most popular search engine, has a 500,000 impressions minimum. This is a very high number of impressions per ad, making the impression rate structure very expensive.

In terms of click-through rates, some sites charge you for how many people click your ad, not how many people see the ad. This payment structure is also quite rare. Click-through rates can range from a few cents to $1.00 per instance.

Another advertising method is banner exchange. A banner exchange is a good way to experiment with banner advertising without involving the large cost of paid advertising. The concept behind an exchange is simple, you allow other members of the exchange to post their banners on your site, and, in return, your banner gets posted on the sites of other members.

The drawback is, of course, having a banner on your page that can pull a user away before he or she has seen your site. There are, however, many advantages to using a banner exchange. Some exchanges let you target specific sites; this is important in effective banner advertising.

Some also offer a high ratio of exchange—you get two views for every one you display—and many will give you hundreds of "free" views for signing up.

Many exchanges also give you extensive performance statistics, including page impressions and click-throughs. It might be a good idea to use a banner exchange to get a feel for their effectiveness before moving on to paid advertising. Most exchanges don't permit adult entertainment sites to become part of the exchange, but be sure to check into their policies carefully before signing up.

<!--

Some popular Banner Exchange programs include the following:

Microsoft offers banner exchanges through `http://www.bcentral.com/`.

Link Buddies offers a 2:1 display ratio on 468×60 10KB ads at `http://www.linkbuddies.com/`.

-->

Common Design Guidelines

The industry size standard for an ad banner has long been 468×60 pixels, with a maximum weight of 10KB (see Figure A.5). As mentioned earlier, these are changing, so you'll want to check into the details for your particular projects. The most effective banners include some sort of animation to attract the eye.

Find the right consultant

Figure A.5
Common ad banner size.

Some sites require that your banners be smaller, with sizes ranging from 234×60 pixels to 400×40 pixels. Anything smaller than that wouldn't be considered banner advertising.

If you intend to design your banner yourself, you've got to be part graphic designer and part psychologist. But it's not that difficult if you follow a few simple rules.

Animation is important—it is said to increase click-through ratio by 25%—but don't over-animate. Simple, concise animation that doesn't distract from your message is best. It should catch the eye and then allow the user to read the ad.

Include the words "Click Here." As rudimentary as this may seem, new users won't realize that they are reading a hyperlinked ad and won't know how to get to the site that is being advertised. Including the words Click Here tells the user how to find your site and is said to increase the click-through ratio by 15%.

Be clear in what you are advertising. Don't try to trick people into coming to your site. You may get lots of click-throughs, but if the user feels tricked, he or she is less likely to buy your products or services. However, if you offer something free to customers on your Web site, a banner ad is the perfect place to advertise that.

You can use any graphics program to design your banner, just be sure that the output is of the quality you desire. This 468×60 banner will be representing your entire site, so it has to be of extremely high quality. There are also many GIF animation programs you can use to animate your banner. If you feel this is too daunting a task, there are many professional banner designers on the Web that will do it for you for a fee.

Banner Placement

The placement of your banner is of utmost importance if you want effective marketing. Putting a banner for your home renovations site on a teddy-bear collectors Web site will not be effective in drawing the customers you want. Put that same ad on a lumber store Web site and you will increase the effectiveness of your advertising by targeting the people who are most likely to want or need your service.

The most popular spot for banner advertising is on the top 10 search engines. One of the most effective forms of advertising within the search engines is purchasing a word or phrase. Using the Home Renovations site example, you could purchase the phrases "Home Repair" and "Home Renovation."

When a user types those phrases into the search engine, your banner ad will appear at the top of the page of results returned. This type of targeting is not inexpensive, however; it can cost upwards of $10,000!

It is also important to note the placement of your ad within the page itself. Top-of-the-page placement is most popular, but most users will scroll past the top of the page before they are ready to leave a site. Banners placed one-third of the way down the page have a 77% higher click-through rate than ads placed at the top.

Does Banner Advertising Really Work?

Banner ads are an industry standard, you see them everywhere. But how often do you click one? The industry average click-through rate is very low. Nielsen Netratings estimates as of July 2001 reflected 0.28% click-through which is far from spectacular. To get any effectiveness out of banner advertising, you must have a great ad that is specifically targeted to your audience. Without that, you might be better off not using banner ads at all.

OTHER ONLINE MARKETING TECHNIQUES

A number of other online marketing techniques will help you boost traffic to your site. They include e-mail, newsgroups, and offline marketing.

E-mail Marketing

E-mail is the number one reason people connect to the Internet. An e-mail address is becoming almost as important as a phone number as a method of communication. As its popularity grows, so does the opportunity to use it as a marketing tool.

One of the most common ways e-mail is used as a marketing tool is by unsolicited commercial e-mailing. This is similar to sending out flyers in "snail mail" (regular post-mail). This is an extremely ineffective marketing strategy, as most people not only dislike but out and out resent spam.

Spamming has such a negative reputation on the Internet that there are Web sites devoted to getting rid of it, such as Netizens Against Gratuitous Spamming (NAGS; http://www.nags.org/). E-mail users take great offense to receiving unsolicited advertising e-mail, much more so than to receiving flyers with their local newspaper. If you were to send out bulk e-mail, the response would be overwhelmingly negative and would not portray your business as trustworthy.

This shouldn't dissuade you from using e-mail as a marketing tool; there are some excellent and appropriate ways you can use this medium.

Encourage users of your Web site to sign up to receive product or services announcements. You can do this by including the option on a form or guestbook section of your site, and very clearly explaining what it is the site visitor is going to receive (or not receive) in kind. You then have the permission of the recipient, and your advertisement would not be considered unsolicited spam. Always include an easy way for people to unsubscribe to your notices.

Similarly, you can write a newsletter relating to the content on your site that can be sent to people who sign up on your Web site. If you had a site devoted to underground poetry, you could send a weekly newsletter giving some insight into the poets featured on your site in the upcoming week—include a sample of the poetry and then point them to your site for more.

This encourages people who have already visited your site to come back again and again. As with your product or services announcements, it is important to give the subscribers to your newsletter a clear and easy way to unsubscribe.

Another easy way to garner more exposure for your site through e-mail is widely underused, and that is including a signature file with all your e-mail correspondence. For example:

Joe Smith
http://www.homerepair.com/
Quality Home Repair, Free Consultations!

Most e-mail programs let you automate a signature that is placed at the bottom of every e-mail you send out. If your e-mail program doesn't have this feature, you should get in the habit of typing your URL and slogan (if you have one) at the bottom of every e-mail.

Newsgroups

Newsgroups are popular discussion groups. Similar to a bulletin board concept, users post messages that other users read and can then post responses or messages of their own. They are different from chat groups because the messages do not have to be read and responded to immediately. One user can post a message at 8 p.m. one day, and another user can read it hours, or even days, later.

There are thousands of newsgroups on every imaginable topic, and they easily make up the largest discussion group in the world.

Newsgroup users develop strong community ties with the other users of the group and are frequently more experienced Web users.

If you intend to use a particular newsgroup for marketing purposes, it is extremely important for you to become an active user of that newsgroup. If you just post an advertisement out of the blue, it will be written off as spam, and you'll get a negative response.

Using the Underground Poetry Web site example, you could subscribe to the `alt.arts. poetry.comments` newsgroup and start contributing. It's always a good idea to observe a newsgroup for a few days before jumping in with a post.

Different newsgroups have widely different unspoken rules that the users follow. It's just a case of understanding the feel of the group and respecting its community. After you start posting thoughtful or helpful messages, you will become part of the community. Then if you post a message informing the other users that you are having a special chat with a poet, it won't be viewed as spam. It's also a good idea to include your e-mail signature file on your newsgroup posts because it can provide a quick and easy link to your site for other newsgroup members.

Links

The beauty of the World Wide Web is its interconnectivity; you can start out on a home page about *The X-Files*, and a few hyperlinks later you are reading about antique grandfather clocks. The whole concept of the Web is these connections that take you to different places within a Web site and out onto the Web itself.

⇨ *For more information on linking, **see** "Adding Hypertext and Independent Links," **p. 155**, Chapter 7.*

Getting links to your site on other Web sites is an excellent way to get exposure. Just think about how many times you've discovered a new and wonderful site through a link on a site you visited.

Do some searching and find sites that you feel would appeal to your audience and contact the owners of those sites to ask for a link. Some site managers might ask for a fee, but many will do it simply for a reciprocal link. Negotiating links on other Web sites is a fantastic way to broaden your audience and your exposure.

Awards

Web site "awards" proliferate on the Internet; there are literally thousands of awards that are handed out every week. There are Cool Site awards, Wacky Site of the Week awards, and Rodney Dangerfield even has his Respect award. Some Web site owners display the awards they have been given as a badge of honor.

Most awards require that a Web site owner submit his or her site for review and, if deemed worthy, it gets the award. To display the award, the Web site owner must link the award back to the award-giving site. You give the award-giving site a free link by displaying any awards you receive.

Developing an award of your own can be a good way to increase exposure to your Web site. If you had a site that sold specialty cigars, you could develop the Humidor Award and hand it out to the people who devote their home pages to cigar appreciation. This would put a link to your Web site on the sites of your target audience.

Be careful to set a relatively high standard for the sites you award; your award loses its respectability if it's on every site a user visits.

WEB RINGS

Similar to awards, a Web ring is a grouping of sites that provide links to one another. Each member of the Web ring includes a graphic somewhere on their site stating their membership in the ring and providing a link to the next site in the ring.

WebRing at `http://www.webring.org/` has listings of the thousands of operating Web rings. If there isn't one that appeals to you or is appropriate for your site, they also have instructions for managing your own ring.

Careful! You don't want to join numerous rings because the resulting number of graphics and notices can look cluttered and unprofessional. It is also wise to carefully investigate the policies of the Web ring you are joining and the other member sites; you don't want to unknowingly provide a link to an inappropriate Web site.

> `<!--` **Caution**
>
> Web rings can be effective in drawing new users to your site, but they could also pull members away from your site to the next site in the ring. `-->`

OFFLINE MARKETING STRATEGIES

Marketing your site does not end with your online strategies. You must also market your site offline to attract new and regular users.

Watch a television ad for any upcoming movie, and you will notice the Web address for the movie's Web site at the bottom of the screen. Although these sites are basically an addition to the ad campaign surrounding the movie, the same concept can be used for advertising a site that has more business content.

Even talk show staples Sally Jessy Raphael and Oprah have jumped onto the Web-site bandwagon. Sally never ends a show without announcing: "Join me on my Web site at `Sallyjr.com`." Oprah has quite the Web site, too. Sitcoms and dramas have joined the online party as well.

It won't be long before every aspect of the entertainment and business world has a corresponding Web site.

When launching Melanie Doane's album *Adam's Rib*, Sony Canada made online music history by focusing its full marketing campaign on a Web site. The only print ads in the campaign were full color pictures of Melanie with her Web site URL written underneath; no other text appeared in the ads.

It was the first time that the Web site address was the focus of the ad and not simply an addendum.

Although Sony realized the power of the Web as an advertising venue, it knew it would have to initially draw people to the Web site. By using the provocative ads focusing on the Web address and not simply adding it to the bottom of a traditional ad, Sony drew press attention it might not have received otherwise.

Although you might not have the resources to launch a national print ad campaign, there are many things you can include in your offline marketing strategy to increase exposure to your Web site.

If you intend to do a lot of radio, print, and television marketing, it's a good idea to register a domain name. This in itself is a form of marketing; it becomes your brand.

If WebGuys hosted your Antique Teddy Bears Web site, your URL could end up something like `http://www.WebGuys.com/~abc/teddybear.html`. That certainly becomes harder to advertise and less recognizable than if you had registered the domain name `teddybears.com`.

If your Web site is a new addition to your business, announce it to all your current customers. Print up a special announcement and send it out to customers on your mailing list, encouraging them to visit your site.

Let them know if you provide any services on the site that you don't provide offline, such as special online contests, newsletters, or a catalog of products that are only available to online customers. Have your URL printed on all your company literature and letterhead and add it to all your employees' business cards.

Include your URL in all your print advertisements. Encourage people to visit your Web site for more information on your products and services. If you have an intuitive URL, consider placing ads just using the URL. This type of campaign would work for `http://www.HomeRepair.com/` but would not be effective for `http://www.townhall.com/repair.html`.

This same strategy applies to any radio or television ads you use in your advertising campaign—always mention your URL and even integrate your Web site activities into those of your business and current marketing strategies.

If your company regularly participates in trade shows, this is a terrific opportunity to promote your Web site. Bring along a laptop computer, have your Web site up and running in the browser, and encourage people to see what you've got. This is often an effective way to get right to your audience, showing them what you've got, and how it will benefit them.

CASE BY CASE: LEGAL ISSUES ON THE NET

Because copyright and trademark are of a complex nature, I took an opportunity to speak with Jodi Sax, an entertainment attorney and Internet legal consultant. She was able to clarify a number of issues that are of serious import to people working on the Web.

Here's what Jodi had to say about copyright:

"A common issue is that people don't realize that everything that is created under U.S. law has a copyright interest. It doesn't mean that someone has to register, or put a copyright notice on their materials."

The good news, then, is that whatever *original* information you create immediately and without registration or notice, is considered copyrighted. On the other hand, this means that original work belonging to *others* is protected as well—meaning that just because it's out on the Net with or without a copyright notice or registration, does *not* mean it's free for you to use.

"...it doesn't matter whether you credit your source or not—if you copy something and you don't have permission, you're committing copyright infringement."

This made me think of what is referred to as "fair use." As a writer, I often run into a situation where I want to use some section of material in an article or chapter. But fair use is apparently a more complicated issue than what I, and others, might think:

"Fair use is hard to quantify—this is the subject of litigation all the time. Someone might ask: Isn't it true that I can use 50 words without getting in trouble? There's no existing standard as to what constitutes fair use. It's a combination of factors, determined on a case-by-case basis."

Another question I've heard designers ask is whether their HTML markup is copyrighted. Sax describes this as an issue up for discussion these days.

"There are instances of people trying to claim rights to source code. To a certain extent, people can claim a right in that it's creative. But you can't claim an interest in something that is pure, factual information, such as `<a href>`.*"*

What about music on the Net?

"The problem is that everything is so unknown that it really depends upon bargaining power. Music on the Net is a big mess right now. For people that are building a basic home page, remember that anything you put on there has a copyright interest. If you want copyrighted music, you should go to ASCAP or BMI to purchase the license to use that music on your site. In a legitimate business, get a lawyer to help you learn what kinds of licenses you need."

Any final words of wisdom regarding copyright?

"I always tell people it's much better to be safe than sorry. Only copy something if you have permission, otherwise don't do it."

`<!--`

For helpful information on copyright and trademark concerns, visit these sites:

Fair Use issues are defined at `http://fairuse.stanford.edu/`.

Learn about copyright and find forms for registration at `http://www.loc.gov/copyright/`.

Search trademarks for free! Visit `http://www.uspto.gov/`.

If you'd like to license music for use on your site, check with ASCAP, `http://www.ascap.com/` and BMI, `http://www.bmi.com/`.

Visit Jodi Sax at her Web site, `http://www.lawgirl.com/`.

`-->`

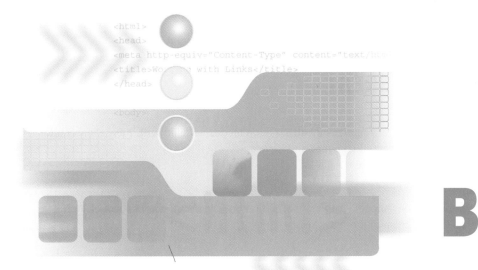

ANNOTATED RESOURCES FOR
WEB DEVELOPERS

B

IN THIS APPENDIX

Web Sites of Interest 564

Mailing Lists 565

Organizations 566

Education and Conferences 567

WEB SITES OF INTEREST

A List Apart

Run by Jeffrey Zeldman, *A List Apart* is a cutting-edge magazine filled with tutorials and information for the standards-oriented designer and developer.

http://www.alistapart.com/

Builder.com

C|NET's entry for Web developers. Targets information on just about every aspect of Web design. Vast resources, links, and great articles.

http://www.builder.com/

Devhead

Ziff-Davis offers up this extremely content-rich developer's site. You'll find news, features, and a wonderful script library for Java applets, JavaScript, and Perl/CGI scripts.

http://www.devhead.com/

IBM's developerWorks Web Architecture Zone

developerWorks offers extensive articles that delve deeply into detail. While there are tips and insights available, the real focus here is coverage on timely development topics with extensive and exhaustive examples for interested developers.

http://www.ibm.com/developerworks/

Hot Source HTML Help

A good source for all HTML help with a good section on DHTML.

http://www.sbrady.com/hotsource/

The HTML Bad Style Page

I rather like it for the fact that it shows you what NOT to do with HTML. Sometimes it is helpful to see a sample of poor workmanship to avoid it.

http://www.earth.com/bad-style/

Lynda.Com

Books, color references, and plenty of wisdom from Web graphics expert Lynda Weinman.

http://www.lynda.com/

Mark Radcliffe's Advanced HTML

Covering a variety of topics—includes helpful HTML hints.

http://www.neiljohan.com/html/advancedhtml.htm

Microsoft Developer Network

An unbelievable variety of information covering Web building and publishing. Lots of community, heavy on Internet Explorer-specific information.

http://msdn.microsoft.com/

Molly.Com

Books, links, and course information.

http://www.molly.com/

The Sevloid Guide to Web Design

A collection of over 100 tips, tricks, and techniques on every aspect of Web design. The tips are sorted into the categories of page layout, navigation, content, graphics, and more.

http://www.sev.com.au/webzone/design.asp

Generally Markup

Tutorials in XML and XSL authoring.

http://www.msxml.com

Web Designers Virtual Library (WDVL)

For years Alan Richmond put together one of the most accessible comprehensive resources for designers and developers. Now it's available via Internet.com.

http://www.wdvl.com/

Webmonkey's How To Guide for Web Developers

A well done, eye-pleasing page that has lots of tutorials and a great sense of humor.

http://hotwired.lycos.com/webmonkey/

Web Page Design for Designers

Explore the possibilities of Web design from the standpoint of a designer.

http://www.wpdfd.com/

Webreference

Vast references, tutorials, and hints about Web design.

http://www.webreference.com/

Webreview

A magazine with very good articles about Web design.

http://webreview.com/

Yale C/AIM Web Style Guide

An excellent, straightforward overview of interface, site design, graphics, multimedia, and, of course, HTML. Now available as a paper book as well.

http://info.med.yale.edu/caim/manual/contents.html

MAILING LISTS

Babble

Geared to advanced Web Design issues, and includes a lively exchange of information, resources, theories, and practices of designers and developers.

http://www.babblelist.com/

WebDesign-L

WebDesign-L is a mailing list community created in early 1997. The list is intended as a forum for those involved in creating the Web—whether for business, for self-expression, or for exploring the possibilities of a new medium.

http://www.webdesign-l.com/

XHTML-L

This forum is here for Web developers, Web designers, Webmasters, document managers, tool builders, integrators, and anyone else with an interest in XHTML to discuss strategies and tactics for making XHTML work.

Discussion of all versions of XHTML (1.0, 1.1, the upcoming 2.0) and their integration with other technologies (HTTP, CSS, MIME, XSLT, CC/PP, and more) is appropriate, as is discussion of XHTML's potential advantages and disadvantages relative to competing formats.

http://groups.yahoo.com/group/XHTML-L/

ORGANIZATIONS

The following organizations are geared toward helping designers inform themselves, organize, and work toward Web design excellence.

The Web Standards Project: WaSP

Dedicated to providing information and a voice in promoting Web recommendations.

http://www.webstandards.org/

World Wide Web Consortium

Standard, standard, who's got the standard? W3C is the first stop for all serious HTML and related technologies students.

http://www.w3.org/

The World Organization of Webmasters

Educational and peer-support resources for Webmasters.

http://www.joinwow.org/

The HTML Writers Guild

The world's largest international organization of Web designers. Offers community, classes, events, and an online bookstore.

http://www.hwg.org/

Association for Women in Computing

A general organization for women in the computer field.

http://www.awc-hq.org/

Webgrrls

The international networking group for women interested in the Internet. Multiple sites by country and city; start at the home page.

http://www.webgrrls.com/

EDUCATION AND CONFERENCES

The following organizations and events offer instruction for Web designers.

Design Workshops of Ojai

Hands-on classes, lectures, training, and seminars organized by Lynda Weinman.

http://www.lynda.com/classes/

DigitalThink

A variety of online offerings, with many oriented toward Web design and programming.

http://www.digitalthink.com/

MegaMind

Public and on-site training for interested individuals and corporations.

http://www.megamind.org/

Thunder Lizard Productions

With a focus on Web, computer graphics, and desktop publishing, Thunder Lizard offers a broad range of high-quality educational events.

http://www.thunderlizard.com/

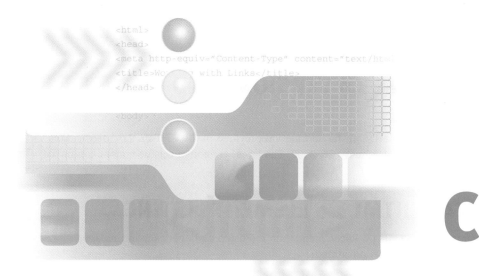

XHTML REFERENCE

IN THIS APPENDIX

Data Types XHTML 1.0 Versions and Specifications   **570**

Alphabetical XHTML 1.0 Element Listing   **570**

Common Attributes   **627**

Intrinsic Events   **627**

Data Types   **628**

DATA TYPES: XHTML 1.0 VERSIONS AND SPECIFICATIONS

This appendix is based primarily on the information provided in the *XHTML 1.0 Specification W3C Recommendation*, dated January 26, 2000. The latest version of this document can be found at **www.w3.org/tr/xhtml1/**.

ALPHABETICAL XHTML 1.0 ELEMENT LISTING

All the elements in the XTML 1.0 Recommendation are listed alphabetically in this appendix, and the following information is presented:

- **Element**—The heading shows at a glance:

  The general notation of the element. For example, `<table>…</table>`.

- **Usage**—A general description of the element.

- **Syntax**—The syntax of the element is given, showing where the attributes and content are placed. *Italicized* information (such as *attributes)* is not part of the element but indicates you should replace that with the values described further in the element reference.

- **Attributes**—Lists the attributes of the element, the actual values allowed or a value data type, and a short description of their effect. Some attributes have the actual values given, such as `shape="rect | circle | poly | default"`, with the default value in **bold**. Others have *italicized* data types, such as `charset="character-set"`. You should refer to the "Data Types" section at the end of this appendix for an explanation of the different data types allowed. Deprecated and Transitional DTD attributes are annotated with an icon. Strict DTD attributes have no icon and are present in the Transitional and Frameset DTDs. No attempt has been made in this reference to identify browser support for a given attribute.

- **Content**—Shows the possible content allowed inside an element, ranging from document data to a variety of other elements.

- **Browsers**—Shows if the element is supported in the top two current browsers (Microsoft Internet Explorer and Netscape Navigator) and the earliest version of the browser supporting the element.

- **Notes**—Relates any special considerations when using the element.

`<!--…-->` Comments

Usage:	An SGML construct used to insert information that is not to be displayed by the browser.
Syntax:	`<!-- content -->`
Attributes:	None

Content:	User text
Notes:	Comments are not restricted to one line and can be any length. The comment close delimiter ("--") and the markup declaration close delimiter (">") are not required to be on the same line as the markup declaration open delimiter ("<!") and the comment open delimiter ("--"). Placing double hyphens inside a comment technically ends the comment and any text after this might not be treated as a comment.
Browser:	MSIE 1; NNav 1

`<!DOCTYPE...>`

Usage:	Version information appears on the first line of an XHTML document in the form of a Standard Generalized Markup Language (SGML) declaration.
Syntax:	`<!doctype top-element availability "registration//organization//type label//language" "uri">`
Identifiers:	`top element`—Top-level element type declared in the DTD. For XHTML documents, this value is `xhtml`. `Availability`—Notes the availability. XHTML documents are publicly accessible objects; therefore this value is `public`. `Registration`—Indicates whether (+) or not (-) the following organization is registered by the ISO. The W3C is not a registered ISO organization. `Organization`—The organization responsible for the creation and maintenance of the DTD. The `W3c` is responsible for all official XHTML DTDs. `Type`—The type of object being referenced. In the case of XHTML, this is the XHTML `dtd`. `Label`—Describes or names the item being referenced. For XHTML 1.0 this refers to the XHTML DTD (Strict, Transitional, or Frameset) being called upon, `xhtml 1.0`, `xhtml 1.0 transitional`, or `xhtml 1.0 frameset` respectively. `Language`—The language of the object. For XHTML, this is `en`, meaning English. `Uri`—Provides the location of the DTD and any entity sets for user agents to download.
Notes:	Mandatory for document to be valid.
Browser:	None appear to process this information.

`<a>...</a>`

Usage:	Defines anchors that might be the source of one link and/or the destination of multiple links.
Syntax:	`<a attributes>content</a>`

Attributes: core—See "Common Attributes" section.

i18n—See "Common Attributes" section.

Events—See "Intrinsic Events" section.

charset="character-set"—Specifies the character encoding of the linked resource. Values (such as iso-8859-1 or us-ascii) must be strings approved and registered by IANA, The Internet Assigned Numbers Authority.

type="content-type"—Specifies the content or media (MIME) type (such as text/xhtml) of the linked resource.

name="data"—Names the current anchor so that it can be the destination of other links.

href="uri"—Specifies the location of the linked resource or anchor. Anchor URIs are identified by a pound sign # before the name value.

hreflang="language-code"—Identifies the language of the linked resource. This attribute might only be used in conjunction with the href attribute.

target="user-defined | _blank | _self | _parent | _top"—Identifies the frame in which the linked resource will be opened:

user-defined—Document opens in the frame designated by the user-defined name that is set by the name attribute of the frame. The name must begin with an alphabetic character.

_blank—Document opens in a new, unnamed window.

_self—Document opens in same frame as the originating link.

_parent—Document opens in the immediate frameset parent of the current frame, or itself if the current frame has no _parent.

_top—Document opens in the full, original window, or itself if the frame has no parent.

rel="link-type"—Defines the relationship between the document and that specified by the href attribute.

rev="link-type"—Defines the relationship between the resource specified by the href attribute and the current document.

accesskey="character"—Assigns an access key (or shortcut key) to the element. When the key is pressed, the element receives focus and is activated.

shape="rect | circle | poly | default"—Defines a region by its shape:

rect—Defines a rectangular region.

Circle—Defines a circular region.

Poly—Defines a polygonal region.

Default—Specifies the entire region.

coords="coordinates"—Defines the position of a shape displayed on screen. All values are of the length data type and separated by commas. The number and order of the coordinates depends on the value of the shape attribute:

rect—left-x, top-y, right-x, bottom-y

circle—center-x, center-y, radius

poly—x1, y1, x2, y2, ..., xn, yn

tabindex="number"—Defines the tabbing order between elements. This is the order (from lowest first to highest last) in which they receive focus when the user navigates through them using the Tab key.

onfocus="script"—Triggered when the element receives focus by either a pointing device (such as a mouse) or tabbed navigation.

onblur="script"—Triggered when the element loses focus by either a pointing device (such as a mouse) or tabbed navigation.

Content:	Zero or more inline elements, to include the following:
	Document text and entities
	Fontstyle elements (tt | i | b | u | s | strike | big | small)
	phrase elements (em | strong | dfn | code | samp | kbd | var | cite | abbr | acronym)
	special elements (img | applet | object | font | basefont | br | script | map | q | sub | sup | span | bdo | iframe)
	Form Control elements (input | select | textarea | label | button)
Notes:	Cannot be nested. Anchor names must be unique.
Browser:	MSIE 1; NNav 1

\<abbr\>...\</abbr\>

Usage:	Indicates an abbreviated form.
Syntax:	\<abbr attributes\>content\</abbr\>
Attributes:	core—See "Common Attributes" section.
	i18n—See "Common Attributes" section.
	events—See "Intrinsic Events" section.
Content:	Zero or more inline elements, to include the following:
	Document text and entities
	Fontstyle elements (tt | i | b | u | s | strike | big | small)
	Phrase elements (em | strong | dfn | code | samp | kbd | var | cite | abbr | acronym)
	Special elements (a | img | applet | object | font | basefont | br | script | map | q | sub | sup | span | bdo | iframe)
	Form Control elements (input | select | textarea | label | button)
Notes:	The content of the element contains the abbreviated form, which is expanded by using the title attribute.
Browser:	In IE 5.0 for the Mac, this will appear as a tooltip.

<acronym>...</acronym>

Usage:	Indicates an acronym.
Syntax:	<acronym attributes>content</acronym>
Attributes:	core—See "Common Attributes" section.
	i18n—See "Common Attributes" section.
	events—See "Intrinsic Events" section.
Content:	Zero or more inline elements, to include the following:
	Document text and entities
	Fontstyle elements (tt | i | b | u | s | strike | big | small)
	Phrase elements (em | strong | dfn | code | samp | kbd | var | cite | abbr | acronym)
	Special elements (a | img | applet | object | font | basefont | br | script | map | q | sub | sup | span | bdo | iframe)
	Form Control elements (input | select | textarea | label | button)
Notes:	The content of the element contains the acronym, which is expanded by using the title attribute.
Browser:	MSIE 5 will display title in a tool tip.

<address>...</address>

Usage:	Provides a special format for author or contact information.
Syntax:	<address attributes>content</address>
Attributes:	core—See "Common Attributes" section.
	i18n—See "Common Attributes" section.
	events—See "Intrinsic Events" section.
Content:	Zero or more inline elements, to include the following:
	Document text and entities
	Fontstyle elements (tt | i | b | u | s | strike | big | small)
	Phrase elements (em | strong | dfn | code | samp | kbd | var | cite | abbr | acronym)
	Special elements (a | img | applet | object | font | basefont | br | script | map | q | sub | sup | span | bdo | iframe)
	Form Control elements (input | select | textarea | label | button)
Browser:	MSIE 1; NNav 1

<applet>...</applet>

Usage:	Includes a Java applet.
Syntax:	<applet attributes>content</applet>
Attributes:	core—See "Common Attributes" section.
	codebase="uri"—Sets the base URI for the applet. If not specified, the default value is the base URI of the current document.

`archive="uri-list"`—List URIs (separated by commas) for archives containing classes and other resources that will be preloaded. This can significantly speed up applet performance.

`code="data"`—Identifies the compiled `.class` file of the applet, to include the path if necessary.

`object="data"`—Names a resource containing a serialized representation of an applet's state.

`alt="text"`—Alternate text to be displayed if the user agent cannot render the element.

`name="data"`—Specifies a name for the applet's instance.

`width="length"`—Sets the initial width of the applet's display area.

`height="length"`—Sets the initial height of the applet's display area.

`align="top | middle | bottom | left | right"`—Aligns the object with respect to context.

`top`—Vertically align the top of the object with the top of the current text line.

`middle`—Vertically align the center of the object with the current baseline.

`bottom`—Vertically align the bottom of the object with the current baseline.

`left`—Float object to the left margin.

`right`—Float object to the right margin.

`hspace="pixels"`—Sets the amount of space to be inserted to the left and right of the element.

`vspace="pixels"`—Sets the amount of space to be inserted to the top and bottom of the element.

Content: One or more `param` elements.

Zero or more block elements, to include the following:

    `p | dl | div | center | noscript | noframes | blockquote | form | isindex | hr | table | fieldset | address`

    Heading elements (`h1 | h2 | h3 | h4 | h5 | h6`)

    List elements (`ul | ol | dir | menu`)

    Preformatted elements (`pre`)

Zero or more inline elements, to include the following:

    Document text and entities

    Fontstyle elements (`tt | i | b | u | s | strike | big | small`)

    Phrase elements (`em | strong | dfn | code | samp | kbd | var | cite | abbr | acronym`)

    Special elements (`a | img | applet | object | font | basefont | br | script | map | q | sub | sup | span | bdo | iframe`)

    Form Control elements (`input | select | textarea | label | button`)

Notes: Either code or codebase attributes must be identified. If both are
                     used, the class files must match.

                     The content of the element is normally given to provide alternate con-
                     tent for user agents not configured to support Java Applets.

                     The `param` element (which resides in the `applet` element content)
                     should come before any other content.

                     Deprecated in favor of the `object` element.

Browser: MSIE 3; NNav 2

`<area />`

Usage: Specifies the geometric regions of a client-side imagemap and the
                     associated link.

Syntax: `<area attributes />`

Attributes: `core`—See "Common Attributes" section.

                     `i18n`—See "Common Attributes" section.

                     `events`—See "Intrinsic Events" section.

                     `shape="rect | circle | poly | default"`—Defines a region by its
                     shape:

                         `rect`—Defines a rectangular region.

                         `circle`—Defines a circular region.

                         `poly`—Defines a polygonal region.

                         `default`—Specifies the entire region.

                     `coords="coordinates"`—Defines the position of a shape displayed
                     onscreen. All values are of the length data type and separated by com-
                     mas. The number and order of the coordinates depends on the value
                     of the `shape` attribute:

                         `rect`—left-x, top-y, right-x, bottom-y

                         `circle`—center-x, center-y, radius

                         `poly`—x1, y1, x2, y2, ..., xn, yn

                     `href="uri"`—Specifies the location of the linked resource or anchor.

                     `target="user-defined | _blank | _self | _parent | _top"`—
                     Identifies the frame in which the linked resource will be opened:

                         `user-defined`—Document opens in the frame designated by the
                         `user-defined` name, which is set by the `name` attribute of the
                         frame. The `name` must begin with an alphabetic character.

                         `_blank`—Document opens in a new, unnamed window.

                         `_self`—Document opens in same frame as the originating link.

                         `_parent`—Document opens in the immediate `frameset` parent of
                         the current frame, or itself if the current frame has no parent.

                         `_top`—Document opens in the full, original window, or itself if the
                         frame has no parent.

                     `nohref`—Specifies that the region has no associated link.

alt="text"—Alternate text to be displayed if the user agent cannot render the element. This attribute is required in XHTML 1.0.
tabindex="number"—Defines the tabbing order between elements. This is the order (from lowest first to highest last) in which they receive focus when the user navigates through them using the Tab key.
accesskey="character"—Assigns an access key (or shortcut key) to the element. When the key is pressed, the element receives focus and is activated.
onfocus="script"—Triggered when the element receives focus either by pointing device (such as a mouse) or by tabbed navigation.
onblur="script"—Triggered when the element loses focus either by pointing device (such as a mouse) or by tabbed navigation.

Notes:	Because the area element has no content to be displayed, an imagemap consisting of one or more area must have alternate text for each area.
Browser:	MSIE 1; NNav 2

\<b\>...\</b\>

Usage:	Displays text with a boldface font style.
Syntax:	\<b attributes\>content\</b\>
Attributes:	core—See "Common Attributes" section.
	i18n—See "Common Attributes" section.
	events—See "Intrinsic Events" section.
Content:	Zero or more inline elements, to include the following:
	Document text and entities
	Fontstyle elements (tt | i | b | u | s | strike | big | small)
	Phrase elements (em | strong | dfn | code | samp | kbd | var | cite | abbr | acronym)
	Special elements (a | img | applet | object | font | basefont | br | script | map | q | sub | sup | span | bdo | iframe)
	Form Control elements (input | select | textarea | label | button)
Notes:	Although not deprecated, the W3C recommends using style sheets in place of this element.
Browser:	MSIE 1; NNav 1

\<base /\>

Usage:	Sets the base URI for the document.
Syntax:	\<base attributes /\>
Attributes:	href="uri"—Sets the absolute URI against which all other URIs are resolved.

target="user-defined | _blank | _self | _parent | _top"—
Identifies the frame in which the linked resource will be opened:

user-defined—Document opens in the frame designated by the
user-defined name that is set by the name attribute of the frame.
The name must begin with an alphabetic character.

_blank—Document opens in a new, unnamed window.

_self—Document opens in same frame as the originating link.

_parent—Document opens in the immediate frameset parent of the
current frame, or itself if the current frame has no parent.

_top—Document opens in the full, original window, or itself if the
frame has no parent.

Notes:	The base element must appear in the head element of the document, before any references to an external source.
Browser:	MSIE 1; NNav 1

<basefont />

Usage:	Sets the base font size.
Syntax:	<basefont attributes />
Attributes:	id="id"—A global identifier.
	size="data"—Sets the font size in absolute terms (1 through 7) or as a relative increase or decrease along that scale (for example +3).
	color="color"—Sets the font color. Colors identified by standard RGB in hexadecimal format (#rrggbb) or by predefined color name.
	face="data"—Identifies the font face for display (if possible). Multiple entries are listed in order of search preference and separated by commas.
Notes:	Deprecated in favor of style sheets.
	Changes to fonts through the font element are resolved against the values specified in the basefont element when present.
	There are conflicting implementations across browsers, and contents of tables appear not to be effected by basefont values.
Browser:	MSIE 1; NNav 1

<bdo>...</bdo>

Usage:	The bidirectional algorithm override element selectively turns off the default text direction.
Syntax:	<bdo attributes>content</bdo>
Attributes:	core—See "Common Attributes" section.
	lang="language-code"—Identifies the human (not computer) language of the text content or an element's attribute values.
	dir="ltr	rtl"—Specifies the text direction (left-to-right, right-to-left) of element content, overriding inherent directionality. This is a mandatory attribute of the bdo element.

Content:	Zero or more inline elements, to include the following:

    Document text and entities

    Fontstyle elements (tt | i | b | u | s | strike | big | small)

    Phrase elements (em | strong | dfn | code | samp | kbd | var | cite | abbr | acronym)

    Special elements (a | img | applet | object | font | basefont | br | script | map | q | sub | sup | span | bdo | iframe)

    Form Control elements (input | select | textarea | label | button)

Notes:	Care should be taken when using the bdo element in conjunction with special Unicode characters that also override the bidirectional algorithm.
	The bdo element should only be used when absolute control over character sequencing is required.
Browser:	MSIE 5

\<big\>…\</big\>

Usage:	Displays text in a larger font size.
Syntax:	\<big attributes\>content\</big\>
Attributes:	core—See "Common Attributes" section.
	i18n—See "Common Attributes" section.
	events—See "Intrinsic Events" section.
Content:	Zero or more inline elements, to include the following:

    Document text and entities

    Fontstyle elements (tt | i | b | u | s | strike | big | small)

    Phrase elements (em | strong | dfn | code | samp | kbd | var | cite | abbr | acronym)

    Special elements (a | img | applet | object | font | basefont | br | script | map | q | sub | sup | span | bdo | iframe)

    Form Control elements (input | select | textarea | label | button)

Notes:	Although not deprecated, the W3C recommends using style sheets in place of this element.
Browser:	MSIE 3; NNav 1.1

\<blockquote\>…\</blockquote\>

Usage:	Designates text as a quotation.
Syntax:	\<blockquote attributes\>content\</blockquote\>
Attributes:	core—See "Common Attributes" section.
	i18n—See "Common Attributes" section.
	events—See "Intrinsic Events" section.
	cite="uri"—The URI designating the source document or message.

Content: Zero or more inline elements, to include the following:
                        Document text and entities
                        Fontstyle elements (tt | i | b | u | s | strike | big | small)
                        Phrase elements (em | strong | dfn | code | samp | kbd | var |
                        cite | abbr | acronym)
                        Special elements (a | img | applet | object | font | basefont |
                        br | script | map | a | sub | sup | span | bdo | iframe)
                        Form Control elements (input | select | textarea | label |
                        button)
Notes: When compared with the a element, the blockquote element is used
                        for longer quotations and is treated as block-level content.
                        Quotation marks, if desired, should be added with style sheets.
                        Normally rendered as an indented block of text.
Browser: MSIE 1; NNav 1

\<body>...\</body>

Usage: Contains the content of the document.
Syntax: content or
                        <body attributes>content</body>
Attributes: core—See "Common Attributes" section.
                        i18n—See "Common Attributes" section.
                        events—See "Intrinsic Events" section.
                        onload="script"—Intrinsic event triggered when the document loads.
                        onunload="script"—Intrinsic event triggered when document
                        unloads.
                        background="uri"—Location of a background image to be displayed.
                        bgcolor="color"—Sets the document background color. Colors identi-
                        fied by standard RGB in hexadecimal format (#rrggbb) or by prede-
                        fined color name.
                        text="color"—Sets the document text color. Colors identified by
                        standard RGB in hexadecimal format (#rrggbb) or by predefined color
                        name.
                        link="color"—Sets the link color. Colors identified by standard RGB
                        in hexadecimal format (#rrggbb) or by predefined color name.
                        vlink="color"—Sets the visited link color. Colors identified by stan-
                        dard RGB in hexadecimal format (#rrggbb) or by predefined color
                        name.
                        alink="color"—Sets the active link color. Colors identified by stan-
                        dard RGB in hexadecimal format (#rrggbb) or by predefined color
                        name.

Content:	Zero or more block elements, to include the following:
	p | dl | div | center | noscript | noframes | blockquote | form | isindex | hr | table | fieldset | address
	Heading elements (h1 | h2 | h3 | h4 | h5 | h6)
	List elements (ul | ol | dir | menu)
	Preformatted elements (pre)
	Zero or more inline elements, to include the following:
	Document text and entities
	Fontstyle elements (tt | i | b | u | s | strike | big | small)
	Phrase elements (em | strong | dfn | code | samp | kbd | var | cite | abbr | acronym)
	Special elements (a | img | applet | object | font | basefont | br | script | map | a | sub | sup | span | bdo | iframe)
	Form Control elements (input | select | textarea | label | button)
	Zero or more block/inline elements to include (ins | del)
Notes:	Style sheets are the preferred method of controlling the presentational aspects of the body.
Browser:	MSIE 1; NNav 1

`<br />`

Usage:	Forces a line break.
Syntax:	`<br attributes />`
Attributes:	core—See "Common Attributes" section.
	`clear="left	all	right	none"`—Sets the location where next line begins after the line break. This attribute is deprecated in favor of style sheets:
	`left`—The next line begins at the nearest line on the left margin following any floating objects.
	`all`—The next line begins at the nearest line at either margin following any floating objects.
	`right`—The next line begins at the nearest line on the right margin following any floating objects.
	`none`—Next line begins normally.
Notes:	The `clear` attribute is deprecated in favor of style sheets.
Browser:	MSIE 1; NNav 1

`<button>...</button>`

Usage:	Creates a button.
Syntax:	`<button attributes>content</button>`
Attributes:	core—See "Common Attributes" section.
	i18n—See "Common Attributes" section.

events—See "Intrinsic Events" section.

name="data"—Defines a control name.

value="data"—Assigns an initial value to the button.

type="button | submit | reset"—Defines the type of button to be created:

button—Creates a push button.

submit—Creates a submit button.

reset—Creates a reset button.

disabled—Identifies that the button is unavailable in the current context.

tabindex="number"—Defines the tabbing order between elements. This is the order (from lowest first to highest last) in which they receive focus when the user navigates through them using the Tab key.

accesskey="character"—Assigns an access key (or shortcut key) to the element. When the key is pressed, the element receives focus and is activated.

onfocus="script"—Triggered when the element receives focus by either a pointing device (such as a mouse) or tabbed navigation.

onblur="script"—Triggered when the element loses focus by either a pointing device (such as a mouse) or tabbed navigation.

Content:	Zero or more block elements, to include the following:
	p | dl | div | center | noscript | noframes | blockquote | hr | table | address
	Heading elements (h1 | h2 | h3 | h4 | h5 | h6)
	List elements (ul | ol | dir | menu)
	Preformatted elements (pre)
	Zero or more inline elements, to include the following:
	Document text and entities
	Fontstyle elements (tt | i | b | u | s | strike | big | small)
	Phrase elements (em | strong | dfn | code | samp | kbd | var | cite | abbr | acronym)
	Special elements (img | applet | object | font | basefont | br | script | map | a | sub | sup | span | bdo)
Notes:	An important distinction between buttons created with the button element and those created by the input element is that the former allows content to be associated with the control.
Browser:	MSIE 4

<caption>…</caption>

Usage:	Displays a table caption.
Syntax:	<caption attributes>content</caption>
Attributes:	core—See "Common Attributes" section.
	i18n—See "Common Attributes" section.
	events—See "Intrinsic Events" section.

align="top | bottom | left | right"—Positions the caption relative to the table:

> top—Places the caption at the top of the table.
> bottom—Places the caption at the bottom of the table.
> left—Places the caption at the left side of the table.
> right—Places the caption at the right side of the table.

Content: Zero or more inline elements, to include the following:

> Document text and entities
> Fontstyle elements (tt | i | b | u | s | strike | big | small)
> Phrase elements (em | strong | dfn | code | samp | kbd | var | cite | abbr | acronym)
> Special elements (a | img | applet | object | font | _basefont | br | script | map | a | sub | sup | span |_bdo | iframe)
> Form Control elements (input | select | textarea | label | button)

Notes: The caption might only be placed immediately following the opening table tag, and only one caption per table is allowed.

Browser: MSIE 2; NNav 1.1

`<center>…</center>`

Usage: Centers content on the page.

Syntax: `<center attributes>content</center>`

Attributes: core—See "Common Attributes" section.
                  i18n—See "Common Attributes" section.
                  events—See "Intrinsic Events" section.

Content: Zero or more block elements, to include the following:

> p | dl | div | center | noscript | noframes | blockquote | form | isindex | hr | table | fieldset | address
> Heading elements (h1 | h2 | h3 | h4 | h5 | h6)
> List elements (ul | ol | dir | menu)
> Preformatted elements (pre)

Zero or more inline elements, to include the following:

> Document text and entities
> Fontstyle elements (tt | i | b | u | s | strike | big | small)
> Phrase elements (em | strong | dfn | code | samp | kbd | var | cite | abbr | acronym)
> Special elements (a | img | applet | object | font | basefont | br | script | map | a | sub | sup | span | bdo | iframe)
> Form Control elements (input | select | textarea | label | button)

Notes: Deprecated in favor of style sheets.

Using the center element is the equivalent of `<div align="center">`, although this method also is deprecated in favor of style sheets.

Browser: MSIE 1; NNav 1

`<cite>`...`</cite>`

Usage:	Identifies a citation or a reference.
Syntax:	`<cite attributes>content</cite>`
Attributes:	core—See "Common Attributes" section.
	i18n—See "Common Attributes" section.
	events—See "Intrinsic Events" section.
Content:	Zero or more inline elements, to include the following:

      Document text and entities

      Fontstyle elements (`tt` | `i` | `b` | `u` | `s` | `strike` | `big` | `small`)

      Phrase elements (`em` | `strong` | `dfn` | `code` | `samp` | `kbd` | `var` | `cite` | `abbr` | `acronym`)

      Special elements (`a` | `img` | `applet` | `object` | `font` | `basefont` | `br` | `script` | `map` | `a` | `sub` | `sup` | `span` | `bdo` | `iframe`)

      Form Control elements (`input` | `select` | `textarea` | `label` | `button`)

Notes:	Usually rendered as italicized text.
Browser:	MSIE 1; NNav 1

`<code>`...`</code>`

Usage:	Identifies a fragment of computer code.
Syntax:	`<code attributes>content</code>`
Attributes:	core—See "Common Attributes" section.
	i18n—See "Common Attributes" section.
	events—See "Intrinsic Events" section.
Content:	Zero or more inline elements, to include the following:

      Document text and entities

      Fontstyle elements (`tt` | `i` | `b` | `u` | `s` | `strike` | `big` | `small`)

      Phrase elements (`em` | `strong` | `dfn` | `code` | `samp` | `kbd` | `var` | `cite` | `abbr` | `acronym`)

      Special elements (`a` | `img` | `applet` | `object` | `font` | `basefont` | `br` | `script` | `map` | `a` | `sub` | `sup` | `span` | `bdo` | `iframe`)

      Form Control elements (`input` | `select` | `textarea` | `label` | `button`)

Notes:	Usually rendered in monospaced font.
Browser:	MSIE 1; NNav 1

`<col>`

Usage:	Groups columns within column groups to share attribute values.
Syntax:	`<col attributes />`
Attributes:	core—See "Common Attributes" section.
	i18n—See "Common Attributes" section.
	events—See "Intrinsic Events" section.

span="number"—Sets the number of columns the col element spans (1 is the default). Each column spanned in this manner inherits its attributes from that col element.

width="multi-length"—Sets the default width of each column spanned by the col element.

align="left | center | right | justify | char"—Horizontally aligns the contents of cells:

> left—Data and text aligned left. This is the default for table data.
>
> center—Data and text centered. This is the default for table headers.
>
> right—Data and text aligned right.
>
> justify—Data and text aligned flush with left and right margins.
>
> char—Aligns text around a specific character.
>
> char="character"—Sets a character on which the column aligns (such as ":"). The default value is the decimal point of the current language.

charoff="length"—Offset to the first alignment character on a line. Specified in number of pixels or a percentage of available length.

valign="top | middle | bottom | baseline"—Vertically aligns the contents of a cell:

> top—Cell data flush with top of cell.
>
> middle—Cell data centered in cell.
>
> bottom—Cell data flush with bottom of cell.
>
> baseline—Aligns all cells in a row with this attribute set. Textual data aligned along a common baseline.

Notes:	The col element groups columns only to share attribute values, not group them structurally, which is the role of the colgroup element.
Browser:	MSIE 3

<colgroup>...</colgroup>

Usage:	Defines a column group.
Syntax:	<colgroup attributes />content
	or
	<colgroup attributes>content</colgroup>
Attributes:	core—See "Common Attributes" section.
	i18n—See "Common Attributes" section.
	events—See "Intrinsic Events" section.
	span="number"—Sets the number of columns in a colgroup (1 is the default). Each column spanned in this manner inherits its attributes from that colgroup element.
	width="multi-length"—Sets the default width of each column spanned by the colgroup element. An additional value is "0*" (zero asterisk), which means that the width of the each column in the group should be the minimum width necessary to hold the column's contents.

align="left | center | right | justify | char"—Horizontally aligns the contents of cells:

left—Data and text aligned left. This is the default for table data.

center—Data and text centered. This is the default for table headers.

right—Data and text aligned right.

justify—Data and text aligned flush with left and right margins.

char—Aligns text around a specific character.

char="character"—Sets a character on which the column aligns (such as ":"). The default value is the decimal point of the current language.

charoff="length"—Offset to the first alignment character on a line. Specified in number of pixels or a percentage of available length.

valign="top | middle | bottom | baseline"—Vertically aligns the contents of a cell:

top—Cell data flush with top of cell.

middle—Cell data centered in cell.

bottom—Cell data flush with bottom of cell.

baseline—Aligns all cells in a row with this attribute set. Textual data aligned along a common baseline.

Notes: The purpose of the colgroup element is to provide structure to table columns.

Browser: MSIE 3

\<dd\>...\</dd\>

Usage: Contains the definition description used in a dl (definition list) element.

Syntax: <dd attributes>content</dd>

Attributes: core—See "Common Attributes" section.

i18n—See "Common Attributes" section.

events—See "Intrinsic Events" section.

compact—Tells the browser to attempt to display the list more compactly.

Content: Zero or more block elements, to include the following:

p | dl | div | center | noscript | noframes | blockquote | form | isindex | hr | table | fieldset | address

Heading elements (h1 | h2 | h3 | h4 | h5 | h6)

List elements (ul | ol | dir | menu)

Preformatted elements (pre)

Zero or more inline elements, to include the following:

Document text and entities

Fontstyle elements (tt | i | b | u | s | strike | big | small)

Phrase elements (em | strong | dfn | code | samp | kbd | var | cite | abbr | acronym)

Special elements (a | img | applet | object | font | basefont | br | script | map | a | sub | sup | span | bdo | iframe)

Form Control elements (input | select | textarea | label | button)

Notes: The dd element might contain block-level or inline content.
Browser: MSIE 1; NNav 1

`<del>...</del>`

Usage: Identifies and displays text as having been deleted from the document
                in relation to a previous version.
Syntax: `<del attributes>content</del>`
Attributes: `core`—See "Common Attributes" section.
                `i18n`—See "Common Attributes" section.
                `events`—See "Intrinsic Events" section.
                `cite="uri"`—A URI pointing to a document that should give reason
                for the change.
                `datetime="datetime"`—Sets the date and time of the change.
Content: Zero or more block elements, to include the following:
                   `p | dl | div | center | noscript | noframes | blockquote |`
                   `form | isindex | hr | table | fieldset | address`
                   Heading elements (`h1 | h2 | h3 | h4 | h5 | h6`)
                   List elements (`ul | ol | dir | menu`)
                   Preformatted elements (`pre`)
                Zero or more inline elements, to include the following:
                   Document text and entities
                   Fontstyle elements (`tt | i | b | u | s | strike | big | small`)
                   Phrase elements (`em | strong | dfn | code | samp | kbd | var |`
                   `cite | abbr | acronym`)
                   Special elements (`a | img | applet | object | font | basefont |`
                   `br | script | map | a | sub | sup | span | bdo | iframe`)
                   Form Control elements (`input | select | textarea | label |`
                   `button`)
Notes: Might serve as a block-level or inline element, but not both at the
                same time. Changes to nested block-level content should be made at
                the lowest level.
Browser: MSIE 4

`<dfn>...</dfn>`

Usage: The defining instance of an enclosed term.
Syntax: `<dfn attributes>content</dfn>`
Attributes: `core`—See "Common Attributes" section.
                `i18n`—See "Common Attributes" section.
                `events`—See "Intrinsic Events" section.
Content: Zero or more inline elements, to include the following:
                   Document text and entities
                   Fontstyle elements (`tt | i | b | u | s | strike | big | small`)

Phrase elements (em | strong | dfn | code | samp | kbd | var | cite | abbr | acronym)

Special elements (a | img | applet | object | font | basefont | br | script | map | a | sub | sup | span | bdo | iframe)

Form Control elements (input | select | textarea | label | button)

Notes:	Usually rendered in italics.
Browser:	MSIE 1

\<dir\>...\</dir\>

Usage:	Creates a multicolumn directory list.
Syntax:	\<dir attributes\>content\</dir\>
Attributes:	core—See "Common Attributes" section.
	i18n—See "Common Attributes" section.
	events—See "Intrinsic Events" section.
	compact—Tells the browser to attempt to display the list more compactly.
Content:	One or more li element, which might contain the following:

List elements (ul | ol | dir | menu)

Zero or more inline elements, to include the following:

Document text and entities

Fontstyle elements (tt | i | b | u | s | strike | big | small)

Phrase elements (em | strong | dfn | code | samp | kbd | var | cite | abbr | acronym)

Special elements (a | img | applet | object | font | basefont | br | script | map | a | sub | sup | span | bdo | iframe)

Form Control elements (input | select | textarea | label | button)

Notes:	Deprecated in favor of unordered lists (UL).
Browser:	MSIE 1; NNav 1

\<div\>...\</div\>

Usage:	Creates author-defined block-level structure to the document.
Syntax:	\<div attributes\>content\</div\>
Attributes:	core—See "Common Attributes" section.
	i18n—See "Common Attributes" section.
	events—See "Intrinsic Events" section.
	align="left | center | right | justify"—Horizontal alignment with respect to context. The default depends on the directionality of the text. For left-to-right it is left and for right-to-left it is right:

left—Text aligned left.

center—Text centered.

right—Text aligned right.

justify—Text aligned flush with left and right margins.

Content:	Zero or more block elements, to include the following:
	p | dl | div | center | noscript | noframes | blockquote | form | isindex | hr | table | fieldset | address
	Heading elements (h1 | h2 | h3 | h4 | h5 | h6)
	List elements (ul | ol | dir | menu)
	Preformatted elements (pre)
	Zero or more inline elements, to include the following:
	Document text and entities
	Fontstyle elements (tt | i | b | u | s | strike | big | small)
	Phrase elements (em | strong | dfn | code | samp | kbd | var | cite | abbr | acronym)
	Special elements (a | img | applet | object | font | basefont | br | script | map | a | sub | sup | span | bdo | iframe)
	Form Control elements (input | select | textarea | label | button)
Notes:	Used in conjunction with style sheets this is a powerful device for adding custom block-level structure.
	Might be nested.
Browser:	MSIE 3; NNav 2

<dl>...</dl>

Usage:	Creates a definition list.
Syntax:	<dl attributes>content</dl>
Attributes:	core—See "Common Attributes" section.
	i18n—See "Common Attributes" section.
	events—See "Intrinsic Events" section.
	compact—Tells the browser to attempt to display the list more compactly.
Content:	One or more dt or dd elements.
Notes:	This element provides the structure necessary to group definition terms and descriptions into a list. Aside from those elements (dt and dl), no other content is allowed.
Browser:	MSIE 1; NNav 1

<dt>...</dt>

Usage:	The definition term (or label) used within a dl (definition list) element.
Syntax:	<dt attributes>content</dt>
Attributes:	core—See "Common Attributes" section.
	i18n—See "Common Attributes" section.
	events—See "Intrinsic Events" section.
	compact—Tells the browser to attempt to display the list more compactly.

Content:	Zero or more inline elements, to include the following: Document text and entities Fontstyle elements (tt | i | b | u | s | strike | big | small) Phrase elements (em | strong | dfn | code | samp | kbd | var | cite | abbr | acronym) Special elements (a | img | applet | object | font | _basefont | br | script | map | a | sub | sup | span | _bdo | iframe) Form Control elements (input | select | textarea | label | button)
Notes:	The dt element might only contain inline content.
Browser:	MSIE 1; NNav 1

<em>…</em>

Usage:	Displays text with emphasis in relation to normal text.
Syntax:	<em attributes>content</em>
Attributes:	core—See "Common Attributes" section. i18n—See "Common Attributes" section. events—See "Intrinsic Events" section.
Content:	Zero or more inline elements, to include the following: Document text and entities Fontstyle elements (tt | i | b | u | s | strike | big | small) Phrase elements (em | strong | dfn | code | samp | kbd | var | cite | abbr | acronym) Special elements (a | img | applet | object | font |basefont | br | script | map | a | sub | sup | span | bdo | iframe) Form Control elements (input | select | textarea | label | button)
Notes:	Usually rendered in italics.
Browser:	MSIE 1; NNav 1

<fieldset>…</fieldset>

Usage:	Groups related controls and labels of a form.
Syntax:	<fieldset attributes>content</fieldset>
Attributes:	core—See "Common Attributes" section. i18n—See "Common Attributes" section. events—See "Intrinsic Events" section.
Content:	One legend element. Zero or more block elements, to include the following: p | dl | div | center | noscript | noframes | blockquote | form | isindex | hr | table | fieldset | address Heading elements (h1 | h2 | h3 | h4 | h5 | h6) List elements (ul | ol | dir | menu) Preformatted elements (pre)

Zero or more inline elements, to include the following:
Document text and entities
Fontstyle elements (tt | i | b | u | s | strike | big | small)
Phrase elements (em | strong | dfn | code | samp | kbd | var |
cite | abbr | acronym)
Special elements (a | img | applet | object | font | basefont |
br | script | map | a | sub | sup | span | bdo | iframe)
Form Control elements (input | select | textarea | label |
button)

Notes: Proper use of the `fieldset` element facilitates user understanding of
the form and eases navigation.

Browser: MSIE 4

<font>...</font>

Usage: Changes the font size and color.

Syntax: `<font attributes>content</font>`

Attributes: core—See "Common Attributes" section.
i18n—See "Common Attributes" section.
`size="data"`—Sets the font size in absolute terms (1 through 7) or as
a relative increase or decrease along that scale (for example, +3). If a
base font is not specified, the default is 3.
`color="color"`—Sets the font color. Colors are identified by standard
RGB in hexadecimal format (#rrggbb) or by predefined color name.
`face="data"`—Identifies the font face for display (if possible). Multiple
entries are listed in order of search preference and separated by commas.

Content: Zero or more inline elements, to include the following:
Document text and entities
Fontstyle elements (tt | i | b | u | s | strike | big | small)
Phrase elements (em | strong | dfn | code | samp | kbd | var |
cite | abbr | acronym)
Special elements (a | img | applet | object | font | basefont |
br | script | map | a | sub | sup | span | bdo | iframe)
Form Control elements (input | select | textarea | label |
button)

Notes: Deprecated in favor of style sheets.
Changes to fonts through the `font` element are resolved against the
values specified in the `basefont` element when present.

Browser: MSIE 1; NNav 1

<form>...</form>

Usage: Creates a form that holds controls for user input.

Syntax: `<form attributes>content</form>`

Attributes: core—See "Common Attributes" section.

i18n—See "Common Attributes" section.

events—See "Intrinsic Events" section.

action="uri"—Specifies the form processing agent that will process the submitted form.

method="get | post"—Specifies the HTTP method used to submit the form data:

get—The form data set is appended to the URI specified by the action attribute (with a question mark ("?") as separator), and this new URI is sent to the processing agent.

post—The form data set is included in the body of the form and sent to the processing agent.

enctype="content-type"—Specifies the content or media (MIME) type used to transmit the form to the server. The default is "application/x-www-form-urlencoded".

onsubmit="script"—Triggered when the form is submitted.

onreset="script"—Triggered when the form is reset.

target="user-defined | _blank | _self | _parent | _top"— Identifies the frame in which the linked resource will be opened:

user-defined—Document opens in the frame designated by the user-defined name, which is set by the name attribute of the frame. The name must begin with an alphabetic character.

_blank—Document opens in a new, unnamed window.

_self—Document opens in the same frame as the originating link.

_parent—Document opens in the immediate frameset parent of the current frame, or itself if the current frame has no parent.

_top—Document opens in the full, original window, or itself if the frame has no parent.

accept-charset="character-set"—Specifies the list of character encodings for input data that must be accepted by the server processing this form.

accept="content-types"—List of content types.

Content: Zero or more block elements, to include the following:

p | dl | div | center | noscript | noframes | blockquote | isindex | hr | table | fieldset | address

Heading elements (h1 | h2 | h3 | h4 | h5 | h6)

List elements (ul | ol | dir | menu)

Preformatted elements (pre)

Zero or more inline elements, to include the following:

Document text and entities

Fontstyle elements (tt | i | b | u | s | strike | big | small)

Phrase elements (em | strong | dfn | code | samp | kbd | var | cite | abbr | acronym)

Special elements (a | img | applet | object | font | basefont |
br | script | map | a | sub | sup | span | bdo | iframe)
Form Control elements (input | select | textarea | label |
button)

Browser: MSIE 1; NNav 1

<frame />

Usage: Defines the contents and appearance of a single frame or subwindow.

Syntax: <frame attributes />

Attributes: core—See "Common Attributes" section.

longdesc="uri"—Links to a resource containing a long description of
the frame.

name="data"—Names the current frame.

src="uri"—Specifies the URI containing the initial contents of the
frame.

frameborder="1 | 0"—Toggles borders to be drawn around the frame.

1—A border is drawn.

0—A border is not drawn.

marginwidth="pixels"—Sets the margin between the contents of the
frame and its left and right borders.

marginheight="pixels"—Sets the margin between the contents of
the frame and its top and bottom borders.

noresize—Prohibits resizing of the frame by the user agent.

scrolling="auto | yes | no"—Determines whether the user agent
provides scrolling devices for the frame:

auto—The user agent provides scrolling devices if necessary.

yes—Scrolling devices are provided even if not necessary.

no—Scrolling devices are not provided even if necessary.

Notes: The contents of a frame must not be in the same document as the
frame's definition.

Browser: MSIE 3; NNav 2

<frameset>...</frameset>

Usage: Defines the layout of frames within the main window.

Syntax: <frameset attributes>content</frameset>

Attributes: core—See "Common Attributes" section.

rows="multi-length"—Defines the horizontal layout, or number of
rows, of the frameset.

cols="multi-length"—Defines the vertical layout, or number of
columns, of the frameset.

onload="script"—Intrinsic event triggered when the document loads.

onunload="script"—Intrinsic event triggered when the document
unloads.

Content:	One or more `frameset` or `frame` elements.
	Zero or one `noframes` element
Notes:	A frameset document contains the `head` element, which is followed immediately by a `frameset`. Content between the `head` and `frameset` will void the frameset. The only place the body element is allowed within a frameset document is within the `noframes` tags.
Browser:	MSIE 3; NNav 2

`<h1>`...`</h1>` Through `<h6>`...`</h6>`

Usage:	The six headings (h1 is the uppermost, or most important) structure information in a hierarchical fashion.
Syntax:	`<hx attributes>content</hx>`
Attributes:	`core`—See "Common Attributes" section.
	`i18n`—See "Common Attributes" section.
	`events`—See "Intrinsic Events" section.
	`align="left	center	right	justify"`—Horizontal alignment with respect to context. The default depends on the directionality of the text. For left-to-right it is `left`, and for right-to-left it is `right`:
	`left`—Text aligned left.
	`center`—Text centered.
	`right`—Text aligned right.
	`justify`—Text aligned flush with left and right margins.
Content:	Zero or more inline elements, to include the following:
	Document text and entities
	Fontstyle elements (`tt | i | b | u | s | strike | big | small`)
	Phrase elements (`em | strong | dfn | code | samp | kbd | var | cite | abbr | acronym`)
	Special elements (`a | img | applet | object | font | basefont | br | script | map | a | sub | sup | span | bdo | iframe`)
	Form Control elements (`input | select | textarea | label | button`)
Notes:	The headings are rendered from large to small in order of importance (1 to 6).
Browser:	MSIE 1; NNav 1

`<head>`...`</head>`

Usage:	Contains elements that provide information to users and search engines as well as containing other data that is not considered to be document content (for example, style and script information).
Syntax:	`content`
	or
	`<head attributes>content</head>`

Attributes:	i18n—See "Common Attributes" section.
	profile="uri"—Specifies the location of one or more meta data profiles.
Content:	One title element, zero or one isindex, and zero or one base elements.
	Zero or more script, style, meta, link, object elements.
Notes:	Information in the head is not displayed (with the exception of the title, which is displayed in the title bar of the browser).
	The title element is required.
Browser:	MSIE 1; NNav 1

\<hr /\>

Usage:	Horizontal rules displayed to separate sections of a document.
Syntax:	\<hr attributes /\>
Attributes:	core—See "Common Attributes" section.
	i18n—See "Common Attributes" section (as per the XHTML 1.0 Specification Errata, 14 April 1998).
	events—See "Intrinsic Events" section.
	align="left | center | right"—Alignment of the hr with respect to the surrounding context:
	left—Rule aligned left.
	center—Rule centered.
	right—Rule aligned right.
	noshade—Renders the hr as a solid color rather than a shaded bump.
	size="length"—Sets the length of the hr.
	width="length"—Sets the height of the hr.
Browser:	MSIE 1; NNav 1

\<html\>...\</html\>

Usage:	The root container of an HTML or XHTML document.
Syntax:	content
	\<html attributes\>content\</html\>
Attributes:	i18n—See "Common Attributes" section.
	version="data"—Specifies the XHTML DTD that governs the current document.
Content:	One head element and one body element if using the Strict or Transitional DTD.
	One head element and one frameset element if using the Frameset DTD.
Notes:	version has been deprecated because of its redundancy with the \<!doctype\> declaration.
Browser:	MSIE 1; NNav 1

`<i>...</i>`

Usage:	Displays italicized text.
Syntax:	`<i attributes>content</i>`
Attributes:	`core`—See "Common Attributes" section.
	`i18n`—See "Common Attributes" section.
	`events`—See "Intrinsic Events" section.
Content:	Zero or more inline elements, to include the following:

Document text and entities

Fontstyle elements (`tt | i | b | u | s | strike | big | small`)

Phrase elements (`em | strong | dfn | code | samp | kbd | var | cite | abbr | acronym`)

Special elements (`a | img | applet | object | font | basefont | br | script | map | a | sub | sup | span | bdo | iframe`)

Form Control elements (`input | select | textarea | label | button`)

Notes:	Although not deprecated, the W3C recommends using style sheets in place of this element.
Browser:	MSIE 1; NNav 1

`<iframe>...</iframe>`

Usage:	Creates an inline frame, or window subdivision, within a document.
Syntax:	`<iframe attributes>content</iframe>`
Attributes:	`core`—See "Common Attributes" section.

`longdesc="uri"`—Links to a resource containing a long description of the frame.

`name="data"`—Names the current frame.

`src="uri"`—Specifies the URI containing the initial contents of the frame.

`frameborder="1 | 0"`—Toggles borders to be drawn around the frame:

    `1`—A border is drawn.

    `0`—A border is not drawn.

`marginwidth="pixels"`—Sets the margin between the contents of the frame and its left and right borders.

`marginheight="pixels"`—Sets the margin between the contents of the frame and its top and bottom borders.

`noresize`—Prohibits the user agent from resizing the frame.

`scrolling="auto | yes | no"`—Determines whether the user agent provides scrolling devices for the frame:

    `auto`—The user agent provides scrolling devices if necessary.

    `yes`—Scrolling devices are provided even if not necessary.

    `no`—Scrolling devices are not provided even if necessary.

align="top | middle | bottom | left | right"—Aligns the object with respect to context:

  top—Vertically aligns the top of the object with the top of the current text line.

  middle—Vertically aligns the center of the object with the current baseline.

  bottom—Vertically aligns the bottom of the object with the current baseline.

  left—Floats object to the left margin.

  right—Floats object to the right margin.

  height="length"—Sets the frame height.

  width="length"—Sets the frame width.

Content: Zero or more block elements, to include the following:

  p | dl | div | center | noscript | noframes | blockquote | form | isindex | hr | table | fieldset | address

  Heading elements (h1 | h2 | h3 | h4 | h5 | h6)

  List elements (ul | ol | dir | menu)

  Preformatted elements (pre)

  Zero or more inline elements, to include the following:

  Document text and entities

  Fontstyle elements (tt | i | b | u | s | strike | big | small)

  Phrase elements (em | strong | dfn | code | samp | kbd | var | cite | abbr | acronym)

  Special elements (a | img | applet | object | font | basefont | br | script | map | a | sub | sup | span | bdo | iframe)

  Form Control elements (input | select | textarea | label | button)

Notes: The content to be displayed is specified by the src attribute. The content of the element will only be displayed in user agents that do not support frames.

Browser: MSIE 3

`<img />`

Usage: Includes an image in the document.

Syntax: <img attributes />

Attributes: core—See "Common Attributes" section.

  i18n—See "Common Attributes" section.

  events—See "Intrinsic Events" section.

  src="uri"—Specifies the location of the image to load into the document.

  alt="text"—Alternate text to be displayed if the user agent cannot render the element.

longdesc="uri"—Links to a resource containing a long description of the resource.

height="length"—Sets the display height of the image.

width="length"—Sets the display width of the image.

usemap="uri"—Associates an imagemap as defined by the map element with this image.

ismap—Used to define a server-side imagemap. The img element must be included in an a element and the ismap attribute set.

align="top | middle | bottom | left | right"—Aligns the object with respect to context:

> top—Vertically aligns the top of the object with the top of the current text line.
>
> middle—Vertically aligns the center of the object with the current baseline.
>
> bottom—Vertically aligns the bottom of the object with the current baseline.
>
> left—Floats object to the left margin.
>
> right—Floats object to the right margin.

border="length"—Sets the border width of the image.

hspace="pixels"—Sets the amount of space to be inserted to the left and right of the element.

vspace="pixels"—Sets the amount of space to be inserted to the top and bottom of the element.

Notes:	Has no content.
Browser:	MSIE 1; NNav 1

`<input />`

Usage:	Defines controls used in forms.
Syntax:	`<input attributes />`
Attributes:	core—See "Common Attributes" section.

i18n—See "Common Attributes" section.

events—See "Intrinsic Events" section.

type="text | password | checkbox | radio | submit | reset | file | hidden | image | button"—Defines the type of control to create.

text—Creates a single-line text input control.

password—Creates a single-line text input control that hides the characters from the user.

checkbox—Creates a check box.

radio—Creates a radio button.

submit—Creates a submit button.

reset—Creates a reset button.

file—Creates a file select control.

hidden—Creates a hidden control.

`image`—Creates a graphical submit button that uses the `src` attribute to locate the image used to decorate the button.

`button`—Creates a pushbutton.

`name="data"`—Assigns a control name.

`value="data"`—Sets the initial value of the control.

`checked`—Sets option buttons and check boxes to a checked state.

`disabled`—Disables the control in this context.

`readonly`—Changes to the control (text and password) are prohibited.

`size="data"`—Sets the initial size of the control.

`maxlength="number"`—Sets the maximum number of characters a user might enter into a text or password control.

`src="uri"`—Identifies the location of the image when the control type has been set to `image`.

`alt="data"`—Provides a short description of the control.

`usemap="uri"`—Associates an imagemap as defined by the `map` element with this control.

`tabindex="number"`—Defines the tabbing order between elements. This is the order (from lowest first to highest last) in which they receive focus when the user navigates through them using the Tab key.

`accesskey="character"`—Assigns an access key (or shortcut key) to the element. When the key is pressed, the element receives focus and is activated.

`onfocus="script"`—Triggered when the element receives focus by either a pointing device (such as a mouse) or tabbed navigation.

`onblur="script"`—Triggered when the element loses focus by either a pointing device (such as a mouse) or tabbed navigation.

`onselect="script"`—The event that occurs when text is selected in a text field.

`onchange="script"`—The event that occurs when a control loses the input focus and its value has been modified since gaining focus.

`accept="content-type"`—A list of content (MIME) types the server will accept for file upload.

`align="top | middle | bottom | left | right"`—Aligns the object with respect to context:

> `top`—Vertically aligns the top of the object with the top of the current text line.
>
> `middle`—Vertically aligns the center of the object with the current baseline.
>
> `bottom`—Vertically aligns the bottom of the object with the current baseline.
>
> `left`—Floats object to the left margin.
>
> `right`—Floats object to the right margin.

Notes:	Has no content.
Browser:	MSIE 1; NNav 1

<ins>…</ins>

Usage:	Identifies and displays text as having been inserted in the document in relation to a previous version.
Syntax:	`<ins attributes>content</ins>`
Attributes:	`core`—See "Common Attributes" section.
	`i18n`—See "Common Attributes" section.
	`events`—See "Intrinsic Events" section.
	`cite="uri"`—A URI pointing to a document that should give reason for the change.
	`datetime="datetime"`—Sets the date and time of the change.
Content:	Zero or more block elements, to include the following:
	`p	dl	div	center	noscript	noframes	blockquote |`
	`form	isindex	hr	table	fieldset	address`
	Heading elements (`h1 | h2 | h3 | h4 | h5 | h6`)
	List elements (`ul | ol | dir | menu`)
	Preformatted elements (`pre`)
	Zero or more inline elements, to include the following:
	Document text and entities
	Fontstyle elements (`tt | i | b | u | s | strike | big | small`)
	Phrase elements (`em | strong | dfn | code | samp | kbd | var | cite | abbr | acronym`)
	Special elements (`a | img | applet | object | font | basefont | br | script | map | a | sub | sup | span | bdo | iframe`)
	Form Control elements (`input | select | textarea | label | button`)
Notes:	Might serve as a block-level or inline element, but not both at the same time. Changes to nested block-level content should be made at the lowest level.
Browser:	MSIE 4

<isindex />

Usage:	Creates a single-line text input control.
Syntax:	`<isindex attributes />`
Attributes:	`core`—See "Common Attributes" section.
	`i18n`—See "Common Attributes" section.
	`prompt="text"`—Displays a prompt for user input.
Notes:	Deprecated in favor of using `input` to create text-input controls.
Browser:	MSIE 1; NNav 1

<kbd>...</kbd>

Usage:	Identifies and displays text a user would enter from a keyboard.
Syntax:	`<kbd attributes>content</kbd>`
Attributes:	`core`—See "Common Attributes" section.
	`i18n`—See "Common Attributes" section.
	`events`—See "Intrinsic Events" section.
Content:	Zero or more inline elements, to include the following:

    Document text and entities

    Fontstyle elements (`tt | i | b | u | s | strike | big | small`)

    Phrase elements (`em | strong | dfn | code | samp | kbd | var | cite | abbr | acronym`)

    Special elements (`a | img | applet | object | font | basefont | br | script | map | a | sub | sup | span | bdo | iframe`)

    Form Control elements (`input | select | textarea | label | button`)

Notes:	Usually displayed with monospaced font.
Browser:	MSIE 1; NNav 1

<label>...</label>

Usage:	Labels a form control.
Syntax:	`<label attributes>content</label>`
Attributes:	`core`—See "Common Attributes" section.
	`i18n`—See "Common Attributes" section.
	`events`—See "Intrinsic Events" section.
	`for="idref"`—Associates the `label` with a previously identified control.
	`accesskey="character"`—Assigns an access key (or shortcut key) to the element. When the key is pressed, the element receives focus and is activated.
	`onfocus="script"`—Triggered when the element receives focus by either a pointing device (such as a mouse) or tabbed navigation.
	`onblur="script"`—Triggered when the element loses focus by either a pointing device (such as a mouse) or tabbed navigation.
Content:	Zero or more inline elements, to include the following:

    Document text and entities

    Fontstyle elements (`tt | i | b | u | s | strike | big | small`)

    Phrase elements (`em | strong | dfn | code | samp | kbd | var | cite | abbr | acronym`)

    Special elements (`a | img | applet | object | font | basefont | br | script | map | a | sub | sup | span | bdo | iframe`)

    Form Control elements (`input | select | textarea | button`)

Notes:	More than one `label` might be associated with a control; however, each `label` is only associated with one control.
Browser:	MSIE 4

`<legend>`...`</legend>`

Usage:	Assigns a caption to a `fieldset` element.
Syntax:	`<legend attributes>content</legend>`
Attributes:	`core`—See "Common Attributes" section.
	`i18n`—See "Common Attributes" section.
	`events`—See "Intrinsic Events" section.
	`accesskey="character"`—Assigns an access key (or shortcut key) to the element. When the key is pressed, the element receives focus and is activated.
	`align="top	bottom	left	right"`—Specifies the position of the legend with respect to the `fieldset`:
	`top`—Places the legend at the top of the fieldset.
	`bottom`—Places the legend at the bottom of the fieldset.
	`left`—Places the legend at the left side of the fieldset.
	`right`—Places the legend at the right side of the fieldset.
Content:	Zero or more inline elements, to include the following:
	Document text and entities
	Fontstyle elements (`tt | i | b | u | s | strike | big | small`)
	Phrase elements (`em | strong | dfn | code | samp | kbd | var | cite | abbr | acronym`)
	Special elements (`a | img | applet | object | font | basefont | br | script | map | a | sub | sup | span | bdo | iframe`)
	Form Control elements (`input | select | textarea | label | button`)
Notes:	The use of `legend` improves accessibility for nonvisual user agents as well as aids general understanding of the form layout.
Browser:	MSIE 4

`<li>`...`</li>`

Usage:	Defines a list item within a list.
Syntax:	`<li attributes>content</li>`
Attributes:	`core`—See "Common Attributes" section.
	`i18n`—See "Common Attributes" section.
	`events`—See "Intrinsic Events" section.
	`type="1	a	a	i	i	disc	square	circle"`:
	`1`—Arabic numbers.
	`a`—Lowercase alphabet.
	`a`—Uppercase alphabet.
	`i`—Lowercase Roman numerals.
	`i`—Uppercase Roman numerals.
	`disc`—A solid circle.
	`square`—A square outline.
	`circle`—A circle outline.
	`value="number"`—Sets the value of the current list item.

Content: Zero or more block elements, to include the following:
                   p | dl | div | center | noscript | noframes | blockquote |
                   form | isindex | hr | table | fieldset | address
                   Heading elements (h1 | h2 | h3 | h4 | h5 | h6)
                   List elements (ul | ol | dir | menu)
                   Preformatted elements (pre)
                 Zero or more inline elements, to include the following:
                   Document text and entities
                   Fontstyle elements (tt | i | b | u | s | strike | big | small)
                   Phrase elements (em | strong | dfn | code | samp | kbd | var |
                   cite | abbr | acronym)
                   Special elements (a | img | applet | object | font | basefont |
                   br | script | map | a | sub | sup | span | bdo | iframe)
                   Form Control elements (input | select | textarea | label |
                   button)

Notes: Used in ordered (ol), unordered (ul), directory (dir), and menu (menu)
                 lists.

Browser: MSIE 1; NNav 1

`<link />`

Usage: Defines a relationship with another document.

Syntax: `<link attributes />`

Attributes: core—See "Common Attributes" section.

                 i18n—See "Common Attributes" section.

                 events—See "Intrinsic Events" section.

                 charset="character-set"—Specifies the character encoding of the
                 linked resource. Values (such as iso-8859-1 or us-ascii) must be
                 strings approved and registered by IANA, The Internet Assigned
                 Numbers Authority.

                 href="uri"—Specifies the location of the linked resource or anchor.

                 hreflang="language-code"—Identifies the language of the linked
                 resource. This attribute might only be used in conjunction with the
                 href attribute.

                 type="content-type"—Specifies the content or media (MIME) type
                 (such as text/xhtml) of the linked resource.

                 rel="link-type"—Defines the relationship between the document
                 and that specified by the href attribute.

                 rev="link-type"—Defines the relationship between the resource
                 specified by the href attribute and the current document.

                 media="media-descriptor"—Identifies the intended destination
                 medium for style information. The default is screen.

target="user-defined | _blank | _self | _parent | _top"—
Identifies the frame in which the linked resource will be opened:
user-defined—Document opens in the frame designated by the
author-defined name, which is set by the name attribute of the
frame. The name must begin with an alphabetic character.
_blank—Document opens in a new, unnamed window.
_self—Document opens in same frame as the originating link.
_parent—Document opens in the immediate frameset parent of
the current frame, or itself if the current frame has no parent.
_top—Document opens in the full, original window, or itself if the
frame has no parent.

Notes:	Might only be used in the head of a document, but any number of link elements can be used.
	Common uses are linking to external style sheets, scripts, and search engines.
Browser:	MSIE 2; NNav 4

\<map\>...\</map\>

Usage:	Specifies a client-side imagemap.
Syntax:	\<map attributes\>content\</map\>
Attributes:	core—See "Common Attributes" section.
	i18n—See "Common Attributes" section.
	events—See "Intrinsic Events" section.
	name="data"—Assigns a name to the imagemap.
Content:	Zero or more block elements, to include the following:
	p | dl | div | center | noscript | noframes | blockquote | form | isindex | hr | table | fieldset | address
	Heading elements (h1 | h2 | h3 | h4 | h5 | h6)
	List elements (ul | ol | dir | menu)
	Preformatted elements (pre)
	or
	One or more area elements
Notes:	Can be associated with img, object, or input elements via each element's usemap attribute.
Browser:	MSIE 1; NNav 2

\<menu\>...\</menu\>

Usage:	Creates a single-column menu list.
Syntax:	\<menu attributes\>content\</menu\>

Attributes: `core`—See "Common Attributes" section.

`i18n`—See "Common Attributes" section.

`events`—See "Intrinsic Events" section.

`compact`—Tells the browser to attempt to display the list more compactly.

Content: One or more `li` elements, which might contain the following:

List elements (`ul` | `ol` | `dir` | `menu`)

Zero or more inline elements, to include the following:

Document text and entities

Fontstyle elements (`tt` | `i` | `b` | `u` | `s` | `strike` | `big` | `small`)

Phrase elements (`em` | `strong` | `dfn` | `code` | `samp` | `kbd` | `var` | `cite` | `abbr` | `acronym`)

Special elements (`a` | `img` | `applet` | `object` | `font` | `basefont` | `br` | `script` | `map` | `a` | `sub` | `sup` | `span` | `bdo` | `iframe`)

Form Control elements (`input` | `select` | `textarea` | `label` | `button`)

Notes: Deprecated in favor of unordered lists (`ul`).

Browser: MSIE 1; NNav 1

`<meta />`

Usage: Provides information about the document.

Syntax: `<meta attributes />`

Attributes: `i18n`—See "Common Attributes" section.

`http-equiv="name"`—Identifies a name with the meta-information, which might be used by HTTP servers gathering information.

`name="name"`—Identifies a name with the meta-information.

`content="data"`—The content of the meta-information.

`scheme="data"`—Gives user agents more context for interpreting the information in the `content` attribute.

Content: Empty

Notes: Each `meta` element specifies a property/value pair. The `name` attribute identifies the property, and the `content` attribute specifies the property's value.

There can be any number of `meta` elements within the `head` element.

Browser: MSIE 2; NNav 1.1

`<noframes>`...`</noframes>`

Usage: Specifies alternative content when frames are not supported.

Syntax: `<noframes attributes>content</noframes>`

Attributes: `core`—See "Common Attributes" section.

`i18n`—See "Common Attributes" section.

`events`—See "Intrinsic Events" section.

Content:	User agents will treat content as in the body element (excluding `noframes`) if configured to support the `noframe` element. Otherwise:

Zero or more block elements, to include the following:

    `p | dl | div | center | noscript | noframes | blockquote | form | isindex | hr | table | fieldset | address`

    Heading elements (`h1 | h2 | h3 | h4 | h5 | h6`)

    List elements (`ul | ol | dir | menu`)

    Preformatted elements (`pre`)

Zero or more inline elements, to include the following:

    Document text and entities

    Fontstyle elements (`tt | i | b | u | s | strike | big | small`)

    Phrase elements (`em | strong | dfn | code | samp | kbd | var | cite | abbr | acronym`)

    Special elements (`a | img | applet | object | font | basefont | br | script | map | a | sub | sup | span | bdo | iframe`)

    Form Control elements (`input | select | textarea | label | button`)

Notes:	The `noframes` element can be used within the `frameset` element.
Browser:	MSIE 3; NNav 2

`<noscript>…</noscript>`

Usage:	Provides alternative content for browsers unable to execute a script.
Syntax:	`<noscript attributes>content</noscript>`
Attributes:	`core`—See "Common Attributes" section.
	`i18n`—See "Common Attributes" section.
	`events`—See "Intrinsic Events" section.
Content:	Zero or more block elements, to include the following:

    `p | dl | div | center | noscript | noframes | blockquote | form | isindex | hr | table | fieldset | address`

    Heading elements (`h1 | h2 | h3 | h4 | h5 | h6`)

    List elements (`ul | ol | dir | menu`)

    Preformatted elements (`pre`)

Zero or more inline elements, to include the following:

    Document text and entities

    Fontstyle elements (`tt | i | b | u | s | strike | big | small`)

    Phrase elements (`em | strong | dfn | code | samp | kbd | var | cite | abbr | acronym`)

    Special elements (`a | img | applet | object | font | basefont | br | script | map | a | sub | sup | span | bdo | iframe`)

    Form Control elements (`input | select | textarea | label | button`)

Notes:	The content of the element should only be rendered if the user agent does not support scripting.
Browser:	MSIE 3; NNav 3

`<object>…</object>`

Usage:	Includes an external object in the document such as an image, a Java applet, or other external application.
Syntax:	`<object attributes>content</object>`
Attributes:	`core`—See "Common Attributes" section.

`i18n`—See "Common Attributes" section.

`events`—See "Intrinsic Events" section.

`declare`—Indicates the object will be declared only and not instantiated.

`classid="uri"`—Used to locate an object's implementation.

`codebase="uri"`—Sets the base URI for the object. If not specified, the default value is the base URI of the current document.

`data="uri"`—Identifies the location of the object's data.

`type="content-type"`—Specifies the content or media (MIME) type (such as `application/mpeg`) of the object identified by the `data` attribute.

`codetype="content-type"`—Identifies the content type (MIME) of the data to be downloaded.

`archive="uri"`—List URIs (separated by spaces) for archives containing classes and other resources that will be preloaded. This could significantly speed up object performance.

`standby="text"`—Provides a message to be displayed while the object loads.

`height="length"`—Sets the display height of the object.

`width="length"`—Sets the display width of the object.

`usemap="uri"`—Associates an imagemap as defined by the `map` element with this object.

`name="data"`—Assigns a control name to the object for use as part of a `form`.

`tabindex="number"`—Defines the tabbing order between elements. This is the order (from lowest first to highest last) in which they receive focus when the user navigates through them using the Tab key.

`align="top | middle | bottom | left | right"`—Aligns the object with respect to context:

    `top`—Vertically aligns the top of the object with the top of the current text line.

    `middle`—Vertically aligns the center of the object with the current baseline.

    `bottom`—Vertically aligns the bottom of the object with the current baseline.

    `left`—Floats object to the left margin.

    `right`—Floats object to the right margin.

border="pixels"—Sets the width of the border drawn around the object.

hspace="pixels"—Sets the amount of space to be inserted to the left and right of the element.

vspace="pixels"—Sets the amount of space to be inserted to the top and bottom of the element.

Content: One or more param elements.

Zero or more block elements, to include the following:

  p | dl | div | center | noscript | noframes | blockquote | form | isindex | hr | table | fieldset | address
  Heading elements (h1 | h2 | h3 | h4 | h5 | h6)
  List elements (ul | ol | dir | menu)
  Preformatted elements (pre)

Zero or more inline elements, to include the following:

  Document text and entities
  Fontstyle elements (tt | i | b | u | s | strike | big | small)
  Phrase elements (em | strong | dfn | code | samp | kbd | var | cite | abbr | acronym)
  Special elements (a | img | applet | object | font | basefont | br | script | map | a | sub | sup | span | bdo | iframe)
  Form Control elements (input | select | textarea | label | button)

Notes: Might appear in the head, although it will generally not be rendered. In such cases it is wise to limit object elements in the head to those with content not requiring visual rendering.

The object content is meant to be rendered by user agents that do not support the specified type of object.

object elements can be nested, allowing the author to provide the same object in various forms in a preferred order.

Browser: MSIE 3

`<ol>...</ol>`

Usage: Creates an ordered, or numbered, list.

Syntax: <ol attributes>content</ol>

Attributes: core—See "Common Attributes" section.

i18n—See "Common Attributes" section.

events—See "Intrinsic Events" section.

type="1 | a | a | i | i":

1—Arabic numbers.

a—Lowercase alphabet.

a—Uppercase alphabet.

i—Lowercase Roman numerals.

i—Uppercase Roman numerals.

`compact`—Tells the browser to attempt to display the list more compactly.

`start="number"`—Sets the starting number of the ordered list.

Content:	One or more `li` element
Notes:	When the `start` attribute is a number and the list type is non-numeric, the `start` value refers to that number in the sequence of non-numeric values.
	Nested lists are allowed.
Browser:	MSIE 1; NNav 1

`<optgroup>...</optgroup>`

Usage:	Used to group `option` elements within a `select` element.
Syntax:	`<optgroup attributes>content</optgroup>`
Attributes:	`core`—See "Common Attributes" section.
	`i18n`—See "Common Attributes" section.
	`events`—See "Intrinsic Events" section.
	`disabled`—Disables these controls for user input.
	`label="text"`—Labels the option group.
Content:	One or more `option` elements.
Notes:	All `optgroup` elements must be specified in the `select` element and cannot be nested.
Browser:	None at this time.

`<option>...</option>`

Usage:	Specifies choices in a `select` element.
Syntax:	`<option attributes>content</option>`
Attributes:	`core`—See "Common Attributes" section.
	`i18n`—See "Common Attributes" section.
	`events`—See "Intrinsic Events" section.
	`selected`—Sets the option as being preselected.
	`disabled`—Disables these controls for user input.
	`label="text"`—Provides a shorter label for the option than that specified in its content.
	`value="data"`—Sets the initial value of the control.
Content:	Document text.
Notes:	If the `label` attribute is not set, user agents will use the contents of the element as the option.
	`option` elements might be grouped in an `optgroup` element.
Browser:	MSIE 1; NNav 1

`<p>...</p>`

Usage:	Defines a paragraph.
Syntax:	`<p attributes>content</p>`
Attributes:	`core`—See "Common Attributes" section.
	`i18n`—See "Common Attributes" section.
	`events`—See "Intrinsic Events" section.
	`align="left	center	right	justify"`—Horizontal alignment with respect to context. The default depends on the directionality of the text. For left-to-right it is `left`, and for right-to-left it is `right`:
	`left`—Text aligned left.
	`center`—Text centered.
	`right`—Text aligned right.
	`justify`—Text aligned flush with left and right margins.
Content:	Zero or more inline elements, to include the following:
	Document text and entities
	Fontstyle elements (`tt | i | b | u | s | strike | big | small`)
	Phrase elements (`em | strong | dfn | code | samp | kbd | var | cite | abbr | acronym`)
	Special elements (`a | img | applet | object | font | basefont | br | script | map | a | sub | sup | span | bdo | iframe`)
	Form Control elements (`input | select | textarea | label | button`)
Notes:	Cannot contain block-level elements.
Browser:	MSIE 1; NNav 1

`<param />`

Usage:	Specifies a set of values that might be required by an object at runtime.
Syntax:	`<param attributes />`
Attributes:	`id="id"`—A unique identification of the element.
	`name="data"`—Defines the name of a runtime parameter required by an object (such as `width`).
	`value="data"`—Sets the value required by the runtime parameter previously identified and named.
	`valuetype="data	ref	object"`—Identifies the type of runtime parameter being used in the `value` attribute:
	`data`—Indicates the `value` will be passed to the `object` implementation as a string.
	`ref`—Indicates the `value` is a reference to a URI where runtime values are stored.

object—Indicates that the value identifies an object in the same document. The identifier must be the value of the id attribute set for the declared object.

type="content-type"—Specifies the content or media (MIME) type (such as application/mpeg) of the object when the valuetype attribute is set to ref (but not date or object).

Content: Empty

Notes: Multiple param elements are allowed in either the object or applet elements but must immediately follow the opening tag.

Browser: MSIE 3; NNav 2

\<pre>...\</pre>

Usage: Displays preformatted text, which normally includes extra whitespace and line breaks.

Syntax: \<pre attributes>content\</pre>

Attributes: core—See "Common Attributes" section.

                i18n—See "Common Attributes" section.

                events—See "Intrinsic Events" section.

                width="number"—Identifies the desired width of the preformatted content block.

Content: Zero or more inline elements, to include the following:

                Document text and entities

                Fontstyle elements (tt | i | b | u | s | strike)

                Phrase elements (em | strong | dfn | code | samp | kbd | var | cite | abbr | acronym)

                Special elements (a | br | script | map | a | span | bdo | iframe)

                Form Control elements (input | select | textarea | label | button)

Notes: The use of tabs in preformatted text is strongly discouraged because of the possibility of misaligned content.

Browser: MSIE 1; NNav 1

\<q>...\</q>

Usage: Designates text as a short quotation.

Syntax: \<q attributes>content\</q>

Attributes: core—See "Common Attributes" section.

                i18n—See "Common Attributes" section.

                events—See "Intrinsic Events" section.

                cite="uri"—The URI designating the source document or message.

Content:	Zero or more inline elements, to include the following:
	Document text and entities
	Fontstyle elements (tt | i | b | u | s | strike | big | small)
	Phrase elements (em | strong | dfn | code | samp | kbd | var | cite | abbr | acronym)
	Special elements (a | img | applet | object | font | basefont | br | script | map | a | sub | sup | span | bdo | iframe)
	Form Control elements (input | select | textarea | label | button)
Notes:	When compared with the blockquote element, the q element is used for shorter quotations not normally requiring a line break and is treated as inline content.
	The browser should automatically insert quotation marks around the content of a q element.
Browser:	MSIE 4

<s>...</s>

Usage:	Displays text as strikethrough.
Syntax:	<s attributes>content</s>
Attributes:	core—See "Common Attributes" section.
	i18n—See "Common Attributes" section.
	events—See "Intrinsic Events" section.
Content:	Zero or more inline elements, to include the following:
	Document text and entities
	Fontstyle elements (tt | i | b | u | s | strike | big | small)
	Phrase elements (em | strong | dfn | code | samp | kbd | var | cite | abbr | acronym)
	Special elements (a | img | applet | object | font | basefont | br | script | map | a | sub | sup | span | bdo | iframe)
	Form Control elements (input | select | textarea | label | button)
Notes:	Although not deprecated, the W3C recommends using style sheets in place of this element.
Browser:	MSIE 1; NNav 3

<samp>...</samp>

Usage:	Identifies and displays sample output from a computer program, script, and so on.
Syntax:	<samp attributes>content</samp>
Start/End Tag:	Required/Required

Attributes:	core—See "Common Attributes" section.
	i18n—See "Common Attributes" section.
	events—See "Intrinsic Events" section.
Content:	Zero or more inline elements, to include the following:
	Document text and entities
	Fontstyle elements (tt | i | b | u | s | strike | big | small)
	Phrase elements (em | strong | dfn | code | samp | kbd | var | cite | abbr | acronym)
	Special elements (a | img | applet | object | font | basefont | br | script | map | a | sub | sup | span | bdo | iframe)
	Form Control elements (input | select | textarea | label | button)
Notes:	Usually displayed with monospaced font.
Browser:	MSIE 1; NNav 1

<script>...</script>

Usage:	Inserts a script into the document.
Syntax:	`<script attributes>content</script>`
Attributes:	charset="character-set"—Specifies the character encoding of the linked resource. Values (such as iso-8859-1 or us-ascii) must be strings approved and registered by IANA, The Internet Assigned Numbers Authority.
	type="content-type"—Specifies the content or media (MIME) type (such as text/javascript) of the script language.
	language="data"—Specifies the scripting language through a predefined name.
	src="uri"—Identifies the location of an external script.
	defer—Indicates to the user agent that no document content will be output by the script and it might continue rendering the page.
Content:	Script expression
Notes:	Might appear any number of times in the head or body of the document.
	If the src attribute is present, the user agent loads an external script. Otherwise, the content of the element is treated as the script.
Browser:	MSIE 3; NNav 2

<select>...</select>

| Usage: | Creates a menu whose choices are represented by option elements, either separately or grouped into optgroup elements. |
| Syntax: | `<select attributes>content</select>` |

Attributes:	core—See "Common Attributes" section.
	i18n—See "Common Attributes" section.
	events—See "Intrinsic Events" section.
	name="data"—Assigns a name to the control.
	size="number"—If represented by a scrolling list box, this sets the number of choices to be displayed at one time.
	multiple—Allows multiple selections.
	disabled—Disables these controls for user input.
	tabindex="number"—Defines the tabbing order between elements. This is the order (from lowest first to highest last) in which they receive focus when the user navigates through them using the Tab key.
	onfocus="script"—Triggered when the element receives focus by either a pointing device (such as a mouse) or tabbed navigation.
	onblur="script"—Triggered when the element loses focus by either a pointing device (such as a mouse) or tabbed navigation.
	onchange="script"—The event that occurs when a control loses the input focus and its value has been modified since gaining focus.
Content:	One or more optgroup or option elements.
Notes:	Must contain at least one option or optgroup element.
	All optgroup elements must be specified in the select element and cannot be nested.
Browser:	MSIE 1; NNav 1

\<small\>...\</small\>

Usage:	Displays reduced-size or smaller text.
Syntax:	\<small attributes\>content\</small\>
Attributes:	core—See "Common Attributes" section.
	i18n—See "Common Attributes" section.
	events—See "Intrinsic Events" section.
Content:	Zero or more inline elements, to include the following:
	Document text and entities
	Fontstyle elements (tt | i | b | u | s | strike | big | small)
	Phrase elements (em | strong | dfn | code | samp | kbd | var | cite | abbr | acronym)
	Special elements (a | img | applet | object | font | basefont | br | script | map | a | sub | sup | span | bdo | iframe)
	Form Control elements (input | select | textarea | label | button)
Notes:	Although not deprecated, the W3C recommends using style sheets in place of this element.
Browser:	MSIE 3; NNav 1.1

...

Usage:	Creates author-defined inline structure to the document.
Syntax:	`<span attributes>content</span>`
Attributes:	`core`—See "Common Attributes" section.
	`i18n`—See "Common Attributes" section.
	`events`—See "Intrinsic Events" section.
Content:	Zero or more inline elements, to include the following:

> Document text and entities
> Fontstyle elements (`tt` | `i` | `b` | `u` | `s` | `strike` | `big` | `small`)
> Phrase elements (`em` | `strong` | `dfn` | `code` | `samp` | `kbd` | `var` | `cite` | `abbr` | `acronym`)
> Special elements (`a` | `img` | `applet` | `object` | `font` | `basefont` | `br` | `script` | `map` | `a` | `sub` | `sup` | `span` | `bdo` | `iframe`)
> Form Control elements (`input` | `select` | `textarea` | `label` | `button`)

Notes:	Used in conjunction with style sheets, this is a powerful device for adding custom inline structure.
Browser:	MSIE 3; NNav 4

<strike>...</strike>

Usage:	Text displayed as strikethrough.
Syntax:	`<strike attributes>content</strike>`
Attributes:	`core`—See "Common Attributes" section.
	`i18n`—See "Common Attributes" section.
	`events`—See "Intrinsic Events" section.
Content:	Zero or more inline elements, to include the following:

> Document text and entities
> Fontstyle elements (`tt` | `i` | `b` | `u` | `s` | `strike` | `big` | `small`)
> Phrase elements (`em` | `strong` | `dfn` | `code` | `samp` | `kbd` | `var` | `cite` | `abbr` | `acronym`)
> Special elements (`a` | `img` | `applet` | `object` | `font` | `basefont` | `br` | `script` | `map` | `a` | `sub` | `sup` | `span` | `bdo` | `iframe`)
> Form Control elements (`input` | `select` | `textarea` | `label` | `button`)

Notes:	Deprecated in favor of style sheets.
Browser:	MSIE 1; NNav 1.1

...

Usage:	Displays text with a stronger emphasis in relation to normal text than that of the em element.
Syntax:	`<strong attributes>content</strong>`

Attributes:	`core`—See "Common Attributes" section.
	`i18n`—See "Common Attributes" section.
	`events`—See "Intrinsic Events" section.
Content:	Zero or more inline elements, to include the following:

     Document text and entities

     Fontstyle elements (`tt | i | b | u | s | strike | big | small`)

     Phrase elements (`em | strong | dfn | code | samp | kbd | var | cite | abbr | acronym`)

     Special elements (`a | img | applet | object | font | basefont | br | script | map | a | sub | sup | span | bdo | iframe`)

     Form Control elements (`input | select | textarea | label | button`)

Notes:	Usually rendered in boldface font.
Browser:	MSIE 1; NNav 1

`<style>…</style>`

Usage:	Creates stylesheet rules for use in the document.
Syntax:	`<style attributes>content</style>`
Attributes:	`i18n`—See "Common Attributes" section.
	`type="content-type"`—Specifies the content or media (MIME) type (such as `text/css`) of the style language.
	`media="media-descriptor"`—Identifies the intended medium (such as `screen`) of the style information.
	`title="text"`—Offers advisory information about the element.
Content:	Stylesheet rules
Notes:	Any number of `style` elements might be present, but they must be in the head element only.
	Browsers that do not support the element should not render its contents. Style sheet rules may be enclosed in comments to hide styles from older browsers.
Browser:	MSIE 3; NNav 4

`<sub>…</sub>`

Usage:	Displays text as subscript (lower in vertical alignment) in relation to surrounding text.
Syntax:	`<sub attributes>content</sub>`
Attributes:	`core`—See "Common Attributes" section.
	`i18n`—See "Common Attributes" section.
	`events`—See "Intrinsic Events" section.
Content:	Zero or more inline elements, to include the following:

     Document text and entities

     Fontstyle elements (`tt | i | b | u | s | strike | big | small`)

Phrase elements (em | strong | dfn | code | samp | kbd | var | cite | abbr | acronym)

Special elements (a | img | applet | object | font | basefont | br | script | map | a | sub | sup | span | bdo | iframe)

Form Control elements (input | select | textarea | label | button)

Browser: MSIE 3; NNav 1.1

\^{…\}

Usage: Displays text as superscript (higher in vertical alignment) in relation to surrounding text.

Syntax: \^{content\}

Attributes: core—See "Common Attributes" section.

i18n—See "Common Attributes" section.

events—See "Intrinsic Events" section.

Content: Zero or more inline elements, to include the following:

Document text and entities

Fontstyle elements (tt | i | b | u | s | strike | big | small)

Phrase elements (em | strong | dfn | code | samp | kbd | var | cite | abbr | acronym)

Special elements (a | img | applet | object | font | basefont | br | script | map | a | sub | sup | span | bdo | iframe)

Form Control elements (input | select | textarea | label | button)

Browser: MSIE 3; NNav 1.1

\<table>…\</table>

Usage: Creates a table.

Syntax: \<table attributes>content\</table>

Attributes: core—See "Common Attributes" section.

i18n—See "Common Attributes" section.

events—See "Intrinsic Events" section.

summary="text"—Text explanation of table structure and purpose for nonvisual user agents.

width="length"—Sets width of entire table.

border="pixels"—Sets the width of a border drawn around the table.

frame="void | above | below | hsides | lhs | rhs | vsides | box | border"—Specifies which borders around the table are visible:

void—No sides visible.

above—Top side only.

below—Bottom side only.

hsides—Top and bottom only.

          lhs—Left side only.

          rhs—Right side only.

          vsides—Left and right sides only.

          box—Top, bottom, left, and right sides.

          border—Top, bottom, left, and right sides.

rules="none | groups | rows | cols | all"—Specifies which interior lines of the table are visible:

          none—No rules visible.

          groups—Rules appear between row groups and column groups only.

          rows—Rules between rows only.

          cols—Rules between columns only.

          all—Rules visible between rows and columns.

cellspacing="length"—Determines the spacing between cells.

cellpadding="length"—Determines the space between cell content and its borders.

align="left | center | right"—Aligns the table with respect to the page. Left-to-right is the default inherited directionality, but this can be overridden using the dir attribute:

          left—Table aligned left.

          center—Table centered.

          right—Table aligned right.

bgcolor="color"—Sets the background color for cells in the table. Colors identified by standard RGB in hexadecimal format (#rrggbb) or by predefined color name.

Content:	Zero or one caption element
	Zero or more col or colgroup elements
	Zero or one thead element
	Zero or one tfoot element
	One or more tbody or tr elements
Notes:	The table element has no content by itself but relies on other elements to specify content and other formatting attributes.
Browser:	MSIE 2; NNav 1.1

\<tbody\>…\</tbody\>

Usage:	Groups table rows into a table body.
Syntax:	\<tbody attributes\>content\</tbody\>
Attributes:	core—See "Common Attributes" section.
	i18n—See "Common Attributes" section.
	events—See "Intrinsic Events" section.

          align="left | center | right | justify | char"—Horizontally aligns the contents of cells:

          left—Data and text aligned left. This is the default for table data.

          center—Data and text centered. This is the default for table headers.

right—Data and text aligned right.

justify—Data and text aligned flush with left and right margins.

char—Aligns text around a specific character.

char="character"—Sets a character on which the column aligns (such as ":"). The default value is the decimal point of the current language.

charoff="length"—Offset to the first alignment character on a line. Specified in number of pixels or a percentage of available length.

valign="top | middle | bottom | baseline"—Vertically aligns the contents of a cell:

top—Cell data flush with top of cell.

middle—Cell data centered in cell.

bottom—Cell data flush with bottom of cell.

baseline—Aligns all cells in a row with this attribute set. Textual data aligned along a common baseline.

Content:	One or more tr elements.
Notes:	Must contain at least one table row.
	The tfoot and thead elements should appear before the tbody element.
Browser:	MSIE 4

<td>...</td>

Usage:	Specifies a table cell's data or contents.
Syntax:	<td attributes>content</td>
Attributes:	core—See "Common Attributes" section.

i18n—See "Common Attributes" section.

events—See "Intrinsic Events" section.

abbr="text"—An abbreviated form of the cell's content.

axis="data"—Organizes cells into conceptual categories.

headers="idrefs"—Associates the content of a cell with a previously identified header.

scope="row | col | rowgroup | colgroup"—Defines the set of data cells for which the header provides header information:

row—Header information provided for the rest of the row.

col—Header information provided for the rest of the column.

rowgroup—Header information provided for the rest of the row group (as defined by a thead, tbody, or tfoot element) that contains it.

colgroup—Header information provided for the rest of the column group (as defined by a col or colgroup element) that contains it.

rowspan="number"—Sets the number of rows spanned by the current cell. The default is 1.

colspan="number"—Sets the number of columns spanned by the current cell. The default is 1.

`align="left | center | right | justify | char"`—Horizontally aligns the contents of cells:

  `left`—Data and text aligned left. This is the default for table data.

  `center`—Data and text centered. This is the default for table headers.

  `right`—Data and text aligned right.

  `justify`—Data and text aligned flush with left and right margins.

  `char`—Aligns text around a specific character.

`char="character"`—Sets a character on which the column aligns (such as `":"`). The default value is the decimal point of the current language.

`charoff="length"`—Offset to the first alignment character on a line. Specified in number of pixels or a percentage of available length.

`valign="top | middle | bottom | baseline"`—Vertically aligns the contents of a cell:

  `top`—Cell data flush with top of cell.

  `middle`—Cell data centered in cell.

  `bottom`—Cell data flush with bottom of cell.

  `baseline`—Aligns all cells in a row with this attribute set. Textual data aligned along a common baseline.

`nowrap`—Disables automatic text-wrapping for the cell.

`bgcolor="color"`—Sets the background color for cell. Colors identified by standard RGB in hexadecimal format (#rrggbb) or by predefined color name.

`width="pixels"`—Recommended cell width.

`height="pixels"`—Recommended cell height.

Content:
: Zero or more block elements, to include the following:

  `p | dl | div | center | noscript | noframes | blockquote | form | isindex | hr | table | fieldset | address`

  Heading elements (`h1 | h2 | h3 | h4 | h5 | h6`)

  List elements (`ul | ol | dir | menu`)

  Preformatted elements (`pre`)

  Zero or more inline elements, to include the following:

  Document text and entities

  Fontstyle elements (`tt | i | b | u | s | strike | big | small`)

  Phrase elements (`em | strong | dfn | code | samp | kbd | var | cite | abbr | acronym`)

  Special elements (`a | img | applet | object | font | _basefont | br | script | map | a | sub | sup | span | _bdo | iframe`)

  Form Control elements (`input | select | textarea | label | button`)

Notes:
: Cells defined by `td` might be empty.

Browser:
: MSIE 2; NNav 1.1

`<textarea>…</textarea>`

Usage:	Creates an area for user input with multiple lines.
Syntax:	`<textarea attributes>content</textarea>`
Attributes:	`core`—See "Common Attributes" section.
	`i18n`—See "Common Attributes" section.
	`events`—See "Intrinsic Events" section.
	`name="data"`—Assigns a name to the control.
	`rows="number"`—Sets the number of visible rows or text lines.
	`cols="number"`—Sets the number of visible columns measured in average character width.
	`disabled`—Disables this control for user input.
	`readonly`—Prohibits the user from making changes to the control.
	`tabindex="number"`—Defines the tabbing order between elements. This is the order (from lowest first to highest last) in which they receive focus when the user navigates through them using the Tab key.
	`accesskey="character"`—Assigns an access key (or shortcut key) to the element. When the key is pressed, the element receives focus and is activated.
	`onfocus="script"`—Triggered when the element receives focus by either a pointing device (such as a mouse) or tabbed navigation.
	`onblur="script"`—Triggered when the element loses focus by either a pointing device (such as a mouse) or tabbed navigation.
	`onselect="script"`—The event that occurs when text is selected in a text field.
	`onchange="script"`—The event that occurs when a control loses the input focus and its value has been modified since gaining focus.
Content:	Document text.
Notes:	The content of the element serves as the initial value of the control and is displayed by the user agent.
Browser:	MSIE 1; NNav 1

`<tfoot>…</tfoot>`

Usage:	Groups a table row or rows into a table footer.
Syntax:	`<tfoot attributes>content</tfoot>`
Attributes:	`core`—See "Common Attributes" section.
	`i18n`—See "Common Attributes" section.
	`events`—See "Intrinsic Events" section.
	`align="left	center	right	justify	char"`—Horizontally aligns the contents of cells:
	`left`—Data and text aligned left. This is the default for table data.
	`center`—Data and text centered. This is the default for table headers.

      `right`—Data and text aligned right.

      `justify`—Data and text aligned flush with left and right margins.

      `char`—Aligns text around a specific character.

`char="character"`—Sets a character on which the column aligns (such as `":"`). The default value is the decimal point of the current language.

`charoff="length"`—Offset to the first alignment character on a line. Specified in number of pixels or a percentage of available length.

`valign="top | middle | bottom | baseline"`—Vertically aligns the contents of a cell:

      `top`—Cell data flush with top of cell.

      `middle`—Cell data centered in cell.

      `bottom`—Cell data flush with bottom of cell.

      `baseline`—Aligns all cells in a row with this attribute set. Textual data aligned along a common baseline.

Content:	One or more `tr` elements.
Notes:	The table footer contains table data cells that describe the content of the columns above it.
	Must contain at least one `tr`.
Browser:	MSIE 3

`<th>…</th>`

Usage:	Specifies a table cell as being an information, or header, cell.
Syntax:	`<th attributes>content</th>`
Attributes:	`core`—See "Common Attributes" section.
	`i18n`—See "Common Attributes" section.
	`events`—See "Intrinsic Events" section.
	`abbr="text"`—An abbreviated form of the cell's content.
	`axis="data"`—Organizes cells into conceptual categories.
	`headers="idrefs"`—Associates the content of a cell with a previously identified header.

`scope="row | col | rowgroup | colgroup"`—Defines the set of data cells for which the header provides header information:

      `row`—Header information provided for the rest of the row.

      `col`—Header information provided for the rest of the column.

      `rowgroup`—Header information provided for the rest of the row group (as defined by a `thead`, `tbody`, or `tfoot` element) that contains it.

      `colgroup`—Header information provided for the rest of the column group (as defined by a `col` or `colgroup` element) that contains it.

`rowspan="number"`—Sets the number of rows spanned by the current cell. The default is 1.

`colspan="number"`—Sets the number of columns spanned by the current cell. The default is 1.

align="left | center | right | justify | char"—Horizontally aligns the contents of cells:

left—Data and text aligned left. This is the default for table data.

center—Data and text centered. This is the default for table headers.

right—Data and text aligned right.

justify—Data and text aligned flush with left and right margins.

char—Aligns text around a specific character.

char="character"—Sets a character on which the column aligns (such as ":"). The default value is the decimal point of the current language.

charoff="length"—Offset to the first alignment character on a line. Specified in number of pixels or a percentage of available length.

valign="top | middle | bottom | baseline"—Vertically aligns the contents of a cell:

top—Cell data flush with top of cell.

middle—Cell data centered in cell.

bottom—Cell data flush with bottom of cell.

baseline—Aligns all cells in a row with this attribute set. Textual data aligned along a common baseline.

nowrap—Disables automatic text-wrapping for the cell.

bgcolor="color"—Sets the background color for the cell. Colors identified by standard RGB in hexadecimal format (#rrggbb) or by predefined color name.

width="pixels"—Recommended cell width.

height="pixels"—Recommended cell height.

Content: Zero or more block elements, to include the following:

p | dl | div | center | noscript | noframes | blockquote | form | isindex | hr | table | fieldset | address

Heading elements (h1 | h2 | h3 | h4 | h5 | h6)

List elements (ul | ol | dir | menu)

Preformatted elements (pre)

Zero or more inline elements, to include the following:

Document text and entities

Fontstyle elements (tt | i | b | u | s | strike | big | small)

Phrase elements (em | strong | dfn | code | samp | kbd | var | cite | abbr | acronym)

Special elements (a | img | applet | object | font | basefont | br | script | map | a | sub | sup | span | bdo | iframe)

Form Control elements (input | select | textarea | label | button)

Notes: Header cell usually rendered in boldface font.

Browser: MSIE 2; NNav 1.1

<thead>...</thead>

Usage:	Groups a table row or rows into a table header.
Syntax:	`<thead attributes>content`
	or
	`<thead attributes>content</thead>`
Attributes:	core—See "Common Attributes" section.
	i18n—See "Common Attributes" section.
	events—See "Intrinsic Events" section.
	`align="left	center	right	justify	char"`—Horizontally aligns the contents of cells:
	`left`—Data and text aligned left. This is the default for table data.
	`center`—Data and text centered. This is the default for table headers.
	`right`—Data and text aligned right.
	`justify`—Data and text aligned flush with left and right margins.
	`char`—Aligns text around a specific character.
	`char="character"`—Sets a character on which the column aligns (such as `":"`). The default value is the decimal point of the current language.
	`charoff="length"`—Offset to the first alignment character on a line. Specified in number of pixels or a percentage of available length.
	`valign="top	middle	bottom	baseline"`—Vertically aligns the contents of a cell:
	`top`—Cell data flush with top of cell.
	`middle`—Cell data centered in cell.
	`bottom`—Cell data flush with bottom of cell.
	`baseline`—Aligns all cells in a row with this attribute set. Textual data aligned along a common baseline.
Content:	One or more `tr` elements.
Notes:	The table header contains table data cells that describe the content of the columns below it.
	Must contain at least one `tr`.
Browser:	MSIE 3

<title>...</title>

Usage:	Identifies the contents of the document.
Syntax:	`<title attributes>content</title>`
Attributes:	i18n—See "Common Attributes" section.
Content:	Document text
Notes:	The `title` element is required and is located within the `head` element.
	The title is displayed in the browser window title bar.
Browser:	MSIE 1; NNav 1

`<tr>`…`</tr>`

Usage:	Defines a row of table cells.
Syntax:	`<tr attributes>content</tr>`
Attributes:	`core`—See "Common Attributes" section.
	`i18n`—See "Common Attributes" section.
	`events`—See "Intrinsic Events" section.
	`align="left	center	right	justify	char"`—Horizontally aligns the contents of cells:

      `left`—Data and text aligned left. This is the default for table data.

      `center`—Data and text centered. This is the default for table headers.

      `right`—Data and text aligned right.

      `justify`—Data and text aligned flush with left and right margins.

      `char`—Aligns text around a specific character.

`char="character"`—Sets a character on which the column aligns (such as `":"`). The default value is the decimal point of the current language.

`charoff="length"`—Offset to the first alignment character on a line. Specified in number of pixels or a percentage of available length.

`valign="top | middle | bottom | baseline"`—Vertically aligns the contents of a cell:

      `top`—Cell data flush with top of cell.

      `middle`—Cell data centered in cell.

      `bottom`—Cell data flush with bottom of cell.

      `baseline`—Aligns all cells in a row with this attribute set. Textual data aligned along a common baseline.

`bgcolor="color"`—Sets the background color for a table row. Colors identified by standard RGB in hexadecimal format (#rrggbb) or by predefined color name.

Content:	One or more `th` or `td` elements.
Notes:	No table data is supplied by this element; its sole purpose is to define structural rows of table cells.
Browser:	MSIE 2; NNav 1.1

`<tt>`…`</tt>`

Usage:	Displays text as Teletype or monospaced font.
Syntax:	`<tt attributes>content</tt>`
Attributes:	`core`—See "Common Attributes" section.
	`i18n`—See "Common Attributes" section.
	`events`—See "Intrinsic Events" section.
Content:	Zero or more inline elements, to include the following:

      Document text and entities

      Fontstyle elements (`tt | i | b | u | s | strike | big | small`)

      Phrase elements (`em | strong | dfn | code | samp | kbd | var | cite | abbr | acronym`)

Special elements (a | img | applet | object | font | basefont | br | script | map | a | sub | sup | span | bdo | iframe)

Form Control elements (input | select | textarea | label | button)

Notes:	Although not deprecated, the W3C recommends using style sheets in place of this element.
Browser:	MSIE 1; NNav 1

\<u>...\</u>

Usage:	Displays underlined text.
Syntax:	\<u attributes>content\</u>
Attributes:	core—See "Common Attributes" section.
	i18n—See "Common Attributes" section.
	events—See "Intrinsic Events" section.
Content:	Zero or more inline elements, to include the following:

Document text and entities

Fontstyle elements (tt | i | b | u | s | strike | big | small)

Phrase elements (em | strong | dfn | code | samp | kbd | var | cite | abbr | acronym)

Special elements (a | img | applet | object | font | _basefont | br | script | map | a | sub | sup | span | _bdo | iframe)

Form Control elements (input | select | textarea | label | button)

Notes:	Deprecated in favor of style sheets.
Browser:	MSIE 1; NNav 3

\<ul>...\</ul>

Usage:	Creates an unordered (unnumbered) list.
Syntax:	\<ul attributes>content\</ul>
Attributes:	core—See "Common Attributes" section.
	i18n—See "Common Attributes" section.
	events—See "Intrinsic Events" section.
	type="disc	square	circle"—Sets the style of bullets in an unordered list:
	disc—A solid circle.
	square—A square outline.
	circle—A circle outline.
	compact—Tells the browser to attempt to display the list more compactly.
Notes:	Nested lists are allowed.
Content:	One or more li elements
Browser:	MSIE 1; NNav 1

`<var>...</var>`

Usage:	Identifies and displays a variable or program argument.
Syntax:	`<var attributes>content</var>`
Attributes:	`core`—See "Common Attributes" section.
	`i18n`—See "Common Attributes" section.
	`events`—See "Intrinsic Events" section.
Content:	Zero or more inline elements, to include the following:
	Document text and entities
	Fontstyle elements (`tt` | `i` | `b` | `u` | `s` | `strike` | `big` | `small`)
	Phrase elements (`em` | `strong` | `dfn` | `code` | `samp` | `kbd` | `var` | `cite` | `abbr` | `acronym`)
	Special elements (`a` | `img` | `applet` | `object` | `font` | `basefont` | `br` | `script` | `map` | `a` | `sub` | `sup` | `span` | `bdo` | `iframe`)
	Form Control elements (`input` | `select` | `textarea` | `label` | `button`)
Notes:	Usually displayed in italics.
Browser:	MSIE 1; NNav 1

COMMON ATTRIBUTES

Four attributes are abbreviated as `core` in the preceding sections:

- `id="id"`—A global identifier.

- `class="data"`—A list of classes separated by spaces.

- `style="style"`—Style rules information.

- `title="text"`—Provides more information for a specific element, as opposed to the `title` element, which entitles the entire Web page.

Two attributes for internationalization (`i18n`) are abbreviated as `i18n`:

- `lang="language-code"`—Identifies the human (not computer) language of the text content or an element's attribute values.

- `dir="ltr | rtl"`—Specifies the text direction (left-to-right, right-to-left) of element content, overriding inherent directionality.

INTRINSIC EVENTS

The following intrinsic events are abbreviated `events`:

Support for intrinsic events in Netscape Navigator is limited to the 1.0 and above versions, and is only applicable to form elements, links, and images.

- `onclick="script"`—A pointing device (such as a mouse) was single-clicked.

- `ondblclick="script"`—A pointing device (such as a mouse) was double-clicked.

- onmousedown="script"—A mouse button was clicked and held down.

- onmouseup="script"—A mouse button that was clicked and held down was released.

- onmouseover="script"—A mouse moved the cursor over an object.

- onmousemove="script"—A mouse was moved within an object.

- onmouseout="script"—A mouse moved the cursor off an object.

- onkeypress="script"—A key was pressed and released.

- onkeydown="script"—A key was pressed and held down.

- onkeyup="script"—A key that was pressed has been released. intrin

DATA TYPES

Table A.1 summarizes and explains the data types used in the information in this appendix.

Table A.1   Data Types

Name	Description
character	A single character or character reference from the document character set.
character-set	Specifies the character encoding. Values (such as iso-8859-1 or us-ascii) must be strings approved and registered by IANA, The Internet Assigned Numbers Authority.
color	Colors are identified by standard RGB in hexadecimal format (#rrggbb) or by predefined color name (with corresponding hex value) shown here: black = "#000000" silver = "#c0c0c0" gray = "#808080" White = "#ffffff" maroon = "#800000" red = "#ff0000" purple = "#800080" fuchsia = "#ff00ff" green = "#008000" lime = "#00ff00" olive = "#808000" yellow = "#ffff00" navy = "#000080" blue = "#0000ff" teal = "#008080" aqua = "#00ffff"
content-type	Content types, also known as MIME types, specify the nature of the resource (such as "text/xhtml" or "image/gif").

Table A.1   Continued

Name	Description
data	A sequence of characters or character entities from the document character set.
datetime	Legal datetime strings follow the following format: `yyyy-mm-ddthh:mm:sstZd`. `yyyy` = four-digit year. `mm` = two-digit month (`01` = January, and so on). `dd` = two-digit day of month (`01` through `31`). `t` = beginning of time element. The `"t"` must appear in uppercase. `hh` = two digits of hour (`00` through `23`) (am/pm *not* allowed). `mm` = two digits of minute (`00` through `59`). `ss` = two digits of second (`00` through `59`). `tZd` = time zone designator. The time zone designator is one of the following: `Z`—indicates UTC (Coordinated Universal Time). The `"Z"` must be uppercase. `+hh:mm`—indicates that the time is a local time that is `hh` hours and `mm` minutes ahead of UTC. `-hh:mm`—indicates that the time is a local time that is `hh` hours and `mm` minutes behind UTC. A valid datetime is `1998-06-13t19:30:02-05:00`
id	An identifier token that must begin with a letter (A–Z or a–z) and might be followed by any number of letters, digits (0–9), hyphens (`-`), underscores (`_`), colons (`:`), and periods (`.`).
idref	A reference to an ID token defined by other attributes.
idrefs	A space-separated reference list to ID tokens defined by other attributes.
language-code	A language code that identifies a natural language spoken, written, or otherwise used for the communication of information among people. Computer languages are explicitly excluded from language codes. Language codes are identified by a primary code (such as `en`) followed by a hyphen and a two-letter subcode (such as `-us`) that identifies the country if necessary. The complete language code is: `en-us` for the U.S. version of English.
length	A value representing either a number of pixels (such as `100`) or a percentage of available space (such as `%50`).
link-type	A space-separated list of link types: `alternate`—Designates substitute versions for the document in which the link occurs. When used together with the `lang` attribute, it implies a translated version of the document. When used together with the `media` attribute, it implies a version designed for a different medium (or media). `appendix`—Refers to a document serving as an appendix in a collection of documents. `bookmark`—Refers to a bookmark. A bookmark is a link to a key entry point within an extended document. `chapter`—Refers to a document serving as a chapter in a collection of documents. `contents`—Refers to a document serving as a table of contents. `copyright`—Refers to a copyright statement for the current document. `glossary`—Refers to a document providing a glossary of terms that pertain to the current document. `help`—Refers to a document offering help. `index`—Refers to a document providing an index for the current document. `next`—Refers to the next document in a linear sequence of documents. `prev`—Refers to the previous document in an ordered series of documents. `section`—Refers to a document serving as a section in a collection of documents. `start`—Refers to the first document in a collection of documents.

Table A.1 Continued

Name	Description
	`stylesheet`—Refers to an external stylesheet. This is used together with the link type `alternate` for user-selectable alternate stylesheets.
	`subsection`—Refers to a document serving as a subsection in a collection of documents.
	`user-defined`—Relationship defined by the content author. If used, the `profile` attribute of the `head` element should provide explanatory information.
media-descriptor	A comma-separated list of recognized media descriptors:
	`all`—Suitable for all devices.
	`aural`—Intended for speech synthesizers.
	`braille`—Intended for Braille tactile feedback devices.
	`handheld`—Intended for handheld devices (small screen, monochrome, bitmapped graphics, limited bandwidth).
	`print`—Intended for paged, opaque material and for documents viewed onscreen in Print Preview mode.
	`projection`—Intended for projectors.
	`screen`—Intended for nonpaged computer screens.
	`tty`—Intended for media using a fixed-pitch character grid, such as Teletypes, terminals, or portable devices with limited display capabilities.
	`tv`—Intended for television-type devices (low resolution, color, limited scrollability).
multi-length	A value representing either a number of pixels (such as `100`), a percentage of available space (such as `%50`), or a relative length designated by an integer followed by an asterisk: "`i*`". The "`i`" is a proportional modifier of any remaining space that will be divided among relative length elements. For example, if there are 120 pixels remaining and competing relative lengths of 1*, 2*, and 3*, the space would be allocated as 20, 40, and 60 pixels respectively.
name	An identifier token that must begin with a letter (A–Z or a–z) and might be followed by any number of letters, digits (0–9), hyphens (-), underscores (_), colons (:), and periods (.).
number	A number composed of at least one digit (0–9).
pixels	An integer representing a number of pixels.
script	Script data. This is not evaluated as XHTML markup but passed as data to the script engine. Value is determined by scripting language.
style	Stylesheet rules. This is not evaluated as XHTML markup. Value is determined by style language.
text	Text that is meant to be read and understood by the user.
URI	A Uniform Resource Identifier, which includes Uniform Resource Locators.

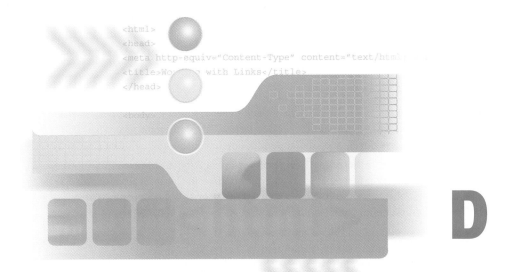

CSS2 REFERENCE

IN THIS APPENDIX

Style Sheet Properties   632

STYLE SHEET PROPERTIES

If you've looked into the details of cascading style sheets-Level 1, much of this appendix will look familiar. However, there are a large number of properties that you won't recognize. CSS22 has taken style sheets to a new level, and this appendix details all the new additions.

Currently, CSS1 is implemented in Netscape Navigator 4+, Opera 3.0+, and Microsoft's Internet Explorer 4+. CSS2 implementation is available to a certain degree in the Internet Explorer 5.0 and Opera 4.0+ browsers, and expected in Netscape's 6.0 browser as it becomes available. CSS2 is a W3C recommendation and can be found at `www.w3.org/TR/REC-CSS2/`.

The properties in this appendix are grouped into areas according to their function. In many cases, one property affects another and I've tried to present them in a logical order. The property groups include the following:

- Text

- Colors and backgrounds

- Fonts

- Box model

- Visual formatting and positioning

- Generated content and lists

- Tables

- Paged media

- Aural style sheets

<!--
Neither Internet Explorer or Netscape have fully implemented CSS in either the first or second level. For a regularly updated, comprehensive look at style sheet properties and browser support, see Eric Meyer's Safe CSS Properties table in `style.webreview.com/`.
-->

<!--
All properties that are new to the CSS2 specification are marked with an asterisk right after the property name.
-->

Selectors

Selectors are the tag elements defined at the beginning of a style sheet definition that tell the browser where to apply the style. After the selector, the style definition is included within curly brackets. In this example, BODY is the selector.

```
BODY {color: blue}
```

Several selectors can be grouped together if they are separated with commas.

```
H1, H2, H3 {font-family: san-serif}
```

In place of selectors, you can use the * wildcard. This example applies a font size style to all tags on the page:

```
* {font-size: 14pt}
```

Another wildcard character is the > sign. This tells the browser to search for child selectors within a certain parent. This example applies the style only to LI elements with OL lists:

```
OL > LI {list-style-type: decimal}
```

Using class selectors, you can apply different styles to the same tag. A period and a name follow a general selector and the style is applied to the tag whose `class` attribute matches the class name. The following example applies the style to any H2 tags that have the `class` attribute equal to `"myBlue"`.

```
H2.myBlue {background-color: blue}
<H2 class="myBlue">This header has a blue background.</H2>
```

Selectors also can be identified by the `id` attribute using the # character. The following example matches the style to any tags whose ID attribute is `"duckie"`.

```
#duckie {border-color: yellow}
```

Pseudo Classes

To access the control of elements that aren't referred to by normal tags, CSS2 defines several pseudo classes. An example is the first line of a paragraph. HTML and XHTML have no way of identifying this element, so a pseudo class called `:first-line` is used. All pseudo classes have colons in front of them. They are located after a selector like the following:

```
P:first-line {color: red}
```

The following are identified pseudo classes in CSS2:

- `:first-child`—This is the first child element of another element.
- `:link`—These are links that have not yet been visited.
- `:visited`—These are visited links.
- `:hover`—This is an element that the cursor is currently over.
- `:active`—This is the currently activated link element.
- `:focus`—This is the element that has the focus.
- `:lang`—This defines the current language.
- `:first-line`—This is the first formatted line of a paragraph.
- `:first-letter`—This is the first letter of a paragraph.
- `:before`—This positions content to come before an element.
- `:after`—This positions content to come after an element.

Rules

Rules are used to access files and documents located outside of the current document. There are five rules defined in CSS2, and all of them begin with the @ character: @charset, @font-face, @import, @media, and @page.

Properties

Properties are the main descriptors of the style sheet language. They appear within brackets and include the property name and a value separated by a colon. Some properties can include more than one value. These values are typically separated by a single space.

Text

The text properties include aligning properties such as text-align and word-spacing, as well as style-altering properties such as text-decoration and the new text-shadow properties.

text-indent

Description:	Defines the length of the indent applied to the first line of text in a block.
Values:	Any valid length—Can include negative values. Default is 0.
	Any valid percentage.
	inherit—Takes the same value as its parent.
Example:	P {text-indent: 40px}

text-align

Description:	Defines how an inline box of text is aligned.
Values:	left—Aligns text to the left.
	center—Aligns text to the center.
	right—Aligns text to the right.
	justify—Justifies the text.
	Any valid string—Defines a string on which table cells will align.
	inherit—Takes the same value as its parent.
Example:	P {text-align: right}

text-decoration

Description:	Defines decorations added to the text of an element.
Values:	none—(default) Applies no text decoration.
	underline—Underlines the text.
	overline—Puts a line over the text.
	line-through—Strikes out the text.
	blink—Causes the text to blink.
	inherit—Takes the same value as its parent.
Example:	P {text-decoration: underline}

text-transform

Description:	Defines capitalization effects to the text of an element.
Values:	none—(default) Applies no capitalization.
	capitalize—Capitalizes the first letter of each word.
	uppercase—Capitalizes all letters.
	lowercase—Converts all letters to lowercase.
	inherit—Takes the same value as its parent.
Example:	H3 {text-transform: uppercase}

text-shadow*

Description:	Describes values to create a text shadow effect. Several lists of shadow values can be included and must be separated by commas. Each separate shadow effect value list must include offset values and can include a blur radius and color.
Values:	none—(default) Applies no shadow effect.
	color—Color of text shadow.
	First valid length—Horizontal distance to the right of the text. Negative values are to the left of the text.
	Second valid length—Vertical distance below the text. Negative values are above the text.
	Third valid length—Text shadow blur radius.
	inherit—Takes the same value as its parent.
Example:	H1 {text-shadow: blue 5px 5px 3px, yellow -2px -2px 3px}

letter-spacing

Description:	Defines the space between text characters.
Values:	normal—(default) Applies normal text spacing for the used font.
	Any valid length—The length of the space between letters.
	inherit—Takes the same value as its parent.
Example:	P {letter-spacing: 0.3em}

word-spacing

Description:	Defines the space between words.
Values:	normal—(default) Applies normal text spacing for the font being used.
	Any valid length—The length of the space between letters.
	inherit—Takes the same value as its parent.
Example:	P {word-spacing—1.3em}

white-space

Description:	Defines how to handle whitespace in an element.
Values:	normal—(default) Collapses whitespace if necessary to fit boxes. This is the same as how HTML handles whitespace.
	pre—Treats all whitespace literally as it appears in code.
	nowrap—Collapses all whitespace.
	inherit—Takes the same value as its parent.
Example:	P {white-space: pre}

Colors and Backgrounds

Adding colors and backgrounds to elements creates a visually stimulating Web page. Style sheets include many properties that give your page the zing it needs.

color

Description:	Defines the text color.
Values:	Any valid color—Colors the text.
	inherit—Takes the same value as its parent.
Example:	P {color: green}
	P {color: rgb(0, 255, 0)}

background-color

Description:	Defines the background color of an element.
Values:	Any valid color—Colors the background.
	transparent—(default) Makes the element's background transparent.
	inherit—Takes the same value as its parent.
Example:	DIV {color: blue}
	DIV {color: rgb(0, 0, 255)}

CSS2 Provides Color Access

CSS2 provides access to all the colors used by a viewer's system. All properties that use color can reference the system colors using the following keywords: ActiveBorder, ActiveCaption, AppWorkspace, Background, ButtonFace, ButtonHighlight, ButtonShadow, ButtonText, CaptionText, GrayText, Highlight, HighlightText, InactiveBorder, InactiveCaption, InactiveCaptionText, InfoBackground, InfoText, Menu, MenuText, Scrollbar, ThreeDDarkShadow, ThreeDFace, ThreeDHighlight, ThreeDLightShadow, ThreeDShadow, Window, WindowFrame, and WindowText. For example, the color property set to MenuText would use the same color as the menu text your system uses.

---

background-image

Description:	Defines the background image of an element.
Values:	none—(default) Sets no background image.
	Any valid URL—URL of the background image.
	inherit—Takes the same value as its parent.
Example:	H1 {background-image: url("texture3.gif")}

background-repeat

Description:	Defines the direction that the background image is tiled.
Values:	repeat—(default) Background image repeats both horizontally and vertically.
	repeat-x—Background image repeats only horizontally.
	repeat-y—Background image repeats only vertically.
	no-repeat—Background image doesn't repeat.
	inherit—Takes the same value as its parent.
Example:	BLOCKQUOTE {background-repeat: repeat-x}

background-position

Description:	Defines the upper-left corner position of the background image. Single values set the horizontal distance and default the vertical offset to 50%. Several keywords can be combined.
Values:	First valid length—Horizontal distance the background image is placed from the left edge. Accepts negative values.
	Second valid length—Vertical distance the background image is placed from the top edge. Accepts negative values.
	First valid percentage—Percent of the element box the background image is offset from the left edge. Default is 0% or upper-left corner.
	Second valid percentage—Percent of the element box the background image is offset from the top edge.
	top—Positions the background image along the top edge.
	center—Positions the background image in the center of the element box.
	bottom—Positions the background image along the bottom edge.
	left—Positions the background image along the left edge.
	right—Positions the background image along the right edge.
	inherit—Takes the same value as its parent.
Example:	BLOCKQUOTE {background-position: top center}

background-attachment

Description: Defines whether the background image is fixed to the window or scrolls with the document.

Values: scroll—(default) Background image scrolls along with the window.
                    fixed—Background image is permanently fixed to its location.
                    Background image repeats only horizontally.
                    inherit—Takes the same value as its parent.

Example: body {background-attachment: fixed}

background

Description: Shorthand property for defining all background properties at once.
                    If not included, a property is set to its default value.

Values: background-color—Background color value.
                    background-image—Background image value.
                    background-repeat—Background repeat value.
                    background-attachment—Background attachment value.
                    background-position—Background position value.
                    inherit—Takes the same value as its parent.

Example: P {background: blue url("texture3.gif") repeat fixed top right}

Fonts

Font control adds style and flair to your Web pages whether you change the family, size, or weight.

font-family

Description: Defines a font to use for the element's text. It can include several font families separated by commas. The list order defines the priority.

Values: Font name—Font to use to render the text. Fonts with more than one word need to be in quotes.
                    Generic font name—Generic font class to use to render the text. Generic fonts include the following: serif, sans-serif, cursive, fantasy, and monospace.
                    inherit—Takes the same value as its parent.

Example: BODY {font-family: "Times Roman", courier, serif}

font-style

Description:	Defines a font style, such as italic or oblique.
Values:	normal—(default) Uses the normal font style.
	italic—Uses an italic font style.
	oblique—Uses an oblique or slanted font style.
	inherit—Takes the same value as its parent.
Example:	SPAN {font-style: italic}

font-variant

Description:	Defines whether a font is rendered using small caps.
Values:	normal—(default) Uses the normal font style.
	small-caps—Renders the font in small caps.
	inherit—Takes the same value as its parent.
Example:	H4 {font-variant: small-caps}

font-weight

Description:	Defines how thick text appears.
Values:	normal—(default) Uses the normal font thickness.
	bold—Uses a bold font weight.
	bolder—Uses a bolder font weight.
	lighter—Uses a lighter font weight.
	100–900—Number indicates the font thickness. 100 is the lightest (same as lighter), 400 is normal, 700 is bold, and 900 is bolder.
	inherit—Takes the same value as its parent.
Example:	H1 {font-weight: bolder}

font-stretch*

Description:	Defines the font's width.
Values:	normal—(default) Uses the normal font width.
	wider—Increases the width by one over current setting.
	narrower—Decreases the width by one over current setting.
	ultra-condensed—Defines the tightest width setting.
	extra-condensed—Looser than the preceding value.
	condensed—Looser than the preceding value.
	semi-condensed—Looser than the preceding value.
	semi-expanded—Wider than normal.
	expanded—Wider than the preceding value.
	extra-expanded—Wider than the preceding value.
	ultra-expanded—Defines the widest setting.
	inherit—Takes the same value as its parent.
Example:	BODY {font-stretch: condensed}

font-size

Description: Defines the size of the font.

Values: Absolute size—Uses keywords to express font size. Values include xx-small, small, medium (default), large, x-large, and xx-large.

Relative size—Uses relative keywords to express font size. Values include larger and smaller.

Any valid length—Defines the absolute font size. Negative values are not accepted.

Valid percentage—Defines the percent increase or decrease from the parent font size.

inherit—Takes the same value as its parent.

Example: BODY {font-size: 16pt}

font-size-adjust*

Description: Defines an aspect ratio to maintain when sizing fonts. This enables users to adjust for the text height when resizing.

Values: none—(default) Font's aspect ratio ignored.

Any valid number—Number representing the aspect value for the font.

inherit—Takes the same value as its parent.

Example: P {font-size-adjust: 0.45}

font

Description: Shorthand property for defining all font properties at once. If not included, a property is set to its default value.

Values: font-style—Font style value.

font-variant—Font variant value.

font-weight—Font weight value.

font-size—Font size value.

line-height—Line height value.

font-family—Font family value.

inherit—Takes the same value as its parent.

Example: BODY {font: italic bold 16pt 110% impact Garmond sans-serif}

Box Model

All elements are enveloped in a box made from the actual content, padding, border, and margins. Learning how to control these properties helps as you lay out your pages.

<!--
The font property can also use system fonts defined by the system. Valid values include caption, icon, menu, message-box, small-caption, and status-bar. For example, a font property set to menu would use the same font properties that the menus on your system use.
-->

margin-top, margin-right, margin-bottom, margin-left

Description:	Defines the margin width for the designated side.
Values:	Any valid length—Number representing the width of the margin. Default is 0.
	Any valid percentage—Percentage of window to use for the width of the padding.
	inherit—Takes the same value as its parent.
Example:	P {margin-top: 20px}

margin

Description:	Shorthand property for defining margins for all sides of an element at once. This property can include one to four values. One value sets only all margins to that value. Two sets the top and bottom to the first and the left and right to the second. Three values set the top to the first, left and right to the second, and the bottom to the third.
Values:	margin-top—Width of the top margin.
	margin-right—Width of the right margin.
	margin-bottom—Width of the bottom margin.
	margin-left—Width of the left margin.
	inherit—Takes the same value as its parent.
Example:	BODY {margin: 20px 30px 5px}

padding-top, padding-right, padding-bottom, padding-left

Description:	Defines the padding width for the designated side. Padding separates the text from the border.
Values:	Any valid length—Number representing the width of the padding. Default is 0.
	Any valid percentage—Percentage of window to use for the width of the padding.
	inherit—Takes the same value as its parent.
Example:	P {padding-top: 20px}

padding

Description:	Shorthand property for defining padding widths for all sides of an element at once. This property can include one to four values. One value sets all padding widths to that value. Two sets the top and bottom to the first and the left and right to the second. Three values set the top to the first, left and right to the second, and the bottom to the third.

Values: padding-top—Width of the top padding.

                     padding-right—Width of the right padding.

                     padding-bottom—Width of the bottom padding.

                     padding-left—Width of the left padding.

                     inherit—Takes the same value as its parent.

Example: BODY {padding: 20px 30px 5px}

border-top-width, border-right-width, border-bottom-width, border-left-width

Description: Defines the border width for the designated side. The border comes between the padding and margin.

Values: thin—Creates a thin weight border.

                     medium—(default) Creates a medium weight border.

                     thick—Creates a thick weight border.

                     inherit—Takes the same value as its parent.

Example: P {border-top-width: 10px}

border-width

Description: Shorthand property for defining border widths for all sides of an element at once. This property can include one to four values. One value sets all border widths to that value. Two sets the top and bottom to the first and the left and right to the second. Three values set the top to the first, left and right to the second, and the bottom to the third.

Values: border-top-width—Width of the top border.

                     border-right-width—Width of the right border.

                     border-bottom-width—Width of the bottom border.

                     border-left-width—Width of the left border.

                     inherit—Takes the same value as its parent.

Example: BODY {border-width: 20px 30px 5px}

border-top-color, border-right-color, border-bottom-color, border-left-color

Description: Defines the border color for the designated side. The border comes between the padding and margin.

Values: Any valid color—Specifies the border color.

                     inherit—Takes the same value as its parent.

Example: P {border-top-color: rgb(255, 0, 255)}

border-color

Description:	Shorthand property for defining border colors for all sides of an element at once. This property can include one to four values. One value sets all border colors to that value. Two sets the top and bottom to the first and the left and right to the second. Three values set the top to the first, left and right to the second, and the bottom to the third.
Values:	border-top-color—Color of the top border.
	border-right-color—Color of the right border.
	border-bottom-color—Color of the bottom border.
	border-left-color—Color of the left border.
	transparent—Makes the borders transparent.
	inherit—Takes the same value as its parent.
Example:	BODY {border-color: blue red pink}

border-top-style, border-right-style, border-bottom-style, border-left-style

Description:	Defines the border style for the designated side. The border comes between the padding and margin.
Values:	none—Specifies no border style.
	hidden—Also specifies no border style, but acts differently for tables.
	dotted—Creates a series of dots.
	dashed—Creates a series of dashed lines.
	solid—Creates a solid, non-breaking line.
	double—Creates two parallel, solid, non-breaking lines.
	groove—Creates a 3D carved-style border.
	ridge—Creates a 3D raised-style border.
	inset—Creates a 3D inset-style border.
	outset—Creates a 3D outset-style border.
	inherit—Takes the same value as its parent.
Example:	P {border-top-style: double}

border-style

Description:	Shorthand property for defining border styles for all sides of an element at once. This property can include one to four values. One value sets all border styles to that value. Two values set the top and bottom to the first and the left and right to the second. Three values set the top to the first, left and right to the second, and the bottom to the third.
Values:	border-top-style—Style of the top border.
	border-right-style—Style of the right border.
	border-bottom-style—Style of the bottom border.
	border-left-style—Style of the left border.
	inherit—Takes the same value as its parent.
Example:	BODY {border-style: double solid}

border-top, border-right, border-bottom, border-left

Description:	Shorthand properties for defining several border properties at once for the designated side. Each separate property applies to its named side. The following definitions use the top.
Values:	border-top-width—Width of the top border.
	border-top-style—Style of the top border.
	border-top-color—Color of the top border.
	inherit—Takes the same value as its parent.
Example:	P {border-top: thin double blue}

border

Description:	Shorthand property for defining borders for all sides of an element at once. The values are applied equally to all sides of the element.
Values:	border-width—Width of the border.
	border-style—Style of the border.
	border-color—Color of the border.
	inherit—Takes the same value as its parent.
Example:	BODY {border: 4px solid red}

outline-width*

Description:	Shorthand property for defining outline widths for all sides of an element at once. This property can include one to four values. One value sets all outline widths to that value. Two values set the top and bottom to the first and the left and right to the second. Three values set the top to the first, left and right to the second, and the bottom to the third.
Values:	thin—Creates a thin weight border.
	medium—(default) Creates a medium weight border.
	thick—Creates a thick weight border.
	inherit—Takes the same value as its parent.
Example:	BODY {outline-width: 20px 30px 5px}

outline-style*

Description:	Shorthand property for defining outline styles for all sides of an element at once. This property can include one to four values. One value sets all outline styles to that value. Two values set the top and bottom to the first and the left and right to the second. Three values set the top to the first, left and right to the second, and the bottom to the third.
Values:	none—Specifies no border style.
	dotted—Creates a series of dots.
	dashed—Creates a series of dashed lines.

solid—Creates a solid, non-breaking line.

double—Creates two parallel, solid, non-breaking lines.

groove—Creates a 3D carved-style border.

ridge—Creates a 3D raised-style border.

inset—Creates a 3D inset-style border.

outset—Creates a 3D outset-style border.

inherit—Takes the same value as its parent.

Example: BODY {outline-style: double solid}

outline-color*

Description: Property for defining outline colors. This property can include one to four values. One value sets all outline colors to that value. Two values set the top and bottom to the first and the left and right to the second. Three values set the top to the first, left and right to the second, and the bottom to the third.

Values: Any valid color—Specifies the border color.

invert—(default) Inverts the colors of the outline.

inherit—Takes the same value as its parent.

Example: BODY {outline-color: blue red pink}

outline*

Description: Shorthand property for defining outlines. The values are applied equally to all sides of the element.

Values: outline-width—Width of the outline.

outline-style—Style of the outline.

outline-color—Color of the outline.

inherit—Takes the same value as its parent.

Example: BODY {outline: 4px solid red}

Visual Formatting and Positioning

The display property provides a way to define elements for the style sheet. Once defined, the position properties can place the elements exactly where you want them to go.

display

Description: Defines the type of display box the element creates. These different types of boxes interact differently with each other as they are laid out on a page.

Values: inline—(default) Creates an inline display box.

block—Creates a block display box.

list-item—Creates a list-item inline display box.

marker—Creates generated content to appear before or after a display box. Only used with the :before and :after pseudo elements.

none—Creates no display box. The element has no effect on the overall layout.

run-in—Creates a box like a block display box depending on its location.

compact—Creates a box like an inline display box depending on its location.

table, inline-table, table-row-group, table-column, table-column-group, table-header-group, table-footer-group, table-row, table-cell, table-caption—Creates a table display box matching the property name.

inherit—Takes the same value as its parent.

Example: P {display: block}

position

Description: Defines the positioning method to use.

Values: static—(default) Defines a normal box using default HTML layout.

relative—Positioned box is offset from its normal layout position.

absolute—Positioned box is offset from its containing box's position and they don't effect the layout.

fixed—Positioned box is offset like the absolute model, but is fixed in the browser window and doesn't move when the window is scrolled.

inherit—Takes the same value as its parent.

Example: IMG {position: absolute}

top, right, bottom, left

Description: Defines the offset width from the designated edge.

Values: auto—(default) Enables the browser to select an offset width to position all elements.

Any valid length—Number representing the width from the edge.

Any valid percentage—Percentage of window to offset from the edge.

inherit—Takes the same value as its parent.

Example: UL {top: 20px; right: 40px}

width

Description: Defines the width of a display box.

Values: auto—(default) Enables the browser to select a width for the display box.

Any valid length—Number representing the width of the display box.

Any valid percentage—Percentage of window to use for the display box width.

inherit—Takes the same value as its parent.

Example: BLOCKQUOTE {width: 260px}

min-width*, max-width*

Description: Defines the minimum or maximum widths of a display box.

Values: Any valid length—Number representing the minimum or maximum widths of the display box.

Any valid percentage—Percentage of window to use for the minimum or maximum widths.

none—No width limit, applies only to the max-width property.

inherit—Takes the same value as its parent.

Example: BLOCKQUOTE {min-width: 100px; max-width: 400px}

height

Description: Defines the height of a display box.

Values: auto—(default) Enables the browser to select a height for the display box.

Any valid length—Number representing the height of the display box.

Any valid percentage—Percentage of window to use for the display box height.

inherit—Takes the same value as its parent.

Example: BLOCKQUOTE {height: 260px}

min-height*, max-height*

Description: Defines the minimum or maximum heights of a display box.

Values: Any valid length—Number representing the minimum or maximum heights of the display box.

Any valid percentage—Percentage of window to use for the minimum or maximum heights.

none—No height limit, applies only to the max-height property.

inherit—Takes the same value as its parent.

Example: BLOCKQUOTE {min-height: 100px; max-height: 400px}

line-height

Description: Defines the line spacing for an element box.

Values: normal—(default) Enables the browser to set the value to fit all elements on the page.

Any valid length—Number representing the height of the display box.

Any valid percentage—Percentage of window to use for the box height.

Any valid number—Number times the font size height.

inherit—Takes the same value as its parent.

Example: BLOCKQUOTE {line-height: 2.2}

vertical-align

Description: Defines the vertical positioning inside a line box.

Values: baseline—(default) Aligns the box's baseline to its parent baseline.

middle—Aligns the box's middle to its parent's baseline.

top—Aligns the box's top with the top of the line box.

bottom—Aligns the box's bottom to its parent's baseline.

sub—Aligns the box's text to be at subscript level to its parent's baseline.

super—Aligns the box's text to be at superscript level of its parent's baseline.

text-top—Aligns the box's top to the top of the parent's text.

text-bottom—Aligns the box's bottom to the bottom of the parent's baseline.

Any valid length—Defines the distance to raise the box's level. Negative values lower its level.

Any valid percentage—Percentage to raise the box's level. Negative values lower its level.

inherit—Takes the same value as its parent.

Example: BLOCKQUOTE {vertical-align: super}

float

Description: Defines whether the display box should float to the left or right.

Values: none—(default) The display box doesn't float.

left—Causes the display box to float to the left and content flows to the right.

right—Causes the display box to float to the right and content flows to the left.

inherit—Takes the same value as its parent.

Example: IMG {float: right}

clear

Description: Defines whether content appears adjacent to the side of float box or not.

Values: none—(default) Content not constrained next to float boxes.

left—Content doesn't appear to the left of a float box.

right—Content doesn't appear to the right of a float box.

both—Content doesn't appear to the left or right of a float box.

inherit—Takes the same value as its parent.

Example: IMG {clear: both}

overflow*

Description: Defines whether a display box is displayed when it overflows the element's box.

Values: visible—(default) The overflowed box is visible and not clipped.

hidden—The overflowed portion is clipped.

scroll—The overflowed portion is clipped and any scrollbars are made visible.

auto—Enables the browser to determine whether overflowed areas are clipped.

inherit—Takes the same value as its parent.

Example: PRE {overflow: visible}

clip*

Description: Defines the clipping area for overflowed sections.

Values: auto—(default) Causes the clipping region to have the same size and location as the element's box.

rect(top, right, bottom, left)—The clipping area is defined by the offsets from the top, right, bottom, and left length values.

inherit—Takes the same value as its parent.

Example: BLOCKQUOTE {clip: rect(5px, 4px, 2px, 4px)}

visibility

Description: Defines whether an element is visible.

Values: visible—Makes the element visible.

hidden—Makes the element hidden, but it still effects the layout.

collapse—Same as hidden, except when used on tables.

inherit—(default) Takes the same value as its parent.

Example: IMG {visibility: visible}

z-index

Description: Defines the stacking order for elements.

Values: auto—(default) Causes the element box to accept the same stacking order as its parent's box.

Any valid integer—An integer value representing the stacking order. Lower values have a lower stacking order.

inherit—Takes the same value as its parent.

Example: IMG {z-index: 3}

cursor*

Description:	Defines how the cursor looks when moved over an element.
Values:	auto—(default) Cursor determined by the browser.
	crosshair—Cursor resembles a crosshair.
	default—Cursor is the default cursor for the user's system.
	pointer—Cursor resembles a pointer indicating a link.
	move—Cursor indicates that something is to be moved.
	e-resize, ne-resize, nw-resize, n-resize, se-resize, sw-resize, s-resize, w-resize—Cursor indicates a corner position.
	text—Cursor text.
	wait—Cursor indicates the system is busy.
	help—Cursor indicates a help location.
	Any valid URL—URL of a cursor file.
	inherit—Takes the same value as its parent.
Example:	IMG {cursor: pointer}

direction*

Description:	Defines the writing direction for text blocks.
Values:	ltr—(default) Sets writing direction from left to right.
	rtl—Sets writing direction from right to left.
	inherit—Takes the same value as its parent.
Example:	BODY { direction: ltr; unicode-bidi: embed}

unicode-bidi*

Description:	Enables the text writing direction to be changed.
Values:	normal—(default) Doesn't enable other writing directions.
	embed—Enables writing direction to be set using the direction property.
	bidi-override—Enables writing direction to be set using the direction property. Applies to additional blocks.
	inherit—Takes the same value as its parent.
Example:	IMG {unicode-bidi: embed}

Generated Content and Lists

With these properties, you have control over the style of your list boxes and how the numbers or bullets are presented. They make it easy to have your list count by twos starting from seven.

content*

Description:	Used with the :before and :after pseudo elements to generate content.
Values:	Any valid string—String to appear before or after the element.
	Any valid URL—URL to an external file to appear before or after an element.

counter()—Defines a counter with a name to insert the value controlled by the counter-increment and counter-reset properties.
open-quote, close-quote—Enables quote marks to be included. Used with the quotes property.
no-open-quote, no-close-quote—Inserts no quote marks.
attr()—Inserts the value of an attribute for the element.
inherit—Takes the same value as its parent.

Example: PRE:after {content: "thank you and good-night."}

quotes*

Description: Defines the pairs of quotation marks to use for each level of embedded quote marks.

Values: First valid string—Pair of characters to use for the outmost quotation marks.
Second valid string—Pair of characters to use for inner quotation marks.
none—No quote marks are created.
inherit—Takes the same value as its parent.

Example: Q {quotes: '"' '"' '<' '>'}

counter-increment*

Description: Increases the value of the specified counter.

Values: none—(default) Counter is not incremented.
Counter name and valid number—Identifies the counter and accepts an integer value that counter is incremented. Negative values are valid.
inherit—Takes the same value as its parent.

Example: H1 {counter-increment: MyCounter 2}

counter-reset*

Description: Resets the value of a specified counter.

Values: none—(default) Counter is not reset.
Counter name and valid number—Identifies the counter and accepts an integer value that the counter is reset. Negative values are valid.
inherit—Takes the same value as its parent.

Example: H1 {counter-reset: MyCounter 2}

marker-offset*

Description: Defines the distance between a list marker (such as a bullet) and the text.

Values: auto—(default) Enables the browser to determine the spacing.
Any valid length—The space between a marker and the text.
inherit—Takes the same value as its parent.

Example: H1 {marker-offset: 12px}

list-style-type

Description: Defines the list style to be applied to the list markers.

Values: disc—(default) Creates a disc-shaped bullet.

circle—Creates a circular-shaped bullet.

square—Creates a square-shaped bullet.

decimal—Numbers lists using decimal numbers, beginning with 1.

decimal-leading-zero—Numbers lists using decimal numbers padded with a zero, such as 01, 02, 03, and so on.

lower-roman—Numbers lists using lowercase Roman numerals.

upper-roman—Numbers lists using uppercase Roman numerals.

hebrew—Numbers lists using Hebrew numerals.

georgian—Numbers lists using Georgian numerals.

armenian—Numbers lists using Armenian numerals.

cjk-ideographic—Numbers lists using ideographic numerals.

lower-latin, lower-alpha—Uses lowercase ASCII characters.

upper-latin, upper-alpha—Uses uppercase ASCII characters.

lower-greek—Uses lowercase Greek characters.

hiragana—Uses Japanese hiragana characters.

hiragana-iroha—Uses Japanese hiragana iroha characters.

katakana-iroha—Uses Japanese katakana iroha characters.

none—No marker is used.

inherit—Takes the same value as its parent.

Example: OL {list-style: upper-alpha}

list-style-image

Description: Defines the image of a list marker.

Values: none—(default) Sets no marker image.

Any valid URL—URL of the marker image.

inherit—Takes the same value as its parent.

Example: UL {list-style-image: url("bullet3.gif")}

list-style-position

Description: Defines the location of the list box markers.

Values: inside—Markers appear within the element box.

outside—(default) Markers appear outside the element box.

inherit—Takes the same value as its parent.

Example: H1 {list-style-position: inside}

list-style

Description:	Shorthand property for defining all list style properties at once. If not included, a property is set to its default value.
Values:	list-style-type—Marker type.
	list-style-position—Marker position.
	list-style-image—Marker image.
	inherit—Takes the same value as its parent.
Example:	UL {list-style: circle inside url("bullet4.gif")}

Tables

Table control is new to CSS2. These properties enable you to define the style, spacing, and layout of your tables.

caption-side*

Description:	Defines the position of a table caption relative to the table.
Values:	top—(default) Positions the caption at the top of the table.
	right—Positions the caption to the right of the table.
	bottom—Positions the caption at the bottom of the table.
	left—Positions the caption to the left of the table.
	inherit—Takes the same value as its parent.
Example:	TABLE {caption-side: top}

table-layout*

Description:	Defines how the table is laid out.
Values:	auto—(default) Enables the browser to decide how to lay out the table.
	fixed—Tables are laid out using a fixed method.
	inherit—Takes the same value as its parent.
Example:	TABLE {table-layout: fixed}

border-collapse*

Description:	Defines how the table borders are displayed.
Values:	collapse—(default) Collapses the table cell borders into a common border.
	separate—Keeps each table cell's border separated.
	inherit—Takes the same value as its parent.
Example:	TD {border-collapse: separate}

border-spacing*

Description:	Defines the spacing between table borders. Only one length value applies equally to both horizontal and vertical directions.
Values:	First valid length—Defines the horizontal width separating table cell borders.
	Second valid length—Defines the vertical width separating table cell borders.
	inherit—Takes the same value as its parent.
Example:	TABLE {border-spacing: 4px}

empty-cells*

Description:	Defines how to render the border of empty cells.
Values:	show—(default) Enables the borders of empty cells to be seen.
	hide—Hides the borders of empty cells.
	inherit—Takes the same value as its parent.
Example:	TABLE {empty-cells: show}

speak-header*

Description:	Enables a screen reader to speak table headers.
Values:	once—(default) Causes the header to be spoken only once for each column of cells.
	always—Causes the header to be spoken each time for a column of cells.
	inherit—Takes the same value as its parent.
Example:	TABLE {speak-header: once}

column-span*

Description:	Defines the number of columns to span.
Values:	Any valid number—The number of columns to span. Default is 1.
	inherit—Takes the same value as its parent.
Example:	TD {column-span: 3}

row-span*

Description:	Defines the number of rows to span.
Values:	Any valid number—The number of rows to span. Default is 1.
	inherit—Takes the same value as its parent.
Example:	TD {row-span: 3}

Paged Media

These properties enable you to split your page content into predefined pages that output correctly to a printer or external device.

size*

Description: Defines the size and orientation of a page.

Values: auto—(default) Enables the browser to determine the page size.

First valid length—Sets the page width.

Second valid length—Sets the page height.

landscape—Sets the page orientation to landscape.

portrait—Sets the page orientation to portrait.

inherit—Takes the same value as its parent.

Example: P {size: 8.5in 11in portrait}

marks*

Description: Enables printed pages to have crop and cross marks.

Values: none—(default) No printing marks are included.

crop—Displays crop marks.

cross—Displays registration marks.

inherit—Takes the same value as its parent.

Example: P {marks: crop cross}

page-break-before*

Description: Defines the page breaks for a page.

Values: auto—(default) Enables the browser to determine the page breaks.

always—Always forces a page break before a box.

avoid—Avoids placing a page break before a box.

left—Always forces a page break before a box so that the next page is on the left.

right—Always forces a page break before a box so that the next page is on the right.

inherit—Takes the same value as its parent.

Example: P {page-break-before: avoid}

page-break-after*

Description: Defines the page breaks for a page.

Values: auto—(default) Enables the browser to determine the page breaks.

always—Always forces a page break after a box.

avoid—Avoids placing a page break after a box.

left—Always forces a page break after a box so that the next page is on the left.

right—Always forces a page break after a box so that the next page is on the right.

inherit—Takes the same value as its parent.

Example: P {page-break-after: avoid}

page-break-inside*

Description: Defines the page breaks for a page.

Values: auto—(default) Enables the browser to determine the page breaks.

avoid—Avoids placing a page break within a box.

inherit—Takes the same value as its parent.

Example: P {page-break-inside: avoid}

page*

Description: Identifies a page with a name.

Values: auto—(default) Enables the browser to identify pages.

Any valid name—Gives a page a name. The name can be any string.

Example: P {page: Mypage}

orphans*

Description: Defines how many sentences can be left at the bottom of a page before starting a new one.

Values: Any valid number—An integer defining the number of sentences that must be left on the bottom of a page. Default is 2.

inherit—Takes the same value as its parent.

Example: P {orphans: 4}

widows*

Description: Defines how many sentences can be left at the top of a new page.

Values: Any valid number—An integer defining the number of sentences that must be left on the top of a page. Default is 2.

inherit—Takes the same value as its parent.

Example: P {widows: 4}

Aural Style Sheets

As a way to define Web pages for individuals with visual handicaps, or provide audio information for hands-free environments such as automobiles, aural style sheets enable designers to specify how screen readers interpret Web pages.

<!--
Aural style sheets are not well supported. As such, there are very few examples of them in use.
-->

volume*

Description:	Defines the loudness of text read by a screen reader.
Values:	Any valid number, 0–100—An integer ranged between 0 and 100 with 0 being minimum and 100 being maximum.
	Any valid percentage, 0–100—A percentage increase or decrease from the current value.
	silent—No sound emitted.
	x-soft—Quietest level of sound, same as 0.
	soft—Quiet level of sound, same as 25.
	medium—(default) Normal level of sound, same as 50.
	loud—Loud level of sound, same as 75.
	x-loud—Loudest level of sound, same as 100.
	inherit—Takes the same value as its parent.
Example:	BODY {volume: soft}

speak*

Description:	Defines how the words are spoken.
Values:	normal—(default) Words are spoken normally.
	none—Words are not spoken.
	spell-out—Words are spelled letter by letter.
	inherit—Takes the same value as its parent.
Example:	ACRONYM {speak: spell-out}

pause-before*

Description:	Causes a pause before the element is read.
Values:	Any valid time—The amount of time to pause before reading the element.
	Any valid percentage—The percent to pause before reading the element.
	inherit—Takes the same value as its parent.
Example:	SPAN {pause-before: 500ms}

pause-after*

Description:	Causes a pause after the element is read.
Values:	Any valid time—The amount of time to pause after reading the element.
	Any valid percentage—The percent to pause after reading the element.
	inherit—Takes the same value as its parent.
Example:	SPAN {pause-after: 500ms}

pause*

Description: Shorthand property for setting the pause-before and pause-after the element is read. If only one time or percent value is given, it applies to both before and after.

Values: First valid time—The amount of time to pause before reading the element. Second valid time—The amount of time to pause after reading the element. Any valid percentage—The percent to pause before reading the element. Any valid percentage—The percent to pause after reading the element. inherit—Takes the same value as its parent.

Example: SPAN {pause: 500ms 300ms}

cue-before*

Description: Causes a cue before the element is read.

Values: Any valid URL—URL of an audio file to play before reading the element. none—No audio is played before the element is read. inherit—Takes the same value as its parent.

Example: SPAN {cue-before: url("bell.wav")}

cue-after*

Description: Causes a cue after the element is read.

Values: Any valid URL—URL of an audio file to play after reading the element. none—No audio is played after the element is read. inherit—Takes the same value as its parent.

Example: SPAN {cue-after: url("bell2.wav")}

cue*

Description: Shorthand property that causes a cue before and after the element is read. If only one URL is given, it applies to both before and after.

Values: First valid URL—URL of an audio file to play before reading the element. Second valid URL—URL of an audio file to play after reading the element. none—No audio is played before the element is read. inherit—Takes the same value as its parent.

Example: SPAN {cue: url("ding.wav") url("dong.wav")}

play-during*

Description: Defines an audio file to be played in the background while text is being read.

Values: Any valid URL—URL of an audio file to play in the background while reading the element.

mix—Mix the current audio with the parent audio file and play both together.

repeat—Repeat the audio until all the text has been read.

auto—(default) Enable the parent element's audio to continue to play.

none—No background audio is played.

inherit—Takes the same value as its parent.

Example: BODY {play-during: url("chatter.wav") mix}

azimuth*

Description: Defines the spatial location of an audio file horizontally around the listener's head.

Values: Any valid angle—An angle value between 0 and 360 degrees. Negative values are not allowed.

left-side—Sound from the left side of the head, or 270 degrees.

far-left—Sound from the distant left of the head, or 300 degrees.

left—Sound from the left of the head, or 320 degrees.

center-left—Sound from the center left of the head, or 340 degrees.

center—Sound from the center of the head, or 0 degrees.

center-right—Sound from the center right of the head, or 20 degrees.

right—Sound from the right of the head, or 40 degrees.

far-right—Sound from the distant right of the head, or 60 degrees.

left-side—Sound from the right side of the head, or 270 degrees.

leftwards—Sound moved to the left of the current location.

rightwards—Sound moved to the right of the current location.

behind—Sound moved to behind the head at that location.

inherit—Takes the same value as its parent.

Example: H1 {azimuth: left-side}

elevation*

Description: Defines the spatial location of an audio file vertically around the listener's head.

Values: Any valid angle—An angle value between 90 and -90 degrees. Negative values are allowed.

below—Sound from below the head, or -90 degrees.

level—Sound from the front of the head, or 0 degrees.

above—Sound from above the head, or 90 degrees.

higher—Sound moved up from the current location.

inherit—Takes the same value as its parent.

Example: H1 {elevation: above}

speech-rate*

Description: Defines how quickly the element text is read.

Values: Any valid number—The speaking rate in words per minute.

x-slow—80 words per minute.

slow—120 words per minute.

medium—(default) 180–200 words per minute.

fast—300 words per minute.

x-fast—500 words per minute.

faster—Causes the words to be read faster than the current speed, adds 40 words per minute.

slower—Causes the words to be read slower than the current speed, subtracts 40 words per minute.

inherit—Takes the same value as its parent.

Example: BODY {speech-rate: fast}

voice-family*

Description: Defines the voice type to use to read the element's text. It can include several voice families separated by commas. The list order defines the priority.

Values: Voice name—Voice to use to read the text.

Generic voice name—Generic voice class to use to read the text.

Generic voices include: male, female, and child.

inherit—Takes the same value as its parent.

Example: BODY {voice-family: Bob, male}

pitch*

Description: Defines the pitch of the element text.

Values: Any valid frequency—The pitch in Hertz (Hz).

x-low—Lowest pitch.

low—Low pitch.

medium—(default) Average pitch.

high—Higher than normal pitch.

x-high—Highest pitch.

inherit—Takes the same value as its parent.

Example: BODY {pitch: high}

pitch-range*

Description: Defines the pitch range of the element text as its read.

Values: Any valid number—A value between 0 and 100 that defines the pitch range. The default, 50, is normal inflection.

inherit—Takes the same value as its parent.

Example: BODY {pitch-range: 50}

stress*

Description:	Defines the stress of the element text as it's read.
Values:	Any valid number—A value between 0 and 100 that defines the pitch range. The default, 50, is normal.
	inherit—Takes the same value as its parent.
Example:	BODY {stress: 50}

richness*

Description:	Defines the richness of the element text as it's read.
Values:	Any valid number—A value between 0 and 100 that defines the pitch range. The default, 50, is normal.
	inherit—Takes the same value as its parent.
Example:	BODY {richness: 50}

speak-punctuation*

Description:	Defines how punctuation is spoken.
Values:	code—Punctuation is spoken literally.
	none—Punctuation is not spoken.
	inherit—Takes the same value as its parent.
Example:	BODY {speak-puncuation: code}

speak-numeral*

Description:	Defines how numbers are spoken.
Values:	digits—Numbers are spoken as individual digits.
	continuous—Numbers are spoken as a full number.
	inherit—Takes the same value as its parent.
Example:	SPAN.phone {speak-numeral: digits}

INDEX

Symbols

7-bit ASCII encoding, 438

8-bit character encoding, 438

8-bit character sets (ISO), 45

32-bit character set, 438

A

a element, 571-573

A List Apart.com Web site, developer resources, 385, 564

A-Prompt accessibility validator, 433

abbr element, 113, 573

abbreviations and accessibility (acronym element), 430-431

absolute links, 158-159, 163

abstract modules (XHTML)
  core
    Applet, 455
    Hypertext, 455
    List, 455
    Structure, 455
    Text, 455
  forms
    Basic Forms, 456
    Forms, 456
  media/scripting
    Base, 457
    Client-side Image Map, 457
    Frames, 457
    Iframe, 457
    Image, 456
    Intrinsic Events, 457
    Legacy, 458
    Link, 457
    Meta-information, 457

    New Identification, 457
    Object, 457
    Ruby, 457
    Scripting, 457
    Server-side Image Map, 457
    Style Attribute, 457
    Stylesheet, 457
    Target, 457
  tables
    Basic Tables, 456
    Tables, 456
  text extension
    Bi-Directional Text, 456
    Edit, 456
    Presentation, 456

accessibility
  abbreviations (acronym element), 430-431
  documents, building, 424-431
  frames
    building, 243-244
    NOFRAMES tag, 242-243
  HTML 4.0 recommendation, 26
  laws
    American with Disabilities Act of 1990, 420
    international policies, 421-422
    Rehabilitation Act of 1973, 420
    Workforce Investment Act of 1998, 420-421
  links
    tab order additions, 426-428
    title attribute, 424-426

  tables, 242, 428-429
  testing, 432-433
  validators
    A-Prompt, 433
    Bobby, 433
    WAVE, 433
  Web Accessibility Initiative (WAI), 422-423

accessing embedded objects, 341

acronym element, 113, 574
  abbreviations and accessibility, 430-431

action element (forms), 270-271

ActiveX components, embedded objects, 326

adaptive palette, graphics optimization, 281

adding
  applets to documents (object element), 330-331
  audio to Web pages (embed element), 308-309
  horizontal rules in paragraphs, 152-153
  images
    documents (object element), 329-330
    Web pages, 282-285
  Java applets to documents (applet element), 332-335
  menu lists to forms, 260-263
  paragraphs (p tag), 115-117
  radio buttons to forms, 258-260

scripts to pages (script element), 403-407

streaming audio (RealServer G2), 316-318

streaming video
HTTP, 316-318
RealServer G2, 316

tab order to links (accessibility issues), 426-428

text fields in forms, 254-256

video to Web pages (embed element), 308-309

additive synthesis (hexadecimal colors), 63-64

address element, 574

Adobe GoLive, FTP capabilities, 543-544

Adobe LiveMotion, 321

Adobe Premiere, 322

Adobe Systems Web site, 281

Advanced Streaming Media Format (ASF), 322

advertising
awards, 559
banners
click-throughs, 553-554
CPM, 553-554
design guidelines, 555-556
flat fees, 553-554
impressions, 554-555
page views, 553-554
placement of, 556
pricing structure, 554-555
e-mail, 557
links, 558
newsgroups, 558
offline strategies, 559-560
search engines, 549
checking on submissions, 553
listing methods, 550
rankings, 551-553
site submissions, 551
target audiences and demographics, 548-549
Web rings, 559

align attribute
hr tag, 152
img element, 284-288
table tag, 188
td tag, 204
values, 125-126

aligning
headers, 125-126
multiple images in Web pages, 295-298
paragraphs, 125-126
table cells, 203-205
table rows, 202-203

alink attribute (body element), 142

alt attribute (img element), 284, 288-290

AltaVista Web site, 549

alternate character sets, labeling, 51-54

alternate content views, creating (XSLT), 505-506

American Demographics Web site, 549

Americans with Disabilities Act of 1990, 420

analog audio files, digitizing, 303-304

analog-to-digital (A/D) converter, 303-304

anchor element
a element, 571-573
attributes
href, 156-158
name, 156-158
target, 156-158
image linking, 299
links, 156, 158
Using a Standard Link code listing (7.1), 157-158

animation in banner ads, 556

ANSI.org Web site, ASCII resources, 439

antialiasing PNG images, 279

Apple QuickTime, 308-310, 322

Apple Web site
font utilities, 448
QuickTime Player, 308-310

applet element, 331, 574-576
attributes
archive, 331
code, 331
codebase, 331
name, 331
object, 331
code listings, Combining object and applet Elements for Cross-Browser Compatibility (13.3), 335-336
combining with object element (cross-browser support), 335-336
Java applets, adding to documents, 332-335

Applet module (XHTML), 455

applets
documents, adding (object element), 330-331
embedded objects, 326

applications (XML)
ChemML, 536
GedML, 536
Health Level-7 (HL7), 536
ICE (Information and Content Exchange), 536
MathML, 536
MISTI (Missile Industry Supply-change Transaction Infrastructures), 536
Real Estate Transaction Standard (RETS), 536
RosettaNet, 536
SAE J2008, 536
SMIL, 536

applying XSLT style sheets, 495-496

archive attribute
applet object, 331
object element, 329

area element, 576-577

Arial font (style sheets), 372

artifacts in JPEG images, 278

ArtToday Web site, stock photos, 547

ASCAP (American Society of Composers, Authors, and Publishers), 547, 561

Ask Dr. Web Web site, 385

assigning classes, style sheet selectors, 361-363

Association for Women in Computing Web site, organization resources, 566

attributes, 627
  case-sensitivity, Mixed Case in HTML 4.01 (Listing 5.1), 106
  documents, 32
  minimization, 248
  properties, 103-104
  table tag
    align, 188
    border, 188
    cellpadding, 188, 192-195
    cellspacing, 188, 192-195
    colspan, 195-198
    rowspan, 198-201
    summary, 188
    width, 188-189
  tags
    case-sensitivity, 106
    quoting, 107-108
  td tag
    align, 204
    valign, 204
    width, 204
  values, 104-105
  XML
    documents, 534-535
    tags, quoting, 108
  XSL-FO
    background-color, 487
    background-image, 487
    border-bottom-width, 487
    border-left-color, 487
    font-family, 487
    font-weight, 487
    height, 487
    max-height, 487
    min-height, 487
    text-align, 487

attributes (XML DTDs), 475-476

audiences (target market), 548-549

audio
  digitizing, 303-304
  file creation, 303-304
  file formats
    AVI (Audio/Video Interface), 307
    downloading, 306-307
    MIDI (Musical Instrument Digital Interface), 307
    MPEG 3 (Motion Picture Expert Group), 307-308
    RMF (Rich Music Format), 307
    streaming, 306
    WAV (Windows Audio/Video), 307
  files sizes versus sampling rates, 306-307
  hardware requirements, 303
  plug-ins (audio)
    Apple QuickTime Player, 310
    Beatnik Player, 310
    Microsoft Windows Media Player, 310
    Netscape Navigator support, 309
    Real Player, 310
    selection criteria, 311
  resources
    Beatmik Web site, 308
    MacMusic Web site, 305
    Pure Digital Audio Web site, 305
  sampling rates versus file sizes, 306-307
  software tools
    Cool Edit, 304
    DigiDesign Pro Tools, 304
    Macromedia SoundEdit 16, 304
    Sound Forge, 305
    Waves Audio Track, 305
    streaming format
      adding (HTTP), 316-318
      adding (RealServer G2), 316
      creating, 312-315
    Web pages, adding (embed element), 308-309

aural attribute (link element), 175

aural style sheets, 656-661

authoring resources, WaSP versus W3C, 28-29

autoplay attribute (embed element), 309

AVI (Audio/Video Interface), 307-308

B

b element (bold), 123-124, 577

Babblelist.com Web site, mailing list resources, 565

background attribute (body element), 142

background property (style sheets), 384-386

background-color attribute (XSL-FO), 487

background-image attribute (XSL-FO), 487

backgrounds
  colors, 142
  style sheets, 384-386

banners
  click-throughs, 553-554
  CPM, 553-554
  design guidelines, 555-556
  effectiveness, 556
  exchange programs
    Link Buddies, 555
    Microsoft bCentral, 555
  flat fees, 553-554
  impressions, 554-555
  page views, 553-554
  placement, 556
  pricing structure, 554-555

base element, 577-578

Base module (XHTML Basic), 457, 462

basefont element, 143, 578

Basic Forms module (XHTML Basic), 456, 462

Basic Tables module (XHTML Basic), 456, 462

bdo element, 578-579

Beatnik Player, 308-310

Beatware e-Picture Pro, Shockwave tool, 321

bgcolor attribute (body element), 142

Bi-Directional Text module (XHTML), 456

big element (large font), 125, 579

BizTalk Web site, DTD listing, 537

block elements, 101

blockquote element, 113, 579-580

BMI Web site, 561

Bobby accessibility validator, 433

body element, 580-581
    attributes
        alink, 100, 142
        background, 100, 142
        bgcolor, 100, 142
        link, 100, 142
        text, 100, 142
        vlink, 100, 142
    document part, 96, 100
    HTML 4.01 conformance component, 36-37

border attribute
    FRAMESET tag, 226
    img element, 284-286
    table tag, 188

border-bottom-width attribute (XSL-FO), 487

border-left-color attribute (XSL-FO), 487

borderless frames, 221
    coding, 234-235
    Web browser support, 233-234

Boutell.com Web site, Mapedit utility, 341

br tag, 581
    code listings
        Using the Break Tag in HTML (6.4), 117-118
        Using the Break Tag in XHTML (6.5), 118

braille attribute (link element), 173-175

Builder.com Web site, developer resources, 564

building
    accessibility in documents, 424-431
    forms, 253-269
    frames
        two-column page, 224-225
        with accessibility, 243-244

bulk e-mailing, NAGS (Netizens Against Gratuitous Spamming), 557

bulleted lists (unordered), 126-129
    attributes, 140-141
    code listings
        Adding Extra Space Between List Items (6.10), 129
        An Unordered List in XHTML (6.9), 127-129
        Bulleted List in HTML 4.01 (6.8), 127
    elements
        li, 126-129
        ul, 126-129
    nesting, 134-140

button control (forms), 251

button element, 581-582

C

caption element, 178, 182, 582-583

captions in tables, creating, 182-183

car navigation systems, XHTML modularization, 453

Cascading Style Sheets (CSS). *See also* CSS
    CSS1, 632
    CSS2, 632
    properties, 632-634
        azimuth, 659
        background, 638
        background-attachment, 638
        background-color, 636
        background-image, 637
        background-position, 637
        background-repeat, 637
        border, 644
        border-bottom, 644
        border-bottom-color, 642
        border-bottom-style, 643
        border-bottom-width, 642
        border-collapse, 653
        border-color, 643
        border-left, 644
        border-left-color, 642
        border-left-style, 643
        border-left-width, 642
        border-right, 644
        border-right-color, 642
        border-right-style, 643
        border-right-width, 642
        border-spacing, 654
        border-style, 643
        border-top, 644
        border-top-color, 642
        border-top-style, 643
        border-top-width, 642
        border-width, 642
        bottom, 646
        caption-side, 653
        clear, 648-649

clip, 649
color, 636
column-span, 654
content, 650-651
counter-increment, 651
counter-reset, 651
cue, 658
cue-after, 658
cue-before, 658
cursor, 650
direction, 650
display, 645-646
elevation, 659
empty-cells, 654
float, 648
font, 640
font-family, 638
font-size, 640
font-size-adjust, 640
font-stretch, 639
font-style, 639
font-variant, 639
font-weight, 639
height, 647
left, 646
letter-spacing, 635
line-height, 647-648
list-style, 653
list-style-image, 652
list-style-position, 652
list-style-type, 652
margin, 641
margin-bottom, 641
margin-left, 641
margin-right, 641
margin-top, 641
marker-offset, 651
marks, 655
max-height, 647
max-width, 647
min-height, 647
min-width, 647
orphans, 656
outline, 645
outline-color, 645
outline-style, 644-645
outline-width, 644
overflow, 649
padding, 641-642
padding-bottom, 641
padding-left, 641
padding-right, 641
padding-top, 641

page, 656
page-break-after, 655-656
page-break-before, 655
page-break-inside, 656
pause, 658
pause-after, 657
pause-before, 657
pitch, 660
pitch-range, 660
play-during, 658-659
position, 646
quotes, 651
richness, 661
right, 646
row-span, 654
size, 655
speak, 657
speak-header, 654
speak-numeral, 661
speak-punctuation, 661
speech-rate, 660
stress, 661
table-layout, 653
text-align, 634
text-decoration, 634
text-indent, 634
text-shadow, 635
text-transform, 635
top, 646
unicode-bidi, 650
vertical-align, 648
visibility, 649
voice-family, 660
volume, 657
white-space, 636
widows, 656
width, 646-647
word-spacing, 635
z-index, 649
pseudo classes, 633
rules, 633
selectors, 632-633
Cast.org Web site, Bobby
accessibility validator, 433
CDH Media Wizard, audio file
converter tool, 312
cellpadding attribute (table
tag), 188, 192-195
cells in tables, vertical alignment, 203-205
cellspacing attribute (table
tag), 188, 192-195

center element, 583
Early Example of HTML
That Uses the center
Tag (Listing 1.1), 12
character data in XML documents, 529
character encoding
7-bit ASCII, 438
8-bit, 438
32-bit, 438
ASCII reference, 439
Demoting Character
Encoding in the XML
Prolog (Listing 18.1),
440-441
international documents,
438-441
Unicode 16-bit, 438
Unicode reference, 439
character entities (DTDs), 473
examples of, 79-80
Greek letters, 69, 73-76
ISO 8859-1, 69-73
markup-significant, 69,
76-77
mathematical, 69, 73-76
symbols, 69, 73-76
Character Entities module
(XHTML), 458
character sets
alternate, labeling, 51-54
code listings
An HTML 4.01
Transitional
Document with
Character Set Defined
(2.6), 50
An XHTML 1.1
Document with
Character Set Defined
(2.7), 50-51
documents, clearly labeled
encoding requirement,
48-49
Greek characters, 47
internationalization, 48
ISO, 45-46, 68-69
math symbols, 47
symbols, 47
Unicode, 45
UTF-8, 69

charset attribute (link element), 175-176

checkbox control (forms), 250

checkboxes in forms, creating, 256-258

ChemML standard (XML), 536

cite element, 112, 584

class selectors (style sheets), 359
   assigning, 361-363
   Working with Classes (Listing 14.4), 361-363

classid attribute (object element), 328

clearly labeled encoded documents, 48-49

click-throughs (banners), 553-554

Client-side Image Map module (XHTML), 457

client-side imagemaps, 336

client-side parsers (XSLT), 489-490

client-side scripts (DOM), 402

clients, addressing DTD usage, 83-84

Clients from Hell – Learn to Deal with Devilish Personalities, 84

CMS (content management systems), 85-86

CNET Web site, client relations, 84

code attribute (applet object), 331

code element, 112, 584

code listings
   A Basic Table (8.1), 181-182
   A Dynamic Table (8.17), 210-211
   A Linked Style Sheet (14.3), 355-358
   A Table-Based Layout (1.4), 15-20

A Valid Warning-Free Document (2.11), 57-58

Adding an Image to HTML Page (11.1), 283

Adding Cellpadding (8.6), 192-193

Adding Color to Text with the font Element (6.20), 147-148

Adding Extra Space Between List Items (6.10), 129

Adding Line Height (15.4), 383-384

Adding Streaming Video (12.2), 317-318

An Aspirin Bottle Broken Down to Components (22.1), 517

An HTML 4.01 Document for Japanese with Character Set Labeled Correctly via meta Tag (2.8), 52

An Invalid Document (2.10), 56-57

An Ordinary XHTML Table (21.4), 498-499

An Unordered List in XHTML (6.9), 127-129

An XHTML 1.0 Document for Korean with Character Set Labeled Correctly via XML Prolog (2.9), 53-54

An XHTML 1.1 Documents That Conforms to Public DTD (2.5), 44

An XML File Written According to garage.dtd (20.2), 471-472

An XSLT Style Sheet (21.5), 500-501

Authoring Borderless Frames-This is Invalid XHTML (9.2), 234

Authoring Borderless Frames-This is Valid HTML (9.3), 235

Authors Will Close Their Paragraph Tags (6.2), 116

Bulleted List in HTML 4.01 (6.8), 127

Cellpadding and Spacing Together (8.8), 194-195

Class and Grouping (14.5), 365-367

Column Grouping (8.4), 184-185

Combining object and applet Elements for Cross-Browser Compatibility (13.3), 335-336

Combining Rows and Columns (9.5), 240-241

Conforming XHTML 1.0 Transitional Document with XML Declaration (2.4), 42-43

Creating a Nested List in HTML (6.14), 137-138

CSS Syntax for Two-Column Layout (15.7), 392

Defining Attributes in Every Cell (8.14), 204-205

Definition List in HTML (6.12), 132-133

Definition List in XHTML (6.13), 133-134

Demonstrating the Use of Relative and Absolute Links (7.2), 163

Demoting Character Encoding in the XML Prolog (18.1), 440-441

Drop-Down Menu (16.2), 410-411

Early Example of HTML That Uses the center Tag (1.1), 12

Embedded Style with Face, Size, and Color (15.2), 379-380

Embedding Streaming Audio (12.1), 317

Examining a Document for Structural Integrity (5.2), 108-109

Example of XML Document That Is Free of Presentational Markup (1.5), 21

Exploring Font Sizing in HTML (6.18), 144-146

Fixed and Dynamic Cells (8.18), 211-212

Fixed, Left-Margin Design with Spacer Graphics Included (8.16), 207-209

Floating Image and Dynamic Text (11.2), 292

Following HTML 4.01 Conformance Requirements and Recommendations (2.3), 36-37

Forcing and Preventing Character Joining (18.4), 446-447

forms, Using optgroup for Logical Option Grouping (10.3), 262-263

Frameset with sizing attributes (9.1), 227

How Using the font Element with Its Attributes Works (6.22), 151-152

HTML Markup for Fixed, Left-Margin Table (8.15), 206-207

Improper Nesting of Elements in Poorly Formed Markup (2.1), 33-34

Intrapage Linking (7.3), 167-168

Linked, Embedded, and Inline Styles Applied to Same Page (14.1), 347-349

Linking to an Alternate Document (7.8), 174-175

Linking to External Script (16.1), 406-407

Mixed Case in HTML 4.01 (5.1), 106

Mixing Types of Nested Lists (6.16), 139-140

New XSLT Style Sheet (21.7), 505-506

Paragraphs in XHTML (6.3), 116-117

Proper Nesting of Elements in Well-Formed Markup (Listing 2.2), 34-35

Properly Nesting Lists (6.15), 138-139

Results of Applying XSLT Style Sheet to Listing 21.6 (21.8), 507-508

Right-Aligned Floating Image and Dynamic Text (11.3), 292-295

Row Attributes Are Often Inconsistent (8.13), 202-203

Sample XSLT Document for Presenting Chapter from Online Book (21.2), 492-493

Simple DTD for Describing Cars in Garage (20.1), 470-471

Simple Way to Describe Book Chapter in XML (21.1), 491-492

Sophisticated Frameset Design (9.4), 237

Spanning Columns (8.10), 196, 198

Spanning Rows (8.12), 199-201

Stacked Tables (8.19), 214-215

Standard Table with Rows and Columns (8.9), 195-196

Styling Text with Bold, Italic, and Underline (6.7), 123-124

Table with Rows and Cells (8.11), 198-199

Text Decoration and Background Settings (15.5), 385-386

Three-Column Layout with a Dynamic Center (15.6), 389-391

Using a Single p Tag Before a Paragraph in HTML (6.1), 115

Using a Standard Link (7.1), 157-158

Using Cellspacing (8.7), 193-194

Using fieldset and legend elements (10.2), 251-252

Using link and Related Attributes to Assist Search Engines (7.9), 175-176

Using link Element for Navigation (7.6), 173-174

Using object Element to Place an Image in Document (13.1), 330

Using object Element to Specify Java Applet (13.2), 330-331

Using Ordered Lists (6.11), 130-131

Using Relative Sizing for Fonts(6.19), 146-147

Using rev Attribute for Reverse Navigation (7.7), 174

Using Table Headers (8.3), 183-184

Using Tables for Their Intended Purpose (1.3), 14-15

Using the @import Rule for Graceful Degradation of Layouts (15.8), 395-396

Using the Break Tag in HTML (6.4), 117-118

Using the Break Tag in XHTML (6.5), 118

Using the caption Element in Table (8.2), 182-183

Using the face Attribute with the font Element in HTML (6.21), 148-149

Using the font Element (6.17), 143-144

Using the font-weight Property in a Header (15.3), 380-381

Using the Label Attribute (10.1), 251

Using the lang and xml-lang Attributes in HTML 1.0 (18.2), 443

Using the link Element in HTML 4.01 (7.4), 172

Using the link Element in XHTML (7.5), 172-173
Using the pre Element (6.6), 121-122
Using the pre Tag to Format Tabular Data (1.2), 13
Using the style Element (14.2), 353-355
Using thead, tfoot, and tbody Elements (8.5), 186-187
Working with Classes (14.4), 361-363
Working with Text Direction (18.3), 444-446
XHTML Basic Document Template (19.1), 463
XHTML Created By Applying XHTML Style Sheets to XML Document (21.3), 495-496
XHTML Document Linked to Layout CSS (15.8), 393
XHTML File Produced by Preceding XSLT File (21.6), 502-504

codebase attribute
    applet object, 331
    object element, 328
codetype attribute (object element), 328
coding
    borderless frames, 234-235
    frames
        margins, 227-228
        resize controls, 227-228
        scroll controls, 227-228
    framesets, sophisticated design, 237
    JavaScript, 403-407
CoffeeCup.com Web site, Image Mapper utility, 341
col element, 179, 584-585
colgroup element, 179, 184-185, 585-586
color attribute (font element), 144, 147-148
color depth, graphics optimization, 281

color palette, graphics optimization, 281
color property in style sheets, 374-380
color reduction, graphics optimization, 281
colors, 636
    authoring combinations, 64
    fonts (style sheets), 374-380
    GIF images, 276
    hexadecimal, 63-64, 148
    representations, 63
    text
        alink attribute, 142
        background attribute, 142
        bgcolor attribute, 142
        link attribute, 142
        text attribute, 142
        vlink attribute, 142
    Web pages, selection guidelines, 147-148
    Web-safe, 65
colspan attribute (table tag), 195-198
columns
    combining with rows in framesets, 240-241
    dynamic size, 228
    frames, 222
        building, 224-225
    relative size, 228
    tables
        grouped, 184-185
        spanning, 196-198
comment tagging (JavaScript), 409
compliance mode (Internet Explorer 6.0), 40
conformance
    documents, 32
    Following HTML 4.01 Requirements and Recommendations (Listing 2.3), 36-37

HTML 4.01 documents
    body element, 36-37
    declarative header section, 36-37
    Document Type Declaration (DOCTYPE), 36-37
W3C Web site resources, 32
XHTML 1.0 documents
    DOCTYPE declaration, 38-39
    Frameset DTD, 37-39
    namespace, 37-39
    root element, 37-39
    Strict DTD, 37-39
    Transitional DTD, 37-39
    XML declaration, 39-43
XHTML 1.1 documents
    DOCTYPE definition, 43-44
    HTML root element, 43-44
    modularization, 43-44
    namespace designation, 43-44
    namespace restrictions, 43-44
constraints in well-formed XML documents, 525-526
content models (XML DTDs), 474-475
content uploads
    FTP (File Transfer Protocol), 542
    testing, 544-545
controller attribute (embed element), 309
controls (forms), 248
    button, 251
    checkbox, 250
    file, 250
    hidden, 250
    image, 251
    password, 250
    radio, 250
    reset, 250
    submit, 250
    text, 250

Cool Edit audio editor, 304

coords attribute (map element), 336

copyright law
ASCAP Web site, 547
publishing guidelines, 547
resources
ASCAP, 561
BMI Web site, 561
Fair Use Web site, 561
U.S. Copyright Office Web site, 561

core modules (abstract type)
Applet, 455
Hypertext, 455
List, 455
Structure, 455
Text, 455

Corel Web site, 281

count( ) function (XPath), 507

CPM (cost-per-thousand), banners, 553-554

creating
audio files, 303-304
hardware requirements, 305
captions in tables, 182-183
checkboxes in forms, 256-258
document templates (Homesite 5), 58-60
headers in tables, 183-184
links in style sheets, 172-173
reset buttons (forms), 267-269
streaming audio, 312-315
streaming video, 315
submit buttons (forms), 267-269
tables, 179-182
fixed-width, 190-191, 206-209
targets in frames, 229-230
text areas (forms), 264-266
XHTML Basic documents, 464-465
XML documents, 523
XSLT style sheets, 491-496

CSS (Cascading Style Sheets), 10, 346, 370, 632
code listings
CSS Syntax for Two-Column Layout (15.7), 392
Three-Column Layout with a Dynamic Center (15.6), 389-391
Using the @import Rule for Graceful Degradation of Layouts (15.8), 395-396
XHTML Document Linked to Layout CSS (15.8), 393
containment hierarchy, 349-350
css/edge Web site, 399
CSS1, 632
CSS2, 632
development of, 10, 346-347
dynamic effects, 396, 399
Eric Mayer on CSS, 87
HTML 4.0 recommendation, 26
inheritance, 349-350
layouts
degrading in Netscape Navigator, 394-396
Web site resources, 386
MeyerWeb.com Web site, 346
properties, 632-634
azimuth, 659
background, 638
background-attachment, 638
background-color, 636
background-image, 637
background-position, 637
background-repeat, 637
border, 644
border-bottom, 644
border-bottom-color, 642
border-bottom-style, 643
border-bottom-width, 642
border-collapse, 653
border-color, 643
border-left, 644
border-left-color, 642
border-left-style, 643
border-left-width, 642
border-right, 644
border-right-color, 642
border-right-style, 643
border-right-width, 642
border-spacing, 654
border-style, 643
border-top, 644
border-top-color, 642
border-top-style, 643
border-top-width, 642
border-width, 642
bottom, 646
caption-side, 653
clear, 648-649
clip, 649
color, 636
column-span, 654
content, 650-651
counter-increment, 651
counter-reset, 651
cue, 658
cue-after, 658
cue-before, 658
cursor, 650
direction, 650
display, 645-646
elevation, 659
empty-cells, 654
float, 648
font, 640
font-family, 638
font-size, 640
font-size-adjust, 640
font-stretch, 639
font-style, 639
font-variant, 639
font-weight, 639
height, 647
left, 646
letter-spacing, 635
line-height, 647-648
list-style, 653
list-style-image, 652
list-style-position, 652
list-style-type, 652
margin, 641

margin-bottom, 641
margin-left, 641
margin-right, 641
margin-top, 641
marker-offset, 651
marks, 655
max-height, 647
max-width, 647
min-height, 647
min-width, 647
orphans, 656
outline, 645
outline-color, 645
outline-style, 644-645
outline-width, 644
overflow, 649
padding, 641-642
padding-bottom, 641
padding-left, 641
padding-right, 641
padding-top, 641
page, 656
page-break-after, 655-656
page-break-before, 655
page-break-inside, 656
pause, 658
pause-after, 657
pause-before, 657
pitch, 660
pitch-range, 660
play-during, 658-659
position, 646
quotes, 651
richness, 661
right, 646
row-span, 654
size, 655
speak, 657
speak-header, 654
speak-numeral, 661
speak-punctuation, 661
speech-rate, 660
stress, 661
table-layout, 653
text-align, 634
text-decoration, 634
text-indent, 634
text-shadow, 635
text-transform, 635
top, 646

unicode-bidi, 650
vertical-align, 648
visibility, 649
voice-family, 660
volume, 657
white-space, 636
widows, 656
width, 646-647
word-spacing, 635
z-index, 649
pseudo classes, 633
rules, 633
selectors, 632-633
three-column layout, creating, 387-391
two-column layout, creating, 392-393
typography, 370
backgrounds, 384-386
font element, 370
font families, 371
italics, 382-383
properties, 373-384
text decorations, 384-386
versions, 347
versus
XSL, 486
XSL-FO, 486
visual effects, 396, 399
W3C Web site, visual formatting resources, 90
Web site resources, 385
XHTML, implementing with, 498-502
css/edge Web site, 399
Cute FTP utility, 543

D

Dartmouth University, Fetch utility development, 543
data attribute (object element), 328
data types, 570, 628-630
colors
combinations, 64
hexadecimal, 63-64
representations, 63
Web-safe, 65

length values
percentages, 65
pixels, 65
relative sizing, 65
media descriptors, 78
MIME
primary, 66
subtype, 66
script data, 78
style data, 78
URIs
elements, 62-63
examples, 62-63
dd element, 132-134, 586-587
declarations
DOCTYPE (DTDs), 468
style sheets, 359
XML documents, 526-527
Conforming XHTML 1.0 Transitional Document with XML Declaration (Listing 2.4), 42-43
Web browsers, rendering problems, 39-40
declarative header section, HTML 4.01 conformance component, 36-37
declare attribute (object element), 329
decorative fonts (style sheets), 371
dedicated FTP packages, 543
default templates (XSLT), 495
definition lists, 131-134
code listings
Definition List in HTML (6.12), 132-133
Definition List in XHTML (6.13), 133-134
elements
dd, 132-134
dl, 131, 133-134
dt, 132-134
degrading CSS layouts (Netscape Navigator), 394-396

del element, 587

demographics
American Demographics
Web site, 549
marketing information,
548-549

deploying XHTML Basic documents, 464-465

deprecated elements, 32

Design Workshops of Ojai
Web site, 567

designing
banner ads, 555-556
dynamic tables, 210-212
fixed-width tables with
dynamic designs, 211-212
frames
advantages, 236
appropriate uses,
236-237
disadvantages, 236
tables
guidelines, 216-217
layouts, 179-182
Web pages, text guide-
lines, 153-154

DesktopPublishing.com Web
site, typography resources,
152

developers
accessibility
international law,
421-422
U.S. law, 420-421
Web Accessibility
Initiative (WAI),
422-423
attribute quoting, 107-108
authoring practices, non-
conformance problems,
11
current methods, 8
document structure, trou-
bleshooting, 108-109
early HTML usage, 10
early methods, 8
proper authoring prac-
tices, 9

software limitations, 8
text, design guidelines,
153-154
WaSP versus W3C, 28-29

Devhead.com Web site,
developer resources, 564

devices
compatibility, XHTML 1.0
recommendation, 28
XHTML Basic, 459

dfn element, 112, 587-588

DHTML (Dynamic HTML),
402
disadvantages, 402
features, 402
Netscape layer element,
403

DigiDesign Pro Tool audio
editor, 304

digital television, XHTML
modularization, 452

DigitalThink Web site, 567

digitizing audio files, 303-304

dir attribute (object element),
329

dir element, 588

Director Gallery Web site, 319

directories
advertising on, 549
checking on site sub-
missions, 553
rankings, 551-553
site submissions, 551
listing methods, 550

dithering, graphics optimization, 282

div element, 588-589
inline style sheets, 351-352

dl element, 131-134, 589

DocBook DTD, 537

Doctor HTML Web site, 546

DOCTYPE declaration
(DTDs), 468, 527-528
components, 468-469
document part, 96-97
formal public identifiers
(FPIs), 469

root element, 469
values, 87-88
XHTML 1.0 conformance
component, 38-39
XHTML 1.1 conformance
component, 43-44

DOCTYPE switching (DTDs),
88-89

Document Object Mode. *See*
DOM

Document Style Semantics
and Specifications
Language (DSSSL), 22

Document Type Declaration.
See DOCTYPE

Document Type Definitions.
See DTDs

documents
accessibility
abbreviations (acronym
element), 430-431
building, 424-431
links, tab order addi-
tions, 426-428
links, title attribute,
424-426
tables (summary ele-
ment), 428-429
testing, 432-433
attributes, 32
case-sensitivity, 106
authors, 32
body element, 96, 100
alink attribute, 100
background attribute,
100
bgcolor attribute, 100
link attribute, 100
text attribute, 100
vlink attribute, 100
character sets
alternate, 51-54
An HTML 4.01
Document with
Character Set Defined
(Listing 2.6), 50
An XHTML 1.1
Document with
Character Set Defined
(Listing 2.7), 50-51

Greek characters, 47
internationalization, 48
ISO 8859-1 (Latin), 46
math symbols, 47
symbols, 47
clearly labeled encoding,
48-49
conformance components
(HTML 4.01), 32
body element, 36-37
declarative header sec-
tion, 36-37
Document Type
Declaration (DOC-
TYPE), 36-37
conformance components
(XHTML 1.0)
DOCTYPE declaration,
38-39
Frameset DTD, 37-39
namespace, 37-39
root element, 37-39
Strict DTD, 37-39
Transitional DTD, 37-39
XML declaration, 39-43
conformance components
(XHTML 1.1)
DOCTYPE definition,
43-44
HTML root element,
43-44
modularization, 43-44
namespace designa-
tion, 43-44
namespace restrictions,
43-44
deprecated elements, 32
DOCTYPE declarations,
96-97
DTDs
elements, 33
attributes, 103-104
block, 101
empty, 103
Improper Nesting of
Elements in Poorly
Formed Markup
(Listing 2.1), 33-34
inline, 101
non-empty, 102

Proper Nesting of
Elements in Well-
Formed Markup
(Listing 2.2), 34-35
values, 104-105
head element, 96-99
content attribute, 99
http-equiv attribute, 99
name attribute, 99
html element, 96
dir attribute, 98
lang attribute, 98
images, adding, 282-285
Java applets, adding
(applet element), 332-335
link element, 99
markup, 529
meta element, 99
obsolete elements, 33
pop-up windows, creating
(JavaScript), 411-413
rendering (HTML 4.0 rec-
ommendation), 26
script element, 99
scripts, adding (script element), 403-407
special characters, 45-46
structure
Examining a Document
for Structural Integrity
(Listing 5.2), 108-109
troubleshooting,
108-109
style element, 99
tags, case-sensitivity, 106
templates, creating
(Homesite 5), 58-60
three-column layout, creating with CSS, 387-391
two-column layout, creat-
ing with CSS, 392-393
user agents, 33
validation, 33
A Valid Warning-Free
Document (Listing
2.11), 57-58
An Invalid Document
(Listing 2.10), 56-57
incentives (XHTML), 28
pros/cons, 55
RealValidator tool, 54

role of, 54-55
XHTML requirement,
54
well-formed rules, 27, 33
XHTML Basic
creating, 464-465
deploying, 464-465
structural guidelines,
463
XML
attributes, 534-535
body construction,
528-529
character data, 529
creating, 523
declarations, 526
declarations in stand-
alone documents, 527
DOCTYPE, 527-528
markup, 529
entities, 530
tags, 529-530
markup entities, 533
root element, 523
rules, 522-523
well-formedness,
523-525
constraints, 525-526

Dogpile Web site, 549

DOM (Document Object
Model), 402

domains, name registration
cost, 542

downloading
audio files, formats,
306-307
video files, formats, 306

drop-down menus, creating
(Listing 16.2), 410-411

DSSSL (Document Style
Semantics and
Specifications Language),
22

dt element, 132-134, 589-590

DTD modules (XHTML), 455
Character Entities, 458
Modular Framework, 458
Module Implementations,
458
Support, 458

DTDs (Document Type
Definitions), 10, 33, 82, 468
attributes
common types, 475
default types, 476
BizTalk Web site listings,
537
case-sensitivity issues, 58
code listings
*An XML File Written
According to
garage.dtd (20.2),
471-472*
*Simple DTD for
Describing Cars in
Garage (20.1), 470-471*
content models, 474-475
declarations for XML, 472
development of, 468
DOCTYPE declarations, 87,
468-469
switching, 88-89
values, 87-88
entities
character, 473
declaring, 473
parameter, 473-474
general features, 82
HTML 4.01 recommenda-
tion, 27
markup, structure versus
semantics, 479
rendering modes
differences, 89-90
Quirks, 89-90
Strict, 89-90
SGML rules, 468
Strict XHTML 1.0/1.1 rec-
ommendation, 28
structure of, 472
syntax, 468-472
*attributes (XML DTDs),
475-476*
character entities, 473
*content models (XML
DTDs), 474-475*
*parameter entities,
473-474*
XML declarations, 472

uniqueness, HTML 4.0
recommendation, 26
usage guidelines, 82-83
*adding to older site, 84,
90-91*
client concerns, 83-84
site redesigns, 85
visual editors, 85-86
XHTML version 1.0
extending, 480-483
Frameset, 477
recommendation, 27
Strict, 477
Transitional, 477-479
XML, 470-472
advantages, 519
disadvantages, 520
DOCTYPE, 527-528
external subsets, 518
internal subsets, 518
vocabularies, 518-519
dynamic effects (CSS), 396,
399
dynamic frame design,
238-241
Dynamic HTML. *See* DHTML
dynamic sizes
columns, 228
rows, 228
dynamic table designs,
188-189
combining with fixed-
width designs, 211-212
creating, 210-211
dynamic text wrapping, 291
Floating Image and
Dynamic Text (Listing
11.2), 292
Right-Aligned Floating
Image and Dynamic Text
(Listing 11.3), 292-295

E

e-mail
advertising, 557
mailto links, creating,
169-171

ECMAScript, 409
Edit module (XHTML), 456
element names (XML), 522
element selectors (style
sheets), 359
element types (DTDs),
532-533
elements, 570
a element, 571-573
abbr element, 573
acronym element, 574
address element, 574
anchor, image linking, 299
applet
archive attribute, 331
code attribute, 331
codebase attribute, 331
*Java applet additions,
332-335*
name attribute, 331
object attribute, 331
applet element, 574-576
area element, 576-577
attributes, 627
b element, 577
base element, 577-578
basefont element, 578
bdo element, 578-579
big element, 579
blockquote element,
579-580
body element, 580-581
br element, 581
button element, 581-582
caption element, 582-583
center element, 583
cite element, 584
code element, 584
col element, 584-585
colgroup element, 585-586
dd element, 586-587
del element, 587
dfn element, 587-588
dir element, 588
div element, 351-352,
588-589
dl element, 589
documents, 33
dt element, 589-590
em element, 590

embed
    autoplay attribute, 309
    controller attribute, 309
    height attribute, 309
    loop attribute, 309
    pluginspage attribute, 309
    width attribute, 309
empty, 115-116
events, 627-628
fieldset element, 590-591
font element, 591
    style sheets comparison, 370
form element, 591-593
frame element, 593
frameset element, 593-594
h1 to h6 elements, 594
head element, 594-595
hr element, 595
HTML
    caption, 178, 182
    col, 179
    colgroup, 179, 184-185
    table, 178, 187-189
    tbody, 178, 186-187
    td, 178, 203-205
    tfoot, 178, 186-187
    th, 178
    thead, 178, 183, 186-187
    tr, 178
html element, 595
i element, 596
iframe element, 596-597
img, 282-283
    align attribute, 284-288
    alt attribute, 284-290
    An Imagemap Using the img element (Listing 13.4), 337-338
    border attribute, 284-286
    height attribute, 284-285
    hspace attribute, 284, 290-291
    scr attribute, 284
    vspace attribute, 285, 290-291
    width attribute, 284-285

img element, 597-598
Improper Nesting of Elements in Poorly Formed Markup (Listing 2.1), 33-34
input element, 598-599
ins element, 600
isindex element, 600
kbd element, 601
label element, 601
legend element, 602
li element, 602-603
link element, 603-604
map element, 604
menu element, 604-605
meta element, 605
noframes element, 605-606
non-empty, 115-116
noscript, 407
noscript element, 606
object, 326-328
    applets, adding, 330-331
    archive attribute, 329
    classid attribute, 328
    codebase attribute, 328
    codetype attribute, 328
    data attribute, 328
    declare attribute, 329
    dir attribute, 329
    id attribute, 329
    images, adding, 329-330
    lang attribute, 329
    name attribute, 329
    standby attribute, 329
    style attribute, 329
    tabindex attribute, 329
    title attribute, 329
    type attribute, 329
    usemap attribute, 329
    Using the object element to Create Imagemaps (Listing 13.5), 339-340
object element, 607-608
ol element, 608-609
optgroup element, 609
option element, 609
p element, 610
param element, 610-611
pre element, 611

img element, 597-598
Proper Nesting of Elements in Well-Formed Markup (Listing 2.2), 34-35
q element, 611-612
s element, 612
samp element, 612-613
script
    JavaScript placement, 403-407
    language attribute, 403
    scr attribute, 403
    type attribute, 403
script element, 613
select element, 613-614
small element, 614
span element, 351-352, 615
strike element, 615
strong element, 615-616
style element, 616
sub element, 616-617
sup element, 617
table element, 617-618
tbody element, 618-619
td element, 619-620
text styles
    b, 123-124
    big, 125
    i, 123-124
    small, 125
    strike, 125
    tt, 125
    u, 123-124
textarea element, 621
tfoot element, 621-622
th element, 622-623
thead element, 624
title element, 624
tr element, 625
tt element, 625-626
u element, 626
ul element, 626
var element, 627

em element, 112, 590
embed element
    attributes, 480-483
        autoplay, 309
        controller, 309
        height, 309
        loop, 309
        pluginspage, 309
        width, 309

audio, adding to Web pages, 308-309
defining, 480-483
extending to XHTML version 1.0, 480-483
video, adding to Web pages, 308-309

embedded objects
  accessibility guidelines, 341
  ActiveX components, 326
  applets, 326
  imagemaps, 326
  images, 326
  multimedia, 326
  object element, 326
  past problems, 326

embedded scripts, 402

embedded style sheets, 347-350, 353-355

empty elements, 115-116

encoding
  documents
    clearly labeled requirement, 48-49
    Greek character set, 47
    internationalization character set, 48
    ISO 8859-1 (Latin) character set, 46
    math symbol character set, 47
    symbol character set, 47
  video files, 305

end tags (XML), 529-530

entities (DTDs)
  character, 473
  declaring, 473
  naming (XML), 533
  parameter, 473-474
  unparsed (XML), 535
  XML markup, 530

Eric Mayer on CSS, 87

events, 627-628

exact palette, graphics optimization, 281

Excite Web site, 549

extending XHTML DTDs, 480-483

Extensible Hypertext Markup Language. See XHTML

eXtensible Markup Language. See XML

Extensible Stylesheet Language. See XSL

external style sheets, code example, 355-358

F

face attribute (font element), 144, 148-152

Fair Use Web site, 561

fantasy fonts (style sheets), 371-373

Fetch program utility, downloading, 543

fieldset element (forms), 251-252, 590-591

file control (forms), 250

files, uploading
  FTP (File Transfer Protocol), 542
  testing, 544-545

Fixed frame design, 238-241

fixed-width tables, 188-189
  combining with dynamic designs, 211-212
  creating, 190-191, 206-209

flat color images, GIF recommendation, 277

flat fees (banners), 553-554

float property, two-column layouts, creating (CSS), 392-393

floating frames. See I-frames

floating images, 291-295
  Floating Image and Dynamic Text (Listing 11.2), 292
  Right-Aligned Floating Image and Dynamic Text (Listing 11.3), 292-295

fo-block tag (XSL-FO), 487

fo-external-graphic tag (XSL-FO), 487

fo-inline tag (XSL-FO), 487

fo-list-block tag (XSL-FO), 487

fo-list-item tag (XSL-FO), 487

fo-list-item-body tag (XSL-FO), 487

fo-list-label-body tag (XSL-FO), 487

fo-simple-link tag (XSL-FO), 487

fo-title tag (XSL-FO), 487

font element, 591
  attributes
    color, 144, 147-148
    face, 144, 148-152
    size, 144-147
  code listings
    Adding Color to Text with the font Element (6.20), 147-148
    Exploring Font Sizing in HTML (6.18), 144-146
    Using Relative Sizing for Fonts (6.19), 146-147
    Using the face Attribute with the font Element in HTML (6.21), 148-149
    Using the font Element (6.17), 143-144
    Using the font Element with Its Attributes Works (6.22), 151-152
  development, 12
  machine-resident fonts, 149-151
  problematic issues, 143
  style sheets comparison, 370
  Web browser support, 370

font families (style sheets), 371-372

font-family attribute (XSL-FO), 487

font-size property (style sheets), 373-374

font-style property (style sheets), 382-383

font-weight attribute (XSL-FO), 487

font-weight property (style sheets), 380-381

fonts
  CSS, 638-640
  international documents
    Chinese example,
    436-437
    Hindu example, 436-437
    requirements for view-
    ing, 436-437
    utilities, 447-448
  machine-resident considerations, 149-151
  relative sizing, 146-147
  sizing, 144-146
  utilities
    Apple, 448
    Fonts 'n' Things, 448
    Keyman for Windows,
    448
    Macromedia
    Fontographer, 448
    Microsoft, 448
    SILkey for Mac, 448
  Web browser support, 370

Fonts 'n' Things Web site, 448

forcing line breaks (br tag), 117-118

foreign policies, site accessibility, 421-422

form element, 249, 591-593

Formal Public Identifiers (FPIs), 58
  DOCTYPE declaration (DTDs), 469

forms
  application technologies, 248
  building, 253-269
  checkboxes, creating, 256-258

code listings
  Using optgroup for
  Logical Option
  Grouping (10.3),
  262-263
  Using the fieldset and
  legend elements
  (10.2), 251-252
  Using the Label
  Attribute (10.1), 251
controls, 248
  button, 251
  checkbox, 250
  file, 250
  hidden, 250
  image, 251
  password, 250
  radio, 250
  reset, 250
  submit, 250
  text, 250
elements
  action, 270-271
  fieldset, 251-252
  form, 249
  input, 249
  isindex, 251-253
  label, 251
  legend, 251-252
  method, 270-271
  option, 250
  select, 249
  textarea, 249
function of, 248
menu lists
  adding, 260-263
  optgroup element,
  262-263
radio buttons, adding, 258-260
relationship between visitors and host, 248
reset buttons, creating, 267-269
submit buttons, creating, 267-269
text areas, creating, 264-266
text fields, adding, 254-256

Forms module (XHTML), abstract type
  Basic Forms, 456
  Forms, 456

FPIs (formal public identifiers), 469

frame element, 593

FRAME tag, 223-225
  attributes
    frameborder, 226
    marginheight, 226
    marginwidth, 227
    name, 227-230
    noresize, 227
    scr, 227
    scrolling, 227
    target, 229-230
    title, 227

frameborder attribute
  FRAME tag, 226
  FRAMESET tag, 226

frames
  accessibility
    building, 243-244
    issues, 242-243
  advantages, 220
  borderless, 221
    coding, 234-235
    Web browser support,
    233-234
  columns, building, 222-225
  design issues
    advantages, 236
    appropriate uses,
    236-237
    disadvantages, 236
  disadvantages, 220
  dynamic design, 238-241
  Fixed design, 238-241
  framesets, function of, 223-224
  I-type, 241-242
  legal use of, 244-245
  links, implementing, 228
  magic targets, 228-233
  margins, coding, 227-228
  resize controls, coding, 227-228

rows, 222
scroll controls, coding,
    227-228
targets, 221
    creating, 229-230
    implementing, 228
    magic, 228-233
two-column page, build-
    ing, 224-225
XHTML specification, 220

Frames module (XHTML),
457

Frameset DTDs
    HTML 4.0 recommenda-
        tion, 26
    XHTML 1.0 conformance
        component, 37-39, 477

frameset element, 593-594

FRAMESET tag, 223-225
    attributes
        border, 226
        cols, 226
        frameborder, 226
        framespacing, 226
        rows, 226

framesets
    combining rows and
        columns, 240-241
    function of, 223-224
    legal use of, 244-245
    sophisticated design, cod-
        ing, 237
    XHTML specification, 223

FrontPage, FTP capabilities,
543-544

FTP (File Transfer Protocol)
    editors
        Adobe GoLive, 543-544
        FrontPage, 543-544
        *Macromedia
            Dreamweaver, 543-544*
    programs
        Cute FTP, 543
        Fetch, 543
        WS_FTP, 543
    uploading files, 542-543
    URI scheme, 63

G

GEDCOM (GEnealogical Data
    COMmunication), 536

GedML standard (XML), 536

GEnealogical Data
    COMmunication (GED-
    COM), 536

GIF (Graphics Interchange
    Format)
    color limitations, 276
    images, selection criteria,
        277
    lossless compression, 276
    popularity of, 277
    run-length encoding, 277
    versus PNG, 279

GIMP Web site, graphics
    optimization tool, 281

globalization and interna-
    tional documents, 437-438

Gopher protocol, URI scheme,
63

graphics
    adaptive palette, 281
    color depth, 281
    color palette, 281
    color reduction, 281
    design guidelines, 276
    directories, 283
    dithering, 282
    exact palette, 281
    file formats, 276
        GIF, 276-277
        JPEG, 278
        PNG, 279
    file sizes, 276
    img element, 282-283
        align attribute, 286-288
        alt attribute, 288-290
        border attribute, 286
        height attribute, 285
        *hspace attribute,
            290-291*
        *vspace attribute,
            290-291*

indexed color, 281
    optimization tools
        Adobe Systems, 281
        CorelDraw, 281
        *GNU Image
            Manipulation Program
            (GIMP), 281*
        Paint Shop Pro, 281
        Ulead, 281
    tables, inserting, 207-209
    Web pages, adding,
        282-285

Graphics Interchange Format.
    See GIF

Greek character set, 47

Greek letter character enti-
    ties, 69, 73-76

grids in tables, creating,
195-196

grouped columns in tables,
    creating, 184-185

grouping style sheets,
364-365

Guggenheim Museum Web
    site, 299

Guide to Cascading Style
    Sheets Web site, 385

H

h1 tag, 119-120, 594

h2 tag, 119-120, 594

h3 tag, 119-120, 594

h4 tag, 119-120, 594

h5 tag, 119-120, 594

h6 tag, 119-120, 594

handheld devices, XHTML
    modularization, 452

hardware
    audio files, creating, 303
    video files, creating, 303

head element, 594-595
    content attribute, 99
    document part, 96-99
    http-equiv attribute, 99
    name attribute, 99

header tags
  h1, 119-120
  h2, 119-120
  h3, 119-120
  h4, 119-120
  h5, 119-120
  h6, 119-120

headers
  aligning, 125-126
  automatic left-alignment, 120
  size usage, 120
  tables, creating, 183-184

Health Level-7 (HL7) application, 536

height attribute
  embed element, 309
  img element, 284-285
  XSL-FO, 487

hexadecimal colors, 148
  additive synthesis, 63-64

hidden control (forms), 250

hidden fields (forms), 270-271

HL7 (Health Level-7) application, 536

Homesite 5, document templates, creating, 58-60

horizontal alignment of table rows, 202-203

horizontal rules
  hr tag
    align attribute, 152
    noshade attribute, 152
    size attribute, 153
    width attribute, 153
  paragraphs, adding, 152-153

Hot Source HTML Help Web site, 564

HotBot Web site, 549

hr element, 595

hr tag (horizontal rule), attributes
  align, 152
  noshade, 152
  size, 153
  width, 153

href attribute (anchor element), 156, 158

hreflang attribute (link element), 175-176

hspace attribute (img element), 284, 290-291

HTML (Hypertext Markup Language), 8
  authoring versus markup, 9
  CSS (Cascading Style Sheets), 10
    development, 346-347
  current recommendation, 20-21
  documents, structure of, 10
  DTDs, case-sensitivity, 58
  early features, 10
  elements
    applet, 331-335
    caption, 178, 182
    col, 179
    colgroup, 179, 184-185
    map, 336
    object, 326-331
    table, 178, 187-189
    tbody, 178, 186-187
    td, 178, 203-205
    tfoot, 178, 186-187
    th, 178
    thead, 178, 183, 186-187
    tr, 178
  evolution of, 9-21
  international documents, language attribute, 441-442
  intrinsic events
    onblur, 408
    onchange, 408
    onclick, 407
    ondblclick, 407
    onfocus, 408
    onkeydown, 408
    onkeypress, 408
    onkeyup, 408
    onmousedown, 408
    onmousemove, 408
    onmouseout, 408
    onmouseover, 408
    onmouseup, 408
    onreset, 408
    onselect, 408
    onsubmit, 408
    onunload, 407
  introduction of, 23
  markup versus authoring, 9
  melding with XML, 22
  nonconformance issues
    error correction difficulties, 11
    interoperability difficulties, 11
    style inconsistencies, 11
  original DTD, 10
  original intent of, 9-10
  presentation elements
    center element, 12
    font element, 12
    tables, 12-20
  regulation of, 20-21
  renegade aspects of, 20-21
  SGML roots, 9
  text versus design constraints, 9-20
  versus XML, 21, 521
  versus XSL-FO, 486

HTML 2.0, introduction of, 23

HTML 3.2, introduction of, 23

HTML 4.0
  features
    accessibility, 26
    CSS, 26
    document rendering, 26
    internationalization, 26
    unique DTDs, 26
  versus HTML 4.01, 27
  W3C recommendation, 26

HTML 4.01
  An HTML 4.01 Document for Japanese with Character Set Labeled Correctly via meta Tag (Listing 2.8), 52
  An HTML Document with Character Set Defined (Listing 2.6), 50
  Following HTML 4.01 Conformance Requirements and Recommendations (Listing 2.3), 36-37
  W3C recommendation, 26

HTML Bad Style Page Web site, developer resources, 564

html element, 595
  dir attribute, 98
  document part, 96
  lang attribute, 98

HTML Writers Guild Web site, organization resources, 566

HTTP (Hypertext Transfer Protocol)
  streaming audio, adding to Web pages, 316-318
  streaming video, adding to Web pages, 316-318
  URI scheme, 63

Hy-Time, 514

hyperlinks, managing, 545
  automatic methods, 546-547
  manual methods, 546

hypermedia, 156, 164-165

Hypertext Markup Language. *See* HTML

Hypertext module (XHTML Basic), 455, 462

I

i element, 123-124, 596

I-frames (inline), 241-242

IANA.org Web site, MIME registered character set values, 439

IBM
  developerWorks Web site, 564
  SGML usage, 514

ICE (Information and Content Exchange), 536

id attribute (object element), 329

ID selectors (style sheets), 359

iframe element, 596-597

Iframe module (XHTML), 457

image control (forms), 251

Image module (XHTML Basic), 456, 462

imagemaps
  client-side, 336
  code listings
    An Imagemap Using the img element (13.4), 337-338
    An Imagemap Using the object element to Create Imagemap (13.5), 339-340
  embedded objects, 326
  map element
    coords attribute, 336
    name attribute, 336
    nohref attribute, 336
    shape attribute, 336
  server-side, 336
  utilities
    CoffeeCup Image Mapper, 341
    LiveImage, 341
    Mapedit, 341
  Web page example, 337

images
  anchor element, hot linking, 299
  code listings, Adding an Image to HTML Page (11.1), 283
  copyright guidelines, 547
  design guidelines, 276
  directories, 283
  documents, adding (object element), 329-330
  embedded objects, 326
  file formats, 276
    GIF, 276-277
    JPEG, 278
    PNG, 279
  file sizes, 276
  floating, 291-295
  Guggenheim Web site, 299
  img element, 282-283
    align attribute, 286-288
    alt attribute, 288-290
    border attribute, 286
    height attribute, 285
    hspace attribute, 290-291
    vspace attribute, 290-291

linking, 299
links, setting, 159, 164-165
Louvre Web site, 299
multiple, aligning, 295-298
Museum of Modern Art (MOMA) Web site, 299
optimization tools
  Adobe Systems, 281
  CorelDraw, 281
  GNU Image Manipulation Program (GIMP), 281
  Pant Shop Pro, 281
  Ulead, 281
San Francisco Museum of Modern Art (SFMOMA) Web site, 299
Virtual Library Museum Web site, 299
Web pages, adding, 282-285

img element, 282-283, 597-598
  attributes
    align, 284-288
    alt, 284-290
    border, 284, 286
    height, 284-285
    hspace, 284, 290-291
    scr, 284
    vspace, 285, 290-291
    width, 284-285

imported style sheets, 351

impressions (banners), 554-555

indexed color, graphics optimization, 281

Information and Content Exchange (ICE), 536

InformIT Web site, FTP tools, 543

InfoSeek Web site, 549

inline elements, 101

inline fonts (style sheets), 371-372

inline frames. *See* I-frames

inline style sheets, 347-352

input element (form), 249,
598-599
  alt attribute, 249
  checked attribute, 249
  hidden field attribute,
    270-271
  maxlength attribute, 249
  name attribute, 249
  scr attribute, 249
  size attribute, 249
  type attribute, 249
  value attribute, 249

ins element, 600

inserting whitespace in documents, 119

international documents
  character encoding,
    438-439
      via MIME, 439-441
  difficulty in U.S. creation,
    436
  fonts
    Chinese example,
      436-437
    Hindu example, 436-437
    requirements for view-
      ing, 436-437
    utilities, 447-448
  HTML 4.0 recommenda-
    tion, 26
  language attribute,
    441-443
  terminology
    globalization, 437-438
    internationalization,
      437-438
    localization, 437-438
    multilingual site devel-
      opment, 437-438
  text elements
    direction, setting,
      444-446
    handling, 444
    joining controls,
      446-447
    line height, 444

International Standards
  Organizations. See ISO

internationalization character
  set, 48

Internet Explorer
  borderless frame support,
    234
  CSS support, 346
  Macromedia Flash sup-
    port, 320
  object element, rendering
    capabilities, 327-328
  q element support, 114
  style sheet resources, 368
  style sheet support, 386
  version 6.0, compliance
    mode, 40
  XSLT parsing, 489

intrapage links
  code listings, Intrapage
    Linking (7.3), 167-168
  creating, 165-168
  screens per page, 168

intrinsic events, 627-628
  onblur, 408
  onchange, 408
  onclick, 407
  ondblclick, 407
  onfocus, 408
  onkeydown, 408
  onkeypress, 408
  onkeyup, 408
  onmousedown, 408
  onmousemove, 408
  onmouseout, 408
  onmouseover, 408
  onmouseup, 408
  onreset, 408
  onselect, 408
  onsubmit, 408
  onunload, 407
  scripts, defined actions
    through Web browsers,
    407

Intrinsic Events module
  (XHTML), 457

isindex element (forms),
  251-253, 600

ISO (International Standards
  Organization), 25
  8-bit character sets, 45
  8859-1 character set
    (Latin), 46

character sets, 68-69
  language codes, two-
    character listing, 66-68
  Web site, 25, 68

ISO 8859-1 character entities,
  69-73, 438

ISPs (Internet service
  providers), 542

italicizing text (style sheets),
  382-383

J - K

JASC Web site, graphics optimization tool, 281

Java applets, adding (applet
  element), 332-335

Java Boutique Web site, 331

JavaScript, 402
  code listings
    Drop-Down Menu (16.2),
      410-411
    Linking to External
      Script (16.1), 406-407
  code placement, 403-407
  comment tagging, 409
  ECMAScript, 409
  function of, 408
  JScript, 409
  origins, 409
  pop-up windows, creating,
    411-413
  popular uses, 409
  rules, 409
  uses, 409

Joe Cartoon Web site, 319

joining characters in international documents, 446-447

Joint Photographic Experts
  Group. See JPEG

JPEG (Joint Photographic
  Experts Group)
  artifacts, 278
  file extension, 278
  images, selection criteria,
    278
  lossy compression, 278

JScript, Microsoft implementation of JavaScript, 409

kbd element, 112, 601

Keyman Web site, font utilities, 448

keywords, search engine rankings, 551-552
  Metaspy Web site, 552
  spam prevention, 553

L

label element (forms), 251, 601

labeling alternate character sets, 51-54

lang attribute (object element), 329

language attribute
  international documents, 441-443
  script element, 403

language codes (ISO), two-character listing, 66-68

layer element, creating, 403

leading and fonts (style sheets), 383-384

Legacy module (XHTML), 458

legend element (forms), 251-252, 602

length values
  percentages, 65
  pixels, 65
  relative sizing, 65

li element, 126-129, 602-603

line breaks
  forcing (br tag), 117-118
  whitespace, inserting, 119

line-drawn images, GIF recommendation, 277

line-height property (style sheets), 383-384

link attribute (body element), 142

Link Buddies Web site, banner exchanges, 555

link element, 603-604
  alternate documents, pointing to, 174-175
  attributes, 171
    aural, 175
    braille, 175
    charset, 175-176
    hreflang, 175-176
    media, 171
    rel, 171
    rev, 171
    title, 171, 175-176
    tty, 175
    type, 171
  code listings
    Linking to an Alternate Document (7.8), 174-175
    Using link Element for Navigation (7.6), 173-174
    Using rev Attribute for Reverse Navigation (7.7), 174
  document part, 99
  navigational uses, 173-174
  search engines, defining information for, 175-176

Link module (XHTML Basic), 457, 462

linked style sheets, 347-358
  A Linked Style Sheet (Listing 14.3), 355-358
  XHTML usage of, 351

linking images (anchor element), 299

links (hyperlinks)
  absolute, 158-159
  advertising, 558
  anchor element, 156-158
  code listings
    Using a Standard Link (7.1), 157-158
    Using the link Element in HTML 4.01 (7.4), 172
    Using the link Element in XHTML (7.5), 172-173

color selection, 147-148

colors, 142

frames
  creating, 229-230
  implementing, 228

images, setting, 159, 164-165

intrapage
  creating, 165-168
  screens per page, 168

link element
  alternate documents, pointing to, 174-175
  attributes, 171
  navigational uses, 173-174

mailto, creating, 169-171

managing, 545
  automatic methods, 546-547
  manual methods, 546

PDF documents, setting, 159

reciprocol, 164

relative, 158
  creating, 160-164

sound files, setting, 159

style sheets, creating, 172-173

tab order additions, accessibility, 426-428

title attribute, accessibility, 424-426

Word documents, setting, 159

List module (XHTML Basic), 455, 462

The List Web site, 542

lists
  attributes
    type, 140-141
    value, 140-141
  bulleted, 126-129
    li element, 126-129
    nesting, 134-140
    ul element, 126-129
  definition, 131-134
    dd element, 132-134
    dl element, 131-134
    dt element, 132-134

function, 126
indentation, 126
nesting, 134-140
numbered, 130-131
whitespace, 126

Live Image imagemap utility, 341

live Web sites
  links, 545
    automatic management, 546-547
    manual management, 546
  testing, 544-545

localization and international documents, 437-438

loop attribute (embed element), 309

lossless compression (GIF), 276

lossy compression (JPEG), 278

Louvre Web site, 299

Lycos Web site, 549

Lynda.com Web site, developer resources, 564

M

Macintosh computers, resident fonts, 149-151

MacMusic Web site, audio resources, 305

Macromedia Director, 319

Macromedia Dreamweaver, FTP capabilities, 543-544

Macromedia Flash, 319-321
  disadvantages, 321
  interface, 321
  Internet Explorer support, 320
  level of difficulty, 321

Macromedia Fontographer, 448

Macromedia Homesite Editor, DOCTYPE options, 96-97

Macromedia Shockwave, 319-321

Macromedia SoundEdit 16, 304

Macromedia Web site, font utilities, 448

magic targets
  frames, 228-233
  names, 79, 230-233

mailto links, creating, 169-171

map element, 604
  attributes
    coords, 336
    name, 336
    nohref, 336
    shape, 336

Mapedit imagemap utility, 341

margins in frames, coding, 227-228

Mark Radcliffe's Advanced HTML Web site, 564

marketing
  awards, 559
  banners
    click-throughs, 553-554
    CPM, 553-554
    design guidelines, 555-556
    flat fees, 553-554
    impressions, 554-555
    page views, 553-554
    placement, 556
    pricing structure, 554-555
  e-mail, 557
  links, 558
  newsgroups, 558
  offline strategies, 559-560
  search engines, 549
    checking submissions, 553
    listing methods, 550
    rankings, 551-553
    site submissions, 551
  target audiences, 548-549
  Web rings, 559

markup, 529
  documents (XML), 529
    attributes, 534-535
  entities (XML), 530, 533
  tags (XML), 529-530

markup-significant character entities, 69, 76-77

master families. *See* font families

math symbol character set, 47

mathematical character entities, 69, 73-76

MathML standard (XML), 536

max-height attribute (XSL-FO), 487

media attribute (link element), 171

media descriptors, 78

media types, 66

media/scripting modules (abstract type)
  Base, 457
  Client-side Image Map, 457
  Frames, 457
  Iframe, 457
  Image, 456
  Intrinsic Events, 457
  Legacy, 458
  Link, 457
  Meta-information, 457
  New Identification, 457
  Object, 457
  Ruby, 457
  Scripting, 457
  Server-side Image Map, 457
  Style Attribute, 457
  Stylesheet, 457
  Target, 457

MediaTec Web site, LiveImage utility, 341

MegaMind Web site, educational resources, 567

menu element, 604-605

menu lists
    forms, adding, 260-263
    optgroup element, 262-263
meta element, 99, 605
Meta Information module
    (XHTML Basic), 462
META tag, search engine
    rankings, 551-553
Meta-information module
    (XHTML), 457
meta-languages
    SGML, 514-515
    XML, 513, 518-519
Metaspy Web site, site
    search resource, 552
method element (forms),
    270-271
MeyerWeb.com Web site, CSS
    resources, 346
Microsoft Advanced
    Streaming Media Format
    (ASF), 322
Microsoft bCentral Web site
    banner exchanges, 555
    listing services, 550
Microsoft Web site
    font utilities, 448
    typography resources, 152
    Windows Media Player,
        310
Microsoft Windows Media
    Player, 310
MIDI (Musical Instrument
    Digital Interface), 307
MIME (Multipurpose Internet
    Mail Extensions), 66
    international documents,
        character encoding,
        439-441
    primary type, 66
    registered character set
        values, 439
    subtype, 66
    types for RealMedia files,
        316
min-height attribute (XSL-
    FO), 487
minimizing attributes, 248

MISTI (Missile Industry
    Supply-change Transaction
    Infrastructures), 536
MMX (Multimedia
    Extensions), 302
Modular Framework module
    (XHTML), 458
modularization (XHTML), 452
    1.0 recommendation, 28
    1.1 conformance compo-
        nent, 43-44
    abstract modules, 455
        core, 455
        forms, 456
        media/scripting,
            456-458
        tables, 456
        text extension, 456
    affected devices
        car navigation systems,
            453
        desktop browsers, 453
        digital television, 452
        handheld devices, 452
        printers, 453
        smart phones, 452
        two-way pagers, 453
    DTD modules, 455
        Character Entities, 458
        Modular Framework,
            458
        Module
            Implementations, 458
        Support, 458
    family member character-
        istics, 458-459
    function of, 454
    intended effects, 453-454
    introduction of, 23
modules (XHTML Basic)
    Base, 462
    Basic Forms, 462
    Basic Tables, 462
    Hypertext, 462
    Image, 462
    Link, 462
    List, 462
    Meta Information, 462

Object, 462
    Structure, 462
    Text, 462
Molly.com Web site, devel-
    oper resources, 565
monospace fonts (style
    sheets), 371
MPEG (Motion Picture Expert
    Group), 308
MPEG 3 (Motion Picture
    Expert Group), 307-308
MSDN (Microsoft Developers
    Network) Web site
    developer resources, 564
    style sheet resources, 368
multilingual site develop-
    ment, international docu-
    ments, 437-438
multimedia
    embedded objects, 326
    forms, 302
    Intel processor improve-
        ments, 302
    MMX (Multimedia
        Extensions), 302
    software tools, 302
        Adobe LiveMotion, 321
        Macromedia Director,
            319
        Macromedia Flash,
            319-321
        Macromedia
            Shockwave, 319
multiple images, aligning on
    Web pages, 295-298
Museum of Modern Art
    (MOMA) Web site, 299

N

NAGS (Netizens Against
    Gratuitous Spamming) Web
    site, 557
name attribute
    anchor element, 156-158
    applet object, 331
    FRAME tag, 227-230
    map element, 336
    object element, 329

namespaces, XHTML 1.0 conformance component, 37-39, 43-44

naming entities (XML), 533

nested lists, code listings
   Creating a Nested List in HTML (6.14), 137-138
   Mixing Types of Nested Lists (6.16), 139-140
   Properly Nesting Lists (6.15), 138-139

nesting
   lists, 134-140
   tables, 213-214

Net Crucible Web site, 489

Netscape LiveScript, 409

Netscape Navigator
   audio/video plug-ins, support list, 309
   borderless frames, support of, 234
   CSS layouts, degrading, 394-396
   CSS support, 346
   layer element creation, 403
   object element, rendering capabilities, 327-328
   q element support, 114
   style sheet support, 386

Netscape Netcenter Web site, listing services, 550

New Identification module (XHTML), 457

New York Public Library Web site, redesign example, 90-91

newlines, XML processors, 531

newsgroups, advertising medium, 558

Nielsen Netratings, banner ad effectiveness, 556

noframes element, 605-606

NOFRAMES tag, 242-243
   accessibility issues, 243-244

nohref attribute (map element), 336

non-empty elements, 115-116

nonbreaking spaces (paragraphs), 119

normalization, XML entity resolution, 531-532

noscript element, 407, 606

numbered lists (ordered), 130-131
   attributes, 140-141
   ol element, 130-131
   Using Ordered Lists (Listing 6.11), 130-131

O

OASIS Web site, 537

object element, 607-608
   applets, adding to documents, 330-331
   attributes
      archive, 329
      classid, 328
      codebase, 328
      codetype, 328
      data, 328
      declare, 329
      dir, 329
      id, 329
      lang, 329
      name, 329
      standby, 329
      style, 329
      tabindex, 329
      title, 329
      type, 329
      usemap, 329
   code listings
      Combining object and applet Elements for Cross-Browser Compatibility (13.3), 335-336
      Using object element to Place in Document (13.1), 330
      Using object element to Specify Java Applet (13.2), 330-331
      Using the object element to Create Imagemap (13.5), 339-340
   combining with applet element, cross-browser support, 335-336
   compliance test suite, 328
   embedded objects, 326
   images, adding to documents, 329-330
   introduction of, 326
   rendering capabilities
      Internet Explorer, 327-328
      Netscape Navigator, 327-328
   use of, 328
   W3C recommendation, 328

Object module (XHTML Basic), 457, 462

objects, embedded, accessibility guidelines, 341

oblique typeface (style sheets), 382-383

obsolete elements in documents, 33

offline marketing, 559-560

ol element, 130-131, 608-609

onblur intrinsic event, 408

onchange intrinsic event, 408

onclick intrinsic event, 407

ondblclick intrinsic event, 407

onfocus intrinsic event, 408

onkeydown intrinsic event, 408

onkeypress intrinsic event, 408

onkeyup intrinsic event, 408

online validation service (W3C), 109

onmousedown intrinsic event, 408

onmousemove intrinsic event, 408

onmouseout intrinsic event, 408

onmouseover intrinsic event, 408

onmouseup intrinsic event, 408

onreset intrinsic event, 408

onselect intrinsic event, 408

onsubmit intrinsic event, 408

onunload intrinsic event, 407

Opera Software Web site
 q element support, 114
 XSL-FO usage essay, 488

optgroup element, 609

optimizing graphics
 adaptive palette, 281
 Adobe Systems tools, 281
 color depth, 281
 color palette, 281
 color reduction, 281
 CorelDraw tool, 281
 dithering, 282
 exact palette, 281
 GNU Image Manipulation
  Program (GIMP), 281
 guidelines, 280
 indexed color, 281
 Paint Shop Pro tool, 281
 Ulead tools, 281

option element (form), 250,
 609

ordered lists. *See* numbered
 lists

Organization for the
 Advancement of Structured
 Information Standards
 (OASIS), 537

P

p element, 115-117, 610
 code listings
  *Authors Will Close
   Their Paragraph Tags
   (6.2)*, 116
  *Paragraphs in XHTML
   (6.3)*, 116-117
  *Using a Single p Tag
   Before a Paragraph in
   HTML (6.1)*, 115

page views (banners),
 553-554

paragraphs
 adding, 115-117
 aligning, 125-126

horizontal rules, adding,
 152-153
nonbreaking spaces, 119
p tag, 115-117
rendering, 117

param element, 610-611

parameter entities (DTDs),
 473-474, 478-479

parsed data (XML), 522-523

parsers
 XML element types,
  532-533
 XSLT, 489
  client-side, 489-490
  server-side, 490

password control (forms), 250

PCs (personal computers),
 resident fonts, 149-151

PDF documents, links, setting, 159

percentage-width tables,
 188-189

Photodisc Web site, stock
 photos, 547

photographic images, Web
 site sources, 547

phrase elements (structured
 text), 112
 abbr, 113
 acronym, 113
 cite, 112
 code, 112
 dfn, 112
 em, 112
 kbd, 112
 samp, 112
 strong, 112
 var, 113

pixels
 frame measurements, 222
 length values, 65

plagiarism and site content,
 547

plug-ins
 audio
  *Apple QuickTime
   Player, 310*
  Beatnik Player, 310

  *Microsoft Windows
   Media Player, 310*
  Real Player, 310
  selection criteria, 311
 video
  Apple QuickTime, 310
  Beatnik Player, 310
  *Microsoft Windows
   Media Player, 310*
  Real Player, 310
  selection criteria, 311

pluginspage attribute (embed
 element), 309

PNG (Portable Network
 Graphics)
 antialiasing, 279
 public domain format, 279
 versus GIF, 279
 W3C specification, 279

pop-up windows, creating
 (JavaScript), 411-413

Portable Network Graphics.
 See PNG

position( ) function (XPath),
 502-504

pre element, 611
 preformatted text, 121-122
 uses, 123
 Using the pre Element
  (Listing 6.6), 121-122

preformatted text
 code listings, Using the
  pre Element (6.6),
  121-122
 pre element, 121-122
 uses, 123

presentation elements, HTML
 evolution, 12-20

Presentation module
 (XHTML), 456

presentational attributes (img
 element)
 align, 286-288
 alt, 288-290
 border, 286
 height, 285
 hspace, 290-291
 vspace, 290-291
 width, 285

printers, XHTML modularization, 453

processors (XML)
  newlines, 531
  unparsed entities, 535
  whitespace, 531-532

properties
  CSS, 632
  style sheets
    background, 384-386
    color, 374-380
    font-size, 373-374
    font-style, 382-383
    font-weight, 380-381
    grouping, 364-367
    line-height, 383-384
    text decoration, 384-386

proportional-width tables, 188-189

publishing sites
  copyright guidelines, 547
  FTP (File Transfer Protocol), 542-543
    Adobe GoLive, 543-544
    FrontPage, 543-544
    Macromedia Dreamweaver, 543-544
  links, 545
    automatic management, 546-547
    manual management, 546
  testing, 544-545

Pure Digital Audio Web site, audio resources, 305

Q - R

q element (quotation element), 113, 611-612

QuickTime video format, 308

Quirks Mode, DTD DOCTYPE declarations, 87-89

quotation elements (structured text), 112
  blockquote, 113
  HTML, 107-108
  q, 113
  XHTML, 108
  XML, 108

radio buttons (forms), 250, 258-260

rankings (search engines), 551-553

Real Estate Markup Language (RELML), 536

Real Estate Transaction Standard (RETS), 536

Real Player, 310

Real Producer, 322

Real Publisher, 322

real-world applications (XML)
  ChemML, 536
  GedML, 536
  Health Level-7 (HL7), 536
  ICE (Information and Content Exchange), 536
  MathML, 536
  MISTI (Missile Industry Supply-change Transaction Infrastructures), 536
  Real Estate Transaction Standard (RETS), 536
  RosettaNet, 536
  SAE J2008, 536
  SMIL, 536

RealMedia files, MIME types, 316

RealNetworks Web site
  Real Player, 310
  streaming audio resources, 312
  streaming video resources, 312
  video tools, 306

RealProducer
  streaming audio, creating, 312-315
  streaming video, creating, 312, 315

RealServer G2
  streaming audio, adding to Web pages, 316
  streaming video, adding to Web pages, 316

RealValidator tool, 54

reciprocol links, 164

redesigning Web sites, DTD selection, 85

Rehabilitation Act of 1973, 420

rel attribute (link element), 171

relative links, 158
  code listings, Demonstrating the Use of Relative and Absolute Links (7.2), 163
  creating, 160-164

relative sizes
  columns, 228
  rows, 228

relative sizing
  fonts, 146-147
  length values, 65

RELML (Real Estate Markup Language), 536

rendering modes (DTDs), 89-90

reset buttons (forms), 250, 267-269

resize controls in frames, 227-228

resources
  education
    Design Workshops of Ojai, 567
    DigitalThink, 567
    MegaMind, 567
    ThunderLizard, 567
  mailing lists
    Babblelist.com, 565
    WebDesign-L, 566
    XHTML-L, 566
  organizations
    Association for Women in Computing, 566
    HTML Writers Guild, 566
    W3C, 566
    Web Standards Project, 566
    Webgrrls, 566
    World Organization of Webmasters, 566

Web sites
  A List Apart.com, 564
  Builder.com, 564
  Devhead.com, 564
  Hot Source HTML Help, 564
  HTML Bad Style Page, 564
  IBM developerWorks, 564
  Lynda.com, 564
  Mark Radcliffe's Advanced HTML, 564
  Molly.com, 565
  MSDN, 564
  Sevloid Guide to Web Design, 565
  Web Designers Virtual Library, 565
  Webmonkey, 565
  Webreference, 565
  Webreview.com, 565
  Yale C/AIM Style Guide, 565
result trees (XSLT), 489
RETS (Real Estate Transaction Standard), 536
rev attribute (link element), 171
RMF (Rich Music Format), 307
root element
  XHTML 1.0 conformance component, 37-39
  XHTML 1.1 conformance component, 43-44
RosettaNet, 536
rows
  combining with columns in framesets, 240-241
  dynamic size, 228
  frames, 222
  relative size, 228
  tables
    horizontal alignment, 202-203
    spanning, 198-201

rowspan attribute (table tag), 198-201
Ruby module (XHTML), 457
rules in style sheets, 359
run-length encoding (GIF), 277

S

s element, 612
SAE J2008, 536
samp element (phrase element), 112, 612-613
sampling rates (audio) versus file sizes, 306-307
San Francisco Museum of Modern Art (SFMOMA) Web site, 299
sans serif fonts (style sheets), 371
Saxon XSLT parser, 490
Scalable Vector Graphics (SVG), 454, 487
scr attribute
  FRAME tag, 227
  img element, 284
  script element, 402-403
screen readers, link element usage, 173
script element, 613
  attributes
    language, 403
    scr, 402-403
    type, 403
  document part, 99
  JavaScript, placement, 403-407
script fonts (style sheets), 371
Scripting module (XHTML), 457
scripts
  client-side, 402
  code listings, Linking to External Script (16.1), 406-407
  data, 78

Document Object Model (DOM), 402
ECMAScript, 409
embedded, 402
intrinsic events, 407
JavaScript
  A Drop-Down Menu (Listing 16.2), 410-411
  comment tagging, 409
  origins, 409
  pop-up window creation, 411-413
  popular uses, 409
  rules, 409
JScript, 409
noscript element, 407
scroll controls, frames, coding, 227-228
scrolling attribute (FRAME tag), 227
search engines
  advertising on, 549
    checking on site submissions, 553
    rankings, 551-553
    site submissions, 551
  AltaVista, 549
  code listings, Using link and Related Attributes to Assist Search Engines (7.9), 175-176
  Dogpile, 549
  Excite, 549
  HotBot, 549
  InfoSeek, 549
  link element, defining information for, 175-176
  listing methods, 550
  Lycos, 549
  Yahoo!, 549
select element (form), 249, 613-614
selecting
  DTDs, guidelines, 82-86, 90-91
  images
    for GIF compression, 277
    for JPEG compression, 278

selectors, 632-633
  classes
    assigning, 361-363
    working with Classes
      (Listing 14.4), 361-363
    style sheet component,
      358
      class type, 359
      element type, 359
      grouping, 364-367
      ID type, 359

serif fonts (style sheets), 371

Server-side Image Map module (XHTML), 457

server-side imagemaps, 336

server-side parsers (XSLT),
  490

setting links
  images, 159, 164-165
  PDF documents, 159
  sound files, 159
  Word documents, 159

Sevloid Guide to Web Design
  Web site, 565

SGML (Standard Generalized
  Markup Language), 9
  DTD development, 468
  general features, 10
  HTML roots, 9
  introduction, 23
  meta-language, 514-515
  structured methodology,
    10
  users
    IBM, 514
    U.S. government, 514
  W3C Web site resources,
    10
  XML subset, 513-515

shape attribute (shape element), 336

Shareware.com Web site, FTP
  tools, 543

Shockwave.com Web site, 319

SILkey for Mac Web site, font
  utilities, 448

site developers
  authoring practices, non-conformance problems,
    11
  current methods, 8
  early HTML usage, 10
  early methods, 8
  proper authoring practices, 9
  software limitations, 8
  text design guidelines,
    153-154
  WaSP versus W3C, 28-29

sites, uploading (File Transfer
  Protocol), 542

size attribute
  font element, 144-147
  hr tag, 153

sizing
  banner ads, 555-556
  fonts, 144-146
    style sheets, 373-374
  frames
    columns, 222
    rows, 222

small element (small font),
  125, 614

smart phones, XHTML modularization, 452

SMIL (Synchronized Markup
  Integration Language), 23

Sonic Foundry Web site, 305

sound files, links, setting, 159

Sound Forge audio editor, 305

source trees (XSLT), 489

spam (e-mail advertising),
  557

span element, 615
  inline style sheets, 351-352

special characters, 45-46

Special Edition Using XML,
  22, 513

stacking tables, 214-215

standalone documents (XML),
  527

Standard Generalized Markup
  Language. See SGML

standby attribute (object element), 329

start tags (XML), 529-530

streaming audio, 306
  Adding Streaming Video
    (Listing 12.2), 317-318
  creating, 312-315
  Embedding Streaming
    Audio (Listing 12.1), 317
  HTTP, 316-318
  RealServer G2, 316

streaming media
  Adobe Premiere, 322
  Apple QuickTime Player,
    322
  Microsoft Advanced
    Streaming Media Format
    (ASF), 322
  Real Producer, 322
  Real Publisher, 322
  User Datagram Protocol
    (UDP), 311-312
  VivoActive Player, 322

streaming video, 306
  creating, 312, 315
  RealServer G2, 316-318

Strict DTDs
  HTML 4.0 recommendation, 26
  XHTML 1.0 conformance
    component, 37-39, 477
  XHTML 1.0/1.1 recommendation, 28

strike element
  (strikethrough), 125, 615

strong element, 112, 615-616

Structure module (XHTML
  Basic), 455, 462

structured text
  phrase elements, 112
    abbr, 113
    acronym, 113
    cite, 112
    code, 112
    dfn, 112
    em, 112
    kbd, 112
    samp, 112
    strong, 112
    var, 113

quotation elements, 112
  blockquote, 113
  q, 113
subscript elements, 112-114
superscript elements, 112-114
style attribute (object element), 329
Style Attribute module (XHTML), 457
style data, 78
style elements (text), 616
  b, 123-124
  big, 125
  code listings, Styling Text with Bold, Italic, and Underline (6.7), 123-124
  document part, 99
  HTML/XHTML support, 124
  i, 123-124
  small, 125
  strike, 125
  tt, 125
  u, 123-124
style sheets
  aural style sheets, 656-661
  benefits, 347
  browser support, 347
  cascade, 347-349
  code listings
    Adding Line Height (15.4), 383-384
    Class and Grouping (14.5), 365-367
    CSS Syntax for Two-Column Layout (15.7), 392
    Embedded Style with Face, Size, and Color (15.2), 379-380
    Linked, Embedded, and Inline Styles Applied to Same Page (14.1), 347-349
    Three-Column Layout with a Dynamic Center (15.6), 389-391
    Using the @import Rule for Graceful Degradation of Layouts (15.8), 395-396
    Using the font-weight Property in a Header (15.3), 380-381
    XHTML Document Linked to Layout CSS (15.8), 393
  components, 358-359
    properties, 358
    selectors, 358-363
    values, 359
  containment hierarchy, 349-350
  CSS
    CSS1, 632
    CSS2, 632
    properties, 632-661
    pseudo classes, 633
    rules, 633
    selectors, 632-633
  declarations, 359
  embedded, 347-355
  font categories
    decorative, 371
    fantasy, 371
    inline, 371-372
    monospace, 371
    sans serif, 371
    script, 371
    serif, 371
  grouping, 364-367
  imported, 351
  inheritance, 347-350
  inline, 347-352
  Internet Explorer, Microsoft resources, 368
  layout, 386
  linked, 347-351, 355-358
  links, creating, 172-173
  rules, 359
  syntax, 358-359
  Text Decoration and Background Settings (15.5), 385-386
  three-column layout, creating, 387-391
  two-column layout, creating, 392-393
  typography, 370
    backgrounds, 384-386
    font element, 370
    font families, 371
    italics, 382-383
    properties, 373-384
    text decorations, 384-386
  user defined, 351
  W3C resources, 347, 368
  Web Review Style Sheet Reference Guide, 368
  Web site resources, 385
  XSLT
    applying, 495-496
    creating, 491-496
Stylesheet module (XHTML), 457
sub element (subscript element), 114, 616-617
submit buttons (forms), 250
  creating, 267-269
  Macintosh platform, 268
  Windows platform, 268
subscript elements (structured text), 112-114
summary attribute (table tag), 188
  accessibility, 428-429
sup element (superscript element), 114, 617
superscript elements (structured text), 112-114
Support module (XHTML), 458
SVG (Scalable Vector Graphics), 454, 487
symbol character set, 47, 69, 73-76
Synchronized Markup Integration Language. *See* SMIL
Syntrillium Web site, Cool Edit tool, 304

T

tab order, links (accessibility issues), 426-428

tabindex attribute (object element), 329

table element (HTML), 178, 617-618
  attributes, 187-189
    align, 188
    border, 188
    cellpadding, 188, 192-195
    cellspacing, 188, 192-195
    colspan, 195-198
    rowspan, 198-201
    summary, 188
    width, 188-189

tables
  accessibility issues, 242
  captions, creating, 182-183
  cells, vertical alignment, 203-205
  code listings
    A Basic Table (8.1), 181-182
    A Dynamic Table (8.17), 210-211
    A Table-Based Layout (1.4), 15-20
    Adding Cellpadding (8.6), 192-193
    Cellpadding and Spacing Together (8.8), 194-195
    Column Grouping (8.4), 184-185
    Defining Attributes in Every Cell (8.14), 204-205
    Fixed and Dynamic Cells (8.18), 211-212
    Fixed, Left-Margin Design with Spacer Graphics Included (8.16), 207-209
    HTML Markup for Fixed, Left-Margin Table (8.15), 206-207
    Row Attributes Are Often Inconsistent (8.13), 202-203
    Spanning Columns (8.10), 196-198
    Spanning Rows (8.12), 199-201
    Stacked Tables (8.19), 214-215
    Standard Table with Rows and Columns (8.9), 195-196
    Table with Rows and Cells (8.11), 198-199
    Using Cellspacing (8.7), 193-194
    Using Table Headers (8.3), 183-184
    Using Tables for Their Intended Purpose (1.3), 14-15
    Using the caption Element in Table (8.2), 182-183
    Using the pre Tag to Format Tabular Data (1.2), 13
    Using thead, tfoot, and tbody Element (8.5), 186-187
  columns, spanning, 196-198
  creating, 179-182
  CSS, 653-654
  design guidelines, 216-217
  development of, 12-20
  dynamic designs
    combining with fixed-width designs, 211-212
    creating, 210-211
  elements
    caption tag, 178, 182
    col tag, 179
    colgroup tag, 179, 184-185
    table tag, 178, 187-189
    tbody tag, 178, 186-187
    td tag, 178, 203-205
    tfoot tag, 178, 186-187
    th tag, 178
    thead tag, 178, 183, 186-187
    tr tag, 178
  fixed-width designs, combining with dynamic designs, 211-212
  grids, creating, 195-196
  grouped columns, creating, 184-185
  headers, creating, 183-184
  nesting, 213-214
  rows
    horizontal alignment, 202-203
    spanning, 198-201
  stacking, 214-215
  summary element, accessibility, 428-429
  widths
    fixed, 188-191, 206-209
    percentage, 188-189
    proportional, 188-189

Tables module (XHTML), abstract type
  Basic Tables, 456
  Tables, 456

tags
  attributes
    case-sensitivity, 106
    minimization, 248
    properties, 103-104
    quoting, 107-108
    values, 104-105
  case-sensitivity, Mixed Case in HTML 4.01 (Listing 5.1), 106
  FRAME, 223-225
    frameborder attribute, 226
    marginheight attribute, 226
    marginwidth attribute, 227
    name attribute, 227-230
    noresize attribute, 227
    scr attribute, 227
    scrolling attribute, 227
    target attribute, 229-230
    title attribute, 227
  FRAMESET, 223-225
    border attribute, 226
    cols attribute, 226
    frameborder attribute, 226
    framespacing attribute, 226
    rows attribute, 226

META, search engine
rankings, 551-553
NOFRAMES, 242-244
XML
end, 529-530
nesting levels, 516-517
start, 529-530
syntax, 515-516
XSL-FO
fo-block, 487
fo-external-graphic, 487
fo-inline, 487
fo-list-block, 487
fo-list-item, 487
fo-list-item-body, 487
fo-list-item-label, 487
fo-simple-link, 487
fo-title, 487
XSLT, 488

target attribute
anchor element, 156-158
FRAME tag, 229-230

target audiences, demographics, 548-549

Target module (XHTML), 457

target names, 79

targets (frames)
creating, 229-230
implementing, 228

tbody element (HTML), 178,
186-187, 618-619

td element (HTML), 178,
203-205, 619-620
attributes
align, 204
valign, 204
width, 204

Telnet, URI scheme, 63

templates
default (XSLT), 488, 495
documents, creating
(Homesite 5), 58-60

Temple University Web site,
WAVE accessibility validator, 433

testing Web site accessibility,
432-433

text
aligning, 125-126
basefont element, 143
colors
alink attribute, 142
background attribute,
142
bgcolor attribute, 142
link attribute, 142
text attribute, 142
vlink attribute, 142
design guidelines, 153-154
font element
color attribute, 147-148
face attribute, 148-152
problematic issues, 143
size attribute, 144-147
headers
automatic left-
alignment, 120
h1 tag, 119-120
h2 tag, 119-120
h3 tag, 119-120
h4 tag, 119-120
h5 tag, 119-120
h6 tag, 119-120
size usage, 120
line breaks, forcing (br
tag), 117-118
paragraphs, adding (p
tag), 115-117
phrase elements, 112
abbr, 113
acronym, 113
cite, 112
code, 112
dfn, 112
em, 112
kbd, 112
samp, 112
strong, 112
var, 113
preformatted text
pre element, 121-122
uses, 123
quotation elements, 112
blockquote, 113
q, 113
style elements
b, 123-124
big, 125
HTML/XHTML support,
124

i, 123-124
small, 125
strike, 125
tt, 125
u, 123-124
subscript elements,
112-114
superscript elements,
112-114
whitespace, inserting, 119

text areas (forms), 264-266

text attribute (body element),
142

text control (forms), 250

text decoration property
(style sheets), 384-386

text elements in international
documents
direction, setting, 444-446
Forcing and Preventing
Character Joining
(Listing 18.4), 446-447
handling, 444
joining controls, 446-447
line height, 444
Working with Text
Direction (Listing 18.3),
444-446

text extension modules,
abstract type
Bi-Directional Text, 456
Edit, 456
Presentation, 456

text fields (forms), adding,
254-256

Text module (XHTML Basic),
455, 462

text-align attribute (XSL-FO),
487

Text-Encoding Initiative
(TEI), 514

textarea element (forms), 249,
264-266, 621

tfoot element, 178, 186-187,
621-622

th element, 178, 622-623

thead element, 178, 183,
186-187, 624

three-column layouts, creating (CSS), 387-391

ThunderLizard Web site, educational resources, 567

title attribute
FRAME tag, 227
link element, 171, 175-176
object element, 329

title element, 624

tools (multimedia)
Adobe LiveMotion, 321
Macromedia Director, 319
Macromedia Flash, 319-321
Macromedia Shockwave, 319

Totalnews Web site, legal controversy regarding frameset usage, 244-245

tr element, 178, 625

trademarks, U.S. Trademark Office Web site, 561

transformation trees (XSLT), 489

Transitional DTDs
HTML 4.0 recommendation, 26
XHTML 1.0 conformance, 37-39, 477
parameter entities, 478-479
section dividers, 477-478

transitioning DTDs to older sites, 84, 90-91

trees (XSLT)
child nodes, 489
element nodes, 489
result, 489
root nodes, 489
source, 489
transformation, 489

troubleshooting document structure, 108-109

tt element (teletype), 125, 625-626

tty attribute (link element), 175

two-column layouts, creating (CSS), 392-393

two-way pagers, XHTML modularization, 453

type attribute
link element, 171
lists, 140-141
object element, 329
script element, 403

typefaces, applying to text, 148-152

typography (style sheets)
backgrounds, 384-386
font element comparison, 370
font families, 371
italics, 382-383
properties, 373-384
resources
DesktopPublishing.com, 152
Microsoft, 152
text decorations, 384-386

U

u element (underline), 123-124, 626

U.S. Copyright Office Web site, 561

U.S. Department of Justice Web site
ADA resources, 420
Section 508 resources, 420

U.S. Trademark Office Web site, 561

ul element (bulleted lists), 126-129, 626

Ulead Web site, graphics optimization tool, 281

Unicode 16-bit character set, 438

Unicode character sets, 45

Unicode.org Web site, 439

Uniform Resource Identifiers. See URIs

unordered lists. See bulleted lists

unparsed data (XML), 522-523

unparsed entities (XML), 535

uploading content
FTP (File Transfer Protocol), 542
testing, 544-545

URIs (Uniform Resource Identifiers)
elements, 62-63
examples, 62-63
schemes
FTP protocol, 63
Gopher protocol, 63
HTTP protocol, 63
Telnet protocol, 63

URLs (Uniform Resource Locators)
absolute links, 158-159
relative links, 158
creating, 160-164

usemap attribute (object element), 329

user agents, 33

User Datagram Protocol (UDP), streaming media, 311-312

user defined style sheets, 351

UTF-8
character sets, 69
encoding, 438

V

validating documents, 33
A Valid Warning-Free Document (Listing 2.11), 57-58
An Invalid Document (Listing 2.10), 56-57
pros/cons, 55
role of, 54-55
XHTML requirements, 54

valign attribute (td tag), 204

values (style sheets), 359
grouping, 364-367

var element, 113, 627

VBScript, 402

vertical alignment of table cells, 203-205

video
  encoding, 305
  file formats
    Apple QuickTime, 308
    AVI (Audio/Video Interface), 308
    downloading, 306
    MPEG (Motion Picture Expert Group), 308
    streaming, 306
  hardware requirements, 303-305
  plug-ins
    Apple QuickTime, 310
    Beatnik Player, 310
    Microsoft Windows Media Player, 310
    Netscape Navigator support, 309
    Real Player, 310
    selection criteria, 311
  streaming format
    adding (HTTP), 316-318
    adding (RealServer G2), 316
    creating, 312, 315
  Web pages, adding (embed element), 308-309

Virtual Library Museum Web site, 299

visual editors, Web authoring, DTD selection, 85-86

visual effects (CSS), 396, 399

VivoActive Player, 322

vlink attribute (body element), 142

vspace attribute (img element), 285, 290-291

W

W3C (World Wide Web Consortium), 24
  component terminology
    deprecated, 26
    forbidden, 26
    obsolete, 26
  formation of, 24
  function of, 24
  HTML 4.0 recommendation, 26
  HTML 4.01 recommendation, 26
  members, 24
  primary benefits, 25
  recommendations, 24-25
  specifications, 24-25
  versus WaSP, 28-29
  XHTML 1.0 recommendation, 26
  XHTML 1.1 recommendation, 26

W3C Web site
  conformance definitions, 32
  CSS visual formatting resources, 90
  data management information, 62
  document validators, 54
  DOM-related resources, 402
  HTML, introduction of, 23
  HTML 2.0, introduction of, 23
  HTML 3.2, introduction of, 23
  HTML 4.0 versus HTML 4.01, 27
  international accessibility updates, 422
  module-based XHTML, introduction, 23
  online validation service, 109
  organization resources, 566
  original HTML DTD, 10
  PNG specification, 279
  regulation of HTML, 20-21
  SGML
    introduction, 23
    resources, 10
  style sheet resources, 347, 368
  SVG resources, 487
  Web Accessibility Initiative (WAI), 422-423

XHTML
  introduction of, 23
  modules, 455

XHTML Basic, introduction of, 23

XML
  introduction of, 23
  related standards, 512

XPath specification, 494

XSL recommendation resources, 486

XSL-FO recommendation resources, 486

XSLT
  common elements, 491
  namespaces, 488

WAP (Wireless Application Protocol), 488

WAP Forum Web site, 488

WaSP (Web Standards Project), 29, 566

WAV (Windows Audio/Video), 307

WAVE accessibility validator, 433

Waves Audio Track audio editor, 305

Waves Web site, 305

Web Accessibility Initiative (WAI)
  testing guidelines, 432-433
  W3C project objectives, 422-423

Web browsers
  audio/video plug-ins
    Apple QuickTime, 310
    Beatnik Player, 310
    Microsoft Windows Media Player, 310
    Real Player, 310
    selection criteria, 311
  borderless frames, level of support, 233-234
  colors, Web-safe, 65
  cross-compatibility, combining applet and object elements, 335-336
  CSS, levels of support, 346, 386

DOM interface, 402

DTDs

   DOCTYPE declarations, 87-88

   DOCTYPE switching, 88-89

font element, text/link colors, 147-148

font support, 370

HTML document structure, 10

Internet Explorer 6.0, compliance mode, 40

q element support, 114

"Quirks Mode", 87-89

rendering modes, DTD differences, 89-90

script actions, intrinsic events, 407

style sheets, level of support, 347

XHTML modularization, 453

XML

   declarations, rendering problems, 39-40

   support, 22

Web Designers Virtual Library Web site, 565

Web pages

  audio files

    adding (embed element), 308-309

    creating, 303-304

    hardware requirements, 303

  fonts

    machine-resident considerations, 149-151

    view support in browsers, 370

  images

    adding, 282-285

    floating, 292-295

  intrapage links

    creating, 165-168

    screens per page, 168

  multiple images, aligning, 295-298

  streaming audio

    adding (HTTP), 316-318

    adding (RealServer G2), 316

    creating, 312-315

  streaming video

    adding (HTTP), 316-318

    adding (RealServer G2), 316

    creating, 312, 315

  text, design guidelines, 153-154

  video files

    adding (embed element), 308-309

    hardware requirements, 303-305

Web Review Style Sheet Reference Guide, 368

Web rings (advertising), 559

Web Site Garage Web site, 546

Web sites

  A List Apart.com, 385, 564

  accessibility

    abbreviations, acronym element, 430-431

    international policies, 421-422

    links, tab order additions, 426-428

    links, title attribute, 424-426

    tables, summary element, 428-429

    testing, 432-433

    Web Accessibility Initiative (WAI), 422-423

    Workforce Investment Act of 1998, 420-421

  Adobe Systems, graphics optimization tools, 281

  advertising

    awards, 559

    banners, 553-556

    e-mail, 557

    links, 558

    newsgroups, 558

    offline strategies, 559-560

    search engine rankings, 549-553

    site submissions, 551

    target audiences, 548-549

    Web rings, 559

  AltaVista, 549

  American Demographics, 549

  ANSI.org, 439

  Apple, font utilities, 448

  ArtToday, 547

  ASCAP, 547, 561

  Ask Dr. Web, 385

  Association for Women in Computing, 566

  Babblelist.com, 565

  Beatnik, 308

  Beatware.com, 321

  BizTalk, DTD listing, 537

  BMI, 561

  Boutell.com, 341

  Builder.com, 564

  Cast.org, 433

  CDH, 312

  CMS usage, 85-86

  CNET, client relations, 84

  CoffeeCup.com, 341

  Corel, 281

  CSS layout resources, 386

  css/edge, 399

  current development methods, 8

  Design Workshops of Ojai, 567

  DesktopPublishing.com, 152

  developers

    authoring nonconformance, 11

    early HTML usage, 10

    proper authoring practices, 9

    software limitations, 8

    WaSP versus W3C, 28-29

Devhead.com, 564

DigiDesign, 304

DigitalThink, 567

Director Gallery, 319

Doctor HTML, 546

documents

  additions, DTD selection, 84, 90-91

  attributes, 103-105

  block elements, 101

  body element, 96, 100

  DOCTYPE declarations, 96-97

  empty elements, 103

  head element, 96-99

  html element, 96-98

  inline elements, 101

  link element, 99

  meta element, 99

  non-empty elements, 102

  script element, 99

  style element, 99

  syntax, troubleshooting, 108-109

Dogpile, 549

early development methods, 8

Eric Meyer's Safe CSS Properties, 632

Excite, 549

Fair Use, 561

files, uploading (FTP), 542

Fonts 'n' Things, font utilities, 448

frames

  advantages, 220

  borderless, 221

  disadvantages, 220

  targets, 221

framesets, legal use of, 244-245

GIMP, graphics optimization tools, 281

Guggenheim Museum, 299

Guide to Cascading Style Sheets, 385

Hot Source HTML Help, 564

HotBot, 549

HTML Bad Style Page, 564

HTML Writers Guild, 566

IANA.org, 439

IBM developerWorks, 564

InformIT, 543

InfoSeek, 549

ISO, 25

  language codes, 68

JASC, graphics optimization tools, 281

Java Boutique, 331

Joe Cartoon, 319

Keyman, font utilities, 448

Link Buddies, banner exchanges, 555

links, managing, 545-547

The List, 542

live testing, 544-545

Louvre, 299

Lycos, 549

Lynda.com, 564

MacMusic, 305

Macromedia, 304, 448

mailto links, creating, 169-171

Mark Radcliffe's Advanced HTML, 564

marketing, search engine submissions, 553

MediaTec, 341

MegaMind, 567

MeyerWeb.com, CSS resources, 346

Microsoft, 152, 448

Microsoft bCentral, 550, 555

Molly.com, 565

MSDN (Microsoft Developers Network), 564

multimedia

  Intel processor improvements, 302

  software tools, 302

Museum of Modern Art (MOMA), 299

NAGS (Netizens Against Gratuitous Spamming, 557

Net Crucible, 489

Netscape Netcenter, 550

New York Public Library, redesign example, 90-91

OASIS, 537

Opera Software, XSL-FO usage essay, 488

Photodisc, 547

publishing, copyright guidelines, 547

Pure Digital Audio, 305

RealNetworks

  streaming audio resources, 312-313

  streaming video resources, 312

  video tools, 306

redesigns, DTD selection, 85

San Francisco Museum of Modern Art (SFMOMA), 299

Sevloid Guide to Web Design, 565

Shareware.com, 543

Shockwave.com, 319

SILkey for Mac, font utilities, 448

Sound Foundry, 305

statistics tools, 548

Syntrillium, 304

Temple University, 433

ThunderLizard, 567

Totalnews, 244-245

U.S. Copyright Office, 561

U.S. Department of Justice, ADA resources, 420

U.S. Trademark Office, 561

Ulead, graphics optimization tools, 281

Unicode.org, 439

Virtual Library Museums, 299

VivoActive, 322

W3C (World Wide Web Consortium), 566

  conformance resources, 32

  DOM-related resources, 402

  HTML 4.0 versus HTML 4.01, 27

international accessibility updates, 422
online validation service, 109
original HTML DTD, 10
PNG specification, 279
SGML resources, 10
style sheets resources, 347
SVG resources, 487
WAI objectives, 422-423
XHTML modules, 455
XPath specification, 494
XSL recommendation, 486
XSL-FO recommendation, 486
XSLT common elements listing, 491
XSLT namespaces, 488
WAP Forum, 488
WaSP (Web Standards Project), 29, 566
Waves, 305
Web Designers Virtual Library, 565
Web Review, 368
Web Site Garage, 546
Web Standards Project, 566
WebDesign-L, 566
Webgrrls, 566
Webmonkey, 565
Webreference, 565
Webreview.com, 565
WebRing.org, 559
World Organization of Webmasters, 566
XHTML-L, 566
XingTech, 312
Yahoo!, 549
Yale C/AIM Style Guide, 565
Web Standards Project. See WaSP
Web-hosting services, 542
Web-safe colors, 65
WebDesign-L Web site, mailing list resources, 566
Webdings font, 371

Webgrrls Web site, 566
Webmonkey Web site, 565
Webreference Web site, 565
Webreview.com Web site, 565
WebRing.org Web site, 559
weight (font style sheets), 380-381
well-formed documents, 33
XML constraints, 523-526
whitespace
adding to bulleted lists, 129
inserting, 119
lists, creating, 126
XML markup, normalization, 531-532
width attribute
embed element, 309
hr tag, 153
img element, 284-285
table tag, 188-189
td tag, 204
Wingdings font, 371
Wireless Application Protocol. See WAP
Wireless Markup Language (WML), 454, 486
Word documents, links, setting, 159
Workforce Investment Act of 1998, 420-421
World Organization of Webmasters Web site, 566
WS_FTP program, FTP utility, 543

X - Y - Z

XHTML (Extensible Hypertext Markup Language)
attributes, mandatory quoting, 108
basis for HTML 4.01 recommendation, 27
code listings
An Ordinary XHTML Table (21.4), 498-499
An XSLT Style Sheet (21.5), 500-501
Using the lang and xml-lang Attributes Together in XHTML 1.0 (18.2), 443
CSS development, 346-347
development of, 22
DTDs
case-sensitivity, 58
extending, 480-483
ease in learning, 23
elements
case-sensitivity, 107
object, 326-331
frames specification, 220
Frameset DTDs, 477
frameset specification, 223
implementing
with CSS, 498-502
with XSLT, 498-502
implications of extensibility, 515
international documents, language attribute, 443
interoperability, 23
introduction of, 23
linked style sheets, 351
modularization, 452
abstract modules, 455-458
affected devices, 452-453
DTD modules, 455, 458
family member characteristics, 458-459
function of, 454
intended effects, 453-454
smart phones, 452
W3C HTML Working Group, 455
Strict DTDs, 477
style sheets, W3C Web site resources, 368
syntatical strictness, 23
Transitional DTDs, 477
parameter entities, 478-479
section dividers, 477-478

XHTML 1.0
  code listings
    An XHTML 1.0 Document for Korean with Character Set Labeled Correctly (Listing 2.9), 53-54
    Conforming XHTML 1.0 Transitional Document with XML Declaration (2.4), 42-43
  device compatibility, 28
  documents
    validation incentives, 28
    well-formed, 27
  W3C recommendation, 26
XHTML 1.1
  code listings
    An XHTML 1.1 Document That Conforms to Public DTD (2.5), 44
    An XHTML Document with Character Set Defined (2.7), 50-51
  modularization, 28
  W3C recommendation, 26
XHTML Basic
  affected devices, 459-460
  body markup examples, 461
  documents
    conformance guidelines, 463
    creating, 464-465
    deploying, 464-465
  goals, 459
  introduction, 23
  modules
    Base, 462
    Basic Forms, 462
    Basic Tables, 462
    Hypertext, 462
    Image, 462
    Link, 462
    List, 462
    Meta Information, 462
    Object, 462
    Structure, 462
    Text, 462

supported features
  forms, 460
  images, 460
  style sheets, 460
  tables, 460
  text, 460
unsupported features
  frames, 461-462
  imagemaps, 461-462
  scripting, 461-462
XHTML-L Web site, mailing list resources, 566
XingTech, audio file tools, 312
XML (eXtensible Markup Language), 21, 512
  advantages in development, 513
  attributes, mandatory quoting, 108
  code listings
    An Aspirin Bottle Broken Down to Components (22.1), 517
    Example of an XML Document That Is Free of Presentational Markup (1.5), 21
  conformity, 21
  customization, 21
  declarations
    Conforming XHTML 1.0 Transitional Document with XML Declaration (Listing 2.4), 42-43
    Web browser rendering problems, 39-40
    XHTML 1.0 conformance component, 39-43
  development of, 21
  disadvantages in development, 22
  documents
    attributes, 534-535
    body construction, 528-529
    character data, 529
    creating, 523
    declarations, 526-527

    DOCTYPE, 527-528
    markup, 529
    tags, 529-530
    markup entities, 529-530, 533
    root element, 523
    rules, 522-523
    well-formedness, 523-525
    constraints, 525-526
  DTDs
    advantages, 519
    disadvantages, 520
    external subsets, 518
    internal subsets, 518
    vocabularies, 518-519
  elements
    case-sensitivity, 106
    name guidelines, 522
  flexibility, 21
  introduction of, 23
  melding with HTML, 22
  meta-language, 513, 518-519
  nesting levels, 516-517
  parsed data, 522-523
  parsers, element types, 532-533
  processors
    newlines, 531
    unparsed entities, 535
    whitespace, 531-532
  Scalable Vector Graphics (SVG), 454
  SGML subset, 513-515
  Special Edition Using XML, 513
  structure
    logical structure, 529-530
    physical structure, 530
  Synchronized Multimedia Integration Language (SMIL), 454
  syntatical rigor, 21
  syntax, 515-516
  tags
    nesting levels, 516-517
    syntax, 515-516
  unparsed data, 522-523
  versus HTML, 21, 521
  vocabularies, 518-519
  W3C standards, 512

Web browser support, 22
Wireless Markup
  Language (WML), 454
XHTML extensibility of,
  515
XHTML modularization,
  453-454
XPath, 486, 494
  count( ) function, 507
  expressions, syntax,
    497-498
  functions, syntax, 497-498
  position( ) function,
    502-504
  predicates, 502
  syntax, 497-498
XSL (Extensible Stylesheet
  Language)
  versus CSS, 486
  W3C recommendation, 486
XSL Formatting Objects. *See*
  XSL-FO
XSL Transformations. *See*
  XSLT
xsl-apply-templates tag,
  494-495
xsl-comment tag, 502
XSL-FO (XSL Formatting
  Objects), 486
  attributes
    background-color, 487
    background-image, 487
    border-bottom-width,
      487
    border-left-color, 487
    font-family, 487
    font-weight, 487
    height, 487
    max-height, 487
    min-height, 487
    text-align, 487
  controversial use of, 488
  tags, 486
    fo-block, 487
    fo-external-graphic, 487
    fo-inline, 487
    fo-list-block, 487
    fo-list-item, 487
    fo-list-item-body, 487

    fo-list-item-label, 487
    fo-simple-link, 487
    fo-title, 487
  versus CSS, 486
  versus HTML, 486
  W3C recommendation, 486
xsl-for-each tag, 507-508
xsl-output tag, 494
xsl-sort tag, 502-504
xsl-strip-space tag, 494
xsl-stylesheet tag, 494
xsl-templates tag, 494-495
xsl-value-of tag, 495
XSLT (XSL Transformations),
  486
  alternate content views,
    creating, 505-506
  applications for, 488
  code listings
    New XSLT Style Sheet
      (21.7), 505-506
    Results of Applying
      XSLT Style Sheet to
      Listing 21.6 (21.8),
      507-508
    Sample XSLT Document
      for Presenting
      Chapter from Online
      Book (21.2), 492-493
    Simple Way to Describe
      Book Chapter in XML
      (21.1), 491-492
    XHTML Created By
      Applying XHTML
      Style Sheets to XML
      Document (21.3),
      495-496
    XHTML File Produced
      by Preceding XSLT
      File (21.6), 502-504
  common elements listing,
    491
    xsl-apply-templates,
      494-495
    xsl-comment, 502
    xsl-for-each, 507-508
    xsl-output, 494
    xsl-sort, 502-504
    xsl-strip-space, 494

    xsl-stylesheet, 494
    xsl-templates, 494-495
    xsl-value-of, 495
  document structure,
    491-493
  namespaces, 488
  parsers, 489
    client-side, 489-490
    Internet Explorer com-
      pliance, 489
    Saxon (Java-based), 490
    server-side, 490
  style sheets
    applying, 495-496
    creating, 491-496
  syntax, 491
  tags, 488
  templates, 488, 495
  trees
    child nodes, 489
    element nodes, 489
    result, 489
    root nodes, 489
    source, 489
    transformation, 489
  uses, 488
  XHTML, implementing
    with, 498-502
  XPath
    predicates, 502
    syntax, 497-498
    usage of, 494

Yahoo! Web site, 549
Yale C/AIM Style Guide Web
  site, developer resources,
  565